June 15, 1970

To Lois DeYoung

from

The University of Akron
Alumni Association.

Thanks for all the many
things you do for us!

A Centennial Publication by
George W. Knepper

New Lamps for Old

One Hundred Years of Urban Higher Education
at The University of Akron

To those who have contributed as learner,
teacher, administrator, or friend, to the
fulfillment of the purpose of Buchtel College
and The University of Akron.
Fiat Lux

Contents

Foreword

A centennial history is an appropriate way to acknowledge the accomplishments of a century, but in an institution as complex as a university it is at best a partial instrument. Space and time limitations dictate that the author pass over large amounts of material that might seem of first importance to others were they to make the selection. It is ironic that the chief activity of the University—the teaching-learning process—is least open to description and analysis, for only rarely does a perceptive student or a sensitive teacher leave an account of what he sought to accomplish in the classroom and whether or not he found what he sought. These difficulties lead some writers of university history to rely almost exclusively on administrative history. I have attempted to avoid this distortion by relating classroom and extracurricular activities that were typical of each period, and I have done so in relation to each chronological period rather than in separate topical treatment. If this makes for modest repetition, it avoids the greater error of treating the University story as a sequence of discrete activities, each of a self-contained nature.

An effort has been made to show the close working relationship that Buchtel College and The University of Akron have had with the City of Akron. Even during the formative years of the denominational school this relationship was much in evidence and, of course, with the advent of the Municipal University, a very self-conscious connection developed. This connection is a major theme of the book; a secondary theme describes the effort to preserve the liberal arts core in the curriculum while new professional programs were vying for strength and attention.

No effort has been made to produce an encyclopedic account that lists the name of every person who contributed in some fashion to the institution's development. Nor have I felt compelled to name every group and describe every function. The choices made were mine, and I must bear the responsibility for omissions that may distress some readers. The alternative, however, was to clutter the work with overabundant detail to the point where the main thrust of the history would be lost.

In the ten years that have elapsed since the project was initially outlined and the first material collected, I have enjoyed and profited from the assistance of many persons. A centennial history was a long-time dream of Vice President Emeritus Donfred H. Gardner who did so much to initiate the project and who eased me into it from the beginning. President Norman P. Auburn gave his endorsement and warm support to the idea and put at my disposal any material to which I required access. During five of the years through which this work progressed I served as Dean of the Buchtel College of Liberal Arts, and my "boss" during that time, the then Senior Vice President and Provost, Dominic J. Guzzetta, was generous and understanding in allowing me to arrange my summer schedule to make room for research.

The help of the University Archivist, Dorothy Hamlen, was essential in carrying this work forward. She not only answered a multitude of questions, but she put in orderly arrangement the basic research materials that now form the University Archives which is in part an outgrowth of this project. The University Librarian, Mr. H. Paul Schrank, provided me with excellent working facilities, and his staff was most gracious, especially the staff of the Circulation Department who protected me from interruption. Mrs. Ruth Clinefelter, Social Sciences Librarian, made many special investigations and gave me the benefit of her extensive knowledge of the early years. Other libraries that provided generous service include the Akron Public Library, the Western Reserve Historical Society Library, the Ohio Historical Society Library, the Rutherford B. Hayes Library, the Knox College Library, the Meadville Theological School Library, the St. Lawrence University Library, and the Universalist Historical Collections in the Tufts University Library.

I have talked formally and informally with scores of persons who were intimately involved in the life of the school. I cannot mention them all, but I would like to single out for special thanks Mrs. Lydia Voris Kolbe and her sister, Miss Marian Voris, Mrs. Agnes Whiton Simmons (deceased), Dean Emeritus Charles Bulger, Mr. Bert Polsky, and Mr. Chester Conner whose delightful student diary proved so valuable. Among those still active on campus, Dr. Thedore Duke, Head of the Classics Department, gave me much valuable information and insight which stemmed from his unparalleled knowledge of obscure portions of the early record. My colleague, Dr. Warren Kuehl, Head of the History Department, gave generously of his experience with university histories and also helped by arranging my schedule to advantage. Mr. Ken MacDonald, Director of Sports Information, gave me useful material about intercollegiate athletics.

In the early stages of the work, Mr. Marshall Keith Clark performed admirably as my research assistant and demonstrated great skill and tenacity in working through some of the more onerous sources. A special thanks is due my former secretary, Mrs. Marilyn Young Gibson who spent long hours typing and arranging notes and preliminary copy. Others who assisted in this work were Mrs. Ruby Gwinn, Mrs. Bernice Gualteri, Mrs. Marcia Labbe, and Mrs. Eleanor Steinle. Mrs. Martha Bell typed the final manuscript.

The entire manuscript was read by my sister, Miss Nancy Knepper, who protected me from many errors of style and form, and by Mr. Robert Sartoris, Director of Publications, whose sharp eye for error and exaggeration saved me from embarrassment. I have profited greatly from the comments of Donfred Gardner who read the entire manuscript and had the grace to let me say what I was inclined to say. His sense of proportion and acute critical judgment have saved me from the abyss. My wife, Phyllis, has endured endless stories and ideas with good humor and a sure sense of balance, and for this, along with a supportive interest in the work, I thank her!

This is an "official" history only in the sense that I was given every support and encouragement to do the work. No one, officially or unofficially, has attempted in any way to direct my telling of the story. For this restraint, I express my admiration and thanks. The interpretations and evaluations are mine alone, and whatever shortcomings or injustices some might find in the book are my responsibility.

George W. Knepper

AKRON, OHIO
OCTOBER, 1969

A note on sources

Much of the material used in this account is now in the University Archives located in the University Library. Research notes compiled for this book, filed both chronologically and by subject, are also in the archives. In spite of the 1899 fire that destroyed many records of Old Buchtel, the basic institutional records are reasonably complete and include the Minutes of the Board of Trustees (Directors), faculty and committee minutes, some financial records, and all of the standard publications including catalogs, presidents' reports, class schedules, year books, brochures, programs of special events, and so forth. A full run of the *Buchtelite* and of the alumni publications proved essential. One of the most valuable sources was the *Akron Beacon Journal* which is available on microfilm in unbroken sequence from the earliest days of Buchtel College to the present. Its accounts, and those of other Akron newspapers, do much to flesh out the rather sterile reporting found in official minutes.

Only one previous published account treats extensively with the University's history. In 1922, The Alumni Association published *Fifty Years of Buchtel,* edited by Dean A. I. Spanton who gathered contributions from many authors, most of whom were former students or faculty members. Several unpublished Master's theses in the University Library were helpful, particularly those written by Ruth Clinefelter (library), Donald Louthan (city charter), and Stuart Terrass (finance). Standard local histories, especially those by Lane, Olin, and Grismer, contain supporting material concerning community developments.

Since word of this book has circulated, a slow but steady flow of interesting and valuable historical material has been sent to the archives by former students, faculty, and friends. Some photographs have been among this material and have added to the fine collection of old pictures in the archives. Thus the record is being constantly enriched, and those who, in the future, make searches for historical material will find a well ordered repository of illuminating source material.

I

Mr. Greeley lays a cornerstone

By any decent measure, Independence Day should be sunny and bright in keeping with the spirit of new beginnings that marked the birth of our nation. It was disappointing, therefore, when Tuesday, July 4, 1871, dawned dark and rainy; it appeared there would be no firecrackers, no festivities, no fun. Among those most concerned were Mr. Henry Blandy of Zanesville, President of the Day for the cornerstone-laying ceremonies scheduled to take place at eleven o'clock on the grounds of Buchtel College, and General George W. McNeil, Chief Marshal of the great parade which was to proceed from the center of Akron's commercial district on Howard Street to the College grounds on Middlebury Street (now Buchtel Avenue) near the city's edge. It was to be the greatest celebration held in the little city in the 45 years since its founding by General Simon Perkins.

At the Akron depot on Mill Street, a succession of special trains unloaded hundreds of passengers from throughout Ohio. Most of these, being of the Universalist persuasion, had come to see the dream of their denomination realized in the building of a college where their sons and daughters could receive an education in the liberal Christian tradition. Others had been lured by the special rates the railroads offered for the occasion so that "hundreds of people who would not otherwise have done so, came for the sake of the ride."[1] By eleven o'clock, when the last train disgorged its passengers, there were at least 5,000 strangers in Akron who had to find their way as best they could along streets already thronged with thousands of local citizens. It was a festive throng despite the rain, for there was much to divert it. Band music and frequent salutes were constant reminders that this was a special day. Indeed, the Excelsior Gun Squad had welcomed the Glorious Fourth at midnight with a rousing 20 gun salute, while the Buckeye Gun Squad "showed their good sense by waiting until sunrise when their cannon thundered forth 37 times."

The local dignitaries, having taken stock of the weather, decided to postpone the ceremonies until two o'clock in the afternoon. As this decision was announced, the skies cleared, and the sun came out to dry the land and relieve the frustration that had been building in the crowd. The visitors were further cheered by lunch. The basket dinner planned for Grace Park had been washed out, but a cooperative crowd was shepherded into Phoenix, Empire, and Temperance Halls where there was "an abundance of provisions" spread on hastily erected tables. Hundreds of visitors were accommodated at the Empire House while the Knights Templar, Marble's Band, and the 29th Ohio Volunteer Infantry held a grand banquet in Commerce Hall.

By two o'clock the procession was formed on Howard Street. There were 22 units in the parade, among them several bands, the G. A. R., Masons, Odd Fellows, Knights of Pythias, the Father Matthew Temperance Society, the clergy, city officials, and "citizens." Turning east on Market Street, the parade moved up the hill to Elm Street (now College Street) where it turned right and proceeded to the College grounds. With bands playing and banners flying it was a colorful sight. Not even an interruption "caused by two drunken men in a buggy breaking into the ranks near the railway bridge and scattering people right and left," spoiled the spirit of the marchers, although the incident probably gave the Father Matthew Temperance Society something more to think about. Many banners, decorations, and mottoes hung along the line of march. One, which attracted considerable attention, read:

Greeley for President, Buchtel for College,
Akron for Enterprise, Beauty and Knowledge.

A great throng awaited the procession on the College grounds. In order to keep this crowd quiet, several local dignitaries made short speeches. Among them was General Lucius V. Bierce, the "Hero of Windsor," avenger of the *Caroline,* many times Mayor of Akron, lawyer, historian, state senator, philosopher, investor, philanthropist, champion of the underdog, and Akron's most colorful citizen.[2] The cornerstone was to be laid according to traditional Masonic ritual, and as soon as the procession reached the College grounds, the Masons gathered in their proper places. Reverend Everett L. Rexford of Columbus, one of the prime movers in the founding of the school, then delivered a prayer. Earnest as he was, the good Reverend probably would have prayed even more fervently than he did for the well-being of the College had he foreseen that within seven years he would be its president.

The officers of the Grand Lodge of Ohio then proceeded with the ceremonies under the direction of Mr. A. H. Newcomb, Grand Master. The three-foot-square cornerstone was properly laid. It bore the inscription:

Centenary of Universalism

in

America

1870

This Stone Laid July 4th, 1871

By A. H. Newcomb, G. M., F. & A. M.

A. L. 5871

A cavity in the stone contained a casket filled with church publications, the *Akron Daily Beacon* and other newspapers, the Bible, a history of the College enterprise, a list of officers of the College and of the participating Masons, and samples of American coins. With the singing of "The Origin of Buchtel College," written by an Akron man, W. Milton Clarke, the placement of the stone was complete. The crowd eased forward in anticipation as the speaker, a plain, grandfatherly man, rose on the platform.

Horace Greeley, editor of the *New York Tribune,* was an ideal choice to present the principal address. He had been the center of attention since his arrival the evening before when he was greeted at the depot with "a spontaneous ovation by thousands who gathered . . . to catch a glimpse of the great philosopher."[3] He had helped educate the people of the west through his columns which were often reprinted in local newspapers. He had been a critic of Lincoln's conduct of the Civil War, and now he was a critic of the Republican organization that dominated national politics under the administration of President U. S. Grant. He was soon to challenge that administration by becoming a candidate for the presidency of the United States. Tradition has it that Akron was first in expressing support of these ambitions because of the banner suggesting "Greeley for President" that hung along the parade route and because of the lyrics of Clarke's song that had suggested:

And when a full report is made

Of this great celebration,

Remember that the Tribune's head

May head this glorious nation.

But if this thing should fail to be,

It sure would be a pity,

For the White House is his proper place

And not in New York City.[4]

Greeley's national reputation was not his only qualification as a speaker. He was a Universalist, and it was appropriate indeed that the new college should be honored by one of its own.

Before beginning his address, Greeley made some informal remarks which have been repeated in substance by many observers of the college scene down to our own day:

Allow me now to say a few words in reference to the education inculcated by our Colleges at large. It is too superficial for the age. People do not grudge

*money for education provided they know that they secure what they pay for,
yet they fear that they are not now receiving in proportion to the expenditures.*

Although there had been a great advance in the world in every department of
human endeavor, he said, "there has not been a corresponding stride in the curriculum of college studies." He hoped to see the day when the college would
"graduate a great and glorious body of young and earnest men in engineering,
science, and a hundred different pursuits, where knowledge is of great benefit to
human kind." In that time of rigid classical curricula, this was a bold position to take.
Now, a hundred years later, we take satisfaction that this worthwhile aspiration has
come to fruition.

While the young Reverend Mr. Rexford shielded him from the hot sun with
an umbrella, Greeley launched into his topic, "Human Conceptions of God as They
Affect the Moral Education of Our Race." In a strong voice that belied his 60 years
and recent illness, Greeley developed the thought that "a vivid conception of God's
active presence, and conscious, intelligent interest in human affairs, is indispensable" to the moral education and development of the human race. In the education
of the intellect man has made great strides, but there remain those who blend "the
knowledge of a Humboldt with the ethics of a Dick Turpin," and their number
"seems to be increasing." To offset this trend, education should be grounded in
religion. Greeley's peroration could serve today as a fitting guide for this university:

> *This, then, I apprehend, is the proper work of the College: to appreciate, and
> measure, and undistrustfully accept and commend, the gigantic strides which
> Physical Science is making in our day, yet be not swept away by them; . . .
> to welcome all that is true and beneficent in the impetuous currents of modern
> thought, but not exaggerate their breadth and depth, nor accept their direc-
> tion as authoritative and final; to proffer a genial and gracious hospitality to
> whatever is nobly new, yet hold fast, and from time to time assert, . . . that
> no discoveries in science, no advances in human knowledge . . . and no
> conclusion of philosophy, [can] ever equal in importance that simple affirma-
> tion of the untaught Judean peasant who long ago perceived and proclaimed
> that GOD IS LOVE!*

The speech was well-received by the crowd which then called repeatedly for
John R. Buchtel whose generosity had made the College possible. He responded in
"one of his off-hand unreportable speeches." With great feeling he thanked those
who had participated in the day's events. He pledged that the College which was
to bear his name would be an institution of honor and pride to Akron and the state.
It would be "first class" in every respect. He reassured the orthodox among the
crowd who looked askance at the Universalist brand of Christianity: "We don't
intend to pull a shingle from a single church, but will unite in suppressing evil and
building up the morals and character of the city." These remarks were greeted with
"thunderous applause." The ceremony was now complete, and the parade reformed
and made its way back to Howard Street.[5]

If the bright, balmy weather that succeeded the morning's drabness seemed
a good omen for the College, the genuine enthusiasm and concern of the crowd was
a propitious sign of the kind of support the College would need in days to come.
Many of those gathered on the College grounds were reluctant to leave. A large
number of them made their way the short distance to Mr. Buchtel's house where
they gathered outside. During the evening hours, Horace Greeley received a steady
stream of visitors who crowded around to shake his hand. Reverend E. L. Rexford
remembered the scene 50 years later:

> *Mr. Greeley sat in a large easy chair under one of the great evergreens at the
> northeast section of the lawn. It was an inspiring scene when the old farmers
> of Summit County and surrounding counties came by the hundreds to shake
> his hand, while many said, "Mr. Greeley, you educated me politically through
> the columns of the Tri-bune"—they divided the name of the paper in this way
> —and Mr. Greeley would bow and smile in his fatherly way, and sometimes
> would say, "Well, well, I hope I did not lead you wrong," or words similar.*

It was a memorable event when people of all classes came to honor him and the occasion.[6]

At 8:30, Babcock's Band came by to serenade the crowd. Toasts were proclaimed from the front steps of Mr. Buchtel's residence. Greeley himself responded to the toast, "The Centenary of Universalism in America," by directing his remarks to the mistake made by the evangelical churches in cutting the Universalists off from the main body of Christianity so that they were made to appear as a sect when they were actually a part of that great Christian body that worshipped God. "We of the Universalist faith are out of the great body of Christian churches at the present time, not because we deserve to be, but because they say we are not orthodox. Our case is similar to that of members of colored churches. Being denied admission to churches of their white brethren, they build for themselves. So we, denied admission to the churches of our orthodox brethren, build for ourselves." After explaining and lauding Universalist views, Mr. Greeley bade all to hope and trust that in the time to come acts would be done in love and faith as they were when John Murray first commenced to preach Universalism in America in 1770.

More toasts, more responses, more band music. One toast, "To Buchtel College, geographically occupying the highest eminence in the great State of Ohio," introduced a misconception that was later perpetuated in the College catalog. When this misinformation was discovered, the catalog was amended to read that Akron was a "healthy city" which fact would tell the reader, in that day of malarial fevers and ague, that it was located on high, well-drained land.[7]

Mr. Buchtel was again called by the crowd. He expanded on his earlier statements to reassure those who were not comfortable about the Universalist persuasion. When the matter of a college was first broached to him in a letter from Reverend George Messenger of Springfield, said Mr. Buchtel, he wrote in reply that he would give $25,000 for the location of such an institution in Akron, but he would have done the same for any college, under whatever auspices. He was proud to think that the institution would not graduate Methodists, or Baptists, or Universalists, but *men,* and he was willing to sacrifice his very life to the success of the College. He had no antipathy toward any church in the city. When he hired a man, he did not inquire into his religion, but into his qualifications to do the duty that he required of him. This institution was to qualify men for work, "and *women too,*" for he wanted them to be on equal terms with the men (cheers!); and one end of the College was for ladies, the other for gentlemen, and one end was exactly like the other (laughter). He believed in educating all, both black and white, of both sexes.

The day's festivities closed on this felicitous note. The special trains had departed long ago returning the tired visitors to their homes. The throng at the Buchtel residence dispersed. Next day work continued on the great College building. It would take more than a year to complete; but it had been a grand start to an enterprise that was to fulfill nearly every good wish that had speeded its beginning.

NOTES

[1] Unless indicated otherwise, details of the cornerstone-laying ceremonies were taken from *The Akron Daily Beacon,* (hereafter *Daily Beacon*), July 5, 1871. It was from this source that material was gathered for the account in Albert I. Spanton, ed., *Fifty Years of Buchtel 1870–1920* (Akron, 1922), pp. 10–15, (hereafter Spanton, *Fifty Years*).

[2] An account of Bierce's life and activity may be found in George W. Knepper, ed., *Travels in the Southland, 1822–23: The Journal of Lucius Verus Bierce* (Columbus, 1966), pp. 3–46.

[3] *Daily Beacon,* July 5, 1871.

[4] Spanton, *Fifty Years,* pp. 12, 21.

[5] *Daily Beacon,* July 5, 1871.

[6] Rexford to Spanton, circa 1920, University of Akron Archives (hereafter referred to as UArch), VF (History), printed in Spanton, *Fifty Years,* p. 14.

[7] *Buchtel College Catalogue, 1878–79,* p. 12. Campbell's Hill (elev. 1550 ft.), just east of Bellefontaine, is Ohio's highest point. The highest point in modern Akron is located at the corner of Newton and Brittain Road.

The Incorporators and Trustees of Old Buchtel College, 1872. John R. Buchtel may be seen in the driver's seat of the carriage at left.

II

Ohio Universalists build a College

The laying of the cornerstone for the College building occurred just four years after the Ohio Universalist Convention decided to build a school in Ohio. The Universalists were comparatively late in arriving at this decision, since nearly every major Christian denomination had built at least one college in the state prior to 1871. Several denominationally inspired or controlled colleges were within a few hours journey from Akron: Wooster was run by Presbyterians, Hiram by Disciples of Christ, Mount Union and Baldwin University (later Baldwin-Wallace) were under Methodist influences. And although they had no direct denominational connections, Western Reserve was close to Presbyterian influences while Oberlin was indebted to Congregationalists. If Methodists, Presbyterians, and others had taken pains to see that their children received an education in surroundings that were theologically and morally safe, the Universalists might well follow their lead. So pervasive was this denominational drive to found colleges in the Buckeye State that "by 1860, Ohio had more institutions of higher learning than the German Empire."[1]

The Universalists were not so hypersensitive to theological considerations as were most denominations. Instead of subscribing to an elaborate creed that defined beliefs in every phase of life and thought, they were content to base their commitment on the short, highly generalized Winchester Confession adopted in 1803:

Article I   *We believe that the Holy Scriptures of the Old and New Testaments contain a revelation of the character of God, and of the duty, interest and final destination of mankind.*

Article II   *We believe that there is one God, whose nature is love, revealed in one Lord Jesus Christ, by one Holy Spirit of Grace, who will finally restore the whole family of mankind to holiness and happiness.*

Article III   *We believe that holiness and happiness are inseparably connected, and that believers ought to be careful to maintain order, and practice good works; for these things are good and profitable unto men.*[2]

This uncomplicated statement gave shelter to a wide variety of beliefs, and the "liberal religion," as they were fond of calling it, permitted Universalists to exercise an unusual amount of tolerance. Their neighbors in trinitarian churches were distressed by this lack of orthodoxy. As we have noted, the reassuring remarks that John R. Buchtel and Horace Greeley made at the cornerstone-laying ceremonies attest to their recognition of this distrust. Especially unsettling to the orthodox was the Universalist teaching of ultimate salvation for all men, a doctrine that struck fear into the hearts of those who preferred to dwell upon man's sinful depravity which, for many, could be expunged only by eternal hellfire.

Whatever threat the Universalists may have posed to the orthodox on theological grounds, they posed none in the seats of temporal power. "Without representation . . . on bench and bar and boards of trade," most Universalists were persons of modest means—preeminently farmers and small tradesmen.[3] In contrast to the comfortably fixed, influential, urban-centered Unitarians with whom they shared the "liberal religion," the Universalists were rural in large part. They regarded themselves, wryly, as the "poor country cousins" or the "disreputable twin brother" of the Unitarians. Although they were not scorned by the Unitarians, other upper-class religious groups tended to look down on them and often referred to them as "atheists."[4]

The Universalists did not fight back effectively. They had no narrow theological position to defend. Rather than seeking converts from the more orthodox bodies, they sat back and afforded a religious haven for those who were disenchanted with more conservative and restrictive doctrines. Even if they had been inclined to press a counterattack against the trinitarian churches, the Universalists lacked the resources to do it successfully. Organized along congregational lines, they had no effective central authority to direct their united efforts. Such coordination as was achieved was through the state conventions and the general convention. Although these bodies spoke on matters of concern to the entire denomination, they had no police power to force local congregations to follow their lead. And although the Universalists could boast numerous periodicals and papers, none of them were widely influential outside the denomination.[5]

It follows from these conditions that Universalism grew slowly in America. In the late nineteenth century, only New England, New York, Ohio, and Illinois could boast any substantial number of communicants. Since they did not proselyte, their numbers would not increase rapidly but, immersed as they were in the mainstream of American life, sharing its values and opportunities, they were determined to offer their children good educational benefits.

Fearing that their children were being indoctrinated in schools operated by other denominations, the Universalists started to found schools in pre-Civil War days as a defensive measure. Seminaries and academies were built in New England and in New York State. A few small ventures of this kind were attempted in the west, but the only effort that flourished in Ohio, even briefly, was the Western Liberal Institute at Marietta, founded by Reverend George Weaver who was later to play a role in the history of Buchtel College through his pastorate at the Universalist church in Akron.[6]

Prior to the founding of Buchtel College, the Universalists had established three other colleges, each with a theological school attached. The first, founded in 1852, was Tufts College in Medford, Massachusetts. Medford was very near Boston, which was the closest thing the Universalists could boast to a center of denominational activity.[7] The second college was established at Canton, New York, and was named St. Lawrence in recognition of its location in the valley of that great river. In the west, Lombard College was started in Galesburg, Illinois just a few years before Buchtel College made its appearance.

The Civil War put a stop to the founding of additional Universalist schools, but shortly after the cessation of hostilities a renewed flow of organizational energy was evident among Ohio Universalists. Reverend Andrew Willson, Chairman of the Committee on Education of the Ohio Universalist Convention, was conscious of a growing feeling among the brethren favoring a school in Ohio. This sentiment came to a focus at the state meeting in June, 1867, when it was evident that some of the Ohio money which was going elsewhere might be used to better advantage closer to home. For some years the Ohio Convention had given support to Lombard College. One recent gift had been for $20,000, enough to support a modest school establishment in Ohio. Money was also going to St. Lawrence. In his report to the Convention, Andrew Willson stated that "it is every day becoming more apparent . . . that our young men and women need an institution nearer home, where they may receive instruction by those who are fully imbued with the spirit of our faith," and he recommended that the committee be instructed "to prepare a plan for the establishment of a State Seminary, and report the same at the next session of the State Convention."[8] Willson's report was received enthusiastically, and his committee set about at once to prepare a plan.

When the Convention reconvened a year later in Dayton, the plan was approved. It called for a subscription of some $50,000 from Ohio Universalists. Once the money was subscribed, a state seminary would be established in that town or city offering at least $10,000 in additional funds. The next year, at Springboro, the Ohio

Convention reaffirmed its intention of establishing a denominational school (although it no longer referred to a "State Seminary") "whenever a suitable location may be secured and requisite funds pledged."[9]

This action excused the Ohio Convention from participating in a general canvass for $200,000 ordered by the Universalist General Convention to create a permanent fund commemorating the arrival in New Jersey of John Murray who, in 1770, first preached the faith in America. It is this connection that is recognized by the inscription on the cornerstone of old Buchtel Hall: "The Centenary of Universalism in America, 1870."

Fund raising, as every college president knows, requires ingenuity, tenacity, and tireless energy. The Ohio Universalists were fortunate in securing these qualities in the Reverend Henry Miller of Dublin, Indiana, who was hired to carry out the solicitation of funds. He was to start his work on January 1, 1870; but Miller was zealous in the cause, and well before that date had already acquired a good start toward the $50,000 goal. The fund raising was completed in the spring. But the Reverend Mr. Miller was charged with another task as well; he was to work with the Committee on Education to select a location for the new school.

It proved easier to raise $50,000 than it did to select a site. Three towns had made serious bids for the school—Oxford, Kent, and Mt. Gilead. Oxford was eliminated because it already had a surfeit of schools. Kent was rejected because periodic flare-ups of fever gave it a reputation as an "unhealthy place." This left Mt. Gilead as the prime contender, and it had much to offer. It was centrally located in the state; it was situated on high ground and was reported to be a healthy place; it had a strong Universalist congregation; and its businessmen quickly subscribed the $10,000 required by the Ohio Convention. With his penchant for closing the deal, Henry Miller was about to recommend that the town's offer be accepted.

Andrew Willson was not yet willing to concede the prize to Mt. Gilead. Since Kent was his parish, Willson was understandably disappointed that it had lost out, but he thought there was a chance of securing the school for the vigorous city of Akron, just 12 miles from Kent.

This thriving young manufacturing city of some 10,000 people boasted an impressive number of highly talented and successful entrepreneurs who were philanthropically inclined. Long before the Civil War, Akron had a strong Universalist church. Its congregation was possibly as prestigious a group as the young town could then boast. Contrary to the general condition within the denomination, Akron's congregation had its share of powerful and influential members. However, internal dissension had split the membership. Its property was sold which left the Universalists in Akron without a church.

Among those with Universalist sympathies was John R. Buchtel, President of the Buckeye Mower and Reaper Works and a public-spirited citizen. He was known to Willson; at least the records of Willson's Kent congregation show that Mr. and Mrs. Buchtel were affiliated with the church for several months early in 1870.[10] Late in 1869, Mr. Buchtel had been approached by persons interested in securing the school for Akron. While he expressed sympathy for the project, he made it clear that he intended to give his money to the development of a free public library for Akron. The matter appeared to be closed, but quite unconsciously a new momentum was building.

The Universalists of Akron, though lacking a congregational organization, met frequently for services. Often they were addressed by a visiting minister. On Sunday, January 9, 1870, Reverend Henry L. Canfield spoke to the Universalists gathered in Empire Hall. The weather was bitterly cold, and Canfield was grateful for an invitation to share the hospitality of Mr. Avery Spicer, a life-long adherent of the "liberal religion." That evening Spicer's two daughters, their husbands, and Mr. Sanford M. Burnham, the Summit County Auditor, stopped by for a visit. The entire company was interested in the Ohio Convention's work toward establishing a school, and since Canfield was close to this work, he was in a position to inform his host of the progress being made.

During the discussion a conviction developed within the group that Akron was

JOHN RICHARDS BUCHTEL

the proper location. They felt that the ideal site for the school would be on the grounds of the old Spicer Hill Cemetery, soon to be abandoned. It was located on high ground, with a commanding view to the west. Beyond, in a shallow valley, Akron lay stretched in a narrow north-south band along the Ohio Canal.

In addition to having confidence in the Spicer Hill site, the group was certain that John R. Buchtel was the proper person to provide the financial support required to secure the school for Akron. Nothing in surviving accounts indicates whether or not anyone in the group knew of any previous attempt to interest Mr. Buchtel, but it seems likely that Mr. Canfield did for he was aware of the fact that Akron had been considered as a location. In any event, they talked themselves into a state of considerable enthusiasm about Akron's prospects. As Canfield described it, "we built a 'Castle in the air' and called it a Universalist Academy."[11]

The next morning, while still enthused, Canfield wrote to the Reverend Henry Miller, "Don't decide upon a location for the school till you have been to Akron again, for I am strongly of the opinion that there is something worth looking after."[12] In his reply, Miller said that he had already called a meeting of the Committee on Education at Columbus, and he thought Mt. Gilead would probably be chosen at that time. However, if Akron people had a proposition to make, let them write or send a delegation to the meeting. Apparently Akron sent a delegation, and their presentation was effective enough to delay a decision until Miller and the Committee on Education could visit Akron.

Meanwhile, Miller had learned of the strong friendship between John Buchtel and the Reverend George Messenger, a retired Universalist minister from Springfield. Miller persuaded Messenger to write to Mr. Buchtel on behalf of the school project. Buchtel later claimed that Messenger's letter was responsible for turning the course of his thinking. He became enthusiastic about the project and changed his financial arrangements to benefit the proposed school. During this transition the committee visited Akron and went away pleased with what they saw and heard.

From the beginning, the Ohio Convention assumed that the school they were planning was to be an academy or a seminary. But Akron already had a fine central high school, the capstone of a system of public education which, upon its inception in the "Akron School Law" of 1847, had established a pattern later adopted throughout the state and much of the nation. Mr. Buchtel and his associates could see no need for an academy that would largely duplicate the work of the high school, and they apparently had little interest in a seminary. "Give us a college," they said to the Reverend Mr. Miller to which he replied, "A College it shall be, but you must pay for it accordingly. If you desire a college in the city of Akron, Summit County must give $60,000."[13]

Miller's bargain was hard but realistic. The spirit of Akron was up to the challenge. Buchtel led the way with a pledge of $25,000 toward the endowment fund and $6,000 toward the building fund. It took the combined efforts of 100 individual and 13 business contributors to match his gift, but all told a total of $62,000 was subscribed for the college.

This subscription settled the question of location. On May 31, 1870, the Trustees of the Ohio Universalist Convention and the Committee on Education met at the Summit County Courthouse in Akron where, by resolution, they constituted themselves "Corporators" of the "Universalist Centenary School of Ohio." After authorizing ten other persons to act with them as corporators, the enlarged body voted unanimously to locate the college in Akron. Nine of the corporators were clergymen and eight were laymen. Of the latter, six were Akronites identified as "resident freeholders of Summit County."

The corporators then took the legal steps required to establish the college as a functioning unit. They selected a name—"Universalist Centenary School of Ohio" having been simply a working title used to inaugurate the enterprise—they adopted articles of association and a seal; they elected a Board of Trustees into whose hands they delivered all property including the $62,000 in subscriptions and 2.6 acres of real estate constituting the Spicer Hill Cemetery plus some modest accretions of land adjacent to it between Carroll and Middlebury Street (now Buchtel Avenue). They then adjourned after instructing the Board of Trustees to meet the next day, June 1, to elect officers and adopt by-laws.[14]

A spirit of optimism and cooperation had moved these men as they transacted their business, but they did have a significant difference of opinion on one important item—the naming of the college. Some thought that since the money Ohio raised for the college was to be considered the state's effort to honor the centenary of Universalism in America, the school should be named "Murray College" or "Murray Centennial College" to preserve the name of the denomination's founder in America. From the first, some favored "Buchtel College," but others expressed the fear that this name would be corrupted by detractors into "Bucktail College." A compromise, "Buchtel Universalist College," pleased no one.

The resolution of this problem was described years later by Reverend Henry Canfield who was present at the meeting as a corporator and trustee:

> *Finally, it was decided to ask Mr. Buchtel if he had any wish or choice in the matter of a name for the college. He was called in, and the question was put in plain words, "Mr. Buchtel, have you anything to suggest, or any wish to express, with regard to the name the college shall bear?" "Gentlemen," said he, "this is to be your college, not mine. I mean to help it financially as I may be able. If I live and am prospered I intend to give the college someday one hundred thousand dollars. You may call the college what you please." It was moved at once [by Henry Blandy] and voted unanimously that the institution be known as "Buchtel College."*

If Canfield had stopped at this point, most readers would probably jump to what seems an obvious conclusion. But it is a mistake, either literally or historically, to hang a man on circumstantial evidence as Mr. Canfield makes clear:

> *If anyone reading these lines is moved to say or think that John R. Buchtel bought the name of the college for himself, let me say that such person has no just conception of the spirit of the occasion. If we had felt that he had made a bid for the name, it would have been given reluctantly, if at all.*[15]

Mr. Buchtel, said Canfield, was a "great-hearted man" who, though he enjoyed the esteem and good opinion of others, was "not in the market to purchase applause." Denied the privileges of any but the most rudimentary education, he took pleasure in helping others acquire what he had been denied.

The work of the corporators was approved enthusiastically by the Ohio General Convention held in June, 1870, in Kent. Resolutions honoring the accomplishment passed unanimously. One of the resolutions gave a vote of confidence to the founders and to Mr. Buchtel by gratefully recognizing "the wisdom that gives the Institution his name."[16]

The trustees who gathered on June 1 to organize and transact the College's business included many of the men who had acted as corporators. Of the 18 trustees, 7 were Akron men, and within six months an eighth would be added to their number. Thus, from the beginning a most significant percentage of the trustees were local men. Since the officers of the Board were most often Akronites, and since it was easier for the College authorities to seek decisions from trustees who were at hand rather than scattered throughout the state and beyond, and since Akron money weighed heavily in the financing of the enterprise, it is safe to say that Akron men, laymen all, tended from the first to wield a disproportionate weight in the management of the College's affairs. Thus early were sown seeds which, when come to fruition, would produce a college organized around local rather than denominational interests. Indeed, if there is one theme of central importance that runs throughout the institution's lifetime, it is the fact that the College and its sheltering community were of use to each other, depended on each other. The school responded to local pressures and desires even while a private denominational college. Once it reached the status of municipal university, the interaction was direct, self-conscious, and nearly all-embracing as one might expect. The surprising thing is that this pattern was set from the school's earliest years.

Akron was a remarkably vital city during most of the late nineteenth century. It was blessed with an extraordinary concentration of enlightened entrepreneurs whose organizational and financial talents enabled them to build an astonishing variety of business and industrial enterprises, some of which became the largest of their kind in the world. These men were an interesting lot: among them were many who had contributed to the original college subscription.

There was, for example, Lewis Miller, inventor of farm machinery, associate of John R. Buchtel in the Buckeye works, founder of Chautauqua, trustee and staunch supporter of several Methodist colleges, churchman, and father-in-law of Thomas A. Edison. Ferdinand Schumacher, the "Oatmeal King," was another. A German immigrant who built a milling empire, he was an avid worker for temperance and lost a great deal of money in support of a utopian scheme to found a temperance town in Harriman, Tennessee, but this did not deter him from life-long support of "cold-water" societies. He served the College for a quarter century as trustee.

Another of Akron's strong men was Ohio Columbus Barber, king of the match industry and organizer of the Diamond Match combine. When he became annoyed at the attempt of the city fathers to impose a modest tax on his business property, he left Akron and founded a new town adjacent to it on the southwest. Developed by professional planners, Barberton was unique in that it enjoyed instant prosperity, but its place in the sun was short-lived. Barber contributed modest sums to the College from his vast personal fortune. Many others achieved industrial leadership; men like the Merrills, Hills, and Robinsons in clay products, tile, and sewer pipe; the Werners and Saalfields in publishing; Pflueger in fishing tackle; John Seiberling in farm machinery and various other enterprises; and a young M.D. who came to town in 1870 to start a rubber factory, Dr. Benjamin Franklin Goodrich.

At the time these men were riding high, Akron was a rapidly growing city. The majority of its citizens in 1870 had origins in Connecticut of whose "Western Reserve" Akron was a part, in the other New England states, in New York, Pennsylvania, and downstate Ohio. These substantial folk drove out the drifters and "blacklegs" who were much in evidence when Akron was just a small canal town. To their enterprise were added the skills of a large German element that started to arrive in the 1830's and 40's. These hard-working and disciplined people added much to the business life of the community, but of equal importance were their characteristic cultural contributions, such as singing groups, gymnastic clubs, newspapers, and bands. A substantial sprinkling of Irish and immigrants from the British Isles rounded out the population. The great influx of persons from the rural south and the somewhat smaller influx from southern and eastern Europe had not yet arrived. When they did, it would change the economic and political tone of Akron with consequences that we shall examine later. This, then, was the fertile ground on which the College was planted, full of promise but in need of careful cultivation.

When the Board of Trustees set about electing officers, it must have been evident to all that John R. Buchtel was "a natural" for the presidency. It is customary for colleges to eulogize their founders and chief contributors, and some probably have to stretch the truth a good deal in order to make a case for their man, but John R. Buchtel can stand on his record. The men who elected him as their leader knew what they were doing. To them he was not just the principal contributor of funds; he was a rational, experienced businessman who always made time for supporting his city through involvement in its many activities. His philanthropy was well known although he made no show of it. In today's language, John Buchtel was a "responsible" citizen blessed with that rarest of qualities, temperate good sense. His contributions to the little College named in his honor were so varied and so vital that one can say without exaggeration that he assured its very existence from its founding until his death in 1892.

John Buchtel's story is clearly within the "rags to riches" tradition that we like to think of as typically American. Born January 18, 1820, on a small farm in Green Township, then in Stark, but now in Summit County, he was raised on hard work.[17] He was of medium height, broad across the shoulders, physically powerful and tough but of a peaceful disposition. In later years he wore a beard, the kind known as "chinwhiskers." His full head of hair stayed with him to the end of his life. He was forceful and somewhat blunt in manner and speech, but this bluntness was tempered by a cheerful outlook. To an unusual degree he had the ability to get the job done, whatever it was, and to enlist others in his support. He was a natural leader who stood at the head of his men and outworked them while maintaining the cheerful good spirits that made his company attractive. Early in life he demonstrated a kind of perseverance that would be called stubbornness had it been less constructive, and there were numerous times when every bit of that perseverance was required to keep the College alive.

In a society that still placed more value on what a man could do than on his formal educational credentials, John Buchtel was not unduly handicapped, but he deeply regretted his lack of formal education. It has been said that he could scarcely write his own name at age 21. This may be an exaggeration, but his spelling and grammar in his few surviving letters leave no doubt as to certain fundamental educational deficiencies. Like so many self-made men of his time, his lack of learning seemed to fill him with determination to see that others had the chance to secure the education he had missed.

As a young man, John was given 100 acres of farmland by his father on condition that he pay off a $700 encumbrance on the property. This he successfully did, and with his stake in life secured he married Miss Elizabeth Davidson, whose family had come to the Akron area from Pennsylvania some years earlier. The Buchtels had no children.

John sold his farm in order to purchase 210 acres later known as the Thornton farm, a tract that covered an area south of Exchange Street in the vicinity of modern Thornton Street. There his use of advanced agricultural techniques produced crops superior to those of his skeptical neighbors. Selling out at a profit, he next bought 1,000 acres from Colonel Perkins on what is now the near west side of Akron and once again proved the skeptics wrong by farming and lumbering it profitably.

It appears that he was about to move again, this time to a large farm he had purchased in LaPorte County, Indiana, when he was offered a job as salesman for Ball, Aultman Company of Canton, manufacturers of the Ohio mower and reaper. In 1864 he helped persuade that company to open an independent branch operation in Akron where the "Buckeye," an improved machine invented by Lewis Miller, would be manufactured. He supervised construction of the plant and took charge as its president. In large part through his influence, Akron became one of the world's foremost producers of farm machinery, a position it was to hold until the International Harvester consolidation absorbed what was left of this industry which had largely moved west to be nearer the market. Buchtel helped to develop a number of industries that served the farm machinery industry: an iron company, rolling mill, knife works, twine factory and chain works. Concurrently he helped form a bank which was to be important in financing Akron's industrial growth.

John Buchtel's most spectacular business venture was the purchase and development of 2,000 acres of mineral lands in southern Ohio for the Akron Iron Company, in which he had an interest. In 1876–77 he personally directed the development of the coal and iron ore resources in the Hocking Valley and the erection there of what was, for a few years, the largest blast furnace in Ohio. He also supervised the building of a company town to house the immigrant labor brought in from southern and eastern Europe, and with his usual thoughtfulness he donated land for a Catholic church, an opera house, and a cemetery. It was an unusually habitable and well-ordered company town, and in recognition for his role in making it so, the inhabitants named their town Buchtel. Though it has been transformed through the years, Buchtel, Ohio is still on the map. In 1887, while working strenuously in the Hocking Valley, John Buchtel suffered a stroke which paralyzed his lower body. He spent the last five years of his life in a wheel chair.

As he prospered in business, John Buchtel spent an increasing amount of time serving in various public capacities. For many years he was a trustee of Portage Township which at that time embraced most of Akron. He was a leading spirit in the Akron Library Association and helped convert its resources into a free public library in 1877. He served many years as Treasurer of the Summit County Agricultural Society. He was Moderator of the newly re-formed Universalist congregation. And through it all he made generous donations to virtually every church and worthy cause in Akron and beyond.

Mr. Buchtel joined the Republican party in its formative years. He was a strong supporter of the Union and its war effort, raising money tirelessly to pay bounties for volunteers, in this fashion warding off the necessity of imposing the unpopular draft laws in Akron. He did not serve in the army, not even as a "hundred day" man in 1864 when many of his Akron associates were rushing to the defense of Washington. Rather he paid a substitute, one W. S. St. John, a fifer, who served in his stead.

After the war, Buchtel served as a presidential elector and dutifully cast his ballot in 1872 for U. S. Grant. If this distressed Horace Greeley, who was also running for president, Buchtel made up for it somewhat by abandoning the Republican party temporarily to run for the state office of Secretary of State on the Prohibitionist ticket. Some scoffers and doubters questioned his zeal in the prohibitionist cause since it was rumored that he kept wine on his table and let slip an occasional oath. Just what such mild profanity had to do with prohibition is not clear. At any rate, he lost the election and never again tried for elective office.

Improbable though it was, Buchtel's greatest contribution was made in the role of college builder. His central part in the development of Buchtel College will unfold in succeeding pages, but it should be noted that concurrently with its founding and establishment, John Buchtel was playing an important role in the building of Ohio's land grant college established by the state legislature under an act of March 22, 1870. He was appointed by Governor Hayes to serve on the Board of Trustees of this newly established Ohio Agricultural and Mechanical College. In making the appointment, the Governor asked his advice on the convening date for the first board meeting. In typical fashion Buchtel urged convening the group at the first opportunity "to give . . . all the time possible to make a judicious location of the college. . . ."[18] Hayes followed this advice and called the trustees together early in the summer at which time they elected Buchtel to the three-man Executive Committee, in whose hands rested the responsibility for launching the project. He remained on the Executive Committee until his retirement from the board in 1874. Commenting on this election, the *Akron Daily Beacon* wrote: "of the executive ability of the Board, as a whole, we have no knowledge . . . but if they possess but a tithe of the energy and business sagacity and activity that the people of this city and county know Mr. Buchtel to possess, the people of the State may be . . . well assured that the work will be pursued to a speedy and successful conclusion."[19]

Buchtel was certainly a plausible choice to serve as trustee of the agricultural and mechanical school. As an experienced farmer, mechanic, and businessman, he presumably knew some of the elements involved in training men for these pursuits even though he learned his lessons by doing rather than by reading. The world of politics being what it is, it is probable that his Republican activities appealed to the Governor, and his prohibition sympathies would please the Governor's wife, the gracious "Lemonade Lucy" soon to earn national attention for her refusal to serve alcoholic beverages in the White House.

In his Columbus work, John Buchtel drew upon his concurrent experience in starting a college in Akron. He was instrumental in selecting the Neil farm north of Columbus as the site for the A & M school. A spring of sweet water attracted him to that site, and years later when he was confined to a wheelchair as an invalid, he returned to the campus for a visit and asked to be carried down to the spring where he drank with pleasure from its waters. It was upon his recommendation that an Akron architect, Jacob Snyder, was chosen to design the first building. And strange as it may seem for an unlettered man who had been both farmer and mechanic, he led the fight in the Board to make the curriculum broad and inclusive rather than restricting it to the agricultural and mechanical fields which were, of course, the chief mission of the land grant A & M schools. That he and his associates built well is evident in the history of accomplishment of that little school now grown to giant size as The Ohio State University.

He had his hand in one final college venture. Possibly through his land holdings in LaPorte County, Indiana, Buchtel was acquainted with John Purdue who was soon to play an important part in establishing the school that bears his name. Buchtel contributed $1,000 and encouragement (and possibly advice) to the cause.[20] In turn, John Purdue supported a $1,000 scholarship at Buchtel College for many years. It is remarkable indeed how much of permanent importance resulted from George Messenger's letter asking his friend John Buchtel to consider aiding a Universalist school seeking to be born.

The other officers of the Buchtel College Board of Trustees were able and influential men. Sanford Burnham, who played an important part in securing the College for Akron, was recognized for his business capabilities through election to the position of Secretary. To find a Treasurer, the Board went outside its own body to select one of the key business figures in Akron, George W. Crouse. Having served in several public offices including County Auditor, Treasurer, President of City Council, State Senator, and United States Congressman, Crouse was well known and highly regarded in Republican party circles. He was a good friend and political associate of William McKinley and the party strategists behind him, men like Mark Hanna, and his successor, Charles Dick of Akron. He had an outstanding business career. At the time of his election as Treasurer of the College he was Secretary of the Buckeye Company where John Buchtel was boss. Later Crouse would take over the presidency of the works. He was heavily involved in many industrial enterprises and financial institutions. If he had a fault in the business sense, it was that he trusted men who proved unworthy of that trust with the result that late in his life he faced the humiliation of bankruptcy action.[21]

Crouse's greatest service to Akron business was performed somewhat unwittingly. Through his efforts a broadside announcing Akron's advantages as an industrial location was printed and distributed. One of these circulars, so it is said, chanced to fall into the hands of Dr. B. F. Goodrich who then determined to look up Mr. Crouse to see if financing could be arranged in support of a small factory for the manufacture of rubber products. Crouse put him in touch with the right people. Both he and Mr. Buchtel put $1,000 into the capital fund of $13,400 required to open the plant, and Akron's premier industry was here to stay, although its shaky beginnings made that fact anything but obvious at the time. Crouse later served as a trustee of Buchtel College for 25 years, ten of them as President of the Board.

Of the other local members of this first Board, Colonel George Tod Perkins, grandson of Akron's founder, made his money in real estate, banking, and the rubber industry where he served as President of the B. F. Goodrich Company. Much admired for his brilliant Civil War record, he was a regular contributor to the College. Mr. Edwin P. Green was a lawyer, public officeholder in Akron, booster of the public school system which he served as an examiner, organizer of the Akron Public Library, and Judge of the Court of Common Pleas. Mr. John F. Seiberling was another of that remarkable breed of practical men of affairs. As a young man he had invented the "Excelsior" mower and reaper with a "dropper" attachment, and then set up manufacturing facilities to produce the machine, finally locating in Akron in 1865. Four years later he withdrew from his Akron company and started small scale production of the "Empire," a wholly new machine which he had designed. Finally he consolidated his former company under new control and financing and started producing the "Empire" on a large scale, thus becoming Mr. Buchtel's chief business competitor in Akron. He was deeply involved in many other local enterprises, and his talented sons were later to start the Goodyear Tire and Rubber Company which rose to primacy in the industry. Seiberling's $5,000 gift was second only to Buchtel's in securing the subscription for the College.

Still another influential Akronite on the Board was Newell D. Tibbals, Judge of the Court of Common Pleas from 1875 to 1883. His 39 years as trustee made him second only to the Reverend Andrew Willson who served 40 years. Another of the original trustees was Avery Spicer whose role in establishing the College has been mentioned.

Finally, Alvin C. Voris should be identified with the Akron men on the first Board even though he joined the group six months late as a replacement for a deceased member. This former Major General had the distinction of being one of the few Union soldiers ever to see Stonewall Jackson in retreat. As a judge and lawyer, Voris was one of Akron's influential citizens who performed a useful service in his quarter century on the Board.

As one would suspect, these men were strong trustees, confident in their judgment and not inclined to seek much direction from the Ohio Convention to whom they were responsible for conducting the College's affairs. The Convention's interests were very much on the mind of the clergy who sat on the Board, however. Each of them was well versed in the spirit and history of the venture and whole-hearted in support of it.

The weakest link in the Board membership consisted of those laymen who were not Akronites. This is not to say, or imply, that they were any less talented or qualified, but in the course of business it was natural for the College authorities to deal with those men whose Akron residence made them easy of access. In the 1870's it was difficult to communicate quickly with persons some miles away. As would be true of later presidents of the College, those who early headed the school found comfort and support close at hand. Conversely, the non-Akron trustees must have felt somewhat left out of things even though their opinions were solicited through letters. A chart helps show graphically how much the continuity of operation resided in the hands of local men.

ORIGINAL APPOINTEES: YEARS OF SERVICE ON THE BOARD OF TRUSTEES

Akron Laymen		Universalist Ministers		Non-Akron Laymen	
John R. Buchtel	22	Henry Canfield	23	Dorsey Anger	3
Sanford Burnham	15	John Cantwell	11	Henry Blandy	3
E. P. Green	25	George Messenger	2	John Cochrane	1
George T. Perkins	27	E. L. Rexford	8	Charles Foster	½
John Seiberling	2	Andrew Willson	40	Oscar Haymaker	2
Avery Spicer	11	(replacing G. Messenger,		James Pierce	5
Newell Tibbals	39	deceased)		Philip Wieland	7
Alvin Voris	25				
(replacing C. Foster,					
deceased)					
166 years		**84 years**		**21½ years**	

Once organized, the Board adopted by-laws which provided for the annual election of officers, provided for one, two, or three-year terms, established a self-perpetuating clause, required a written annual report to the Ohio Universalist Convention accounting for its actions throughout the year, and provided for amendment to the by-laws by a two-thirds vote of the members present. With these fundamentals taken care of, the Board could now turn its attention to the manifold problems of putting up a building, recruiting a faculty, hiring a president, and publicizing the new institution so that students would be attracted to it.

While the trustees were organizing for business, the initial steps were being taken to establish the College building on its site. We may be accustomed to think of building frustrations as peculiarly a product of our own age, but in every construction project on the campus, starting with the first, it has been necessary to overcome problems and unforeseen circumstances. None of these obstacles, however, has been as exotic as that which confronted the first Buchtel College Board.

As we have noted, the College was to be located on the old Spicer Hill Cemetery. From the beginning of burials on this plot (about 1813), there had been complaints about its inadequacy. The plot had probably been selected in the first place because it was on higher ground than surrounding property and thus would presumably drain well. However, the soil tended to hold water which percolated through the loose soil covering new graves and collected in the graves themselves, and there it stayed. The thought that the recently departed might be lying in a pool of water was distressing to contemplate, but burials continued nevertheless as long as there was no suitable alternative.

Shortly after the Civil War the Akron Rural Cemetery (popularly known as Glendale) underwent extensive development—indeed it was made into a garden spot with a brook, two duck ponds, ornate bridges, quiet paths—and it apparently had the additional advantage of being well-drained. As early as March, 1870, therefore, bodies were being exhumed from Spicer Cemetery for transfer to Akron Rural.[23] Old Miner Spicer himself was disinterred, and when a slide on his coffin was pushed back, there was the Major, as well preserved as when put into the grave 15 years earlier, a condition that brought comfort to his family.[24]

Miner Spicer and his wife, Hannah, had given title to the cemetery plot to the Spicer Cemetery Association in November, 1851.[25] On September 14, 1870, "all lands belonging to the Spicer Hill Burying Place, formerly known as the Spicer Cemetary [sic] Association. . . ." were conveyed by quit-claim deed to Buchtel College for a consideration of one dollar, thus voiding the original deed from Miner Spicer and his wife, this deed stating that the land was "to be used for a Burying ground and for no other use or uses whatsoever."[26]

Removal of the bodies proceeded slowly until February, 1871, when the *Daily Beacon* reported: "The removal of human remains from Spicer Hill Cemetery, in order to prepare that ground for the erection of Buchtel College, promises to go on rapidly now that the city council has passed the ordinance by which the unclaimed dead bodies can be removed. . . . The committee appointed by the council . . . will have all it can do to remove such dead bodies as are unclaimed. They intend purchasing a lot in Glendale and place all such in it."[27] By March 8, all the bodies except two were removed. Grading for the College building was to commence soon.[28]

One wonders how thoroughly the job of vacating the graves was performed. Frank Payne, Class of '84, recalled years later "that gruesome day when . . . mother and I, went to the graveyard on Spicer Hill to see them dig up the relics of our dead for removal to Glendale Cemetery." He goes on to say: "I remember the early years of the college, before the trees were planted and when every rainfall gouged out deep runnels in the clayey soil and disclosed full many a human bone."[29] Vincent Tomlinson's most vivid memory of his first year at Buchtel (1872) was the "exhuming of graves" on campus.[30] In all, at least 64 bodies were transferred.[31] The ground was cleared to the satisfaction of the Board, and on March 15, 1871, ground was broken for the College building.

Meanwhile, the trustees had discussed the proposed College building and had requested various architects to submit plans. Those submitted by Mr. Thomas W. Silloway of Boston were selected, a fact that gratified the *Boston Advertiser* which noted that "eastern experience and talent" had been chosen.[32] At a meeting in December, 1870, Mr. Silloway explained his plans to the trustees following which they all went out to the College grounds and "determined the exact location of the proposed new building."[33] Construction was entrusted to Noah Carter of Akron.

Work progressed rapidly. No records remain to tell us what the building cost, but it has been estimated that a building fund of some thirty to forty thousand dollars was raised for this purpose.[34] However, it was soon apparent that this would not be sufficient, principally because the fund had been raised at a time when the planners assumed that the College building would be of modest proportions. Mr. Silloway's plans called for a far more elaborate and extensive building which so captured the trustees' enthusiasm that they resolved to seek an additional $30,000 to complete the building in its extended form. They approved a scheme whereby Universalist churches through their women's societies, Sunday School classes, and other organizations might furnish rooms in the building at an estimated cost of $50 each.[35] However, the cost must have been much greater than these figures would suggest. It is known that Reverend Henry Miller, the fund raiser, was campaigning vigorously for funds until his resignation in April, 1872, after which time the work was carried on by Reverend D. C. Tomlinson. In all, it is estimated that between $160,000 and $200,000 was spent on the building and its furnishings.[36]

In the long run this excessive cost was to prove harmful since Universalists who gave generously to the building were not so easily persuaded to give again to the support of the College, even when its need became desperate. Judging by his conduct to date, and having some awareness of how he was to meet every other financial need of the College, it is probable that John R. Buchtel was principally responsible for urging this extension of plans. It is known that he was in the thick of this project, for on the same day that the cornerstone was laid, the Board adopted a resolution thanking him for "the ability he had exercised in pursuing the building of the college."[37]

By September, 1872, the great building was complete except for some interior finishing work. It loomed over Akron and dominated it in a manner unmatched by any other building before or since. This massive structure—240 feet long, 54 feet wide, and five stories high—was symmetrical in design, its center section crowned by a blunt tower and flanked on each side by narrow towers through which entrances led into the building.[38] Identical wings extended to the east and west of the center section. Architecturally it was described as a combination of Doric, Gothic, and Norman. This marriage of disparate styles evidently pleased the Victorian eye for its "beauty" was often noted by students and visitors alike. The current generation would not find much to admire in it.

The largest amount of space was assigned to student rooms. Although changes were constantly being made in the internal arrangements, the building could house 150 students in reasonable comfort. The east end (East Hall) contained rooms for young men and the west end (West Hall) contained rooms for young ladies. These accommodations were described as "light, airy, and ample, furnished with . . . modern and most improved conveniences."[39] Rooms for lectures, recitations, music, "apparatus," library, and other instructional modes were located on the two lowest floors as were the College offices. A dining room, kitchen, gymnasium, storage, and utility rooms were located in the basement. A large chapel which could seat several hundred was situated on the fourth floor in the center of the building. From the beginning of occupancy there were frequent changes in room arrangement as old functions gave way to new.

The building was blessed with a fine supply of cold, pure well water. It was heated by steam, a relatively safe and clean method. Gas lights provided illumination, and it is a miracle of sorts that the building was spared a disastrous fire as long as it was since this gas was generated in the building under conditions that left much to be desired from a safety standpoint. In later years gas was supplied by a local company.

Since the grounds around the building had not been landscaped when the first arrivals appeared for class, the huge building looked stark and forbidding. Within a few years, however, its outlines mellowed as trees, lawns, and walks gave form to its surroundings. Throughout its 27 years it remained by far the most impressive structure that most of its occupants had ever seen.

NOTES

[1] Merle Curti and Roderick Nash, *Philanthropy in the Shaping of American Higher Education* (New Brunswick, 1965), p. 43.

[2] [George S. Weaver], *Autobiography of George Sumner Weaver, D.D.: A Sketch of a Busy Life* (Schenectady, 1965), p. 111.

[3] Ernest S. Bates, *American Faith; Its Religious, Political, and Economic Foundations* (New York, 1946), p. 403.

[4] *Ibid.*

[5] L. B. Fisher, *A Brief History of the Universalist Church for Young People,* 4th ed., rev. (n.p., [1913?]), has information regarding various publications.

[6] Weaver reported "much dissatisfaction among my people [in Marietta] with the Presbyterian teachers in the academy and college on account of their disposition to proselyte among the Universalist students." Weaver's advice to his people: "Then have a school of your own." It took $6,000 to put up a building and start the academy. (Weaver, *Autobiography,* p. 39).

[7] Russell E. Miller, *Light on the Hill: A History of Tufts College 1852–1952* (Boston, 1966) tells of the founding of Tufts against the general background of the Universalist position regarding education.

[8] Spanton, *Fifty Years,* pp. 1–2.

[9] *Ibid.,* p. 2.

[10] Charles R. Walker, ed., *One Hundred Years of Liberal Religion in Kent, Ohio: 1866–1966, First Universalist Church* (n.p., [1967?]).

[11] Spanton, *Fifty Years,* p. 5. Spanton has told the story of the College's founding in considerable detail, much of which he secured from letters addressed to him by participants in the endeavor and from newspaper clippings. Most of this material is now in The University of Akron Archives, VF (History).

[12] Spanton, *Fifty Years,* p. 5.

[13] *Ibid.*

[14] *Ibid.,* p. 7.

[15] *Ibid.,* pp. 8–9.

[16] *Ibid.,* p. 9.

[17] In the early 1920's there was considerable debate about the year of John R. Buchtel's birth. Apparently there were plans to celebrate the one hundredth anniversary of his birth in 1920, but then the investigations of a professional tracing firm found evidence (which, unfortunately is not revealed in the records) that he was born January 18, 1822, so Founder's Day, 1922, was set aside to commemorate his centennial year. If 1820 was not his birth year, it is strange that Buchtel made no effort to have it corrected in his lifetime, for there were public references made to 1820 as the birth year at a time when he could have protested were it in error. His tombstone in Glendale Cemetery carries 1820 as his birth date. Additional biographical data can be found in Spanton, *Fifty Years,* pp. 24–38.

[18] Buchtel to Hays *[sic],* April 25, 1870, Rutherford B. Hayes Memorial Library MSS Collection (Fremont, Ohio).

[19] *Akron Daily Beacon,* Jan. 9, 1871. For Buchtel's work on the board of the land-grant college see *First Annual Report of the Board of Trustees of the Ohio Agricultural and Mechanical College. . . .* (Churches, 1872), p. 3 *et seq.*

[20] Buchtel's connection with Purdue was related in the Purdue University *Handbook,* ca. 1956. Efforts to trace the connection more fully have been unsuccessful.

[21] "Proceedings of the Crouse examination, 1903," are in UArch. Biographical sketches of prominent Akronites of the nineteenth century can be found in Samuel A. Lane, *Fifty Years and Over of Akron and Summit County* (Akron, 1892), hereafter referred to as Lane, *Akron.*

[22] Spanton, *Fifty Years,* pp. 298–9.

[23] UArch., box 37/3/117.

[24] Lane, *Akron,* p. 233.

[25] UArch., box 37/3/117.

[26] Quit-claim deed, September 14, 1870, *ibid.*

[27] *Akron Daily Beacon.* Feb. 21, 1871.

[28] *Ibid.,* Mar. 8, 1871.

[29] *Alumni Quarterly,* II, no. 3.

[30] *Ibid.,* V, no. 2.

[31] UArch., box 37/3/117.

[32] Board Mins., I, 9–10; *Boston Advertiser* reprinted in *Akron Daily Beacon,* Feb. 2, 1871.

[33] Board Mins., I, 9–10.

[34] Spanton, *Fifty Years,* p. 221.

[35] Board Mins., I, 12–13.

[36] Spanton, *Fifty Years,* pp. 15–16.

[37] Board Mins., I, 11.

[38] A description of the building can be found in the *Buchtel College Catalogue* (1872).

[39] *Ibid.* The interior arrangements of old Buchtel Hall at various times in its existence have been studied in meticulous detail by Professor Theodore Duke who has in his possession a typescript of his work, including floor plans.

PRESIDENT SULLIVAN McCOLLESTER (1872–78)

III

The first decade (1870–1880)

The selection of a president is a critical task for a college at any time, but special significance attaches to the choice of the first man to serve in that role. As the trail blazer, he is in a position to set precedent and define the nature of his office. One would think, therefore, that finding the first president of Buchtel College would be a long and arduous task. This was not the case, primarily because the church-related schools of a century ago tended to believe that any competent clergyman within the ranks of the sponsoring denomination was likely to have most of the qualities required for the job.

The position appeared to be well defined. A president was to preside over the faculty. The faculty, in turn, was charged with determining the curriculum, standards, and discipline of the institution. The president served as a court of appeals from faculty disciplinary decisions, raised money, and publicized the school by preaching and speaking in churches, conventions, and denominational meetings. He was assisted in fund raising by a financial secretary and by the trustees. He was also expected to teach, usually mental and moral philosophy or something of ethical import. He presided at daily chapel exercises, commencements, and special events, and he was also expected to preach Sunday sermons, at least occasionally. It was important that he be cultured, well read and travelled, and that he command respect if not affection.

In nearly every way, the man secured for the presidency measured up quite well to these expectations even though he was the trustees' second choice. In January, 1872, the Committee on Officers and Teachers learned that Reverend Doctor Thayer, one of the best known Universalist ministers in the east, had declined the position. It then commissioned Mr. Henry Blandy, who was going east on business, to be a committee of one to visit New England and procure a suitable man for the presidency.[1] Blandy conferred with leaders of the denomination and decided to recommend Reverend Sullivan McCollester, pastor of the Universalist church in Nashua, New Hampshire, and a man experienced in educational matters.

McCollester was invited to Akron where he was interviewed by the committee to "the eminent satisfaction of all present." At its March meeting the Board adopted unanimously a committee recommendation that McCollester be appointed President of Buchtel College.[2] He was notified of his appointment and invited to take a seat with the Board. "After some talk and promises on the part of the Board that they would stand by him in his endeavors to make Buchtel College a first-class institution of learning," McCollester accepted the position.[3]

It appeared the Board had chosen well. Sullivan McCollester was born in Marlboro, New Hampshire in 1826. He was a graduate of Norwich University and the Harvard Divinity School. He had served as principal of four different academies and seminaries in New England. For three years he had been Commissioner of Education for the state of New Hampshire. He contributed regularly to Universalist publications, many of his articles describing his extensive travels.[4] He was married and had a young son, Lee, who later was to have a distinguished career as a Universalist minister and as Dean of Crane Divinity School at Tufts, where he exerted a benevolent influence on the ministerial students who passed through its corridors.

The McCollesters arrived in Akron in June. They were guests in the Buchtel's home until the President's House could be made available. McCollester used the summer to plan a curriculum, work out a schedule prospectus, and assist (the trustees took the lead) in recruiting a faculty. When school opened on September 11, these tasks were accomplished, and the new enterprise was underway.

No school can afford to miss an opportunity to acknowledge publicly its great occasions, and so, on September 22, Buchtel College let the world know that it was in business by dedicating the new building and by installing Sullivan McCollester in office.[5]

Like the College itself, the great new building was named for John R. Buchtel, whose money and concern supported its construction at every step. He personally took charge of many of the myriad details that accompany any building venture. His enthusiastic involvement was so obviously a product of genuine interest, rather than a function of his role as President of the Board, that his associates felt it natural to name the building Buchtel Hall. Among the many speeches, a short talk by the architect, Mr. T. W. Silloway, struck a prophetic note. He foresaw the time when the College would have a place of first importance in an enlarged and prosperous Akron. Silloway then presented the keys to the building to Mr. Henry Blandy representing the trustees.

The morning ceremonies were followed by the inauguration of Sullivan McCollester. He was installed as "President of the Faculty," a title that connotes a more restricted role than that played by college presidents nowadays.

John Buchtel read the president's charge of office, following which McCollester delivered his inaugural address, "The Educational Demands of the Nation." He emphasized the College's duty to train the body of the student, to teach him to think, and most important, to discipline his conscience and strengthen his will. Only in this fashion could the College strengthen democracy which was its true mission. In the Natural Sciences one found further revelations into the wonders of God's creation which needed careful study, as did language, literature, history, and philosophy. "Our colleges," he declared, "have not any too much breadth and depth of character. It would be a sad mistake to cut short their curriculum, thinking that the young could gain true intellectual honors and religious emolument in some other way than by running in the long and beaten track." He called for quality instruction: "Some bearing the name of college are not even first class academies. Ripe scholarship can no more be the outgrowth of these second rate institutions than oaks and elms can be the products of hot houses." He urged that "minds be so instructed in this Institution that, as they shall go out from it into the varied callings of life, they will prize most of all their individuality in the sight of God."[6]

By the time these ceremonies took place, classes had been in session for more than a week. On September 11, 46 collegiate and 171 preparatory students had been on hand for the beginning of classes. And what an assortment they were! The largest contingent were Universalists. A majority came from Akron and the small towns immediately around it. Most of the Akron students lived at home, but those from Cuyahoga Falls, Mogadore, Copley, East Liberty, and other places now an easy 15 minute drive from campus found it necessary to room and board in the College building or in a nearby home. A young lady from Cuyahoga Falls lived with the McCollesters in the President's House on campus. The Buchtels had students staying with them from time to time. Some students lived in faculty homes.[7]

The first students to arrive at Buchtel College were the Parmenter brothers, Charlie and Fred. They had made the long journey from Vermont to enroll in the new College. They were farm boys who took kindly to the informal reception with which they were met. It must have relieved their parents when Fred wrote that "Mr.

Buchtel is a jolly good fellow. He is full of fun and always seems to be as happy as a clam in high water. He has invited us to come down to his house and get all the apples and grapes we wanted."[8] Three weeks later Fred reported, "Saturday we went out to copla (Copley) swamp with the president of the college and Mr. Buchtel to shoot pigeons. We got eight pigeons and a squirel [sic] and was only gone from here three hours and it is four miles out there."[9]

When Fred was not feeling well, President McCollester brought him a dose of iron tonic and advised him to exercise. This led Fred to explain to his parents that McCollester was "a pretty good physician as well as a minister."[10] On the whole, the brothers were pleased with their classmates even though a few were "pretty high boys." Their only complaint was the time-honored one of food: "so far the only trouble is they don't do what they should by way of board. We have pretty poor fare in the victuals line so far but I guess they will do better after they get straightened round a little. If they don't we shall come home—that is all."[11]

Personal attention from the president and from Mr. Buchtel was not unusual, for both were uncommonly humane in their regard for their charges. McCollester was in the habit of visiting sick students at night to reassure them that someone cared. John and Elizabeth Buchtel were openhanded, dispensing food and support, including loans, to students who were in effect a substitute family for this childless couple. Mr. Buchtel, "that benevolent saint," as one coed remembered him, "was everywhere with cheerful helpfulness, a willing godfather to us all."[12]

For many years each class at Buchtel had students from the homes of some of Akron's prominent families. Often these young people took their preparatory work at Buchtel Academy and then went on to an eastern school or to a well-known college elsewhere for their baccalaureate work. Some, however, completed their collegiate course at Buchtel. There was no better way to tie the College to the community. One of the first two students to complete the tough classical course was Edwin Voris, son of General Alvin C. Voris, a trustee of the College and well known Akron lawyer. Edwin had a distinguished business and professional career in Akron. His daughter, Lydia, would later marry Professor Kolbe's son, Parke, and thus become first lady of Buchtel College when he assumed the presidency in 1912. Associations of this kind bound an increasing number of Akron's leaders to the College and had much to do with the shift in emphasis that would take the College out of the Universalist orbit and into Akron's.

The majority of the students did not come from prominent families, however. They came from rural areas, small towns, and farms. For many of them the tuition of $30 per year was a forbidding sum as was the $10 annual room rent and the board bill of $5 per week. The latter included heat, light, and washing. Charges for the preparatory courses were essentially the same, although calculated by the term instead of the year. From the beginning students formed boarding clubs to reduce costs. The College encouraged those who could afford it to room and board in the College building, for at no time did it accommodate all the students it had been designed to hold. Income was lost when the dormitories were but partially filled.[13]

There were great variations in age and maturity in the early student groups. The young men particularly exhibited a wide range from ten-year-old Vincent Tomlinson,[14] who was a first-year prep student, to mature adults—including at least one Civil War veteran, Albert White, who came to Buchtel in 1873 with the distinction of having been the youngest boy to serve in the Union armies. As a nine-year-old drummer boy, he had been through several campaigns.[15] Clearly this disparity in maturity caused many problems, but we shall look at those matters and other aspects of student life in later chapters.

The faculty that had been assembled to instruct the new student body was small. Its talents were diversified, however, and this was fortunate. Had it not been so, they would never have been able to handle all the different courses and levels of study that Buchtel offered its first students. Only seven faculty members were on hand to teach two collegiate courses (degree programs), two preparatory courses, a normal course, and various "irregular" student programs. As Professor of Intellectual and Moral Philosophy, President McCollester was the leader of this faculty. One would assume that in his presidential dignity he would teach seniors or, at the very least, collegiate students. In fact, the first year he taught reading to prep students, a condition that seemed remarkable to young Vincent Tomlinson who was later to remark, "Why the president of a college should teach reading to a first year prep is beyond me."[16] The answer was simple enough; the need existed, and the president was more interested in meeting needs than in holding himself aloof from such mundane chores.

Of the seven faculty members, Miss Louden and Mr. Persons gave full time to preparatory courses. Prep students were also enrolled in some classes offered in the collegiate department. As the faculty was enlarged and as the curriculum became better structured, this shifting of faculty duties across divisional lines lessened.

There is an ethnocentrism at work in little colleges that is responsible for each claiming a particular excellence for its faculty, or at least for certain members of the faculty. Skeptics have scoffed at these claims saying they represent a romanticized illusion that grows with the years. The further removed one is from his college days the more virtue he is apt to ascribe to his old professors. The professoriate of Yale in the late nineteenth century has been described by Henry Seidel Canby and by "Billy" Phelps in rather uncomplimentary terms on the whole.[17] And since Buchtel College liked to compare itself with Yale in the quality of its work, one might assume it would try to emulate Yale in the type of teacher it sought. But it did not. The strong practical bent of men like John Buchtel, added to the humane concern characteristic of McCollester, led the College to seek out "teachers" in preference to "scholars" if, by the latter term, one means a person who places his own investigations ahead of his responsibility for transmitting knowledge in the classroom.

What we refer to as "teaching" is a process whereby a knowledgeable and experienced person seeks to impart some of his enthusiasm and competence in a subject to a "learner." Most of the effort in this process is the learner's. Therefore, a good teacher is adept at discovering what it takes to stimulate the learner to make the necessary effort. It could be said that a good teacher is a good motivator. Further, he recognizes that what motivates one student will not always motivate another and he is required, therefore, to know enough about students, either as types or as individuals, to know what it takes to stimulate them.

This is the truth recognized by Hermon Kelley, Class of '79, a distinguished Cleveland attorney who had studied at a number of institutions in America and abroad:

> *The great teacher must be able through his personality to assume a compelling intellectual leadership. He must not simply know his subject; he must know his pupils. He must feel keenly and see clearly their difficulties. Above all, he must be willing and able to give not only the best that is in his subject, but what is even more important, the best that is in himself.*[18]

When graduates made a distinguished record in their fields of activity and then claimed that they owed it all to some respected professor who taught them to think, or who showed them how exciting chemistry could be, who are we to gainsay them? In teaching as in war, the only measure of success is in the outcome of the engagement, and if a competent young man or woman wishes to attribute his success to his teacher or his college, we should have the grace to believe him. Indeed, it is only in recent years that the so-called "behaviorists" have made the academic world uncomfortable with this assumption. In the late nineteenth century there would have been little doubt of the propriety of the observation.

There is every likelihood that one will find on most campuses a few outstanding teachers who exert a lasting influence on students. The little faculty assembled during President McCollester's tenure contained such persons. A few, like Nehemiah White, Professor of Ancient Languages, served but briefly and then moved on—in White's case, to the presidency of Lombard College.[19] More significant, however, were the remarkable men who had a formative influence on nearly everyone who sat at their feet and whose tenure was long enough to affect several student generations. Such a man was Carl F. Kolbe who gave the College 33 years of service and a son who was to serve it with distinction as its president.

Born and educated in the German Empire, Kolbe had served as a bandmaster in the Union armies during the Civil War. He came to Akron to publish the *Akron Germania,* a German-language newspaper, but he was persuaded by Mr. Buchtel to accept the position of Professor of Modern Languages in which role he was "to teach our boys and girls Dutch." At the end of the first college term, Kolbe resigned from the faculty because the work was so time-consuming that he couldn't do justice to his publishing venture. He was swayed from this course by the bulldozing tactics of John Buchtel who appeared at Kolbe's door before six o'clock one bitterly cold morning. "Professor," said Buchtel, "I want you to come right back to college, and make college work your life's work." Buchtel wouldn't even step in out of the cold to discuss it, saying "there's nothing to consider; you make up your mind right here and now to return and remain with us in college." And Kolbe did, earning the universal regard and affection of his students, some of whom called him "umlaut," but never in his hearing.[20]

In September, 1875, Charles M. Knight arrived on campus to start a career of unparalleled service, giving of himself and his substance to the College throughout a long life. Born in Vermont, he was too young to enlist in the Union army, but farm work, schooling, and employment with the railroads then being pushed across the western plains filled his early years. After special training in physics and chemistry, he came to Buchtel to take charge of all science instruction. After 1884 he taught only physics and chemistry and, from 1907 on, chemistry only. He introduced laboratory work to Buchtel. He directed his students in the renovation of a basement room into a science laboratory, and he was one of the first college teachers to insist that lab work was essential to science instruction. In those days when chemistry was taught more as a cultural subject than as a narrowly professional one, Knight was best remembered for his ability to show how chemistry related to daily life and activity. Often he employed illustrations derived from his own research and from his industrial consulting. He was as much admired for his thoughtful concern for his students, even long after they had graduated, as he was for the clarity of explanation that did so much to lead some to—and others through—the complexities of science. Of his many other contributions, more will be said later.

Elias Fraunfelter, former Captain in the Union armies, was another good teacher. His mathematics classes were appreciated by many whose natural propensities would have led them to avoid that subject were it not required. Fraunfelter was of the "hard but fair" school so often admired by serious students. He valued imagination over rote learning with the result that his students often credited him with a big assist in preparing them for careers. As one of them expressed it:

> *I attribute most of the small success I have had in this world to those men who taught me to think. Among these, Professor Fraunfelter—not the mathematician, but the man and the teacher—will always have my deepest gratitude and affection.*[21]

Fraunfelter left Buchtel to become Superintendent of the Akron Public Schools where he continued to be a constructive force for education.

In March, 1873, the Board took steps to regularize faculty positions. Chairs were established in intellectual and moral philosophy, ancient languages and comparative philology, chemistry and physics, geology and mineralogy, mathematics, modern languages, and in rhetoric, English literature, and belle lettres.[22] The first endowment for a chair had been received four months earlier when Mrs. George Messenger gave $25,000 for the Messenger Professorship of Mental and Moral Philosophy in memory of her husband. Mr. Buchtel came forward with $20,000 for a "Woman Professorship" on condition that the women of the state raise a corresponding amount. This gift must surely have been one of the first in the nation to be specified to such an end. In 1875 The Pierce Professorship was endowed by Mrs. Chloe Pierce, widow of one of the corporators.[23]

While the trustees were considering faculty welfare, they were also considering their duties. The president was to "distribute the labor of professor and teachers," requiring of them five hours a day, and if he thought it necessary, full time each day of "regular exercises" in the College.[24] Apparently the Board was dissatisfied with some faculty performances, for at the end of the first school year three were fired, no reasons being stated for the action. At the same time a committee was appointed "to have charge of the selection of professors (chair holders) and teachers upon consultation with the president."[25] This direct involvement of the trustees in the selection of teaching personnel was doomed to failure as anyone who knows the academic world might guess. Laymen do not have the same set of priorities as academicians when it comes to selecting faculty. It is possible that this involvement contributed to internal strains that would soon show up in the tight little world on Spicer Hill.

As noted, the first group of students to assemble at Buchtel represented a broad spectrum of academic background and need. Nearly everyone who applied seems to have been accepted into some program, and much improvisation was necessary to make a suitable place for all. Most of this burden fell to the president who assumed the functions now delegated to the Director of Admissions and the Registrar. There must have been times, as McCollester labored over schedules, when he asked himself what he was doing there. If that thought crossed his mind, he was not the last of the school's presidents to indulge in such speculation.

The heart of the collegiate program was the four-year Classical course which led to the Bachelor of Arts degree.[26] A strong three-year secondary school preparation was required to meet the admission standards for this program. Minimum preparation consisted of Latin and Greek grammar and "prosody," some familiarity with selected writings of Xenophon, Homer, Caesar, Virgil, Cicero, the *Aeneid,* algebra to equations of the second degree, English grammar, United States history, ancient and modern geography. Except for a lighter emphasis on mathematics, these admission standards were essentially the same as those of Yale and other recognized centers of excellence against which Buchtel measured herself.

Once embarked upon the Classical course, the young scholar could look forward to two years of intensive work in Latin and Greek, to French, German, and English with work in the latter taking the form of rhetoric, themes, declamations, oral and written reviews, and "voice culture." Also to be mastered were mathematics through the calculus, physiology, zoology, botany, geology, mineralogy, field surveying, chemistry, natural philosophy, intellectual philosophy, logic, "moral science," Greek and Roman history, English literature, political economy, mechanics, astronomy, and Guizot's *History of Civilization.* As long as Buchtel College remained, this curriculum was essentially unchanged although the elective system made possible a modest amount of flexibility in the Classical course after 1882. At any given time, only a minority of the collegiate students were in this course.

For the less well-prepared students—or the less solvent or ambitious—a two-year Philosophical course was offered. Its requirements were much the same as those for the Classical course without the Latin and Greek. In 1873 it was lengthened to three years and in 1875 to a full-fledged four-year course. Briefly it was identified as a Philosophical and Engineering course. By 1878 four terms of Latin were added to the requirement. The Bachelor of Philosophy degree marked completion of this course.

A Scientific course, started in 1873 as a three-year program, was lengthened to four in 1875. By 1878 it was the only collegiate course which did not require Latin, and as the title would indicate, more time was spent on the natural and physical sciences. The degree Bachelor of Science was awarded to those who completed this course, and for many years to come it was looked upon patronizingly by those who felt that the Bachelor of Arts was the only degree of merit.

For each college course there was a corresponding preparatory course. In addition, students who wished to teach could meet state requirements by taking a two-year Normal course offered in the preparatory department. It is interesting to note that then, as now, it was all too often assumed that those who were to teach did not need as extensive, diversified, and demanding a training as that required in many other programs. There were a number of students whose preparation did not fit exactly any course of study, so they were classified as "irregular" students, and their programs were individually tailored.

After the first few years the curricular offerings were established, although they didn't remain that way for any extended period. It is not possible to give a confident answer to those who want to know how Buchtel's graduates compared with those of established schools. One might cite the success with which they moved on through professional and graduate schools at good universities as evidence of adequate preparation. It can be said with certainty, however, that in the face of many difficulties, Buchtel accomplished her curricular shakedown expeditiously, and the solidity of the product was a tribute to all who contributed in that process.

The first faculty and students had little enough to work with despite the large amount of money that had gone into the building and its furnishings. It was not long, however, before some of the "extras" that proved in time to be necessities were obtained by gift or purchase.

Instruction in geology, mineralogy, physiology, zoology, and botany was dependent in part on collections of specimens which could be examined by students. In addition, such collections were wonderful show pieces for public display. Pictures of them looked impressive in the catalog, and they permitted the College to brag about its fitness to offer instruction in the sciences. In the summer of 1873, President McCollester donated a collection of natural history specimens valued at $2,000. This gesture was evidence of his genuine concern that the College be "first class."[27] Many others gave mementos and collections of modest proportions to the College. Among the donors was General Bierce whose collections of fossils, minerals, and other natural phenomena had been significant enough to cause the Smithsonian Institute to send out a cataloger to record his treasures. The General had an even more significant gift to make, however.

Central to any significant academic activity in our day is a library adequately supplied with the books, periodicals, and scholarly tools which are essential to original investigation. General Bierce was responsible for the excellent start that Buchtel College was able to make toward the accumulation of a library collection. He gave $4,964 for the purchase of books and the fitting up of a suitable room to house them. In addition, he presented many volumes from his own considerable library. Bierce knew the value of books. As a desperately poor student trying to make his way through Ohio University in 1819, he took $1.25 that he had managed to accumulate, and with it he bought three books which he donated to the library of the Athenian Literary Society of which he was a member.[28]

An "elegant and spacious room" was converted into a library for the "many volumes of valuable books" the College claimed. There was "space for still more," but it would be a long time indeed before the library was again the focus of beneficence. Of course the library was treated as a showpiece and was open to students for one hour each week so that they might admire the collection. The day had not yet arrived at Buchtel when professors would assign projects requiring the use of its resources. Such reading as was done outside textbooks took place in the two reading rooms— one for gentlemen, one for ladies—each "well supplied with newspapers and magazines."[29]

In gratitude for the General's splendid gifts, the trustees gave his name to the library. In later years, when the library was housed in a separate building, the collection retained the name "Bierce Library." It is a matter of regret to some alumni and friends of the University that the name Bierce was discarded in 1961, when the library building and collection were given the bland designation "University Library."

As the 1872–73 school year drew to a close, preparations were made for Buchtel's first commencement. This ceremony was the great event of the college year. It would grow more elaborate each year until the endurance and patience of faculty, students, and guests wore thin. It is astonishing to the present generation to observe the stamina that enabled participants and visitors to survive events stretched out over several days. These included student examinations before an august examining committee, musical presentations, poems, declamations, prayers, sermons, and, of course, the degree candidates' orations, the commencement speech, and the awarding of degrees.

Not all of these events came off well. A bored and critical reporter described in unflattering terms the initial event of that first commencement—an address "The Romance of the World's Youth," delivered by Professor A. H. Welsh:

> *The Professor . . . took his position behind the stand and for the next hour and a half, more or less, amused himself by reading some words in a monotonous, rapid and jumbled up manner which was now and then embellished with certain spasmodic jerkings of the upper extremities, and once or twice his voice was raised above the droning monotone, and at such times he spoke so forcibly that he might have been heard in the back part of the room if there had been anyone there to listen.*[30]

Apparently not all of Buchtel's faculty were great teachers. Whether or not this performance had anything to do with it, Professor Welsh was soon replaced on the faculty by Elias Fraunfelter.

The graduation exercises were held in the evergreen-decorated chapel on July 9. The Bachelor of Science degree was conferred upon Susie Chamberlain, James Pierce, Charles Saxe, and Anna Sisler for successful completion of the two-year philosophical course. Not until 1875 would there be a graduate of the four-year classical course to receive the Bachelor of Arts degree. Another first at this commencement was the awarding of an honorary Doctor of Divinity degree to Reverend Willard Spaulding, a Universalist minister from Massachusetts.[31]

To award collegiate degrees in the chapel of a great college building, amid a throng of appreciative well-wishers, just six years after the dream of a Universalist school was first advanced by the Ohio Convention was an accomplishment of a high order. It had been a great day!

To the current generation, student life during the 1870's seems rather grim, circumscribed as it was by restrictive rules and regulations. As a matter of fact, it seemed somewhat grim to many of those who had to endure it. In assessing the outlook of students on matters of behavior and social usage, it is well to keep in mind some of the characteristics of the period.

It has been argued that American innocence died on the fields of Gettysburg. Like most such generalizations, this one is overdrawn. The old slogans and moral imperatives that had driven Americans forward were still operative in the late nineteenth century. An articulate minority may have expressed disenchantment with much of American life, but the majority believed that they were living in an age of opportunity and that each man's capacity for seizing it rested upon his character and righteousness.

Behavior was still beholden to the Calvinist conscience. It was still possible for a "decent fellow" to have genuine concern for the state of his neighbor's soul. The Universalists and their fellow practitioners of the religious ethic regarded such overt signs of weakness as smoking, drinking, swearing, and failure to attend Sunday services as cause for concern if not alarm. Frank Wieland, Class of '90, remembered when, from the window of the Kappa room, a student was observed smoking a cigarette. "He was from Oil City, Pennsylvania, a Godless place," said Wieland, "and he did not know that smoking was considered sinful at Buchtel. The Kappa meeting broke up in outraged disorder. At luncheon one of their number wept tears in her soup at man's depravity."[32]

Young men talked earnestly together about how they could help a classmate become a "true fellow." Yet, underneath it all, boys would be boys, and it was unnatural for a group of them to sustain this piety for any length of time. It was not long before the Buchtel boys found a variety of ways to enliven their spirits without endangering their souls. In the last two decades of the nineteenth century, the mood of the College mellowed as the initial religious zeal that had inspired its foundation became less and less a part of the lives of those who studied there.

The College minimized chances for deviant behavior by requiring that every candidate for admission furnish a reliable certificate of good moral character. Frequently these certificates originated with the student's local pastor or a former teacher. Once admitted to Buchtel, the student found himself in a society closely hedged about with rules and regulations which were indistinguishable in spirit from those he would have encountered in any denominational college of the time. Even the public colleges were precise in their definition of what constituted responsible student conduct.

Among the rules that restrained high spirits at Buchtel was the old dependable: "No student shall fire gunpowder in the college building or on the premises, or engage in card playing or any form of gambling in the college or in the city, or visit liquor saloons or billiard rooms, or commit injuries upon the person or property of any student." There were rules designed to deter the destructive impulses that possess the young from time to time: "No student is allowed to take or remove furniture from the rooms; to mark, cut, drive nails into the buildings; to throw anything to or from the windows; to spit upon the floors, or in any way deface the college property." This catch-all rule was supported by others designed to prevent boisterousness or scuffling in the rooms and halls, to keep students out of the kitchen, bakery, storeroom, or other places of possible delights, to prevent the illegal entry of the building by means of forged keys, and so forth. Then there were the usual regulations designed to keep the sexes at bay from one another: "Young men and young women are not allowed to take walks or rides together without permission;" or another, "At all public exercises given in the college chapel, the young men will occupy the east side and the young women the west side."[33]

Anyone who remembers his own student days can recall that rules present a certain challenge which makes the pleasure of circumventing them all the more satisfying. This does not necessarily mean that those who ignore the rules are "bad" or have a block of sorts on authority symbols (although there are such individuals in any sizable student group). Rather, high spirits and an inability to allow the threat of future punishment to deter them from the pleasure of the present coup prompt them to match wits with those who have challenged them. Rules are defied because they are there.

It would be a distortion, however, to leave the impression that most students were so affected. At any time, those who challenged authority with any regularity were in a pronounced minority, but they were the ones whose deeds were recorded and remembered since they provided peaks of vicarious excitement for the conventional majority who would not risk deviation from the behavior expected of them.

Rules were enforced by means of demerits, suspension, or expulsion. In nearly all cases the faculty had to review the circumstances and rule upon them. The time and attention involved seem misplaced to this generation; indeed, it seemed misplaced to some observers of that day as in the case of a couple of students, "among the best in the college," who had appropriated a mattress from an unoccupied room. When it was repossessed by the angry steward, they reappropriated it to their use. "This complicated case was submitted to the grave consideration of the president and by him brought before the faculty, who spent many hours deliberating what should be done to the offending students. All of which goes to show that some action should be taken to relieve the faculty of these weighty responsibilities in order that they may have time for the proper teaching of their classes."[34] Under the demerit system, a sliding scale of offenses and punishments was introduced. It is of interest now principally because it reveals the nature of the most common transgressions, and it provides modest insight into the scale of values of a time when missing a Sunday church service cost four demerits while missing class cost but two.

Criminologists have long taught that the threat of punishment does not deter certain persons from law-breaking. The fertile and inventive student mind was often put to work outwitting the faculty since the latter maintained order and meted out punishment when appropriate. A disproportionate share of the disciplinary burden fell to the unmarried faculty who lived in the dormitories. Outwitting these watchdogs of student deportment was a constant challenge.

Most of the tricks employed to make life hideous for the faculty were standard on any campus of that time. A cow was led to an upper floor and then proved to be all but impossible to get down; a large wagon was carried in parts to the roof where it mysteriously appeared, fully assembled; bed slats were ridden down stairs; sacks filled with water were dropped down the stairwell or on the heads of those who passed too close to the outside of the building; air was blown into the gas lines shutting off the lights; large rocks from the geology cabinet were rolled down the stairs, as were cannon balls which had been heated over a gas jet until they were hot enough to blister the hand of anyone unwary enough to pick them up.

Chapel exercises were favorite targets for student pranks. The working day started at these services and they afforded a splendid opportunity for the ingenious prankster to produce effects before a wide audience, since the president customarily presided, the faculty sat in dignity upon the platform, and all students were present. The pranks ranged from the amusing to the disruptive. One morning the president raised a box-like cover that was kept over the Bible, and a chicken emerged, crowing his discontent. On another occasion all of the furniture was removed from the chapel. This not only accomplished the happy result of postponing exercises for that morning, but lent a continuing excitement to the college scene while the perpetrators of the deed were tracked down and punished.

The Board of Trustees kept close watch over student morality and conduct. In July, 1874, President McCollester was requested to appear before them to answer many questions concerning the moral condition of the institution. The chief concern was coeducation. Two years later similar questions prompted a special Board meeting with the faculty to discuss "the vexed question of permitting young men to wait upon female students of the Institution under any circumstances whatever."[35] It was finally agreed that the faculty might grant permits in special cases, on petition, to students deserving consideration. The absence of further concern would seem to indicate that the problems of fraternization between the sexes had been worked out to the satisfaction of the trustees—at least for the moment. Indeed, in July, 1876, a special committee reported to the Board that the College work was being conducted in excellent fashion, with good discipline, solid work, and a high level of moral and religious outlook. The committee commended President McCollester as "a superior man for the position he occupies."[36] It is surprising, therefore, that McCollester submitted his resignation within a year of this report. There is no way to determine exactly what motivated his decision, since this information was not made part of the record, but we can reconstruct the circumstances of 1877–78 in such a way as to suggest an answer.

No educational institution born in nineteenth-century America could be in business long without experiencing a survival crisis brought on by one of the periodic economic depressions or panics that erupted every few years throughout the century. Buchtel College, it appeared, had been started at a propitious time. The remarkable economic and industrial expansion of the North following the Civil War was fully shared in by Akron. The city was driving ahead in every important civic endeavor, and the spirit of optimism was there for all to see. This thriving town and vigorous citizenry impressed Reverend George Weaver, who arrived in 1873 to take the pulpit of the newly organized Universalist congregation:

> *Akron . . . won at once my interest. It was a brisk young city of some 20,000 inhabitants, enterprising in business, public spirited, large minded, up to date, and bound to win. It had caught the spirit of Mr. Buchtel. He was its representative man.*[37]

That same year, however, the short but sharp economic crisis known as the "Crime of '73" hit Akron with enough force to create concern for the stability of the prosperity, and it contributed to a mounting sense of anxiety at Buchtel College. The large sums raised for the school had temporarily drained the chief sources of support within Universalist ranks. Even the local money that had enabled the Ohio Convention to realize its dream was turned off temporarily until the economic picture cleared.

In 1872 Reverend H. F. Miller resigned as Financial Secretary of the College and was replaced by Reverend D. C. Tomlinson who continued the practice of seeking money mainly in Ohio. There is no evidence that at this time the College followed the rather general practice among western colleges of seeking funds in the east. Western Reserve, for example, had agents in the east almost continuously from its founding in 1826.[38] But then, most schools did not have a John R. Buchtel to sustain them with money, shrewd management, and great devotion through their first 22 years.

When the trustees reviewed the financial situation in July, 1874, they found an indebtedness of $29,400 on the books. Some of this resulted from default on pledge payments triggered by the economic panic. It cannot be attributed to ineffective management, although the expansive mood of these building years had in it the risk of over-extension. Mr. Buchtel offered to pay $9,400 of the deficit on condition that friends of the College pay the remainder within one year.[39] This was a typical Buchtel offer, designed to elicit the support of others in the cause by hooking his own generous contribution to their expected participation. The matching grants of the federal government and of certain foundations so common in the mid-twentieth century were predicated on the same self-help principle.

Mr. Buchtel's offer was quickly accepted, but the records do not reveal whether or not the fund-raising effort succeeded. Judged by conditions of the period 1875–79, one would assume it did not, for during that time the College owed some $50,000, much of it to banks at 10 percent interest. Things were so tight that the Messenger Fund, an endowment, was used for operating expenses while Mr. Buchtel took out $25,000 of insurance on his life for the benefit of the fund.[40] Andrew Willson, who had taken over as financial secretary in 1875, called this the College's "most trying financial experience" and later claimed that only he and Mr. Buchtel knew how close it came to closing its doors.[41]

By 1876, Akron business was reviving. The old Ohio Canal was experiencing its best year since the railroads had cut severely into its revenues some 20 years before. The equivalent of six large trains of coal was shipped daily to Cleveland, and about 30 boatloads of "wheat, lumber, brick, and other merchandise" flowed through the port each day.[42]

There was a lag, however, between Akron's business revival and the renewing of financial support for the College. In 1877 President McCollester was still lamenting that "the principal want of Buchtel College is money."[43]

Perhaps it was the lack of money that discouraged McCollester, for in June, 1877, he submitted his resignation. The trustees refused to accept it. They were pleased with his work and urged him to stay on. He agreed to stay temporarily, but there appeared to be little doubt that he would leave eventually.[44]

McCollester did not appear discouraged by the work going on in the institution. He reported that the year 1876–77 was the most "progressive" since the founding: the curriculum was sound, the students were abler and better fitted for college work, especially those from the Akron high school with their "excellent rank in scholarship and moral deportment." There was progress to report in each department.[45] Every report made during McCollester's administration praised him for his work, so he apparently was satisfying those who were looking.

There seems to be little question that McCollester's resignation resulted from a split that had developed between the College and the Universalist congregation. This is ironic, for McCollester had organized the local congregation in 1872, John Buchtel was its Moderator, and the group met in the College chapel for Sunday services. Reverend George Weaver, pastor of the congregation, was well thought of, but one wonders if he or his parishioners did not resent the too close ties with the College.

One thing is clear: Buchtel students were the medium of controversy. The president had said of 1876–77 that "outsiders have let the College alone or have not been disposed to listen to disaffected students or floating rumors which might be used to the detriment of the Institution."[46] Among the "disaffected students" may have been the son and daughter of the pastor. Mr. Weaver allowed his daughter to withdraw from Buchtel to return to St. Lawrence where she had been enrolled previously, and his son was permitted to choose Tufts College because he wanted to attend a "more noted institution." "Some of my parishioners," said Weaver, "were displeased with my allowing the children to go elsewhere to finish their college courses. So the pleasantness of my pastorate was quite interfered with."[47] In 1920, Reverend E. L. Rexford, then over 90 years of age, added more explanation:

> Early in the year 1877, May, Mr. Buchtel wrote me that trouble had arisen in the college and church affairs at Akron. Some 60 students in the college had petitioned the Board of Trustees for the resignation of President McCollester and among the petitioners were two of the children of the pastor of the church, Dr. Weaver (?).
> This created a feeling of alienation between the president and the pastor and their friends. This chasm deepened and broadened 'til the church people withdrew from the college chapel where they had held services and went down town to a school building and held their meetings there. . . . Mr. Buchtel wrote me that nothing could be done by way of union. The president wanted to resign. The pastor had resigned or would resign.'[48]

On June 25, 1878, the Board of Trustees reluctantly accepted the resignation President McCollester had seen fit to re-submit. "I have loved and still love the College," he said, and the warm interest he continued to take in its accomplishments throughout his long life is evidence to it. At commencement with the "Akron Class of '78," so called because all five of its members were locals, President McCollester was given "an elegant gold watch and chain" as a memento.[49] In 1908 Buchtel College would honor this humane man with the honorary Doctor of Letters degree. He continued to write widely about his travels and produced several books about them. He died in his home town of Marlboro, New Hampshire on May 22, 1921, at the age of 94. He had been an admirable pace-setter.

"Aunty" Brown and the Old Shoe

Sullivan McCollester recommended that his successor in the presidency be Reverend Everett L. Rexford, one of the most distinguished men in the denomination although just 37 years old. John R. Buchtel concurred in this assessment and also appears to have paved the way for Rexford's appointment to the dual role of President of Buchtel College, for which position he was unanimously chosen in June, and Pastor of the Universalist church which duties he assumed in September.[50]

Few persons had entered as fully into the life of the young College as he, and none was more aware of its history, its problems, its promise. As a member of the Committee on Education of the Ohio Convention, he had helped select Akron as the site and had served as a corporator. From the beginning he had been a member of the Board of Trustees. He delivered the first commencement address in 1873 and the following year was honored with the Doctor of Divinity degree. Born in Harmony, New York in 1842, he graduated from St. Lawrence before serving pastorates in Cincinnati, Columbus, and San Francisco. This vigorous, positive, handsome minister appeared to be a perfect choice.

He entered his new work with enthusiasm. Some changes started or contemplated by President McCollester were brought to fruition. To secure more funds, tuition was charged on a term-payment plan that raised the total to $40 for a three-term year. Board in the College building cost $2.75 a week for food only, and this amount could be reduced if a student joined a boarding club where he could eat well for $1.75 a week. Students who roomed in the College building were strongly urged to eat there and, as before, were required to furnish their own quilts, comforters, sheets, towels, napkins, pillow cases, and toilet soap.

It would be inappropriate, even an injustice, to write of the room and board arrangements without mentioning Mrs. Lucinda Brown, known to generations of Buchtelites as "Aunty Brown," who made it her task in life to help young people secure an education. The widow of a Universalist minister, she had commenced her career of support and concern for students at the Clinton Liberal Institute run by the Universalists of New York State. She visited Akron in 1878 and there met Mr. Buchtel at the College commencement. Hearing of her great work in New York, Mr. Buchtel determined that she must come to Akron and offered her a house, rent-free, at 268 Carroll Street, plus $100 to defray expenses. In one of the rare letters from him that have been preserved, Mr. Buchtel deals with additional arrangements:

"Mrs. L. W. Brown

August 4, 1878

> *Your kind letter of the 22 July come duly to hand I was glad to here from you. Great to here that you are encouraged in your nobell work. I believe that you will meet with good success. I have no doubt but that satisfactory arrangements can be made for you to accomadate all the students that you can attend to. I have 50 acres of land near by. Should you want 5 or 10 acres for the boys to work on to rais vegatabells you can have it hoping that you may succeed I remain*

John R. Buchtel"[51]

For Aunty Brown it was the beginning of a long career working on behalf of Buchtel students, and she never forgot the man whose generosity made possible the carrying on of her mission in life. Of John R. Buchtel she said: "He was my benefactor in ways that would make a volume if written out in detail. It is to John R. Buchtel that I am indebted for my pleasant home place and the pleasant duties that have occupied me for 30 years."[52] What Aunty referred to as "pleasant duties" consisted of hard work of the housekeeping variety plus the wide range of church, charitable, and neighborly activities she was so heavily involved in.

On September 10, 1878, she arrived in Akron from western New York with eight boys and two girls in tow. They carried ticks filled with straw secured from Mr. Buchtel's farm; some stayed in the College building, and some were guests of the Reverend Mr. Tomlinson who once had been Aunty's pastor in Perry, New York, and whose sons were the first to call her "Aunty." Once things were under control at the house on Carroll Street, some 16 students at a time roomed and boarded there and shared in the work. This busy activity led someone to call the house the "Beehive," but it was soon to be renamed the "Omnibus." Finally, William Couden, reminded of the old lady that lived in a shoe who had so many children she didn't know what to do, started calling it the "Old Shoe," and this name stuck. Indeed, in 1905 the house was replaced by a new one which was promptly named the "New Shoe."

It is hard to measure the good that a selfless person can do. That Aunty Brown was a constructive influence on many generations of students is abundantly clear from their testimonies. The help she constantly received from others—cereal and flour from Mr. Schumacher's mills, food products and straw from Buchtel's farm, coal from Mr. Pendleton—indicates that her work was recognized and appreciated. She was 95 years old when she died in 1917. A bronze plaque which hung for many years in Bierce Library said of her: "Aunty Brown . . . for 40 years wise counselor, generous giver, and devoted mother to the boys and girls of Buchtel."

In addition to their concern for the physical welfare of students, President Rexford and the faculty found it desirable to suggest certain clarifications regarding the moral and religious climate of the school. There is evidence that the College was moving toward a somewhat broader interpretation of the student's religious responsibilities. The catalog for 1878–79 declared: "While the college is under the auspices of a religious denomination, there are no restrictions imposed upon the exercise of religious opinions." And again, "While the college aims to be religious it is, in its internal economy, in no sense sectarian. Religious opinions are respected but not talked."[53]

The need to define the school's position may have been the outgrowth of the acrimony that lay behind the McCollester-Weaver split. There was no loosening of the rules requiring students to attend daily chapel exercises and Sunday services at "whatever church their parents or guardians may elect." And as for conduct, the

PRESIDENT EVERETT REXFORD (1878–80)

trustees decided at this time that scholarships would be granted only on condition that the recipients abstain wholly from alcoholic beverages and tobacco. It is clear that Buchtel College was going to permit a student to think whatever he would about religion and morality, but he had to act along lines that guaranteed at least a surface adherence to orthodox expectations.

Everett Rexford was not president long enough to develop a style or an educational philosophy that we can identify with him. The closest he came was to extol individuality—the development of individual character—as the work of the College.[54] He thought that one of the most questionable phases of college life was its tendency to put a "uniform stamp" on graduates. He did not attack directly the rigid curriculum then in vogue, but since Buchtel took her first steps toward the free elective system of course selection just two years after Rexford left office, one wonders if his exaltation of the right to be different might not have prepared the way.

The new president proved to be an able administrator and organizer. Some confusion was eliminated by separating the preparatory work from the collegiate. Each professor (chair-holder) was to be responsible for the administration of his own "department," but he retained his voice and vote in matters of concern to the entire faculty. The preparatory school had been a "source of embarrassment" to the president since a preparatory instructor with little or no experience had been able to "neutralize" the vote of a professor of great experience, even on questions that pertained exclusively to College interests. Therefore, the faculty was split into a College faculty and a preparatory faculty.

Initially the preparatory instructors were upset by the separation which implied a second-class academic citizenship: "We have received no communication, nor formal recognition, from the college faculty during the year," they lamented. But the initial feeling of exclusion did not keep the preparatory faculty from reporting in 1879 that "our work has been more systematic and uniform than before, and the separate organization seems to be beneficial."[55]

As a further efficiency, the College faculty was divided into committees—classification, courses of study, rules and regulations, discipline, printing and advertising, ways and means, and conference—thereby relieving the faculty as a whole from delving into unnecessary detail on every issue.

The Normal Department, thought Rexford, was a department in name only. In his view, the best teacher training resulted from the student meeting state requirements in the preparatory school and, in addition, observing competent instructors in action. If the Normal Department were to continue, and the president was sure it could be useful, then it should be strengthened.

Rexford was a realist. He knew that the College had no business trying to be all things to all people. There were not enough instructors on the teaching force, he said, to warrant the catalog invitation to pursue elective studies. A short-lived literary course was abolished by joint action of the faculties. In 1876 the Ohio Convention had asked that a Department of Theology be established and had been informed that it was beyond the College's resources at that time.[56] Continuing expressions from influential Universalists favoring a theology program were discouraged by Rexford.

Student deportment was another area of college life requiring adjustment. The faculty abolished the demerit system. Its demise, said Rexford, resulted from the same phenomenon that usually undermined such systems—the miscreant student paid little attention to demerits until he reached the point at which the next demerits earned would result in suspension or expulsion. "It has been decided not to advertise such a margin for irregularities and excess," the president reported.[57] The faculty found that direct punishment inflicted for each offense was superior to the demerit system.

Just who was responsible for regarding the Saturday night dancing parties as a disciplinary problem isn't known. They had been a feature of college life since the beginning but now they were to be discontinued because they were "a source of complaint among both the parents and students on account of the general tendency to divert the mind from studious habits."[58] Maybe the parents believed this, but it is a little hard to credit the students with such premature solemnity. At any rate, socials on alternate Saturdays were substituted. Students were generally well behaved with one notable exception. Two young gentlemen of the College were found locked in the "sleeping quarters" of one of the young ladies. "Certain grave questions growing out of this circumstance" were referred to the trustees because the faculty could not agree on any course of action.[59] Unfortunately, the Board's solution to the "grave questions" was not made a matter of record.

While Rexford contributed organizing skill to the College, he also served it well by doing much to heal the breach between the College and the local Universalist congregation. Perhaps the fact that the congregation now had its own building—a brick structure on the northwest corner of Mill and Broadway—removed one source of tension. Ferdinand Schumacher was the principal donor to the building fund. As with every fund-raising effort, John R. Buchtel contributed generously. Since they were both on the College Board of Trustees at this time, their gifts provided a visible sign that support of the church was not incompatible with support for the College.

It is interesting that Dr. Rexford should be the vehicle of reconciliation, for he was uncommonly quick to rise to any challenge and throw himself headlong into debate. Charles Wright, Class of '80, characterized him in striking imagery: "With positive convictions and exceptional dialectic skill, controversy was the very breath of his nostrils. Like the ocean petrels, he seemed at times to hover by choice over the stormiest waters, and it behooved an opponent to be well equipped who encountered him in debate."[60] Now most of President Rexford's contests were waged in denominational papers and magazines, but on at least one occasion, he took on local opposition in an exchange that is revealing.

Dr. Rexford preached a sermon in February, 1879, commenting upon the reported death-cell conversion of a convicted murderer named McGill. Rexford protested against the quickness with which the Christian churches were wont to ascribe salvation to the perpetrator of a heinous crime because he had "repented" and at the same time assign the victim of the crime to hell because she was living a sinful life at the time she died.[61] The newspaper account of the sermon, which Rexford acknowledged was a correct account, drew comment from an Episcopalian clergyman, the Reverend Mr. Ganter, who was much exercised at Rexford's remarks. In the exchange of letters that followed, the ground of argument shifted in part to Rexford's role as President of Buchtel College: "With . . . justice," wrote Ganter, "might I charge Buchtel College an 'Undenominational College,' with the denominational opinions of its accredited head and representative." To this, Dr. Rexford replied:

> *You address one of your letters "To Rev. Dr. Rexford, President of Buchtel College." Allow me to say that the sermon you undertook to criticise was preached by me not in my capacity as President of Buchtel College, but in my capacity as pastor of the Universalist Church. . . . I defend [my original] effort as pastor of the church and not as President of Buchtel College. Buchtel College is not engaged in religious controversy.*

To this, Mr. Ganter replied: "Dr. Rexford: According to your own confession, you are pastor of a church one hour and President of Buchtel College the rest of the week. When do you cease to be President? How do you do it? Do you resign every time you preach?" He goes on to ask, "Is there anything . . . more absurd as a statement and weaker as an excuse, than being both President and pastor, you abused the 'Christian world' as pastor, while as President you had no sort of responsibility in the matter. Possibly you have a double personality."

Rexford continued to draw the distinction in his roles, but it is apparent that the combination left him open to the sort of criticism that Ganter had levelled. A pastor as outspoken as Rexford was certain to find his words represented as illuminating the position of Buchtel College, and the efforts he made to discount that connection indicate that the consequences could be serious should it appear to the public that the conduct of the College was not in fact "undenominational" as was claimed. Rexford had the grace to recognize that this confusion was apt to persist as long as he held both positions. Since he was clearly more interested in pulpit work than in the management of college activities, he chose wisely in submitting his resignation in 1880 to become pastor of the newly established Universalist church in Detroit.

He had accomplished much of importance. In 1879, a campaign was launched to raise money to pay off the large debt. Financial agents were appointed in Ohio, Indiana, Michigan, part of Illinois, western Pennsylvania, and western New York. They raised some $60,000, a sum sufficient to return the College to solvency.[62] In two years, therefore, the faculty had been reorganized, student rules revised, the breach with the local congregation healed somewhat, and the College returned to solvency. When Orello Cone arrived in 1880 to administer the College, he found a solid operation of good reputation among the Universalist faithful and with the Akron community. This is Rexford's tribute.

NOTES

[1] Board Mins., I, 15.

[2] *Ibid.,* 16–18.

[3] *Ibid.,* 16.

[4] Spanton, *Fifty Years,* p. 45.

[5] An account of the day's activities is bound in Buchtel College Publications, 1872–76, in UArch.

[6] *Ibid.,* pp. 5–11.

[7] Catalog, 1872–73.

[8] F. Parmenter to parents, Akron, Sept. 10, 1872, UArch., box 39/4/140.

[9] *Ibid.,* Oct. 1, 1872.

[10] *Ibid.,* Oct. 6, 1872.

[11] *Ibid.,* Sept. 15, 1872.

[12] Ella Pitcairn to Miss Weeks, Pasadena, Dec. 28, 1933, UArch., VF (History).

[13] Catalog, 1872–73, p. 15.

[14] *Alumni Quarterly*, V, no. 2.

[15] *Buchtelite*, Nov., 1889.

[16] *Alumni Quarterly*, V, no. 2.

[17] Henry Seidel Canby, *Alma Mater; the Gothic Age of the American College* (New York, [1936]); William Lyon Phelps, *Autobiography, with Letters* (New York, 1939).

[18] Spanton, *Fifty Years*, p. 194.

[19] Faculty sketches are drawn from a variety of sources, but Spanton, *Fifty Years*, pp. 52, 189–200 contains material on the faculty treated in this chapter.

[20] *Ibid.*, p. 30.

[21] *Ibid.*, p. 195.

[22] Board Mins., I, 26.

[23] *Ibid.*, pp. 25, 27, 36.

[24] *Ibid.*, p. 26.

[25] *Ibid.*, p. 29.

[26] Anyone interested in following in detail the evolution of course and admission requirements can find this information in the annual catalogs.

[27] *Daily Beacon*, July 2, 1873.

[28] Knepper, ed., *Bierce Journal*, pp. 1–42 for details of Bierce's career. Among the memorabilia he presented to the College was a sword taken from the body of a Major Hume, shot and killed by irregular "patriot" troops under Bierce's command during an illegal invasion of Canada in December, 1838. For Bierce's gifts to the College, see Ruth W. Clinefelter, "History of Bierce Library of The University of Akron," pp. 32–37, unpublished master's degree thesis, UArch.

[29] Board Mins., I, 28–29; Catalog, 1872–73.

[30] *Daily Beacon*, July 8, 1873.

[31] Spanton, *Fifty Years*, p. 412.

[32] *Ibid.*, p. 339.

[33] These rules appear in Catalog, 1872–73, p. 14, with modifications in subsequent catalogs.

[34] Spanton, *Fifty Years*, p. 360.

[35] Board Mins., I, 30, 42.

[36] *Ibid.*, 42.

[37] Weaver, *Autobiography*, p. 67.

[38] Curti and Nash, *Philanthropy*, p. 54.

[39] Board Mins., I, 31.

[40] *Ibid.*, 35.

[41] Spanton, *Fifty Years*, p. 217.

[42] *Daily Beacon*, Sept. 16, 1876.

[43] President's Annual Report, 1877, bound in Buchtel College Publications, 1872–78. Hereafter the President's Annual Report, which appears under a variety of titles over the years, will be cited as President's Report, with the appropriate year indicated.

[44] Board Mins., I, 53–4.

[45] *Ibid.*, 55.

[46] President's Report, 1877.

[47] Weaver, *Autobiography*, p. 73.

[48] Rexford to Spanton, ca. 1920, UArch., VF (History).

[49] Board Mins., I, 53, 60; UArch., VF (Commencement).

[50] Rexford to Spanton, ca. 1920, UArch., VF (History); Board Mins. I, 60.

[51] UArch., VF (Buchtel, John R.).

[52] UArch., box 2/2/120.

[53] Catalog, 1878–79, p. 11.

[54] Board Mins., I, 67.

[55] Buchtel Academy Minutes, UArch., box 1/2/123.

[56] Board Mins., I, 41.

[57] *Ibid.,* 67.

[58] *Ibid.,* 71.

[59] *Ibid.*

[60] Spantón, *Fifty Years,* p. 55.

[61] The entire correspondence is in a reprint titled, *A Too Easy Heaven for Criminals a Premium on Crime. The Ganter-Rexford Correspondence in the McGill Case,* in Buchtel College Publications, 1876–82, UArch.

[62] Spanton, *Fifty Years,* pp. 217–18.

Buchtel College looms over John Buchtel's Buckeye Works.

IV

Buchtel's golden age (1880–1890)

For the third time in eight years the Board faced the task of finding a president. A committee headed by John R. Buchtel first considered William D. Shipman for the position. A graduate of Buchtel, Class of '77, Shipman was the first person to earn a Master's degree in course from the College (1880). Although he was not a clergyman, he had been active in Universalist affairs. Shipman declined to become an active candidate for the position, however, so the committee turned elsewhere.

Before leaving the presidency, Dr. Rexford had recommended as his successor the distinguished professor of Biblical Languages and Literature of the St. Lawrence Theological School, Reverend Orello Cone. It was to him that the committee now turned, and after a summer's correspondence that failed to establish clearly any rapport between Cone and the committee, the trustees offered the position to him.[1]

Orello Cone was in no hurry to accept. With typical impatience, Mr. Buchtel urged him to make an immediate decision, even offering to let him stay at the Buchtel residence and use the horses and carriage free of charge if he would decide affirmatively.[2] To everyone's apparent surprise, Cone refused the offer, but he had not reckoned with the tenacity of Buchtel once that stubborn man's mind was set. A meeting of the two men was arranged to take place in the publishing house of the *Christian Leader* in Boston. Mr. Buchtel's secretary, A. B. Tinker, wrote the Reverend Mr. Cantwell of the selection committee, "I fear Dr. Cone's opinions of Mr. Buchtel have been poisoned, but hope he may be persuaded to come on and time will cleanse his opinions." If any such difficulties existed they were resolved at the meeting of the scholar and the blunt business man. Dr. Cone accepted the call to Akron.[3]

The appointment of Orello Cone to the presidency was widely hailed in the Universalist press. He was well known in the denomination because of his teaching and writing, and before his career at Buchtel was completed, no one in the Universalist world of the late nineteenth century would exceed him in accomplishment and reputation in scholarly work. His writing in the field of Biblical criticism and commentary established him in the international world of scholarship where he was recognized as peer of the formidable German critics. While President of Buchtel College he was actively publishing: in 1891, Putnam's of New York published his *Gospel-Criticism and Historical Christianity . . .,* and in 1893 *The Gospel and Its Earliest Interpretations: A Study of the Teaching of Jesus and Its Doctrinal Transformations in the New Testament.* In 1892 he joined two Harvard professors in editing the quarterly *New World,* published in Boston as successor to the defunct *Unitarian Review.* The quarterly declared itself "hospitable to progressive, scientific thought in religion." Among its contributors were George Santayana, Josiah Royce, Lyman Abbott, William James, Paul Elmer More, Mrs. Humphrey Ward, and L. P. Jacks.[4]

It is important to note this intense focus on scholarship because it explains in large part the difficulties that plagued Cone's later years in the presidency, and because it suggests a generalization about the scholar-turned-administrator, an enduring feature of the American educational scene. The man who by temperament and choice builds a scholarly career dedicated to a search for truth, who is contemptuous of sophistry and irrelevance, finds himself out of patience with the unending flow of trivia that crosses his desk as an administrator. Yet, left unattended, academic trivia

The President's House ca. 1890 was overshadowed by Old Buchtel. Crouse Gym is in the right rear next to the remnants of the President's barn.

becomes academic dynamite, so the scholar is trapped into giving serious attention to minutiae that, on the surface, does not warrant much consideration. This aspect of the administrator's activity represents only a fragment of his duties, and yet the scholar is prone to judge the job from this vantage point. In his scholarly investigations he is accustomed to dealing with harassing detail, but there he is in his element and is better reconciled to accepting it as part of the job. Finally, the scholar in his study need cater to no one; the scholar in the presidency must cater to everyone— faculty member, student, trustee, donor, politician, reporter, citizen—or be willing to pay the price his aloofness will inevitably exact from him and from the institution he serves as spokesman.

A little less handsome than his predecessors with his stocky build, mutton chop whiskers, and sober face, Orello Cone was warmly received by the students and faculty at the outset of his tenure. Maria Parsons, who taught English during his presidency, referred to Dr. Cone's 16 years as "good years for Buchtel." He was, she said, an "able, upright, honourable man, a master of six or seven languages, a scholar eloquent of tongue and pen. He loved his study and classroom; he detested cases of discipline."[5]

On September 13, 1880, the new president was inaugurated at ceremonies held in the College chapel before some 300 guests. John R. Buchtel invested Dr. Cone, and in the process repeated once more the erroneous notion that the College stood "upon the highest point of land within the limits of our State."[6] Dr. Cone commenced his inaugural address with the assurance that he had not invited his listeners to hear "large promises of a new order of things or schemes of radical innovation." What a comfortable sound those words have to many in our own time who resent the constant drive for change that permeates contemporary higher education. Cone directed attention to the danger of overdoing the "practical" aspects of education. He was not unaware that a sound education was the best preparation for making one's way in business and the professions, but he utterly rejected any attempt to allow the utilitarian and the material emphasis to outweigh the spiritual. He suggested that any such movement was "reactionary," interesting indeed to consider in light of the tendency of later generations to regard such movement as progressive. This call to keep the focus of higher education on the spiritual was not intended to minimize the accomplishments of American society:

> *Let us not, however, disparage the mighty spirit of this age, which energizes with such amazing force in material enterprises, conquering the powers of nature and making human life on its earthward side so rich and glorious. These are the achievements of intellect, and every new discovery, every triumph over matter is a jewel in its crown of glory. But let us set forth to man the high and divine uses to which all these forces should be put, in the service of which they must be spent in order to lend to them other than a transient and perishable value.*

The mission of the colleges, he continued, "is to furnish the higher education to the

President Orello Cone (1880–96)

utmost possible extent to the sons and daughters of the people." The public schools "are its proper feeders," and to their graduates it throws open its doors.[7]

An appeal was then made to the Universalists to support the school as they should; an equally strong appeal to the people of Akron "to whom the college appeals for sympathy, patronage, and material aid," indicates that Cone learned fast. As with the beginnings of the collegiate project, so now; the College was in every way except sentiment as much the creature of the city in which it flourished as it was the instrument of Universalism in higher education.

The new president got off to a great start. "Dr. Cone is taking hold with willing hands," reported Mr. Tinker, "school opens very buoyantly."[8] A few weeks later Tinker assured Mr. Buchtel, "Dr. Cone will make a good president. He is certainly taking hold as if he meant business."[9] One of the areas he was "taking hold" of was curriculum whose character he had spent so much time discussing in his inaugural address. Keeping the virtues and values of the old classical courses while also giving appropriate attention to the demands of a progressive age for more practically oriented courses, put the College right in the middle of conflicting interests that have pulled upon it to this day.

The well-intentioned attempt to balance the curriculum between courses that train a student to make a living and those designed to acquaint him with the mainstream of western culture has been an enduring one, leading in Cone's day to the beginning of the elective system on this campus and leading in our own time to general education. In the 1880's balance was attained by offsetting the rigidities of the various courses of study with a modest amount of course selection by the student. Now the search for balance takes the reverse pattern; certain core requirements are demanded of all students in an effort to guarantee at least minimal exposure to the mainstreams of our society's development.

During the decade of the seventies, President Eliot of Harvard was leading that school toward a full-fledged elective system.[10] It was accomplished a step at a time. In 1872 subject requirements for seniors were abolished, and the juniors followed in 1879. By 1884 the sophomores were liberated, and the freshmen, too, acquired the right to elect a portion of their studies in 1885. This move toward liberalizing requirements within courses of study was not accomplished peacefully either at Harvard or any other school that developed the elective principle. Trustees, faculty, alumni, and friends of the institution were usually all involved in spirited debate over the relative merits of the reformed curriculum.

Frederick Rudolph's fine history of the American college and university is helpful in giving us information about the process of reform as it unfolded nationally during the late nineteenth century. "Hardly an institution was spared the necessity of considering its own course of study in relation to the reforms that Eliot was carrying out at Harvard," says Rudolph. Most small schools found that discussion of reform centered as much around finance as around intellectual concern. The elective system, in order to be effective, "required an immediate and expensive expansion in faculty, staff, laboratories, and libraries, and while many of the smaller institutions, forced now to compete with the more popular expanding state institutions, indulged in university pretensions, they seldom succeeded in doing more than confusing themselves as to what their assigned role should be." The "intellectual anarchy" of the elective system, coupled with a rising secularism, often meant for the little College "a loss of old purpose without the discovery of new purpose."[11]

From its beginning, Buchtel College had provided courses which could be chosen at the discretion of a student who was not in a prescribed degree program. The "irregular" student, who could thus pick and choose his subjects of study, was given a "certificate of rank and advancement made" upon leaving college.[12]

In 1882 the "elective system" made its appearance in a tentative way. The elective system differed from the earlier electives in that the courses were considered part of the degree requirements and their selection was formalized and not indiscriminate. Buchtel embraced the system with enthusiasm. At the end of the first term of the sophomore year, the student was allowed to elect subjects from any four "courses" he wished to complete his degree requirements. Judging by the Harvard timetable, it is apparent that Buchtel was one of the first colleges to adopt the elective principle in a generous way. One would suspect that there was reasonable satisfaction with the new curriculum, since the catalog of 1887–88 has this to say about the elective system:

> By means of this system, applying as it does to the latter two-thirds of the course, the professors are enabled to extend each department of work considerably beyond the limitations of the ordinary college curriculum, and students are enabled to follow out those lines of advanced study most congenial to them. The experience of several years has proved this method to be satisfactory and successful.[13]

This modification of the curricular structure persisted for nearly 20 years until, in 1900, the three-term academic year was discarded in favor of the two-semester plan, and the final concession to the elective system was made by the substitution of the semester hour for the course as the basis of determining credit toward a degree.[14]

With the elective principle fully established, there came a predictable push on the part of persons interested in introducing new courses of study into the curriculum. We have already noted the attempt to introduce theology and civil engineering in the 1870's. Requests multiplied in the next two decades. In 1882, for example, the Board entertained a recommendation that municipal law be introduced, "possibly as an elective," and the plea was so successful that when instruction started in 1883 with A. B. Tinker as professor, it was made a required subject in all three degree programs.[15] By the 1890's, even photography, still more a technique than an art form, was being taught, which might well serve as evidence that our well known tendency to put everything of potential use or interest into the college curriculum has antecedents that go back further than most realize.[16]

Not everything proposed was accepted even when it had powerful support. In May, 1895, Judge A. C. Voris, long-time trustee, urged his colleagues to establish a school of manual training and industrial arts. The Judge was confident that the city of Akron would cooperate, possibly by endowing a chair to finance the cost of a professor. No action was taken on this request, probably because of the acute financial pinch then hampering the College, but the real significance of the proposal is that it demonstrates how far from the classical curriculum the thinking of a progressive trustee had drifted.[17] When, nearly 70 years later, a Community and Technical College was formed as part of The University of Akron, no one would have believed that its concern with vocational education was much the same as that proposed in Victorian times.

Every major change or reform experienced by a college breeds a host of administrative adjustments. Academic machinery must be put in a condition to perform the new tasks that the institution has set for itself. Prior to the adoption of the elective system, each branch of knowledge taught at Buchtel was under the direction of a "Professor" who occupied a "chair." This "chair" was usually endowed. In some subjects more than one person taught, and those of lesser rank—assistants, instructors, adjunct-professors—were never properly accorded the title "Professor." The elective system, however, introduced a spread of course offerings that could not possibly be handled under the old system. Now, those working together in one area of knowledge were constituted a "department" of instruction, and the courses they taught were offered within the department. The catalog of 1885 first lists a "Summary of Instruction by Departments" and recognizes the following departmental units: physical science, natural science, Greek, modern languages, Latin, English literature, mathematics, mental and moral philosophy, political science, and law. These so-called departments were not the strong, semi-autonomous units so familiar today; modern departmental structure developed on this campus about 1914 and has continued to grow in strength ever since, except for a brief flirtation with the divisional structure in the late 1930's.[18]

Growth of a specialized curriculum brought a commensurate need for new equipment. Ingenuity went a long way toward solving the need for equipment for classroom and laboratory. Dr. Knight had used student help and miscellaneous materials in converting part of the basement of Buchtel Hall into a makeshift laboratory for his work in the sciences. But the champion maker of ingenious props for the use of his classes was undoubtedly Professor Edward Claypole who took over the work in natural science in 1884 (Dr. Knight retaining the work in chemistry and physics which was now designated "physical science"). Claypole's students spent hours collecting specimens for geology and biology and in preparing the simple equipment needed for classroom use and for laboratory experiments. Of course this student participation in the making of the course was the best possible pedagogical device, for it has always been true that the most effective learning takes place when the learner is teacher, or in this case where the learner is the creator and builder of learning devices. Even Claypole could not meet all his needs by ingenuity alone. He secured Board approval in 1892 to spend up to $200 to purchase for the College museum the skeleton of a sloth recently found in Holmes County. Another $275 requested for a plaster cast of a mastodon was withheld, however, but the problem was neatly solved by Judge Green, a trustee, who donated such a cast two years later.[19]

As to the library, not much was done at this time to increase its limited treasures. The old curriculum had stressed recitation from prepared texts; no collateral reading was required or expected of the students. As in the College's first days, library holdings were used primarily to impress visitors and to prove to the world that the institution was a reservoir of knowledge.

Accessions to Bierce Library were painfully slow in the early years. Between July 1, 1891 and March, 1892, for example, only 20 titles were added to the collection.[20] There was not enough activity in ordering and classifying books to keep even one person employed full time. W. D. Shipman held the title "Librarian" starting in 1874 when he was still in his second year as an undergraduate. His successor, Charles Olin, managed the position for eight years, but it didn't take much of his time since he was also serving as secretary and treasurer of the College and its chief business officer, as adjunct-professor of mathematics, and official United States weatherman in Akron. In the long run, of course, the elective system was responsible for an irresistible need to strengthen the library and to make its use an expected part of the student's preparation.

Freeing the curricular structure, as we have noted, required additional faculty. As courses became more specialized, there was a tendency to seek instructors whose training was somewhat more specialized. In Cone's day as in ours certain visible signs of scholarly attainment were sought. Usually the Master's degree was thought to be sufficient evidence of scholarly attainment since American universities had but recently embarked on doctoral training, and it would be some years before schools like Buchtel could secure many professors with that level of formal schooling and training. But at least it was clear what an instructor was being hired to do at Buchtel College. He was to teach. If he also wished to engage in scholarly research in his field, it was done in addition to his teaching duties. It was assumed that the faculty member would be intimately involved in the life of the College. He would take his turn at the various academic and housekeeping duties that befell each member. The single men and women got an extra dose of this involvement since they were to live in the College halls and there serve as monitors.[21] Some managed this gracefully while others left the students with a distinctly bad impression.

There were few Buchtel teachers who were held in contempt by their students. The collegiate and preparatory faculties were generally admired and respected. Much credit for this belongs to Dr. Cone whose standards of selection placed more weight on professional soundness and personal worth than on piety and orthodoxy in Universalist tenets. Since the latter criteria were thought by the public to be adequate, it took considerable courage for the president to put other considerations first. While considering Miss Mary B. Jewett, Class of '76, and a faculty member of Hiram College, for the chair of English literature, Dr. Cone wrote that he was under strong pressure to appoint a Universalist, "but I shall not allow myself to be influenced by the *mere fact* of religious belief or association. I shall recommend the best qualified candidate regardless of Theological opinions."[22] The pressure was strong enough to cause him to write a week later that he would like Miss Jewett to attend the Universalist church as an example for the girls. "Could you give us a part of your heart, at least, in case you should find our preacher acceptable?" he asked wistfully.[23] She could, and she did.

As one of the first Buchtel graduates to be appointed to the faculty, her affable manner, keen enthusiasm for her students, and support of her Alma Mater made her a favorite of students and faculty. In 1892 she resigned and spent the next 18 years in New York in medical study and practice, thus following in the footsteps of her father who was a prominent Akron physician. In 1910 she left medical practice and relocated at Winter Haven, Florida where she turned into a "a Florida cracker, farmer, fruit grower, and in some small way, a social worker."[24]

Other women faculty members made a strong contribution to the College in this period. Dora Merrill, bright, gay, effective in her teaching, was the first to teach history as a separate subject. She resigned in 1892 and paralleled Mary Jewett's career by becoming manager of "several hundred acres" of apple orchards and farms in Emmett, Idaho. This is of interest because it demonstrates the degree to which these were liberated women who could make their way outside the sheltered walls of the College.[25] Such women must have provided the college girls with a model of confident womanhood that was influential in preparing so many of Buchtel's female graduates for active roles in the ministry, medicine, social work, nursing, administrative tasks on national, state, and local levels, and of course, teaching.

In the preparatory departments, Miss Jennie Gifford, Principal of the Preparatory School (1879–98) and teacher in the normal course, was a strong personality. One of her successors, Miss Martha Bortle, of "commanding presence, strong personality, and happy temperament," later entered the ministry and became pastor of a church in Hamilton, Ohio.[26]

The first of the great early triumvirate—Kolbe, Knight, Fraunfelter—to leave was Elias Fraunfelter. His replacement in mathematics was Charles S. Howe. In the six years he spent at Buchtel, Professor Howe made a fine contribution. His favorite subject was astronomy. He secured the funds needed for construction of a small observatory which was built and equipped in 1886–87 for $3,700. Howe's work resulted in making astronomy one of the most popular subjects at Buchtel because "it ceased to be a matter of lecture and textbook routine and in his hands became one of the most interesting, practical, and vital of studies."[27]

It was also due to Howe that Buchtel took her first steps in physical education. He organized the Buchtel Cadets and commenced military drill in the interests of physical fitness. This interest led him to take a prominent part in securing support for the new gymnasium which provided a facility for these activities. All too soon Howe left campus. He accepted a call to the presidency of the young Case School of Applied Science in Cleveland where his organizing talent would continue to be used.

Charles Bates was another who joined the faculty in Cone's administration. He taught Latin in what must have been a unique style. He would have each of the dozen students in his class recite at the same time. In this bedlam he was capable of attending to each recitation, and woe be to the student who tried to put anything over on him. His tall, slender, bearded presence was a familiar sight in East Hall where he roomed for many years.

Possibly the most scholarly member of the faculty—if one takes into account all the characteristics now ascribed to that outlook—was Professor Edward Claypole, an Englishman who came to America because his outspoken support of the views of Darwin and Wallace brought him under attack by the clergy of his homeland. Cone had no concern about his scientific views, but he found it prudent to cover his tracks on the religious issue. "At our last State Convention," he wrote to Claypole, "considerable criticism was expressed, because we did not make the college denominational enough—did not so move it as to make it helpful to the Church." He continued, "I have little sympathy with this tendency . . . I am not in search of a Christian Geologist, but I would like to be able to answer the question [of religious outlook] in case it should be proposed."[28]

Claypole's great contribution to Buchtel was to have each of his students undertake a thorough investigation of a specialized subject within a more general field of study. This was to train them in precision, but even more it was to give them some idea of the charm and discipline of research.[29]

His interests extended beyond the campus. As one of the organizers of the Ohio Academy of Science, he brought the group to Akron in 1892 and they were profitably and pleasurably occupied by trips to collect specimens on Long Lake and in the Cuyahoga Glens.[30] His two daughters were school favorites, and one of them, Edith, Class of '92, became one of the world's outstanding women scientists before her premature death at the University of California. Claypole left for California in 1897 to accept a position at Throop Polytechnic Institute (Cal Tech). His death in 1901 came shortly after he had learned that fire had destroyed Buchtel Hall and the fine collections he had acquired for the College.

The College's success in securing strong faculty members can be attributed to a number of factors. One of the most attractive conditions was the fact that Buchtel's denominational ties were much less onerous and demanding than those usually found in church-related schools of that period. Location is another factor that influences faculty, but it is not possible to say how much weight that carried. However, the bustling city of Akron provided at least as much extracurricular opportunity for faculty as did such towns as Hiram, Alliance, Wooster, Oberlin, and most other Ohio towns that boasted colleges of Buchtel's type. President Cone's scholarly outlook would be attractive. Perhaps salary, then as now a most important consideration, had much to do with it. Low as they were, Buchtel College salaries appear to have been in line with what similar schools paid. Indeed, in 1890 the *Buchtelite* claimed that "Buchtel is said to pay its professor of oratory the largest salary of any in the country."[31] Unfortunately, the writer did not reveal his source of information.

In recounting the successes of the past, it is almost certain that the picture painted is bigger than life. While students have the grace to praise good instruction, they also have the honesty to admit boredom and frustration when faced with inadequate courses or instructors.

The closer the student is to his college experience, the better he remembers those things that could have been improved upon. Despite the inroads made by the elective system in the late nineteenth century, students were still forced to take courses that some would have avoided if possible. This situation bred resentment. Probably no one put his disenchantment with his courses of study any more plainly than Orill Cole, Class of '99, who was in the gypsum business in Toronto. Sixteen years after graduation he had this to say about the relevance of his college courses:

> As in my former business of roofing and fireproofing, I have little opportunity to use the general education received at Buchtel. Occasionally I can use a little chemistry talk when trying to convince an obstinate prospective customer. . . . So far, however, my careful study of the earthworm in college days has not assisted me in increasing the annual dividend. I have never secured an order because I could call one or two butterflies by the first name . . . A general education is hard to estimate just as general publicity advertising is difficult to trace to direct results. I believe, however, if I had an opportunity again to take a college course, I would prefer to prepare along the lines of some specific profession or commercial activity during at least two or three years of the term. This is so manifestly an age of specialists that, unless a student has means, he should utilize his educational days to some extent in direct preparation for competition with trained men in his chosen vocation. [32]

One wonders whether it ever occurred to Mr. Cole that the power with which he stated his case was no doubt enhanced by the work he took at Buchtel. His assessment of the worth of higher education and the direction it should take was in the spirit of the times (1915), although it would have pained Orello Cone to hear general education dismissed so cavalierly.

Still another illustration of student disenchantment should be mentioned since the sentiments are as fresh in 1970 as they were when written in 1892. In the March issue of the *Buchtelite*, the editor observed that some students left college feeling dissatisfied with their courses, and he thought improvements could be made. That this situation existed, he said, was "abundant evidence" that something was lacking "to bind together the student and the college [and] get him interested in the welfare of his alma mater." He suggested that more interest should be taken in the students outside the classroom; that there be more contact with the faculty; and that there be more "occasional talks" from the instructors. [33] Apparently, the same lament now heard from 16,000 students in The University of Akron was then the lament of some 300 students in little Buchtel College.

Despite Buchtel's location in Akron—self-styled "tip top city"—the College was essentially a "country college," having little contact with the town. As one would expect, the town boys regarded the college boys as stuffed shirts while the college boys looked "with rank disfavor" on the local boys. [34] Only an occasional encounter in church, in a place of amusement, or in the infrequent contests between a College nine and a team from the city brought the two together. As the number of local students increased, however, there was a lessening of this isolation, and excursions to the house of a local student for a social or for Sunday dinner were common in the 1890's and thereafter. Until that time, however, life on Spicer Hill went on in a little world of its own when the shift of interest and support tied the College permanently to Akron. Houses were built in the fields and vacant lots adjacent to the campus, especially on the Carroll Street side, as the city gradually surrounded the College grounds.

At the Ohio State Fair, in 1894, the Buchtel football team walloped Ohio State University 12 to 6.

Prior to 1900 the student body was remarkably homogeneous, particularly if one considers only the College students and discounts the preps who were in large part Akronites. While Ohio had always supplied the largest number of dormitory students, eastern states had given way to neighboring states as the main source of out-of-state students. Nearly all who attended Buchtel were from "plain, substantial homes where there was no poverty and no great wealth." In many instances, " the sending of a boy or girl to college meant real sacrifice," wrote Frank Wieland, and the $40 annual tuition was "a colossal and forbidding sum" to many students.[35]

Many of the boys earned their way through school. Some found part-time work on the campus. Ringing the College bell paid tuition for one lucky student, but some of the jobs were less attractive. Tom Prior, for instance, finally quit his job of slopping President McCollester's hogs even though it paid expenses. In 1890, President Cone found it necessary to warn the boys about spending too much time on outside work. The *Buchtelite* approved the president's position saying that "there is time after leaving college to indulge in the greedy, grasping rush after gold, and it does no man harm to isolate himself from it for four years longer."[36]

Student homogeniety extended beyond financial conditions. One would expect to find a preponderance of Universalists in the student body, and this was the case during the College's first years. This proportion steadily diminished, however. A survey made in 1893 revealed that only 62 collegiate students, far less than half, were Universalists, and nearly all the rest were from "evangelical" Protestant denominations. One student was Catholic, two Hebrew, and three listed no preference, which led one observer to state that "religious toleration is carried out at Buchtel in fact as well as in theory."[37] Throughout its 40 years as a private college, this writer can identify just one Negro student at Buchtel, a Mr. A. P. Cook, "Buchtel's worthy colored student" who was in school in 1889 but appears not to have completed a degree program.[38] Likewise few foreign students appear on the register. One of these, Carlos D'Assumpacao of Sao Paulo, Brazil, was a member of the Class of '82. He tried earnestly, but unsuccessfully, to introduce fencing to his Buchtel classmates. More students from distant places probably would have come to Buchtel had the Universalists been more active in foreign missions since this often provided a feeder for foreign students to American colleges.

These students shared some common assumptions that were part of the conventional wisdom of American society in the Gilded Age. Capitalistic business enterprise was in its most aggressive phase. Most American business had been conducted on a somewhat localized or regional scale prior to 1870, but with the creation of great business combinations—trusts, pools, holding companies—business competition reached a peak of intensity that was reflected in the mapping out of national and international combines with monopolistic ambitions. Along with business consolidation came the first attempts to create government regulatory machinery that would provide the consumer some defense against corporate rapacity. Throughout this period, however, the American ethos was clearly geared to the support of "free enterprise," a spirit enshrined in the *laissez-faire* attitude of government. The student editor who wrote of the "greedy, grasping rush after gold" did not imply that his student readers should take no part in it; rather he said "there is time after leaving college" to indulge in it. This attitude, which was probably not unusual among Buchtel students, revealed the conviction that somehow college was a nice interlude before the grubby work of the world had to be faced, and apparently few expected to find much connection between what one learned in college and how one made a living. In our contemporary society, where almost no one seeks learning and culture for their own sake, the separation between college and "life" would be regarded as impractical.

The overwhelming majority of students at Buchtel must have felt in tune with the spirit of their time, if we can judge from an absence of recorded protest against it. On the other hand, some of the symptoms of a disjointed society caught their attention, and much interest was taken in righting certain well defined wrongs. Many students were outspoken in their support of women's suffrage and a number of faculty actively supported the cause.[39] The more bizarre labor abuses of the time were deplored but there is nothing to indicate shock at the 10-hour day, six-day week found in Akron factories, including John R. Buchtel's Buckeye Works. Temperance was a popular cause throughout this period supported alike by students and the "best" families of Akron.

The tolerant social ethic of Universalism could be seen in student attitudes, and this ethic, which gave emphasis to social justice of a rather general kind, was preached by McCollester, Rexford, Cone, and others to whom students listened. One did not find in Universalism that Calvinistic equation of success in this world with godly favor which provided such a motivating force in the evangelical churches. Even such late-comers to Universalism as John Buchtel and Ferdinand Schumacher (whose fortunes were well established before they were attracted to its beliefs) appeared to find more godly purpose in their charities than in the amassing of their fortunes.

It is tempting, of course, to push this point too hard. No one's life is as neatly compartmentalized as this argument implies. The cynic can suggest that it is easy to be charitable if one is securely protected against life's buffetings. Aunty Brown with her widow's mite was clearly within the spirit of giving recognized in Christian tradition. But it seems presumptuous to assume that John Buchtel, who gave away his entire fortune, acted any less within the spirit of Christian charity simply because he had more resources at his disposal to give.

The College students had no argument with Mr. Buchtel's wealth or his stewardship of it. Their argument was not with an economic system that permitted some men to become rich; it was with those who did not play the game fairly—men like Jay Gould, Jim Fisk, "Bet a Million" Gates—or with those who indulged in vulgar displays of wealth during this "Age of Excess."[40]

To the present generation, the students of the late nineteenth century would appear too smug about the world and their part in it. It was pride, however, and not smugness that led to observations such as one made in 1892 in the *Buchtelite:* "the

United States is the only country in the world which spends more money upon education than upon war or preparation for war."[41] Times have changed!

Student life in the dormitories went along its bumpy course. There was always difficulty in keeping the rooms filled with a satisfactory number of students; there were occasional complaints that the rooms were "double occupancy" which was regarded as a hardship by those seeking privacy. In common with every other school, Buchtel experienced problems with the quality of food served its boarders. Shortly after school opened in 1881, Mr. Tinker found it prudent to admit that certain charges against the boarding department were true. "The bread has sometimes been sour, flies have been found in the muffins, the butter has been generally bad, but I doubt the validity of the charge of 'absence of neatness in everything.'"[42] In 1880 a special Board committee was asked to investigate that part of President Rexford's report asking for a more home-like atmosphere for the young ladies in West Hall who appear to have petitioned the president to this effect. They desired a more pleasant and inviting place for socializing other than "the naked and cheerless hall," and in addition to a special waiting room they urged that the hallway be left to those who wish "to dance or skip and play."[43] This sought-for improvement was attained; later publications from the College frequently commented upon the fine quarters fitted out for social affairs and casual gatherings.

Security was another problem associated with the dormitories. Much against the wishes of the College officers, the state had required that fire escapes be erected across the front of Buchtel Hall. As the frequent fires proved, this was an elementary precaution, but there was little doubt that the ugly iron framework spoiled the facade of the building. It also made it possible for prowlers, of whatever motive, to gain access to the dormitory rooms from outside the building.

In the 1890's a series of incidents involving men on the fire escapes outside the ladies' rooms seriously disturbed the College. The business manager, C. R. Olin, reported an incident to the state inspector in November, 1892: "Now again last night some man entered one of the ladies' rooms about 12 or 1 o'clock, and it has so frightened the young ladies rooming there that we shall have to devise some effectual means to prevent the escapes from being thus improperly used. Unless something can be done about this very soon, all of our 40 or so lady roomers are likely to go out of the building . . ."[44] One of the steps taken was to post a guard. In April, Officer Harrison caught the "ghost" who had been using the escapes for his purposes. The "ghost," who lived within a few blocks of the College, was released with a warning.[45] This did not suffice, however, for prowlers continued to use the escapes. A professor charged with visiting a lady student in her room by means of the fire escape strenuously denied it; still other suspects were identified at various times, and Olin outlined to the faculty steps to minimize the problem. These didn't work. In 1898 Professor Egbert with the assistance of some of the girls caught a prowler who had been at his activity for two years.[46] Only the destruction of the building in 1899 ended the problem. This tempts one to speculate that either the monitoring of the building was inefficiently handled, or the young men of the College and neighborhood were unusually audacious, or even that the young ladies covertly offered encouragement and aid to a venturesome swain who wished to pay his respects.

At the same time these nocturnal excursions caused Olin to fear that the young ladies would vacate the West Hall dormitory, plans were afoot to discontinue the use of East Hall as a dormitory for young men and appropriate it to the use of the young ladies. There were three contributing factors behind this decision: the number of boys living in the dormitory was at a low point; it was difficult to persuade the bachelor faculty members to room in the dormitory; and keeping control of the boys took an extraordinary amount of time and resource. In June, 1893, on the recommendation of the president, the Board voted to close East Hall as a boy's dormitory and fit it out as a girl's dormitory as soon as finances would permit.[47] The boys would room in private homes near campus.

Dormitory pranks were not to be confused with moral tone. In the latter respect the College was well pleased with its record. President Cone assured a concerned lady in 1893 that:

. . . so far as the moral tone of our students is concerned . . . no college in Ohio or vicinity surpasses us. This is the reputation which Buchtel has borne for a long time. We do not, it is true, set forth so extensive a code of rules and regulations for the government of our students [for] it has been thought best for the young men and women to depend in large degree upon their sense of honor. At the same time, however, a vigilant care is exercised to eliminate from among them influences that are likely to be bad.[48]

True, there were trying moments. Dr. Cone felt called upon to inform a father of his daughter's behavior:

Adele is excessively forward in her relations with gentlemen, often rude, and sometimes goes to an excess which is dangerous to her reputation for modesty at least. I refer to sitting in a gentleman's lap, or at least on the arm of his chair with her feet across his lap and over the opposite side of the chair. His arm was around her waist. There is no doubt about this, for it has come from a reliable eye witness.

Possibly some of the President's concern grew out of the fact that "Adele indulges in the freest and loudest criticisms of the management . . . and applies opprobrious epithets to those in authority."[49] With this kind of conduct to contend with, it is remarkable that President Cone was the one who recommended turning over East Hall to the "ladies."

Of all the traumas resulting from student behavior, the greatest in Cone's experience must have been that which resulted from the comedy of events centering around Henry Morris. Henry was an exception to the rule about Buchtel students being of humble origins, for his father was a successful Chicago lawyer. Henry was a delicate boy who did not take kindly to being "bounced" in a blanket as per custom. Driven on by his "cranky" mother with her "endless jealousy and suspicion," and by his equally "cranky" father, he had the students who bounced him arrested. After making public apology, the students were released. But students can retaliate against those who flaunt their custom. Henry was promptly dropped as business manager of the College annual. This stimulated a bitter letter from Henry's mother who warned the editor, on behalf of her husband, "that you cross not his path in this world." Henry found it prudent to have a bodyguard with him as he attended campus functions, particularly after he claimed that he lost the annual oratorical contest to a girl because of fraud, and then published his charges which were promptly reprinted in newspapers around the country.[50]

President Cone must have been relieved when Henry withdrew from Buchtel at the end of his third year. He finished his degree at Lombard College. Twenty-five years later, however, after a successful career as an attorney and public service as United States Consul in Ghent, Belgium, he was awarded a Master's degree by Buchtel College. Upon his death, Henry's library of some 20,000 volumes was given to The University of Akron library where it now forms an important part of the collections.

Although Henry Morris was disappointed in his oratorical efforts, it was the annual oratorical contest that led to the emergence of Buchtel College's first student hero, Robert Tucker, Class of '91. As winner of the local contest, Tucker was eligible for the state contest held at Springfield, and there he won first place with his oration, "Democracy the Dominant Idea." A telegram announcing the victory was read to an expectant crowd on the first floor of East Hall whereupon "the whole building rang with the college yell." The ladies joined in the celebration, the College bell pealed, and a bonfire was set ablaze. Then "an immense crowd of boys" set out with horns and drums for the residences of John R. Buchtel, Ferdinand Schumacher, and Joy Pendleton where the good news was announced. The parade went on downtown, "making the night hideous," then returned to campus where a salute was fired. "It was the greatest night in the history of the College," according to the special edition of the *Buchtelite* issued in honor of the event. On arrival in Akron, Tucker made his way triumphantly to the College grounds in a carriage pulled by four white horses, preceded by the Eighth Regiment Band and a crowd of students. The pride engendered by events of this kind was needed by a college that had few moments to stand above the crowd.[51]

There were, of course, a number of special celebrations throughout the academic year which served the purpose of rallying college spirit or simply of providing an outlet for the high spirits that are better released in organized horseplay than in destructive improvisation. Founder's Day was first observed in 1882.[52] It has evolved in form over the years, but its purpose remains to bring honor and recognition to those whose generosity, spirit, and talent were largely responsible for the school's early successes. Class Day was celebrated in connection with the commencement season until 1885. Thereafter the classes voted against it because it ran into commencement activities and the annual Ashton Speaking contest.[53] The latter was given much attention not only because it carried a prize, but also because speaking proficiency was much admired.

At the beginning of the school year, the rivalry between the sophomore and freshman classes could be counted on to enliven things. Throughout most, if not all, of Buchtel's history as a private school, freshmen were required to wear beanies or some distinguishing headgear—a German student cap served the purpose in 1889.[54] Then of course the class rush, or "color rush," between the upper classmen and freshmen gave outlet to high spirits, so much so that periodically it was curtailed lest someone be injured. At the other end of the school year, the seniors held "cremations," solemn ceremonies in which robed seniors carried a representative sample of their textbooks to a funeral pyre burning atop the class stone of '79 and celebrated as the flames liberated them from the tyranny of their lessons.[55] Throughout the year there were spontaneous bonfires and parades to enliven the student's life. Wooden slats from fences or walks in the campus area were often appropriated to kindle a blaze. Just as frequently, the appropriators were required to pay for damages and supply the labor necessary to restore property.

Another outlet for high spirits were the College socials, held weekly in the dining hall, and presided over by the faculty in a manner that precluded undue revelry. The College social was as much a part of the student's social training as it was a chance for him to have fun. Dancing was a principal activity. It may be that, as the catalog claimed, the "influences exerted by the sexes upon each other have been wholly beneficial," but there were limits. In the square dances boys danced with girls, but in the round dances, boys danced with boys and girls with girls. As one who participated said later, "whoever said that dancing is the poetry of motion never saw two men trying to waltz or polka together in the basement of Buchtel." The faculty, he continued, "sat in one corner of the room in icy and lofty seclusion, and eyed us ominously. I think they feared that under the sin-compelling influence of the dance we would lead some husky partner to a bar and buy him a drink."[56]

More popular by far were the class socials. They were usually held in the homes of class members who lived in or near Akron. Since the freshmen had the largest numbers and were the most enthusiastic in their celebrations, it was a point of honor for the upperclassmen to discover the location of the freshmen socials and then steal the refreshments. Seniors rarely held socials on a regular basis, probably because the class was invariably small by that time.

During the winter months ice skating, taffy pulls, and sleigh rides were favorite student diversions. In the warmer months the natural advantages of Buchtel's location gave opportunity for a variety of activities. One former student reminisced about "the many lakes, the beautiful scenery of the Gorge with its famous Fosdick's Inn and chicken and hot biscuit suppers, Gaylord's Grove and its picnic grounds, the Cuyahoga River with its boating, Silver and Long Lakes with their dance pavilions, State Mill with its famous fish fries, the old canal, the chestnut groves and the sugar camps" all of which furnished entertainment and added to the charm of Buchtel's social life.[57] To those of a later generation who know the old Ohio Canal as an open sewer, who have seen the chestnuts succumb to blight and the picnic groves fall before the developer's bulldozer, and who would scarcely risk a swim in the polluted waters of nearby lakes, these earlier delights, now despoiled, create an anguish of spirit that is almost physical in intensity.

In addition to enjoying a more relaxed social life after 1880, the students were showing signs of wanting some form of self-government. It had been difficult for College authorities to find bachelor faculty members who were willing to live in East Hall and monitor the men's conduct. By 1890 the *Buchtelite* was commenting on an absence of supervision over "the men's side of the house." Whether this absence was intentional or not, student self-government was "undoubtedly the wisest policy." In October, 1892 the *Buchtelite* urged that all matters of discipline be referred to a body composed of faculty members and students to be chosen by each class. Later that month, President Cone submitted a plan for "student government" to the executive committee of the Board, and the committee gave the faculty its consent to try the "experiment" for one year.[58] The movement failed to achieve its objective. A year later, President Cone recommended that the young men be turned out of East Hall because it was impossible to maintain order.

From the College's first days, organized student activities provided opportunities for leadership and personal development that the formal curriculum was not geared to provide. The first organizations to make an appearance were the literary societies.[59] A short-lived Greeley Society founded by the men failed to catch on. Distressed, so it is said, by their exclusion from Greeley, the girls formed the Cary Literary Society soon afterward, and with the encouragement of President McCollester, they fitted up a meeting room. The chief activity of these societies was to encourage literacy in all its forms through the performance of readings, orations, "dramatic presentations," debates. Many of these "entertainments" were open to the public; indeed, the first public entertainment performed by college students in Akron was put on in the first college term by the Greeley men and the Cary women. Money raised in this fashion was used for philanthropic purposes and for fixing up the meeting rooms. Not all the efforts of the literary societies were appreciated by the public. Bryant Society for men, founded in 1873, presented a farce which proved to be just that. As the local newspaper reported it:

> *Though the play is extremely laughable in parts, its selection was, to say the least, an unfortunate one, and while Bryant Society has shown itself able to present a programme of literary merit, the public will doubtless be gratified if comedies of the stamp of "Yankee Land" are in the future dispensed with.*[60]

It was a blessing that William Cullen Bryant, the venerable American poet whose name graced the society, was unaware of its efforts. Had he been able to accept their invitation to address the 1878 commencement, he might have learned that not all that was done in his name was meritorious.

In 1883, Bryant Society joined with a portion of the Cary Society to form the Buchtel Union Literary Society. By 1889, only the Everett Society, "a preparatory society for young gentlemen," remained in good health. It continued its activities into the 1890's but eventually succumbed like the others, some of which had such a short existence as to escape notice here, because of the competition of required rhetoricals in chapel, the growth of the fraternity system, and other College activities.

Among these other activities were the debating clubs which made a brief appearance in the nineties. Like the literary societies, they were crowded out of existence by competition from the curriculum on the one hand and competing extracurricular activities on the other. The requirement that students perform publicly at chapel "rhetoricals" or at special times set aside for examination cut into their enthusiasm for additional speaking activities. In 1893, for instance, the Junior Class appeared in the annual Junior Exhibition—open to the public, as were virtually all such affairs—and some 21 essays, orations, and class histories, etc. were dutifully presented on topics ranging from "North American Indians" to "Prohibition vs. the

Keeley Cure." The one oratorical activity that endures to this day, the Ashton Prize Contest, began in 1887 as the result of a gift of $3,000 from Oliver C. Ashton, of Bryan, Ohio, the income from the gift to go for prizes in an annual contest in each of the three upper classes for "excellence in reading and recitation."

In the areas of drama and music where so much is now accomplished, there was little extracurricular activity in the nineteenth century. The only dramatic productions were those sponsored by the literary societies or by the classes for presentation on Class Day or some other appropriate occasion. Most of these attempts at theater were valued more for entertainment than for serious opportunity for acting and dramatic interpretation.

Music had been part of the regular curriculum since the opening of the school, and a number of able faculty members served its interest, particularly Gustavus Sigel who devoted 18 years to it, but there was little in the way of extracurricular musical activity of an organized sort. Early references to a College orchestra are misleading since they appear to refer to temporary groups assembled for particular programs. The earliest mention of a regular choir appears in 1892 when 16 men and women formed a chapel choir in an effort to improve the quality of singing at the daily services. They started out well, but we have no record of how enduring their presence or success was. A "college band" is mentioned from time to time, but it appears to have been an impromptu group to accompany parades and play at athletic contests.

Along with athletics, the activity that captured the greatest interest and devotion of Buchtel students was the fraternity system. The record of Buchtel College and The University of Akron in the annals of the national fraternity system is remarkable, especially so because Buchtel College was small and not blessed with affluent students, while the University is essentially local in its orientation, and thus the fraternities lose the advantage of having most of their men living in the houses on a regular basis. The University's story will come later in this account, but it is predicated on the formative years of fraternity life in Buchtel College.

Although the establishment of national fraternity chapters at various colleges about the country was not a new phenomenon in the 1870's, Buchtel College was among those schools to be well represented in what were still the comparatively early stages of the system's development.[61] In 1873 Eta chapter of Delta Tau Delta was established as Buchtel's first fraternity. It was the fifth chapter in this expanding national fraternity founded some 14 years earlier at Bethany College. In January, 1875, nine Buchtel men were initiated into Phi Delta Theta and were constituted the Ohio Eta chapter, later changed to Ohio Epsilon. Like the Delta Tau Deltas, they fitted out a "suite of rooms," the Phi Delts being located in the Arcade building on Howard Street. There were scarcely enough upperclass men in the College to justify two fraternities since many of the boys had neither the money nor the inclination to join. And, of course, not all were invited. That perennial bane of fraternity life—the "ins" vs. the "outs"—plagued Buchtel fraternity life from the beginning. The fraternities competed with each other in every segment of college life, but they banded together in defending the superiority of the fraternity system whenever threatened from the outside. The constant trumpeting of their virtues created an aura of snobbishness that was galling to the non-frat man.

On Founder's Day, 1882, a new secret society was announced. Eight men joined together in the Lone Star Fraternity, which by 1883 had adopted all the characteristics of the national chapters, including a rented suite of rooms in which to gather. According to local tradition, this is the oldest surviving local fraternity outside of New England, and it still maintains a very active role in campus affairs.

The three fraternities flourished through the 1880's and on into the 1890's but were suddenly and dramatically caught up short in the severe depression of the mid-1890's. The number of men enrolled in the college course dropped alarmingly; there were so few that each chapter was hard-pressed to secure and hold a sufficient number to make operation worthwhile. Delta Tau Delta was so depleted of members that it voluntarily surrendered its charter to the national office in 1895. Although it had served most effectively (Frank Wieland, Class of '90, was its national president

for six years after 1901), the charter was never reinstated, and Buchtel's first fraternity disappeared permanently from campus. In like fashion, Phi Delta Theta surrendered its charter to the national in 1896. Within two years some five of Ohio Epsilon's
remaining members associated themselves together as the Zeta Alpha Epsilon fraternity (local) with the hope that Phi Delta Theta would renew the charter of Ohio
Epsilon and that they would thus be brought back into the national fraternity. The
national was not interested, however, and Zeta Alpha Epsilon was to remain local
until well after the passing of Buchtel College. Lone Star likewise fell inactive in
1896–97. In 1897, seven students petitioned the alumni for the Lone Star charter and
they were accepted and initiated into the fraternity which was then formally incorporated under the laws of Ohio on January 29, 1898.

The course of the women's fraternity (hereafter called sorority) efforts during
the same period ran somewhat smoother. In 1877 three Buchtel girls organized
Lambda chapter of Kappa Kappa Gamma. They met secretly in one of the dormitory
rooms for a while but later transferred their meetings to Cary Hall which continued
to be their home until 1899. Several of their members achieved national office in the
nineteenth century, and in 1886 Lambda Chapter entertained the national convention in Akron using the Phi Delta Theta rooms for the event. By all odds, the most
tragic event associated with the fraternity system at Buchtel was the terrible Kappa
fire of 1890. During a festive social in the sorority room, one of the girls, dancing
about the room in her gauze costume, brushed her tall hat against a gas jet which
immediately set her clothing ablaze. The flames spread instantly to others and to
those who attempted to beat out the flames with their hands. May Steves and Lula
Steigmeyer died that night; six others were badly burned, one later dying of her
injuries. The College was plunged into shock and mourning. Only the bond of shock
and grief held the Kappa chapter together at that moment.

Buchtel's only other sorority before the turn of the century was Delta Gamma
which chartered Eta Chapter on March 15, 1879. A small room in the living quarters
of Buchtel Hall was the DG's first meeting place, but they soon moved into more
spacious quarters on the fifth floor. Buchtel's delegation was one of two that attended
the first national convention in Oxford, Mississippi in 1881. The Akron chapter was
host to the second national convention in 1883. It couldn't have been too large a
gathering since the banquet was well accommodated in the home of Jessie Tibbals.
Again in 1893 Eta chapter invited the national convention to Akron and the meetings
were held in the Universalist church. The sorority journal, *The Anchora,* was started
and first published in Akron under the direction of Eta chapter and remained its
responsibility from 1884 to 1887. These sketches of the beginnings of the fraternity
system at Buchtel serve merely to establish the movement in point of time in the
school's history. An assessment of their role will be made in a later chapter.

Publication activities made an appearance in the early years of the College.[62]
The first serious effort was the *Argo,* a class yearbook published by the Class of '80.
This annual set a format copied by succeeding classes. It contained general information about the College and its personnel, information of the sort normally found in
the College catalog. It had sections devoted to sports, fraternities and sororities,
various student organizations, a class roster, alumni roster, and a good deal of non-
sense of the kind that is intelligible only to those who have lived through common
experiences. A substantial number of business advertisements, many from companies
represented by Board members, rounded out the publication and doubtless made its
existence possible. Two years after the *Argo,* the *Buchtel* was published by the Class
of '82. Class annuals continued with some regularity under that title until 1908.
Following a gap in publication, the Class of '11 published its annual under a new title
—the *Tel Buch*—and this name persists to the present.

The other important publication of the early days was the journal started by A. E. Hyre who, as a sophomore, edited the *Buchtel Record* in 1882. According to Hyre's later account, there was no student interest in a paper so he persuaded "Uncle Johnny Buchtel" to promise half the financial support. The students cooperated by pledging to buy a suitable paper; the faculty cooperated by endorsing the scheme, and on January 18, 1882, the first celebration of Founder's Day at Buchtel, the *Buchtel Record* made its appearance. Hyre was a good businessman as well as editor. With but 54 College students in school and but 63 on the alumni rolls, the paid subscriptions reached 300 copies per month. This venture in private enterprise was successful, and in the spring of 1883 Hyre sold the paper to E. J. Felt, Class of '87, who continued publication until the College bought him out and placed the paper in the hands of the students as a regular activity.[63]

The new paper, now called the *Buchtelite,* was edited by Ed Cone, Class of '89, the president's son. The first issue in April, 1889, was introduced by the editor as filling a need: "For several years past there has seemed to be something lacking in the life of our college. Frequent demands have been made and wishes expressed for a paper."[64] The new venture was to serve the alumni as well as the current student body so that in a sense it was the forerunner of the *Alumni Quarterly.*[65]

The new student paper was organized just in time to take a leading role in the formation of the Ohio Inter-Collegiate Press Association. At the Association's first meeting, at Wooster, May, 1890, the editor of the *Buchtelite* was chosen president of the group that included Wooster, Kenyon, Denison, Ohio University, Western Reserve, and Ohio State.[66]

As is so often the case with fairly new enterprises, once the enthusiasts who start them have left college, it becomes difficult to find others with similar drive and interest to carry on. Already by 1892, editor James Cole would write in his farewell editorial that "with one or two exceptions," it had been "almost impossible to get the students to contribute" material for the paper "while voluntary contributions would have shocked us."[67] Thus it has been throughout much of the *Buchtelite's* long life.

It did not take the Buchtel College boys long to organize their first athletic contest.[68] On October 5, 1872, the College baseball nine played a team from the city. No record remains of the outcome of this initial foray into organized athletics, but it is known that the first intercollegiate athletic contest in Akron took place in 1873. The baseball team of that year played three games with other colleges and one each with an Akron nine and one from Cuyahoga Falls. They won just one of the five contests, besting Wooster 38 to 20. Not until 1879 would they again play more than one game a year; indeed they would not win another baseball game until beating Wooster 22 to 6 in that year. In 1877 the boys had their first experience trying to hit a curve ball. None of them knew just why it was so difficult to hit against the Western Reserve pitcher, but Paul Miller claimed the ball curved away from the batter. This started an argument, for his teammates said it was not possible for the ball to curve. Even Professor Fraunfelter appeared to be skeptical. While out survey- ing on Carroll Street, Gus Guthrie took three surveying poles, set them up in a line, and standing to the south of the first pole, repeatedly threw the ball so that it passed north of the middle pole and south of the pole on the end. This demonstration not only settled the argument, it made Guthrie much in demand as a pitcher.

The games were played on vacant lots across Carroll Street from the campus. Money to purchase bats and balls was secured by passing the hat, and balls were so scarce that play had to be halted whenever the ball was lost in weeds or puddles, for there were no replacements immediately available. Of course, these first baseball games were entirely a student undertaking. The faculty and administration allowed the boys to make their own arrangements and pay their own expenses. In 1890 representatives from Buchtel met with their counterparts from Wooster, Denison, and Ohio State at the Arcade Hotel in Springfield and agreed to form the Ohio Inter-Collegiate Athletic Association. W. B. Baldwin of Buchtel drafted a constitution that resembled one recently adopted for use on the Buchtel campus. The executive committee of the Association had power to draft schedules. An interchange of eligibility lists certified by the faculties was provided. Only a *bona fide* student could compete, that is, one who had "attended at least two college exercises for two weeks prior to the date of the contest." The latitude afforded by this definition of "student" hampered no one seriously.

Football made its appearance in 1891. Prior to that time there were sandlot games, but formation of the Athletic Association gave impetus to the formation of a College team. Buchtel started out by losing to Western Reserve Academy 22 to 6 at Hudson.[69] On November 5, 1891, Kenyon came to Akron to play the first intercollegiate game of football the city had witnessed. The Buchtel boys went down to defeat, 42 to 0.

The team was without a coach, but, in the primitive action of that time, the lack of a coach was not so keenly felt as would be the case in the present day when the game resembles a science. One old-timer who played in the early games described the action some years later:

> The game was a much fiercer proposition than at present. All massed plays were in vogue, including the flying wedge, and when 22 men came together after a five or ten yard start, in a double-V formation, something happened to the men in the front lines of those V's. A man could not be taken out of the game unless he had received sufficient damage to disable him from further participation. Broken arms, legs, noses, shoulders, ribs, etc., were in the inventory of every game.[70]

A big boost was given athletics at Buchtel by the completion of Crouse Gymnasium in 1888 and the development of Buchtel Field in 1892. Property for the latter amounting to four acres was purchased by the Board in 1891 at a cost of $8,700. The field was located four blocks south of the campus at the corner of Kling and Wheeler Streets. Some $3,700 was spent in preparing the grounds and erecting a grandstand that seated 300 people. A running track and tennis courts were part of the facility. The entire area was fenced in. Apparently it was named "Buchtel Field," for it has always gone by that name, yet there is no evidence that it was given the name formally.

The students were delighted with these developments. The new facilities gave impetus to athletics. "Athletics have never run high at Buchtel," wrote the *Buchtelite* editor, "but a revolution has taken place."[71] Buchtel students looked with pity upon Wooster College whose faculty, it was reported, had abolished intercollegiate athletics. This was contrasted unfavorably with the helpful attitude and assistance given Buchtel students by their trustees.

The new athletic grounds were opened October 15, 1892, on the day of the first football game of the season. The College band paraded through Akron's streets followed by the Buchtel and Case teams in wagons. It was Buchtel's last cheering for the day since Case scored a 14 to 9 victory.

It was apparent that if Buchtel were to hold her own with other colleges, her teams must have a coach. The 1892 team was assisted by a Mr. Cook from the Cleveland Athletic Club, and his advice helped make possible victories over Denison and Hiram and also over the Akron Athletic Club in the first Thanksgiving Day game in Akron's history. But a permanent director of athletics was sought by the boys. With Dr. Cone's blessing and his promise to arrange with the Board of Trustees to pay a salary for the director, the boys sought out Mr. John W. Heisman, a recent graduate of Pennsylvania who had coached the undefeated Oberlin team of 1892. Heisman accepted the offer and did splendid work with the baseball and football teams of 1893–94.

The coach's job was far from easy. Buchtel had about 100 boys, a number of whom worked their way through school so that there were scarcely enough left to field a team and almost no scrubs to practice against. The editor of the paper lent his support by indicating that there were some students who would not get on the football team, "but the team must have someone to sacrifice himself for the good of his fellow students and for his college."[72] Just the way he said it had an ominous ring. Under these handicaps Heisman's success, especially with the football team, brightened the athletic promise of Buchtel College.

At this juncture, however, the faculty felt called upon to express its concern, and Mr. Heisman received a letter informing him that, in the judgment of the faculty, "the athletic sports should be for the benefit of the regular student of the college; and that the main object should not be to win in the contests in which the clubs may participate, but to minister to the physical development of those engaged in this exercise."[73] So at the end of the 1894 baseball season Mr. Heisman severed his connection with the College. Strangely enough, he seems to have given the boys one last fling, for many years later he wrote to Charles Bulger, then compiling information for inclusion in Spanton's history, describing a football game played September 5, 1894 against Ohio State University as part of the entertainment of the Ohio State Fair in Columbus.[74] Since it marks Buchtel's only football victory over O.S.U., it might be appropriate to notice the manner of its accomplishment. After playing two twenty-minute halves in burning heat, and the score deadlocked at six points apiece, the teams took a ten-minute rest and then started a "sudden death" overtime period. Heisman himself was playing quarterback and he drove the team to Ohio's four-yard line. There he stopped and made a little inspirational talk to the team. On the next play he stuck the ball squarely in the "breadbasket" of the fullback, Frank Fisher. "Fortunately," said Heisman, "he either saw or felt it—and got it. Then away we all went like mad. I think about every man on the team had his hands on Frank somewhere, for that was in the days when hiking the runner was *the* big thing in the game. I recall I had hold of him by the back of his jersey and was going in front of him. And we all went through together, just like the water of a mill dam when the dam goes out. With a last yank I tore the jersey clear off Frank's back—but what did it matter since we were across?" Since Heisman later coached Georgia Tech and the University of Pennsylvania, it is evident that his Buchtel days made an impression on him since he could recall them in such detail more than 20 years later. It is this same Heisman for whom the trophy annually awarded the country's outstanding college football player is named.

In 1893 the newborn Ohio Inter-Collegiate Athletic Association broke apart in a dispute concerning the eligibility of an Adelbert track man. Buchtel's representatives resigned as a result of the dispute, but the other disputants refused to accept a resignation and insisted on voting to expel Buchtel from the Association. This difference, coupled with the leaving of Heisman, dampened enthusiasm for athletics, and the effort in organized sports was spotty until early in the twentieth century. The editor of the *Buchtelite* was disgusted with the lack of interest. Students, he felt, should give a little time to athletics instead of "talking with the girls in the library, lounging in each other's rooms and running to cheap third class theatres."[75] Not only baseball and football were affected. Tennis, track, and fencing had each made a hesitant appearance on Buchtel's athletic scene, but no sustained effort was made in any of these sports at that time.

Throughout the maturation of the young College, efforts were made to improve the campus and the physical plant. In its first years, Buchtel Hall stood in the center of a construction wasteland. In the seventies and eighties extensive landscaping relieved the barren ugliness. Lawns, trees, shrubbery, and flowers were planted to soften the stark scene. Stone walks were laid and a curving drive was built up to the front of the massive building.[76] Each graduating class left some memento—trees, benches, plaques—which added interest to the grounds.

Among these class mementos, the class stone of '79 remains today as the oldest physical connection with Buchtel College. The larger and more visible stone of the Class of '80, a huge piece of syenite some 90 cubic feet in size, was found on the farm of Colonel Perkins, and with much ingenuity and expense was hauled from its moorings in what is now the near west side of Akron to the College grounds, more than two miles away, where it stands today. The whole dramatic story is told in Spanton's history. When the excavation was dug for the Education Building in 1960, the great rock had to be shifted to its present resting spot just south of Knight Hall. The stone was so heavy and so well imbedded that it tipped the crane whose powerful winches attempted to pull it from its moorings.

Another addition to the College grounds was an enormous ornamental cast iron urn situated on the front lawn. It came from Mr. Buchtel's residence. The urn was planted annually, and it was a familiar sight until its removal in the 1960's when it became apparent that its Victorian character contrasted unhappily with the functionalism of the buildings that were its neighbors.

Around the whole of the improved grounds an elaborate iron fence was erected in 1884.[77] It was ornamental in part, but was also designed to prevent neighborhood boys from using the College grounds as a shortcut on their way to the Akron High School just two blocks away. This effort to prevent paths from being worn in the lawn was no more successful than later attempts.

Briefly, in the 1880's, the campus was disfigured as a result of Buchtel's participation in Akron's first attempt to use electricity for lighting the streets at night. A huge mast, one of three in the city, was constructed atop Buchtel Hall. Its four lamps, each of 4,000 candle power, gave off such a harsh brightness that it annoyed those nearby. This brightness had little penetrating power, however, and the experiment was soon abandoned by the city in favor of suspending street lamps from poles located at street intersections. The disfiguring mast was taken down to the relief of everyone.[78]

The high point of campus improvement in the eighties was the erection of a gymnasium. As early as 1880, some of the boys secured plans from a local architect, Frank Weary, "for a cheap but attractive structure 44 by 66 feet with a bowling alley attached."[79] The cost of this building was estimated at $800. Today, one could not build a garage for that amount, but even this small sum was impossible to raise without support from the Board. The boys' enthusiasm persisted, however, and in 1886–87 a fund-raising campaign was launched under the direction of President Cone. The subscription fund was started by John Buchtel, who offered to give the boys $1,000 if they would carry him in his "invalid" chair to the fourth floor chapel so that he could attend the commencement exercises of 1887. The offer was quickly accepted. On July 4, the executive committee of the Board appointed George W. Crouse and Ferdinand Schumacher to raise $20,000 for the gymnasium. Each of them immediately subscribed $5,000 to the cause, and with a later contribution of another $5,000 from Mr. Crouse, and smaller gifts from others, the money was raised so that ground could be broken by August 15. Arrangements with the architect, Jacob Snyder of Akron, were left to Professors Howe and Jeffords whose efforts had precipitated the formation of the Buchtel Cadets. Equipment was donated by Jonas Pierce of Sharpsville, Pennsylvania. The new structure was formally dedicated on February 22, 1888. Its first event was a dance given by the College girls.[80]

It was named Crouse Gymnasium in honor of the man who had donated about half the required money. "The finest gym west of the Alleghenies," as it was sometimes called, was of brick and stone construction. In addition to the playing floor, it contained a bowling alley, dressing and bathing rooms, a running gallery eleven feet above the gymnasium floor, a small visitor's gallery, and examination and apparatus rooms. This fine facility encouraged the faculty to require physical exercise of all students, and the gym was to be open to students for voluntary exercise during the week.[81] With the completion of Buchtel Field in 1892 and a batting cage alongside the gym in 1893, Buchtel College had sports facilities that compared favorably with those of schools in its class.

The elective system placed a strain on instructional facilities, and President Cone urged the construction of a library building and a science building to relieve it.[82] A fund drive was started on behalf of a science building. It was off to a good start with gifts of $10,000 apiece from George Crouse, Ferdinand Schumacher, and John F. Eddy of Bay City, Michigan. Enough money was raised to start construction on the west end of the campus, but this work had not progressed far when the depression 1893 dealt the College and its supporters a devastating blow. The science building could not be completed beyond its foundation. Seven years later, a portion of that foundation would be used for the new Academy building (later Olin Hall).

Many generous gifts not related to buildings and grounds were made to Buchtel College during the 1880's and 90's.[83] Additional professorial chairs were endowed. The Ainsworth Professorship of Mathematics resulted from a gift of $30,000 from Henry Ainsworth of Lodi, Ohio; Reverend William H. Ryder of Chicago willed more than $32,000 to endow the Ryder Professorship of Elocution and Rhetoric; in 1888 Judge E. P. Green, a trustee of the College, turned over contributions amounting to $10,000 which he had solicited for a library fund. Also in 1888, Reverend Andrew Willson, long-time trustee who had done so much to start the College and locate it in Akron, donated $10,000 to be used for a professorship in theology in the expectation that a theology department would be established. Many other gifts were received for scholarships, general endowment, prizes, and for unspecified purposes. In fund raising and in personal giving, John R. Buchtel led the way as he had in every aspect of the College's life. The termination by death of his support was a turning point for the College which, coupled with the depression, very nearly spelled the end to its efforts.

NOTES

[1] Board Mins. I, 82.

[2] Buchtel to Cone, July 24, 1880, UArch., box 1/1a/130, #7.

[3] Tinker to Cantwell, Aug., 1880, *ibid.*

[4] Frank L. Mott, *A History of American Magazines, 1885–1905* (Cambridge, Mass.; 1957), p. 295.

[5] *Alumni Quarterly,* I, no. 4.

[6] "The Inauguration of Dr. Orello Cone" in Publications of Buchtel College (1880), UArch.

[7] *Ibid.*

[8] Tinker to William Slade, September 16, 1880, TS in UArch., box 1/1a/130 #7.

[9] Tinker to Buchtel, Oct. 25, 1880, TS, *ibid.*

[10] Frederick Rudolph, *The American College and University, A History* (New York, 1962), p. 294.

[11] *Ibid.,* p. 300.

[12] Buchtel College Catalog, 1872.

[13] *Ibid.,* 1887–88.

[14] Spanton, *Fifty Years,* p. 173.

[15] Board Mins., I, 96.

[16] *Buchtelite,* April, 1889.

[17] Board Mins., I, 204.

[18] Spanton, *Fifty Years,* p. 170.

[19] Board Mins., I, 172, 200.

[20] *Buchtelite,* March 20, 1892.

21 Board Mins., I, 82.

22 Cone to Jewett, Apr. 16, 1884, TS in UArch., box 1/1a/130 #7.

23 Same to same, *ibid.*

24 Jewett to Susie Cole, Feb. 16, 1919, UArch., VF (History).

25 *Ibid.*

26 Spanton, *Fifty Years,* p. 157.

27 *Ibid.,* p. 206.

28 Cone to Claypole, Oct. 16, 1883, TS in UArch., box 1/1a/130 #7.

29 Spanton, *Fifty Years,* p. 202.

30 UArch., VF (Claypole, Edward).

31 *Buchtelite,* Nov. 5, 1890.

32 *Alumni Quarterly,* I, no. 3.

33 *Buchtelite,* Mar. 5, 1892.

34 Spanton, *Fifty Years,* p. 332.

35 *Ibid.,* p. 338.

36 *Buchtelite,* Nov. 20, 1890.

37 UArch., VF (History).

38 *Buchtelite,* Dec., 1889.

39 *Ibid.,* various issues 1890 ff.

40 Ray Ginger has applied the title "Age of Excess" to this period.

41 *Buchtelite,* Oct. 5, 1892.

42 Tinker to Slade, Sept. 22, 1881, TS in UArch., box 1/1a/130 #7.

43 Board Mins., I, 79.

44 Olin to W. A. McDonald, Nov. 2, 1892, UArch., box 1/1a/130 #7.

45 UArch., VF (History).

46 Olin to Faculty, June 8, 1894, UArch., box 1/1a/130 #7; *Buchtelite* Nov. 17, 1898.

47 Olin to J. E. Cole, Aug. 12, 1893, TS in UArch., box 1/1a/130 #7.

48 Cone to Mrs. P. Vinton, June 28, 1893, TS in UArch., box 1/1a/130 #7.

49 Cone to F. L. Mathews, Aug. 8, 1885, TS in *ibid.*

50 This unhappy affair can be followed in UArch., box 1/1a/130 #7, and box 39/2/22.

51 Spanton, *Fifty Years,* pp. 290–91; *Buchtelite,* Feb. 22 and May 5, 1890. In May, Tucker finished third in the inter-state contest at Lincoln, Nebraska.

52 *Ibid.,* Jan., 1890.

53 *Ibid.,* May, 1889.

54 *Ibid.,* Nov., 1889.

55 *Ibid.,* Sept., 1889, Mar. 2, 1899.

56 Spanton, *Fifty Years,* pp. 343–44.

57 *Ibid.,* p. 342.

58 *Buchtelite,* Oct. 20, 1890, May 5 and Oct. 5, 1892; Olin to Faculty, Oct. 25, 1892, TS in UArch., box 1/1a/130 #7.

59 A complete account of the College's literary activities is in Spanton, *Fifty Years,* Chapter XIV.

60 Quoted in Spanton, *Fifty Years,* p. 273.

61 A more detailed account of the founding of fraternity and sorority chapters at Buchtel College can be found in Spanton, *Fifty Years,* Chapter XVI.

62 A complete account of Buchtel College publications can be found in *ibid.,* Chapter XV.

63 A. E. Hyre to *Buchtelite,* printed in the issue of Apr., 1889.

64 *Ibid.*

65 *Ibid.*

66 *Ibid.,* June 5, 1890.

67 *Ibid.,* Apr. 5, 1892.

68 Spanton, *Fifty Years,* Chapter XIII, has much detail. The appendix contains scores of every inter-collegiate contest in which Buchtel teams participated.

69 Some students satirically claimed victory (interview with Charles Bulger who knew the

story from some of the participants).

[70] Spanton, *Fifty Years,* p. 242.

[71] *Buchtelite,* Apr. 20, 1890.

[72] *Ibid.,* Nov. 5, 1891.

[73] Spanton, *Fifty Years,* p. 246.

[74] *Ibid.,* pp. 246–50; *Ohio State Journal,* Sept. 5, 1894.

[75] *Buchtelite,* Feb. 8, 1900.

[76] UArch., box 1/1a/130 #7.

[77] Olin to Rittenhouse, Oct. 19, 1892, TS, *ibid.*

[78] Lane, *Akron,* p. 312.

[79] Spanton, *Fifty Years,* p. 231.

[80] *Ibid.,* pp. 230–32.

[81] Buchtel College Catalog, 1887–88, p. 14.

[82] Board Mins., I, 158.

[83] For details see Spanton, *Fifty Years,* Chapter XII.

Old Buchtel College as seen from Union Street.

Old Buchtel in flames, December 20, 1899.

When the fire cooled, little remained to be salvaged.

V

The dark decade (1890–1900)

It has been claimed that John R. Buchtel gave nearly his entire fortune to the College named in his honor. This is only a slight exaggeration. Considering only those gifts whose magnitude is known, the total reaches approximately $471,000. When one adds to that total the unceasing flow of gifts in kind, of expenses assumed for guests of the College, of gifts and loans to students, of untotaled sums for cadet uniforms, books, furniture, rent-free houses for such friends of the College as Aunty Brown, and the assumption of the year-end deficits, it is not at all unreasonable to assume that Buchtel gave half a million dollars to the College.[1]

In the spring of 1887, while supervising the interests of the Akron Iron Company in the Hocking Valley, Mr. Buchtel suffered a "stroke of paralysis." At the time of his attack, Mrs. Elizabeth Buchtel had been an invalid for six years from a similar attack. For the four years of life remaining to her, Mrs. Buchtel and her husband bore their afflictions patiently, apparently never losing interest in the great enterprise in which they had invested so much of themselves.

Elizabeth Buchtel died May 22, 1891. Classes were suspended on that Friday. "We shall miss her happy presence among us," said the student newspaper, "but her long life of earnest, Christian work has written upon our memories a record which time can never erase."[2]

Just a year and a day later—May 23, 1892—John R. Buchtel followed his wife in death. The College was in mourning as indeed was most of the city. A special edition of the *Buchtelite*, bordered in black, recounted details of his career and of his concern for the College. He had lived to see the first student, one of whose parents had attended the institution, make her appearance on campus, thus fulfilling the generational cycle.[3] In his last years he took pleasure in continuing his support of individual students who needed help.

One such student was Frank Pixley, then teaching country school at Copley. He had a keen desire to go to college but no money. Mr. Buchtel's niece described his plight to her uncle who was more than happy "to help a poor boy get an education."[4] Frank Pixley became famous as a librettist, writing the "Prince of Pilsen" and other much-loved operettas, and he gave money to the College for the Pixley Scholarships which are still awarded annually to students who excel in drama and the arts. The benevolence of others in support of the College gave Mr. Buchtel as much satisfaction as his own. When President Cone received a letter from Oliver Ashton announcing his gift to establish the Ashton Prizes for public speaking, he took it to Mr. Buchtel who was "still lying helpless, his work done, and he was overjoyed. Such marks of interest in the college from others," said Cone, "encourage and elate him."[5]

Funeral services were held May 26 in the Universalist church. Eulogies were pronounced by President Cone, who used the parable of the talents as his text, and by Mr. Buchtel's great friend, J. Park Alexander: "What of this man of oak? What of this man of iron? What of this man of steel? Who with all these qualities, with children was a child." Briefer remarks were made by Reverend Andrew Willson, co-worker in founding and sustaining the College, by Ferdinand Schumacher who spoke of his leadership in Akron's business, by Reverend T. E. Monroe, pastor of the First Congregational Church, who recalled Mr. Buchtel's practice of attending commencement ceremonies at the Akron High School and giving scholarships to those whose orations impressed him with their excellence, and finally by Dr. J. S. Cantwell, long associated with the College, who spoke of his "genius for friendship, for charity, for kindness."[6]

If one is of a cynical turn of mind, he might by now think that no man could deserve as much praise as Mr. Buchtel's contemporaries and this historian have placed upon him. But this history recounts the life of a college, and there is no denying the record—Mr. Buchtel and the College were inseparable; the triumph and prosperity of one was the triumph and prosperity of the other. Possibly the best summation of that relationship is found in the memorial statement adopted by the Board of Trustees:

> The history of this College is so closely related to that of Mr. Buchtel that they cannot be separated. When the opportunity to assist in establishing an institution of learning in the city of Akron was offered to him he had the wisdom to embrace it. The more he worked and gave, the more interested he became and the more he desired its growth and prosperity until his life became absorbed in this educational enterprise. To him, more than to any other person are we indebted for the large measure of success that has been realized. His personality was a wonderful power and became the inspiration of noble and generous effort. He will ever be remembered as a prompt, faithful and earnest presiding officer. His influence over the young was almost marvelous and will never perish. Large hearted, with invincible courage, unfaltering faith in humanity, and a quick insight into human nature he was a providential man and we are grateful that he was privileged to be so long and intimately connected with the institution that bears his name.[7]

Two small vanities were denied him: he had hoped that, after his death, the Board would use 20 percent of his last large gift ($174,000) for construction of a building to be known as Elizabeth Buchtel Hall, engraved with the legend, "The wife of John R. Buchtel," and also that his statue would be placed on the College campus.[8] Presumably the depression of 1893 negated the first wish, and the statue, instead of being placed on campus, was placed on his grave in Glendale Cemetery, a grave that he had planned while serving as a Trustee of the Cemetery Association.[9]

At a special meeting of the trustees immediately following John R. Buchtel's death, Ferdinand Schumacher was unanimously elected President of the Board.[10] At the regular annual meeting in June, the Board elected its first woman member, Mrs. Abby Soule Schumacher, to a three-year term. Revised by-laws were also adopted.[11] In 1893 Charles R. Olin was elected Secretary of the Board which, in company with his position as Financial Secretary of the College, gave him complete control of the business management.[12] He performed these tasks with precision, thoroughness, and dedication for many years and provided a continuity of effort in the business end of College operations. Mr. George W. Crouse succeeded Schumacher as President of the Board in 1894 since Schumacher's business interests had been absorbed into the American Cereal Company, a new combine in the milling and cereal industry, which he served from its Chicago offices as its first president. Crouse, like the majority of his associates, was familiar with the College from its earliest days, so it was with a continuity of purpose that the school faced the years immediately following Mr. Buchtel's death.

Although the purpose might be essentially the same as in earlier days, the means of carrying that purpose into execution were seriously strained by financial stress and denominational tensions. As has been mentioned, Buchtel's experience with the elective system in curricular matters paralleled that of similar institutions which adopted the system—the cost of instruction increased. As early as 1884, just two years after the tentative introduction of the elective system, the finance committee of the Board complained that the cost of instruction for 1883–84 had increased 50 percent although attendance increased 100 percent. The committee felt "it ought not to cost much more to instruct three hundred fifty students in this college than to instruct one hundred seventy-five." This was wishful thinking of an extreme kind as any college administrator well knows. The increase in cost, they believed, was caused by adding new departments, "which policy in the future must be confined to cases of absolute necessity."[13] It is amusing to note that the problem of "proliferation of courses" has been with the College almost from the beginning. Those who oppose the cafeteria-style curricular practices of the mid-twentieth century might deduce from this early manifestation of the problem that only a return to prescribed curricula confined within a narrow definition of purpose can successfully halt this process. It is highly unlikely, however, that the clock of history will be turned back in this direction in the foreseeable future.

Despite the trustees' obvious intention of holding tight rein over curricular expansion, the quiet, inexorable pressure that results in course diversification and expansion was at work. In the sciences, physical education, literature and history, art, and music, courses were added and the instructional staff to man them. Supporting costs for facilities and equipment rose commensurately. At this moment of spiralling costs, one of the most severe economic depressions the country had experienced found Buchtel College ill-prepared to meet the emergency. Its greatest benefactor was dead, it had no substantial endowment, the Universalists were unable to offer succour, and Akron wealth was in difficulty.

Akron, indeed, suffered severe financial losses as a result of the depression, but also as a result of the shift in markets and the growth of business consolidations that gutted some of her most profitable industries. The great works of the Buckeye and the Empire farm machinery manufacturers and their many dependent industries in Akron fell victim to the shift in markets to the west. Chicago and vicinity became the new focus of the farm machinery industry, and while this market shift was occurring, a new industrial giant, the International Harvester Company, absorbed much of Akron's remaining effort in the field. In similar fashion, Ferdinand Schumacher's milling operations, seriously weakened by the burning of the "Jumbo Mills" in 1886, were consolidated into the American Cereal Company with headquarters in Chicago. No longer would Akron men reap the principal profits from this industry although the Quaker Oats Company which evolved out of this consolidation maintained large milling operations in Akron for many decades, and still has storage facilities and a small plant at the corner of Broadway and Mill Streets where the Jumbo mill once loomed over the city. In the match industry, Ohio Columbus Barber reigned supreme with his own great combination, the Diamond Match Company. But that important industry and several others in which Barber held the dominant interest moved to the new town of Barberton. The "Match King" continued to make modest contributions to the College although his energies were directed elsewhere. Much of the manufacturing activity of the clay products industry had moved from Akron to be nearer the sources of supply. Although Akron maintained an important stake in this industry, the city no longer dominated it as it had several decades earlier. In the publishing industry, the great house established by Paul Werner, reputedly the largest in the country, fell on hard times. Indeed, the only important industry that was thriving was that newcomer, rubber. The bicycle craze of the nineties gave it a new spurt of vitality. Clearly, local businessmen to whom the College had turned for help on earlier occasions were now preoccupied with their own difficulties and were no longer in a position to come to its aid.

While certain economies had been put into effect as early as 1893, the trustees did not institute drastic savings until 1895. In that year the Board adopted a report submitted by its Committee on Reductions. Even in brief summary this report conveys the seriousness of the financial problem and the degree to which the College's program was overextended in relation to its support. A number of positions were abolished: The chairs of Latin and Greek were consolidated, thereby eliminating one professor; the Chair of Rhetoric and Oratory was combined with the Chair of English Literature and Logic; instructors were discontinued in law, in physics and geometry, and in both men's and women's gymnasium work, and the chemistry assistants were let go. Other salaried positions were abolished: Miss Bortle, preparatory teacher and "lady in charge" of the young women in the dormitories, was released as were the treasurer, the financial agent, and the engineer. The latter's duties were to be performed by the gardener. Salaries were reduced 20 percent for all those earning

$1,300 or more a year and 10 percent for those earning less. The cuts affected all salaried employees; the teachers, the steward, even President Cone who spoke of his salary reduction as a "contribution" to the work of the school. Cuts were made in scholarship appropriations, in library purchases, in money used for acquiring natural history specimens, and the prize awards were limited to the income from their respective funds.

The Board did not adopt all of the committee's recommendations. Most significant of the items not acted upon were recommendations calling for more extensive cutbacks in the work in literature, chemistry, and astronomy. During its study, the committee had examined the courses of 15 of the "best" institutions in Ohio. It found that Buchtel College offered 12 percent more work in literature, 20 percent more in chemistry, and 100 percent more in astronomy than the average of these 15 schools. It would appear that the trustees were quite selective in their pruning. These operational economies were adopted with great reluctance. The trustees read into the minutes their desire that it be known that the cutbacks reflected a financial judgment only and were in no way a commentary on how the parties concerned had performed their work.[14]

Within a year the financial crisis deepened. In March, 1896, the Board issued some $80,000 in bonds secured by a mortgage on all available real estate. This money was to be used to pay certain annuities, to pay the floating indebtedness, and to pay the operating deficit for the current year. The balance remaining was to be turned over to C. R. Olin to meet current expenses. As this was being done, a Board committee prepared a statement to be sent around the state and to those areas from which the school drew support to allay "doubts that are current" as to the continuance of Buchtel College.[15] These doubts were largely the product of the financial crisis, but they were also tied in with a crisis in the College's leadership and in its relations with the Ohio Universalist Convention.

When Everett Rexford left the presidency in 1880 with the conviction that he had healed the breach between the College and the local Universalist congregation, he could not have known how soon the strains would reappear. The quarrels he had experienced were largely over local issues. Students had been the medium of conflict. But during Dr. Cone's administration, the issues broadened. Not only was there conflict with the local congregation, but there was a growing division between the College and the Ohio Convention. The record is fragmentary, but we can piece together what we know with what can plausibly be assumed and thus fashion an outline of the chief elements of strain.

Orello Cone himself was perhaps the principal focus of the widening breach. He was in the forefront of the movement that was making "scientific" and historical criticism of the Bible a subject of scholarly inquiry. The questions raised by this criticism threatened the conservatives within Universalism who, like their trinitarian neighbors, resisted any change in the old truths. Dr. Cone would have to be classed with the liberals in the Universalist brotherhood.

While the liberal-conservative split in Universalist theology contributed to the breach between College and denomination, a broader resentment was directed at Cone because of his resolute attempts to minimize Universalist direction of the College while, at the same time, calling upon the church for increased support. If the Ohio Convention were to lose control over the College, why should Universalists feel any obligation to support it? After all, the College was started to provide a congenial atmosphere for Universalists. A letter appearing in the *Christian Leader* urged that Universalist schools make a more deliberate effort to train students in the Universalist faith. The writer, who signed himself "Old Student," urged that trustees require attendance "at the services of the denomination whose money built and maintains the school." Cone was clearly "rather distasteful to many Universalists throughout the state" because "he did not make the College sufficiently denominational."[16]

Early in his administration Cone had expressed concern about the "backward-ness of Universalists in sending students to the College."[17] He told the trustees that it would be desirable to reach that element among Universalists who were known as "liberals," and he suggested that he visit the Universalist constituency and seek them out.[18] There is no way of determining how successful the effort to attract support from the "liberal" group was, but it is certain that the strain within Universalism—liberal vs. conservative—continued to cause the College concern. As late as 1889, in solicit-ing a contribution from a potential donor, Dr. Cone wrote: "This is the only College which stands for Liberal Christianity in this whole region."[19] Even though Cone's reference was probably to the Universalist practice of referring to their faith as the "liberal religion," his choice of language suggests that the president was inclined to favor the liberals within the "liberal religion."

President Cone's defensiveness about the College's place within the parent denomination was reflected in his conviction that Buchtel did not get as much space and attention in the *Christian Leader* as did Lombard College. His anxiety is trace-able in part to John Buchtel's close attention to publicity for the College. Cone wrote to the editor of the *Leader:* "You have many readers in Ohio, and among them is Mr. Buchtel, who is very sensitive to all that is said or unsaid in the papers about the college for which he has done so much." And then, in a phrase that tells much about Orello Cone's own position: "For myself, I care nothing about the matter of newspa-per notices. But the College is helped and Mr. B. is encouraged by such attentions as I am writing about."[20]

On another occasion, Mr. Buchtel was incensed when the minister of the Akron congregation, the Reverend Elwood Nash, failed to read some College an-nouncements at Sunday services. Since some tension still existed between College and congregation, Nash apparently felt that President Cone had called the oversight to John Buchtel's attention. Cone assured Nash that he had not "set Mr. Buchtel after you," and assured him that the faculty desired "to make the College as helpful to the church as we can consistently with the chief aim of a college which, of course, is not religious."[21]

Elwood Nash had reason to wonder about the College's helpfulness to the church. He had been elected by the Ohio Universalist Convention to a three-year term on the Buchtel College Board of Trustees, but at the conclusion of his term a successful effort was made to keep him off the ballot for re-election. Apparently this was accomplished with the help of Professor W. D. Shipman who was chairman of the Committee on Nominations at the 1890 meeting, but it was the Board rather than the faculty who sought to block Nash. The trustees did not want the pastor of the local congregation to serve with them "in any circumstances."[22] The Board's position caused resentment in the Ohio Convention. As for Mr. Nash, he later became presi-dent of Lombard College and remained a widely respected leader in the Universalist persuasion.

Discontent that had been brewing for some time started, in 1893, to focus on President Cone. From the beginning, he had been unpopular with certain elements concerned with the College. Mr. A. B. Tinker, who combined his work at the College with the position of secretary to Mr. Buchtel, had been one of the first to praise Cone on his arrival in Akron for the manner in which he took over his duties. Just three years later Tinker complained to John Buchtel that the College did not stand up to those who "detract from it in print and speech." Tinker knew what should be done: "I wish you had a good education and was President of the Faculty as well as the Board. It needs a large hearted man there more than it needs an educated one." And if Cone "had more heart he would desire more respect here, and if he had more backbone he would demand it."[23]

During the fall term, 1893, a student petition containing charges against Dr. Cone was presented to the trustees. The petition claimed he was not suitable for the presidency; he was too reticent; he was not a sports enthusiast. The alumni then entered the picture by asking the Board for facts concerning Orello Cone's administration. The trustees' response was to appoint an investigating committee to look into the charges against Dr. Cone, and on December 19, the committee completely exonerated the president "both intellectually and morally."[24] That unfortunate phrasing suggests that someone had judged him to be unfit both "intellectually and morally," but the student charges had been much less telling. One can hardly equate lack of enthusiasm for sports with intellectual or moral failure.

In June, 1895, the Board was again petitioned, this time by 23 alumni who asked for "the resignation of Dr. Cone as President." At the same meeting, another paper signed by some 38 alumni was read. It expressed "their strongest disapproval" of the petition for removal. Another investigating committee was formed.[25] The committee informed the president of both the earlier and the present expressions of dissatisfaction with his administration. Cone thought it would be "a calamity to the College" if he were to resign under the circumstances in which the College found itself at that time. The Board was persuaded that Cone was right and decided to take no action for the moment.[26] Once raised, however, dissent and suspicion would not die. Cone's position deteriorated, and at a special Board meeting in March, 1896, his resignation was accepted.[27]

It is well to spare some sympathy for Orello Cone. He was talked into the presidency in the first place. His hesitation in accepting the initial offer suggests that he suspected he might not have the temperament for the position. He was no politician; his candor upset the Universalists; he lacked the golden touch as a fund raiser. In his last four years the school advanced toward disaster triggered by the twin calamities of a severe national financial depression and the death of John R. Buchtel.

Despite all this, the first 12 years of his administration were as close as Buchtel College ever got to a "golden age." It blossomed out from its constricted beginnings and rose to strengths that made it one of the best schools in the state. Dr. Cone brought certain essential attitudes to the campus without which the school could never have risen above a pedestrian mediocrity. These attitudes were an insistence upon the importance of scholarship, upon high quality work in the classrooms and laboratories, a recognition of the need to embrace new areas of study while retaining the essential portions of the established curricula, and a determination not to subvert academic integrity to denominational demands.

If his elevation of collegiate priorities over denominational priorities seems to indicate insufficient gratitude to the Ohio Universalist Convention, it is well to remember that even as the oversolicitous parent stunts the emotional growth of his child, so the denomination that holds too tightly the college it has created compromises the school's ability to perform its function. By reinforcing the Universalists' tendency to lean but lightly upon their school, President Cone contributed to Buchtel's early rise to maturity.

Upon leaving Akron, Dr. Cone accepted a pastorate in Lawrence, Kansas. Two years later, he was re-called to the Theological School of St. Lawrence University where he filled the chair of biblical studies with honor and distinction until his death in 1905.

As the depression tightened its hold on Ohio, the Universalists sought to look after their own. In June, 1896, Dr. H. L. Canfield presented the Board with a memorial from the Ohio Convention and had it spread upon the minutes. The Convention did not ask that all trustees be Universalist, but they did ask that a majority of the Committee on Instruction be of that denomination. The "lady principal" (of the preparatory school) should be a Universalist and Universalist instructors should be obtained to fill vacancies if competent ones could be secured. Preference should be given to Universalists and their friends in all employment about the building and grounds. The memorial also asked the Board to reconsider the closing of East Hall to the young men, believing "that in spite of boyish pranks" it was better for both the boys and the College that they be in the building rather than scattered around town. The memorial disavowed any narrow sectarian feeling in making these recommendations, but since "more than 90 percent" of all money that had gone into the buildings and endowments had been Universalist money, they felt that they had heretofore asked less than they were entitled to. The memorial concludes: "We have

PRESIDENT CHARLES KNIGHT (1896–97)

no desire to make the college a proselyting institution nor to make its management offensively denominational. We only ask that it shall record the respect due to the people by whose sacrifices it was founded and the church whose interest it was builded to conserve."[28] What the Convention wanted would have been a retrograde step in church-College relationships; and while it is fruitless to argue about just how much of the College's support came from Universalists, we know that in the 18-year period 1878–96, on an average just 36.6 percent of the student body, College and prep, was Universalist and in 1896 only 19.7 percent.[29] The percentage would have been higher if only the College students had been considered. As for financial support, virtually all of the endowment was Universalist money, but in building funds, prize funds, and scholarships the involvement appears to be well below the 90 percent figure cited in the memorial.

Finding a successor to Dr. Cone was most difficult. The presidency of Buchtel College was not so appealing a post as it had been when everything was on an upward track and when the dynamic salesmanship of Mr. Buchtel was backed by his financial support. In order to have time to find the right man for the post, Dr. Charles M. Knight, Professor of Chemistry and Physics, was appointed to the position on an interim basis.

This 20-year veteran of the faculty had all the qualities to make an outstanding president, but he was one of those rare persons who knows his true vocation, and he preferred to return to the classroom and his students at the first opportunity. It was said of Knight that "he would have made an excellent president could he have won his own consent."[30] He provided a steady leadership through that trying year, one which found enrollments down 20 percent. So few men were in the College courses that fraternities and athletic teams ceased operations.

Upon relinquishing the presidency, Knight was awarded an honorary Doctor of Science degree and was also appointed first Dean of the Faculty for which he received an extra stipend of $50 per year. Ironically, the same letter that informed him of these recognitions also informed him that his salary was to be reduced 10 percent.[31]

In April, 1897, the Board met to examine the financial exigencies. It was suggested that endowment funds might be used to meet current expenses. This suggestion was opposed by Mr. Canfield who countered with the thought that classes be suspended for one year during which time endowment income could be applied to payment of the debts. He was confident the Ohio Convention would strongly support his alternative. Canfield's proposal stirred vigorous discussion and was "warmly opposed by a number of the young and newer members of the board as well as by some of the older ones."[32] Nevertheless, a committee was appointed to study the legal implications of closing operations for a year. It reported that this course would involve the College in complications, so Canfield's suggestion was dropped. Rather than see the College close, members of the faculty volunteered a further 10 percent reduction in their salaries for 1897–98. The offer was accepted.[33]

Everyone seemed to turn on the College while it was down. "There is a strong feeling of prejudice . . . among a large number of our citizens against the college," wrote C. R. Olin. "People who share this feeling are only too glad of every opportunity to verify their opinion that the college is an unmixed evil in the community, or that its cost is too great to make it worth while to maintain it." To counter this feeling, thought Olin, the committee to select a new president should act at once. It would take "heroic measures to pull the college through."[34]

On May 20, 1897, Dr. Ira A. Priest, pastor of the Universalist church in Akron, was named President of Buchtel College. He was inaugurated June 24, and assumed his duties on July 1.[35] Born in Mt. Holly, Vermont, in 1856, he had spent his boyhood on a farm, worked his way through Goddard Seminary and Tufts College, and in 1887 earned his B.D. from Tufts Divinity School. That same year he married Miss Eva Hall, an art teacher at Goddard. After serving three pastorates in Massachusetts, Dr. Priest came to Akron in October, 1896. In addition to his pastoral duties, he became chaplain and instructor in ethics and psychology at Buchtel. "Our new President . . . will make a go of it," wrote C. R. Olin to a friend, "if he is half supported by the proper constituency of the college. He is full of courage and zeal for the institution, is very much liked by the students and professors, and is not afraid of work."[36]

Dr. Priest was not so well known throughout the Universalist world as were his three clergymen predecessors. He had not written as much as Sullivan McCollester, nor engaged in theological debate with the ardor and skill of Rexford, nor displayed the scholarly disposition of Cone, but he was claimed by both the liberal and conservative elements within Universalism and his teaching gave him insight into the problems and needs of the College.

He entered the work with gusto; hope was rekindled in the Ohio Convention that events at the College would resume a happier and more profitable course. Rebuilding is a slow process, however, so there was still need to keep faculty salaries well below normal levels (his own salary was set at $2,000 plus use of the President's House), and to economize in every activity. Priest himself took to the field to raise support for the College. "Reference Committees" carried the story of Buchtel's need through those areas from which the school drew students. These efforts were not very successful. The alumni attempted to help by campaigning for some $60,000 to build the science building so long needed, but they were poorly organized, none of them had been in business long enough to have accumulated great wealth, and when they discovered that the College could not meet its regular operating expenses, they lost heart and abandoned the plan. One reason operating expenses could not be met was that it cost the College between $125 and $140 a year to educate a student who paid tuition of but $40 a year.[37]

The road up from the financial depths was uncertain. A rescinding of the action closing East Hall to young men brought that lively element back into the College building and must have pleased the Ohio Convention which had pressed for the move. Student enrollment was up slightly from its nadir in 1896, but several outstanding faculty members left—Claypole, Bortle, Gifford, Stockman, Garrigues—and their positions remained unfilled. Nationally, however, the pall of depression had started to lift by 1898, and rising tensions with Spain distracted the public from familiar troubles closer to home.

When war with Spain broke out, Buchtel was ready to contribute. About 20 present and former students served in the military services. One of them, Fred Haushalter, gave his life. In light of the divided and ambivalent attitudes of students regarding American involvement in Vietnam in the 1960's, it is interesting to note that support of the government was enthusiastic. "There is scarcely another class of American citizens which is so intensely patriotic as the great student body of the numberless schools of the Union," said the *Buchtelite* editor.[38]

The war's effect was transient. But Buchtel's dark decade, ushered in by the tragic fire that left three Kappas dead and others disfigured, was to close with yet another holocaust.

The mood of happy expectation that grips a college just before a holiday was much in evidence at Buchtel on December 20, 1899, the day before the fall term was to close.[39] Doubtless plans had been made for trips home over the holidays. The Delta Gammas were meeting in their room, and a faculty meeting was in progress when, shortly before five o'clock, a man rushed into West Hall shouting that the building was on fire. Evacuation of the building was prompt. Two fire companies were quickly at the scene with their horse-drawn, steam-driven apparatus. Within five minutes of their arrival a general alarm went out bringing to campus Akron's entire department. The blaze seems to have started under the eaves of the roof on the east end of the building, but it spread quickly into a general conflagration. Workmen on their way home dropped their dinner pails and rushed to help faculty, students, policemen, and passersby to remove whatever could be salvaged from the building. Books, furniture, apparatus, College records, whatever could be grabbed, was taken to Crouse gym. At the end of an hour this work had to be stopped because of the hazard, and although no one was killed in the fire, several narrow escapes had forced the police to suspend the removal activities.

The huge structure burned spectacularly, and its death torch lighted the sky so that people for miles around knew of its passing. In the crowd that gathered to watch were many who wept, and it is likely, human kind being what it is, that some were exhilarated with excitement. To hundreds of people presently and formerly associated with Buchtel College, the fire meant loss—loss of property, books, equipment of all kinds, but above all, loss of that focus that visibly represented the College and all it stood for, and it was this, more than any other, that was an irreplaceable loss. After three hours of fierce burning, only the outer shell remained. When daylight came, it stood stark and severe with smoke rising from the smouldering debris.

By daylight thousands of colored handbills were scattered everywhere announcing a meeting in the Universalist church. At nine o'clock on the morning of December 21, students, faculty, and such alumni and friends as could be present heard President Priest praise the expressions of loyalty he had been receiving. He vowed the continuance of the College. George Crouse, President of the Board of Trustees, spoke of the loss felt by Akron and its cooperation in the College's future efforts; Gerald Brown, a senior, and Edson Robinson, a junior, pledged that every student would return and pledged their support. As one young lady described her plight, "I was an Akron girl and I knew that both financially and physically there would be no further education for me if Buchtel did not rise from its ashes."[40] That afternoon, the faculty, local trustees, and a committee from the alumni association met in the President's House. It was decided to finish the year's work, and a committee was appointed to find space for classes.

On December 23, under the leadership of Mr. Crouse, Akron businessmen met in the parlors of the City National Bank and gave their unanimous endorsement to a pledge to raise $50,000 from the citizens of Akron. The Board of Trustees met on December 26 and decided to secure classrooms, to build suitable buildings to house the College's needs, and to secure funds to equip the school and increase the endowment. Secretary Olin estimated that it would take $293,000 to erect the necessary buildings, restore the endowment funds already drawn upon, and secure additional endowment to put the College on a self-sustaining basis. President Priest was relieved of all classroom duties to that he might push the campaign for funds with full vigor. The executive committee of the Board was empowered to look after the housing of students for the rest of the year.

As a result of vigorous action, the new term started January 4, 1900, with a full student attendance standing for chapel services in Crouse gym. The gymnasium now became the center of activity; five classrooms were partitioned off on the main floor and two adjoining rooms were converted to classroom use; the south end of the building was used as a library and chapel, and the basement was converted into chemical and physical laboratories. The east room of the President's House was used as a classroom. Prep students met for their classes in a nearby business establishment. Women dorm students were housed in "Masaldwar," a large house on Union Street just a block from the campus. Miss Warner was the "preceptress" in charge under the same rules that had applied in the old dormitory. The men were housed in private homes.

Thus a splendid recovery of the College's program and spirit was underway immediately. It would be inappropriate for us to dwell overlong on the tragedy, the loss, since the generation that had to live with it did not. For the record, however, a moment of retrospect as to the significance of that great building might be in order. It was, above all, a symbol as all great public buildings should be, of a noble activity that went on within. Americans can understand, even if they do not in large part appreciate, the functional value of building a cathedral that points a spire toward heaven since it serves as a visible reminder of the activity within. Even if old Buchtel Hall was ugly by current standards, it was imposing, it made an impact, it could not be overlooked. Like the pyramids, sheer size was one of the building's assets, and all this has something to do with creating spirit and supportive attitudes,

The loss of the building seemed also to cap a growing inability on the part of the Universalists to sustain their College. If one were to select a point at which the support of the College in terms of students, gifts, and even sentiment switched from the Ohio Convention to the city of Akron, he would do well to consider the fire of 1899. Despite the heavy local involvement in the College, what went before was more Universalist-oriented than community-oriented; the reverse was true thereafter. Although the Ohio Convention generously resolved to raise $100,000 for the College, it was beyond their reach.[41] Finally, the fire deprived the College of much of its history and tradition. Records, books, personal belongings, mementos, all the familiar things were gone. But as long as purpose endures, the past lives even though the setting is new, and those who loved the College, or honored it, set about rebuilding.

Support for the local fund raising effort was gratifying at the beginning. Students and faculty contributed to the building fund and, for the first time in the College's experience, Akron people of humble means contributed in substantial numbers; post office employees secured over $1,000 from a benefit minstrel show; factory girls contributed ten cents a week out of their pay. A fireman pledged $50 while manning a hose at the scene of the blaze; a washerwoman pledged $5; a 12 year old boy pledged $200 and had secured $135 of it within 24 hours.[42] Alumni contributed, of course, as did Universalists from around the country.

The trustees were so encouraged by the response that on March 21, they voted to proceed with construction of a recitation building to cost no more than $50,000. The funds for this building were to come from the subscription money and from insurance on old Buchtel. In addition, the trustees accepted a plan submitted by Professors Knight and Orth on behalf of the faculty. This plan called for a recitation hall, a natural science building, women's dormitories, a building to house the library, chapel, and administrative offices, and a preparatory school building. A power plant isolated from the campus completed the faculty's scheme. The buildings were to be arranged on the periphery of the campus so as to form a quadrangle of sorts. As buildings were constructed over the next two decades, they were placed in positions roughly consistent with the plan.

By far the most urgent need was for a recitation building. A faculty-Board building committee was appointed to oversee construction, and a competition was held for the best building plan and campus arrangement.[43] The winner was Frank

PRESIDENT IRA PRIEST (1897–01)

Weary of Akron who designed a recitation hall to be located just east and south of the original building, at a point where the center lines of College Street and Center Street intersect. The architectural style was "Grecian," with Ionic columns flanking the center doorway which was approached by a flight of marble steps. In the center of the main floor an open court extended to a sky-light and curving staircases extended to the second floor. On the first and second floors were classrooms with faculty offices attached. Administrative offices were located on the first floor. The basement level was almost entirely above ground so that sufficient natural light and ventilation could reach the laboratories located there. This building contains two cornerstones; its own in the northeast corner and the stone from the original Buchtel Hall which was put into the wall of the vestibule of the main entrance.

The College had hoped to have President William McKinley as the speaker for the cornerstone-laying in the spring of 1900, but he was unable to attend. New plans were made to have the President in June, and he tentatively agreed to appear, but troubles in China kept him at his desk in Washington.[44]

The new building was dedicated at commencement time in 1901. It was named Buchtel Hall, like its predecessor, and this gave rise to a confusion of names. It is necessary to specify which Buchtel Hall one is talking about; occasionally the former building is referred to as "Old Buchtel," but that terminology too is compromised because the entire College prior to 1913 is sometimes accorded that name. At any rate, Buchtel Hall is the only building that now remains from Buchtel College days.

While Buchtel Hall was under construction, a new power plant—not "isolated" from the campus as recommended by the building committee—and a building for the preparatory departments were also rising on the west end of the campus. The Academy, as the building housing the preps came to be known, was built on part of the foundation left from the abortive effort at a science building in 1893. It was dedicated with Buchtel Hall in June, 1901.

While new buildings changed the face of the campus, important innovations in academic organization were taking place. In 1899–1900 the elective system assumed its maximum hold on the College.[45] After the freshman year, the student was permitted to elect most of his subjects in any of the degree programs. Since the heavy cutbacks required by the financial stringencies of the 1890's, the curriculum did not contain an excessive number of choices. It was not possible for a collegiate student to fulfill graduation requirements by taking only "snap" courses as might be true today if such a permissive system were employed.

In 1900–01 the semester system was introduced in place of the old three-term system. It is most interesting to note that one of its selling points was that it presumably distributed vacation periods more evenly. Sixty-seven years later, semesters would give way to the quarter system which, ironically, is almost indistinguishable from the old three-term system of the nineteenth century. One of the selling points used in 1967 on behalf of the quarter system was that it would distribute vacation periods more evenly. A cynic might wish to make something of that.

The semester system did give the school a new legacy; the semester credit or semester hour became the unit of academic measurement. A student was now required to attain a certain number of semester credits in order to earn a degree instead of completing a "course"—Classical, Philosophical, or Scientific—as had formerly been the case. With these changes the basic structure of measurement was set for the next seven decades, and only modest changes were made from time to time. A kind of tinkering with the academic machinery is characteristic of colleges since there is always the hope and expectation that somehow, somewhere, someone is going to find a more rational way of measuring student progress and growth. Although many ideas for basic changes are put forth in every generation, seldom does a college break free of the anchor that holds it to the "tried," even though it may not be the "true."

Buchtel College and The University of Akron have followed a middle course; no startling innovation in the measurement of student growth and progress has emanated from its campus, but it has readily embraced at an early stage several of the more promising academic developments from the elective system to the honors concept, general education, student testing and counseling on an organized basis, and the general college concept. When compared to the ideal in measuring student growth and progress, the local practice falls short of the mark; when compared with institutions of similar character, the local record is uncommonly good, reflecting much careful thought and attention to the problem and reasonable adjustment and adaptation in approach.

On June 25, 1901, Dr. Ira Priest resigned. It is impossible to measure his contribution to the school with the same sense of sureness with which one can assess work of others who held that office. At no time during the four years of his tenure can it be said that Buchtel experienced normal days. "Eminently satisfactory to all Universalists of the state," when he came to office at the tag end of a prolonged depression, recovery of the College's fortunes had barely commenced when the tragic fire came very close to destroying the College.[46] That he failed to hold the confidence of some alumni is apparent, however, for in March, 1901, the trustees received a petition from the alumni association calling attention to "the present condition of the College" which, in the alumni view, was not a happy one. Their charges centered around a lack of "concerted, vigorous effort" in fund raising, advertising, business policy, and general aggressiveness. They claimed "a spirit of discord" in the faculty, and an "undercurrent of unrest and lack of confidence" in the student body. "The College Spirit, so essential to the vigorous, healthy life of educational institutions, has been stultified and nearly killed by the abolition of the dormitory system." Finally, the alumni were distressed that no official attempt had been made to keep in touch with them; in short "the 'penny wise and pound foolish' policy predominates, and drifting has taken the place of aggression." The alumni association thought that things might go better if they were represented on the Board of Trustees.[47]

The trustees investigated these charges in several meetings with the president and faculty. The trustees then became entangled in their own indecision. First they suggested that Priest resign, then they apparently reconsidered.[48] Priest tendered his resignation effective June, 1901, and this caused Andrew Willson to move that the trustees request Priest to withdraw his resignation; the motion carried 10 to 3. Priest declined to withdraw his resignation, whereupon it was moved that the trustees accept it. This motion lost 8 to 4 with one abstention. Finally, after considerable debate among the trustees, Mr. Carlton moved to reconsider the motion to accept, and the motion carried unanimously.[49]

First McCollester, then Cone, then Priest; only Rexford escaped the humiliation of being requested to resign, and it may have happened to him had he not beat everyone to the punch. In each case, the principal malcontents were to be found in the student body, the alumni, and within the Universalist fold. Each president suffered from circumstances he could not control. Priest, especially, encountered depression, then fire, and then dissent which clearly drained him of his optimism. He left the presidency and the ministry to enter the business life of Akron.

NOTES

[1] Obituary in *The Akron Beacon and Republican,* May 23, 1892; Spanton *Fifty Years,* p. 34.

[2] *Buchtelite,* June 5, 1891.

[3] *Ibid.,* Apr. 5, 1891, June 5, 1892.

[4] Spanton to S. Schumacher, Aug., 1941, UArch., VF (History).

[5] Cone to Ashton, Oct. 13, 1887, TS in UArch., box 1/1a/130 #7.

[6] *Akron Beacon and Republican,* May 27, 1892.

[7] Board Mins., I, 186–87.

[8] *Ibid.,* I, 173–74.

[9] Lane, *Akron,* p. 254.

[10] Board Mins., I, 168.

[11] *Ibid.,* 181, 174–80.

[12] *Ibid.,* 190.

[13] *Ibid.,* 107.

[14] *Ibid.,* 214.

[15] *Ibid.,* 220–21.

[16] *Christian Leader,* Jan. 11, 1894.

[17] Board Mins., I, 104.

[18] *Ibid.,* 108.

[19] Cone to F. Huidekoper, April 1, 1889, UArch., VF (Cone).

[20] Cone to Dr. Emerson, July 26, 1883, TS in UArch., box 1/1a/130 #7.

[21] Cone to Nash, June 16, 1886, TS in *ibid.*

[22] [H. L. Canfield?], Memoranda, UArch., VF (History).

[23] Tinker to Buchtel, July 16, 1883, TS in UArch., box 1/1a/130 #7.

[24] UArch., VF (Cone).

[25] Board Mins., I, 215.

[26] *Ibid.,* 216–17.

[27] *Ibid.,* 220.

[28] *Ibid.,* 228.

[29] Letter Book F, UArch., box 1/1a/130 #7.

[30] Spanton, *Fifty Years,* p. 91.

[31] *Ibid.;* Board Mins., I, 247–48; Olin to Knight, June 25, 1897, TS in UArch., box 1/1a/130 #7.

[32] Board Mins., I, 232–36; Olin to Willson, Apr. 13, 1897, TS in UArch., box 1/1a/130 #7.

[33] Board Mins., I, 243. Under the new salary schedule, Kolbe, Knight, Bates, and Claypole were paid $1,400 each, Egbert $1,260, Parsons and Gifford $1,050 apiece.

[34] Olin to Stearns, Apr. 14, 1897, TS in UArch., box 1/1a/130 #7.

[35] Board Mins., I, 237; Spanton, *Fifty Years,* p. 93.

[36] Olin to "Friend Robert," June 29, 1897, TS in UArch., box 1/1a/130 #7.

[37] Spanton, *Fifty Years,* p. 94; Olin to Stewart, Aug. 31, 1898, TS in UArch., box 1/1a/130 #7.

[38] *Buchtelite,* Nov. 3, 1898, Mar. 16, 1899.

[39] Accounts of the fire may be found in the *Daily Beacon,* Dec. 21, 1899, the *Buchtelite,* various issues in December, 1899, and thereafter, Spanton, *Fifty Years,* p. 94, and in Mrs. Grace Ewart to N. P. Auburn, October 3, 1960, UArch., VF (History).

[40] Ewart to Auburn, *ibid.*

[41] Board Mins., I, 262–64, 274.

[42] "Buchtel College Opened on Time," Jan., 1900, TS in UArch., box 1/1a/130 #7.

[43] Spanton, *Fifty Years,* p. 98.

[44] Priest to Charles Dick, June 13, 1900, TS in UArch., box 1/1a/130 #7.

[45] Spanton, *Fifty Years,* p. 100.

[46] *Ibid.,* p. 100; Olin to Bartlett, Aug. 25, 1897, TS in UArch., box 1/1a/130 #7.

[47] Petition, Mar., 1901, UArch., VF (Alumni Assoc.).

[48] Board Mins., I, 282–83.

[49] *Ibid.,* 284.

VI

The last stand of a private college
(1900–1913)

In August, 1897, Secretary Olin, who was thoroughly involved in local and statewide Universalist affairs, wrote a letter to the Reverend A. B. Church who was about to assume the pastorate of the Akron church. It was a typically blunt Olin letter, and yet an encouraging one. The disaffection of the congregation had moderated during Ira Priest's pastorate, wrote Olin: "The ladies of the church unfortunately are not all working *together* but they are nevertheless substantially all working for the common interests, and even this was not true one year ago."[1]

If anyone could lead the local congregation to a spirit of cooperation, it was Augustus Church. The chasm that had long existed between orthodox and liberal in the Universalist church was largely spanned by the new minister's genial personality and earnest public spirit.[2] Immediately after his arrival in Akron, Mr. Church was asked to serve Buchtel College as instructor in mental and moral philosophy, and in 1898 he was elected to the Board of Trustees which position he held until his death in 1912. When Ira Priest resigned, the trustees asked Church to serve as acting president until a new man could be secured. Church agreed, and, on August 19, 1901, he reported to the Board in considerable detail that the selection committee was having little success in securing a man for the presidency. Six prospects had been approached, but not one was inclined "to consider the matter favorably." A certain Mr. Griffith who sought the position was refused consideration. The Board thereupon requested Reverend Church to serve as acting president during the school year 1901–02 at a salary of $1,600 plus use of the President's House.[3] He accepted the offer, and when, in March, 1902, further efforts to find a suitable candidate for the presidency failed, he accepted the position on a continuing basis.

Augustus B. Church was born in North Norwich, New York, January 11, 1858. He earned the A.B. and B.D. degrees from St. Lawrence University. Before coming to Akron, he held pastorates in two New England churches and served as secretary of the Board of Education in North Adams, Massachusetts. He was popular with students "because of his earnest spirit and general disposition." Upon hearing of his selection to the presidency, a group of students gathered to cheer him: "Three cheers for Prexy Church. Rah! Rah! Rah!"[4] His hair had turned prematurely white, and with expressive dark eyes under shaggy brows his appearance attracted people to him. But his most noted characteristic was his approachability. He maintained an informality of manner that put people at ease immediately. He was patient, yet he could be firm when there was no time for wavering. Most important for the College, "he kept ever before him the old-fashioned standard that a liberal education is to make men and women and not intellectual machines."[5]

Augustus Church was the first man to hold both of the "presidencies" of the College at the same time. He comes closer, therefore, than any of his predecessors to fulfilling all the duties now ascribed to a college president. By being elected President of the Board of Trustees in 1904, he added responsibility for the business side of the operation to his previous concern for the academic and disciplinary side which were his by virtue of his position as President of the Faculty.[6] His skills in both areas were to be tested in the years ahead, for Buchtel College was mired in a perpetual financial crisis, indeed, in a struggle for survival.

One of the familiar manifestations of financial difficulty was a fall-off in enroll-

Crouse Gym with the Academy Building (Olin Hall) in the background.

Knight Chemical Laboratories where rubber chemistry was first taught.

Carl F. Kolbe Hall housed Bierce Library from 1916 to 1960.

PRESIDENT AUGUSTUS CHURCH (1901–12)

ment. In 1903–04, only 63 students were in collegiate programs.[7] Despite this criti-cally low enrollment, Dr. Church (he received an honorary D.D. from St. Lawrence in 1901, and an LL.D. from Tufts in 1905) pressed the faculty to maintain high scholastic standards. There was to be no compromise with excellence in instruction and student performance. One immediate result of this attitude was the conversion of the preparatory curriculum from a three-year to a four-year program in 1903. Coincidental with this change, the entrance requirement to collegiate work was raised to make a full four-year secondary course mandatory for admission. Although there had been a steady decline in the number of students taking the traditional classical course, the philosophical and scientific courses had been so strong that little was sacrificed in the way of quality education.

The chief deterrent to the classical course was the two years of Greek required for entrance into it, and since few high schools were giving attention to Greek, a Buchtel freshman desiring the classical course usually had to attend the Academy to get the amount required for admission. In 1906, only one student out of a class of 17 earned the B.A. At the same time, however, the student paper boasted that Buchtel credits were fully transferable to Harvard, Tufts, Columbia, Smith, Wellesley, Stan-ford, Colorado School of Mines, Case, Cornell, Penn, Chicago, and Michigan. Then with typical student simplification, the writer extended this evidence to the generali-zation that Buchtel College was on "an equal educational level" with those schools —maybe so, but maybe not.[8]

For all his emphasis on quality education, Dr. Church believed that practical, job-oriented courses had a place in the College curriculum. As long as the chief ends of education were served—the building of character and the acquisition of useful knowledge—what did it matter whether these ends were achieved through the means of classical education or through more prosaic job-related subjects? In this spirit, he recommended in 1903 that the College furnish training along "special lines of economics" with the intent of "looking toward a higher commercial education."[9]

He also recommended that the College attempt to affiliate with some of the best technical schools—Case School for example—so that a student could take a three-year pretechnical course at Buchtel followed by a two-year course at the technical school. However, the faculty was not persuaded that Buchtel would benefit as much as the technical school. They rejected the plan in favor of an attempt to "enrich" Buchtel's offerings so that more students would be induced to spend four years at Buchtel.[10]

The President's suggestions about economics and commercial education produced some response. The Buchtel Commercial School was established early in Dr. Church's administration. It was operated as a special department of instruction in the Academy under the direction of Mr. Harry A. Miller, founder of Miller's Actual Business College in Akron. The courses taught were shorthand, typing, bookkeeping and business, civil service, and insurance.[11] The school had a branch in Barberton.[12] This effort failed because competition from two local business schools was too keen. Its chief interest historically rests in the fact that it was an early effort by the College to make available to the community practical courses that would supply a need for trained personnel in Akron business and industry.

Coincident with the effort in commercial education, a Chair of Economics and History was established in the College, and Professor Oscar E. Olin, formerly Principal of the Academy, was appointed to that chair. This move was an enduring one as economics and history both evolved into regular departments of instruction.[13]

A workable compromise to the problem of preparing arts students for a technical education was worked out in 1904–05 when the College first offered mechanical drawing and descriptive geometry as an alternative to biology for freshmen students in the scientific curriculum and as an elective for upper classmen in other programs. Only six or eight students were expected to exercise this option, and the president was most gratified when 18 students enrolled the first time the courses were offered. Consistent with this development, mathematics and science courses were rearranged to coincide both in extent and time with their equivalents at regular engineering schools. At the end of his junior year, a Buchtel student in the scientific curriculum could transfer smoothly into the best engineering schools in the country.[14]

The faculty considered still other curricular adjustments during the 1903–05 period. They were selective in their approach and refused to recommend all the additions and changes urged upon them by interested parties within the faculty and without. Despite student pleas, the College failed to reinstitute a chair of oratory. Continuing financial stringencies made it necessary to terminate some promising programs of an innovative nature. Since 1899, certain courses had been offered in the community as a kind of extension program. These courses were not available for credit, indeed they were the forerunners of the non-credit informal courses of the present day. They constituted an interesting early example of adult education which, over the years, has become one of the most effective services rendered to the community by Buchtel College and The University of Akron.

In 1909, credit courses were offered in the evening for the first time. Subjects represented were economics, English, French, German, mechanical drawing, and physics. Despite "good enrollment," this effort was discontinued after one year and was not reinstated until the formation of a permanent evening program in 1915. The evening program was not alone in suffering from the financial squeeze. Day classes in art were cancelled for the third time in two decades, and music instruction ceased for the year 1911–12.[15]

One new program that emerged during these years endured and prospered. In the distinctive area of rubber chemistry, the College evolved a program that was uniquely appropriate to its setting. For years Dr. C. M. Knight had served the emerging rubber industry as a consultant. He was intrigued by the interesting chemical problems that rubber presented, but he was also alert to anything that would make the world of chemistry real to his students. For this reason he was particularly keen on the industrial applications of chemistry. He was able to convince the faculty, the president, and the Board that Buchtel College should make a special effort in the direction of rubber chemistry. The new chemistry building that was opened in 1909 contained a special rubber chemistry laboratory and a mixing and preparation room adjacent to it. In these facilities Dr. Knight taught the world's first college courses in rubber chemistry (although rubber was a special topic in Qualitative Analysis as early as 1902), and from this early beginning came a continuing effort that produced some of the world's ablest rubber chemists. The program finally evolved into the Institute of Polymer Science which today provides fundamental research and academic programs in rubber and related fields and makes Akron one of a half-dozen world centers of polymer inquiry.

Curricular change and experimentation were accompanied by changes in the academic machinery. In the fall semester, 1906, the term "credit" which heretofore signified one semester of study with four recitations per week was changed to the present understanding of the term—one "credit" was earned by the student for every hour he spent in recitation or lecture, and for every two hours he spent in laboratory. In 1906 the faculty used "term hour" to describe the unit now called "quarter hour" or "quarter credit."

Starting with the freshman class of 1906, a student had to earn 128 "term hours" (semester credits), to qualify for a baccalaureate degree. Most freshman courses were required: six hours of English, six of mathematics (three of which could be waived for American History or Masterpieces in English), six hours of chemistry or biology, fourteen hours of foreign languages, and one hour of physical education. At the beginning of the sophomore year, the student elected a "major" (field of specialization) leading to a degree. Each "major" required 24 hours of work in a particular field of study. For each "major," there was a required "minor" involving 18 hours of study in a supporting field. In all, the student was committed to at least 75 hours of required course work which left approximately 53 hours which he could employ in elective courses.[16] Thus was set the basic pattern that prevailed until the introduction of the General College and the general education program in 1935.

While these adjustments were being made, the Board voted to eliminate the Ph.B. and B.S. degrees. Only the B.A. was to be awarded by Buchtel.[17] No rationale was given for the move, but status considerations were probably involved since there was a common understanding around the country as to what the B.A. stood for. Professional schools and the emerging graduate schools expressed a preference for candidates holding that degree when considering admission to their programs. For reasons unexplained, however, the trustee's action was not put into effect, but within a few years of the founding of the Municipal University, the Ph.B. degree was abolished and only the B.A. and B.S. remained.

The facilities problems created by the great fire of 1899 were met in part by the construction of new Buchtel Hall and the Academy building in 1900–01. Some students welcomed the change. They had "exchanged discomfort for comfort, endurance for pleasure," and they were proud of the first new buildings of "greater Buchtel."[18] But the character of the school would never be the same unless something could be done to provide dormitories. Having the young men room in nearby homes appeared to work out all right, but the temporary dormitory for women, "Masaldwar," had to be abandoned in 1901, and no suitable replacement was available.[19]

The trustees directed President Church to seek funds for a new women's dormitory. Not until 1904, nearly two years after the president started his fund-raising activities, did the first donations come in. Local people gave some $3,500 to which the Ohio Universalists added $1,000. At that point, Mr. William Pitt Curtis of Wadsworth gave a gift that covered the remaining cost. The little frame building on the Carroll Street side of the campus cost $11,674. It housed 18 women in nine rooms, and it contained a parlor, dining room and kitchen, and sorority rooms. The building was named Curtis Cottage at dedication ceremonies held in conjunction

The Kappas enjoy a picnic and cruise at Long Lake (1890's)

The Reverend Andrew Willson helped establish Buchtel College, and served longer as Trustee (1872–1912) than any other person.

The Lone Stars ca. 1907. Standing on the far right is Hezzleton Simmons; Charles Jahant, a Director of the University, is in the front row, fourth from the left.

with Founder's Day, 1905. It served a wide variety of uses after 1914 until it was torn down in 1958 to make room for an enlargement of the student center.[20]

Early in 1905, it was announced that Andrew Carnegie, after a thorough six-week investigation of the College, had offered a gift of $25,000 for a science building on condition that a similar amount be raised for the permanent endowment. (Mr. Buchtel would have approved!) A spontaneous student demonstration erupted upon receipt of this news, and President Church himself supplied kerosene for the bonfire around which students gathered and cheered.

The additional $25,000 was most difficult to raise. It took nearly a year of intense effort by Dr. Church to raise half the amount needed, and the remainder was not secured until 1908. Ground was broken for the building on commencement day, 1908, and one year from that time it was finished and ready for inspection. Designed by Herbert Briggs, Class of '89, a Cleveland engineer and architect, it cost $30,439. In June, 1908, the Board voted "that in recognition of Doctor Knight's long and distinguished services, the new building be named The Knight Chemical Laboratory, and the name be carved upon a suitable tablet upon the building." Not only had Dr. Knight supported the fund-raising efforts on behalf of the building, but he had supervised the layout of internal spaces, making certain that his prized rubber chemistry labs would be contained therein.[21] It was the first building to be named for a faculty member, and the choice was singularly appropriate.

President Church was also anxious to secure a new administration building so that Buchtel Hall could be used exclusively for classes, but in this he was to be disappointed.[22] Nor did gifts to the library and to the natural science collections keep pace with the earlier experience of the College. However, 600 volumes were received from the estate of Judge E. P. Green, long-time trustee, and zoological specimens were donated by Miss Isabella Green which helped to fill the void in these important instructional materials left by the great fire.[23]

Periodically in the experience of any college significant changes occur in the faculty and administration. When they involve long-time members of the college community, there is a distinct sense that an era is passing. From time to time in the institution's history there have been periods when a number of changes occurred in close succession. One of these shifts in personnel occurred during Church's presidency. In this case, the change was due less to the loss of old-timers than to the acquisition of a half-dozen talented men who were to render exceptional service for decades to come. There was loss, however.

On May 10, 1905, Dr. Carl Kolbe, Hilton Professor of Modern Languages, died at his home of "heart seizure." No one was more closely identified with the College than he. In the sentimental mode of the day, he was referred to as 'Buchtel's most perfect gentleman." The "daily beauty about his life," said a *Buchtelite* writer, influenced those who knew him to do their best.[24] His death occurred on a Wednesday; all classes were suspended for the remainder of the week; the buildings were draped in black; the funeral was held in Crouse Gym. No one's death today would shut down the plant for three days, probably not even for one. No one's passing today would leave such a gap in the life of the campus as did the death of a faculty member who taught virtually every student who entered the College doors, and who was seen daily by the whole College community at chapel, in class, and about the campus and town.

Charles Knight who, like Kolbe, provided a link with the early days of the College would retire shortly after the end of President Church's tenure. As interim President (1896–97), Dean of the Faculty, and Vice President of the Faculty, he performed more administrative chores than any other member of that little faculty. His most enduring services, however, were those a teacher admires—his students made outstanding contributions to teaching and research in the sciences, and his rubber chemistry program opened new fields of investigation to generations of students. Long after his retirement, he donated several lots to the College. They were adjacent to the campus on the east side and contained houses that provided income to the school. He lived more than 90 years and died after spending most of his later years in Florida.[25]

Among those who left the College at this time after long service, special recognition should be given to Professor Charles Bates, for many years the watchdog of East Hall. Maria Parsons, professor of English literature, who resigned in 1905, was both admired and loved by her students. Her affection for them caused her to write long, warmly affectionate letters of reminiscence years after she left Buchtel. Hermas Egbert, Professor of Mathematics, resigned in 1903, but he could not remain away from the College, and in 1917 he returned to his teaching.

In succession to these worthies came a new wave of talent to take up leadership in the College. They will have a place in the continuing story, but it is well to introduce them here briefly.

First in immediate influence was Parke R. Kolbe, Class of '01, who succeeded his father as Hilton Professor of Modern Languages in 1905, but who made a greater contribution as the last president of Buchtel College and the first president of the Municipal University of Akron. Yet another future president started his career during Church's administration. In 1910, Hezzleton E. Simmons, Class of '08, became Dr. Knight's assistant in chemistry and succeeded to the professorship of chemisty upon Knight's retirement in 1913. Simmons' Alma Mater would call him to the presidency in 1933 in another period of deep financial trouble. Albert I. Spanton, Class of '99, was first hired to teach preparatory students, but in 1905 he succeeded Maria Parsons as Pierce Professor of English Literature. He was perhaps best known as "the little dean," for he was barely five feet tall and for a quarter of a century he administered the Buchtel College of Liberal Arts. When he retired from the liberal arts deanship, he was succeeded by Dr. Charles Bulger, Class of '08, who commenced his teaching career in 1910 in the department of Germanic languages.

Along with these men came several influential new faculty members who had not attended Buchtel College. Foremost among them was Oscar E. Olin, Principal of Buchtel Academy (1898–1905), and after 1902 a professor in the collegiate program and ultimately Dean of the Faculty and Vice President of the Faculty. Samuel Orth succeeded Claypole as Professor of Natural Sciences which is interesting because he later earned a Ph.D. degree in political science and became a distinguished professor of that subject at Cornell. Although he served just five years at Buchtel, he contributed excellent ideas on campus planning and finance. Charles Brookover was named as his successor in 1902, and for the next 11 years he contributed strong instruction to the natural sciences. Another 1902 appointee, Joseph Rockwell, succeeded Bates as Professor of Latin; as much as anyone on the faculty, he came to be regarded as the defender of high academic standards. Another important academic development of the early twentieth century was the establishment of a full-time librarian's position. In 1912 Miss Rena Findley became the first to be appointed to the new task, and the beginning of a truly functional library dates from that time.[26]

In the period between the fire and the demise of Buchtel College (1899–1913) there appears to have been a change in student outlook and activities. Many old traditions vanished as, of course, did all those activities and associations connected with old Buchtel Hall and dormitory life. In their place were substituted activities and attitudes that are as easily associated with present outlooks as with the nineteenth century, and yet they were not so similar as to be mistaken for present practices. Thus, Dr. Church's administration was a transition period in student conduct, attitudes, and activities.

One of the first traditions to be modified after the great fire was hazing. Although it had been officially abolished in the 1890's, it continued to be practiced surreptitiously. Tied in with hazing was the requirement that freshmen wear "beanies" or caps denoting their inferior status, but trouble from this source was mild compared to that which erupted during the "color rush" each fall when upperclassmen attempted to keep the frosh from displaying their class colors. Things got out of hand in October, 1903, when the freshmen came to chapel one morning wearing their colors. As the *Buchtelite* saw it; "In the eyes of all upperclassmen, the wearing of the colors by the freshmen is considered the same as placing a chip on the shoulder and daring a man to knock it off." After chapel services, President Church addressed the upperclassmen and told them that the faculty considered the freshmen duly initiated and thus entitled to wear their colors. The upperclassmen did not see it that way, however, and a rush ensued, the freshmen losing their colors. Faculty members took the names of every upperclassman participating and each was immediately notified that he was suspended pending a faculty meeting. Nearly every man in College thus found himself suspended. The faculty wasted no time—how could they, since they had just suspended virtually the whole male student body? Eleven upperclassmen were suspended pending further action and the rest were "acquitted." While the faculty deliberated their fate, the suspended students amused themselves by marching around Buchtel Hall, singing College songs and "celebrating." The issue was finally resolved by joint faculty-student meetings which decided what would constitute a reasonable freshman initiation. The color rush was retained, but only sophomores were to challenge the freshmen henceforth, and since the freshmen outnumbered the sophomores, they more than held their own in subsequent rushes.[27] However, memories are short when campus enthusiasms are ignited, and within a year the agreement was breached.[28]

Another tradition that came under attack was the requirement that all students attend chapel exercises at 8:55 each morning in Crouse gym. In the eyes of some students these exercises had become an "empty farce." They thought chapel should be held one hour each week with some of the "worthy men of Akron" speaking to them.[29] The *Buchtelite* editorialized that the students, if polled, would register slight interest in devotional exercises "except they furnished an opportunity for boning on French verbs" and little more in chapel as a whole. If students attended chapel for its social features—the singing of College songs, a chance to greet friends—why not give part of the time to devotions and make the rest social in nature instead of devoting the full fifteen minutes to "a half-hearted, time-grudging devotion, which is no devotion at all."[30]

In 1912, seven years after these protests were registered, the faculty, on motion of Parke Kolbe, voted to require chapel on Monday, Wednesday, and Thursday. Tuesday and Friday were to be given to student activities for the time being. Buchtel's experience was similar to that of other schools where formal chapel requirements were coming under attack from students.

Also in keeping with the times was a movement to establish a student council. The effort that was made in the 1890's to organize student government was aimed at letting the students assist in policing themselves in the dormitories rather than toward the initiation of constructive programs. In 1907, a student council consisting of four members elected from the College at large and one member of the Academy was instituted with the blessing of the faculty. Its functions were to keep College authorities informed of student sentiment, to see that the faculty gave serious consideration to strong demands made by the student body, to constitute itself "a seminar on college government," collecting information on practices at other schools for the benefit of Buchtel College, and to mediate "frictions" between students and faculty. The council had no budget to control and no standing committees.[31]

Organized student activities proceeded apace. From 1904 to 1914 the *Buchtelite* went literary. It was published monthly in magazine form, and attempted to be more than a news sheet.[32] In 1907 the College annual made a reappearance after a

15-year absence. It was known as the *Buchtel* as were its predecessors, but in 1911 the name was changed to *Tel-Buch,* and so it has remained to the present.[33]

A College band was formed and performed on a more regular basis than the pep bands of an earlier era. Intermittent attempts were made to sustain a glee club. There were transient Glee and Mandolin clubs, but nothing of the sustained effort that characterizes vocal organizations in the present.[34] A student dramatic club was active in the early twentieth century. In 1912 the members presented such a successful outdoor play at commencement time that it became a featured event at the ceremonies. A student-organized Oratorical Association endeavored to keep alive interest in public speaking, but it fell victim to the times. Oratory had lost its primacy as a collegiate activity although the annual prize contests, especially the Ashton, continued to attract considerable interest.[35] The Women's League, which included students, women faculty, and faculty wives, was organized in 1906. Later the League was to be exclusively student in makeup, and it became perhaps the foremost service organization on campus.[36]

Another significant innovation was the formation of Phi Sigma Alpha by the Class of '10. Its membership consisted of the members of that class, the three honor students of each succeeding graduating class, and all members of the faculty who were members of honor societies. This organization, founded with the support of Professor Rockwell, filled the need that Phi Beta Kappa filled on many campuses.[37] It continues to be the premier academic honorary on the University campus, and in recent years repeated efforts have been made to have Phi Beta Kappa recognize it as a colony. These efforts might well have succeeded had they been made early in the century, but they have failed in the mid-twentieth century due largely to the fact that the University is not oriented as heavily toward the liberal arts as Phi Beta Kappa feels appropriate.

In May, 1902, at the urging of President Church, "Tree Day" was introduced. Church had been familiar with this celebration while a student at St. Lawrence. Recitations were dismissed for the day, and each collegiate and preparatory class planted a tree on campus, each group holding a program at the planting site. The entire day was taken up with activities—guest lecturer in the morning, tree-planting ceremonies in the afternoon, and dancing and refreshments after the ceremonies. Ultimately Tree Day evolved into May Day. Obviously the little campus could not accommodate indefinitely all the trees that would be planted over the years had the practice remained unchanged. But tree-planting gave way to May Queen crowning so the problem never materialized.[38]

Fraternity and sorority life made a strong comeback in the early 1900's. Dr. Church was a strong supporter of the societies. "I think, in general," he wrote in 1905, "that fraternity life is beneficial to any young man or woman, and I . . . am not unmindful of the many particular instances where it worked harm, but these instances are usually due to some local or temporary condition."[39] The only new group to form during Church's presidency was Phi Mu sorority. Started in 1907 as a local, Theta Sigma Chi, the chapter went national in 1912, becoming the first chapter of Phi Mu north of Dixie.[40]

Of all the extracurricular activities that typify college life, athletics undoubtedly does more than anything else to focus student sentiment. It is a continuing concern among educators that colleges are so often judged by the success or failure of their intercollegiate athletic teams. And yet, what could be more natural? In addition to the color, drama, and excitement inherent in a good athletic contest, it is the one type of activity that a complete cross section of the public can take an interest in and identify with. A strong and colorful athletic team will call public attention to a college on a magnitude unmatched by any other activity. Because they know this, and because they are often the most rabid fans, college administrators and trustees seldom cut back on any intercollegiate athletic program even though the same amount of money and attention that goes into the program could support a broad intramural program that would serve all students rather than a handful of varsity stars. Many of the stars would never enter a college were it not for substantial inducements from the schools that covet their services.

In time, The University of Akron would have to face up to some of these considerations, but the first years of the twentieth century presented quite a different picture. Until its last few years, Buchtel College's varsity athletic program was student directed. The school provided facilities, but student initiative supplied the organizational effort. The College paid Coach Heisman's salary in 1893–94, but that was an exception. With his leaving, Buchtel varsity athletics lacked continuity of effort until 1908 when the College started to field teams in football, basketball, and baseball on a regular basis. Prior to 1908, the effort was sporadic and ill-organized even though that period produced some of Buchtel's greatest players and most satisfying victories.

In 1901 a new Athletic Association was formed by students. The Association's board of directors supervised the scheduling of games and passed on all expenditures subject to subsequent approval from a faculty-student-alumni Board of Control. Any faculty member, student, or alumnus could be a member of the Association, and every member of an athletic team was required to hold membership.

In response to a student petition, the trustees increased the student incidental fee by one dollar to be used in support of athletics. In 1902 the faculty adopted an eligibility rule which provided that an athlete must be passing at least eight hours of work in the college, academy, the school of art, or the school of music, and he must attend class regularly. Some members of the 1903 basketball team were unable to meet even this simple test and were declared ineligible, much to the disgust of students as yet unfamiliar with the idea that there should be an irreducible minimum in scholarly involvement required of athletes. Protests would not move Dr. Joseph Rockwell, chairman of the faculty committee on athletics, and "a much needed step forward was taken in control of athletics."[41]

A temporary resurgence of optimism accompanied these forward steps. The students attempted to found an athletic league as they had done in 1890. Buchtel joined Mount Union, Hiram, Kenyon, Wooster, and Baldwin-Wallace in the Eastern Ohio College Athletic League designed to promote pure athletics and closer athletic relations, but the liaison failed to endure and the League quickly faded into oblivion.[42] In 1903 the Athletic Association secured the coaching services of the Reverend Alfred Place, pastor of the Fourth Church of Christ and winner of a varsity "C" in football, baseball, and track at the University of Chicago. His influence seems to have been salubrious; judged by his won-lost record he accomplished little, but his leaving in 1904 was a blow to the students who admired him as "just one of the fellows, only a good deal better in every way."[43]

Meanwhile events continued their unpromising course. In 1904 the grandstand and some of the fence at Buchtel Field were destroyed by fire. The loss was $1,200, the insurance $750, and in the desperate financial squeeze there appeared no way to rebuild. Not until the spring of 1912 was the loss reclaimed. In that year Akron businessmen donated the resources for equipping and fencing the field. Student carpenters were given time off to do the fencing, and in two and a half hours they were finished and on their way to Crouse gym where the girls of the Women's League had prepared a "feed." That same year, Crouse gym was repaired and re-equipped, largely through the generosity of George Crouse himself, and Buchtel could again boast suitable athletic facilities as she had in the early 1890's.[44]

In football the dreary story was "no team" due to "lack of interest," or "not enough men in the College," and even "parental objections." Equally dreary was the lack of responsibility displayed by students charged with managing the finances of athletic teams. Year after year the College was embarrassed by unpaid bills resulting from carelessness or from a student manager leaving school without fulfilling his responsibilities. Finally the faculty cracked down and, in 1908, voted "that further intercollegiate athletics be suspended until the deficit in basketball and the probable deficit in baseball be provided for, and that the financial condition of athletics at Buchtel be put before the Student Council for adjustment."[45]

A committee composed of local alumni members of the Board of Trustees conducted an investigation, held open meetings with students, and then recommended that a coach be hired for the coming year.[46] In March, 1909, the trustees voted to hire a director of physical training and athletic coach who would also teach and thus be a faculty member. This position was filled by Clarence Weed who brought order to Buchtel's athletic efforts.[47] He stayed just a year, but a start had been made to put intercollegiate athletics on a sound basis.

The hiring of Frank Haggerty as coach in 1910 marks the point at which the three ingredients essential to a successful program—permanent organization, funds, and professional coaching—were finally put together. While Haggerty took care of the coaching, the organizational work fell to the capable hands of Charles Bulger who assumed the position of faculty manager of athletics in 1910. This work was carried on in addition to his teaching responsibilities. Bulger assumed control over schedule making and the handling of funds, and once he had straightened out these areas, Buchtel's relationship with other schools improved markedly. In 1915, when Fred Sefton came to Akron as director of physical training, he assumed the additional duties of faculty manager of athletics and in this combined capacity functioned in the whole range of activities that are now the province of the Director of Athletics and the Head of the Physical Education Department.[48]

Shining through the disorganization of Buchtel athletics was the successful introduction of basketball as a varsity sport. Dr. Charles Knight, who had seen basketball played in the east, brought the game to Buchtel where it was taken up first by the girls of the academy, and then by the academy boys who organized the first team in 1901.[49] Intercollegiate competition started in 1902 when the Buchtel neophytes went up against an experienced Mount Union team which administered a 120 to 9 drubbing to the local forces, and that in a day when a good team might score only 30 points in a game! The local boys were fast learners, however, and the 1904 season was quite spectacular with Mount Union, Western Reserve, Hiram, the University of West Virginia, and the University of Indiana all falling before the Buchtel onslaught. But the zenith of early basketball experience was the victory over Yale on New Year's day, 1908.

Yale, a national power in those days, offered to play Buchtel if they were guaranteed $200. Team captain Charles Jahant and student manager Lucien King secured permission from the faculty to engage in an agreement to this effect, and with these two men leading the way, every seat in Crouse gym was sold out at reserved seat prices, so that the game made money and basketball became a profitable sport in Akron. The game was all that the spectators had paid for, a hard-fought contest which the unknown Buchtel team won 36 to 30 over its famed opponents. It was a great day for old Buchtel, little dimmed by Yale's 32 to 28 revenge victory the next year.[50]

Buchtel teams often went out of their class in these contests. The 1910 football team won seven of their nine games, but one of the defeats was 51 to 0 at the hands of Notre Dame. Buchtel never made the mistake of playing them again, but it took successive defeats—41 to 0 in 1913 and 75 to 6 in 1914—by the Michigan Aggies (now Michigan State University) to convince the local boys that it was unprofitable to play teams decidedly out of their class. Not until the late 1930's would another attempt be made to run in fast football company.

Coach Haggerty produced fine teams and developed some outstanding players in his five years as coach. The bane of any coach's existence, of course, is the fickle fan, the fair weather friend who is happy with nothing short of an unending string of victories. When some of his later teams failed to perform as well as his first teams, Haggerty became the victim of "the discontent of the student body, the alumni, and the public in spite of his admitted ability as a coach." Some years after his resignation in 1915, he wrote to Professor Bulger: "Since leaving Akron I have refereed five-hundred athletic contests in ten states; coached a national winner in football and a team tied for the professional championship in the same sport. I have yet to see a better football player than [Lee] Jackson, a better pitcher than [Albert] Sidnell, a better all-around athlete than [Joseph] Wilhoyt [sic], or a more conscientious worker than [Guy] Zimmerman."[51]

While Haggerty was still coach, initial steps were taken to secure membership in the Ohio Athletic Conference. Application was made by Dean Fred Ayer in the fall of 1914, and after a year of probation Akron was formally admitted on October 8, 1915. This provided a good athletic home for Akron teams during most of the next 52 years even though the character of the school changed radically. Akron was the exception in a conference that was otherwise composed of small, private colleges and universities.[52]

It is not generally known that Buchtel College experienced a transformation in 1907 from its previous position as a denominational school to a new posture as a private, non-denominational school. The reasons for the change were persuasive; Universalist support in the form of students and money was again at an ebb, and, at this juncture, the Carnegie Foundation for Pensioning Teachers offered to make its program available to Buchtel, but only if the College severed its denominational ties. The story is summed up rather well in the minutes of the Board of Trustees, June 18, 1907. After amending the articles of Buchtel College so as to make the College eligible for the Carnegie Foundation program, the Board adopted the following resolutions:

> *Whereas in view of the changed conditions under which Buchtel College is compelled to maintain her existence and her standing with other colleges, it has been deemed wise and expedient with the full authority and consent of the Ohio Universalist Convention to sever its technical, organic connections with that body in order that the College may participate in the advantages and benefits of the Carnegie Foundation for pensioning teachers. Resolved that this action of the Board desired not to change in the least the policies and purposes of the College relative to the Ohio Universalist Convention but to simply change an inoperative technicality in order that the College in all its active work and its sympathetic relations with the Convention may be stronger and more efficient an institution. Resolved: that this Board hereby records its appreciation of the high responsibility imposed upon this body by the generous and broad-minded action of the Convention regarding the progress and work of the College to the end that the bodies may continue to be of mutual help and strength to each other.[53]*

The trustees then adopted measures making the Board a self-perpetuating body. This change made Buchtel faculty eligible for Carnegie pensions, an act that was judged to be the equivalent of raising their salaries some $500 to $800.[54] It also enabled the school to hold its faculty members, for one of the conditions of a Carnegie pension was that the recipient must serve in one institution for the rest of his career after he had joined the pension plan.

Buchtel was not alone among Universalist colleges in severing connections with the denomination. In 1910 St. Lawrence University severed its ties, except for the Theological School which continued its close affiliation with the New York State Convention. Tufts University, however, retained her Universalist ties intact.[55] If there was any strong reaction against the College's leaving the Universalist fold, none of any moment found its way into the records.[56]

In 1908 a new series of crises commenced which, once their course was run, would find Buchtel College giving way to the Municipal University of Akron, but of course no one saw that far into the future in 1908. The chronic financial squeeze that had plagued the College was at the root of the new difficulties. The Ohio College

Association adopted a requirement in 1908 that member colleges must have a productive endowment of at least $200,000. Buchtel had until December 13, 1910, to bring its endowment up to that amount.[57] Though Buchtel met all other membership standards, her endowment was only $100,000.

It was obvious that another subscription campaign was required, but the trustees decided that as long as they were going after money, they might as well go all out and seek enough to take care of the College's immediate needs. Therefore, in March, 1910, President Church presented plans for a campaign to raise $300,000 of additional endowment. He assured the Board that they would be supported by the Akron Chamber of Commerce which had investigated "the management of the College, its financial needs and the relation of the College to the City of Akron and Summit County."[58]

The first steps in the campaign were taken when school opened in the fall. Student leaders made speeches to citizen groups pointing out that were it not for the local College, many students would be unable to afford a college education. Most Buchtel students, they claimed, planned to work and live in Akron and aid in the city's growth. "Whatever our usefulness may be," they reported, "it will be no small measure due to Buchtel College."[59] By December the students had raised $1,000 among themselves and they were busily canvassing the city. Sixteen committees were at work out of their headquarters in the Windsor Hotel. They were assisted by 100 prominent Akron business and professional men. When all the mopping up was completed, it was found that $98,000 had been pledged by 1,700 people.[60]

This campaign revealed a number of significant things. First, its focus was entirely local. "Buchtel College is, in large degree, a local institution and we have been . . . putting special stress on the local situation and canvassing and soliciting the interest of local people," wrote C. R. Olin to an Akron businessman.[61] Never before had the local connections of the College been emphasized to the exclusion of denominational interests, but of course the severing of the Universalist connection in 1907 pretty well assured that its appeal would have to be local.

Another significant feature of the campaign was that it touched a wide segment of Akron's population. Only relief donations following the fire of '99 came near to matching the broad base of support given this campaign. The Municipal University in later years would successfully use citizen's committees to the same end in fund raising efforts. Yet, despite the broadened base, the largest dollar contribution in this campaign, as in virtually all campaigns, came from a small number of affluent men. George W. Crouse, Frank Mason, and Frank Seiberling accounted for $40,000 of the total. Finally, although the money raised was enough to keep Buchtel in the Ohio College Association, only one third of the goal sought was attained, and the additional money, while essential, was not nearly enough to remove the College from the financial brink on which it had been living for nearly two decades.[62]

Realizing that a broadened base of local support was essential, the Board of Trustees voted to increase their membership from 18 to 25 in order to secure the cooperation of a larger segment of Akron businessmen in the interests of Buchtel College. Five of the additional trustees were to be resident freeholders of Summit County; the College president was to be an *ex officio* member. The plan seems never to have been implemented, however.

By 1912, the last of the old-time trustees had left the Board. One of the last of them, Andrew Willson, had served 40 years, and to cap his contributions to the school he had done so much to start and to foster, he wrote a brief history of Buchtel College to 1905. This history was published as Chapter XII in William Doyle's *Centennial History of Summit County.* The other member of long standing who finished his work in 1912 was George W. Crouse. From the beginning he had rallied local support for the College to which he gave so generously and in whose interests he contributed a quarter century of support. The students recognized his efforts and dedicated the 1911 *Tel-Buch* to him. Crouse died of blood poisoning January 5, 1912, a faithful friend to the last.[63]

The shift in Board membership toward men who were relatively new to their duties and who had weaker ties with the early tradition of the College had an obvious, if unstated, bearing on the course of the school. Whether or not events would have unfolded as they did had the old-timers still been present in force is conjectural, but in 1912 only Carlton, Church, Doyle, and Hidy had experience as trustees before the fire of 1899 changed the character of the College. One can assume that many of the trustees approached their task with no strong sense of indebtedness to the old way of doing things. Their problem was to be survival.

Some of the ambivalence experienced by those who had long served the College is revealed in a letter from C. R. Olin to J. B. Harsh, March, 1912, in which Olin argued first, that Buchtel College was strong in its connections and conscious denominational ties with the Universalists, and second, that Buchtel College was largely supported from outside the denomination and had to continue to rely on outside support.[64] Help would be welcome from any legitimate source.

One unexpected source of help examined by Dr. Church was the possibility of merging Buchtel with Lombard College, its sister institution in Galesburg, Illinois. Lombard was in as much financial difficulty as Buchtel and had considered the possibility of merging with Knox College in Galesburg. Church believed the Universalist schools should stick together, and in March, 1912, he sent a plan of merger to the Lombard trustees. Negotiations lagged, however, and in the summer Parke Kolbe, Dr. Church's assistant, wrote an exceptionally frank letter to a Lombard trustee urging the union. "United we stand, divided we fall," wrote Kolbe. "We must get together for mutual protection and the assurance of a continued existence."[66] Lombard trustees chose not to pursue the merger. They attempted to survive in Galesburg, but failed, ultimately going out of business with some of the school's properties going to Knox College and some to the Meadville Theological School in Chicago.

While the continuing effort to keep the College alive went on in the background, there was a surface prosperity in the fortunes of the institution. The 1912 freshman class of 78 students was 50 percent larger than that of the preceding year and numbered 15 more than the entire collegiate enrollment of 1903 even though entrance requirements had been raised three times and tuition had been raised twice since then.[67] The Academy's enrollment increased 50 percent during the same period.

In 1909 the Academy won recognition for its solid academic efforts by being placed on the accredited list of the North Central Association of Colleges and Secondary Schools.[68] In the collegiate program, an extensive study of the relative standing of the nation's colleges made by Dr. Kendrick C. Babcock, placed Buchtel College in a rank just below the top in a group that included Rochester, Syracuse, Middlebury, Allegheny, Swarthmore, and Pittsburgh. They were described as schools which might belong in the first class (i.e. schools whose graduates did master's degree work in one year's time at first-class graduate and professional schools) were it not that they were young schools with certain records that might be in doubt. In Ohio, only Cincinnati shared Buchtel's rating while Oberlin, Western Reserve, and Ohio State ranked in the first class.[69] With all due reservations about the validity of such efforts at rating, it appears that a neutral observer gave Buchtel good marks for the results of its academic efforts. Secretary Olin summed up the situation very well: "Buchtel College was never in a more flourishing condition so far as its educational work and its local patronage is concerned. The current year [1912] is by far the best it has ever had in this respect but we are squarely face to face with a stone wall so far as its finances are concerned."[70]

Through these difficult years Dr. Church had invested every energy in Buchtel's behalf. His inadequate salary must have caused him some anxiety, in addition to which he felt obliged to assist an old friend in New York State in his business affairs. Apparently, he was giving some thought to resigning in 1908 for these reasons and perhaps others that are not part of the record. It is known that C. R. Olin viewed that possibility with some alarm, but apparently things were reconciled somewhat in June, 1908, when the Board increased the president's salary to $3,000 and continued use of the President's House. Three years later, however, Dr. Church submitted his resignation as President and Trustee of Buchtel College effective June 30, 1911, giving as his reason personal business matters which he felt needed his attention. The trustees were alarmed at the possibility of losing him in a critical period, and at their request he withdrew his resignation. He continued to struggle with the problems of his office until November, 1912, when he died of pneumonia brought on by exhaustion and by a severe cold contracted at a College football game.[71]

No president of Buchtel College enjoyed greater popularity with all segments of the community than did Augustus Church. The faculty responded well to his kindness and patience, students were attracted to him and valued his interest and support of their activities, and no one could better have bridged the gulf which so often separates college from city. Alumni would long remember him as the author of the Alma Mater. "The establishment of The University of Akron with Buchtel College as its center, shortly after his death," said the chronicler of his administration, "was in no small degree made possible of accomplishment by reason of the excellent work that he had done in popularizing Buchtel College with the citizens of Akron."[72]

A special faculty meeting was called to make arrangements for the funeral. Classes were suspended until the day after the funeral, and social activities were suspended for the remainder of the semester. The faculty voted to appoint Dr. C. M. Knight, C. R. Olin, and Dr. Parke Kolbe as an executive committee to care for the College business, and Dr. Knight was recognized as acting president for the second time in his long career. Dr. Knight's health soon required that he be relieved of his acting presidency and of the deanship of the faculty. Parke Kolbe replaced him as acting president, and Oscar E. Olin assumed the deanship.[73]

In the passing of Augustus Church, one might see, symbolically, the passing of Buchtel College. Although it had another year to live as a private school, that year was filled with expectations of change. The late president represented the qualities that characterized the College at its best—loyalty to the Universalists for their support and interest, especially in the early years, a concern for academic excellence and with it a healthy character development, plainness in manner that shunned ostentation, geniality toward a community whose support was vital to the College, and a humane concern that placed people in the forefront rather than power or prestige. The last of Buchtel's pastors-turned-president, Dr. Church would be missed.

There should be little need to summarize the accomplishments of Buchtel College at this point. It might be instructive, however, to pause and review what the school had accomplished in the development of men and women of character and competence, for this is the ultimate test of any educational endeavor. It is the end toward which all the maneuverings of boards, presidents, faculties, and others is directed. Unless the product is worthy, the effort is in vain.

In this day of quantification there exists a subtle predisposition to rate activities by numbers. Judged in these terms alone, Buchtel College does not come off too handsomely. From 1873 through 1913, it awarded baccalaureate degrees to 465 students or an average of little more than 11 per year. Of these, 248 were men and 217 women, an excellent balance for that time.[74] Measured against the record of similar colleges, this is respectable productivity. Buchtel graduates were an elite in a day (1910) when only seven-tenths of one percent of the American people had earned a college degree.[75] Many of the hundreds of students who spent a year or more in the collegiate department without earning a degree made outstanding records in both public and private endeavors.

Buchtel College did not produce a president of the nation, or a governor, Supreme Court justice, Chief of the General Staff, or Nobel Laureate. It did, however, produce a highly talented and competent group of professionals in teaching and education, medicine, law, politics, public service, nursing, scientific agriculture, finance, journalism, scientific discovery, the ministry, the arts, and all kinds of business enterprise.

A substantial number of Buchtel graduates came back to serve their Alma Mater in important tasks. Susie Chamberlain, the first to receive a Buchtel degree, taught English and rhetoric from 1873 to 1887. At least 22 other Buchtel graduates served on the faculty of the College or the Academy. Both Parke Kolbe, Class of '01, and Hezzleton Simmons, Class of '08, served as president, and both married Buchtel girls—Lydia Voris Kolbe and Agnes Whiton Simmons. At least 15 graduates served on the Board of Trustees of Buchtel College or on the Board of Directors of the Municipal University. Two long-time deans of the Buchtel College of Liberal Arts— Albert Spanton, Class of '99 and Charles Bulger, Class of '08—grew up with their College. C. R. Olin and A. B. Tinker performed valuable services in the business management of the school.

Each president who had children of appropriate age sent them to the College. Lee McCollester attended Buchtel but graduated from Tufts, where he later served as Dean of the Crane School of Theology and became one of the best loved men in the Universalist fold. He served Buchtel College as trustee from 1902 to 1913. Ed Cone, Class of '89 was an editor of professional publications, a career toward which he gained a start as the result of his venture in college journalism. Hal Knight and Maurice Knight both finished with the Class of '06, while Ruth Priest and Evelyn Church were members of the Class of '13. Two presidents of the Municipal University, Simmons and Auburn, continued the practice of sending their children to the school they headed. In like manner, many "faculty kids" attended Buchtel; indeed, Carl Kolbe petitioned the Board on two occasions during the salary cutbacks of 1897–98 asking that tuition be waived for his son Parke. Luckily for the future of the institution, the Board saw fit to grant the petition, thus possibly saving for Buchtel the man who ultimately did so much to save the College.

It is neither practical nor possible to detail the accomplishments of each Buchtel alumnus, but an idea of the range of their activities may be set forth in brief compass. Statistics compiled in 1914 on 366 of the 465 graduates of Buchtel College reveal that the largest group, 27 percent, were in activities classified as "commercial," 20 percent were teachers, 9 percent lawyers, 4½ percent physicians, 4 percent engineers, 4 percent continuing students, and then numbers drop off sharply for the ministry, music and art, social work, authors-newspapers, stenographers, and nurse. Of course, there was the ubiquitous category, "married," that claimed 22 percent of the respondents.[76]

These statistics conceal far more than they reveal. In the first place, it is aggravating to anyone whose mind relishes neat and tidy compilations to realize that nearly a fourth of all the graduates are unaccounted for. And even when a graduate is safely pigeon-holed in a job description, an injustice is perpetrated because so many of these talented people performed extracurricular tasks of a demanding and professional nature in community, lodge, service organization, the arts, and many other fields of endeavor. Indeed, it is this rather general competence to contribute that is the most impressive thing about Buchtel graduates. Not that they outstripped graduates of other colleges; there is no way of measuring that. The record of Buchtel is clear, however, its graduates produced.

Among the stories concealed behind our statistics is that of Hermon Kelley, Class of '79, a lawyer, and a very successful one, who took the lead in organizing the Cleveland Museum of Art, one of the nation's cultural treasures. His classmate, Arthur Stearns, was a guiding spirit of the great Cleveland Public Library. And Arthur Coit, Class of '90, probably classified as "commercial," ran one of the world's largest lecture agencies, one that had grown out of the Chautauqua movement whose original support came from Lewis Miller, once John R. Buchtel's associate in the Buckeye Works. Perhaps the most misleading of all categories was "married" which included women who managed extensive land holdings, who were officers in national organizations, who organized state-wide parent's organizations in support of the schools, who were active suffragists, prohibitionists, pacifists, and cause servers.

The Class of '85 had a financial bent. Lillian Acomb Hunter was Treasurer General of the D.A.R.; Charles Olin was long the treasurer of Buchtel College and The University of Akron; D. R. Crissinger, life-long friend of Warren G. Harding, was

Comptroller of the United States Treasury and later was Governor of the Federal Reserve Board. Another presidential friend was Henry Morris who, as we have seen, was appointed by Grover Cleveland to serve as United States Consul in Ghent, Belgium. Nearer home, Will Sawyer, Class of '87, served as Mayor of Akron. Dayton Doyle (1878), Robert Tucker (1891), Frederick Swanson (1904), Dana Reynolds (1905), were among those who served on judicial benches.

Also semi-anonymous in the statistics are those who were creative in more than one field. Joseph James, Class of '94, was listed as "teacher," and that he was. But he found time for original research in addition to his duties as Head of the Chemistry Department at Carnegie Tech. He invented anti-freeze compounds and discovered aldehol, an additive that makes alcohol taste bad without changing the chemical composition. It was particularly useful during prohibition. Willet Hardin, Class of '93, spent a full professional lifetime as a chemist, and then started a journal of commentary about international affairs which he edited until well beyond his ninetieth birthday.

Along with those whose records are known would be found others equally worthy who worked quietly and unobtrusively, contributing to the betterment of their time and place. If the stature of a school is measured in terms of the useful life, Buchtel stands high.

NOTES

[1] Olin to Church, Aug. 10, 1897, TS in UArch., box 1/1a/130 #7.

[2] Spanton, *Fifty Years*, p. 105.

[3] Board Mins., I, 286.

[4] *Buchtelite*, Mar. 20, 1902.

[5] Spanton, *Fifty Years*, p. 106.

[6] Board Mins., I, 344.

[7] Spanton, *Fifty Years*, p. 175.

[8] *Buchtelite*, Apr. 14, 1904, Apr. 6, May 4, 1906.

[9] Board Mins., I, 302.

[10] *Ibid.*, 308.

[11] *Buchtelite*, Nov. 17, 1905.

[12] "Applied Education," circular in UArch., VF (Publications and Circulars).

[13] Board Mins., I, 309.

[14] *Buchtelite*, Sept., 1904, Oct. 15, 1906; Board Mins., I, 316.

[15] *Buchtelite*, 1900–04; Oct., 1909; Board Mins., I, 363.

[16] *Ibid.*, 330; *Buchtelite*, Apr. 10, 1907.

[17] Board Mins., I, 332.

[18] *Buchtelite*, Apr. 18, 1901.

[19] Board Mins., I, 276.

[20] *Ibid.*, 290; Spanton, *Fifty Years*, pp. 109, 234–35.

[21] *Ibid.*, pp. 109–11, 235–36; Board Mins., I, 338; A. B. Church to E. S. Church, Dec. 6, 1909, UArch., box 1/1a/130 #7.

[22] *Buchtelite*, June, 1909.

[23] *Ibid.*, Oct. 23, 1902.

[24] *Ibid.*, May 12, 1905; UArch, VF (Kolbe).

[25] Spanton, *Fifty Years*, pp. 195–200.

[26] Details were selected from *ibid.*, pp. 207, 211; *Buchtelite*, Oct. 13, 1905; Board Mins., I, 320, 323, 328, 245, 347–48, 359; Church to Simmons, July 30, 1906, TS in UArch., box 1/1a/130 #7.

[27] *Buchtelite*, Oct. 8, 22, 1903, Mar. 10, 1905.

[28] UArch., VF (Hazing); *Buchtelite*, May 4, 1906.

[29] *Ibid.*, Mar. 10, 1905.

[30] *Ibid.*, Dec. 15, 1905; UArch., VF (University Council).

[31] *Buchtelite*, Dec. 25, 1907, Jan. 25, 1908.

[32] *Ibid.*, 1903 through 1915.

[33] *Ibid.*, Dec. 25, 1907.

[34] Spanton, *Fifty Years*, pp. 114–15.

[35] *Buchtelite*, Nov. 17, 1905.

[36] Spanton, *Fifty Years*, p. 114.

[37] *Buchtelite*, 1910.

[38] *Ibid.*, Apr. 24, May 22, 1902; Spanton, *Fifty Years*, p. 115.

[39] Church to Grace Telling, Feb. 3, 1905, TS in UArch., box 1/1a/130 #7.

[40] Spanton, *Fifty Years*, pp. 313, 315.

[41] *Buchtelite*, Mar. 14, 28, 1901, Mar. 20, 1902; Spanton, *Fifty Years*, p. 254.

[42] *Buchtelite*, June 26, 1902.

[43] *Ibid.*, May 19, 1904.

[44] Board Mins., I, 310; Spanton, *Fifty Years*, p. 111.

[45] See *Buchtelite*, Oct. 28, 1904, Oct. 13, 1905, Oct. 15, 1906, Oct. 28, 1907; Spanton, *Fifty Years*, 255.

[46] *Buchtelite*, Mar. 31, 1908.

[47] *Ibid.*, Mar. 31, May 25, June 24, 1908, Mar., June, 1909.

[48] Spanton, *Fifty Years*, pp. 256–59.

[49] *Ibid.*, p. 251.

[50] *Ibid.*, p. 252; *Akron Beacon Journal*, Apr. 12, 1953 (hereafter cited as *Beacon Journal*).

[51] Spanton, *Fifty Years*, pp. 261–62.

[52] *Ibid.*, p. 262.

[53] Board Mins. I, 337.

[54] *Ibid.*, 338; *Buchtelite*, June 28, 1907.

[55] *Sixty Years of St. Lawrence* (Canton, N. Y., 1916), p. 3; For Tufts' experience with the Universalists see Russell E. Miller, *Light on the Hill; a History of Tufts College 1852–1952* (Boston, 1966), various pages.

[56] One letter expressed resentment over Carnegie's supposed power to inhibit free speech by denying grants to those who disagreed with him. See *Akron Sunday Times*, Dec. 5, 1910.

[57] Board Mins., I, 349.

[58] *Buchtelite*, 1909–10; Spanton, *Fifty Years*, p. 112; Board Mins., I, 357.

[59] *Buchtelite*, Sept., 1910.

[60] *Ibid.*, Dec., 1910; Spanton, *Fifty Years*, pp. 112–13.

[61] Olin to Starr Piano Co., Nov. 12, 1910, TS in UArch., box 1/1a/130 #7.

[62] *Buchtelite*, Oct., 1910.

[63] Olin to F. W. Albrecht, Jan. 14, 1911, TS in UArch., box 1/1a/130 #7; Board Mins., I, 342, 365; *Tel-Buch* (1911); *Buchtelite*, Jan., 1912.

[64] Olin to Harsh, Mar., 1912, TS in UArch., box 1/1a/130 #7.

[65] Board Mins., I, 373.

[66] P. Kolbe to M. Shutter, July 26, 1912, in UArch., 4/6/VF; Church's plan and additional correspondence is in *ibid*.

[67] *Buchtelite*, Oct. 1912.

[68] *Ibid.*, Apr., 1909.

[69] *Ibid.*, Oct., 1912.

[70] Olin to M. D. Shutter, Dec. 3, 1912, TS in UArch., box 1/1a/130 #7.

[71] Board Mins., I, 347, 364, 366, 375.

[72] Spanton, *Fifty Years*, p. 107.

[73] Minutes of the Faculty Council, Nov. 18, 1912, UArch., box 17/2/122 #1 (hereafter cited as Council Mins.); Board Mins., I, 375.

[74] Spanton, *Fifty Years*, pp. 405–10.

[75] Department of the Interior, *Bureau of Education, Bulletin*, 1919, No. 90, Vol. III (Washington, 1921), p. 699.

[76] *Buchtelite*, May, 1914.

VII

"Something almost providential;" Buchtel College becomes the Municipal University of Akron

Few things cling so tenaciously to life as do institutions directed by talented and devoted men, determined to fulfill the mission upon which they are embarked. From the vantage point of half a century, one can now clearly see that, by 1913, Buchtel College had run her span of years as a denominational and private institution, and that the infusion of vitality which resulted from the tapping of new resources ordained that the College's work would be perpetuated in the new Municipal University. Old denominational affiliations, controls, and financial support had been cast off; but much of Old Buchtel remained: the faculty and administration, the nucleus of the newly enlarged student body, the campus with its buildings and traditions, the determination to maintain excellence while broadening the availability of higher education.

What had transpired in the 41 years since the College had opened its doors that accounts for the choice—adjust or die—that had to be made in 1913? Recall that at no time did the College reach a secure level of financial strength and support, for the Universalists, while utterly sincere in their desire for a first-rate college, were unable to provide funds to support adequately the fledgling institution. Remember also that only John R. Buchtel gave munificently of his means. Others were generous, but they didn't have as much to give nor was their dedication as total as his. As in any marginal business operation, every national or regional depression or panic was reflected in hard times for Buchtel College. But at least this can be said of her financial troubles; she survived under circumstances that have killed institutions less ably handled.

One of the untold stories of American education concerns the large number of schools that failed, schools that had no alternatives when pressed to the limit. Buchtel's experience was far from unique. The novel feature of her story is that when the final crisis ensued, there were astute men who saw a plausible alternative and took advantage of it, even though it involved a complete change of character, not in order to extend the death throes of a college they thought was dying, but rather to infuse a new vigor into it so that they might perpetuate the advantages it had brought to generations of students and to the city of Akron.

Old Buchtel, live thou proudly on,
Beneath thy founder's name.

(Lulu Weeks Knight, "The College on the Hill")

It now seems the most natural thing in the world that the trustees of Buchtel

President Parke Kolbe (1913–25)

College, hard pressed to meet their obligations, should turn for help to the city whose interests they increasingly served. The idea that the financial resources of Akron might be used to salvage the hilltop College set in its midst did not spring full grown in 1913. The vicissitudes of town and gown relationships have been recounted in previous chapters. It would probably be too strong to characterize it as a "love-hate" relationship such as one finds in a family, but there is no doubt that local money, even though it was largely local Universalist money, kept the College alive in some periods of crisis. Then there were times of distress when "the community took the College for granted, smiling benevolently over its prosperity, but apparently not appreciating its times of adversity—not indifferent, only thoughtless."[1] Earlier we identified the great fire of 1899 as the turning point in College-community relations; after that cataclysmic event, local solutions were sought, ultimately to the exclusion of Universalist solutions, when the fate of the institution hung in the balance.

The ashes of old Buchtel Hall had scarcely cooled before suggestions began to be directed toward ways of refinancing the College and even of relocating it. Covetous eyes were cast by at least one person on an 80-acre tract that the Perkins family had recently given the city for a park. Professor S. P. Orth who, along with Dr. Charles Knight served as faculty representative to a committee to plan Buchtel's rebuilding, suggested that the campus be relocated on city-owned land located west of the city proper. There is no record of the reaction engendered by this proposal, but Professor Orth apparently was not reluctant to suggest extreme measures, since he next investigated the possibility of securing city tax support for the College. He conferred with Akron attorneys and was told that a special act of the legislature would be required.[2] The denominational tie was still intact in 1900, so the matter was dropped. The College was rebuilt on the old site and financed from private gifts and insurance. However, a seed had been planted; many times during the frustration of the long struggle for endowment funds (1908–12), President Church must have longed for the municipal connection. We know, at least, that he "had the plan long in thought," but his premature death forestalled any move in that direction.[3]

Parke R. Kolbe was certainly the right man in the right place at the right time. Colleges generally make extended searches for the properly qualified man whenever the need arises to select a new president, but there are times when it is apparent to nearly everyone concerned that he is available on the spot. Such was the case with Parke Kolbe in 1913.

In a very real sense, he grew up with Buchtel College. His father, the most beloved of Buchtel's early teachers, occasionally brought little Parke to class, and the bright four-year-old lad would "astound" the class with his precocious fluency in German—and why not, since that was all that was spoken at home. In turn, we are assured that Parke was "astounded" by some of the German he heard the students recite.

Upon completing the A.B. in 1901, Parke Kolbe succeeded his father as Professor of Modern Languages upon the latter's death in 1905. For the next seven years, he taught, travelled, and carried on research for his doctorate which he earned, *magna cum laude,* from Heidelberg University in 1912. Returning from Germany that year, Dr. Kolbe was appointed Professor of German Language and Literature, but, as he did not have a full teaching assignment, he was given duties which would now be embraced under the title of Assistant to the President.[4] He was, therefore, more than casually acquainted with the duties and responsibilities of the College president, and he gained additional insight into the work as a member of the faculty committee asked to carry on temporarily following Dr. Church's sudden death.

On February 4, 1913, the Buchtel College Board of Trustees unanimously elected Parke R. Kolbe President of Buchtel College. His wife, Lydia Voris Kolbe, recalled that Dr. Kolbe, not quite 32 years of age, accepted the appointment with equanimity.[5] To most men in academic life this appointment would be less than alluring. The fact that the new president could view the situation without panic, and that he could express a genuine hope and confidence for the future, indicate his quality. Indeed, he had been an active candidate for the position, although C. R. Olin thought some opposition to him might arise because "he is not a church man." Olin pointed out that Kolbe had "secured three promises of $100,000 conditional on half a million being raised." However, it was "altogether likely that he would not be willing to continue in his present position if someone else were appointed president."[6]

Within four days of his appointment he announced that $100,000 had been raised and another $100,000 pledged toward a hoped-for endowment of half-a-million dollars. Despite this apparent progress, he commented that Buchtel might have to move (he did not say where or how) unless the remaining amount was raised. He also reiterated the point that Buchtel was no longer affiliated with the Universalists. Without additional funds, the College would have to limit enrollment; just five weeks later the Board announced that only 200 students would be accepted in September. In summarizing the state of affairs, the new president called upon Akron to "give from her prosperity" to aid the College in its growth.[7]

Commenting upon Kolbe's statement, the *Akron Beacon Journal* said editorially that there were enough wealthy people in Akron to put up the $300,000 still needed.[8] True though this may have been, there were local problems of such magnitude in the spring of 1913 that citizens who might have worked to save Old Buchtel were preoccupied.

The city was in the early stages of an unprecedented boom in her economy and population. The rapid development of the automobile and the truck made rubber tires much sought after. The pneumatic tire had been invented, giving an enormous shot in the arm to the rubber tire industry. International tensions suggested that if hostilities broke out in Europe, American industry would have great expansion possibilities. In 1913 not many were yet of the opinion that the United States herself would become embroiled in a world war, but, of course, when that circumstance did come to pass four years later, the demand for rubber products skyrocketed, and Akron factories couldn't keep up with the demand.

By 1913 thousands of laborers were flocking to Akron where the new jobs in the rubber shops (familiarly referred to as the "gum mills") paid good wages. Akron's population of 70,000 in 1910 had swelled to 100,000 in just three years, and the peak of the flood was not then in sight. No longer was Akron the quiet, well ordered town of the nineteenth century when it had appeared so attractive to visitors. Jerry-built structures popped up in unlikely places; houses were rushed to completion on little lots that should never have held anything bigger than a garage. Residential areas in walking distance of the factories or the downtown business district were over-built, leaving the city with a heritage of confusion that has not been totally reconciled to this day. Fortunately, Akron did not go in for tenement apartments, thus saving untold misery for the future, but people were allowed to build houses in their own backyards, or in blind courts, with no thought to the need for open space or clear access to property. And there was no concern by the majority for schools, playgrounds, or aesthetics—they were too busy making money.

Even this frantic building could not keep up with demand. Many landladies followed the "warm bed" policy whereby a man would rent a bed for eight hours. At the end of that time, he left and another took his place. Thus the bed could be rented three times in every 24 hours. While this arrangement sufficed for bachelors, it was clearly inadequate for families.

A retired member of the University faculty recalled that when he arrived in Akron in 1917 to assume his newly acquired teaching position, there was not a room to be had in the city. Only the sympathy of a hotel manager who allowed his small family to stay in the bridal suite at regular rates saved this faculty member from spending his first night in the Akron depot. Along with scores of others, he went to the newspaper offices to try to intercept landladies coming to place ads for rooms.[9]

Akron's prosperity was not reflected adequately in support for Buchtel College or the municipal university that supplanted it. The city had developed in a fairly stable manner following the Civil War, but now it was overrun by newcomers who had no ties to Akron. Many of them were single men. Much of their money went for food and drink, for entertainment, and for expensive clothing, especially silk shirts which were a fad of the moment. Indeed Akron had a reputation nationally as a quick-money town where factory workers wore silk shirts.

For most of the workers flocking to Akron, "home" was a tired farm or a moribund mining town in the depressed areas of southern Ohio, West Virginia, Kentucky, Tennessee, and points south. Many held intense loyalties to the places from which they had come. The city was alien, a place in which to make a lot of money in a short time. A number of the more provident saved their wages for a time and then went home to spend their savings. When their money ran out, they could always return to Akron and make more.

To a large extent, therefore, Akron was becoming a city of transients, and like footloose people everywhere, they saw little point in contributing to a city that they were in for the moment only. As a result, taxes lagged, collections were difficult, the cost of extending and maintaining city services increased dramatically, and the problems of running an orderly city were enormous.

To these general considerations might be added those special circumstances that made Buchtel's appeal a rather hollow-sounding one in the spring of 1913. In February, a great strike swept Akron rubber factories. Since this was the first significant strike in that booming young industry, it was especially disconcerting to the city. Waves of red-ribboned strikers surged through the streets in an unhappy frame of mind. They were encouraged and inflamed by the exhortations of "Big Bill" Haywood and other crack organizers of the I.W.W., the "Wobblies," considered by most persons of property to be part of an "international conspiracy of anarchy." To lessen the chance of violence, Mayor Frank Rockwell ordered the saloons closed. A group of non-sympathizers calling themselves the Citizens Welfare League donned yellow armbands and, carrying "billies" issued by the sheriff, kept guard on the downtown streets. On March 31 the last of the strikers returned to work, but the care and strain of the last seven weeks overshadowed the crisis at Buchtel College.

As if to compound problems for the city and school, Akron was innundated in

March by torrential rains that dropped some nine and a half inches of water on frozen ground within a 36-hour period. The water raced off Akron's hills with great force, and once the water reached the Ohio Canal, the Little Cuyahoga, and other natural gathering places, it surged in flood. Buildings were smashed, property destroyed, the locks on the canal were washed out, ending once and for all its commerce-carrying days and working costly problems on those industries that depended on the canal as a water source. These twin blows—strike and flood—distracted Akron from Buchtel's plight and ruined any hope the trustees may have had of acquiring from local sources the additional $300,000 essential to a continuation of the College's work.[10]

This was for Buchtel College "one of the most critical hours in her entire history," and, as we have seen, there had been several. The new president's principal task was to convince Akron that the College was by this time much more a local than a Universalist institution. The break with the Ohio Universalist Convention in 1907 had simply confirmed the shift away from denominational involvement. By 1913 only 16 of the 180 collegiate students were from Universalist families. The overwhelming majority of both collegiate and prep students lived in Akron and Summit County.[11] Parke Kolbe realized that unless Akron could be persuaded to take the school as its own, the College would die, and all that had been accomplished would be but a distant memory. If private money was not available in sufficient quantity to save the College, perhaps public money could be secured.

There is no doubt that Parke Kolbe was familiar with the arguments favoring city tax support for the College. Municipal colleges and universities were never very numerous, but the pattern was already well established in this country long before 1913. If there is anything unique about Buchtel's experience, it lies in the unusual circumstance of a private, denominational school being converted through its own initiative into a public, secular institution. Miss Marian Voris, Parke Kolbe's sister-in-law, remembers that one morning at breakfast he read a story in the *Cleveland Plain Dealer* about the municipal universities in Cincinnati and Toledo and observed that a municipal university of this type would answer the needs of Buchtel.[12] Once the idea was implanted in his mind, Parke Kolbe would be the most determined and resourceful of all the advocates of a transition to municipal status.

At the Board meeting of April 14, 1913, President Kolbe submitted a proposal that Buchtel College, including all physical properties and endowment, be offered to the City of Akron to be operated as a municipal university. On motion of Mr. Frank Seiberling it was voted unanimously to make this proposition to the city through its Charter Commission, then at work drafting a charter.[13] The proposal read in full:

To the Charter Commission of the City of Akron:

> *Gentlemen: During its existence of more than forty years, Buchtel College has performed a most important work in this community, and it should be looked upon as an institution to be permanently maintained among us. As an evidence that the college has a rightful and permanent place among our municipal institutions, we call attention to the fact that the attendance has trebled during the last decade, and that this increase is due largely to the increased attendance of local students. Unfortunately, the increase in our endowment has not kept pace with the increase in attendance, with the result that the present sources of income are insufficient to enable the college to carry on its work satisfactorily.*

> *Therefore, we, the Board of Trustees of Buchtel College, representing the corporation in its corporate capacity, do offer and propose hereby, to transfer, turn over, and convey to the City of Akron, Ohio, the entire plant and endowment of Buchtel College and Academy on the terms and conditions hereinafter set forth. We will pay and discharge all the present indebtedness of the college; and the residue set over to the city will have a value of about $400,000, of which about $150,000 will be in interest-producing endowment, but subject to a few small annuities not exceeding the sum of $1,845.65 per year, payable to certain donors during their lives, and further subject to the granting of certain free scholarship privileges as requested by the original*

donors of scholarship funds or their descendants. The College is now and has been for some years wholly free from all denominational control and influence, and will be so turned over to the City of Akron.

This offer is conditioned as follows:

1. That the City of Akron will devote perpetually the plant and funds thus turned over to it, to the uses of a municipal college or university, to be called the College (or University) of the City of Akron, with the provision that in case of the development of several colleges, schools, or departments, the department of Liberal Arts shall retain the name of "Buchtel College of Liberal Arts," thus forming a department of a university in the same manner as Adelbert College forms a part of Western Reserve University, or as McMicken College forms a part of the University of Cincinnati.

2. That the endowment fund turned over to the city shall be maintained as an endowment and not diverted from that purpose, and that only the income thereof shall be used for the support of the college or university.

3. That if a Charter be adopted for the City of Akron, it will provide in adequate terms for the maintenance of the college or university. The present laws on the subject relating to municipal colleges and universities as provided in sections 7902 to 7922 of the General Code . . . will be deemed adequate.

4. The charter of the City shall provide for the government of the institution by a separate Board of Trustees to be chosen and perpetuated under city control in a manner to be determined by you, with a provision, however, that fitting representation on the Board of Trustees be assured to the present organization of the Alumni of the College.

The Charter Commission devoted much of its meeting on April 15 to this offer. A three-man committee, which included Professor O. E. Olin, was appointed by the Charter Commission to investigate the Buchtel offer and acquaint the commissioners with the nature of a municipal university and the services it could perform.[14] To this end, President C. F. Dabney of the University of Cincinnati spoke to the commissioners, discussing in detail the workings of a municpal university; but of greater importance than this was the stress he placed upon the key selling point for this type of an institution—a municipal university, supported by tax funds, could provide inexpensive education for students who, by living at home, could afford a higher education that would ordinarily be beyond their means. The city would flourish according to the skills and competence of her people; civic progress would flow from a more highly educated citizenry.[15] It was a statement of the Jeffersonian creed translated into an urban setting.

On May 6, 1913, the Akron Charter Commission reported favorably on the offer of the Buchtel College trustees. Expressing pleasure at this action, the *Beacon Journal* reminded its readers that they were being offered a bargain. The College was valued at $400,000. The cost of maintaining operation for one year was $48,000, and the estimated income for the municipal school would amount to $60,000, leaving a favorable balance of $12,000. This balance, said the *Beacon Journal,* would be used to start a course in cooperative engineering. The newspaper further stated that the College currently had 19 full-time faculty members serving 13 departments of instruction. The degrees granted were Bachelor of Arts, Bachelor of Philosophy, and Bachelor of Science. In the last decade 498 students had entered the collegiate program (143 of them graduated). Seven reasons were then listed to explain why a municipal university would prove advantageous to the city.[16]

Despite support from the *Beacon Journal* and the initial enthusiasm of the Charter Commission, there were difficulties ahead for proponents of the plan. A modest opposition to the municipal university idea had risen, and even though the university provision in the charter would have been voted on separately, the commissioners feared that this issue might jeopardize acceptance of the larger charter.

Rather than risk defeat, the commissioners passed the Buchtel offer to city council on May 14 with the recommendation that it be placed on the ballot for direct vote of the people.[17] It was fortunate for Buchtel College that the commissioners acted with such caution, for on August 28, 1913, the newly prepared city charter was narrowly defeated at the polls.[18] Those responsible for the College's future could afford a small sigh of relief that its fate was not tied in with the charter.

Before the commissioners passed over the Buchtel offer they took the extraordinary step of appointing a committee of six influential citizens (the Committee of Six) to consider four vital questions to which there must be satisfactory answers if the voters were to be convinced of the wisdom of supporting a municipal university. These questions were: 1) Could the levy for the municipal university be incorporated in the city tax duplicate, under existing tax laws, without taking needed funds from city departments and from the Board of Education? 2) Would the expense of maintaining a university become a burden on the city in years to come? 3) What would be the maximum cost to the taxpayer? and 4) What advantages would the city receive in the cooperation of the university with city departments?[19]

For a time, it was feared that the Committee of Six would make an adverse report since there was some possibility that the city tax rate for 1914 would reach the limit of 15 mills, beyond which the Gregory Act, allowing a tax of .55 mills for a municipal university, would become inoperative.[20] This fear proved groundless.

On July 28, the Committee of Six made its report to the Charter Commission. After "mature and careful investigation and deliberation," they unanimously recommended that Akron City Council be requested to accept Buchtel College as the nucleus of a municipal university, for the benefit of Akron, or provide for submitting the question to the electors of Akron. The committee was confident that there were satisfactory answers to each of the four questions it had been asked to investigate. The investigation revealed that 1) state law permitted a levy of .55 mills for municipal university purposes only, and money thus raised could not be used for any other purpose, therefore, the proposed levy could be incorporated in Akron's tax duplicate; 2) money expended for education was "the best investment which any community can make," so the tax would not be a "burden;" 3) the maximum cost to the taxpayer for maintaining a municipal university would be 55 cents per $1,000 appraised property valuation; and 4) the advantages which a city could hope to derive from a municipal university were "almost unlimited." Eight such advantages based upon the experience of the University of Cincinnati were then listed.[21]

While the city awaited this report, the *Beacon Journal* devoted considerable space to the advantages which a municipal university would have for Akron.[22] Some had to do with the costs to the student which would provide "free higher education to Akron's sons and daughters—rich or poor." This would be accomplished at "small cost to the taxpayer." A municipal university would attract a "desirable class of citizens" to Akron, suburban communities would be more willing to annex themselves to Akron to benefit from free tuition, and "free" practical and technical training to boys would stimulate Akron business and industry. Furthermore, asked the *Beacon,* why import trained technical personnel for local industries if they can be trained inexpensively at home? A municipal university could cooperate with the high schools and provide a stimulus to high school attendance as happened in Cincinnati. Such a democratic institution, controlled by local citizens, would make possible a higher education under home influence. Finally, the university could perform many services for the city. Based upon the experience of Cincinnati, one might expect university professors to undertake chemical and microscopic work for the hospitals, make analyses and tests for the city purchasing and engineering departments, serve as experts on water works problems, train Akron teachers, give psychological tests to public high school children, maintain a municipal reference library and supply information to city officials and councilmen, and cooperate in matters of taxation, census taking, collection of historical information, and supervision of civil service examinations.

Through the month of June, other endeavors were made to inform the citizens. Akron labor organizations were not enthusiastic about Buchtel's offer to the city until Professors Olin and Knight addressed representatives of 20 labor organizations and corrected certain erroneous impressions, including one that the city was to pay $450,000 for the College. So persuasive were Olin and Knight that the Central Labor

Union, at its meeting of July 29, unanimously endorsed the proposal that the city take over the College.[23]

Another group to whom special attention was directed was the Ohio Universalist Convention, then in annual session in Akron. Although there was no legal ground on which the denomination could act to forestall the change, proponents of the scheme wanted to have the understanding and support of this group. In a short speech to the Convention, President Kolbe restated the reasons why the Board of Trustees had unanimously entered upon the course they had taken. He reviewed the financial status of the College, the enrollment shift from denominational to local sources, and the measures taken by Dr. Church to preserve the College. He further asserted that the Board's action would have been approved by John R. Buchtel and by Dr. Church had they been alive. The "threatened letter of protest" from the Convention did not materialize.[24]

Further efforts to influence Akron voters were made in June and included an address, "The City Mind," delivered to the Buchtel College alumni by the Reverend Dr. Simon. He discussed the needs of a city and the reasons why a municipal university was the best method of training future civic leaders.[25] The College reprinted and circulated Viscount Haldane's famous address, "The Civic University," which outlined the aims, work, and needs of city universities.[26] To these efforts at persuasion was added a note of implied coercion when President Kolbe announced that the quota of 200 students, set by the board as an economy measure, was nearly assured for September. If the city would accept Buchtel's offer, said Kolbe, the larger resources available to the College would enable it to "expand with the needs of the city and . . . take care of local young people for a long time to come."[27]

City Council, meanwhile, had been concerned to find the best method of handling the Buchtel offer as referred to it by the Charter Commission on May 14. The Committee of Six had endorsed acceptance of Buchtel's offer either by council vote or by popular vote.[28] Most councilmen, while in favor of accepting the offer, felt that this decision should be made by all the people. Therefore, on July 28, council passed an ordinance requiring a popular vote on the issue at the September primaries. Special ballots reading "Shall Buchtel College be accepted by the City of Akron?" were to be used.[29]

A number of complications soon arose. It was discovered that council had acted illegally on July 28, since an issue of this nature could be placed on the ballot only through an initiative petition; that is, a definite percentage of the registered voters of Akron would have to sign petitions requiring election officials to place the issue on the ballot for popular vote at the next general election. To add embarrassment, the county auditor had gone to Columbus to consult with state tax commissioners about the legality of a half-mill levy for the maintenance of a municipal university. He found that the levy was legal, but it would be necessary for city council to enact the levy immediately if taxes were to be collected for these purposes in 1914.[30] Since the acceptance issue could be placed on the September ballot only through initiative petition, and since that was a time-consuming process, the Summit County Budget Commission decided that the levy could not be made unless council would take hurried action and accept the Buchtel offer for the city. If council were to do this, the people of Akron would have 30 days to petition for a referendum vote on council's action. The budget commission promised that should council accept Buchtel's offer, they would approve the half-mill tax levy required for operating funds.[31]

On August 20, in the midst of these developments, the trustees formally offered Buchtel College to Akron City Council; this offer closely paralleled the earlier one made to the Charter Commission.[32] Five days later, council passed ordinance No. 4050 accepting the trustee's offer "to transfer and convey the entire property, assets and endowments of [Buchtel] College to the City of Akron for a municipal university." The trustees having complied with all the commitments on their part of the transaction, council agreed to abide by the conditions set forth in the Buchtel offer. The mayor and solicitor were instructed to "examine, approve, and receive all the necessary deeds, conveyances and other instruments necessary to receive and perfect the title" to the College property, and to take all other necessary steps to effect the transfer. The ordinance was to be in force "from and after the earliest period allowed by law." It was signed by George C. Jackson, President of the Council, and by Ira Priest, Clerk of the Council, whose feelings must have been stirred at thus seeing the old College he once headed directed into new channels. Mayor Frank Rockwell signed the ordinance on August 26.[33] Ordinance No. 4050 was accompanied by Ordinance No. 4039 which levied a half-mill tax in support of the Municipal University. Both ordinances were to take effect September 24, 1913.[34]

Thus the dream of many men came to fruition; "Old Buchtel" was saved in the life of a new University. Credit for this saving act must go to the Buchtel Board of Trustees, to progenitors of the movement such as Dr. Church and Professor Orth, to cooperative faculty members like Dr. C. M. Knight, C. R. Olin, and O. E. Olin, and to leaders of community sentiment—the city administration, the Charter Commission and its Committee of Six, and to the newspapers. Clearly, however, Parke R. Kolbe emerges preeminent as the key mover of this transfer. Speaking in 1924 about the transfiguration of Buchtel College, Kolbe's good friend and fellow educator, Chancellor Samuel Capen of the University of Buffalo, said: "I don't need to tell [you] who was the moving spirit, because you know it as well as I do."[35] It is proper now, more than half a century after the event, to remind ourselves that Parke Kolbe's enlightened vision of the expanded role Buchtel might play has redounded to the advantage of thousands of men and women whose influence for constructive action radiates from the hilltop campus to far places of the world.

Each September, college campuses across America experience a rebirth. Empty buildings reverberate with sound; classrooms, laboratories, and libraries accept a new generation of users; campus walks come alive with the indolent and the inquiring, the confident and the confused. A spirit of new beginnings permeates the crisp days.

For returning Buchtelites, the sense of anticipation must have been sharpened by the decisive changes in prospect. In the first issue of the student paper, the editor said well what was in the minds of many:

> *It is with mingled emotions that Buchtel students regard this vital change in the control of their college. We who have spent a year or more at Buchtel cannot meditate over the matter without a feeling of regret that "Old Buchtel" is to lose something of her individuality as a privately endowed institution. Yet there can be no question that the students and faculty of Buchtel as a body are heartily in favor of the change, for they foresee in the not distant future a greater institution, a university of which we shall be proud to call ourselves alumni.[36]*

The events of the ensuing months seemed to justify this confidence.

The University considers December 15, 1913, to be its true birthday. It was on that day that Mayor Rockwell officially appointed the new Board of Directors of the Municipal University of Akron. He had discussed the appointments with President Kolbe over a period of 10 weeks. Kolbe had recommended George W. Crouse, Jr., F. M. Cooke, A. A. Kohler, F. A. Seiberling, J. P. Loomis, W. B. Baldwin, M. I. Stevenson, F. W. Albrecht, and himself. On November 24, Mayor Rockwell made public the names of the men he intended to appoint as soon as the property of the College was turned over to the city. This early announcement was made in the hope that it would expedite the turnover.[37] Of the list recommended by Kolbe, all were appointed except Crouse and Albrecht whose places were assigned to C. C. Carlton and W. A. Putt. Seven of the new directors had served as Buchtel Trustees; six of them—Kolbe, Baldwin, Cooke, Kohler, Carlton, and Putt—were alumni of Buchtel College.

The new Board held its first official meeting December 16, 1913, to confirm action that they had already agreed to in unofficial meetings. Parke Kolbe was elected Chairman and C. R. Olin Clerk of the Board.[38] It is interesting to note that the Municipal University continued the practice that started with A. B. Church of having the same man serve as President of the University and also Chairman of the Board. Though certain efficiencies in operation might have resulted from this union, it was obviously not wise to perpetuate this practice once the University had grown to considerable size since educational institutions, like the government itself, require checks and balances to assure that public rather than personal interests are being served.

By-laws were adopted at this meeting. The school was to be known officially as The Municipal University of Akron and, in keeping with the conditions set by the Buchtel College Trustees, the college of liberal arts was named the Buchtel College of Liberal Arts. Of all the by-laws, perhaps the most meaningful to students provided that tuition in the Buchtel College of Liberal Arts "shall be free to all students whose parents are residents of Akron." In other business transacted at this meeting, deeds to the property of Buchtel College were accepted by Mayor Rockwell and City Solicitor Taylor.

Many other considerations came before the new Board, including plans to broaden the scope of the University along lines promised in the rationale for creating a municipal university. A dean of engineering was to be selected immediately so that he could set about organizing a college and make preparations to enroll a freshman class in September. A Bureau of Research was to be created to assist small manufacturers who could not afford their own chemical laboratories. The Bureau of City Tests was designed to relieve the city of this activity. Since no effort would be made to encourage non-residents of Akron to attend the university, Curtis Cottage could be converted into a domestic science building.[39]

Clearly the school was to direct more of its energies toward practical and applied fields, but this shift was only partly the result of the new commitment to municipal education. It was just as much the reflection of the times, for in American education, universities were branching out into all sorts of new efforts in applied fields, efforts that would have been judged inappropriate a decade or two earlier. Even Buchtel College had moved in this direction under Dr. Church by establishing programs in commerce, enhancing teacher training, trying to establish evening and extension programs, and inaugurating a highly specialized study program in rubber chemistry. The new University was better structured to deal with this educational trend than Old Buchtel had been.

The new University fulfilled, in a general way, the promises that had been made to the Charter Commission, the City Council, and the voters of Akron. Undoubtedly there were persons who expressed disappointment at the school's inability or unwillingness to press ahead in a particular area of endeavor, but the larger commitments were honored and the greater prophecies fulfilled. Within a few years the Municipal University was offering an impressive list of services to Akron.

The College of Engineering was established in 1914 under the leadership of Dean Frederic E. Ayer, formerly of the University of Cincinnati. It adopted the cooperative plan of alternating class assignments with actual work experience on the job. This new college was closely involved with local industries who received the benefits of student labor and the pick of well qualified graduates while the student was paid for learning skills that would be useful to him professionally. The College of Engineering also tested paving and building materials for the city, and engineering students assisted in surveying city property.

Also started in 1914 was the Bureau of Industrial Research under the direction of Dr. C. M. Knight. It was to assist "smaller manufacturing concerns which do not employ a permanent chemist," and its services were available on a fee basis. Factories were reported to have shown "great interest" in the work. The Bureau of City Tests, directed by Arden Hardgrove, Class of '11, was transferred to the campus where it performed all chemical and physical testing for the city—tests of coal, paving materials, building material (to this extent it appears to have overlapped some of the work done by the engineering people), bacteriological tests for the Board of Health, and tests useful to the police department in solving criminal cases. Specialized public health training was offered through the Department of Biology. City playground activities were supervised in part by the Department of Physical Training. Sociology students were used by Judge Lytle to survey living conditions of wards of the court. Political Science contributed useful materials toward a municipal research library. The School of Home Economics was established in 1914 and cooperated in community projects from the beginning.

A wide selection of special courses, each serving some specific community need, was offered in the evening. Among them were courses for scoutmasters, social workers, typists, Y.M.C.A. workers, and teachers of "Americanism" who were to prepare immigrants for naturalization. Some of these were credit courses, and some were not. The regular evening program that offered courses for credit started in 1915, but in these early years of the University it had not yet assumed the settled character that marked it in the 1920's.

Other services provided for Akronites included a resurrection of the effort in commercial education. In the early twenties, the Department of Commerce would begin to train men and women for local businesses, and the Teachers College would be established to prepare teachers, most of whom would be employed in Akron. Finally, music lessons, dramatic productions, and lectures were available to the public through the University, although in this, as in some other nascent activities, the effort was small.[40]

If the Municipal University could not reach every objective within a few years of its organization, it was due in part to the community's inability to supply the financial support that would have made more rapid and thorough development possible. After the first blush of enthusiasm wore off, a considerable amount of criticism was directed at the school. The *Beacon Journal,* without whose effective service in educating the public to the advantages of the Municipal University scheme the whole business might have been stillborn, became highly critical of the administration when in May and June, 1915, the Board of Directors requested a substantial increase in the money City Council directed to the uses of the University. The *Beacon* attributed the increase to the "high cost of professors," claiming that the present faculty would get excessive increases in salary, and that there was no need to hire as many new faculty as President Kolbe had been doing since the rate of expansion did not justify this.[41]

The *Beacon*'s ire was directed at President Kolbe. His claim that the newspaper had misrepresented the proposed budget, and his refusal to disclose the salary schedules of Buchtel College—an act which forced the paper to base its stories of unwarranted increases on speculation—seem to have contributed substantially to the vigor of the attack.[42] "The great trouble with Dr. Kolbe apparently is that he believes that he is already the head of a great school, instead of a small one supported by public funds of a mighty hard-up city," the Beacon lamented.[43] Kolbe liked to compare the University he was trying to build with the relatively vigorous Ohio University, but the *Beacon* claimed that Hiram College was a better benchmark. The *Beacon* had a lot to learn about college presidents and how they gauge their needs. It is obvious that the image of struggling Old Buchtel was at this moment more congenial to some of Akron's citizens than was the ambitious dream of an ever-expanding university of the first class serving the growing needs of an expanding Akron, self-styled "City of Opportunity" —that was the way the President of the Municipal University had to talk![44]

Relentlessly the newspaper bored into the University's expenditures. Special attention was paid to the salary of the most highly paid faculty member, Dean Ayer of the College of Engineering. As "J. W. W." put it in a letter to the editor printed on page one under a two-inch headline:

I note your articles in regard to University of Akron salaries. In my opinion, the salary of the dean of engineering is way out of proportion to what it should be, still he wants an increase and he has been here just one year. I am told he does little teaching and rides around from shop to shop visiting his co-operative students. Does a co-operative department pay? Why should we taxpayers pay him so much?[45]

Following this lead, the *Beacon* stated that there was some question as to the merits of the co-op system. Some long-time faculty members had been struggling for years to come within sight of a $2,000 salary goal, and, said the paper, they did not like to see a new man in so far ahead of them. Furthermore, some faculty thought that the arts were being slighted to the benefit of engineering, hinting that this "school to train rubber specialists" profited while the rest of the University was giving general training for life at lower compensation. Though the *Beacon* favored having engineering in the curriculum, it felt that program was "too highly financed with too little work to do."[46]

On May 27, 1915, the *Beacon Journal* editorial displayed a tone of betrayed innocence that the city had taken over a "great financial burden" when there had been no necessity for it to do so. "In fact," said the editor, "those who took the time to think about it must have realized as we do now, that it was committing the city to something the cost of which might easily get out of all proportion to the benefits received." He then proceeded to make an argument so pessimistic in tone that, had it been made in the summer of 1913, it might well have doomed the city's takeover of Buchtel College. It is well to recall that the Committee of Six had examined the expense of maintaining a university and had concluded that such expense could not become a "burden" since money expended for education was the "best investment any community could make."[47]

After weeks of blind speculation, the *Beacon* found itself in luck. Triumphantly it printed the news that its suspicions had been confirmed—"salaries were whooped up, the minute it was assured that the city was to pay the bills." This tentative confirmation came from "taxpayers who are familiar with the old management" and who had disclosed the Buchtel salary schedule because they were "not in favor of a headstrong course of extravagance" even though they were reputed to be in full sympathy with the University. The *Beacon's* figures showed that salaries more than doubled in the period 1913–16. "No wonder Dr. Kolbe refused to make the records public. We understand his reluctance now perfectly," crowed the paper.[48]

Of course, what no one was saying in print was that the offer of the College to the city would never have been made had not Buchtel salaries been so wretched and general solvency so perilous. The *Beacon* evidently forgot that the city was to *improve* this situation, and that immediate and dramatic measures were required. As is inevitable in such moments, the Board and administration probably promised more than they could produce immediately in improved conditions for faculty and students, since they saw how imperative it was to sell the idea. To do this required strong faculty and student support or else townspeople might feel there was some question about the need.

In late July, sweet reasonableness was returning to city-campus relationships —at least on the surface. The University's budget requests for 1916, were slashed by city council by some $10,000.[49] By January, 1916, three new appointments to the Board of Directors put the alumni in the minority, an action the *Beacon* regarded as a hopeful sign. By March budget requests for operation in 1916–17 were being discussed with council, and the Board of Directors was commended for presenting in advance "a statement of the school's needs in an open manner," rather than "trying to conceal a salary boost as the old board did."[50]

What lessons can be drawn from this crisis in the young University's career? Obviously, one is that in virtually every human undertaking, the first surge of enthusiasm wears thin as once poorly perceived reality rises to be dealt with. It is apparent that the administration was utterly sincere in its desire to make Akron a "first-class" university (the same terminology, incidentally, used by the Ohio Universalists on the founding of Buchtel College), but to do this required a level of spending that seemed fabulous to persons unfamiliar with the high cost of quality education. The University people had to realize that their needs were bound to be evaluated as part of the total needs of the city, a city whose financial health was poor and whose needs were enormous. As Akron's population exploded, nearly tripling from 70,000 in 1910 to 208,000 in 1920, even a stunted imagination could see the legitimacy of the city government's plight. There was also, of course, the lesson that the advantages which the University would provide the city were not as immediate, as tangible, as large, or as dramatic as some hoped they might be. It would be fair to say that the marriage of College and community had been consummated, the honeymoon was over, and a long range adjustment to the new partnership was in the process of being forged. These adjustments once made, the relationship was never again threatened by dissolution until, by mutual agreement, the University assumed state status in 1967.

In a sense, the long transition period which had started during Dr. Church's presidency terminated about 1920. Although Akron was billed nationally as "the fastest growing city in America" (or sometimes in less modest moments, the "world"), the student body grew at an even greater rate. The 198 day students of 1913 had given way to 508 day students and an additional 509 evening students by 1919–20. In the decade 1910–20, The Municipal University of Akron, with a growth rate of 240 percent, led Ohio colleges. This figure would have been much greater if evening students had been counted. During the period 1914–20, the annual budget more than doubled to $145,758, while the tax support for the University dropped from .5 of a mill to .38. The number of full-time instructors grew during this same decade from 20 to 32. Two new buildings were added—Carl F. Kolbe Hall housing Bierce Library and the Engineering Lab—and several major campus improvements were underway by 1920.

The Academy and its prep students are not counted in these statistics since it had been a casualty of the transition. As a public institution, the Municipal University of Akron was expected to draw students from public high schools. No public money was available for a University high school. President Kolbe was charged with the task of phasing out the last class. The Academy ceased operations in June, 1914, but since it would be a real hardship to ask last-year students to transfer, instructors from the College faculty taught and tutored some 13 preps who, on June 16, 1915, became the last to receive diplomas from Buchtel Academy. The Academy building was converted to the use of the College of Engineering in 1914.[51]

Through this period of shifting emphasis, Buchtel's high academic standards were maintained by the Municipal University. One of Parke Kolbe's first acts in 1914 was to apply for membership in the North Central Association of Colleges and Secondary Schools, the same agency that had put Buchtel Academy on its accredited list in 1909. For the first time in its history, the North Central suspended its rule that member schools have an annual income of $100,000 or more—Akron's income at the time being only $65,000. A combination of high academic standards and an assured income through municipal tax support were considered grounds for this move.[52]

A fear frequently expressed during the transition period was that the Municipal University would be so eager to accommodate every local need that it would overemphasize the applied "bread and butter" courses. An examination of salaries, equipment purchases, and other basic expenses for the period 1914–20, provides some evidence that the new programs, especially engineering, were receiving a disproportionate share of the resources. There were mitigating circumstances, however. It is always a little more expensive to equip a new technical program than it is to maintain one that has already passed through the period of initial investment.

Further, one of the truisms of the academic world is that it costs much more to train an engineer than it does to produce a philosophy major, a classicist, or a history major. It would be difficult indeed to demonstrate that there was any effort to downgrade the liberal arts with respect to the new practical curricula.

It is true that Parke Kolbe was ambitious and aggressive in pushing new programs. He was eager to have the Municipal University assume its full range of services to Akron. But in his zeal he came close at times to trying too much in light of the resources available to the school. One example will suffice.

In February, 1914, Kolbe wrote to Professor Sleeter Bull, Class of '09, of the Department of Animal Husbandry at the University of Illinois, soliciting his advice on the wisdom of Akron's starting a program in agriculture. It now seems a singularly inappropriate area to consider given the location of the school and the rampant industrialization of Akron, but the United States of 1914 could still boast agriculture as its largest business, by far, and more than half of the population lived on farms and in the towns that served them. Kolbe indicated that Mr. Ohio Columbus Barber, the "Match King," and a frequent contributor to Buchtel College, would turn over his model farm to be used as an agricultural laboratory if the Board would provide "a professor of Agriculture." Kolbe then asked: 1) Would Barber's farm be a fitting place; 2) how much could one man do in developing agricultural courses; 3) what courses would Bull suggest under these conditions; and 4) was the whole plan practicable? Bull's answer on February 5 was cautious; the farm must have separate management; the program outlined by Kolbe was more than one man could handle. Unspoken, yet very much present between the lines, was Bull's lack of interest in undertaking such a task.[53] Fortunately, the matter was dropped.

Concern over the viability of the liberal arts interest was premature. With such articulate and courageous spokesmen on campus as A. I. Spanton, O. E. Olin, and Charles Bulger advancing the cause from administrative positions, and with strong support from Joseph Rockwell in ancient languages, Frank Sturtevant in English, Max Morris in mathematics, Sidney Lockner in mathematics and physics, Hez Simmons in chemistry, Amon Plowman in biology, Elizabeth Thompson in history, there was little chance that the arts and sciences would languish at the expense of applied courses. A more serious threat to the general health and well being of the arts and sciences would arise in the 1930's, but that story will unfold in due course.

The great semi-centennial celebration of 1920 marked the end of an era. Hundreds of graduates of Old Buchtel mingled with the young University alumni during the celebration. One of the original incorporators of the College, Dr. H. L. Canfield, then past 90 years of age, came from Los Angeles, and Buchtel's second president, Dr. Everett L. Rexford, was on hand to be greeted by his young successor and namesake, Parke Rexford Kolbe.[54] The main address on this occasion was delivered by Dr. Samuel Capen, an educator whose initial acquaintance with Buchtel College was made in 1886 when he had visited the campus with his father, then President of Tufts. Dr. Capen emphasized the "complete change of structure and purpose" that the University had experienced. "There is something almost providential about this metamorphosis," he said, and because this process had occurred the institution was in a "position of exceptional strength" to meet the demands of a social order radically different from that of a generation earlier.[55]

Four years later when Dr. Capen again visited Akron, this time to introduce Parke Kolbe as the new president of the Association of Urban Universities, he asked:

I wonder if you people in Akron realize exactly what has happened in your midst in the last ten years in the development of this institution? I had known Buchtel College ever since I was a little boy, and I think it is fair to say that no one would have expected that out of Buchtel College could have come in so short a time, an institution of such comprehensiveness, of such direct public service; an institution that perhaps more than any other represents our idea of the function of a municipal university.[56]

Old Buchtel, a "country college" which had served so well the needs of its time and place, lived on in its worthy successor, The Municipal University of Akron, devoted to the task of serving an urban people.

NOTES

[1] Spanton, *Fifty Years*, p. 92. For differences that separated town and gown, see *ibid.*, pp. 101, 107, 332.

[2] *Ibid.*, p. 97.

[3] *Christian Science Monitor*, Apr. 8, 1914.

[4] Mrs. Lydia Voris Kolbe's statement to the author, July, 1961. There is no definition of Dr. Kolbe's additional duties in the official records.

[5] Board Mins., I, 376; Mrs. Kolbe's statement to the author, July, 1961.

[6] C. R. Olin to M. D. Shutter, Dec. 3, 1912, TS, in UArch., box 1/1a/130 #7.

[7] *Beacon Journal*, Feb. 8, Apr. 19, 1913.

[8] *Ibid.*, Feb. 10, 1913.

[9] Ross Durst to author, (*ca.* 1961).

[10] The best source for accounts of the strike and flood is the *Beacon Journal*. A convenient summary can be found in Karl Grismer, *Akron and Summit County* (Akron, [1952]), pp. 366-75.

[11] Spanton, *Fifty Years*. p. 120.

[12] Personal interview, June 27, 1961.

[13] Board Mins., I, 379-81. The official text of the offer is printed in *Beacon Journal*, Apr. 15, 1913, and in Spanton, *Fifty Years*. pp. 122–24.

[14] *Beacon Journal*, Apr. 16, 1913. In addition to Olin, Dayton A. Doyle, a Buchtel trustee, and Clyde F. Beery, later a director of the Municipal University, served on the commission. See Donald Louthan, "Akron Writes and Adopts a Home Rule Charter," unpublished MA thesis (1964), p. 27.

[15] *Beacon Journal*, Apr. 26, 1913.

[16] *Ibid.*, May 7, 1913 for the report of the commission; May 10, 1913 for the analysis of advantages.

[17] *Ibid.*, May 15, 1913. The Buchtel offer was a "hot potato" for the commission to deal with according to Louthan ("Home Rule Charter," p. 36).

[18] Louthan, "Home Rule Charter," p. 56; Opponents of the charter are identified in *ibid.*, Chapter III.

[19] Spanton, *Fifty Years*, p. 125.

[20] *Beacon Journal*, June 17, 1913.

[21] *Ibid.*, July 18, 1913; Spanton, *Fifty Years*. pp. 125–27.

[22] From July 7 to July 25, 1913, the *Beacon Journal* ran a series of articles each devoted to one or more advantages which Akron would realize from a municipal university.

[23] *Ibid.*, June 4, July 30, 1913.

[24] *Ibid.*, June 12, 1913.

[25] *Ibid.*, June 19, 1913. The speech is printed in Parke R. Kolbe, compiler, *A History of the Establishment of the Municipal University of Akron* (Akron, 1914), pp. 27–36.

[26] *Beacon Journal*, June 18, 1913.

[27] *Ibid.*, June 24, Aug. 6, 1913.

[28] *Ibid.,* July 28, 1913; Spanton, *Fifty Years,* p. 127.

[29] *Ibid.,* p. 127; *Beacon Journal,* July 29, 1913.

[30] Kolbe, *History,* pp. 15–16.

[31] *Beacon Journal,* Aug. 11, 1913.

[32] Spanton, *Fifty Years,* p. 128.

[33] *Ibid.,* pp. 127–29; Kolbe, *History,* pp. 16–19.

[34] Spanton, *Fifty Years,* p. 129.

[35] Proceedings, Tenth Annual Meeting of the Association of Urban Universities, TS in UArch., VF (History).

[36] *Buchtelite,* Sept., 1913.

[37] Kolbe to Rockwell, Sept. 23, 1913, TS in UArch., VF (History), and unidentified note, Nov. 24, 1913 in UArch., VF (Board of Directors).

[38] Board Mins., II, 2–3.

[39] Board Mins. (1913–24), pp. 7–9. Unofficial board meetings were held Dec. 3, 9, and 13. Business transacted at these meetings was given legal reenactment Dec. 15, 1913.

[40] *Beacon Journal,* Feb. 24, Apr. 14, June 18, Aug. 25, Sept. 9, 25, 1914, and Jan. 2, 1917. See also Spanton, *Fifty Years,* pp. 129–35.

[41] *Beacon Journal,* May 24, 1915.

[42] Kolbe did give some general comparisons of Buchtel College and Municipal University salary schedules, but the information was not specific enough to satisfy the *Beacon Journal* (*ibid.,* May 25, 1915). For Kolbe's charge of misrepresentation see *ibid.,* May 26, 1915.

[43] *Ibid.,* May 27, 1915.

[44] *Ibid.*

[45] *Ibid.,* June 7, 1915.

[46] *Ibid.*

[47] *Ibid.,* May 27, 1915.

[48] *Ibid.,* June 21, 1915.

[49] *Ibid.,* July 20, 1915.

[50] *Ibid.,* May 14, 1915.

[51] Spanton, *Fifty Years,* pp. 132–34; Board Mins. (1913–24), p. 7.

[52] *Beacon Journal,* May 24, 1914.

[53] Kolbe to Bull, Feb. 3, 1914, and Bull to Kolbe, Feb. 5, 1914 in UArch., VF (History-letters).

[54] Spanton, *Fifty Years,* p. 19.

[55] *Ibid.,* p. 140.

[56] Proceedings, TS in UArch., VF (History).

The "War to End War" comes to the campus

The "Great War," as World War I was called by a generation that had yet to experience a greater one, brought a drastic, if brief, restructuring of campus programs and emphases. It can best be treated as a separate episode in the University's life, since it produced an abberation in the normal tenor of things, following which the campus returned to a more normal and familiar path, when some civilian concerns, temporarily in suspended animation, were reinfused with vitality.

Although there had long been signs that the United States was drawing closer to involvement in the European war that commenced in 1914, the campus community shared in the general shock when the break with Germany and the Central Powers came in April, 1917. There had been minor irritations—disrupted faculty travel plans and delayed shipments of laboratory chemicals from Germany—that had brought the war home for some in a most modest way, but by March the *Buchtelite* was clamoring for organized drill and military training on campus, citing Yale as an example of a school that was already drilling a volunteer company. If war did come, said the paper, Akron men would be better prepared if they had experienced military training.[1]

On April 9, the faculty voted to require military training for all male students except conscientious objectors. Drill was to be held from 4:00 to 5:30 on Monday, Wednesday, and Friday afternoons. Professor G. A. Bennett who had spent seven years in the Wisconsin militia was in charge, assisted by Coach Fred Sefton and Virgil Rogers, a student.[2] Drill got under way in May with about 160 men participating.[3]

Enthusiasm among the students was high. At a mass meeting on April 10, they commended President Kolbe and his associates for their stand on war preparedness. Kolbe addressed the students, assuring them that there was no reason to call off athletics unless the men were called into active service. Men in the senior class called into service at a time when they had passed all their academic work would be given their diplomas just as if they had stayed in school until graduation with the Class of '17. Kolbe's own idea of how to meet the crisis was clear enough. "While I believe in military training for all college students especially at this time, I heartily agree . . . that the students [should] be trained for a year, at least, before they are sent to the front." He went on: "I believe that the man who goes to the front knowing just how to use a gun and who is familiar with military tactics is infinitely more useful as a soldier than the untrained man, and in addition he stands a good chance of joining the ranks as a commissioned officer if he is backed up by a year of thorough drill, such as we plan to give here."[4]

The ladies could not be ignored when it came to preparedness. The coeds formed a Red Cross unit to learn to make bandages, care for the injured, and "to encourage the men taking part in military drilling." Dr. A. B. Plowman, an authority on first aid and hygiene, and Sarah Stimmel, a home economist, were to direct this Red Cross effort.

Once initial zeal and fervor wore off it was a different matter, of course, to persuade students that there was something useful to be gained from drill. In the spring semester drills, the men had no equipment to carry or use, no uniforms to display, and spirit soon sagged, discipline was lax, and cutting grew to considerable proportions. There were some other activities in which patriotic students could find an outlet for their zeal (or was it just possible that some welcomed relief from scholarly routine?). In response to a request from Mayor Laub, students signed with the Akron Home Guard. They were to be prepared to quell riots or disorders. During 1917–18 the Home Guard, equipped with uniform and gun, patrolled the dam at Lake Rockwell, source of Akron's water supply. No doubt it was easier to convince students that the Home Guard effort was in earnest than it had been to sell them on voluntary drill.[6] During the summer, however, President Kolbe requested the federal government to equip the University for regular military training beginning in the fall semester.[7] Compulsory drill was instituted as planned and continued until the student trainees were absorbed into the Student Army Training Corps in 1918.

Other parts of the war effort reached the University. Mr. C. L. Knight, County Food and Crop Commissioner, issued a call on April 17 for high school and college boys to work on farms to enhance wartime food supplies. The next day, the faculty urged the program along by granting full credit to students thus engaged on the same basis that credit was awarded to those who enlisted in military service. Food shortages attracted the energies of Dr. Kolbe who accepted the chairmanship of the Akron branch of the Food Conservation League, a body pledged to save food, eliminate waste, and limit luxury.[8] In another area of cooperation with the war effort, the University offered a course in telegraphy for the War Department. Students in this program were obligated to enter government service when called. Six men took the course.[9]

While initiating special war service programs, the University's regular programs had to be served as well. Naturally, one of the greatest concerns was that enrollments would drop off to such a low level that drastic cuts in operations would have to be made. This situation did not develop for two reasons; certain students were deferred until the completion of their degree programs, and the federal authorities established a unit of the Student Army Training Corps on the Akron campus.

On order of Secretary of War Newton D. Baker, engineering students were exempted from the draft although they were required to take military training and enter the engineering reserve corps upon graduation. Emphasis in engineering courses shifted from the theoretical to the practical. Despite this ruling, many engineering students joined with those from other fields in volunteering for service.[10]

It is outside the scope of this study to follow student war experiences. However, it helps keep the student image of war in mind to look at one example of it as revealed in a letter from a student, David Darrah, to Professor Thompson from his billet with the A. E. F. in France. "I find myself wondering . . . how I was ever satisfied with what seems trivial occupations of peace," said Darrah who had been a pacifist prior to the war. "But since being here in France I have changed my mind on a number of things, and I am not so sure now that despite the pinched faces of children, the sad faces of women and the maimed bodies of men, you see on the street, that there has not been something added to France and England and all these other nations that, except for the war, would not have existed." As Darrah saw it: "I hope that this will be the last war, but at the same time when *very very* near to war one cannot help, when he philosophizes on conditions, but feel that war may, after all, be a function of society that cannot be dispensed with."[11] One familiar with the rapidity with which students can shift their ground will sense the poignancy of a young idealist getting his baptism in a hard world.

On the home front, the University had its own wartime traumas. On April 23, 1918, Mr. W. H. Eager, a member of the Board of Directors wrote the following letter to Dean A. I. Spanton who was acting as president during Dr. Kolbe's absence from campus.

*"As acting head of the university, I am addressing this letter to you.
[Recently] one of our professors of the University had his class in Chapel
singing a German song in German . . .*

I am not one of those who advocate the utter destruction of German text books and elimination of German from our schools; I feel that it is imperative for us to know the German language to beat the Huns in the present war; we cannot be as effective unless we know the language that he speaks and reads and writes.

I feel such text books should be carefully scrutinized to see that they are proper but I do not consider it necessary, patriotic or proper at the present time to go beyond this point and songs in the German language are absolutely unnecessary, unwise and unpatriotic.

As this information has come to me as Director of the University I feel it is my duty to place the matter before the Board but before doing so I would like to obtain the exact facts from you."[12]

Spanton replied immediately. The class in question, he wrote, was Professor Bulger's and was at the point of its work where the German lyric was emphasized, and it was customary to sing some of the lyrics. It being the time of the year when this was usually done in class, "Professor Bulger . . . put the matter up to the class itself, leaving it with them to decide whether the custom should be followed out this year." The class was all in favor, especially since no patriotic songs were to be included. The students remained a short time after assembly for that purpose. Spanton had heard of this and told Professor Bulger that it was "injudicious" under conditions then current. Dr. Bulger replied that it was reasonable to assume that it was not the right time and assured Spanton that nothing of the kind would happen again. "Of Professor Bulger's thoro-going Americanism and loyalty I have no doubt whatever," wrote Spanton; "anyone on the hill who has talked with Professor Bulger since the United States entered the war well knows that there is nothing pro-German about him." As for Spanton, his position now that the United States was at war was, "He, who is not for us, is against us."[13]

While the singing of German songs was an isolated incident, the teaching of the German language and literature was an emotion-charged issue across the nation, and it caused continuing problems for the directors. In April, 1918, Secretary Olin presented a communication from the Alsace-Lorraine Benevolent Union requesting that the teaching of German be discontinued, at least for the duration of the war. The resolution was tabled after discussion.[14]

A compromise solution came in January, 1919, when the Board accepted a faculty recommendation that German "be continued in the college as an elective." Although the faculty normally controlled curricular matters, Kolbe asked the directors to add a proviso that no class in beginning German would be given unless 15 or more students elected the subject (lowered to 10 in February, 1930). The amended proposal was adopted unanimously.[15]

It is a little difficult to see what Kolbe had in mind by his suggestion. Was he so strong in his support of the cause of the United States that he wished to suppress the teaching of German? Such an explanation is impossible when one remembers the good sense and judiciousness he brought to matters, even under stress. His own heritage and professional interest would indicate to him above all others that there was little to fear from the teaching of German. Perhaps the most plausible explanation would be to assume that Kolbe recognized tendencies among certain Board members to act with vigor against the teaching of German, and he felt that by adding a little to the faculty recommendation he could convince those persons that he was "solid" on this question. And further, any battles in the future over teaching German might as well not be fought for the sake of a mere handful of students. At this same meeting, the directors voted to merge the Department of German with French and Spanish to form a new Department of Modern Languages, and placed Professor Bulger at the head of the new department.[16]

The voluntary efforts made by the University to prepare its students for war experiences, and its efforts to support instruction in areas of national importance became much more formalized in the spring of 1918 and thereafter. On May 15, the first unit of 100 soldiers of the Mechanics Training Corps arrived on campus, the first of four units trained at Akron in the summer of 1918. Akron was the only small school selected to train units of the corps, and the reason is self-evident when one considers that the unit sent here was the Tire Repair Division. These men were raw recruits drawn from many states. They were quartered in Crouse gym and ate in a one-story mess hall hastily erected next to the new engineering lab (now the northern portion of Simmons Hall). The trainees received eight hours of instruction and two hours of drill each day. In addition to classroom work on the campus, the trainees went on inspection trips through the rubber companies and did practical work for two weeks at the Goodrich, Goodyear, Firestone, or Miller tire factories.[17]

In August, the directors renewed the contract with the War Department to extend this program for nine months.[18] The University was to construct barracks and a latrine west of Crouse gym where three old houses were to be razed, but the program was phased out before the barracks was actually constructed. In all, some 500 men were trained as tire repairmen, a significant contribution to an army that increasingly moved on wheels. This training, said Kolbe, "wasn't the kind of work exactly that the colleges had been doing, it wasn't exactly higher education" as we were accustomed to think of it. But in another sense, it was "the highest kind of education" because it served directly the nation's need.[19]

Dr. Kolbe soon found himself an expert in devising training programs. He was called to Washington for special work with the Bureau of Education which could foresee that some means must be found to prevent suspension of college programs during the war. In devising a program for the colleges, Kolbe and his associates sought to avoid creating a special, privileged class of men, and also to avoid measures that would in any way hinder the government's plans for ending the war as speedily as possible. The result of their deliberations was the Student Army Training Corps (S.A.T.C.).[20]

Each college in the country having more than 100 able-bodied male students over 18 was to become a training site for the Army. This branch of the service could not produce the 6,000 new officers it required monthly without help from other agencies. Enlistment in the S.A.T.C. was voluntary; but a volunteer became a member of the United States Army, subject to active duty at the call of the President of the United States. Only in an extreme emergency, however, was a student to be called prior to reaching age 21. Army officers provided military instruction for the cadets. Students currently in college could volunteer for the program, but draftees were also to be put into the program. Cadets lived under regimented, army conditions. The University would house and feed them; they were to wear uniforms at all times; they were subject to military discipline; and they could go home on leave only if their commanding officer approved. For all this, they were to draw a private's pay of $30 a month.[21]

On August 17, 1918, Akron was officially designated by the War Department as a training center for the S.A.T.C., and the Board promptly contracted to lease the Bashaw Garage Building at the corner of Mill Street and College Street. The garage was converted into a barracks to accommodate the anticipated 300 S.A.T.C. cadets and also 100 tire repair trainees.[22]

The first group of cadets—273 trainees under the command of Captain A. E. Aub—was inducted into the service on October 1 in an "impressive" ceremony on the campus. This Akron unit was organized and functioning in a very short time in contrast with the haphazard experiences on many other campuses because the college authorities cooperated fully in the undertaking. In a busy day that ran from first call at 5:45 A.M. to taps at 10:00 P.M., the students followed a program of course work that included mathematics, chemistry, English composition, military hygiene, surveying, map making, war aims, and military law.[24]

The new program was just underway when the armistice of November 11, 1918 brought it to a halt even though the War Department insisted the program would be maintained.[25] The Board discontinued S.A.T.C. on December 9, cancelling the lease on the Bashaw Garage and winding up the program. Those men not participating in the S.A.T.C. had been required to take military drill, and they were also released from their obligation at this time. But President Kolbe was convinced that the University should try to secure a unit of the newly formed Reserve Officer Training Corps (ROTC) and steps were soon taken to implement this plan.[26]

Most of the S.A.T.C. personnel were demobilized in early December, but a flu epidemic that hit the barracks just before this date held things up. The main flu attack came at Thanksgiving when all the trainees were on 24-hour passes. The campus had been quarantined when the epidemic first struck Akron. Civilian students were banned from the campus, but the cadets continued to meet their classes until the Thanksgiving outbreak. A few of the local cadets were allowed to go to their homes, reporting only for formations. Some of the cadets volunteered for hospital duty as did some of the coeds to their own considerable peril. Four men died, and only the untiring care of the medical officer, Lt. Gottlieb, and his volunteer assistants prevented an even worse situation.[27] With the waning of the epidemic, demobilization was completed by December 23, with some 145 students who had come to Akron solely for S.A.T.C. now returned to their homes.[28]

The campus returned to normal. The academic calender, divided into three equal terms for the army programs, was returned to the semester plan in 1919.[29] Engineers had gone off co-op during the S.A.T.C. program, and they returned to this feature of their program in 1919. The varsity teams had continued to play during the war years with the exception of the 1918 baseball season. And although sororities had maintained their social programs through this period, the fraternities had had to close. Now they could reopen, and college social life revived.

A summing up of the University's war involvement can accomplish no more than to call attention to projects, programs, and activities that were set down in the record. Many personal sacrifices and contributions went unrecorded in this, as in every great crisis.

We must start with those who entered the service of their country. The University was represented in the fighting forces by six faculty members, 98 students and alumni, and 255 members of the S.A.T.C.[30] At least 25 served as commissioned officers, while many others were in the non-commissioned ranks. The highest ranking officer claimed was Brigadier-General William S. Scott who was a Buchtel student in 1875–76. Miss Mary Gladwin, Class of '87, rendered unparalleled service as a war nurse. For four years she labored under tense and dangerous circumstances in Serbia and elsewhere. Her heroism was recognized by her Alma Mater when it awarded her an honorary doctor's degree. Two men died for their country—Lieutenant Thomas J. Quayle and Private Thomas B. Welker, both killed on the battlefields of France.

The services of Dean Ayer and of F. H. Nestell in assuming complete responsibility for the housing and feeding of the student soldiers, the efficient work of C. R. Olin in handling the financial affairs of the S.A.T.C., and Dean Spanton's administration of the University during President Kolbe's absence on war service in Washington are all deserving of special praise. The devoted efforts of many coeds in Red Cross work, nursing during the flu epidemic, and in general helpfulness should be acknowledged, plus the fact that they took their relegation to second place on campus during the army training programs with good grace.[31]

A brief summary of work contributed by the various academic departments will serve to give some idea of the totality of involvement the campus experienced in the war effort. Biology, with the cooperation of Professor Hopkins of Kent State Normal College, gave a course in military hygiene; the War Issues course was given by Dr. MacAyeal in cooperation with the Departments of History and Social Sciences; the History Department also offered a course in Current Events Since 1916; the Departments of English and Classics co-ordinated their work with that of the course on War Aims; Modern Languages adapted their offerings to the special needs of the wartime curriculum; Engineering offered courses in surveying and map making, supervised the co-op work periods of the tire repair trainees, conducted a course for automobile repair men, and cooperated with Akron industries engaged in war work; Chemistry prepared students in the areas of chemical warfare, established a testing program in tires for the U. S. Government, and, in cooperation with engineering deparments, aided Akron industries when called upon; the School of Home Economics assisted with food conservation studies, gave canning demonstrations, and worked with many war-related community interests; the Athletic Department's service in drill and military training was a major contribution; the Social Sciences Department cooperated with a number of local agencies to prepare volunteer workers for home service to the families of soldiers and sailors. Thus all segments of the University felt the effects of wartime service to greater or lesser degree.

When the war was over the campus returned to normal pursuits with few regrets. But there were many persons who were concerned lest the nation again be caught unprepared in some future engagements. President Kolbe who was writing a book, *The Colleges in War Time and After,* for D. Appleton and Co., was aware of plans to establish on a permanent basis a Reserve Officer Training Corps, and he early urged the Board of Directors to apply for a unit.[32] ROTC was established at Akron February 1, 1919 and was to be continued for the academic year 1919–20. Captain Adolph Unger was the commanding officer of the unit. About 40 liberal arts students and 40 engineers had elected to take the drill. In the fall, cadets were to spend five hours a week in ROTC, three of them in military science and two in physical education. The course was made compulsory for freshmen men beginning September, 1919, and thereafter for sophomores also.[33] In later years this stipulation was to cause extensive discontent and opposition. These plans made in the spring, 1918, were jeopardized when the government recommended that the program be dropped at Akron because there were far fewer than the minimum 100 students enrolled, but Lt. Anderson of the staff explained in Washington that the lack of men was due to the fact that most of the men had previously been in the service or in S.A.T.C. and that prospects were bright for the fall semester, 1919. He was convincing, and the unit remained.[34]

As a final bit of business concerned with World War I, the Board of Directors offered space on the campus to the Mayor's committee for devising a suitable soldier's memorial—possibly a Soldier's Memorial Hall "to serve the uses of the community and particularly of the various patriotic and military interests, as well as of the students of the University itself."[35] The primary argument for constructing the building on the campus was that the University had taken a prominent role in war work.

Although this particular plan was never realized, the University did eventually provide the memorial site. In 1923, a new concrete grandstand seating 6,000 people was erected at Buchtel Field. It was officially dedicated in October as The Memorial Stadium. A bronze tablet, gift of the Athletic Association, and inscribed with the names of 304 Summit County heroes who had lost their lives in the war, was placed on the wall near the main entrance.[36] Years later the stands were torn down, and Akron's World War I memorial was no more.

NOTES

[1] *Buchtelite,* Jan. 18, 1916.

[2] *Beacon Journal,* Apr. 10, 1917; *Alumni Quarterly,* II, no. 8.

[3] *Akron Times,* May 4, 1917. Spanton says drill was voluntary until the fall semester. 1917, but this conflicts with all other sources (*Fifty Years,* p. 383).

[4] *Beacon Journal,* Apr. 10, 1917.

[5] *Ibid.,* Apr. 7, 10, 1917.

[6] *Ibid.,* Apr. 13, 24, 1917; *Buchtelite.* Oct. 5. 1917; Spanton, *Fifty Years,* p. 383.

[7] Board Mins. (1913–24), p. 87.

[8] *Beacon Journal,* Apr. 17, 18, 20, 1917.

[9] *Ibid.,* Sept. 29, 1917; Board Mins. (1913–24), p. 93; *Buchtelite,* Dec. 19, 1917.

[10] *Ibid.,* Dec. 7, 1917; *Beacon Journal,* Dec. 10, 1917.

[11] *Buchtelite,* Dec. 7, 1917.

[12] Eager to Spanton, Apr. 23, 1918, UArch., 4/7/VF.

[13] Spanton to Eager, Apr. 24, 1918, *ibid.*

[14] Board Mins. (1913–24), p. 106.

[15] *Ibid.,* p. 125.

[16] *Ibid.,* pp. 126, 146. Buchtel College had a professorship of modern languages from an early time.

[17] *Buchtelite,* May 21, 1918; *Beacon Journal,* Apr. 18, 1918.

[18] Board Mins. (1913–24), p. 115.

[19] *Beacon Journal,* June 5, 1918.

[20] Spanton, *Fifty Years,* p. 385; Board Mins. (1913–24), p. 106. Civilian students promptly dubbed the S.A.T.C. the "Saturday Afternoon Tea Club."

[21] *Buchtelite,* May 21, 1918; *Beacon Journal,* July 31, Aug. 19, Sept. 3, 1918.

[22] *Ibid.,* Sept. 10, 1918; The lease was for $2,000 a month. Board Mins. (1913–24), p. 117.

[23] *Beacon Journal,* Oct. 1, 3, 19, 1918.

[24] *Ibid.,* Oct. 19, 1918; *Buchtelite,* Nov. 2, 1918.

[25] *Beacon Journal,* Nov. 14, 1918.

[26] Board Mins. (1913–24), p. 121; *Beacon Journal,* Oct. 17, 1918.

[27] Spanton, *Fifty Years.* p. 390; *Beacon Journal,* Oct. 24, Nov. 29, 1918; *Buchtelite.* Nov. 2, Dec. 14, 1918, Jan. 8, 1919.

[28] *Ibid.,* Jan. 22, 1919.

[29] *Ibid.,* Nov. 2, 16, 1918, Jan. 8, 1919; Board Mins. (1913–24), pp. 111, 138.

[30] *Buchtelite.* Nov. 14, 1919.

[31] Spanton, *Fifty Years,* pp. 378, 379, 385.

[32] *Buchtelite,* May 2, 1919.

[33] *Beacon Journal,* Mar. 14, 1919; Board Mins. (1913–24), pp. 127–28; *Buchtelite,* Jan. 8, Mar. 21, 1919.

[34] *Ibid.,* Oct. 3, 1919.

[35] Board Mins. (1913–24), p. 123.

[36] *Buchtelite,* Apr. 4, 1919, Oct. 12, 1923; *Akron Sunday Times,* Oct. 14, 1923.

Examinations are painful in any age.

IX

"Prepare students for the practicality and competition of life" (1913–1924)

Shortly after the conclusion of World War I, there was a widespread desire on the part of Americans, including Akronites, for a return to that "normalcy" that an Ohio President, Warren Gamaliel Harding, popularized. For the University, "normalcy" meant reinstituting appropriate programs and casting off adjustments to wartime exigencies. The only inheritance from the war years was a nursing course and an ROTC program which kept uniformed trainees drilling on the campus. For a brief period, veterans were sent to the University under contract with the Veteran's Rehabilitation program of the United States government which paid for the schooling of disabled veterans. This program was phased out in 1924 at the University's request because of excessive red tape.

The most visible impact that peace had on the campus was the swelling enrollment. There were almost no barriers to admission for an Akron student. Tuition was free in liberal arts, most could live at home, and little beyond a high school diploma was required to satisfy admission requirements. As noted earlier, in a study of Ohio college growth in the decade 1910–20, the Municipal University of Akron headed the list with an enrollment increase of 240 percent. This figure counted day students only, and if one adds to that figure the number of full-time equivalents taking evening work, the enrollment increase would be even more dramatic.[1]

This influx of students pleased certain University officials. It appeared to confirm their confidence that Akron was changing rapidly from a small college to a large university. The increase was attributed to increased interest in collegiate work, to propaganda put out by the army urging the value of education to the nation, to the desire of students to enhance their earning power, and to students who would normally have gone away to college now finding it necessary to secure their education more cheaply at home.[2] The last phenomenon was the result of the sharp depression that swept the country in 1920–21.

Akron was hit unusually hard by this economic crisis. The rubber industry was grossly overextended as a result of the phenomenal boom of the preceding decade, and the recession caught the major operators by surprise. Control of some Akron rubber companies shifted to New York bankers.[3] Many of the smaller firms folded. Industries dependent upon rubber suffered severely. Akron had become a one-industry town to an unhealthy degree, and when that industry was sick, Akron was sick. Thousands of men were laid off on the production lines, and this was followed by substantial lay-offs of white-collar workers. There was a great exodus of workers who left Akron to return to the rural, small-town life they had come from originally.

The strange paradox of University enrollment flourishing while the economy of the community was in crisis would be repeated in the 1930's. This circumstance has led some local people to claim that the University flourishes whenever the economy is in trouble, but that claim is clearly excessive and one dimensional. As a tax-assisted institution, the University could not possibly be immune to the general economic health of Akron and the nation. To flourish, a university needs much more than rising enrollments, especially when most of the newcomers paid no tuition.

As enrollment increased far more rapidly than facilities, overcrowding became endemic on the Hilltop. The *Buchtelite* conjured up a familiar picture for its readers:

Perched on the windowsills, the Freshman drummed a steady tattoo against the wall with his heels.

"Keep your feet on the floor," barked the instructor, his brow furrowed with deep lines as he struggled with the pile of papers before him.

"Can't do it sir. Ain't long enough," piped up the Freshman.

"Sit in a chair," growled the instructor.

Then he paused and looked around. Every chair was full. Along the walls drooped lines of students, patiently waiting. And packed on each windowsill, others perched, elevated but uncomfortable.

Such was the condition which prevailed after the beginning of the 1921–22 academic year.[4]

President Kolbe reported "great additions" to faculty and equipment during 1921, but these were insufficient to meet the needs of the larger student body. Classes which normally would have had 30 students now had as many as 80.[5] It was clear that the University could not go on indefinitely opening its doors to all comers.

In December, 1921, the president received an opinion from the City Law Director that the Board of Directors could restrict the number of freshmen admitted to the University.[6] Through the winter and spring, the directors considered the possibility of imposing limitations. They were concerned that 28 percent of the freshman classes had more students than they should under standards common in American higher education. For the moment, however, they took no action.

Conditions continued to grow worse. As the academic year 1922–23 got under way, the deans reiterated to President Kolbe their pleas that enrollment be limited. Those who had reveled in bigness were having second thoughts. In October, Dr. Kolbe submitted the most recent figures to the Board:

STUDENT ENROLLMENT		
College or Department	1921-22	1922-23
Buchtel College of Liberal Arts	372	416
Curtis School of Home Economics	29	44
Engineering	139	156
Commerce	63	94
Teachers College	72	103
Total	675	813

This increase of more than 20 percent represented day students only. In 1921 evening enrollment was double what it had been the previous year, and the numbers continued to rise yearly.

Apparently students and faculty were still in favor of allowing enrollment to increase without limitations and restrictions. This attitude was related to a hope and expectation that enrollment pressure would force the construction of new buildings. Naturally the directors would also have liked new buildings, but the prospects did not look favorable. Rumors that the admission of non-Akron students would be restricted were poorly received by many students and faculty, and by some administrative officers. Out-of-town students, said one student observer, made the institution "broader" and gave it a "cosmopolitan atmosphere." Limit enrollment to townspeople and the institution is reduced "to the level of a mere high school," he said.[8]

The directors voted to seek authority from the Ohio Legislature to permit Akron citizens to vote on a bond issue for capital improvements. If this request were denied, the Board would ask the city to enact a special, limited tax for capital purposes. Pending the outcome of this plea, the directors agreed to limit the 1923 freshman class to the same number admitted in 1922. First priority was to go to Akron students. Evening classes were to be rearranged to take the overflow from day classes. Registration at mid-year (January, 1923) was limited in all departments except engineering by the capacity of freshman courses to receive new students.[9]

Once limitation of enrollment was established, no one seemed happy with it. Dr. Kolbe and Dean Spanton saw the necessity for it but hoped it would not endure. Dean Ayer was strongly opposed to limiting enrollment of non-Akronites in engineering because he believed that most of his graduates stayed in Akron and took jobs with local firms. Professor Simmons thought out-of-town students added much to school spirit. Nevertheless, further limitations appeared likely. In the spring of 1923, the Faculty Council's executive committee recommended that freshman class sections be limited to 35 students and that enrollment in each subject be set at limits to be determined by the deans. The directors adopted these proposals in March.[10]

The pressure was relieved somewhat when school opened in September, 1923. Freshman enrollment had declined modestly due to two circumstances. First, the economy was healthy enough to provide jobs for high school graduates so they had an alternative denied many in the preceding years. Second, new entrance requirements had been adopted by the University. No grade below 80 percent (C) earned in the last two years of high school would be accepted. Students with grades below that level could request permission to take entrance examinations in the subjects in which they were delinquent. Relatively few applicants had to take the special exams, although it is probable that would-be applicants were deterred from applying if their grades did not measure up to expectations.[11]

Naturally, many of the problems resulting from overcrowding could have been ameliorated if the University had had more operating money to hire additional teachers and take other steps that would have eased the strain. The problem was not simply too little space, it was also that there were more students in a class than the faculty thought proper for optimum teaching effectiveness—the student-teacher ratio was awry.

In the absence of additional public money, the directors started to impose student fees. They were first directed entirely at the non-resident (non-Akron) student. In 1920 it cost a non-resident liberal arts or home economics student $150 a year in fees and tuition to attend the University. This figure was up by $50 over the previous year. Even so, the actual cost of educating a student at that time was about $235 a year. Thus, the non-resident was paying only 65 percent of the cost of his education. Fees for non-resident engineers went up from $80 to $120 per year. No reason was stated for this disparity among colleges, although it seems obvious that it must have represented an attempt to encourage enrollment in engineering. The disparity was greater than would appear on the surface since engineering education tends to be more costly than the other fields. Fees for non-residents were raised again in 1922, to $160 for engineers and $200 for other students.[12]

In these years only some 16 percent of the student body were subject to these fees. No matter how much they were raised, not enough additional money was brought in to meet the needs. The situation was made more grave by the failure of the City Budget Commission to allocate to the University the maximum amount of millage permissible under state law. The 1914 tax rate in support of the institution had been .5 of a mill, but that rate had dropped by 1921 to .475 of a mill, which was insufficient to provide for increased needs. In 1923 the City Budget Commission authorized the maximum levy permitted by state law (.55 mills) because enrollment increases, coupled with a decline in the Akron tax duplicate as a result of the depression, made it mandatory that the University receive the full amount allowable.[13]

In 1922, Dr. Kolbe proposed to the Board a six-point program for increasing revenues. First was an increase of tuition for non-resident students, and this was accomplished as noted. Second, more rigid residence requirements were to be imposed on students claiming free tuition. Third, state legislation allowing Akron to add public money to the University's support was to be sought. Fourth, state legislation to permit the Municipal University to charge Akron students a fee equal to that charged residents of Ohio at the state university should be encouraged. Fifth, private funds should be solicited. Sixth, an "endowment association" to solicit and receive bequests should be formed.

Kolbe used some statistical data to buttress his proposals. In its first nine years as a Municipal University, Akron's student enrollment increased from 198 to 2,096 (many of the latter being part time). The ratio of full-time students to full-time faculty increased by 8.6 to 17.5. Total University expenditures tripled, and the city tax duplicate tripled during that nine-year period. But the University tax rate (the millage allotted to it each year by the City Budget Commission and City Council) decreased slightly while the total city, school, and county tax rate for all local purposes increased from 12.6 to 20.4 mills. The University's annual cost per student decreased by about one-third. The 1922 figure of $207.12 per student was too low for best academic results and compared unfavorably with other municipal universities. And finally, the rapid rise in student-teacher ratios had reached a point where further increase would impair teaching efficiency.[14] The needs were obvious and pressing; the Board supported Kolbe's assessment of what needed to be done, and they pushed ahead on all six points of his program.

During this period of financial stringency, Kolbe was spared the criticisms that had earlier been directed at his handling of financial matters. The *Akron Press* thought the University handled the taxpayers' money well and asserted that an endowment of sufficient size would solve most of its immediate problems. It would also make the University "independent of the whims of politicians with different tax plans." The only other alternative that seemed plausible, said the *Press*, would be for Ohio to adopt Governor Vic Donahey's recommendation that all tax and debt-limitation laws be repealed, thus allowing communities "home-rule" in the matter of taxation and debt creation.[15] Neither of these suggestions was realistic: the voters of Ohio were not about to adopt Donahey's plan, and Akron wealth, such as it was in the 1920's, was not ready to build an endowment for the Municipal University.

The most significant and far-reaching development in the search for revenue resulted from an amendment to the state law governing tuition at state universities. The amendment permitted municipal universities to charge resident students fees equal to those charged residents of Ohio at the Ohio State University. The Board of Directors promptly enacted a "maintenance fee" of $30 per year for all students, resident and non-resident alike, who entered the University in September, 1923, or thereafter. This new fee replaced a $15 "incidental fee" that continued in effect for students enrolled prior to September, 1923.

The new legislation and fee increase came just in time. The amount realized from the city tax duplicate in 1924 was no greater than that of 1923. Only the new fee increase permitted the Board to balance the budget for 1924.[16]

In his efforts to find additional revenue, President Kolbe took the first step to secure funds from the State of Ohio. In the winter of 1923–24, he met with the presidents of the municipal universities of Cincinnati and Toledo. The presidents agreed to request the state legislature to consider the following adjustments in financing: 1) the sinking fund for bond issues for municipal purposes should be placed outside the .55 mill limitation; 2) the teacher's colleges of the municipal universities should receive state aid since the burden they carried would otherwise fall upon the state normal schools; and 3) the rate chargeable to municipal universities for Workmen's Compensation Liability should be reduced.[17] Variations on these themes would occupy the municipal university presidents and their successors until the 1960's.

The troubled financial climate of 1920–24 was largely responsible for financial policies and practices that stayed with the Municipal University throughout its existence. These practices included keeping non-resident fees at a level that paid about half the actual cost of educating the student; charging a "maintenance fee" of all students; seeking the maximum tax millage allowable under existing laws; charging laboratory and other "incidental" fees; and seeking private sources of revenue for endowment and special purposes. The attempt to secure help from the State of Ohio would serve as a model for later administrations to follow, as would the practice of cooperation with Cincinnati and Toledo in this quest. And another important practice initiated in this period would be repeated over the years—City Council was persuaded to issue bonds for capital improvements. The amounts were small, but the improvements that sprang from this money enabled the University to keep its head above water during the floodtide of student enrollment.

Buchtel College, unlike the Municipal University, had but one source of capital funds—private donations. The Buchtel Trustees were able to turn over to the city a physical plant consisting of Buchtel Hall, Crouse gym, Curtis Cottage, the Academy building, Knight Chemical Laboratory, the President's House (later called Phillips Hall), the heating plant, and Buchtel Field. Only "Old Buchtel" Hall and the astronomical observatory had disappeared from the campus. Naturally this plant, adequate in 1913 for the 198 collegiate students plus the prep students, would be inadequate for the 2,500 students of 1924. Just two small buildings had been added during Dr. Kolbe's administration, but his inability to do more along this line was not for lack of trying.

A significant addition to the campus was the construction of a library building in 1915–16. This was made possible through the generosity of Mr. Frank Seiberling who transferred a gift of $20,000 to this cause from the endowment fund. Mr. Frank Mason contributed $10,000 in similar fashion.[18] Ground was broken on the southeast corner of the campus during commencement exercises in June, 1915. The new building, named Carl F. Kolbe Hall in honor of Buchtel's respected language teacher, was ready for students just a year later. The book collection, still known as the Bierce Library, numbered about 15,000 volumes. Since the new building was designed to hold 40,000 it appeared that growth space had been allowed. Although poorly arranged by modern standards, it was a stylish building for its time. A large room for men and another for women were arranged as informal lounges to provide a much-needed gathering place for students. It was hoped that these rooms, forerunners of the student union, would help unify the student body and help dissipate "differences and dissentions among fraternities and other campus organizations."[19] This building, much modified and with an annex added, would serve until 1960 when it was razed to provide room for the present library building.

The first building made possible by the Board's new methods of financing was the engineering laboratory. In March, 1916, the directors considered asking City Council to authorize a $100,000 bond issue to erect and equip an engineering building to accommodate the new college. By May, however, the directors had modified their request and lowered it to $50,000 in recognition of the critical state of the city's finances. Bonds in this amount were issued in July and, within a year, the new lab was ready in its location—adjacent on the south to the engineering recitation building (the Academy building).[20]

The Board had ambitions for additional buildings, and to this end they adopted a development plan that described a method for fulfilling the basic scheme for campus improvement drawn up in 1900. Now, some two decades later, the directors requested City Council to issue $150,000 in bonds to provide an addition to the engineering lab, to remodel the Academy building for physics and biology, to modernize the power plant, and to erect a grandstand and dressing rooms at Buchtel Field. In the fall of 1920, Council issued bonds in the full amount.[21]

Work started immediately, and within a year all but the grandstand project were completed. Engineering students, urged on by Dean Ayer, had cleared the site of their building addition by tearing down the old wooden barracks on the southwest corner of the campus. When the engineering lab addition was complete, all engineering classes were centralized in that building and the old Academy building was quickly modified to meet the needs of physics and biology. The building was given a new name in 1921—Olin Hall—in honor of the great contributions made to Buchtel College and the Municipal University by Charles R. Olin and Oscar E. "Daddy" Olin. Contrary to a common assumption, the two were not closely related and came to Akron by quite separate paths.

With the installation of new boilers campus needs could be met until a new building spurt following World War II overtaxed their capacity. A two-story workshop was constructed. It also housed the ROTC armory and was a familiar place to generations of cadets. Finally the first section of the grandstand was built, but not until 1923 was the Alumni Memorial Stadium completed.[22]

Many space needs still had to be met since the total amount of new instructional space added was minimal. Some persons were of the opinion that a new gymnasium was the first requirement. At the time, they could not have known that people would still be saying that 30 years later.[23] In May, 1923, President Kolbe submitted a plan outlining building needs of $750,000 which he felt would meet the requirements of the next seven years. The directors authorized him to present these plans to the City Administrator, but nothing came of this effort.[24] Meanwhile, other sources of building funds were explored, including another appeal to the Carnegie Foundation, this time on behalf of an engineering classroom and laboratory building, but the appeal was unsuccessful.[25] Indeed, no new buildings or significant remodeling would occur for the next 13 years, even though Dr. Kolbe warned that "no ingenuity can long defer the time when new buildings must be built."[26]

One reason that enrollment skyrocketed in the new Municipal University was the addition of many new courses and degree programs which spread the appeal of a college education to a much broader group of potential students. Although some of the new programs have been mentioned briefly, it is necessary to look more closely at their beginnings, for these programs represented important additions to the University's mission.

The College of Engineering was in some respects President Kolbe's proudest achievement. That may seem odd for a man whose background and training were so concentrated in the humanities and arts. But Kolbe appears to have found a home in matters concerning engineering and technical education as his career, both before and after leaving Akron, demonstrates. It is clear that much local support for the municipal university idea came from those most interested in engineering.

The College of Engineering was established in January, 1914, so that an immediate start could be made to hire a dean, assemble a faculty, prepare a curriculum, and secure a student body. A special announcement of the faculty and program of the new college was printed and circulated; and when classes opened in September, there were 29 men enrolled in the college. One of the attractive—and still novel—features of the program was the cooperative plan whereby the engineering student spent considerable time on a job in some engineering-related activity. Two students held one job so that while one was on the job, his partner was in class. Every two weeks the pair traded places. At the completion of each two-week job session the student had to report to the dean on some phase of his work. Discharge from the job meant dismissal from school. The first firms to employ the co-op students were Goodyear, Firestone, Goodrich, and Miller rubber companies, Akron Rubber Mold, Adamson Machine Company, Williams Foundry and Machine Company, and various railroads.[27]

Some skeptics thought co-op engineering was being oversold. Dean Ayer was committed to its advantages and, from time to time, brought them to the public's attention. Co-op work taught students to get along on the job with other men; students could see in the shop the practical applications of problems they had studied in the classroom; they matured by performing a responsible job; they came into contact with various branches of engineering and thus had an opportunity to decide what type of engineering they wished to pursue.[28] However, the Dean did not emphasize one reason the co-op program was so popular with students: they were paid for their work. How many students are paid for fulfilling degree requirements? In 1922 the co-ops averaged 47 cents an hour in wages, with pay ranging from 30 cents to a high of 90 cents an hour. Even freshmen were placed on co-op except when the depressions eliminated many jobs. This happened in 1921 when no freshmen could be placed, but the following year there were more jobs than students.[29] Years later, engineers did not co-op until their third (pre-Junior) year.

It was a proud day for the Municipal University and the city when the first engineering graduate, John S. Kennedy, received the Bachelor of Civil Engineering degree at the 1918 commencement. The first degree in mechanical engineering was awarded in 1919 as was the first degree in manufacturing production (industrial engineering). In 1922 James E. Lynn received the first degree awarded in electrical engineering.[30]

The success of this college was due in large part to the determination of Parke Kolbe and the directors' willingness to provide the funds required. Principal credit, however, should go to Dean Fred Ayer and the faculty he assembled. Fred Ayer was a graduate of Lafayette College and held positions with several industrial firms before joining the faculty at Cincinnati in 1906 as Instructor in Civil Engineering. There he was thoroughly imbued with the co-op engineering plan pioneered by Dean Herman Schneider. Indeed, it was his knowledge of the co-op plan that appealed to Akronites who thought it an attractive educational scheme and very much in keeping with the "practical" orientation of the Municipal University.

Ayer was a favorite among students because he was outspoken and colorful. He favored the "rough and ready" image of the engineer, supported the students in their pranks when others wished to censure them, and looked out for their interests in a manner that created an *esprit* among engineers that was unmatched by any other group of undergraduates. He was the first faculty member to deliberately break an unwritten expectation that faculty members of the Municipal University would live in Akron. He moved to Tallmadge.[31]

For many years, Ayer administered such commercial courses as the University offered. He wished to put commerce students on the co-op plan, and in preparation for that possibility, he secured a position as a bathrobe salesman in O'Neil's department store. "I want to get the atmosphere of the retail business," he said. "I want to come face to face with the practical problems that my students will be called on to solve daily. Too many college instructors feel that all they need is an observational experience." However, said the dean, "I know that they need practical experience; they must know the work their students are doing from that point of view."[32] Ayer's experience earned him the student nickname "Bathrobe King."[33]

In his later years, Dean Ayer sported a wispy Van Dyke beard which did nothing to detract from his image. He liked creative writing, but his one novel, *Call the Doctor,* a satire on college life, will never rate as enduring literature; yet he would rather have tried and failed than let the opportunity pass.

Not everyone in an academic community loves or respects an outspoken person and there were those who were not amused by Dean Ayer. When one measures his success in starting a professional school under great limitations, however, and the manner in which he built it into an important unit of the University, there can be little quarrel with the fact that he performed his job well. And when one notes further the many and varied services he performed for the larger community, on campus and off, he deserves acclaim for his contributions.

Coincident with the beginning of a program in engineering was the development of the Curtis School of Home Economics. Dr. Kolbe took close personal interest in this work, for it afforded "practical" training for girls, in keeping with the service ideal of the Municipal University. Miss Sarah Stimmel was hired from Ohio State to direct the school housed in Curtis Cottage. In February, 1914, Kolbe took a trip through the east where he hoped to get ideas that would make the home economics program the "peer of any college course in the land." He might better have gone west instead, for, with the exception of Cornell and Penn State, which he did not visit, the premier schools of home economics were located in the land grant universities west of the Appalachians and the Mississippi.

Miss Stimmel proved to be a good organizer. Some 28 students entered in September, 1914, instead of the 12 anticipated; but the school grew slowly. Apparently Akron girls were not yet oriented toward home economics. The first degrees were awarded by the Curtis School in 1916 to Irene Willson and Bessie Proehl. Despite small numbers, Curtis graduates secured important positions in the developing fields of dietetics, child development, institutional management, and others.

A most popular aspect of the program was the practice of allowing girls in child care classes to take charge of a real baby. When started in 1924, so many Akron mothers volunteered their children to be cared for that the school was over-whelmed.[34] One of the great unrealized aims of the home economics program at Akron is the establishment of a regular child care center even though, one suspects, the mothers of 1970 would be just as eager as the mothers of 1924 in providing little clients. An offshoot of the home economics program was the establishment of the first cafeteria on campus. Twenty-five patrons could be accommodated at one time in Curtis Cottage where they were served foods prepared by the girls in their laborato-ries. No one was reported to have suffered from being part of the experimental process.[35]

Still other courses of an applied nature were started in the University's first years. Business administration and commerce were added as new efforts in 1916 when Mr. G. E. Bennett was hired as Professor of Business Administration.[36] Akron's boom economy of the time was in search of trained business people, and a recent session of the Association of Urban Universities, attended by Parke Kolbe, had em-phasized the importance of this kind of training.[37] The new courses were initially unconnected with the College of Engineering, although they were taught in conjunc-tion with the engineering curriculum. Business students, of whom there were six in the first year (1916–17), took the same courses as engineers except that they sub-stituted accounting and "co-ordination" for certain engineering courses.

For the first time in the country, business students went on a co-op program.[38] The first group found employment with Firestone, Goodrich, and the Whitman-Barnes Company. The co-op program was discontinued during the war years, but when it was re-established, Akron became the only school in the country, except Antioch, to place women in a co-op program as was the case with coeds in the commerce courses.[39]

In 1921, the Department of Commerce and Administration was formed and placed in the jurisdiction of the Dean of the College of Engineering. This arrange-ment was made "in order to preserve a distinction between the cultural functions which is [sic] the province of the college of liberal arts and the vocational function now lodged separately in the College of Engineering and Commerce." By 1922, the "School of Commerce," as a division of the College of Engineering, offered three different programs: a four-year course in commerce and administration, a four-year course in secretarial science, and a five-year co-op course in industrial engineering which "dealt with the human side of engineering."[40] That same year, the first Bache-lor of Science in Commerce and Administration degree was awarded.[41]

A specialized part of the commerce curriculum emerged in 1921 with the establishment of secretarial courses. A two-year program leading to a certificate of proficiency and a four-year program leading to a degree were offered, and the first graduate of the latter program was Helen Pouchot who received the Bachelor of Secretarial Science degree in 1923.[42]

Another postwar development in curriculum was the beginning of a nurses' training program. The acute shortage of nursing help in the war period had demon-strated the need for a supply of trained personnel to serve the growing public needs. Akron adopted the "Vassar Plan" whereby some 20 weeks of theoretical and techni-cal subject matter was studied at the University, followed by practical training in local hospitals. The plan has been modified many times through the years, but Akron has maintained a connection of some sort with nurses' training to the present time. Since 1967, of course, the College of Nursing has provided direction to this effort.[43]

By any measure, one of the most critical of the professional curricula devel-oped in the early 1920's was the teacher training program. Until late in the nine-teenth century, school teachers seldom received special training in the methods of pedagogy. Instruction was often given by persons who were just slightly ahead of those they taught. Upon graduation from high school, many young men taught for a brief period in little country schools as a way of subsisting until they could find something more remunerative to do. And many young women of similar academic background made teaching a career. However, the growing professionalism of late nineteenth-century America inspired the development of courses and requirements that led to "certification" to teach in the public schools. Generally the state controlled certification requirements and set itself up through state law as the guardian of the public interest in education.

From its founding, Buchtel had offered a two-year "normal" course to prepare teachers for the public schools. Normal work was offered in the preparatory department and it was regarded, both then and later, as an inferior course unworthy of equal status with the more demanding academic programs. Still, the normal course apparently served its purpose of helping students prepare for certification, and it undoubtedly turned out some good teachers, for the "art of teaching" is a gift, and those who possess it are seldom corrupted by an inferior training program. Clearly, however, not everyone who tries to teach is gifted, and it is in the interest of society to insist that they have some professional guidance toward proficiency in their field of work.

At the same time that the Buchtel faculty was urging that the normal course either be strengthened or done away with altogether, the State of Ohio was in the process of forming new normal schools at Kent and Bowling Green. This development, in 1910, called attention to the importance being placed on professional training for teachers. In her straitened circumstances, Buchtel College could do little to improve her effort in this line, but it was vital to the new Municipal University to do its work well in this area.

A crisis developed in 1914 in relation to the University's ability to implement the new state requirements in teacher training. New subjects were to be taught, and these would require more instructors, but also a supervised teaching experience (practice teaching) was to be required for certification. The State Department of Public Instruction informed Akron of the need to meet these new requirements and told President Kolbe that Akron would be placed on the list of accredited teacher training schools once she could meet them. Since Akron had no university school, Kolbe asked Superintendent Hotchkiss of the Akron Public Schools to cooperate in providing practice teaching opportunities in the city schools. Hotchkiss was unwilling to do so, but Kolbe found President McGilvrey of the Kent State Normal School entirely willing to assist.[44] Kolbe, therefore, recommended to his directors that, for the school year 1915–16, Akron attempt to arrange a cooperative course with Kent for the training of high school teachers. The directors approved.[45]

This initiative persuaded Hotchkiss to reconsider. In December, 1915, Kolbe announced that a combined course in teacher training involving the University and the Perkins Normal School (operated by the Akron Board of Education) had been worked out to the satisfaction of the State School Commissioners. Under the agreement a student had two options. Either he could take three years at the University and a fourth at Perkins, or he could take four years at the University and a fifth at Perkins. The former program led to a B.S. degree from the University and certification in elementary education from the state, while the latter program led to the same degree but with state certification in either elementary or secondary education.[46]

World War I caused a temporary cessation of interest in adjusting teacher training programs. Shortly after the close of hostilities, however, a committee of the Board was charged with responsibility for examining means for closer cooperation between the University and the public school system in Akron.[47] The work of the committee and other interested parties resulted in a plan whereby the University and the Akron Board of Education agreed to transform the Perkins Normal School into the Teachers College of the Municipal University of Akron. Teachers College was to be financed jointly by the Akron Board of Education and the University, and responsibility for its program was to reside with President Kolbe and the Superintendent of Akron schools—at that time Mr. Carroll Reed. The agreement clearly stated that the principal task of Teachers College was to prepare teachers for the *Akron* schools although that emphasis would be dropped within a few years.[48] One feature of the agreement that did not turn out well was that the Akron Board of Education would provide the college with a dean. After conferring with Superintendent Reed, Kolbe recommended the appointment of Walter J. Bankes who had been in charge of Perkins Normal for some years. Bankes' salary was paid by the Akron Board of Education.[49]

The agreement opened the entire Akron public school system to students of

Teachers College. All their training, including practice teaching, could take place in close proximity to the University. This gave Akron students an advantage in later years for they were never far from the campus while students in the normal colleges often had to go considerable distances to find practice teaching positions.

The popularity of the new arrangement was reflected in a doubling of enrollment in teacher training courses in little more than a year's time. The popularity of the new program grew in part out of the practice of paying practice teachers $2.50 per day for their work in the schoolrooms. In addition, they received eight credits for that part of their degree program. Another boost came from the special courses offered in non-degree subjects such as "trade" (apparently a kind of industrial arts) and "Americanization." Some 28 faculty members from both within and without the Teachers College staff were employed to a limited extent in the special courses.

The State Department of Public Instruction was favorably impressed by these adjustments in Akron's teacher training program. The Superintendent of Public Instruction called it the best course in Ohio.[50] The State Board of School Examiners informed Dean Bankes: "You have adopted one of the sanest methods of the development of teachers. The courses contain all of the theory necessary for a good teacher to possess and from the description of the different courses we feel that the instruction would be highly practical."[51] The new programs produced their first graduates in June, 1922, when five women were awarded the Bachelor of Education degree. In 1923 a Master's program was started in the Teachers College, and in 1924 the M.A. in Education and the M.S. in Education were both awarded for the first time.[52]

The beginning of Master's level work added impetus to the development of an extensive evening program designed to appeal to Akron teachers then in service. In the early 1920's nearly one-half of the Akron teaching force was enrolled in one or more extension (evening) course. This influx led to a doubling of evening enrollment—from 500 in 1920 to nearly 1,000 in 1921.[53] As Akron profited from student interest in the new program so it profited from the absorption into Bierce library of the books from Perkins Normal.[54] For the first time Akron had a modest collection in the field of pedagogy.

In another new development that is traced to Teachers College, Akron prospered. A summer session was started in 1922 primarily to accommodate teachers. In the first year about 75 percent of the 221 students were teachers.[55] Through the years, summer session enrollment has been heavier in Teachers College than in any other program. The summer session was self-supporting from the first.[56] Years later, the "profit" made on summer programs would be used to help maintain a good salary base for the faculty, but this aspect of University operation was much debated later on when the initial practice of paying the faculty equitably for its summer instruction was changed.

In 1923 the re-negotiation of the agreement between the Board of Directors and the Akron Board of Education set up conditions that were sustained until the depression made a drastic change necessary in the early 30's. In this re-negotiation, the joint control of the Teachers College was confirmed. The college faculty was to consist of the Perkins faculty plus members of other faculties of the University "giving prerequisite or prescribed courses which are expressly arranged for students expecting to become teachers." Faculty salaries were to be paid by the Board of Education while the University was to furnish classrooms, offices, absorb overhead, and carry routine operating costs.[57] When the University took over exclusive support and control of Teachers College it was a strong unit in the University structure that had served, and would continue to serve, Akron well.

The new programs in engineering, home economics, business and commerce, secretarial science, nursing, and education were the best possible evidence to the community that those directing the course of the University were providing every possible avenue to the students interested in training for the specialized tasks of the day. As in earlier periods of curricular expansion—the 1880's and the decade 1900–10, for instance—requests were made of the University to initiate programs it was unable to attempt. To the end of his administration, Dr. Kolbe was aggressive in his pursuit of new fields of service for Akron, and only a lack of money prevented him from accommodating other community interests in campus programs.

Early in the 1920's the University had been asked to establish professional curricula in law and in pharmacy. These expensive programs were beyond the institution's resources; indeed, so critical was the shortage of funds in 1924 that a moratorium had to be placed on even routine additions to existing programs.

Even in these straitened conditions the Board listened sympathetically to any proposal that promised to be self-supporting. It was possible to start short courses to accommodate special interests such as the Library Board which wanted a four-month course in library training. The directors approved this request on condition that at least ten students register and that each pay the $10 incidental fee. This effort proved abortive, however.[58] Some years later, short courses designed to service limited special interests became an established part of the "informal course" program, and in this way confusion with the regular degree curricula was avoided.

In view of the amount of effort and resources poured into the new vocational and professional programs at the University, it may seem incongruous that a commentator, writing about this phenomenon in 1920, could say: "It is a significant fact that in the rapid growth of the Municipal University of Akron the addition of other schools and departments has in no wise lessened the popularity and the growth of Buchtel College of Liberal Arts. In spite of an ever-increasing interest in vocational training and specialized courses, the dominant demand is still for the broad and fundamental education offered by the college over which Dean Spanton presides."[59]

One reason for this continuing interest in the liberal arts is apparent to anyone acquainted with the nature of college curricula. Freshman requirements in English, mathematics, science, and other fields taught in the liberal arts had to be taken by all students regardless of their later specialization. And even in the specialized programs, much of the advanced work was taken in regular arts and sciences subjects.[60] Engineers took mathematics, physics, and chemistry from instructors in the regular science departments. Home economists, business majors, and education students each took many courses offered in arts and sciences departments. This "service function" of the arts and sciences departments, therefore, permitted them to join in the growth of the University's effort even though these departments did not experience a proportionate growth in the number of students electing a major in an arts and sciences department.

An assessment of the arts and sciences is further complicated by the fact that some major programs in this academic arm of the University are vocationally oriented. What could be more "practical," or "applied," or "vocational" than rubber chemistry? Yet this program, offered in the Buchtel College of Liberal Arts, flourished under the direction of Professor Hez Simmons who wisely made every effort to keep the course of study useful to future employers of these chemistry majors. While engaging in a good deal of theoretical work, rubber chemistry students were involved in solving many practical problems in the lab. These problems were referred to them from small companies around the world. As with the co-op engineer, the rubber chemist left the University with his hands already dirty from the tangible tasks of his specialty.[61]

Rubber chemistry is a marked example of vocationalism in the arts and sciences, but consider also the growth of the "combination course" which permitted a student to take three years of pre-law or pre-medicine at Akron and then transfer directly into an accredited professional school with which Akron had a working agreement. Such agreements were maintained primarily with Ohio State and with Western Reserve.[62] Even though the course work taken by students in these programs was in the best arts and sciences tradition, there is no doubt that the final objective was professional-vocational, and the student was no less involved in "training" for his ultimate job than was the home economist or the engineer. If there is a difference worth pursuing between vocationalism in an "applied" field and vocationalism in an arts and sciences program, it would appear that the difference lies in the self-consciousness with which the student in an applied or vocational curriculum regards his task as preparation for a specific career.

If the liberal arts interest suffered during the rush toward specialized, vocationally oriented curricula, it was a selective suffering. The greatest change took place in the area of classical language and literature, an area that formerly was all-important to Buchtel College. In 1915, Greek was deleted from the curriculum even though it remained in the catalog. A plan was then instituted to offer Greek every other year to the small number of students desiring it. This lack of continuity was the final death knell to a field of study that had once ruled supreme over every college curriculum in America. One of the reasons President Kolbe advanced for this devlopment was that students were more interested in practical subjects that would "fit them for life."[63] Commenting on this development, the local newspaper recognized that deemphasis of Greek and other cultural subjects reflected a "transition period in college curricula and educational values."[64] But the newspaper made more of a defense for the values of Latin and Greek than did officers of the University! The latter's comments seemed more concerned with confirming what popular taste was demanding. And while the public would be served—and in a municipal university *should* be served—it was sad for some faculty to see the academicians rush to preside over the passing of a great tradition, sparing no more regret than can be spared yesterday's sports hero who hasn't thrilled anyone lately. In place of the old language requirements, the faculty in 1921 set a new one that compelled a student wishing a degree from the Buchtel College of Liberal Arts to complete a minimum of five years of foreign language including work taken in secondary school and the University, with no less than two years to be taken in the University.[65]

In other curricular areas problems and concerns that habitually plague faculty came in for their share of attention. The faculty repeatedly urged the English Department to bring students to a more effective level in the use of language. The department would respond periodically with yet another plan for ameliorating the situation only to hear the familiar plaint repeated shortly afterward.[66] No doubt in self-defense, the English Department used the argument still favored, that it was the collective responsibility of the entire faculty to require literate performances on tests and papers. A good argument it is, but the problem endures.

The new areas of practical emphasis got overwhelming student approval. By the 1920's, America was beyond the "Gothic Age" of the American college, and few seventeen-year olds could have been convinced that education of the "whole man," or "education for life" was nearly as relevant and significant as a practical education that trained one to make a living. The *Buchtelite* editor spoke for many when he said that colleges were often "islands isolated from the practical, day-to-day experiences of life." A student entering college was retiring from the world for four years. It was a serious indictment of American universities, thought the editor, that "they don't prepare students for the practicality and competition of life." But Akron was not as guilty as others:

> *Our Alma Mater gives its sons an unequalled opportunity of finding out what men are like outside the classroom and the text book. Our situation near the heart of a busy industrial city; the fact that many of the undergraduates are working their way through school; the co-operative plan in use by the engineering school; and the fact that the greater part of the student body live at home and come in daily contact with non-academic life—all contribute to the making of college graduates who are on better than even terms with the rest of the world, both in spite of and because of their sheepskins.[67]*

A final curricular development of interest in the early 1920's was the concept of "honors courses" or, as it was often called, honors work. The movement grew out of a belief that the better student was insufficiently "stretched" by traditional courses taught in the traditional manner. Challenged by a more demanding, comprehensive, or enriched course in lieu of the regular course in a given subject, he would respond by performing beyond his usual levels of accomplishment. The principal impetus for this concept came from President Aydelotte of Swarthmore College. Since Akron, like old Buchtel, was alert to new educational ideas, it was receptive to the possibilities of honors work.

In June, 1921, the faculty accepted a definition of "honors courses" that described them as designed "to acquaint the student with the fundamental principles and methods of independent investigation and study. Since the chief aim of such courses will be to teach the student *how to learn,* rather than to teach him *concrete facts,* these courses shall not be counted for credit toward any degree."[68] This definition contains the interesting implication that concrete facts add up to a degree. In the practical environment that characterized the Municipal University in that period, there was never any chance that students would be attracted to work that brought them no closer to their degrees. The program met with "a cool reception" as few students expressed interest.[69]

Concurrent with discussion of honors work was an interest shown in independent study. Dean Ayer expressed a concern of some faculty when he claimed that freshmen were working harder than seniors and that the reverse should be true. The amount of work expected of students in their senior year, said Ayer, was no more than that required in the freshman year. His remedy was "to increase the amount of unsupervised work which a student must do" in his upper-class years.[70] However, nothing significant was developed in the area of independent study although much lip service was given to its reputed benefits, and has been even to the present.

Of much greater interest to students than independent study was the standard by which their course performance was measured. The grading system came in for periodic comment. The *Buchtelite* said that the best plan, "from an undergraduate's way of looking at the matter," was "to make scholarship and not the number of questions a student can answer correctly without hesitation the basis of grades." In May, 1923, the Faculty Council enacted a letter system of grading which was thought to reflect more accurately a student's standing with respect to other students. The A through F system is still is use.[71]

One final adjustment to the academic machinery should be mentioned in connection with developments in the early years of the Municipal University. Since 1914 the faculty had expressed concern about requirements for graduate work and the Master's degree. They voted in January, 1914, to require one year's residence of all students, including Buchtel graduates, who were candidates for the Master's degree. When the growth of Teachers College brought a greatly increased demand for graduate work, the Faculty Council realized it was time to re-formulate the requirements for a Master's degree.[72] A faculty committee was assigned this task, and its efforts resulted in the first consistent and orderly definition of graduate work that the University produced. This report, made in 1922, marks the beginning of graduate work on a level consistent with today's outlook. It would be many years, however, before any significant number of graduate degrees were awarded in fields other than education and rubber chemistry.

NOTES

1 Spanton, *Fifty Years,* pp. 133, 178.

2 President's Report, 1921, p. 3; *Buchtelite,* Sept. 23, 1921.

3 A good account of the fate of Akron's rubber industry can be found in appropriate chapters of Howard and Ralph Wolf, *Rubber: A Story of Glory and Greed* (New York, 1936).

4 *Buchtelite,* Sept. 23, 1921.

5 *Beacon Journal,* Oct. 4, 1922.

6 Board Mins. (1913–24), p. 183.

7 *Ibid.,* p. 197.

8 President's Report, 1923, p. 3; *Buchtelite,* Oct. 11, 1923.

9 *Beacon Journal,* Oct. 12, 1922; *Buchtelite,* Jan. 10, 1923.

10 *Ibid.,* Oct. 18, 1922; Board Mins. (1912–24), p. 207.

11 President's Report, 1923, p. 4; *Ibid.,* 1924, p. 3; *Beacon Journal,* Sept. 11, 1923; *Buchtelite,* Feb. 8, 1922.

12 *Beacon Journal,* Feb. 24, 1920; Spanton, *Fifty Years,* p. 133; *Buchtelite,* Dec. 13, 1922; *Catalog, 1921, 1923.*

13 *Buchtelite,* Dec. 23, 1922; President's Report, 1924, p. 4.

14 *Ibid.,* pp. 8–9.

15 *Akron Press,* Jan. (?), 1923.

16 *Buchtelite,* Mar. 21, 1923; President's Report, 1923, pp. 4, 10.

17 Board Mins. (1913–24), p. 230.

18 *Ibid.,* pp. 35, 36.

19 *Beacon Journal,* Apr. 7, Nov. 9, 1915, June 23, 1916; *Buchtelite,* Apr. 7, 1916; Spanton, *Fifty Years,* p. 135.

20 *Ibid.,* p. 236; Board Mins. (1913–24), pp. 62, 68.

21 *Buchtelite,* Nov. 5, 12, 1920; Board Mins. (1913–24), p. 162.

22 *Ibid.,* p. 169; President's Report, 1921, pp. 3, 5.

23 Spanton, *Fifty Years,* p. 266.

24 Board Mins. (1913–24), p. 215.

25 *Ibid.,* p. 231.

26 *Beacon Journal,* Mar. 22, 1924.

27 *Catalog, 1914,* Supplement; *Beacon Journal,* Feb. 9, 1916.

28 *Buchtelite,* Apr. 19, 1922.

29 *Ibid.,* Dec. 13, 1922; Board Mins. (1913–24), p. 197.

30 *Ibid.,* pp. 111, 134.

31 Biographical material drawn from a variety of sources; see, for example, *Beacon Journal,* Jan. 6, 1914.

32 *Buchtelite,* Dec. 13, 1922.

33 *Ibid.,* Dec. 12, 1923.

34 *Beacon Journal,* Feb. 18, 1914.

35 *Buchtelite,* Oct. 15, 1914, March 6, 13, 1924.

36 Board Mins (1913–24), p. 52.

37 *Beacon Journal,* Nov. 20, 1915.

38 *Buchtelite,* Oct. 12, 1916; President's Report, 1921, p. 4.

39 Board Mins. (1913–24), p. 201; *Beacon Journal,* Dec. 16, 1924.

40 *Buchtelite,* April 19, 1922.

41 Board Mins. (1913–24), p. 193.

42 *Ibid.,* May 26, 1920; Board Mins. (1913–24), p. 216.

43 *Buchtelite,* Oct. 1, 1920.

44 Board Mins. (1913–24), pp. 20, 27, 34.

45 *Ibid.,* p. 55.

46 *Beacon Journal,* Jan. 13, 1916.

47 Board Mins. (1913–24), p. 106.

48 *Beacon Journal,* Feb. 16, 1921. Perkins Normal was started by the Akron School Board in the 1890's to supply trained teachers to the Akron Schools. (Minutes of the Akron School Board, 1896–97, located at the Akron Board of Education offices).

49 Board Mins. (1913–24), p. 170.

50 *Buchtelite,* Sept. 23, Nov. 4, 1921.

51 *Ibid.,* Oct. 14, 1921.

52 Board Mins. (1913–24), pp. 193, 241.

53 President's Report, 1921, p. 4.

54 *Buchtelite,* Sept. 23, 1921.

55 *Ibid.,* June 7, 1923.

56 President's Report, 1922, pp. 4–5; *Beacon Journal,* Sept. 5, 1923.

57 Board Mins. (1913-24), p. 219; *Beacon Journal,* Sept. 17, 1924.

58 Board Mins. (1913–24), p. 163.

59 Spanton, *Fifty Years,* p. 138.

60 *Buchtelite,* Oct. 25, 1915.

61 *Ibid.,* June 13, 1923.

62 *Ibid.,* Mar. 21, 1919.

63 *Beacon Journal,* Oct. 7, 1915.

64 *Ibid.,* Oct. 11, 1915.

65 Council Mins.; May 16, 1921.

66 General Faculty Mins., Feb. 6, Oct. 24, 1922.

67 *Buchtelite,* June 13, 1923.

68 Council Mins., June 6, 1921.

69 *Buchtelite,* June 13, 1923.

70 *Ibid.,* May 24, 1922.

71 *Ibid.,* Feb. 15, 1915; Council Mins., May 22, 1923.

72 *Ibid.,* Jan. 13, 23, 1914.

Campus scene in winter (1950's).

"No other profession
more truly useful to the world"

The evolution of collegiate administration provides an interesting study of institutional growth. Buchtel College's experience was fairly typical of its time, and had it continued its course through the twentieth century it would have continued to evolve in a pattern that was at once similar to, and yet far removed from, the pattern taken by the Municipal University. The administration of Buchtel College consisted originally of John R. Buchtel as President of the Board of Trustees running the business end of things, even to the extent of recruiting faculty, and Sullivan McCollester taking care of virtually everything else. McCollester's duties as President of the Faculty included personal oversight of student conduct, health, registration, and general well-being, while the faculty busied itself with the details of each student's academic record and made recommendations in disciplinary cases. The president was soon relieved of a few of his duties; and the college steward and matron took over some housekeeping details, and the college secretary relieved him of others. The treasurer was an official of the Board and was responsible to Mr. Buchtel and his fellow trustees rather than to the president.

The complexity of this structure increased with time, and in Orello Cone's administration, some functions formerly managed by Mr. Buchtel—faculty recruitment for example—were now performed by the president. Fund raising had been largely the province of the financial secretary, responsible to the Board, but now it became a responsibility of the president. Another significant step in the evolutionary process occurred in 1904 when Augustus Church was elected President of the Board of Trustees in addition to his duties as President of the College. This move united the business management of the College with its academic management in a formal way. The Clerk of the Board and chief business officer of the college, Mr. C. R. Olin, no longer served two masters since the entire management was in the hands of Dr. Church. Upon assuming the presidency in 1913, Parke Kolbe assumed the dual role pioneered by Church, and he retained it as President of the Municipal University of Akron and Chairman of the Board of Directors, the latter role being relinquished in 1916.

Kolbe was a strong executive; indeed one gets the impression that he would not have shared managerial control gladly. He was an "idea man" who could produce original solutions to Akron's problems or suggest innovative procedures along lines as yet untried, but he was also remarkably adept at borrowing techniques and ideas from others. Throughout most of his administration he was unusually successful at marshalling the support he needed from others—notably the Board of Directors and city officials—to carry out his programs. Predictably, his efforts resulted in a growing complexity of organization that required the help of administrative officers charged with specific responsibilities. A brief look at these assistants and their responsibilities reveals how relatively complex the institutional structure had become in a brief span of years following the emergence of the Municipal University, and also how much of the academic machinery that evolved during those years still exists virtually unchanged.

On the academic side, the evolution of specialized administrative functions has an inevitable logic. For every new college within the University there had to be a dean to take charge of the multitudinous details of faculty recruitment and development, curriculum, student advisement and discipline, and all related activities. Albert Spanton who had been Dean of the Faculty in old Buchtel College became Dean of the Buchtel College of Liberal Arts in the Municipal University.[1] By 1921 the college he presided over had more than twice as many students enrolled as Buchtel College had in her entire collegiate program in 1913. During President Kolbe's absences from campus in the spring of 1918, and again in 1919, Dean Spanton was Acting President and acquitted himself well. Dean Ayer was responsible for the engineering and commerce programs, but he also took on many general University tasks. Dean Bankes directed the Teachers College and had other responsibilities in the University. Professor O. E. Olin held the title Vice-President of the Faculty, but all it involved was presiding at University functions during the president's absence.[2]

For the time being there were no divisions of function in the business office. C. R. Olin took care of it all. Such positions as Auditor, Purchasing Agent, and the managers of specific operations were yet to evolve. An important innovation occurred in 1916 when the president's secretary, Miss Gladys Weeks, was appointed Registrar and spent half-time at the task of maintaining student academic records.[3]

Another specialized administrative role was created in 1915–16 with the introduction of a permanent evening program. Initially, courses were scheduled from 5 P.M. to 6 P.M., and it was expedient to have someone to manage the program on behalf of the faculty and deans. Professor Lockner was first appointed to this task. He was succeeded by Professor Simmons under whose direction the program expanded consistently in quantity and quality.

Maintenance of the physical plant and grounds was another important activity that was requiring full-time supervision in place of the more casual procedures of the past. One of Kolbe's last recommendations before leaving the presidency was to establish the position of Superintendent of Buildings and Grounds.

One of the most successful of the new Municipal University's liaisons with the city was the transfer to the campus of the Bureau of City Tests. Much of the credit for this was due to the work of Mr. Arden Hardgrove, Director of the City Testing Bureau. He was much more thoroughly involved in the total work of the University than his successors were to be, and his position was accorded an importance that it lost once the zeal of Parke Kolbe to serve the city had been pushed somewhat into the background as other considerations required attention.

An important development in 1914 was the appointment of Mrs. Elizabeth A. Thompson as Dean of Women and Assistant Professor of History in the newly organized Department of History. A long-time teacher at the Akron High School, Buchtel Academy, and College, she was well known and highly regarded in the community.[4] The new position, Dean of Women, was necessary as the school went to municipal status because the position of lady preceptress or matron, which had sufficed for the Buchtel girls, disappeared with the private school. Now virtually all girls in the University would live at home, but they still needed the personal and social counseling and control that traditionally have been the Dean of Women's function. At the conclusion of Kolbe's tenure in office a similar service would be provided for the men.

With the growth of the faculty, the developing specialization of activity that kept one department removed from another, and the collapse of the intimacy that had characterized faculty-administration relationships in Buchtel College, the need arose for a restructuring of the University so that faculty opinion and advice could be brought to bear effectively on problems that were part of their concern and responsibility. By 1916 a Faculty Council was functioning.[5] This Council consisted of a select group of the general faculty that met monthly to take action in the name of the faculty. Tradition has it that this plan was introduced on the recommendation of Dr. Kolbe who was familiar with a similar plan in effect at Reed College. The general faculty continued to meet infrequently. In June, 1922, Kolbe described another faculty reorganization. The general faculty, he said, had "grown too large to busy itself with details of administration and legislation," and for that reason its meetings should be reduced in number. The general faculty of all full-time academic employees would meet only at the beginning and end of each academic year. The Faculty Council would serve "as the general legislative body of the university on matters concerning two or more colleges or on matters of general university policy." The Executive Committee of the Faculty Council was to "represent, and . . . act in emergency cases for, the Faculty Council" in the intervals between regular meetings of that body.

Four college faculties were recognized: Buchtel College and Curtis School, Engineering and Commerce, Teachers College, and the "extension faculty" (including evening program faculty). Each college faculty was to include all persons teaching six hours or more in their respective colleges, except for the extension faculty, whose membership included all faculty teaching in the program. Each college faculty was to meet monthly and have its minutes referred to the Executive Committee for further reference to the Faculty Council of matters that might concern general University policy.[6] With few basic modifications, the Faculty Council and the Executive Committee arrangement have continued to serve the purpose for which they were established. What worked adequately for the faculty of 1922, however, does not work so successfully for the much larger and more anonymous faculty of the 1960's. As this is being written, restructuring of the Council and Executive Committee into a more effective and more representative framework has just been completed.

The faculty of the Municipal University grew considerably in its first decade, but its growth failed to keep pace with the need; the student-faculty ratio grew progressively worse. Money, of course, was the chief problem. There was never enough of it to permit the University to employ an optimum number of teachers. By 1925, those faculty who, by the length of their tenure and by the importance of their contribution, are of particular interest to the historian were generally of two kinds. First were the old guard, carryovers from Buchtel College, and a strong group indeed. Mention of them has already been made, but an additional word on some is in order here.

Parke Kolbe and C. R. Olin brought to the central administration of the University backgrounds exceptionally rich in the traditions and spirit of Buchtel College. Neither was constrained by his ties with the past from pushing ahead most vigorously in new directions. Olin had a longer effective connection with the school than anyone else on the faculty, having entered the preparatory curriculum in 1879 from which time he was continuously associated with the institution in some capacity or other. By 1925 he had relinquished the teaching of mathematics which he had long pursued on a part-time basis. He continued his role as weather observer and the fidelity of his trust gave Akron one of the most complete sets of weather records in the state.

Albert Spanton, a contemporary of Kolbe's as a student and as a beginning instructor in the collegiate program, was another who carried the best traditions of Buchtel College into the Municipal University. He taught several years in the preparatory program before assuming the professorship of English and Rhetoric in 1905. Few teachers were more admired than he. Many of his students remember with affection, amusement, or embarrassment their enforced classroom portrayals of some Shakespearian character. When some sobersides read Falstaff, or some brawny football player enunciated Romeo's appeals to Juliet, an indelible impression was created in student memories. This technique may appear better calculated to amuse than to instruct, but by their own testimony, the students who experienced this treatment remembered more than their temporary discomfiture; they remembered something of Shakespeare, and of Spanton.

Hezzleton Simmons and Charles Bulger, like Kolbe and Spanton, had been contemporaries at Buchtel College as students and as fledgling teachers. "Hez" Simmons is more often remembered for the presidency that he assumed in 1933 rather than for his teaching role; but he was, by every account, an enthusiastic teacher of chemistry, especially rubber chemistry. Upon the retirement of C. M. Knight in 1913, Simmons carried the chemistry program forward most effectively. He published in the field of rubber chemistry and was much sought after by industry.[7] Faculty raiding by industry is not a new phenomenon.[8] Simmons had at least four offers to take more lucrative positions with various rubber companies, but in each case he stayed with the teaching he loved. The outside offers helped, to be sure, for each was countered by a raise in salary. Charles Bulger also refused the chance to make more money by moving out of teaching when he turned down an offer to become business manager of City Hospital.[9] Like Simmons, who spent a great amount of time in various administrative chores, Bulger was frequently involved in useful duties outside his classroom. Mention has been made of his success as faculty manager of athletics in bringing order out of the chaos that had typified Buchtel athletics prior to his organizing efforts. Bulger recovered nicely from the restrictive outlook toward German studies that had dominated the wartime atmosphere. Highly respected as a "tough but fair" teacher of German, many students later knew him as Spanton's successor as Dean of the Buchtel College of Liberal Arts.

Perhaps the student favorite of the twenties was Oscar E. Olin, better known as "Daddy" Olin. He came to Buchtel in 1898 to serve as Principal of the preparatory school, but by 1905 he had transferred his effort entirely to the collegiate curriculum. For many years he taught just about all the College offered in the social sciences and philosophy. Daddy Olin was not a profound scholar, nor was he particularly original in his insights, but he had the invaluable gift for synthesizing, in a convincing way, much of what man has learned about himself. In the classroom and on the platform, Olin was as much preacher as teacher. He was ordained in the Universalist ministry, and, like Albert Spanton, regularly filled pulpits in the Akron area. He performed over 100 marriages for former students, and he took a continuing interest in their welfare. He was a good public servant; in 1913 he was a member of the Akron Charter Commission and played an important role in guiding the transfer of Buchtel College to the city. In 1917, his *History of Akron and Summit County* was published. It is one of the better efforts at local history.

Upon reaching the retirement age of 70 in 1922, the directors voted to retain "Daddy" in active service.[10] As an earlier evidence of their esteem, he received the rare honor in 1920 of being awarded the honorary LL.D. degree in recognition of 50 years of teaching, and in 1921 he was recognized jointly with C. R. Olin in having the Academy building renamed Olin Hall. At age 71 he was interviewed by a *Buchtelite* reporter and assured the young man that he did not feel old. His secret for keeping healthy and vigorous, he said, was that "life has always been interesting to me." He loved his work and his fellow men, kept regular habits of eating and sleeping, and for years walked four to six miles a day. He read and studied and felt that his capacity for learning increased with his age. He believed the mind had great power over the body, and "if a man looks on the bright side of things no trouble can mar his happiness for long." As for teaching: "There is a great joy in the knowledge of the good that a teacher is constantly doing for humanity. There is no other profession in which one can be more truly useful to the world."[11] Would that this credo were more widely endorsed by the teaching profession.

Joseph C. Rockwell, Professor of Latin and Greek, was another who carried over from Buchtel College to the Municipal University. He was a most worthy successor to Charles Bates. Known irreverently as "Goat" Rockwell because of his whiskers, he was respected by student and colleague alike. Although their appointments did not pre-date the establishment of the Municipal University, Fred Ayer in engineering, Sarah Stimmel in home economics, Fred Sefton in physical education, Carita McEbright in oratory, and Arden Hardgrove in the testing bureau would be counted with the faculty veterans in 1925.

In addition to the veterans, many faculty appointed early in the Municipal University's life were to serve for long periods and were well known to many student generations. Ross Durst (engineering), Fred Householder (physics), Richard Schmidt (chemistry, later Registrar), Dr. Earl Crecraft (political science), Raymond Pease (English), Fred Griffin (mechanical engineering), Miss Will Lipscombe (mathematics), David Anderson (chemistry, later Director of the Testing Bureau), Marjorie Mitchell (English), Ulysses Vance (English and journalism, and long-time University Editor), and Walter Kraatz (biology) were all appointed between 1918 and 1924.[12]

In 1924, a young man not long out of Princeton was hired as Instructor in History. Donfred H. Gardner thus started a career at the University that in terms of influence on students and faculty alike has seldom, if ever, been matched on this campus. The story of his accomplishments is interwoven with developments yet to be discussed.

In 1920, Mr. Francesco DeLeone was employed on a part-time basis to give instruction in music. He soon became the full-time director of music and brought real musicianship and much favorable recognition to the University. His most interesting accomplishment was the composition of an American opera, *Alglala*. This story of the American Indians had its premiere in the Akron Armory in April, 1924. Leading roles were sung by Edward Johnson and Mabel Garrison of the Metropolitan Opera Company who gave up engagements in London to perform in the Akron premiere. The work was well received, the critics were kind, but it did not catch on sufficiently to endure in musical literature. DeLeone composed many other works. His vital, productive musicianship stimulated the musical life of Akron.[13]

Other faculty members appointed during these years gave briefer service to the University. Some had substantial accomplishments to their credit including Lawrence McDermott, Professor of Commerce and Administration, who wrote a *Military History of the United States* published by Macmillan, which was virtually alone in its field of surveying the entire military record of the United States.[14] Some teachers were remembered for such special traits as Dr. Edgar Dehn's penchant for writing examination questions in political economy in rhyme. One sample will suffice:

When the veil of truth you've lifted:
Can a tax on rent be shifted?[15]

The evening and part-time faculty numbered some talented people. Perhaps the best known was Dr. Lloyd C. Douglas, pastor of the First Congregational Church, but better known as the author of numerous best-sellers of Biblical fiction.

As president Kolbe said in 1924, "The number of buildings that a college adds each year is not the surest index of its growth. The development of a strong faculty —not only strong in numbers but high in caliber—is a matter too likely to be overlooked. In planning for the growth of the university we should look to the problem of strengthening our faculty."[16] This, of course, is exactly where the emphasis belonged.

The conditions of employment for faculty changed from time to time. In 1915 the directors adopted President Kolbe's recommendation that, in the future, no faculty member in the Buchtel College of Liberal Arts be advanced beyond the rank of Instructor unless he had the Master's degree. The following year the work load was defined. Each full-time faculty member was to teach a "term hour load" of 18 hours per semester, with the objective of reducing the load to 16 hours ultimately. No instructor was to teach more than 25 hours per week whether in classroom, laboratory, or elsewhere. All extension (evening) instruction was to be done by members of the regular teaching staff wherever possible. Such work was to be counted in the regular term-hour load and no overtime pay was to be granted for this work. In estimating the term-hour load, a one-hour evening course was to be counted as the equivalent of two hours regular day work and two consecutive hours of evening work was to be counted as three hours of regular work. Policies governing leaves of absence, compensation for outside work by faculty members, and requirements for attendance at commencement ceremonies were legislated during this period.[17]

And what of faculty salaries and welfare during the first decade of the Municipal University? Once the smoke had cleared in the dispute between the *Beacon Journal* and President Kolbe over the proper course for the University to follow in faculty salary development, wartime inflation had taken hold and price increases outran salary increases causing the faculty considerable alarm. In June, 1918, the Board announced a $200 increase to virtually all full-time employees, to meet the "greatly increased cost of living."[18] In 1919 the faculty successfully petitioned the Board for an increase but the directors could not support the 30 percent requested; instead they granted $300 increases.[19] The next year the faculty tried again, this time requesting $400 per person, but no action was taken to meet the request.[20] The Board was in a bind since the City Budget Commission had fixed the tax levy for the University in 1920 at only .38 of a mill which would produce about $25,000 less than the University requested.[21] Maximum salaries were fixed that year at $3,600 for full professors, $2,800 for assistant professors, and $2,200 for instructors. Extra compensation could be earned at that time for evening teaching. By 1923 the highest paid professor without administrative duties was Hezzleton Simmons at $4,200 per year, and that figure would have been considerably lower had he not been granted raises above the normal amount to keep him at the University when others were bidding for his services. At the same time, President Kolbe's salary was fixed at $6,500 plus use of the President's House.[22]

These salaries were not unreasonable in the least, but in view of the public character of the University, any mention of professors' salaries was likely to bring a complaint from some taxpayers that the salaries were too high.

Not only were the salaries modest, there were few additional benefits. In 1921 Akron entered the State Teacher's Retirement Pension System. Participation by the faculty was optional for those already in the employ of the University but mandatory for all new employees. The maximum pensionable salary in 1921 was $2,000, allowing a maximum pension of not more than $1,000; this was clearly inadequate.[23] An effort was made to provide life insurance under a group plan, but the City Law Director ruled "that the matter of group life insurance as outlined . . . is not a legal expenditure of public funds under present legislation."[24] And of course this was before hospitalization plans were available to public employees, so the total benefits program for the faculty and other employees was minimal in the extreme. Such were conditions in the faculty after 12 years of striving to fulfill the promise of the Municipal University.

The commencement of 1925 was held in Central High School's auditorium— the first time the ceremonies were held off campus. Crouse gym was no longer able to accommodate the crowd. The two-block walk from the campus to Central was a familiar one to generations of Akron students waiting the day when the campus would again boast an assembly hall large enough to accommodate its public exercises. (In exchange for the use of the auditorium, the University offered the facilities of Buchtel Field to Central High's athletic teams which were without practice fields.[25]) The commencement speaker was Dr. George Zook, Assistant to the United States Commissioner of Education in Washington, D.C., and a specialist in the problems and administration of higher education in this country. He was a strong advocate of the municipal university concept and frequently referred to Akron as an example of what could be accomplished with this approach.[26] Many other educators around the country also looked to the University as a leader in municipal education, and Dr. Kolbe was frequently asked for advice with regard to the establishment and operation of such schools. Wichita, for example, intended to transform Fairmount College into a municipal university on the Akron model.[27]

Probably not many of the persons assembled at the commencement ceremonies realized that they were being addressed by the next president of the University. But they were, for Parke Kolbe had submitted his resignation in order to accept the presidency of Brooklyn Polytechnic Institute. After one year as President of Buchtel

College and 11 as the head of the Municipal University, he was leaving on the same note on which he began—serve the community, expand the effort, extend the impact of the College to every facet of community life and need. In his final report to the Board of Directors he urged "more cooperation with civic and social agencies," better cooperation with local industries through cooperative courses, evening courses, and research in rubber chemistry. Within the University he urged development of the health and recreation program including better physical examinations, corrective work for physical defectives, and intramural athletics. He urged an enlargement of the administrative group to include a full-time Director of the Evening School, a Dean of Men, full-time Registrar, Superintendent of Building and Grounds, and a reorganization of the business office. He urged a School of Practical Arts for young women to include work in home economics, secretarial science, and industrial arts. A larger library including a municipal reference library was needed as was a larger non-resident student body to supply trained persons for local industry "and to develop college spirit." An art museum and a conservatory of music were required to develop the cultural life of Akron. Many new courses and degree programs should eventually be offered including law, two-year technical courses for men (probably in cooperation with the public schools), botany and geology, graduate work through the Master's degree in liberal arts and the sciences, and finally, a rubber research institute. He thus foresaw many new areas of activity that have been undertaken by the University since that time.[28]

With the success and recognition that he enjoyed, and with innumerable ideas and plans in mind, why did Parke Kolbe decide to leave his Alma Mater for new academic circles? One important consideration was that he had the wisdom to see that he had little new to add to what he had already given through the years. No matter how successful a college president may be, there comes a time when everyone has heard him make the same pleas in the same manner so many times that they stop listening. Even an excellent administrator loses his effectiveness when he has to plead unendingly with the public for money and support. This need for money suggests another probability in Kolbe's decision. He was backed against a wall by state legislation limiting to .55 of a mill the amount of municipal tax support the University could acquire. It wasn't enough to sustain the present effort satisfactorily let alone sustain the expansion Kolbe foresaw. And he had tried repeatedly, but without success, to get the law changed.

Possibly another important factor was the changed composition of the Board of Directors. It was quite a different group from the Buchtel College Trustees, and from the directors of the first days of the Municipal University. Many of the men from the transition period had left the Board, including Frank Seiberling who announced to an alumni gathering that he would soon move into his "little shack" on North Portage Path, and since that was outside the city limits in 1915, he felt he should resign as a director. Kolbe lost his seat on the Board when his term expired in 1920. Some friends who knew him well suggest that Kolbe was distressed by what he considered to be his inability to carry the thinking of the directors with him on his plans for the University. At the end, controversy was already heating up over the issue of relocating the campus out on the west side of Akron on land donated by Ed Good, an Akron businessman. Kolbe was a strong supporter of the proposed move, and sentiment being what it is, it is not unlikely that his stand made him *personna non grata* with those who wanted the campus to remain as it had always been. For these reasons and possibly others that do not appear in the records, Parke Kolbe left Akron with the affection, admiration, and fervent good wishes of a generous cross-section of its citizenry.

A relaxed and genial man, Kolbe had a great number of friends in the community and on the faculty. In a sense, he had grown up with many of the men who were directing the destiny of Akron and its business, industrial, and professional life. As an Akron girl of the influential Voris family, Mrs. Kolbe brought still another circle of support to the University effort.

The campus, until about 1920, was still a self-contained community. There was the ill-defined but recognized "pecking order" in campus society where office and rank had the effect of distinguishing among men. Nearly all the faculty lived within the immediate campus neighborhood. Most of them attended the Universalist church, and Sunday morning brought a flow of dignified faculty traffic—enlivened with irrepressible children—down College Street and Mill Street to the Universalist church at the corner of Mill and Broadway, where each had his accustomed pew. Professor Knight sometimes drove his electric car. Often the trip to church was made by streetcar via a line that ran in front of the campus and on down College Street. After morning services, there would sometimes be a dinner at the church, or on pleasant days a group would set off on a picnic at one of the many unspoiled picnic groves in the area.

The Kolbes led this little world in a way that caused them to be remembered with affection. It was still possible in those times for the president of the University to take off on a week-end hiking jaunt to southern Ohio with his faculty cronies of the "Blister-Foot Club." In the summertime it was not uncommon to find the president and some of his faculty on a fishing expedition. Is it any wonder that in this close environment the faculty developed a real sense of loyalty to the institution? To a greater extent than could ever be true later, there was a sense of shared enterprise, of belonging, of familial closeness with all its advantages and disadvantages. But that day was closing in 1920; mobility was soon to triumph.

And what of the heritage that Kolbe left Akron? He had largely inspired and presided over the critical transition of Buchtel College to the Municipal University of Akron. He had formulated a clear notion of the task of the Municipal University by observing successful plans—Cincinnati, for instance—by conferring constantly with educators around the nation, and by his own ingenuity and that of his faculty. He organized well; he operated by persuasion rather than coercion; indeed, he had nothing with which to coerce people if he had wanted to, the only exception being the threat to close enrollments so that the student body could be held to manageable size in the face of the community's unwillingness or inability to provide construction funds to meet critical space needs. In the long view there can be no doubt about the fact that he redeemed the pledge, shared by the Board, to make the University of direct service to the city.

Those who knew the story of higher education in America—Samuel Capen or George Zook, for example—were amazed at the comprehensiveness of the new University's commitment. Dr. Kolbe also kept the University in the mainstream of higher education by seeing that it affiliated with appropriate national and regional educational associations, and that it secured accreditation in each of its academic endeavors where some outside agency customarily put its stamp of approval on those schools performing up to standards. Thus Akron was accredited by the North Central Association of Secondary Schools and Colleges (1914), the Association of American Colleges, the Ohio College Association, the Association of Collegiate Alumnae (1920), and the National Collegiate Athletic Association (1914).[29] Dr. Kolbe, along with President Dabney of Cincinnati, founded the Association of Urban Universities (1914), now an influential academic association.[30]

The critical period of establishing a multi-purpose University was successfully surmounted. The school had been brought safely through the disruptions of World War I, the fantastic growth of Akron with its accompanying problems, the sharp depression of 1920–21, and various lesser trauma. At Kolbe's leaving every sign pointed toward a growing acceptance of the University as a cornerstone of Akron's life. This feeling was summarized in the *Akron Alumnus* of January, 1925:

> *To a greater degree than ever before in the history of the university, citizens of Akron, civic organizations, public officials, and business men of the city have been supporting various activities of the municipal institution and cooperating in numerous ways to help place the University of Akron before the citizens.*[31]

Thus did the continuity of this invaluable effort appear to be assured.

NOTES

[1] Board Mins., I, 376.

[2] *Ibid.*

[3] Board Mins (1913–24), p. 72.

[4] Spanton, *Fifty Years,* p. 185.

[5] Council Mins., 1916.

[6] *Ibid.,* Oct. 24, 1922.

[7] *Buchtelite,* May 6, 1921.

[8] See, for example, offers made to Akron faculty in 1919, *ibid.,* Sept. 19, 1919.

[9] Board Mins. (1913–24), p. 194.

[10] *Ibid.,* p. 193.

[11] *Buchtelite,* Apr. 18, 1923.

[12] These appointments can be found in Board Mins. (1913–24), various pages.

[13] *Buchtelite,* Apr. 3, 10, 1924.

[14] *Ibid.,* Jan. 23, 1924.

[15] *Ibid.,* Feb. 7, 1924.

[16] *Ibid.,* Jan. 17, 1924.

[17] Board Mins. (1913–24), pp. 11, 31, 65, 111, 205.

[18] *Ibid.,* p. 112.

[19] *Ibid.,* p. 142.

[20] *Ibid.,* p. 153.

[21] *Ibid.,* p. 139.

[22] *Ibid.,* p. 202; President's Report, 1920, p. 7.

[23] President's Report, 1921, p. 3; Board Mins. (1913–24), p. 174.

[24] Board Mins. II, 11.

[25] *Ibid.,* 12.

[26] *Akron Alumnus,* XI, no. 9.

[27] *Buchtelite,* Mar. 19, 1925.

[28] President's Report, 1925, pp. 10–11.

[29] *Beacon Journal,* Mar. 24, 1914; *Buchtelite,* Nov. 2, 16, 1914, Apr. 23, 1920.

[30] *Ibid.,* Nov. 16, 1914; Board Mins. (1913–24), p. 10.

[31] *Akron Alumnus,* XI, no. 4.

Curtis Cottage, completed in 1905, served Buchtel College and the municipal university in several capacities from dorm to classroom, playing a prominent role in campus life during the 1920's and '30's.

XI

College students are
"No worse than anyone else"

The reaching out of the new Municipal University into fields and interests far removed from those of Buchtel College had an influence on the student body—its character, organization, social outlook, scholarship, and spirit—but these differences were of degree, not of kind. The differences that existed were largely environmental. The 17-year-old Akron freshman of 1925 was not a much different person than his Buchtel counterpart of 1913, but the society he lived in was changed by war, depression, prohibition, and shifting social mores. His immediate society, centered on the campus, was also changed by the widened mission and the heterogeneity of the Municipal University. Just as the familial pattern of faculty behavior started to disintegrate in the early twenties, so the inward-facing ties among students were sundered as their society moved from social cohesiveness toward increased anonymity.

In a previous chapter we touched briefly on the general enthusiasm among Buchtel students for the changeover to municipal status. "In less than a year," said one student observer, "we have had the unique experience of leaving college and going to a university, without changing our addresses."[1] The address may have remained unchanged, but an important consideration to students was what to do about changing school colors, songs, and yells? Would the titles of the *Buchtelite* and *Tel-Buch* be appropriate any longer? On these matters the editor of the *Buchtelite* advised a go-slow approach; nothing "radical" should be done immediately, he said, since it was wise to avoid premature change. The name Buchtel was an honored one, and "as many mementoes as possible" should be retained while the new University was growing out of the old College.[2]

The "gold and blue" of Buchtel College continued to grace University events, but in the heat of battle during an athletic contest there was a fair chance that a spontaneous "yea Buchtel" would be followed by a self-conscious "yea Akron." Although yells were soon changed to conform to the new school name, not much appears to have been done to change songs until 1923 at which time the cheerleaders pushed a movement to substitute "Akron" for "Buchtel" in school songs, since the former represented all the colleges of the University while the latter was associated with the College of Liberal Arts only. Parke Kolbe was not in favor of changing the existing songs, fearing that John R. Buchtel would be forgotten. He suggested that new songs be composed to honor the University, and he showed the way with his "Men of Akron", one of the more solid local efforts at song writing.[3] In 1924 the alumni initiated a contest to secure new lyrics for the "Alma Mater." Selection of a new "Alma Mater," they said, music as well as lyrics, should involve "the whole university body, students alumni and faculty."[4] Nothing came of opening this door, and after repeated attempts to change it in the past 45 years, students still sing "Close beside Cuyahoga's waters . . ." to the tune of the Cornell Hymn.

College spirit is a tenuous thing. It seems to be more real and more compelling in the memories of old grads than it ever was in fact. This feeling derives in part from the tendency to remember longest and most vividly those things that were amusing or pleasant. In time, memory erases from its slate the long hours of boredom, moments of panic, lapses of duty that might have occurred with more frequency than the college dance, fraternity party, or conference championship that sticks in the memory. The old grad almost wills himself to believe that he was a sport and that life was delicious in good old college days.

The "lack of spirit" that was a perpetual lament on Akron's campus grew from the fact that Akron students were more involved in the "real" world and were not confined to the fringes of serious adult activity as were the students of a small, relatively isolated, dormitory college. Even in the most vigorous days of old Buchtel, it was difficult to get enough students interested to field athletic teams, or to produce the school paper. Of course the talent pool was pretty thin, especially for an activity as rough as football which was simply too destructive for many students. Even though it has been exaggerated in memory, there was *more* school spirit, *more* sense of belonging in Buchtel than in the Municipal University. There is no modern counterpart of that intensity of contact that marked the day when students lived together, ate together, and attended classes with *all* of their classmates, each of whom was taking practically the same subjects as all his fellows, and each of whom had the same instructors. They could play upon the conscience (or patience) of the slacker to make him perform for the College in a way that could not be matched after 1899.

The lack of effective dormitory space after the great fire was probably the strongest single factor contributing to a lack of spirit during Parke Kolbe's administration. Until the Student Center was built in the late 1930's, there was no really satisfactory place for students to gather. Efforts to provide space in the Library after 1916, or in Crouse gym, did not answer the need. "Bennie's Beanery" as Ben Miller's restaurant at the corner of Mill and College Streets was called, was the student "hang-out" in the early days of the Municipal University. It was but one of a number of campus eating places which found a spot in student memory, and even the well-equipped Student Center of later days never succeeded in keeping all of the students on campus.

Every generation of Akron students was familiar with complaints about lack of school spirit. In 1917, for instance, a student observed that his contemporaries seemed to think that all college consisted of was "going to school in the morning, attending classes, going back home, and studying for a repeat performance the next day."[5] In 1923 the *Buchtelite* editor applied the charge of "provincialism" to the student body, but his successor scoffed that anyone would bother to trot out that old complaint which was "almost a tradition of the university."[6]

There were the usual signs of life that erupted from time to time to dispel the picture of a docile, non-participant student body. The *Beacon Journal* lamented that many students, including those at Akron, considered four years of college as years of "high social life and merryment."[7] The writer may have been referring to signs of high spirits such as marked the pajama parade through downtown Akron before the Case game in 1913 when 75 students marched onto the stage of the Colonial Theater to the accompaniment of the house orchestra, delivered an impromptu performance of "In My Harem," and marched out to a burst of appreciative applause. Or maybe it was concern about students who put salts in the drinking water or those who stole music racks from chapel. Certainly no points were won by the students who interrupted the freshman party in 1915 by cutting the wires to Crouse Gym, stealing donuts, and rolling a 50-gallon barrel of cider down the drive onto Carroll Street where it ripped a fender off an auto.[8]

Along with these pranks, the hazing that is sometimes mistaken for spirit continued to cause problems. Freshmen were visible; they had to wear "glaring yellow caps with a green stud in the center" in 1913. Two years later it was hats of gold and blue. In 1925, after a wartime lapse, freshman men wore green jockey caps and girls wore arm bands.[9] Elaborate "Freshman rules" were published from time to time until 1924 when they were reduced to a minimum.[10] Along with these rules some other traditions passed; the old watering trough was removed in 1922 from its spot on Buchtel Avenue where many a "kicking, squirming, writhing thing of greenish hues" had been dumped.[11]

Amid declining enthusiasm for class rivalries, a new rivalry of modest dimension was building. The engineers, those "grimy workmen and ink-stained clerks from the west end of the campus," were at odds with the liberal arts students whom they characterized as "stuck-ups" taking easy courses and running school activities for their own benefit.[12] In later years this rivalry was largely channeled into the activities surrounding Engineer's Day.

College spirit, class rivalries and student pranks are phenomena peculiar to the student's experience within the confines of his campus. It is worth a moment to look at the broader picture that society presented during and after World War I, for students are influenced by the prevailing fashions of society at large even though they tend, at the same time, to construct a campus subculture peculiar to themselves.

There was little time to mourn the fate of "dissolute youth" during the busy war years. Some students of that period apparently saw themselves as superior in certain respects to their predecessors. The editor of the *Buchtelite* probably slandered the Buchtel College crowd when he wrote in May, 1918, that "present day students are of a higher mentality than their predecessors." They "took life more seriously" than the earlier group "because they were not the offspring of wealthy parents and would have to earn their own living." It certainly would have amused the great majority of Buchtel students to discover that they were offspring of wealthy parents, and the Ohio Universalist Convention may be excused a wry smile. Not content with this mild slander, the editor compounded things by arguing that "the students of yesterday . . . only desired the honor of having gone to college, not the knowledge to be gained." This new phenomenon, "the present-day student," was more carefully dressed, his clothes were neat, his walk was better, his shoulders were square, his head was held high, and the old pipe or cigarette was missing! Shades of Jack Armstrong! The editor then weakened his position by describing the "student of yesterday" in terms that must have been all but irresistible to his readers. This student was attired in a big sweater, oversized trousers, small cap or large hat, and a pipe. He affected a slouchy "devil-may-care-walk" with which "he swaggered all over the sidewalk" which caused town folks to refer to him as "one of them worthless good-for-nothings from the hill."[13]

The invoking of prohibition as national policy had little effect on the Akron campus. The Universalists had been staunch in the temperance and prohibition movements. There was still a strong Universalist legacy on the campus. There was no tradition of drinking in fraternity houses or at parties. As a matter of fact, smoking was still beyond the pale of acceptable campus conduct, and a movement in 1914 to allow smoking on campus failed to get the two-thirds favorable majority needed to pass, 100 students voting for it, 100 against. One interesting argument against smoking asserted that it would show a "lack of respect for the girls." Some things do change after all.[14]

Since student drinking and smoking were not serious enough to be criticized by the public, what was? Dancing, of course, and jazz. It had been a long time since boys danced with boys and girls with girls, as was the requirement at the socials held in old Buchtel in the 1870's. The nation was sufficiently aroused about the questionable propriety of new dance styles that the *Literary Digest* found it profitable to publish articles about them including, apparently, a poll of college presidents regarding their attitudes toward new dances. Parke Kolbe wrote the *Digest* that "the young people of our colleges are morally sound" and he emphasized that college students were "no worse than anyone else." He felt that certain "improper" forms of dancing were "a passing fad."[15]

Students defended the new dances as "merely a reflection of the trend of the times." If the new dancing was improper it was because the dancing public's morals were declining, but there was confidence that most University of Akron students would observe good taste in dancing. While recognizing that the new dances would "appear extreme to the older generation," it was evident that the new dances were "just as graceful and pretty to watch as the old ones when they are danced properly and within bounds." The dances referred to were the "Shimmy" and the "Toddle." As for criticism of jazz, the music desired by young people, said a student commentator, was a reflection of the times, and young people did not want old-fashioned music played by an old-fashioned orchestra.[16] How familiar it all sounds to ears attuned to the fashions of the 1960's.

Parke R. Kolbe, Charles Bulger, and "Hez" Simmon compare notes.

The "Little Dean", A. I. Spanton, and Oscar E. "Da Olin.

Charles R. Olin

Student opinion was sought on the changes in taste and fashion because these things frequently emanated from college campuses. But what of the "revolution in morals" that was supposedly sweeping American society? Student opinion on that topic is interesting since many of the same opinions are being expressed today by the grandchildren of the Akron students of 1922. A few summations of student opinion taken from the *Buchtelite* of May 10, 1922, may be pertinent.

Only continual restraint causes excesses; when a man is not overly restrained, he will do right naturally. If a man is allowed to follow his own desires, the idea of 'sowing his wild oats' will become less attractive to him.

Morality depends upon the state of the mind. Things which would have been considered immoral 25 years ago need not be considered so at the present time.

People are franker. They do in the open things which used to be done on the sly. Although we may be affected by the hectic age in which we live, there is nothing fundamentally wrong.

There is a laxness of morals in the present day. Parents and the churches have lost their influence over the present generation.

The present-day generation is degenerating. The kind of reading people want is shown by the demand for sensational magazines. The sex question is the basis for novels. We are moving toward an age similar to the one after Shakespeare's time when literature became so 'disgustingly frank' that Englishmen reacted strongly against it. I think that in our effort to disregard conventions we have gone to extremes.

Then there was the problem of women's place in the world. The "modern woman" who "smokes, drinks, and pets a little" was at the heart of the discussion since it was recognized that, compared with men, the women of America lived under a more restrictive code, any bending of which was regarded as posing a fundamental threat to established standards.[17]

Buchtel girls did not run with a "fast" crowd, nor did most of their Akron sisters. Being largely middle-class in origin and outlook, they did not adopt the practices that were put forward as fashionable in high society or in the entertainment world. Most of the college girls were more interested in establishing their *right* to certain liberties of conduct and action than they were in taking full advantage of those liberties. One coed summed up most of the attitudes her classmates held concerning the role of "modern women." Woman, she wrote, was "neither any better nor any worse than she was." But society no longer demanded that a woman "be a clinging vine, or sweetly submissive. Society no longer places her in a glass cage." Women wanted to accomplish things in society just as men did. They wanted to enter into more phases of society and assume responsibility. As to modern woman's dress, "Woman has never dressed more sensibly, more hygienically and more economically than she does today."[18]

As always when hard-pressed by criticism of their youth and its accompanying enthusiasms, the students sought out the views of "Daddy" Olin. He didn't fail them. Of young people he said:

They get a lot of relish out of life. True, their grandfathers and grandmothers didn't say, 'Oh, Hello,' when they met each other; they didn't ride wildly thru the streets in Fords or bicycles, and they probably would have perished at the mere thought of riding in an airplane, but they surely did miss a lot of life.

There was "absolutely nothing" wrong with young people. They had "changed greatly," but they were "just as earnest, more active, more efficient, and they possessed more initiative than the young people of 50 years ago." Such a blanket endorsement must have been music to the student's ears.[19]

With all their problems, new enthusiasms, and introspection, students were still students. It was not surprising, therefore, that they continued and expanded their activities, clubs, and interests into new fields and into new versions of former activities. To understand student life in these times it is necessary to look briefly at these developments.

Student activities grew in number and variety with the University. As new fields of specialization were opened in the curriculum, students added departmental clubs and college honoraries to the extracurricular program. The Buchtel College of Liberal Arts had its honorary, Phi Sigma Alpha, and now the engineers organized their honorary, OHM. Another honorary society made a brief appearance in the liberal arts college when junior men of high scholastic record who took part in extracurricular activities were initiated into Lance and Helmet (1922). More important, however, was the formation of Theta Circle of Omicron Delta Kappa, national men's honorary, on May 3, 1922. Other honoraries founded in the 1920's were: Theta Phi, commercial (1921); Pi Kappa Delta for men (1922); Sigma Upsilon, men's literary (1922); Eta chapter of Phi Sigma, biology (1921); Kappa Delta Pi, education (1925); Phi chapter of Sigma Tau, engineering (1924); student branches of the American Society of Mechanical Engineers (1924), American Society of Electrical Engineers (1926), and American Society of Civil Engineers (1926); Pi Gamma Nu, social science (1925); Chi Delta Phi, women's literary (1925); Tau Delta Beta, men's music (1928); and Scabbard and Blade (1925). Akron was only the second non-state university to have a Scabbard and Blade, national military honorary for advanced cadets in ROTC. Local honoraries were Delta Epsilon Chi, men's chemistry (1927), and Mu Phi Omega, music (1928).[20]

Political clubs made their first appearance since Buchtel boys had organized "Cleveland and Hendricks" clubs in 1884. In 1920, the Student's Republican Club was founded through the efforts of the Republican Party organization. Little did the party organizers realize that the Akron campus was to produce in Ray Bliss a distinguished chairman of the state and national Republican Committee in years to come.

In still another area of student life, a brass band was formed in 1922.[21] Previous bands had been short-lived, but this one paved the way for an enduring organization. The first Akron literary magazine, the *Acheronic,* made its appearance in 1924 and sold 500 copies. It was supported by four literary organizations (there presently is one), the R.L.S. Quill Club, Literature Club, Sigma Upsilon, and Alpha Phi Gamma. No continuity of effort has been made in the literary publications field although sporadic productions have appeared through the years.[22] The *Buchtelite* changed in 1914 from a monthly journal to a bi-weekly newspaper. Newsgathering was in the hands of the students, and they got direction through journalism classes established in 1913 and expanded into a laboratory course in 1916.[23]

With the development of student activities an effort was made in 1921 to centralize control and to protect the name and credit of the University. For these purposes the Faculty Council adopted a "plan for the organization of all student activities under a business manager and general rules governing University organizations."[24] This was a stop-gap arrangement since control was soon taken over by the Dean of Men (later the Dean of Students) and finally by the Extracurricular Activities Committee of the University Council, but these developments were still in the future.

As an indication that the students and faculty saw merit in judicious participation in extracurricular activities, an honor-point system for recognizing students who served the University by their participation was started by the Student Council. The purpose of this system was to encourage students to participate in college activities as part of their growth. It was part of the effort to make students "well-rounded," and this unfortunate term often got in the way of a laudable effort to help students develop social skills through campus activities. The faculty's contribution was a rating scale under which a student who amassed 12 points a year was awarded an "Akron Honor Key" which came to be known simply as an "A" key. This honor is still coveted as it was from its inception.[24]

In addition to new organizations there were attempts every few years to establish new traditions. Few of them "took", however. Traditions grow out of a long usage and not out of self-conscious, artificial efforts to create a long usage. One of the innovations of the early twenties that did catch on was the Military Ball, first held in November, 1921.[25] The continuous existence of an ROTC unit practically guaranteed a continuation of this effort. Not so successful, however, was Hello Day when students pinned on name tags and went about meeting their classmates. Loud Tie Day, a carry-over from Buchtel College's Loud Day, had a short life span. On a more serious level, authorities persuaded the Mayor to set aside one day as Akron University Day. First held in 1924, it was hoped that it would become a traditional observance in conjunction with Founder's Day. An extensive evening program at the Armory featured a variety program put on by University talent for the citizens of Akron.[26] It was in part, of course, a public relations venture, but it died an early death, although sporadic attempts along the same line have been made from time to time.

The most important development in student activities was the evolution of student government. The idea that students could learn most effectively about the processes of government by helping to govern themselves was at the root of the movement. This spirit was quite in contrast with the "student power" philosophy of the late 1960's. In supporting the movement, Professor Sibley write in 1915, "The choice in a college is between an aristocracy on the one hand or a democracy on the other. Student self-government is merely an effort to apply the democratic principle in the affairs of the college body."[27]

The senior class of 1915 drew up a student government constitution modeled on that of Western Reserve, and in April the students voted 160 to 20 to adopt this constitution which provided membership from each class on a Student Council, with seniors having the most and freshmen the fewest members. At least two senior representatives had to be non-fraternity. Women had to be represented. The Student Council was to take charge of elections, inter-class activities, petitions to the faculty, mass-meetings (ominous note), establishment of customs, college colors, appeals to the student body for money to support student activities, deciding disputed elections, and hearing charges of cheating brought against students and recommending penalties when appropriate.[28] The Executive Committee of the Faculty Council generally reviewed the penalties meted out by the Student Council, and in cases of disagreement, the faculty prevailed, but generally on the side of leniency. This Student Council plan worked much better than the abortive efforts at student government attempted in Buchtel College because some real responsibility was attached to it. The council's most important responsibility, perhaps, was to hear charges of dishonesty growing out of the "honor system" then in effect.

The "honor system" was one of those educational innovations that works in a particular setting when all the conditions are favorable, but then gets spread abroad by its enthusiasts and is adopted by others who do not have proper conditions for success. The system had many variations as practiced around the country, but the common pattern was to require each student to sign a pledge on all written tests and lessons that he neither recieved nor gave any aid. Faculty no longer monitored examinations, since all students were on their honor. When President Kolbe received a communication from Swarthmore College in 1913 requesting information about Buchtel's experience, if any, with the honor system, he replied that no demand for this system "was ever made either by the faculty or students of Buchtel." He further stated that "no trouble has been had with the giving of examinations to the students."[29] The closely knit society of Buchtel College before 1899 was precisely the atmosphere in which the honor system had the best chance of success. But it was not tried locally until it was too late; that is, the diffuse character of the student body and its spread through many different academic fields plus the loosening of the *esprit de corps* that bound Buchtel students to common values made it unlikely that an honor system would work after 1920.

In April, 1914, the faculty discussed the "alleged prevalence of cheating in the institution."[30] No action was taken to change conditions until 1916 when the faculty granted the request of the sophomore class of engineers that they be permitted to operate on the honor system.[31] After World War I, the system was introduced throughout the University and immediately the alarm was sounded that some students were not living up to their pledge.[32] Apparently the system was popular, however, for in March, 1920, the students voted 182 to 11 in favor of retaining it.[33] In the previous fall semester, two men had been dropped from school for violating the system, and five other students had hours added to their graduation requirements for offenses. Three students charged with violations were acquitted. The father of a freshman coed was so incensed in one of these cases that he threatened to take legal action against the University, but the Board of Directors backed the penalty meted out by the faculty in this case.[34]

In most, if not all, cases of cheating under the honor system, the initial judgment of guilt or innocence was made by the Student Council. If judged guilty, the student's penalty was set initially by the Student Council. The Faculty Council or the Executive Committee reviewed the penalty, sometimes upholding it, sometimes reducing it; but if they ever increased the penalty assessed by the Student Council, there is no record of it. In 1922, the *Buchtelite*'s editor complained that the penalties assessed were too lenient. Predictably, the Student Council defended their handling of these cases, and one member said council "did not want to go to extremes such as expelling students as this might do great harm to students who later realized the seriousness of their acts in violating the Honor System."[35]

By 1924, President Kolbe was beseiged with so many student complaints that he suggested, in an open letter to the Student Council, that the members promote "a fair and impartial student discussion of the usefulness and effectiveness of the Honor System at the University of Akron today." It was Kolbe's opinion that the "great majority" of Akron students were "essentially honest." Campus opinion was divided: many students thought reports of cheating were exaggerated, but many looked upon the system "as a huge joke" or "bunk" as one member of Student Council put it.[36]

The honor system was abolished in March, 1924. A vote revealed that 54 percent of the 469 students polled had witnessed instances of cheating during that academic year. Taking this to mean that students were opposed to reporting violations, Student Council by a vote of 8 to 2 recommended to the faculty that the system be abolished. The faculty accepted the recommendation. Council president Edwin Kregenow said "It was not right for students to cheat in examinations, and then perjure themselves by signing the pledge." One supposes the good president really meant that it wasn't right to cheat in the first place.

Kolbe was reluctant to dispense with the system. "The abolition of the Honor System does not mean that the students are less honorable than they were seven years ago," he said, "but it does mean that the student body has grown so large that it is difficult for students to enforce their own system." Examinations were now once more supervised by the faculty, and discipline was returned to the deans to enforce on behalf of the faculty. So ended a noble but futile experiment on the Akron campus.[37]

In assessing student life at Akron, it is helpful to keep in mind that a large proportion of students worked while going to school. This had been true, of course, even during Buchtel College days; but in those times the amount of work engaged in tended to be less time-consuming, and it seldom took the student far from the campus. The Municipal University opened its doors to a somewhat wider spectrum of students, many of whom thought it natural that they should work their way through school, and they weren't too particular about the hours or convenience of the job. A survey of Akron University students in 1916 revealed that nearly one-fourth were entirely self-supporting and that 35 percent would have been unable to attend college had there been no University of Akron. Some 45 percent of the students depended entirely upon their families for support although 42 percent came from families with annual incomes of less than $1,500.[38]

During the war years many students and faculty members worked in local industry. In his annual report of 1920, President Kolbe said the institution had largely recovered from "the disorganization of the war period" and student and faculty attitudes and scholarship were showing distinct improvement. "The result can be attributed to economic readjustments so that faculty and students no longer are attracted to industrial work."[39] Also in 1920, Professor Charles Bulger published an article in *School and Society* discussing the favorable aspects of students holding jobs while attending school. Although the classroom work of the student was not always of high quality, he was learning initiative, perseverance, self-confidence, reliability, how to get along with people, how to handle men, and how to work hard at what he undertook. At the same time, however, a report compiled by Dean Spanton showed that many working students left college because their working schedules were too heavy.[40]

Faculty opinion, while generally sympathetic to the need for students to work part-time, was largely opposed to their working a full shift. Dean Fred Ayer's assessment just about describes the outlook assumed by those responsible for student loads and academic progress through the years. He did not approve of students working a full eight-hour day. Such a student could not devote sufficient effort to his studies. He felt the average college man lacked the judgment to regulate adequately his own affairs and that the college should feel itself responsible for the health and welfare of the student and thus regulate his affairs for him. The college should regulate the number of credit hours a working student could carry. Ayer believed the majority of students working in factories did so to obtain more spending money, and the College of Engineering had recently limited to 10 hours the amount of credits carried by a students working a full shift, regardless of his academic standing.[41]

The students themselves showed some pride in the fact that many worked long hours and still succeeded in obtaining decent grades in their class work. The 100 students employed by Goodyear, at nearly every job in the plant, some involving hard, dirty work, refuted Thomas Edison's charge that college men were afraid of such work, or so said the *Buchtelite* in February, 1923.

In characteristic fashion, some of the working students created their own organization, "The Owls," open to those who worked a full shift while attending school and who maintained an average above the all-University grade average. Members were to have passed at least 72 credits and have worked full shifts for three years. The purpose of the group was to discuss mutual problems, advise working students, discourage those who did not need to from working while in school, and gain a little recognition for their efforts.[42] Anyone familiar with students could predict the outcome of this well meant effort. First the Owls lowered their membership requirements, and then they disappeared all together. With the exception of the truly unusual character who seems to be able to accomplish everything he puts his mind and energies to, most students who work a full shift and attend school do not have the time, energy or interest to sustain casual organizations.

Allow a problem to lie around a university long enough and somebody will eventually write a research paper about it. In compiling data for a Master's thesis in 1924, Jacob Nagle discovered that the grades of full-time students who worked were five percent higher than the grades of those who didn't. Most of the University graduates who had worked their way through school thought the experience was valuable to them. More than half of the working students felt there was a loss in participation in extracurricular activities, but a considerable number did participate and 11 of 18 "A" key winners were "working" students.[43]

Ultimately, the University established sensible controls over student employment, even going to considerable trouble to help find jobs for students who needed work. A Student Self Aid department was functioning as early as 1915. It was a casual sort of operation replacing an earlier student employment bureau run by a student manager. One pronounced influence that outside work experience had on student life was to minimize the "ivory tower" tone of the campus. Akron students, then and now, do not experience to the same degree as students in a small-town, dormitory school, the dichotomy between their campus society and the larger society of which it is but a fragment.

NOTES

[1] *Buchtelite,* Jan., 1914.

[2] *Ibid.*

[3] *Ibid.,* Oct. 21, Nov. 7, 1923; For lyrics of "Men of Akron" see Spanton, *Fifty Years,* p. 141.

[4] *Akron Alumnus,* X, no. 5.

[5] *Buchtelite,* Nov. 12, 1917.

[6] *Ibid.,* Apr. 4, 1923, Oct. 23, 1924.

[7] *Beacon Journal,* Sept. 6, 1915.

[8] *Buchtelite,* Jan., 1914, Nov. 11, 1921; *Beacon Journal,* May 22, 1915.

[9] *Buchtelite,* Jan., 1914, Oct. 1, 1915, Apr. 16, 1920; *Akron Alumnus,* XII, no. 1.

[10] See, for example, *Buchtelite,* May 24, 1922, Feb. 14, Dec. 12, 1923, Feb. 21, 1924.

[11] *Ibid.,* Mar. 8, 1922.

[12] *Ibid.,* Feb. 14, 1924, Jan., 1919.

[13] *Ibid.,* May 21, 1918.

[14] *Beacon Journal,* Dec. 7, 1914; *Buchtelite.* Nov. 2, 1914.

[15] *Ibid.,* Feb. 25, 1921.

[16] *Ibid.*

[17] *Ibid.,* Nov. 5, 1926.

[18] *Ibid.,* May 31, 1922.

[19] *Ibid.,* Jan. 25, 1922, Oct. 14, 1921.

[20] See appropriate issues of the *Buchtelite* (1921–28).

[21] *Ibid.,* Nov. 15, 1922.

[22] *Ibid.,* Mar. 6, 20, June 5, 1925.

[23] *Beacon Journal,* Sept. 22, 1914, Feb. 8, 1916.

[24] Council Mins., Feb. 21, Apr. 3, 17, 1921; *Buchtelite.* May 31, 1922.

[25] *Ibid.,* Nov. 18, 1921.

[26] *Ibid.,* Apr. 18, May 2, 1923, Dec, 18, 1924, Jan. 8, 1925.

[27] *Ibid.,* Apr. 15, 1915.

[28] *Ibid.,* Apr. 15, May 1, Oct. 1, 1915.

[29] *Akron Evening Times,* Mar. 5, 1913.

[30] Council Mins., Apr. 21, 1914.

[31] *Akron Evening Times,* Mar. 9, 1917.

[32] *Buchtelite,* Dec. 12, 1919.

[33] *Ibid.,* Mar. 12, 1920.

[34] Council Mins., Jan., Feb. 4, 1920; Board Mins. (1913–24), p. 151.

[35] *Buchtelite,* Mar. 15, 22, 1922.

[36] *Ibid.,* Mar. 6, 20, 1924.

[37] *Ibid.,* Mar. 26, May 22, 1924; President's Report, 1924, p. 5.

[38] *Buchtelite,* Mar. 17, 1916.

[39] President's Report, 1920, p. 5.

[40] Bulger's article quoted in *Buchtelite,* Mar. 12, 1920; *ibid.,* Sept. 24, 1920.

[41] *Ibid.,* Apr. 11, 1923.

[42] *Ibid.,* May 2, Nov. 28, 1923.

[43] *Ibid.,* Mar. 20, 1924.

George Zook and the relocation effort (1925–1933)

In his letter of resignation as President of the Municipal University of Akron, Parke Kolbe had written that he would "hesitate to leave" the work with which he had been so closely identified "were I not confident that the experimental stage of the Municipal University is now past and the institution firmly established in the hearts of Akron's people."[1] It was imperative that the momentum be maintained, and in Dr. George Frederick Zook, those enthusiasms needed to carry on the missionary work of municipal higher education in Akron were obviously present. Long before his formal inauguration on January 22, 1926, Dr. Zook was hard at work on the implementation of the vision he shared with Parke Kolbe.

The new president said that he came to Akron because he believed that education properly belonged "in the hands of public institutions." Elaborating on this theme, he continued:

> *Our type of school has a fine spirit of public service which a privately owned one usually lacks. Every institution, like every business, should have the desire to serve the public. I like the complex problems of a city and think it is a mistake to establish a college in a small, isolated town which takes the student away from contact with real questions. I believe the remoteness of many colleges is partially responsible for the criticism often made of the college graduate that he is not prepared for any real work.*[2]

During the eight years of his presidency, Dr. Zook had this ideal of service at the forefront of his thought and action. It is difficult to imagine that anyone could be found for the presidency who would be as totally dedicated as Parke Kolbe to the purposes of municipal higher education, but in George Zook, that man was found.

George Frederick Zook was the product of public higher education. Born in Kansas in 1885, he earned baccalaureate and master's degrees from the University of Kansas. He completed his Ph.D. degree in history at Cornell in 1915. He taught Modern European History at Penn State and Cornell universities before entering government service during World War I. His work in government centered on matters concerning communication and higher education. In his last assignment before accepting the Akron presidency, Dr. Zook was head of the division of higher education in the United States Bureau of Education, and in this capacity he traveled extensively, both at home and abroad, so that he was uncommonly well acquainted with the diversity and character of higher education. He was sedate in appearance and temper, cool in his administrative judgments, unflappable in personal demeanor. He was liked and respected, but it was not easy to establish a warm relationship with him. Mrs. Zook was a *grande dame* who brought dignity and a strong sense of propriety to her role as first lady of the University. The Zooks, in short, were well equipped by background and outlook to perform their new roles in Akron.[3]

In his inaugural address, President Zook outlined a brilliant prospectus for building a "vigorous youth" among educational institutions into a great university geared to provide unparalleled services as "a great center of community service." Important as was this objective, of equal importance was the hope that the university

President George Zook (1925–33)

would become "a civic monument" that would "stir the imagination deeply." In bringing these hopes to reality, said Zook, "it would be preferable to build the greater University of Akron on a new and much larger site, provided the necessary funds may be secured from both public and private sources."[4] Thus he introduced his stand on the issue that was to absorb the major portion of his energies for the next three-and-a-half years.

The question of relocating the campus had arisen from time to time ever since the great fire of 1899. The campus was so hemmed in by residential building that it had no place to expand. At least two sites on Akron's west side had been proposed as proper places to rebuild the College. Neither proposal had received serious consideration. In transferring the assets of Buchtel College to the City of Akron, the trustees stipulated that they expected the school to remain where it was.

By the early twenties, however, the growth of the city had forced a change in character in the residential environment of the campus while a concurrent growth in enrollment taxed existing facilities to capacity. The first official mention that the University might become seriously involved in an effort to relocate came in President Kolbe's annual report for 1924 in which he observed that Mr. J. Edward Good, an Akron businessman, had donated his farm of 180 acres to the city. The farm lay just west of Hawkins Avenue on the outskirts of Akron. Kolbe indicated that land for expansion "may be vitally necessary in 10 to 20 years for future growth," although "the present six acres will be adequate for a student body twice the size of the present one." He went on to say that "the proposal that a part of the Good farm be reserved to university purposes has been placed before the proper authorities by the University Directors." This action resulted from deliberations by the directors and other concerned parties throughout the summer and fall of 1924.[5]

During these conferences, President Kolbe and certain directors met with Mayor Rybolt, Mr. Good, and his legal counsel. Mr. Good wanted the University to be located on part of the property he had donated. The architect who was drawing plans for a municipal golf course on the land was instructed to draw preliminary plans for locating the University on part of the site.[6] As plans went forward, opposition started to rise against changing the University's location.

The *Beacon Journal* opposed relocation at that time and summarized some of the arguments against it. Previous bond issues for the University's benefit represented substantial outstanding debts. As of November, 1925, the total indebtedness of the University from previous bond issues was $359,000. Interest charges and installments which were coming due on Akron's total bonded debt would leave little revenue for current city operations. The *Beacon* felt that "the time is at hand when there should be no more dream projects to pile the mountain of debt any higher." Furthermore, the present site was "ideal, historic and central," and it was senseless to junk "the splendid equipment and buildings as if they were so many worn out mills."[7] Very soon additional arguments would be used against the scheme. It was assumed by opponents that the tax in support of the Municipal University would be increased, but they failed to reckon with the limitations invoked by state law. A popular argument was that the new location would be hard to get to from most parts of the city, although in 1926, Mr. E. B. Atchley of the Northern Ohio Traction and Light Co. asserted that his company would provide adequate transportation to the proposed site should the move be made.[8]

In the spring of 1925, Superintendent of Schools, Carroll R. Reed, proposed a plan that would take care of the most persistent obstacle to a move—what should be done with the abandoned campus. Since the public school system of Akron was congested, Reed proposed that the existing University plant be converted into a single, large high school for Akron, and the existing high schools be made into junior highs. The purchase price paid by the Board of Education could supply much of the cost of relocating the University.[9] President Kolbe quickly endorsed the plan, commenting that "the taxpayer's school dollar will work twice as much." Since money must be spent on public school construction anyhow, dollars used to purchase the University plant would result in a new high school as well as in a new University.[10] One important point not commented upon was the obvious need to rehabilitate the University buildings before they would be suitable to the needs of the high school, and not much was said about where this money was to come from. Superintendent Reed's plan was received enthusiastically by Mayor Rybolt, who thought it was "very obvious that the university cannot expand in its present location." A bond issue would be necessary to secure funds to relocate the University, but the time was not yet at hand when the voters would approve such an issue. The mayor declared that in a few years new bond issues might be feasible, since the county auditor was reappraising property and the lower tax rate resulting therefrom might encourage people to support a University bond issue.[11]

While the mayor tempered his support with a dose of realism, enthusiasts pushed ahead; among them were students whose enthusiasm sometimes outran their prudence. In the fall of 1925 the editor of the *Buchtelite* supported Superintendent Reed's plan. He was not too concerned with how the old campus was to be disposed of or how the money to pay for the new was to be found. A new University should be built "at any cost" out of "justice" to students of the city of Akron.[12] While the student paper continued to endorse the move, the directors were moving quietly until they had a better idea of the prospects.

Quite literally, they investigated where they were going, since a number of locations were put forward for consideration once it was known that there was a chance the University might relocate. A committee on sites was appointed by the chairman of the Board. They considered and rejected the Adamson estate off East Avenue, a site off Merriman Road, and another near the High Level Bridge on the north side of the city. While the committee was out looking over these spots, a committee of the Akron Board of Education was inspecting University buildings to try to determine how they might be used should the Board acquire them in the future. The University committee on sites made its report to a special meeting of the directors in March, 1927. The committee recommended the Good Park site, supplemented by a 12-acre strip on the east, fronting on Hawkins Avenue. The

Board took no action at this meeting, however.

President Zook now pressed vigorously on the need for new buildings. In convincing detail he outlined the impossible space squeeze and argued that since new buildings should go on "another, and much larger site," all divisions of the University except the Evening School should move as soon as possible. "The question as to whether the university should be moved to a new site has been discussed freely during the last three years before numerous civic organizations and by hundreds of friends interested in the development of the university," he said. "I believe that public opinion has gradually crystallized in the direction of this policy. I am convinced, therefore, that a decision on this matter is of far greater importance than anything else."[14]

At a meeting held April 17, 1928, the Board of Directors unanimously approved a resolution:

> *That it is the opinion of the board that the university should be moved to the Edward Good Park site, including the 12-acre tract between the park and Hawkins Avenue, provided this 12-acre tract can be secured to the university without cost to the City or the university, and provided further that the City Council will appropriate about 60 acres from the easterly end of the park adjoining the 12-acre tract, to be used for university purposes from time to time as in the opinion of the Board of Directors of the university it may be needed.*[15]

The resolution was generally well received, although the directors took no action on the vexing question of funds for relocating the campus.

President Zook believed that private donations would determine the course that financing the relocation would take. If a substantial amount of money was given to the effort, it would reduce the amount that would have to be sought from the voters.

The key problem at this early stage was the acquisition of the 12-acre tract between Good Park and Hawkins Avenue. This was the proposed location for the initial building effort. The Akron City Council assured that expansion room would be available as needed by presenting the University with the 60 acres adjoining the 12-acre plot on April 24, 1928.[16] Four different parties owned parts of the 12 acres. Negotiations with the owners were complicated by the fact that there was no sign in 1928 that this property would be available without cost to the city or to the University.

Once construction started on the new campus, the directors intended to proceed a step at a time and build only as there was a need for new buildings. The transfer of operations from the old campus to the new would be gradual and in Zook's estimate might take as long as 10 years. The evening session and certain short courses might remain permanently on the old campus, since Zook was convinced that a central location was essential to the success of this kind of operation. Other people's plans were held in abeyance pending a more definite move by the University. The Akron Board of Education was holding off constructing a vocational school in the hope that the Engineering Building might become available in the near future.[17]

Among the faculty and student body, the Board's determination to move to Good Park met with great enthusiasm, and why not, given the incredible crowding that forced all to work in conditions of minimal efficiency? Even though great things can be accomplished in minimal physical surroundings, there are limits to the inconvenience a long-suffering faculty will put up with, even when their efforts seem to be producing good results. Zook was not merely "crying wolf" when he spoke of Akron's limitations. He was widely acquainted with college campuses across the land and had much experience as an examiner of colleges seeking to meet the standards of accreditation that the North Central Association maintained in its 19-state area. Indeed, Dr. Zook must have shuddered when he imagined the embarrassment he would experience should some of the people he had criticised for inadequate facilities come to his own campus and there find even greater inadequacies.

In the professional literature of that day, educators had arrived at a figure of

200 square feet per student as the minimum amount of instructional space needed to carry on a quality educational program in a college or university. Akron had less than 100 square feet per student. As so often happens in the educational world, the figures evolved: 150 square feet came to represent the minimum requirement, and 88 square feet represented Akron's condition.[18] And this later tabulation was even more discouraging when one discovers that the square footage at Akron included hallways, closets, and attics which were being used for classroom space. It was thought for a time in 1928 that the Teachers College would be unable to operate at all for lack of space, but the timely addition of room in Spicer School made it possible to continue this vital part of the University's mission.

And why shouldn't the students seek relief? Of the many student organizations and activities, only Women's League was operating on the campus because space was at such a premium. School spirit, that much debated phenomenon, never too much in evidence on the campus as a whole, had been dealt a severe blow by the over-crowding and accompanying restrictions. The announcement of the imminent move did more than anything else could have to stimulate student enthusiasms anew. Even those who were against it—and there were probably a few—now had the pleasure of expressing their discontent against a real, solid, worthy issue.

Unless new buildings were constructed immediately, enrollment would have to be limited. Initial steps in this direction involved raising admission requirements in order to restrict enrollment. To be eligible for admission to the freshman class, a student had to have an 83 percent (a low "B") average for all work taken in his last two years of high school. This requirement, initiated in 1926, was as high as any in the state at that time, and it caused President Zook to say with some anxiety, "That should not be for a municipal university, but there was nothing else to do."[19]

The intellectually geared-up student body was willing and able to help with the proposed relocation of their campus. Immediately following the directors' decision to move, President Zook announced that the students would hold a fund-raising drive. "The students must now help. I want every student to have a share in the new university," he said.[20] Their response was prompt. "Pleading our case before a jury of 220,000 people," said the editor of the *Buchtelite*, "is a matter not to be accomplished in a day; nevertheless there are over 1,100 students in our Alma Mater who should each and every one become self-appointed salesmen."[21]

A campaign was quickly set to raise $25,000 among the students and faculty, this money to be used toward the cost of a gymnasium on the new campus. Jerome Taylor was general chairman. Under his direction the men captained by Eugene Warner competed against the women captained by Sarah Apel. Evening students conducted a separate drive, but their contributions went into the total. Close to 90 percent of the student and faculty contributed some $26,469, a fantastic record compared to anything previously tried in the way of student-faculty fund-raising. Victory in this campaign was celebrated on May Day when a float parade led celebrators on a three-mile pilgrimage to the Good Park site where the day's festivities were held.[22]

Concurrent with the student-faculty drive, plans were laid for a major effort by the alumni association to raise $200,000 to be used for a new Buchtel Hall on the Good Park campus. Up to this time, no municipal university had raised such a sum from alumni donors, but the campaigners were heartened by the success of the student-faculty effort, and they pressed ahead under the general chairmanship of Bert Polsky and his chief solicitor, Rodney Sutton, Class of '21. The campaign was organized with exemplary thoroughness. It got off to a good start with subscriptions of $10,000 each from Bert Polsky, John Thomas, P. W. Litchfield, and Frank Mason. The alumni campaign raised about $150,000, nearly all of it in Akron. When added to the student-faculty total, a little over $175,000 of the $200,000 was secured. Although the campaign fell short of the goal, it was by far the most successful private fund-raising effort in the school's history to that time.[23]

Enthusiasm continued to rise as word was received that Akron's sister institutions had done well at the polls with bond issues in the fall of 1928. Toledo was to receive $2,000,000 for relocation of its campus in a setting quite similar to Good Park, and Cincinnati was to get $1,200,000 for expansion. On March 5, 1929, Akron City Council authorized the purchase of 21 acres of land at the corner of Hawkins and Mull Avenues adjoining the 60 acres previously allotted to the University. On this parcel it was proposed to locate the main entrance to the new campus and the buildings that the public would use for general cultural activities such as the auditorium, art gallery, and library. The city would pay $7,000 of the cost of the land in 1929 from the general fund, and the remaining $40,000 was to be part of a bond issue to be on the ballot in the November election.[24] The final obstacle in securing the new campus site was overcome in May when John Thomas and P. W. Litchfield authorized the use of $15,300 from their gifts to the alumni campaign toward the purchase of the 12-acre tract on Hawkins that was the key to the new campus development.[25]

On July 25, the Board of Directors unanimously adopted a resolution calling for issuance of $3,000,000 in bonds of the City of Akron "for the J. Edward Good Park and adjoining land." Of the amount requested, $2,000,000 was to be used for building construction, $700,000 for development of the site, and the remainder for utilities, equipment, land purchase, and related needs.[26] The bonds were requested immediately, but they were not to be floated in a unit, the expectation being that they would be disposed of at the rate of $1,000,000 per year for three years. Nor were the structures for which these funds would be used too well defined, although it was expected that a major classroom building would be built on the highest knoll, and in close juxtaposition to this a chemistry building, engineering building, and gymnasium, the latter also serving temporarily as an assembly hall.[27]

In order to clear the legal considerations underlying relocation, the Board of Trustees of Buchtel College assembled once again in Akron to remove all restrictions on the use of the campus site. Dr. Parke Kolbe, President of Brooklyn Polytechnic, presided, and C. R. Olin served as secretary. Also present were former trustees A. A. Kohler, F. W. Albrecht, George W. Crouse, Jr., W. B. Baldwin, John R. Smith, and James Ford. Three former trustees were unable to attend—A. H. Noah, H. S. Firestone, and F. A. Seiberling. The three vacancies were filled by President Zook and two directors of the University. By resolution, the Trustees of Buchtel College then abandoned all rights, restrictions, and qualifications concerning property holdings entrusted to the Municipal University of Akron.[28] This action confirmed the opinion rendered earlier by City Law Director, H. M. Hagelbarger, in his private capacity as a lawyer that the sale of the buildings and grounds would be legal.[29]

The Buchtel Trustees cleared the way for action, but no definite decision on the disposal of the campus and buildings had yet been made. The possibilities included turning over some of the buildings to the Board of Education for a vocational school, or converting buildings to the uses of a library or art museum (which seemed to be talking at cross purposes with Zook's avowed intention of securing places for such cultural facilities on the new campus.) There seemed to be little doubt that the athletic field could be sold and the proceeds used to construct an athletic plant on the new site.

During the summer and fall of 1929, support for the bond issue came from a variety of local organizations. Both the *Akron Beacon Journal* and the *Akron Times-Press* now supported relocation as did the Akron Ministerial Association, Akron Missionary Union, Akron Council Knights of Columbus, Akron Automobile Dealers, Akron Bar Association, Akron Council for Home and School League, Akron Chamber of Commerce, and the united women's organizations of Akron. A strong cross-section of Akron's business and industrial leaders spoke in support of the move, none more enthusiastically than Mr. Good himself who said Akron would become a "world center of learning some day" because there was not "a better advertised city in America. Even if we penetrate the jungles of Africa," he continued, "although the natives may be somewhat ignorant of the pronunciation, these dusky natives have at least heard of Akron."[30] The problem, however, was not persuading Africans, but Akronites.

Everything that ingenuity could contrive was employed to secure a favorable vote on campus relocation and the supporting bond issue. Everyone at the University was expected to help. A mimeographed "Historical Survey of the University of Akron" was placed in the hands of faculty members so each would be adequately informed when questioned about the school's condition.[31] A study of the home background of Akron students was printed in the *Beacon Journal* to demonstrate how completely the University served the plain citizen who could claim no special influence in the community. Of the students reporting, 460 were sons and daughters of rubber workers, skilled tradesmen, and farmers; 459 of salesmen, teachers, managers, contractors, merchants, clerks; 49 of doctors, lawyers, dentists, ministers; 31 of retired parents.[32]

To further persuade the doubting that a need existed for more space, statistics were compiled to show that, since 1913, Akron's population had increased 172 percent and taxable property 332 percent, while during that same period day enrollment increased 534 percent, in addition to which there were 1,983 evening and 539 summer students in 1928–29 where there had been none in 1913. Meanwhile, campus floor space had increased only 57 percent. Figures showing the combined investment value of buildings, equipment, and grounds in proportion to each student revealed Akron on the bottom of a list of Ohio colleges.[33]

The public was brought to the campus. Various civic organizations were taken on tour, and on October 18 an open visitor's day was held so the public could see for itself the temporary physics lab in the attic of Olin, other attics and hallways being used as classrooms, crumbling bricks in Phillips Hall (formerly the President's House) and in Crouse gym. The latter, indeed, had become dangerous; falling bricks had already injured the eye of one student and narrowly missed hitting a mathematics instructor, as a result of which the decorative towers were removed from the roof. For those who could not or would not come to the campus, a film of the crowded conditions was shown in Akron theaters.

More research was done to convince the public of the wisdom of the move. Travel time to the new campus was studied. It would take, on the average, some 4.7 minutes longer for students to reach the Good Park site than it took them to reach the present location of the campus. Also, for those who drove, traffic congestion was less on the city outskirts. For those dependent on public transportation, the local street railway company announced it would provide service to the new campus. Dr. Zook, meanwhile, had figured out that it would cost the University $377,000 to buy land adjacent to the campus on its present block for expansion purposes. The value of remaining ground around Buchtel Field which might be used for expansion was $155,000. Thus, he reasoned, it would be cheaper to expand the University on the new site than on the present one.[34]

Other arrangements to educate the public to the University's need included a speaker's bureau of faculty and student participants, window displays in downtown stores, radio broadcasts of University activities and broadcast appeals by Akron's prominent citizens, University Sunday in Akron churches, and house to house canvasses of voters by student volunteers. Indeed, the students were so busy that homecoming activities were dispensed with. A final effort, frequently emulated in later years, was the manning of the polls in each precinct by students who passed out literature to the voters.[35] This tremendous organizational effort was Dr. Zook's responsibility, and he was able to call upon dedicated help from Sherman Schumacher, Class of '27, who organized the campaign forces, Perth Killinger who served as Schumacher's assistant, Professor Donald Hayworth who assumed responsibility for the tours and the speaker's bureau, and Professor Harold Queen who had charge of radio broadcasting.

It would be nice to think that the need of the University was so self-evident that no organized opposition would be made to the proposed move and its supporting bond issue. Such is never the case when money and sentiment are joined in an issue. Yet the only overt organized opposition came from the North Akron Board of Trade which favored expansion of the University in its present location or some other central location. The Board of Trade's position carried weight since two city councilmen were members of the organization. One of them, Wade DeWoody, was quoted as saying that if people "want golf courses, athletic fields, drives and a large campus they can find schools close to Akron that have them. Akron University should be developed for people who cannot afford either time or money to go to these other schools."[36] The president of the organization, Elmer Green, said that if the present campus didn't have room for sufficient expansion, the University should build higher, as was done in Pittsburgh, rather than spreading out. Dr. Zook answered the latter suggestion effectively when he told the Republican Club that state law forbade the construction of college and university buildings over five stories high. He quoted cost figures to show that Pittsburgh's "Cathedral of Learning" had cost more than twice as much per cubic foot as the estimated building cost at Good Park.[37]

But it was one of Buchtel's own who kept up a running fire against relocation. William T. Sawyer, Class of '87, was an enthusiast. When he championed a cause, or opposed one, he went all out. He was also a sentimentalist about Old Buchtel, having written fondly about his student escapades at the College which he later served as a trustee. Former Mayor of Akron and a real estate developer, he was well known in the area. He charged that the University could not legally be moved from its present site since the plant was to be "perpetually" used as a municipal university.[38] Cletus Roetzel of the Board of Directors and President Zook said Sawyer's charges were unfounded since the Buchtel Trustees had removed these restrictions in July.[39] Sawyer countered that some of the Buchtel Trustees were "tricked" into releasing the University from the restrictions placed on it in 1913. He then claimed that people who had purchased property near the present campus thinking the University would stay there would lose from 25 percent to 50 percent of their property's value if the campus were moved.[40]

Others supported Sawyer in letters to the editor of the local papers which might well have given some anxiety to those favoring relocation. There were many more letters opposing relocation than favoring it. The chief reasons cited for opposing the plan were high taxes and a fear that $3,000,000 would be only the beginning of a long string of money requests. A strong desire for keeping the University centrally located was much in evidence. A fear that the school would become an elite school for "west hill" was another reservation that one imagines was not articulated as often as other points. There was even some feeling in these letters that the city should not furnish higher education at the expense of the working people, and two letter writers questioned whether there was much value in a college education. Persons predisposed to think along these lines would be unconvinced by President Zook's statement that "those who protest against the cost of education are wrong, for education costs nothing." They were not prepared to accept his truism that education is "a community investment" and that "it is the lack of education that is costly."[41]

These small clouds on the generally bright horizon of public opinion were fused into a solid overcast by events quite outside the University. On "Black Thursday," October 24, 1929, the New York Stock Exchange experienced the first heavy tremor of the "crash" that led to the most serious and prolonged depression the United States had ever witnessed. In the month of October alone, stock values listed on the New York Exchange declined by 32 billion dollars, or some 37 percent. But coming just 12 days before the vote on the University bond issue, the panic focused voter concern on rising taxes and debt burdens so that even those not previously concerned became true believers.

On election day the voters of Akron soundly defeated the University bond issue by a vote of 18,923 favorable to 22,475 opposed, the margin of defeat being even greater than appears, for the issue needed a 55 percent favorable vote to pass. Two other money issues on the ballot lost by considerably larger margins, and in the election post mortem the *Beacon Journal* suggested that the University issue would have passed had it been the only money issue. Akron, said the *Beacon,* had the "incurable habit" of loading down every ballot with bond issue proposals and Akron citizens "distinctly want a holiday from further debt making."[42] President Zook agreed with L. E. Judd, editor of the *Akron Times-Press,* on the causes of failure at the polls. First, it was an inopportune time to present the issue to the voters; second, there was an unusually high degree of unemployment in Akron; and third, the recent collapse of the stock market shook confidence. Judd estimated that the stock market crash cost the University about 11,000 votes.[43]

Brave words concealed the bitter disappointment on campus. The needs of the University were real and acute, and there was nothing to say but "Of course we'll cope with conditions and triumph over them." At an assembly in the Palace theater, the day after defeat, John Turner, a student, ran up to President Zook on the stage and told him that the students should not be patted on the back for their part in the campaign because it was their job and they would be willing to do it again when necessary, a sentiment confirmed on behalf of the student body by the *Buchtelite,* which saw a "new era" of student unity growing out of common efforts in the campaign.[44]

It is fortunate we cannot read the future with precision. Had the supporters of relocation known then that the financial crises of 1929 were but the first of a succession of devastating, paralyzing blows against material progress and accomplishment, they could not have held to the hope that sustained them in their disappointment. Even at the end of the year when President Zook recapitulated the events of the campaign in his annual report to the Board, he had not seen enough of the depression to lose hope.

It is yet too early to make a definite statement as to what should be our immediate course. Circumstances may alter the details of our plans but the needs of the university are so apparent and so widely appreciated as to make it certain that they will be met as soon as the economic situation makes a better turn. There is every evidence that the university, through contacts with individual citizens, is more popular with people of the city than ever before.[45]

The last to give up hope were the students. Relocation had top priority in the list of accomplishments the *Buchtelite* outlined for 1930–31. The paper cited a successful private fund-raising drive by John Carroll University and local support for large Y.M.C.A. and Y.W.C.A. buildings as evidence that a similar approach should be used to secure money for relocation. At the same time, they welcomed the news (or rumor) that plans were being laid for another campaign. In 1932 the paper was calling for alumni to support and aid construction of a new campus and even argued that the depression should "stimulate" the building of a new campus since it could be a public works project. Slowly the last student hope disappeared. In a rather poignant gesture, May Day, which had been celebrated on the Good Park site since 1928, was held there for the last time in 1935, the last remnant of University activity on these once-promising acres.[46]

It is easy to speculate about the "might have beens" had the campus been relocated at Good Park. A large number of those associated with the University continued to lament this lost opportunity for many years. It is evident that even had the bond issue passed in 1929, financial conditions in the thirties were not conducive to selling bonds or financing construction. Only through public works projects can one visualize a realistic possibility for building a new campus. In the late 1950's and early 1960's, however, the great physical development of the campus in its central location promised for the first time to offset the longing for more spacious grounds. Urban renewal opened the door to better days on the old site, and now, with the prospect that the University will continue to be the pacesetter for the redevelopment of Akron's central city, its present location seems a blessing.

One final price had to be paid for this attempt at relocation. The uncertainty about campus location delayed any chance for new construction on the existing campus. As late as 1933–34, the Board of Directors delayed a decision for a proposed utility building because some directors felt a new building would end all hope of relocating. The Board's building committee was to consider further any plan for expanding the plant on its present site before abandoning the proposal to build a new plant on the west side.[47]

The Good Park issue focused attention and enthusiasm on problems of space and facilities. These were indeed critical, and first priority properly went to their consideration. Underlying this period of buildup to the election of 1929, however, were the same basic financial considerations about securing adequate operating funds that had been a principal concern ever since the Municipal University came into being. President Zook demonstrated understanding of the financial needs and, so far as one can judge at this distance, he put forward every reasonable plan for relieving severe strains upon the operating budget.

One piece of good fortune for those charged with running the University's business was the adoption of the Dinsmore-Laughead Bill by the state legislature on April 21, 1927. This bill gave municipal universities authority to manage their own funds. All funds from taxation and endowment were to be placed in the university treasury under the management of the trustees. Formerly the City Auditor handled these funds, and the school had to go through considerable red tape to secure its money. The Board of Directors assumed control and custody of all funds at their January meeting in 1928.[48]

The basic financial strain of the late twenties to the student was that each year he was paying a higher percentage of the cost of his education. Conversely, public tax sources were paying a smaller percentage of the cost each year, a pattern that had existed since World War I. In 1921, for example, public tax money supplied 88.3 percent of the cost of operation while in 1929 public tax money accounted for only 50 percent.[49] Since there was a negligible amount of money from endowments, increased costs were met by a steady increase in student fees—from $20 per year in 1921 to $50 per year by 1926. State law, of course, prohibited the University from charging residents of Akron for instruction in academic departments, so income from the maintenance fee had to be applied to expenses other than instruction. As Dr. Zook pointed out, it was impossible to raise fees indefinitely without violating state law.[50]

Underlying this practical matter of securing operating funds was a philosophical question of considerable moment. If, as many citizens thought, the student was the principal beneficiary of his college education, then it was plausible to expect him to pay the largest share of its cost. However, the Municipal University was conceived as an institution for the upgrading of the life of the entire community. When it was performing its task well, it produced graduates whose skills were needed to man the business, industrial, professional, and social activities of the city, and it also rendered many direct services that would otherwise not exist at all or would cost the city more to secure were these services not available at the University. There never was, nor will there ever be, complete agreement on this matter among the citizenry at large, but there was no doubt about where George Zook stood.

The president was foursquare behind the premise that the Municipal University's mission was to serve the community. To those who believed that any student capable of paying should be required to bear the entire expense of his education he said, "I do not believe this position is sound at all because it does not take into account the benefits to society of an educated citizenry and the investment which the municipality may therefore rightfully be expected to make." It was with reluctance, therefore, that he condoned student fee increases, and he reconciled necessity with philosophical outlook by rationalizing increases in 1927 as not having "caused any real hardship or prevented young men and women from attending the university."[51]

The only sources of funds other than local taxes and fees were state and private sources. Repeatedly, over the years, Dr. Kolbe and Dr. Zook called for a systematized solicitation of endowment money. Akron, it would seem, should have citizens of wealth who were willing to contribute to the University, but this supposition overlooks some key considerations. In the first place, few cities in the nation had as many growing pains as Akron which had inherited costly problems from the boom of 1910–20. As a result of its fantastic growth, the city had enormous needs for money, and its citizens were already taxed heavily. In addition, many philanthropic interests stood as high or higher than the University in the priorities of Akron's wealthy. After all, the University was clearly a public responsibility. Fund solicitations for the Y.M.-C.A. and Y.W.C.A. were popular with private givers because they filled a real need in the community, they were in harmony with the prevailing social outlook of the twenties, and they had no public money to rely on. A TB hospital, churches, and many other worthy causes seemed to attract the attention of the private givers. Many of Akron's wealthy citizens had suffered serious setbacks in the depression of 1920–21 which had hit the overextended rubber industry with particular force, and they had become cautious in the handling of their resources.

Despite these problems, an Endowment Fund Association was created in 1926 to "solicit and receive gifts of money from private individuals for buildings for special purposes and the general endowment of the university." The Association was modeled upon the successful Cincinnati plan. A pamphlet was issued annually listing the principal needs that endowment money would be used for.[52] In 1926, $835,000 was sought for new buildings. The 1929 pamphlet listed 53 sponsors with C. W. Seiberling serving as president; included were most of Akron's industrial and business leaders, several clergymen, and even a young lawyer named Wendell Wilkie who had not yet risen to the fame he later achieved.[53] The editor of the *Beacon Journal* pointed out that Akron's income from endowments was "almost nonexistent, ranking at the bottom of the rest of the nation's universities." That was where Akron was to stay for the time being despite the fund-raising effort.[54]

The other potential source of income was the state. Yearly efforts were made by the presidents of Akron, Cincinnati, and Toledo to convince the legislature that state support was needed, especially in teacher training, but even their most promising effort, which occurred in 1931 when State Senator Robert Taft introduced legislation to this purpose, failed to materialize.[55] Indeed, the argument used by the presidents—that the education of school teachers is a function of the state—very nearly boomeranged against them when critics suggested that all teacher training be placed in the state schools. As to the legitimacy of state subsidization to municipal universities, the schools were already receiving a modest amount of state money for training teachers in vocational rehabilitation.

The budgetary squeeze experienced during the thirties would have hurt the University under any circumstances, but it was especially acute as a result of action taken by the Akron Board of Education to stop payment of the annual subsidy they had given the University for training its teachers. The school board paid the University $34,000 per year for operating Teachers College. In June, 1930, however, the school board gave notice that it would discontinue the subsidy and, indeed, did remove it from the budget for 1931. This produced a real crisis and raised the issue as to whether the Teachers College, enrolling 307 day and 537 evening students, was "to be given up or modified seriously for want of $34,000 per year."[56]

One way out of the impasse would be to levy a tuition fee over and above the maintenance fee then charged Teachers College students. This was permissible under state law since tuition restrictions pertained to the liberal arts program only. Such action in the Teachers College would raise the question as to whether similar action should be taken in other "technical divisions" of the University—engineering and commerce, for instance. Cincinnati, Akron's model in municipal education, did charge tuition in engineering and commerce as well as in medicine and law, and there was a distinct possibility that they would embrace teacher's training in their tuition scheme should the annual attempt at securing a state subsidy again fail. Having pointed out this path to the directors in his annual report, Dr. Zook once again affirmed his faith in the role of the Municipal University:

I cannot view this suggestion at The University of Akron with any enthusiasm at the present time. The students are already paying a substantial proportion of the cost of their education. We are in the midst of a period of economic depression where lack of employment makes it more difficult than formerly for many students or their parents to make the modest payments necessary to secure a college education. To be sure, these payments are only a fraction of what is necessary for students who attend college elsewhere; but we should be very careful to make the university accessible to all aspiring young men and women in Akron who demonstrate their ability and willingness to profit by it. Ability and an earnest desire for self-improvement, not money or the lack of it, should be the key to the university's classrooms and laboratories.[57]

After prolonged consideration, the Board resolved on June 10, 1931, that Teachers College rendered an important service to the student, but also to the city. "Through economies and reduction of expenses," declared the resolution, it was the intention of the directors "to conduct the work of Teachers College on the highest possible plane consistent with the reduced income of the university."[58] No special tuition was to be charged, and even in financial extremity, no fee discrimination was to be imposed upon this important activity.

At the same meeting, a contract was executed with the Board of Education which permitted the University to use part of Spicer School for classrooms and offices, to use Central High School's auditorium free of charge, to assign cadet teachers to the public schools, to have access to demonstration schools, and to carry out testing programs for the Board of Education. In return, the University would allow Central High the use of Buchtel Field.[59] This settlement endured with little modification for many years. Not everyone was happy about the situation, however. The *Beacon Journal* suggested eliminating Teachers College because it was difficult to support with tax money; there were already plenty of teacher's colleges in the state, especially Kent, and the Teachers College was "the center of irritation between the university and the public schools."[60] No little part of that irritation focused on the person of the Dean of Teachers College, Walter Bankes.

Dean Bankes was the stormy petrel of the campus in the late twenties. He was inherited by the University in 1921 when Perkins Normal School, which he then headed, was absorbed into the University as Teachers College. From time to time throughout his tenure, the teacher training program he headed was rated very high in the state, as in 1929 when the Ohio State Board of Education rated it one of the four best teacher training programs in Ohio among some 41 schools.[61]

There are not any specific references in the record that would indicate disagreements between Dr. Zook and Dean Bankes with respect to the program of the college except what one may infer from Bankes' occasional statements that he would be happy to carry out Dr. Zook's wishes with respect to the college if he but knew what they were. It may be that Bankes was unhappy at Zook's recommendation in 1928 that the two and three-year programs of teacher training be abandoned since the need for teachers could be met with those holding a four-year degree. Some disagreement along these lines could be at the root of Zook's alleged feeling that Bankes did not maintain rigorous enough standards and that he was more interested in numbers than in quality. But if one accepts the state's ratings of the work accomplished, it would appear that Akron's program of teacher training was superior to the general level of that time.

It is far more likely that the disenchantment Zook acquired for Bankes centered around Bankes' personal and community activities. Some of these caused Zook and the University considerable embarrassment. Soon after Dr. Zook assumed the presidency, he received a letter from Professor Leonard, Director of the School of Education, Columbia Teachers College, complaining that Dean Bankes published "ideas, data, and even sentences and phrases" from Leonard's article in a scholarly publication "without giving appropriate credit." Leonard thought "it will do no harm for you to know that the dean of one of your most important colleges is professionally unreliable, at least so far as appropriating the materials of other workers in the profession is concerned."[62] Such charges could only have been most disturbing to Dr. Zook who brought the matter to Bankes' attention.[63] This was not a happy introduction to the relationship between the two men.

Dean Bankes' professional life became further entangled as a result of the publication in 1930 of a pamphlet, *The Teacher Tells a Story*, written by Miss Ellen F. Sullivan. At the time her pamphlet was published, Miss Sullivan, a teacher for 18 years, claimed that a conspiracy existed between President Zook and Akron's Superintendent of Schools, Thomas W. Gosling, to remove Dean Bankes as head of the Teachers College. Dr. Zook denied any such conspiracy. Her pamphlet proposed to demonstrate that her alleged difficulties in securing bachelor's and master's degrees from the University and her unsuccessful efforts to gain the principalship of an elementary school were the result of a campaign to get rid of Bankes.

Miss Sullivan contended that an anti-Bankes campaign started when the University president was given sole power to appoint the head of the Teachers College. She claimed Zook was critical of what he considered to be loose standards in the Teachers College. Superintendent Gosling was supposed to have aided in sustaining this charge by refusing jobs in Akron schools to Teachers College graduates on the grounds that their qualifications were inferior. Gosling, she claimed, recruited teachers through agencies. Miss Sullivan was particularly upset by an apparent reluctance on the part of the registrar to accept Bankes' evaluation of her transfer credits from Kent State Normal School. In appealing to the president, she said that Dr. Zook told her that some "defective machinery" of the University faculty would be removed as a result of her case. Hearing that there was to be a meeting of the Faculty Council to discuss her case, she secured a lawyer and attended the meeting unannounced and uninvited. She and her attorney were barred from the discussion, but the case was resolved in her favor and she was awarded her degrees.[64]

In the meantime, Dean Bankes was coming under fire from other quarters. He was concerned with local politics, and in a highly controversial manner. Miss Sullivan was not alone in accusing him of "being a promoter of Ku Klux Klan activities in the community."[65] Akron was particularly vulnerable to Klan influence because such a large part of her population were recent arrivals from the southern areas of the nation where Klan activities were historically a force in politics. Two Akron mayors, two superintendents of schools, several judges, and other public officials were listed among the Klan membership.

More explosive to Bankes than the Klan connection was the issue of "wets vs. drys" that enmeshed Akron politics in the early thirties. In a speech to the New Voter's Club, meeting at the Y.W.C.A., Bankes, who was president of the Summit County Dry Maintenance League, was quoted as saying "the wets of Ohio are spending $5,000,000 to elect Bulkley. I have the proofs and can substantiate these charges." It was further asserted that in discussing those who were opposed to the 18th amendment to the Constitution of the United States, Bankes said, "Anybody who says anything against the Constitution is a traitor and should be put in jail."[66] Bankes' charge that the "wets" had a $5,000,000 slush fund to elect their candidates was challenged by Dow W. Harter, Democratic candidate for Congress, who said that Bankes stooped to "falsity and vilification."[67]

A municipal university is peculiarly sensitive to the displeasure of any large segment of the citizens who vote its taxes and support its programs. No school has its constituents sitting more directly in judgment. It is little wonder, therefore, that President Zook felt it necessary to oust Bankes from his position as Dean. In a letter dated November 21, 1930, Zook informed Bankes that he would not be reappointed when his contract expired June 30, 1931, and offered him the opportunity to resign.[68] Dr. Zook offered no reasons in public for this action, so one is left to deduce how much of it stemmed from each of the issues here related. The Board of Directors backed President Zook solidly, and it was well that they did.[69] In a conference with Dr. Zook, Bankes made thinly veiled threats about the unhappy repercussions his ouster would have on the University.[70]

Some Akronites saw a conspiracy of sorts in the separation. The thought expressed by a local minister was typical of their attitude:

This is just about what the wet and law-breaking element of Akron threatened during the recent election campaign. Some other ministers feel with me, that such action at this time will be a victory for the enemies of temperance and wish that our university could be spared the charge of yielding to the demands of enemies made by the Dean in Championing the Cause of Prohibition.[71]

The Board received and noted a number of formal communications protesting its action, but it was unmoving.[72] Bankes left the campus in June, and Teachers College was placed in the hands of Albert Spanton who served as Acting Dean until a replacement could be found.

In larger perspective, the Bankes incident is the most dramatic illustration that Akron affords of the difficulty inherent in a teaching or administrative position in the municipal university. If a faculty member or administrator is interested and highly motivated toward involvement in politics, or any other controversial activity, he is soon aware that the president and Board are likely to view any active role in public issues with considerable reservation. An educator who wants also to be a political and social activist will find conditions less to his liking in a municipal university environment than in most private schools, or even in a state school where he is somewhat more shielded from the attention of the voting public. The possibility of retaliation by any large and organized segment of the electorate against the university that harbors persons with ideas that are obnoxious to them is great enough to be intimidating and it is a defect that faculty must live with in a municipal university.

While the Bankes situation held center stage, the financial position of the University fell into a precipitous decline. The budget adopted by the directors in January, 1929 called for expenditures of $413,583, and the budget adopted in January, 1930 totaled $458,178. If all had gone well with the economy, the budgetary increase would have indicated a reasonable growth, but conditions steadily worsened. Tax collections were falling off, and in October, 1930, it was necessary to reduce the budget by $9,392 in anticipation of this fall-off. A downward trend in income was thus well established as a pattern for the next few years.[73]

In 1931, an anticipated tax deficit of $26,000 and loss of another $13,600 from termination of the Board of Education's subsidy of the Teachers College led President Zook to suggest cost-cutting operations. Early in 1931 it was determined not to fill vacancies as they occurred, and after July 1, certain positions both in the teaching staff and other divisions were to be eliminated. At the end of the year, the *Beacon Journal* reported that the University was expected to be able to stand up under the financial difficulties until March 1, 1931, but unless more income was forthcoming by then, drastic retrenchment would be necessary, possibly even to the extent of closing some departments. C. R. Olin pointed out that the further reduction in Akron property taxes that was pending, and an inability to predict closely what revenue would be available from other sources of taxable property, made it most difficult to plan the 1932 budget. He admitted "we do not know which way to turn just now."[74]

As in 1920–21, Akron was unusually hard hit by the depression. With its economy overwhelmingly tied to the rubber industry, and with that industry in trouble, the city suffered from a heavy burden of unemployment and greatly reduced tax revenues. For the University, reality was worse than projection. The anticipated $26,000 loss in tax revenues for 1931 was actually twice that amount ($52,747), and in addition, income from student fees dropped by some $18,000. In fiscal 1932, losses of income to the University amounted to a 22 percent decrease from 1931.[75]

The collection of student fees was much more difficult, and though every reasonable leniency was shown students, no one was granted a degree until all his fees were paid. Despite plummeting tax revenues and other financial difficulties, the Board of Directors recognized the student's problems by approving fee reductions. First to go were the activity fees charged all students other than regular day students; then regular fees for evening and summer work were cut. In September, 1933, the activity fee for full-time students was cut from $15 to $10 and then to $7 a year, and this cut was reflected in the elimination of some student activities—the *Tel Buch* was not published in 1934, for example—and in the reduction of other activities.[76] A deferred fee payment plan was authorized for students who had good credit relations.

A small carrying charge was levied on deferred payments. Bookstore sales fell off as students doubled up on texts or, in some classes, were relieved from the usual purchase of a text because the instructor found a way to dispense with it and thus help the student reduce expenses. Funds deposited by students for R.O.T.C. uniforms, chemistry breakage, and school lockers were frozen because these funds were deposited in a bank that had frozen withdrawals.

Conditions were grim enough to make the hard-pressed student drop out of school altogether. President Zook urged those who could to remain in school. The dropout, he warned, seldom returned to complete his work despite good intentions. His warning was supported by the *Buchtelite* which reminded its readers that it was better to stay in school through difficulties and prepare for a job, than it was to drop out and compete for a non-existent job. In a later chapter we shall see how many of the hard-pressed students were able to hang on through lean times.

The budget anticipated for 1933 totaled $293,000, a decrease of more than $165,000 since 1930.[77] As a result of this decline the cost per student had also fallen steadily since 1930, but the student was paying a larger percentage of the cost of his education.[78] Earlier it was noted that during the supposedly prosperous years of the late twenties the student was paying an increasing share of the cost of his education, and now that the economic cycle seemed to be flowing in the opposite direction he was again paying an increasing proportion of the cost.

President Zook, of course, was charged with the principal responsibility for making ends meet. In the summer of 1932, P. W. Litchfield, an influential member of the Board, wrote Zook that "thinking over the affairs of the university in view of present business and political outlook, I cannot urge too strongly upon you the preparing of an estimate of just exactly what you would do to save 10 percent, 20 percent, 30 percent or 40 percent in running the university next year."[79] Zook had already given considerable thought to cost cutting; indeed, he had written an article in the *Bulletin of the Association of American Colleges* in which he pointed out economies that could be used by depression-hit schools. The University of Akron had, by the fall of 1932, instituted all of these economies:

1. *Do not erect buildings if the money might be used for current expense emergencies or if the new buildings would add to maintenance costs without corresponding income.*

2. *Reduce or postpone general maintenance charges.*

3. *Reduce or postpone purchase of permanent equipment.*

4. *Reduce money spent on research and supplementary activities. This money can be used for instruction.*

5. *Reduce unnecessary administrative and clerical personnel.*

6. *Reduce teaching personnel and consolidate course offerings.*

7. *Reduce salaries, if possible, but not below the reduced cost of living.*[80]

These steps appear self-evident to anyone familiar with academic work, but colleges and universities are notoriously loath to cut back, and it takes firm commitment at the top to do all that the situation requires in a financial crisis. At least the people concerned had the comfort of knowing that they were victims of the times rather than the victims of capricious administrative policy. In a sense, when everyone is hurting, no one individual's pain is as hard to bear as it is when he is the exception, a pauper in a prosperous society.

Since instructional salaries were by far the largest item in the University budget, major savings in operating costs had to come from faculty salaries. In that halcyon summer of 1929, faculty salaries stood at an all-time high. Things were so good, relative to former times, that compensation for instructors in the summer session was set at one-sixth of the annual ten month's salary, a level that the University has been unable to match to this day.[81] But, by the summer of 1931, retrenchment had set in. All contracts for reappointment contained a clause that the salary stipulated could be reduced up to 10 percent at the Board's discretion. All employees on indefinite tenure were required to agree to this which, in effect, made tenure a chancy thing.[82] By October it was clearly seen that the full 10 percent reduction of salaries would be required and action to this effect was taken as of October 1.[83] Even some faculty who had firm contracts for 1931–32 prior to the renegotiation of the past summer accepted the 10 percent reduction. Professor Simmons is an example; for his good spirit in accepting the reduction he received a handwritten note from President Zook:

> *Your voluntary acceptance of the 10 percent reduction in salary is an evidence of very fine spirit on your part. In these trying times I appreciate it very much indeed.*[84]

On April 22, 1932, the Board of Directors approved additional salary reductions for all employees to be effective May 1. President Zook had conferred with the Executive Committee of the Faculty Council on the anticipated budgetary deficit, and it was the members' judgment that it would be better to distribute a salary cut at a higher rate of reduction among the existing staff rather than to dismiss a large number of employees. Zook favored this course because he knew that it would be nearly impossible for many of the dismissed faculty to find another place in academic life under prevailing conditions. The reduction was scaled from 25 percent on salaries of $2,000 or more, down to 10 percent for salaries below $1,000. Evening instructors previously unaffected would bear a 10 percent cut this time.[85] All employees on continuing contract accepted the salary reduction.

The rapidity with which conditions worsened is evidenced by the Board's action in June revoking indefinite tenure as a condition of employment. From July 1, all employment and compensation was fixed on a month-to-month basis.[86] The University "must protect itself against being caught with a payroll it cannot meet," explained Zook.[87] He said there was no general complaint against the measure. Additionally, after July 1 no separate pay would be granted for evening teaching, and each faculty member teaching both day and evening course would receive but one check. Each was expected to teach a load to be determined by his dean.[88]

If the professors were bemoaning their lot, some in the community had little sympathy to spare for them. The professors "have no real kick" coming concerning their salary cuts, said the *Beacon Journal.* Even with the cut, their salary scale was higher than if the University were a private school and the president had to go around scrounging funds. Because the University was municipally supported, many professors had jobs who otherwise "would now be nosing around Hoover relief stations lining up for a pick and shovel job in the roads and ditches." The nation's economic plight was intensifying "while these professors were too passively on the job of teaching ethics rather than directing the course of political decisions."[89] Probably under the stress of the moment, the *Beacon's* writer can be forgiven the irrationality of his last point, but the comments are interesting because they point up again that, until very recent times, the outside world has viewed the campus as a privileged society which somehow considered itself above the common herd. What might well have been true some 30 years earlier was no longer true. The shift of attitudes and the rising social consciousness that characterized the twenties was intensified by the psychic pressures of the thirties. Any lingering ideas of faculty superiority, exercised in a little world removed from the hard realities of life, received a final death blow in the egalitarianism of the wartime society of the forties.

As usual, Akron's gadfly, Mr. Gus Kasch, had a specific suggestion for saving public money; combine the offices of President of the University and Superintendent of Akron Schools.[90] It had already been demonstrated in Detroit that such a combination of responsibilities did not work effectively. In that city Wayne University was just emerging in 1933 into a unit separate from the Board of Education and under separate management. In the longer view, Kasch's idea was penny-wise and pound-foolish and it got no substantial backing.

In the spring of 1933 the directors again faced an imminent shortage of funds that would make it impossible to meet the payroll.[91] Secretary Olin pieced things together, almost on a day-to-day basis, but nothing could be done to forestall another salary slice. In May, another 10 percent reduction was assessed those faculty and staff whose salaries exceeded $1,650 while the rest were cut 5 percent. Salaries in the higher brackets were now down 45 percent from the 1931 scale. The nadir was reached in June, 1933 when it became necessary for the University to pay salaries in script. Some $45,000 in tax anticipatory notes had been delivered to Olin by the City Finance Director, and part of this sum went for faculty and staff salaries.[92] Script was rather well accepted by local merchants, and the impact of this form of payment was not as harmful as might otherwise have been the case. When all is accounted for, it must be clear that the University was *in extremis,* and once again it was brought through most difficult times by the diligent efforts of men who would not let it die. The corner was finally turned in the fall of 1933. It was estimated in October that the fiscal year might end with a balance of about $38,000 on hand.[93] Recovery was to be a slow and agonizing process, but at least it appeared that the downward slide had been halted.

NOTES

[1] *Buchtelite,* June 5, 1925.

[2] *Ibid.,* Sept. 22, 1925.

[3] This assessment is based on information from persons who knew the Zooks well and on material in *Akron Alumnus,* Sept. 1925.

[4] *Beacon Journal,* Jan. 22, 1926.

[5] President's Report, 1924, p. 10; Board Mins. (1913–24), p. 242.

[6] *Beacon Journal,* Aug. 19, 1924.

[7] *Ibid.,* Aug. 29, 1924.

[8] *Buchtelite,* Apr. 23, 1925; *ibid.,* Feb. 5, 1926.

[9] *Beacon Journal,* Apr. 14, 1925.

[10] *Buchtelite,* Apr. 23, 1925.

[11] *Ibid.,* Feb. 19, 1926.

[12] *Ibid.,* Nov. 13, Dec. 4, 1925, for example.

[13] The Board of Education committee was composed of Messrs. Hyde, Guinther, and Beck. Board Mins. II, 48.

[14] President's Report, 1926, p. 16.

[15] Board Mins. II, 113.

[16] *Ibid.,* 116–17.

[17] *Beacon Journal,* Apr. 18, 1928.

[18] *Ibid.,* Apr. 18, 1928, Oct. 10, 1929.

[19] President's Report, 1927, pp. 11–12.

[20] *Buchtelite,* Apr. 20, 1928.

[21] *Ibid.,* Apr. 17, 1928.

[22] *Ibid.,* Sept. 17, 1929; President's Report, 1928, pp. 11–12.

[23] *Ibid.*

[24] *Beacon Journal,* March 6, 1929.

[25] Board Mins. II, 149.

[26] *Ibid.,* 161.

[27] *Beacon Journal,* July 26, 1929.

[28] *Buchtelite,* Sept. 17, 1929. Deeds to the Buchtel College campus from Spicer Cemetery Association Trustees, the Spicer heirs, John R. Buchtel, and others donating land, make no

mention that the lands must be used for education. When Buchtel College deeded its property to the City of Akron, the property was conveyed "for the purposes of a municipal university." If not so used, title could revert back only to Buchtel College and not to the original donors of the land. See *Beacon Journal,* Jan. 23, 1927.

[29] Board Mins. II, 87.

[30] *Buchtelite,* May 22, 1928. Endorsements of relocation are found in *ibid.,* and in *Beacon Journal,* various issues.

[31] UArch., VF (History).

[32] *Beacon Journal,* Oct. 4, 1929.

[33] *Ibid.,* Oct. 26, 1929.

[34] *Ibid.,* Oct. 19, 1929; Buchtelite, June 7, Sept. 17, Oct. 4, 1929.

[35] *Beacon Journal,* Nov. 6, 1929.

[36] *Ibid.,* July 27, 1929.

[37] *Ibid.,* Nov. 1, 1929.

[38] *Ibid.,* Oct. 28, 1929.

[39] *Ibid.,* Oct. 29, 1929.

[40] *Ibid.,* Oct. 31, 1929.

[41] Letters appeared in *ibid.,* Oct. 16-Nov. 4, 1929. Zook's position is stated in *ibid.,* Sept. 24, 1929.

[42] *Ibid.,* Nov. 6, 1929.

[43] *Buchtelite,* Nov. 8, 1929.

[44] *Ibid.; Beacon Journal,* Nov. 6, 1929.

[45] President's Report, 1929, p. 13.

[46] *Buchtelite,* Mar. 21, Sept. 16, Oct. 14, 1930, Nov. 5, 1932.

[47] *Beacon Journal,* Nov. 11, 1933.

[48] *Ibid.,* Apr. 1, 1927. Board Mins. II, 103.

[49] *Akron Alumnus,* XIII, no. 5.

[50] President's Report, 1926, pp. 6–7.

[51] *Ibid.,* pp. 7–8.

[52] *Ibid.,* p. 8.

[53] "The Endowment Fund Association of The University of Akron" (1929), in the Simmons Papers.

[54] *Beacon Journal,* Jan. 22, 1927.

[55] *Ibid.,* Jan. 23, 1931.

[56] President's Report, 1930, pp. 7–8.

[57] *Ibid.,* p. 9.

[58] Board Mins. II, 220.

[59] *Ibid.,* p. 230.

[60] *Beacon Journal,* Jan. 7, 1931.

[61] *Buchtelite,* Jan. 14, 1930.

[62] Leonard to Zook, Sept. 30, 1925, UArch., box 4/8a/65.

[63] Zook to Leonard, Oct. 12, 1925, *ibid.*

[64] *The Teacher Tells* is in UArch., VF; *Beacon Journal,* Dec. 19, 1930. Zook's denial is in *ibid.,* Dec. 20, 1930, and Gosling's denial is in *ibid.,* Feb. 4, 1931.

[65] Sullivan, *The Teacher Tells.*

[66] *Akron Times Press,* Oct. 21, 1930 (?), clipping in UArch., box 4/8a/65.

[67] *Ibid.,* Oct. 22, 1930 (?).

[68] Zook to Bankes, Nov. 21, 1930, *ibid.* Bankes claimed that Zook told him that he was "one of the most unpopular men in Akron." (*Beacon Journal,* Jan. 1, 1931.)

[69] Board Mins. II, 205.

[70] *Beacon Journal,* Dec. 31, 1930, Jan. 1, 1931.

[71] J. H. Dutton to Zook, Dec. 9, 1930, UArch., box 4/8a/65.

[72] See, for example, Board Mins. II, 209.

[73] *Ibid.,* 137, 175, 215.

[74] *Beacon Journal,* Dec. 24, 1931.

[75] President's Report, 1932, p. 6.

[76] Board Mins. II, 283, 305; *Beacon Journal,* Jan. 14, 1933; *Buchtelite,* Feb. 15, May 26, Sept. 22, 1933.

[77] Board Mins. II, 291.

[78] President's Report, 1933, p. 11; *Beacon Journal,* May 25, 1933.

[79] UArch., box 4/8a/65.

[80] *Bulletin of the Association of American Colleges* (Fall, 1932).

[81] Board Mins. II, 146.

[82] *Ibid.,* 221.

[83] *Ibid.,* 239.

[84] Simmons Papers.

[85] *Beacon Journal,* Apr. 22, 1932; Board Mins. II, 264, 267.

[86] *Ibid.,* 271.

[87] *Beacon Journal,* July 1, 1932.

[88] Board Mins. II, 271.

[89] *Beacon Journal,* Apr. 23, 1932.

[90] Kasch to Board of Trustees and Akron Board of Education, July 18, 1932, UArch., box 4/8a/65.

[91] Board Mins. II, 298.

[92] *Ibid.,* 301, 317; *Beacon Journal,* May 13, 1933.

[93] *Ibid.,* Oct. 23, 1933.

Politically alert, students participated in local campaigns in the city and on the Hilltop in the '30's.

XIII

Putting the academic program in order

While relocation efforts and financial crisis preempted attention in the late 1920's and early 30's, campus life flowed on behind the scenes much as usual. While some faculty left, others came to take their places; curricula were revised in the endless process of academic tinkering that not even crisis can check; old traditions were perpetuated and new ones made an appearance; student life went on even in the face of serious space limitations.

During President Zook's administration a considerable number of persons who would serve the institution well over a period of many years were added to the faculty. Warren W. Leigh was appointed Professor of Commerce and Administration; Howard Doutt was appointed Instructor in Political Science but would later become head of the Secretarial Science Department; Miss Josephine Cushman was appointed Librarian in 1925, and in 1929 Miss Dorothy Hamlen, Class of '28, became her assistant and ultimately her successor. Mr. Sam Selby, hired as Instructor in Mathematics in 1927, was granted a year's leave to complete his doctorate at Chicago. He then returned to a brilliant teaching career that spanned some 41 years. David King (political science), Howard Evans (education), Harmon O. DeGraff (sociology), and George Hayes (psychology) also joined the faculty during these years.

The arrival of new talent was accompanied by the departure of some old timers. It seemed like the passing of an era when they left. Hermas Egbert, Professor of Mathematics, taught in Buchtel College from 1889 to 1903, then left for other activities only to return again in 1917; he died in 1927. The death, three years later, of Professor Joseph C. Rockwell was much lamented by a campus that regarded him as the embodiment of integrity and high academic standards. "There was a certain combination of staid humor and musty antiquity that made him an outstanding figure in the corridors of Buchtel College," said a student memorialist. "He loved the Grecian and Roman ages of which he taught but better still he loved the civilization about him. As a link between the ancient and the modern his marked consideration and quaint humor enabled him to make unusual headway with students."[1]

Another whose passing in 1931 brought grief to the campus was Mrs. Elizabeth Thompson whose combined roles of Professor of History and Dean of Women had brought her close to many of Akron's students. She was much loved and respected for her "vigorous and alert mind," and her "gracious personality." This "rarely gifted woman" was a great favorite of all Akron for she had long served the whole community.[2]

Professor Amon B. Plowman was another whose death in 1932 created a sense of loss on the campus. One of his duties was lecturing new freshmen on the subject of body care. While ending the lecture to his last group of freshman, Plowman looked gravely at this audience and said, "Now, take the sex urge." At this point a feminine voice impatiently exclaimed, "You take it. I've had enough of it."[3] The good professor was much amused, as well as he should be, by such candor.

It was hard to imagine the campus without an Olin or two busy about the place, but the time that must inevitably come for all arrived in October, 1932 for Charles R. Olin, and four months later, February 15, 1933, for Oscar E. "Daddy" Olin. No one served the College and University as long as C. R. Olin. He had invested 53 years of his life in the school. It is unlikely that anyone will ever match that mark. He was honored by his school with the award of an honorary master's degree in 1909 and again in 1921 when he shared with Oscar Olin the honor of having a building named for him. Though exclusively concerned with business affairs in his later years, "C. R." had taught mathematics for an extended period and had served for decades as the official United States weather observer in Akron, faithfully keeping records which he read from instruments located on the campus.[4] A staunch member and active layman in the Universalist church, much of the remaining spirit of Old Buchtel passed with his death.

Oscar E. Olin, of course, was the particular favorite of generations of students. No one else was ever asked to stay on so long after retirement age as was "Daddy" Olin. He taught until his 78th year and was 81 at the time of his death. Mention has been made elsewhere of his popularity and the reasons for it, and of his contributions to the community as pastor, historian, and public servant. If ever the University could boast a teacher whose whole presence radiated a conviction that education should lead to the health and well being of every aspect of the student's life, "Daddy" Olin was that teacher.

Professional conditions for the faculty were not promising while Dr. Zook was president. The extreme crowding, inadequate facilities, and lack of equipment have been mentioned. But, in addition, it should be noted that library holdings were still inadequate although the size of the collection doubled to 32,500 volumes between 1921 and 1930, and its use tripled.[5] Book purchase budgets were appallingly low. Not until 1925 did the amount of money budgeted for book purchases and binding exceed the amount paid to the highest paid professor. In that year $5,000 was set aside for these purposes while the highest paid professor, without administrative duties, received $4,400.[6] By 1932 the library was in real difficulty. Book binding was not done; books were no longer being purchased for the speech and chemistry departments, and orders were cut drastically in English, the Teachers College, and in the popular book section. Such funds as were available went largely for book purchases, although this reduced the ability of the librarians to maintain periodicals in unbroken series, a condition which had serious consequences with the later emphasis on graduate study.

From the $7,000 budgeted for books and binding in 1930, only $3,500 was available in 1932. The *Buchtelite* suggested that a library fund be raised by securing the donation of excess funds from campus organizations. The idea was endorsed by Student Council and students generally, and by early June, 1932, more than $550 had been collected, heartening evidence that students were concerned about their academic life.[7]

Back to faculty salaries. Akron's salaries compared unfavorably with national averages in every rank from dean through professor to instructor. The average annual salary for an Akron professor in 1925 was $3,020 compared with a national average of $4,000, and though the disparity was not so great in other ranks, it was there.[8] And while the late twenties saw some improvement in faculty salaries, the depression eliminated these gains and then some.

The difficulties of the 1930's led to faculty interest in professional working conditions. In November, 1932, a local chapter of the American Association of University Professors (AAUP) was established on the Akron campus with Professor Charles Bulger elected as first president of the organization.[9] There always has been much misunderstanding about the nature of the AAUP. It is a professional association and not a union. Even professors don't expect it to perform miracles. There was nothing it could do, for example, when indefinite tenure was abolished by the Board in response to the financial crisis of 1932–33, and yet tenure is perhaps the most cherished privilege that AAUP protects. The Akron chapter was not militant then, and thus little of general interest accompanies its activities, but it is a sign of faculty health that a professional association was maintained.

In spite of cramped conditions and pressing financial needs, the proliferation of specialized programs and new departments of instruction went on apace. A Department of Secretarial Science was established in the College of Engineering and Commerce in 1926 five years after secretarial courses were introduced. It offered two- and four-year programs, and also cooperated with Teachers College in preparing teachers of commercial subjects.[10] From the beginning of work in secretarial subjects, the courses had been taught at Central High School, but in the spring of 1930 the classes were moved into the old cafeteria in Curtis Cottage. Also in 1926 a Department of Economics and Sociology was created, the course work in these areas being taken from the Department of Political Science and the Department of Philosophy which now assumed the character by which they would be recognized in the future.[11] The work in economics and in sociology was divided in 1934 and separate departments established in each field.[12] Speech emerged as a separate department in 1928.[13] This active department under Professor Donald Hayworth's direction was in the forefront in developing radio training for its students. An engineering student's five-minute speech, broadcast to an engineer's public speaking class in Buchtel Hall on May 21, 1930, was hailed as the first experiment in college radio speaking classes in the United States.[14] Professor Hayworth believed that a microphone and loudspeaker setup encouraged speech students to make the most of their abilities. Less than a year after this maiden trial, the radio speaking class presented a regular University of Akron Radio Hour every Saturday evening over WADC.[15]

In another adjustment made during this period, the Curtis School of Home Economics was closed and home economics assumed departmental status in the Buchtel College of Liberal Arts.[16] Sarah Stimmel who had administered the school since its inception in 1914 resigned and was replaced by Miss Elsie Maxwell who also served as home economics director for the Akron Public Schools.[17] While home economics waned, other programs prospered. Music offerings increased to such an extent that it appeared a complete music department and a conservatory of music could be established when the campus was relocated.[18] When plans for relocation aborted, the formation of a music department was abandoned for some time. Throughout the late twenties, President Zook continued to press for the establishment of "short courses," one-, two-, or three-year courses in applied and vocational fields, but lack of money and space precluded the establishment of this kind of program which is now embraced in the Community and Technical College.

Much of Dr. Zook's advocacy of short, vocational courses grew out of his strong belief that a municipal university was to serve the total community. He was distressed that space considerations had forced the University to limit the number of new freshmen it could accommodate by raising admission standards beyond those usually thought appropriate for a public university. It was satisfying to note that the average grade level had risen considerably as a result of selective admissions (from 76.8 percent in 1919–20 to 80.95 percent in 1927–28), but there were still hundreds of students who were not given the chance and attention they deserved.[19] The president noted complaints from parents of students who graduated from high school courses other than the college preparatory that their sons and daughters were not prepared to meet the University entrance requirements, and this suggested the possibility of voter resistance at the polls when University measures were at stake.[20]

One of the principal concerns of the administration and faculty was the admission and retention of students. The new enthusiasm in higher education for testing as a means of determining the fate of students was much in evidence on the Akron campus. Dr. George Hayes, Professor of Psychology, urged testing as a means for selecting college students. "Some men," he said in 1927, "are better fitted to be plasterers or plumbers than they are to be executives. Such persons are wasting their time in college."[21]

Psychological tests were part of the students' admission application after 1926. A student who failed to achieve the minimum 83 percent average for his last two years of high school might score high enough on such tests to merit admission. Tests were further used to assist advisers in revising and reducing the scheduled load that probationary students were allowed to carry. This probationary category was a recent innovation replacing the former policy of dropping from school any student who failed to pass a certain required number of credits in a given semester. "I believe," said Dr. Zook, "the new rules are a small beginning toward dealing with students on a more scientific and personal basis."[22]

Still another adjustment of the 1926–27 period that was intended to regularize admission policy was the restructuring of the old Entrance Committee as the Admissions Committee. The Chairman of the Admissions Committee, to be known as the University Examiner, was to bring regularity into admission practices.[23]

As we have noted before, Akron developed an early interest in "honors courses." Although it had students capable of profiting from these geared-up academic programs, other conditions on campus were not promising for their success. The two main deterrents to success were first, many of the students who should have had the opportunity for enrichment in honors sections had to work and thus could not afford the extra time that preparation for honors courses required, and second, there was "lack of time on the part of Heads of Departments" and limited resources in the library and in technical equipment.[24] Nevertheless, Dr. Zook called for greater effort, but honors courses foundered, as did other worthy ideas, under the limitations imposed by the depression.

A great deal of adjustment in the academic program and its degree requirements went on in the years of Dr. Zook's presidency. In April, 1930, the Faculty Council adopted a motion calling for comprehensive final examinations which must be passed by senior candidates for bachelor's degrees. Each department was to determine whether or not to require a comprehensive examination of its seniors. Its purpose was to test the student's ability to unify, correlate, and apply his knowledge in his major. Professor Bulger claimed that students were measured by what they once knew rather than what they knew at graduation, while Dean Gardner said, "The idea of the general final examinations is not to flunk anyone but to make sure they leave the institution with at least a college education."[25] This plan, already widely used throughout the country, was adopted by nearly all departments, at least at the outset. Students protested that the first group of seniors would not have a fair opportunity to prepare for the comprehensives.[26] It was never a popular requirement with the students, although they felt considerable pride, on the whole, once they had successfully surmounted what they regarded as a formidable obstacle to a degree. Teachers College soon abandoned the comprehensive and replaced it with a qualifying examination to be taken at the end of the junior year. Feeling apparently that they must prove the validity of this step, they made the new examination eight hours in length instead of the three hours allotted the comprehensive.[27] This detail is worth notice because it reveals how the academician occasionally equates the length of the trial he devises with its worth. Students have always seen through such sham, but the old torture still endures in hidden corners of academe.

Some students saw the introduction of the comprehensive examination as a means for securing more radical changes in requirements. If comprehensive examinations were to be "a progressive step," then the grading and semester examination methods must first be eliminated. A removal of requirements, examinations, and grades, and the substitution for them of successful completion of comprehensive examinations would "improve the standards of the university."[28] What they were arguing for, in effect, was the system introduced at Chicago by Robert Hutchins which permitted a student to move at his own pace through a series of examinations, the successful passage of which assured the student's ability to manage certain fields. Due to selective admission, Akron students were intellectually capable of adopting the Chicago plan, but the practical limitation already noted made it a most unrealistic concept on the Akron campus.

In 1933 and 1934 adjustments were made to the degree requirements in each college. Teachers College made more room for subject matter courses and proposed awarding the B.S. in Education degree to secondary teachers. Student teachers now had to prepare in three fields instead of the two formerly required. The College of Engineering and Commerce voted to award the bachelor's degree in the respective engineering fields in lieu of the general engineering degree. After adjustments in degree requirements in 1929, the Buchtel College of Liberal Arts added a new Bachelor of Science in Applied Arts degree. In 1930 an attempt to change the University calendar to the quarter system failed to receive committee endorsement. Two years later the grading period was changed from six to nine weeks, and the public posting of student grades was formally discontinued although the practice endured informally for many years. Freshmen requirements in English and mathematics were adjusted in some cases. All these changes are indicative of a considerable amount of thought being given to the kind of education needed by a student in preparation for his adult role. We shall see in a later chapter how these nascent probings coalesced into a unified plan of undergraduate education that placed Akron in the vanguard of American universities and colleges that were trying to bring some sort of order into a chaotic curriculum.

While undergraduate education was properly the main focus of concern in these years, George Zook was anxious to develop a broad program of graduate work. There is little doubt that he would have succeeded had circumstances been favorable, for he saw, perhaps more clearly than any other president of the University, the nature and extent of the commitment this level of work requires. In his annual report for 1928 he noted that the graduate effort was confined largely to Teachers College which produced about 12 master's degrees each year, and to the three fellows in rubber chemistry sponsored by local rubber company fellowships. He thought the social sciences were in a position to move toward graduate work because opportunities existed in the community to support research problems and thesis topics.

In 1931 President Zook appointed a special faculty committee under the chairmanship of Charles Bulger to revise regulations and assess opportunities for additional graduate programs. In that year there were 34 graduate students in the day session—17 in Buchtel College of Liberal Arts, 13 in Teachers College, and 4 in secretarial science.[29] As was true of the undergraduate work, a constant adjustment of graduate requirements was made during the early thirties, but again, the times were against any flowering of graduate activity.

By far the most dramatic venture of the Zook era in the area of graduate research and investigation was the establishment in Akron of the Guggenheim Airship Institute. Akron was the center of the lighter-than-air industry in the United States, thanks to the efforts of the Goodyear Zeppelin Corporation. There was great excitement in the industry over the promise of inexpensive, comfortable, and safe long-distance travel by dirigibles. The Guggenheim Foundation for the Promotion of Aeronautics had made grants to Stanford and the California Institute of Technology for research in lighter-than-air craft, and Dr. Zook was certain that Akron, as center of the industry, should apply to the Foundation to support research in which the University would have a major role. The Board of Directors authorized the grant application, and after the usual adjustment and delay, an appeal was made to the Guggenheim.[30]

The Foundation came through handsomely. In 1929 Akron received $175,000 with which to erect and maintain for five years on the municipal airport of Akron, a building housing a research institute to investigate the problems of lighter-than-air craft. This grant was supplemented by bonds in the amount of $100,000 issued by City Council in October to finance the city's share in the development of the site and building. In addition, the California Institute of Technology was awarded $75,000 with which to establish graduate fellowships and supervise the work of the research institute for a five-year period.[31] The concurrent development of the municipal airport, the great Goodyear Zepplin hangar, and the establishment of a class in aeronautics at the University raised enthusiasm to a high pitch.[32]

The California Institute of Technology was selected to direct the research program because The University of Akron did not have a degree program in aeronautical engineering and was not staffed with people who could handle the work. There was hope in Akron that after the first five-year period elapsed (ca. 1932–37), local talent would be prepared to carry on the research program. The director of the research effort was Dr. Theodore von Karman of Cal Tech, formerly of the Aerodynamisches Institute at Aachen, Germany, and he immediately brought to Akron his former assistant at Aachen, Dr. Theodore Troller, to serve as resident director of the Airship Institute. The research staff consisted of the director, his assistant, and five graduate fellows. Its work was to be devoted exclusively to high level research; it was not to give instruction. Local talent, particularly Dr. Karl Arnstein, Chief Engineer of the Goodyear Zeppelin Corporation, would be consulted as needed; indeed, cooperation with Goodyear was one of the chief reasons that the Institute was located in Akron.[33]

Under the immediate direction of Dr. Troller, the four-story institute building was constructed at the municipal airport. At the suggestion of von Karman, a vertical wind tunnel was installed. For an operation this size, a vertical tunnel was quite an innovation, and in order to publicize the activity von Karman suggested, partly in jest, that a girl parachutist then performing locally with an air show be hired to test the tunnel. She could float in the updraft while the scientists tested the effectiveness of various wind forces on her chute. "Unfortunately," wrote von Karman, "the pretty young aerialist took one startled look into the dark throat of the thirty-foot-long wind tunnel and quickly turned us down." Since the press wanted a picture, a screen was placed over the opening of the tunnel and she posed safely for the cameras.[34] With work completed, the Institute was prepared to carry on its research in 1932.

Among the studies carried on at the Institute were investigations of turbulence and its effect on aircraft. The world's two greatest dirigibles, the *Akron* and the *Macon,* were then under construction in Akron, but they were too far along toward completion to benefit from these studies. Both of the great airships crashed—the *Akron* in the Atlantic off the New Jersey coast, and the *Macon* off the Pacific coast of California—and in both instances turbulence seems to have played a major role.[35]

The death of these two great airships marked the end of effective efforts to make rigid craft a paying proposition. In America efforts would be confined to the building of the famous "blimps" and various non-rigid craft. In Germany, mother of the lighter-than-air industry, the fiery crash of the *Hindenburg* at Lakehurst, New Jersey, coupled with Hitler's antipathy toward the whole activity, spelled the end of these efforts. Thus, by a cruel turn of events, the Guggenheim Institute got started at precisely the time that the operations it was especially designed to facilitate were being phased out. Officials at Cal Tech must have sensed that there was little left in this research effort, for in 1934, at the expiration of the original five-year agreement between Akron and Cal Tech, the latter withdrew from any further connection with the Institute and The University of Akron assumed full operational responsibility for it. The Institute continued to operate under the direction of Mr. Curtis Meyers until the 1940's. Just as the "crash" of 1929 ended Dr. Zook's great plan for campus relocation, so now the crashes of the *Akron* and *Macon,* at opposite ends of the continent, spelled the ultimate doom of his other grand project, an undertaking which had taken courage and imagination to initiate. Zook's efforts were deserving of a better fate.

Concurrent with the rise of enthusiasm for lighter-than-air research at Akron came a swell of student enthusiasm for flying. The University offered courses in both lighter and heavier-than-air theory. In 1929 some 50 students were enrolled in the heavier-than-air course and 25 in the lighter-than-air courses.[36] The heroics of Charles Lindbergh in 1927 and the exciting exploits of Jimmie Collins, a former student at Akron, caught the student imagination. Briefly it appeared that Akron and its University would become national centers of flying instruction and activity, but the demise of the lighter-than-air industry (save for military uses in World War II), and the great depression squelched these prospects. World War II, with its massive infusion of resources into the aircraft industry, found the principal research and manufacturing activities far removed from Akron, even though Goodyear Aircraft produced the lethal Corsair fighters and provided other vital products for the aircraft industry.

Students with a hard-core interest in flying found an outlet in the formation of a glider club in 1931. Impetus for this effort came from Dean Ayer, and most of the student members were engineers. Prominent Akron businessmen contributed to the purchase of a Baker-McMillan Cadet II glider with a 37-foot wingspan. The glider was housed at the Akron airport and was available to student members after they completed instruction in flight theory and other relevant subjects. According to the *Buchtelite,* the only other college club of its kind was at M.I.T.[37] This extracurricular activity, coupled with an aeronautical engineering option in the curriculum, kept alive the interest in flying.

The quality of leadership is often a determining factor in the life and health of an organization. Some institutions carry on almost in spite of the kind of leadership they receive, but in times of crisis most—and one must certainly include universities—are highly dependent upon the skill, communicative ability, imagination, and patience of their leaders. It is not particularly helpful in telling the University's story to try to compare her presidents with each other; as one would guess, each had special strengths that were useful in carrying forward the school's mission, and each had certain limitations. Almost to a man, however, the presidents of the University have been excellent organizers. This capacity for producing order out of the diverse efforts of many persons is essential to good administration. It is indeed a happy circumstance for a university when it is fortunate enough to have at its head a man who has an original turn of mind and a charismatic quality that infuses an excitement for the intellectual life into the faculty and student body.

George Zook lacked charisma, and he was not much for transmitting real excitement to an enterprise—few people are—but he knew what was appropriate to the educational enterprise, and he could express his beliefs in language that rang true to the times. In his annual report for 1932 he summarized some of his thoughts on "The Function of University Education." He subscribed to contemporary criticisms of college education—students failed to get what they, as individuals, needed; they were too interested in extracurricular and outside activities; faculty failed to keep up with the demands of modern life; instruction was traditional instead of useful; college business methods were sloppy and inefficient—but these things would always be true because a college or university was an association of individuals, and, said Zook, "History records that universities have as often been in the rear of progress as in the vanguard." In the last 50 years, Zook continued, universities had been in the vanguard so far as production of material goods was concerned, and the old gap that once existed between academic institutions and the industrial world had largely been eliminated. "Colleges and universities have even gone over to a materialistic conception of life which naturally accompanies so much emphasis upon the production of goods," he wrote. Universities would be better advised to devote themselves to the study of problems of distributing goods.[38]

As for Akron, the University should devote itself primarily to educating a considerable number of young men and women who were capable of being intelligent and conscientious leaders of thought and action. This task must take priority over research, important though that was.[39] This assessment of the University's role was not convincing, however, for it did not identify specific measures whereby the University could be assured of moving closer to the goals the president had identified. Perhaps he assumed that it was the faculty's duty to adjust the academic machinery to attain these goals, and if so he was indeed wise for that was where the responsibility should lie. In this case, a movement aiming toward reform was already under way among the faculty.

Dr. Zook had come to Akron from a position that had exposed him to an overview of American higher education. This valuable knowledge was much sought after by educators around the nation, and throughout his eight-year tenure at Akron, President Zook was constantly called upon to serve on committees, commissions, and all those myriad bodies that proliferate throughout the academic world. Two of his assignments were especially meaningful. First in its impact upon American higher education was his work as Secretary of the Commission on Institutions of Higher Learning of the North Central Association of Colleges and Secondary Schools. In this role he led a study of accreditation standards in the North Central's 19-state area. His chief aide in this work was Dean Donfred Gardner who visited a great number of college and university campuses, assessing them for accreditation purposes and collecting data for a larger study the commission was undertaking.[40] A central office for this purpose was maintained on campus under the capable direction of Howard Doutt. The study resulted in a seven-volume work, *The Evaluation of Higher Institutions,* the first volume of which was written by Dr. Zook and Dean Haggerty of Minnesota and published after Zook had left Akron. The fifth volume in the series was the work of Dean Gardner. In the years before student personnel work was taken over by psychologists, his *Student Personnel Services* was a "bible" for those working in this vital university area.

The second of Zook's assignments, and one that had long-term influence, was his service on the National Educational Advisory Committee. This group presented a report to President Herbert Hoover in November, 1931, recommending the organization of a federal department of education. It is ironic that Dr. Zook voted against this part of the committee's work because he feared that the federal government would ultimately intrude on the autonomy of colleges and universities, overstepping in the process its own self-imposed limits.[41] Zook was soon to become the federal government's chief education officer, although he didn't know it at the time, but it would be many years before educational matters were raised to departmental rank in the federal government.

An expert in educational matters can spend his life on the road if he will, journeying from one place to another dispensing advice to troubled states, communities, school boards, etc. Zook made many trips, among them inspection tours to survey the state systems of California and Georgia. In turn, Akron was visited by those curious to know how an expert ran his own campus. Through his publications, Dr. Zook received requests for information and advice from around the world, including Russia, which apparently was most interested in the municipal university idea.[42] Close connections were maintained with conditions in Detroit as that city was consolidating several educational efforts in the establishment of Wayne University.[43] Toledo expressed interest in Akron's mode of operation.[44] The University of Louisville, a sister municipal institution, was so impressed with Dr. Zook that they offered their presidency to him, but he stayed at Akron, for which good judgment he received a handsome salary increase.[45]

It seemed only a matter of time until an opportunity would come along that would prove irresistible to Dr. Zook. It came in the spring of 1933. George Zook resigned, effective July 15, to accept appointment as United States Commissioner of Education.[46] His decision was widely regretted on campus and in the community. His "finest hour," so far as the students were qualified to judge, came in his farewell address to them at an assembly in June. In a "heart-to-heart" fashion, he talked of the importance that young people held for the world and urged students to strive for a long-range ideal. He briefly rekindled old enthusiasms by telling his audience not to give up hope for a new campus. Once Akron recovered from the economic disasters of recent time, he predicted, it would be glad to turn its attention to a plan for a new University.[47] As things worked out, it is fortunate that his successor did not follow this advice, but no one could have known then how impractical Zook's hopes for a new campus would prove to be.

Even a cool and reserved man must be moved by a standing ovation from students, accompanied by a singing of "Auld Lang Syne." Such was the send-off for President George F. Zook.

NOTES

[1] *Buchtelite,* Feb. 21, 1930.

[2] *Ibid.,* Apr. 10, 1931.

[3] *Ibid.,* Jan. 8, 1932.

[4] *Ibid.,* Nov. 7, 1930, Oct. 17, 1932.

[5] *Beacon Journal,* June 28, 1930.

[6] *Buchtelite,* May 13, 1932.

[7] *Ibid.,* May 13, 17, June 4, 1932.

[8] *Beacon Journal,* Nov. 9, 1925.

[9] *Buchtelite,* Nov. 23, 1932.

[10] Board Mins. II, 37; *Buchtelite,* Feb. 12, 1926, Feb. 18, 1930.

[11] Board Mins. II, 42.

[12] *Ibid.,* 333.

[13] *Ibid.,* 110.

[14] *Beacon Journal,* May 22, 1930.

[15] *Buchtelite,* Dec. 5, 1930.

[16] Board Mins. II, 203.

[17] Dean's Report, Buchtel College of Liberal Arts, 1929–30, bound in University of Akron Publications, 1930.

[18] *Beacon Journal,* Aug. 17, 1929.

[19] President's Report, 1928, p. 8.

[20] *Ibid.,* 1927, p. 11.

[21] *Beacon Journal,* Jan. 19, 1927.

[22] *Buchtelite,* Jan. 7, 1927.

[23] Council Mins., Sept. 27, 1927.

[24] President's Report, 1926, p. 12.

[25] *Buchtelite,* May 9, 1930.

[26] *Ibid.,* Mar. 27, 1931.

[27] *Ibid.,* Nov. 19, 1932.

[28] *Ibid.,* Feb. 25, Mar. 1, 4, 1933.

[29] *Ibid.,* Oct. 9, 1931; Council Mins., May 5, 1931.

[30] Board Mins. II, 67.

[31] President's Report, 1929, pp. 12–3.

[32] *Ibid.,* p. 11.

[33] Board Mins. II, 167, 362, 363; *Beacon Journal,* Nov. 27, 1929; President's Report, 1930, p. 12; *Buchtelite,* Feb. 20, 1929, Oct. 31, 1930, Dec. 8, 1931.

[34] Theodore von Karman and L. Edson, *Wind and Beyond: Theodore von Karman, Pioneer in Aviation and Pathfinder in Space* (Boston, 1967), p. 160.

[35] *Ibid.,* p. 161.

[36] *Beacon Journal,* June 4, 1929.

[37] *Buchtelite,* April 24, Dec. 8, 1931, Oct. 29, 1932.

[38] President's Report, 1932, pp. 9–10.

[39] *Ibid.*

[40] Various interviews with D. H. Gardner between 1948 and the present; Board Mins. II, 50.

[41] *Buchtelite,* Nov. 17, 1931.

[42] *Ibid.,* Sept. 28, 1926. Years later, President Norman P. Auburn would be a frequent visitor to the U.S.S.R. Some of these trips were undertaken for the purpose of securing information about the operation of the Russian education system. His observations were of interest to many persons inside and outside education.

[43] Leslie Hanawalt, *A Place of Light: The History of Wayne State University* (Detroit, 1968), Chapter 6.

[44] *Beacon Journal,* Oct. 2, 1928.

[45] Board Mins., II, 150.

[46] *Ibid.,* 308.

[47] *Buchtelite,* June 7, 1933.

XIV

Survival struggles in the depression

Again it was time to change the leadership of The University of Akron. The mood engendered by the commencement ceremonies in June, 1933, was anticipatory. Those whose memories focused on Buchtel College and the early days of the Municipal University found comfort in the presence of Parke Kolbe, then President of Drexel Institute in Philadelphia, who had come home to deliver the address and to receive the honorary Doctor of Laws degree from his Alma Mater. Had they but known that another old Buchtelite, Professor Hezzleton E. Simmons, was soon to be named president, they would have rested in the confidence that the values of an earlier time would not be forgotten.

In troubled times, there is a strong temptation for an institution to give leadership to a person already familiar with the problems. And so it was in the choice of Dr. Zook's successor. The *Beacon Journal* put its support behind selection of a local man for just that reason. The paper hinted that an outsider might expect too much support from a city already pressed to the extreme by its "lowered income."[1] Under Paul Litchfield's chairmanship, the presidential selection committee quickly recommended the appointment of Hezzleton Simmons, and their recommendation was accepted unanimously by the directors. His salary was $4,000 *below* the starting salary Dr. Zook had received some eight years earlier. Monetarily, at least, the rewards were not proportionate to the responsibilities of the office. The appointment was well received, the *Beacon Journal* editorializing that Simmons was popular, an experienced executive, and thoroughly familiar with the University's problems.[2]

There is no question about his complete identification with the school he was now to lead. In notes for a speech entitled "My Preparation for College," Simmons described how the ministers of his church at LeRoy, Ohio—Ira Priest, Albert Spanton, and "Daddy" Olin—had all been connected with Buchtel College.[3] In 1903 he had packed his suits, overcoat, telescope, some apples and walnuts, and made the three-hour trip to Akron on the Erie Railroad (it now takes 25 minutes by automobile). He paid $1 a week for his room on South Union Street and earned the money for rent and board by waiting on table. His class was the last to be systematically hazed, and Simmons liked the practice because it helped to develop class spirit.

His memories of the "good old days" included the time the faculty banned football—not because it was rough, but because the student-managed enterprise was a source of embarrassment due to unpaid bills and unmet obligations—and the students protested by staging a mock contest on the front campus lawn with the elaborately dressed "Mollycoddles" opposing the equally splendid "Milk-sops" while the referee, attired in a full-dress suit with white tie, maintained the proper aura of gentility. He remembered how the Carnegie gift for a chemistry building in which Simmons was to spend so much time was celebrated by bonfires that denuded the campus area of any lumber that wasn't securely fastened, and some that was.

Simmons graduated with the Class of '08, having been set back by a baseball injury. He had served as an assistant to Dr. Knight in the chemical laboratories while still an undergraduate, then secured a master's degree from the University of Pennsylvania and taught there briefly before returning to Buchtel in 1910. He succeeded Dr. Knight as Professor of Chemistry upon Knight's retirement in 1913. He directed the evening programs for many years, participated in all sorts of quasi-administrative tasks about the campus, served on innumerable committees on campus and in the community, and still found time to gain recognition as an outstanding classroom teacher and a contributor to the literature of rubber chemistry. On at least four occasions, he received attractive offers from industries who coveted his skills, but each time he decided to remain at the College. Like Dr. Knight, he did much industrial consulting. His long service with the rubber division of the American Chemical Society kept him in close professional association with the leading investigators in rubber chemistry.

Throughout his life, Hezzleton Simmons was a strong Universalist. He served on a number of national committees and served as President of the Ohio Convention. His devotion to the College and to the Universalists was greatly reinforced by virtue of his marriage to Agnes Whiton, Class of '06. For many years she edited various directories published by the College and its Alumni Association. Few were as well versed as she in Buchtel College and Akron University lore. No one was more completely a part of the old faculty community than the Simmonses, and they carried this sense of family into their relationships with faculty and administrators. Their summer place at Pointe au Baril, Ontario, where the Fred Ayers and the Parke Kolbes were near neighbors, was seldom without visitors from campus.

Each of us tends to judge a person by the limits of our contact with him so it is not surprising that one can find a variety of opinions among Simmons' former associates as to his management of the presidency, his relationship with the Board, his ability as a fund raiser, and so on. There is general agreement, however, on his approachability, his interest in people, and his sincere concern for the best interests of the University as he saw them. A former associate in the chemistry department wrote shortly after his appointment:

Dear Mr. President,

> *It is a great pleasure for me to be able to address this letter to you in this formal way. This is the last time . . . you will be addressed in this way. In the future I will continue to call you "Hez," in spite of your merited·promotion.*[4]

With enthusiasm the student body welcomed the "new deal" that the University was to receive under its new president. While casting no reflection on Dr. Zook's "highly successful career" as president, students felt that with a new leader the University should react "just as a smoothly working but old machine does at the injection of new parts."[5] Part of the "new deal" was Simmons' determination to maintain an "open door policy" so that he would not lose contact with students. Every president says that he welcomes students in his office anytime his schedule permits. Simmons did nothing to belie his invitation, and students did approach him on all kinds of subjects. This writer remembers how President Simmons helped him secure a summer job by calling the Summit County Engineer—one of his former chemistry students—and telling him he had a boy who needed work. In response to a question from the other end of the line, Simmons said, "I don't know whether he is a Democrat or not." Politics aside, the job was mine. Now, of course, size dictates that the Placement Office, the Student Personnel Office, or some other agency be called upon to help the student in need.

Some of the earliest advice given the new president came from Parke Kolbe who reminded him that "the great job necessary is popularizing the institution in the eyes of Akron people."[6] Simmons believed him: "My aim is to make the city of Akron realize that [a] worthwhile institution exists on the campus. I shall devote my time to raising the spirit of the students, and faculty, and in so doing, raise the spirit of the citizens." And the first step in projecting the University would be through the football team because people were interested in it. Publicity could also be achieved through music, theater, and debate which would "show off the cultural side of our students."[7]

PRESIDENT HEZZLETON SIMMONS (1933–51)

One of the chief purposes of a municipal university, Simmons thought, was to provide inexpensive education for all. But he apparently did not mean that "all" literally, for he frequently asserted that higher education was only for those who could profit from it. Others "shouldn't be exposed to it," for it hurt them and the University and took time and money. In the Municipal University "the student should be trained to be a more useful part of the society in which he lives." The new ideal of the University, said the president, would be to train students to make effective use of leisure time since he was convinced there would be more of it in the near future.[8] Although President Simmons was relatively inarticulate in stating the objectives of a university education, he was most resourceful in finding practical, tangible, overt ways of making students identify positively with the efforts of the faculty and others associated with the enterprise to achieve the maturing that is integral to a successful college experience.

We tend to speak of universities as if their course were determined entirely by their president. No doubt a strong president is the dominant force on campus; his is the voice heard alike by the public and the campus community. He is, however, the employee of the Board of Directors, and should that body take initiative into its own hands that fact can be brought home with immediacy. It was Simmons' experience to find himself the servant of a Board that had not yet reconciled itself to two facts of life—the New Deal was here to stay, and the last chance that the University would relocate at Good Park was gone. It is only fair to admit that what is now clear was much less clear in 1933. Simmons was more inclined than the Board to accept the times and adjust to them. The conflict between the president's position and the Board's is seen most clearly in the struggle to secure financing for a new building.

There had been no new building on Akron's campus since the engineering laboratory was expanded in 1919. With that exception, no new classroom space had been constructed since Curtis Cottage provided a minimal increase in 1906. The conversion of the President's House into Phillips Hall provided a few additional rooms.[9] In addition, Teachers College had the use of some classrooms in Spicer School, but that was a stop-gap arrangement.[10]

It was with a sense of urgency, therefore, that President Simmons reported to the directors in August, 1933, that they might consider applying for building funds under terms of the Federal Relief Act.[11] In October, Simmons brought a specific proposal before the directors. He thought that a utility building housing a gymnasium, theater, assembly hall, swimming pool, and facilities for student activities could be financed from federal work-relief funds as part of a city-wide construction program.[12] Since the building would be self-liquidating from fees, etc., the Board was willing to refer it to the Buildings and Grounds Committee for additional study. This project, said Simmons, would not mean abandonment of plans to build a new campus, since the proposed building would be an asset even if it were decided at some future time to dispose of the present campus and plant.[13] Parke Kolbe endorsed the plan saying that "Other universities throughout the nation have received money from the Federal government for similar purposes and the University of Akron certainly deserves her share."[14] But Cletus Roetzel, Chairman of the Buildings and Grounds Committee, was appropriately cautious, expressing reservations about any new building until the University's intentions with respect to relocation had been worked out. Several directors believed that erection of a new building would mean giving up forever plans to move the campus. The reservations expressed in the Board's November meeting discouraged the students who saw the project "doomed to an untimely and hurried death." They thought plans to relocate the campus were dead. It was something "for our grandchildren to think about."[15]

With the stalling of the utility building project came a plethora of proposals from faculty, students, and others as how best to meet the acute need for space. Simmons was investigating the Public Works Administration (PWA) as a source of building funds. He claimed, probably with justification, that "the University of Akron today uses its entire plant to a greater extent than does any other educational institution in the United States."[16] In February, 1935, the Board finally authorized President Simmons to proceed with efforts to secure a campus building project through PWA.[17] Not all the directors were happy about this. Indeed, at the next meeting Mr. Smoyer stated his belief that the policy of the federal government in projects for relief, such as the building program at the University, was basically unsound, "and this board should not be a party to it." Mr. Litchfield concurred, as did certain other directors. Then in one of those splendid inconsistencies that overcome rational men when principle conflicts with interest, the directors ordered it to be shown that the "sense of the Board" was to continue to pursue a federal grant if monies were available, and they directed the president and the secretary of the Board to continue to seek funds from federal sources.[18]

A period of great frustration followed as first one project, then another, seemed to have a chance at realization. In May the Board approved drawings and specifications for remodeling the engineering building preparatory to getting PWA assistance; then in June they cancelled the contract in favor of a new and broader one. After six meetings in two weeks, the directors signed an agreement with a Chicago firm to carry forward a federal building project which was first intended to embrace a large, centrally located classroom building; then, as this plan was turned down by PWA because its cost was too high, the project was switched to construction of a chemistry building, auditorium, and arts building, joined under one roof, plus a new library and gymnasium. In addition five minor structures would be razed and the remaining buildings remodeled. Funds were to be sought from the Work Progress Administration (WPA) instead of the PWA because fewer strings were attached to their programs.[19] One thing was certain; no one was thinking any longer of relocating the campus. It was clear that if anything were going to be accomplished it had to be done now.

Finally, in November, 1935, the University was informed that it had been awarded money for a large addition to the engineering building and for a retaining wall along the Carroll Street side of the campus. President Simmons had narrowed the grand project outlined by the Board to this modest size when it appeared there was little hope of getting the entire plan approved.[20]

Ground was broken February 4, 1936, for this building which would increase classroom space by more than 50 percent. It contained 25 offices, 15 recitation rooms, two lecture rooms, and laboratories for the physics department. The Alumni Association diverted $65,000 from funds raised for the proposed new campus to provide the local money required while the WPA provided $163,000.[21] Students suggested the building be named after President Simmons since he had led the way in securing it. The Faculty Council passed a resolution commending the president on his tenacity in bringing federal funds to the campus. When opened to classes the next year, however, the building was still known as the engineering building, but the students were not to be denied. In an open letter to the Board of Directors which appeared in the *Buchtelite* on November 18, Student Council formally requested that the building be named for the president, and on December 16 the directors approved "Simmons Hall" as the name of the new building.[22]

Well before Simmons Hall was completed, another mass of red tape enmeshed the president and his associates in their quest for a student activities building to be financed from federal funds. Since 1924, there had been repeated efforts to launch a drive for a student center. The men's and women's lounge rooms built into the basement of the library building had long been usurped for other purposes. They would not have served a student body as large as Akron's in 1935. Every year since 1927, Dean Gardner had called attention to the urgency of the need. Every annual report contained a plea.

The steps leading toward realization of a student activities building started on March 26, 1936, when Omicron Delta Kappa sponsored a meeting to make plans for such a building. Thirty-four campus leaders representing every activity at the University were called together and formed into a Committee of 34. Philip Sherman, President of ODK, was chairman of the Committee of 34 which was broken into four sub-committees to investigate the various functions a student building must provide. Sherman wisely advised the committee to forget about a campaign for funds. Lack of success in the past made the idea "absurd," such a campaign "possibly bringing in a mere $50." Support for the building would have to come from government funds or endowment, said Sherman, but since the endowment was non-existent, the answer was federal money.[23] The student body had already demonstrated overwhelming support of a plan to charge each student an annual $3 activity fee to help amortize the building. But the Board rejected the idea on the grounds that a fee would be more appropriate for operational purposes. The building would not be "on a million-dollar plan" said Dean Gardner, "but anything that will give the students a place to talk and relax in their free time is worth a great deal to all of us."[24]

In June the Board authorized $500 for preparation of plans, and they also had the graciousness and good sense to consider plans submitted by students. Application to the PWA was delayed until the summer of 1938, at which time $67,500 was requested as an outright grant and $82,500 as a loan from PWA. The full $150,000 was granted in October and construction commenced in December.[25] Work was expedited to such an extent that the building was opened in November, 1939. As requested by the students, the building was run by a student crew; Richard Sipes served as the first student manager. This building would never be known as "Dean Gardner Hall," said the *Buchtelite,* but then in a prophetic qualification, "at least not for a long time." The PWA, unlike its bureaucratic brother, the WPA, would not permit the naming of any building after a living person. Gardner would have to wait —until 1966 in fact—for his well deserved recognition.[26]

In his annual report for 1939 President Simmons revealed the never-ending character of this work: "When a person attempts year after year to make a report on the activities of an educational institution he becomes more and more aware of the routine character of the enterprise."[27] Although other urgent needs were still to be met, no more buildings would rise until the post-war years, but the incredibly long drought in new construction had been broken as had the reluctance of the Board to operate under the new modes of financing growing out of federal programs.

From the nadir of 1933, the financial condition of the University moved on a slow, unsteady upward trend. Money impounded in the liquidation of the First Central Trust Company of Akron caused the Board considerable anxiety, as did the fact that the 1934 budget was set about 6 percent under the 1933 budget.[28] This bad news was offset, however, by a surplus of more than $16,000 carried over from 1933, a surplus made possible by the issuance of script. Because of this happy circumstance, the most recent 10 percent faculty salary cut (May, 1933) was restored effective January 1, 1934.[29] For the first time since 1930, a catalog was to be published although it was considerably smaller than earlier ones. Faculty travel policy whereby the faculty member was reimbursed for a portion of the expenses incurred in attending professional meetings was reinstated. The leave policy was modified to include an agreement in writing that the faculty member granted leave would agree to return to Akron for a year. The policy was still prohibitive in that a faculty member on leave was required to pay the cost of his substitute out of his salary.[30]

Setbacks continued to occur even though the trend was upward. In March, 1934, for example, Max Boggs, the University Treasurer, informed the faculty and staff that it was advisable to meet the March and April payrolls "with a payment of 50 percent each month in tax notes."[31] As late as 1938 the Board requested City Council to issue tax anticipatory notes so they could meet payrolls in June, July, and August, and the Council complied. It was even necessary to reinstitute salary cuts in 1939 when those earning more than $1,400 were cut 5 percent because "prior to 1939 the University for several years spent more money than its normal yearly income."[32] Late that same year Simmons reported that curtailment in departmental spending made it likely that the fiscal year could be closed without the necessity for borrowing funds.

These conditions resulted from the University's general financial position which in turn was determined by its level of tax support. That level depended on the city tax duplicate. Akron's tax duplicate had fallen off drastically during the depression; appraisals of property at lower value and delinquent tax payments had, by the end of 1938, deprived the University of more than $100,000 that it should have received. The mood of the city was fearful, and at times ugly, during much of the thirties. Resentments that festered in the rubber shops spilled over into the great sit-down strikes of 1935–38. The plight of those who depended upon public tax money seemed secondary to men who were battling for their more immediate personal interests and needs. The writer was told by one old battler from the picket lines that he and his friends had nothing against Akron University as long as it was a "poor man's school," but they weren't about to support it if admission requirements and costs were raised to the point where a poor boy couldn't get in. The "rich kids," he said, could go away to school if they wished, but "Akron U must remain peon U."

It is to be expected, of course, that in the general malaise of the thirties the University might appear to be an unnecessary luxury the community could ill-afford. A letter from OLDTIMER to the editor of the *Akron Times-Press* contains many of the points raised by its critics. The University, said OLDTIMER, was forced upon the city by a group of "obliging but stupid" City Council members, and it had "lived like a parasite" on the taxpayers ever since. The cost of operating it was partly responsible for the "financial fix" which Akron was in. Money spent on the University over the years would have gone a long way in retiring Akron's bonded indebtedness. Furthermore, he argued, Akron University was not a particularly good school; "Its own students are its loudest knockers, especially night school people." State schools had lower fees, and there were many advantages to going away to a larger state school. Among the advantages were outstanding teachers (few great teachers are found in small municipal schools), better facilities, extracurricular activities, beautiful campus, and being away from "mama's apron strings."

Akron taxpayers, the letter continued, would not likely feel any distress concerning the survival of an institution that has for years been a "white elephant." Rather, taxpayers were concerned about an inadequate garbage collection system, inadequate fire, police, and health departments, excessive public indebtedness, and loss of homes due to inability to pay property taxes. Taxpayers were "fed up" with unnecessary expenses and could not be blamed for trying to get taxes lowered through the proposed charter amendment.[33]

The charter amendment was the issue that called forth this indictment. In the fall of 1935 "a few people with selfish interests," as one University official identified them, succeeded in putting on the ballot a proposal to repeal sections 86 a, b, and c of the city charter.[34] These sections assured the citizens of Akron health, fire, and police protection, street lighting, garbage collection, and the maintenance of public schools. Also included was the guarantee that Akron University would obtain up to 55 hundredths of a mill in city tax support. A citizen's Committee of Eighty was formed to combat this measure, and President Simmons was elected temporary chairman of the group as it organized its campaign. The vote to repeal failed by a three-to-one margin to the great relief of the University community. Since this issue embraced so many vital public services, it is impossible to attribute the victory to the University's popularity with the voters. Nevertheless, the *Buchtelite* liked to think that it showed Akron was "no longer the forgotten university buried in a big industrial city."[35]

Throughout this period of challenge, the trend that had forced students to pay an ever larger percentage of the cost of their education continued. President Simmons liked it no better than George Zook. The situation would have been worse than it was had the University not had the good fortune to participate in the distribution of sales tax monies allocated to the city in 1935. Despite this help, the student was providing 50.5 percent of the University's income in 1938 in contrast to 13 percent in 1914.[36] The *Beacon Journal* warned that Akron was "approaching the limit of progress possible with its restricted support from taxation and student fees." The school's greatest need, continued the editorial, was "the creation of a liberal endowment fund."[37] But conditions for soliciting private money were less promising than they were during the unsuccessful attempts of the previous decade. No private gifts eased the situation, and as each budget from 1936 through 1939 was lower than the previous one, it was clear that financially the school was going backward.[38]

A turning point of sorts was reached in 1939. After many years of effort by concerned parties in Akron, Cincinnati, and Toledo, the state limitation of 55 hundredths of a mill for municipal universities was removed and they could now seek additional operating levies providing tax monies up to one mill.[39] The Board of Directors immediately requested City Council to levy a tax of 33 hundredths of a mill for a period of five years and to submit this levy to the voters in November, 1939. For reasons unexplained, the directors amended their request in August and asked for only 25 hundredths of a mill. City Council approved the amended request and, on November 7, it carried by a narrow margin. Thus the University was assured an increase in operating income of approximately $68,000 a year for five years based on the tax duplicate then current.[40]

In 1941, the budget, exclusive of the Guggenheim Institute, exceeded half a million dollars for the first time. Faculty salaries were raised in the first general increase since before the depression, although the maximum increase was only $200. Expenditures for books and periodicals reached $10,000 that same year, a milestone for the chronically under-nourished library.[41] These modest breakthroughs marked the end of the depression with respect to the financial position of the University.

The stabilization of the financial picture helped stall two threats to the status quo. In 1938, Gus Kasch of Akron introduced a bill into the State Legislature that would have placed municipal universities under state control.[42] The Board of Directors and President Simmons opposed this plan, and they were reassured by the governor that he would not support the legislation. Kasch, who regarded himself as the conscience of the people, had previously suggested that he and two other recently elected members of the Akron Board of Education be named to fill three vacancies on the University Board of Directors.[43] One might gather from these suggestions that Kasch was a little suspicious of the manner in which the University was being run.

The other threat to the status quo that was cleared up after a long period of ambivalence was the possibility of relocation. In January, 1938, the directors adopted provisions for returning legal title to the west side real estate to its former owners.[44]. It seemed the end of a splendid dream. But a happy ending of sorts was in store as campus expansion since 1946 has provided a new plant, and in the process the

University has stepped forward as the pacesetter for the redevelopment of downtown Akron. In keeping with the current mood of higher education, the University's location is ideal with its proximity to the inner city, its resources, and its problems.

During the 1930's a significant shift occurred in administrative roles within the University. Following the death of C. R. Olin in 1932, Mr. Maxwell P. Boggs was appointed Clerk of the Board of Directors and Secretary of the University, a title that was soon changed to Secretary of the Board of Directors and Treasurer of the University.[45] He performed his duties conscientiously and was a strong influence on the president. It was his unhappy responsibility to be the "nay-sayer" during these years of stringent financial control, but with his penchant for finding the humor in things, he managed to remain a student favorite, always ready to enter into a skit or other pleasantry.

The office of Registrar finally came into its own as a full-time operation with the appointment of Professor Richard Schmidt to the position in place of Miss Gladys Weeks who returned to full-time duties as the president's secretary.[46] Miss Weeks, along with Spanton, Bulger, and Simmons, was a veteran whose service went back to Buchtel College days. There is more than a little truth in the old observation that the president's secretary holds the University together.

In 1933, Albert Spanton who had served as Acting Dean of Teachers College since Bankes' departure, requested to be relieved of this position. The directors promptly elected him Vice-President of the University (an honorary position rather than a functioning one) with a salary increase of $1,000.[47] Professor Howard Evans was appointed to the deanship and held that position at the time Teachers College became the College of Education in 1935.[48] Another key administrator who joined the staff at this time was Leslie P. Hardy, formerly with the public school system. Appointed Director of Adult Education in 1934, he soon became the versatile handyman of the administration and was used by President Simmons to solve problems of a diverse nature as they arose.[49] More of Hardy's resourceful contributions appear in a later chapter.

Another change, and a very natural one, occurred in 1938 when Albert Spanton resigned as Dean of the Buchtel College of Liberal Arts "because . . . it is best both for myself and for the university."[50] He remained as teacher and head of the English department. For his long and devoted service to the institution, the University Council, as the old Faculty Council was now known, recommended the honorary degree, Doctor of Literature, be conferred upon him at the 1938 commencement. The new dean was Charles Bulger who, since 1933, had been Dean of Graduate Study.[51] In addition to these responsibilities he was head of the Modern Languages department. Although none of these operations was of great size (there were 110 students working on graduate degrees in 1936–37, for example), it required a good deal of nimbleness to keep up with the various demands thus placed upon one man's shoulders. But Bulger was equal to the task, representing each interest as effectively as limited resources would permit.

Among those who left the University was Marjorie Mitchell, who resigned as Dean of Women in 1937 to assume the presidency of Cottey College for women.[52] Probably no appointee in a university comes under greater scrutiny than a new Dean of Women, but Mitchell's successor, Miss Helen Battrick, seemed to pass the test. Maybe it was due to her capacity for refraining from arbitrary judgment as when asked soon after the appointment what she thought about the new craze among coeds for ankle socks. "Wear them when they're appropriate," she said, "It's up to you to guess when they are appropriate."[53] Whether by design or by accident, it was an observation worthy of a Solomon.

While the administration underwent changes in personnel, President Simmons repeatedly praised the faculty for their "loyalty" to the institution in trying times. It would be easy to read back into those years an interpretation of this "loyalty" that is more appropriate to the present. Faculty mobility of the 1960's has reduced greatly the amount of attachment younger scholars feel toward any given institution. The feeling abroad in the scholarly world is now all too often that the scholar can be lured away from any school at any time if "the price is right." The cynic might say that scholars of the thirties would have been just as mobile, just as ready to leave their university for greener pastures, had there been the opportunity. While it is impossible to refute this charge convincingly, those who work in the history of colleges and universities usually assert that there was a different attitude a generation ago. The young new appointee did not come to his position with one eye cocked for his next job unless he was one of the handful whose compulsion is such that they know their talents will ultimately grace the faculty of a prestige graduate school. Although a few faculty members left Akron for "better" positions from time to time, there was much stability in the faculty until World War II opened the doors of change.

A faculty position at the University during the 1930's was no plum in a material sense. Faculty salaries continued to compare unfavorably with national norms. Akron faculty salaries were well below the median of some 190 institutions. When the 5 percent additional salary cut of 1939 was imposed, President Simmons commented, "I marvel at the loyalty of the faculty to the administration."[54]

One important improvement in conditions of employment was the reinstituting of indefinite tenure in 1937 for those above the rank of instructor who were recommended by the president.[55] In 1935 the Board adopted recommendations from the president that normal retirement age be 65, with the Board exercising an option to continue a person on a year-to-year basis to age 70.[56]

But, of course, longevity is not the critical focus of tenure. The critical concern is that the faculty member be protected from peremptory and capricious action by the administration or the Board in cases where he is exercising his right to be heard on subjects within his competence. Ideally, the tenured professoriate should feel a security that permits it to speak out, even on controversial subjects, without fear of retaliation because of public spite or differences with the university community. Only such an environment will produce the free inquiry and the willingness to take a stand that characterizes a healthy intellectual climate.

Although the depression brought protest in its wake, there were no visible "radicals" on the University faculty during the 1930's. If one can assume that what he reads and hears of faculty views on political, economic, and social conditions is a true reflection of their thinking, one must conclude that the faculty members were very conservative. Certainly many faculty members seemed comfortable with the New Deal and its implications for American Life, but no responsible observer would ever equate sympathy for the New Deal with radical social thought. There wasn't even a Technocrat on the engineering faculty, possibly because Dean Ayer made an impassioned statement decrying the onesidedness of Technocracy's panacea for America. When interviewed by the student press on matters of current social interest, faculty members responded with platitudes which revealed nothing of note.

There is a self-selective process in the hiring of new faculty that tends to keep like-minded people together. Thus, for example, an Oberlin with its reputation as a "liberal" institution attracts "liberal" faculty members and students while, until very recent years, one would not find many denominational schools, or small state schools, attracting faculty members interested in espousing "liberal" or "radical" ideas— unless one counts Populist sentiment "radical." When Akron confronted the prospect in 1938 of hiring a bright young faculty member who "thought otherwise," there was a tendency to back off. This man was well known on the Akron campus from his undergraduate days. He had since earned a Ph.D. from a top-flight school and was teaching in a state university in the west. The head of his department wrote on his behalf to Dean Bulger:

My attention has been called to certain opposition which has developed on your campus to Dr. _____, rumors that attribute to him radical tendencies while an undergraduate . . . No such characteristic has come to my attention either through classroom instructions [sic] or through personal conferences and group discussion. If he had any radical tendencies I would have been apprised of them because in [our state] there are many well-meaning citizens who assume full responsibility as protectors of the young against exposure to radical professors.

My colleagues share my feeling that Dr. _____ is not only a stimulating teacher but also a genuine scholar and a fine man.[57]

Bulger replied that ". . . there was no very vigorous opposition to him; only a rather mild degree of uncertainty." Crossed out in the draft of the letter was the line: "We are perhaps a little over cautious because of some recent experiences."[58] If this cryptic reference was to a faculty member, it does not appear to have found its way into the record. The new faculty member was hired and proved to be the stimulating teacher he was reputed to be, and his only radical tendency was smoking his pipe in class where smoking was forbidden.

This triumph over rumored radicalism was offset by what seemed to be the precipitate firing of Mr. Frank Maturo, an Instructor in Modern Languages, for remarks he allegedly made to a feature writer from the *Akron Beacon Journal*. Maturo was quoted as saying that "men no longer want their women pure."[59] Maturo claimed he had really said "Purity has almost vanished as a masculine ideal of womanhood."[60] In reporting the incident to the Board of Directors, President Simmons revealed that he had received many letters and telephone calls about the statement and had held interviews in his office with parents and representatives of civic groups. He felt that the University had suffered a distinct loss of prestige as a result of the incident. He believed that, in the main, Mr. Maturo had indeed been misquoted, and that the entire controversy had been "unfortunate."[61] Though no action was taken by the directors in February, 1934, when Simmons first brought the matter before them, it was the "sense of the board" that the resignation of Mr. Maturo at the end of the academic year might be a "practical way out" of the situation. This would clarify the University's position and not cause Mr. Maturo "any immediate hardship."[62] In March his services were severed effective July 1, but apparently not much was known of these circumstances until the end of classes since protest against his dismissal did not appear until after the first week of June.[63]

The students came to his defense claiming that it was unfair to dismiss a professor for holding and expressing opinions even though most students might not agree with his opinion. Some students and alumni signed a petition urging his reinstatement.[64] The Board of Directors claimed it had no interest in railroading Maturo; one director said the Board would gladly have heard any remarks Maturo might have cared to make. The *Beacon Journal* editorialized that Akron "loses standing as an intellectual center by gagging its instructors on and off the campus."[65] Since Maturo was not using the classroom to encourage sex freedom, said the editorial, he was unjustly treated by being fired. The writer next charged, without any evidence, that since Maturo's dismissal, University instructors had to submit all speeches to the school "press agent" for censorship. The directors fired Maturo, he continued, after one clergyman and a group of clubwomen demanded his dismissal. To that extent, "one clergyman and a group of clubwomen are running the university."[66] Later attempts by Maturo to secure reconsideration of his case were fruitless. It was a most unheroic episode in the University's experience.

Throughout these times when concerns of interest to the faculty were being considered, the AAUP was little involved. President Simmons was not a member, possibly since the Akron chapter was organized about the time he went into administration, but he claimed sympathy for the ideal of AAUP. He knew that both Dr. Kolbe and Dr. Zook had supported the organization and once told a regional meeting at Toledo, "I would like to have every one of our faculty eligible for membership in AAUP identified with it. This would make it a more effective organization." He went on to say that he would welcome faculty suggestions routed through AAUP relative to promotions.[67] Despite this receptive attitude, the AAUP did nothing to enhance its role as a professional organization; it remained essentially moribund.

In considering faculty working conditions, it is always necessary to keep in mind the conditions of the city. If the advantages of the community are limited, that is one less tie that the university has to attract and hold its faculty. We have already alluded to the condition of Akron during the depression. Physically, the city was in tenuous shape, and although not so apparent at first blush, it was also declining culturally. More than ever, Akron had given up hope of securing for herself the cultural benefits that her more affluent citizens could find in Cleveland. There was no ground swell of popular support for using tax monies to build civic centers, auditoria, exhibition halls, art galleries, and the like, nor was private money interested. In an interview with Fred Barton for *The Akronite*, Francesco DeLeone threatened to move to Cleveland where the opportunity for leading orchestras and training pupils was greater. "Akron has lost some of her fineness," he said. "Remember how we staged *Alglala* a few years ago? Now all the music you hear is a lot of hillbilly stuff over the radio. That's too bad."[68] Culturally, Akron was in a slough.

NOTES

[1] *Beacon Journal*, June 14, 1933.

[2] Simmons to "Harry," July 11, 1933, Simmons Papers; Board Mins. II, 316.

[3] Simmons Papers.

[4] Zimmerli to Simmons, Nov. 1, 1933, *ibid.*

[5] *Buchtelite*, Sept. 22, 1933.

[6] Kolbe to Simmons, Sept. 14, 1933, Simmons Papers.

[7] *Buchtelite*, Sept. 22, 1933.

[8] *Beacon Journal*, July 1, 1933.

[9] A former Akron resident, Miss Harriet Phillips of New York, gave a collection of her paintings, art books, and etchings to the University in 1927. The paintings were largely her own work. They were hung in the former President's House which was renamed Phillips Hall in her honor. See the *Beacon Journal*, Oct. 12, 18, 1927, and also President's Report, 1927, pp. 6–7.

[10] *Ibid*, p. 14.

[11] Board Mins. II, 319.

[12] *Beacon Journal*, Oct. 20, 1933.

[13] *Buchtelite*, Oct. 21, 1933.

[14] *Ibid.*, Oct. 25, 1933.

[15] Board Mins. 11, 328; *Buchtelite*, Nov. 14, 1933.

[16] Board Mins. II, 338; President's Report, 1934, p. 17.

[17] Board Mins. II, 374.

[18] *Ibid.*, 375.

[19] The story can be traced in *ibid.*, 383, 391; *Beacon Journal*, June 13, 22, 24, Dec. 13, 1935.

[20] *Buchtelite*, Dec. 14, 1935; *Beacon Journal*, Nov. 9, 1935.

[21] Board Mins. II, 407; President's Report, 1936, p. 9.

[22] Board Mins. II, 531.

[23] *Buchtelite*, Mar. 28, Apr. 29., May 9, 1936.

[24] *Ibid.*, May 20, 1936.

[25] *Beacon Journal*, May 28, Aug. 16, Oct. 30, 1938; Board Mins. II, 510.

[26] *Buchtelite,* Feb. 10, 1939.

[27] President's Report, 1939, p. 3.

[28] Board Mins., II, 349–50.

[29] President's Report, 1934, p. 11; *Beacon Journal,* Jan. 13, 1934.

[30] *Buchtelite,* Dec. 20, 1933; Board Mins., II, 334; President's Report, 1934, p. 14.

[31] UArch., VF (Finance-salaries).

[32] Board Mins., II, 497; President's Report, 1939, p. 4.

[33] *Buchtelite,* Oct. 9, 1935.

[34] *Ibid.,* Oct. 30, 1935.

[35] *Ibid.,* Sept. 28, Nov. 6, 9, 1935, May 29, 1936; President's Report, 1935, p. 14.

[36] President's Report, 1936, p. 8.

[37] *Beacon Journal,* Jan. 18, 1937.

[38] Board Mins., II, 410, 456, 495, 551.

[39] Representative George Harter of Akron introduced the measure in March, 1939. *Beacon Journal,* March 14, 1939; Board Mins., II, 590.

[40] President's Report, 1938, p. 5; President's Report, 1939, p. 5.

[41] Board Mins., III, 45, 46, 50.

[42] *Ibid.,* II, 494.

[43] *Ibid.,* 404; Kasch to Schroy, Nov. 23, 1935, UArch., box 4/8a/65.

[44] Board Mins., II, 491.

[45] *Ibid.,* 281.

[46] *Ibid.,* 317.

[47] *Ibid.*

[48] *Ibid.*

[49] *Ibid.,* 354.

[50] Dean's Report, Buchtel College of Liberal Arts, 1936–37, bound in University of Akron Publications, 1937.

[51] Board Mins., II, 442, 487, 502.

[52] *Ibid.,* 446.

[53] *Buchtelite.* June 30, 1937.

[54] *Beacon Journal,* April 12, 1938; President's Report, 1938, p. 8.

[55] Board Mins., II, 442.

[56] *Ibid.,* 369.

[57] Senning to Bulger, June 4, 1938, UArch. 21/1/VF.

[58] Bulger to Senning. n.d., *ibid.*

[59] *Beacon Journal,* June 7, 1934.

[60] *Ibid.,* June 9, 1934.

[61] Board Mins., II, 338.

[62] *Ibid.*

[63] *Ibid.,* 340–41.

[64] *Beacon Journal,* June 13, 1934.

[65] *Ibid.,* June 8, 1934.

[66] *Ibid.*

[67] Notes for a talk delivered Dec. 3, 1938, Simmons Papers.

[68] *The Akronite,* III, no. 1, p. 10.

XV

General education and the restructuring of the University

Change in a university curriculum usually comes about in bits and pieces. Seldom does an institution engage in a self-conscious review of its program with the intention of recasting it in its entirety. Naturally many new curricular areas had been added as the University reached out to acquire new fields of specialization, but there is a significant difference between adding new degree programs and courses and creating a fundamentally new educational philosophy for the institution.

In the mid-1930's, the University of Akron embraced "general education." This involved more than simply replacing an old curricular requirement with a new one. It involved recasting the framework of the University so that the entire operation was directed at preserving a unity, a wholeness in the curriculum, in student advisement procedures, and in extracurricular (co-curricular) activities.

"General education" means different things to different people. As practiced at Akron, however, it describes a program aimed at recapturing some of the educational philosophy of an earlier time. In an increasingly specialized world, the curriculum had become overly specialized in response to community demands. The educational effort had become fragmented so that there were no longer those common bonds that had once been the property of *all* college students. It did not seem appropriate that a college graduate in engineering, or commerce, or education could complete his undergraduate work without being exposed to the world's great ideas, its culture, its infinitely complex physical makeup, its institutions, its history. It is an exaggeration, of course, to argue that the student in a vocationally oriented curriculum encountered none of this material. However, it is true that he encountered only a minimal amount of it.

The Akron program had another interest beyond that of producing a "well-rounded" college graduate. It emphasized the necessity of assisting its students to become good citizens. This noble objective—one advocated by Thomas Jefferson—was consistent with Akron's concept of her responsibility as a municipal university. The community needed skilled persons who were also "good citizens," therefore the University should provide not only the skills, but contribute as well to its graduates' competence as citizens.

In the late nineteenth century, as observed in Buchtel College, forward-looking, "progressive" educators were demanding a break with the unity of knowledge represented by the Classical Course and its variations. In a world starting to place a premium on specialized knowledge and competence, the rigidities of the old system seemed to frustrate progress. College had as its purpose the perfecting of a select few for the genteel professions. It was only a happy accident when a student exposed to Greek, Latin, rhetoric, and classical literature (with a bit of mathematics and science for disciplinary value) ended up in business or some other work-a-day activity.

The free elective system broke the old unity, and it was soon followed by courses designed to train students for a particular kind of work—engineering, law, business, etc. In the early years of the Municipal University, Parke Kolbe gathered under its wing every specialized training and service function that could be accommodated. This swing of the curricular pendulum—now freed from traditional re-straints—to the other extreme, is typical of a college in the throes of change.

The key to this new diversification of effort was the rapid discarding of the old admission requirements; first Greek, then Latin, and then, depending on the specialty sought by the student, various other portions of the old classical preparation. Akron shared this abandonment of the classical framework with most other public universi-ties and many private ones as well. The faculty of the University of Chicago, for example, voted in 1916 to abolish Latin as an admission requirement to the B.A. degree program, a move which "meant inevitably the abandonment of the entire system of education of which the classics were a symbol."[1]

The move away from the old unity resulted in a revival of the "generalist-specialist" debate which in one form or another is almost as old as American higher education. Until the twentieth century, the debate was one-sided, favoring the gener-alist position; but the emergence and triumph of the scientific-technological-intellec-tual revolution swung the balance. This "explosion of knowledge" brought the specialist to the fore; and as he cemented his position in the academic world, the generalist sought ways of preventing him from achieving a total take-over of the curriculum. One of the techniques employed to recapture some of the balance was the introduction of general education.

No one can accurately date the first blush of an academic fashion, since much unstructured thought and conversation goes on before ideas become formalized into a program. There are evidences that the general education concept was discussed on the Akron campus at an early stage of its development. During World War I and immediately thereafter, a number of universities, most of them eastern, took an initial, hesitant step toward what were later called "survey courses" which dealt with some broad area of man's experience and concern. Columbia's "Introduction to Civiliza-tion" was perhaps the most emulated course of this kind.

The first record of Akron's faculty hearing about survey courses—an integral part of general education packages—was at the inaugural ceremonies for President Zook held in January, 1926. In his inaugural speech, Dr. Zook addressed himself to the growing concern about the need for a common core of knowledge for the encour-agement of good citizenship. He talked about the "unnatural separation" between the last two years of high school and the first two years of college. Perhaps this break could be bridged by more effective "articulation" between the high schools and colleges.[2] The University of Chicago was groping in the same direction as its faculty labored over the formulation of a college that would prepare students for entrance into the specialized work of the University.

More directly to the point, however, were the remarks of Dr. Charles H. Judd, head of the Department of Education at the University of Chicago, who called attention to the proliferation of courses in response to the growing body of knowl-edge, and to the increasing numbers of students going to college. One of the "promis-ing signs" for mastering this situation, he said, was the appearance of "general survey" courses—general science in the high schools, for instance—and the "college courses which have been so widely discussed and somewhat less widely given since the war, especially in the social sciences, introducing students to the general methods of thinking about the world and man's place in the world." Such courses, he said, "represent an effort to gather up the details with which specialized courses of a more highly technical character have dealt and to make them comprehensible to students who will never have time to pursue numerous specialties."[3]

Late in 1927, Dean Spanton, Dean Bankes, and Professor Warren Leigh re-quested President Zook to call a meeting of the Executive Committee "to consider the introduction of a four hour course in Science Survey and a four hour course in Social Science Survey," to be required of freshmen in the arts curricula, in the Teachers College, and in commerce. These courses were to replace American Gov-ernment. It was further recommended that a director be appointed for each survey course. President Zook referred the matter to the respective deans.[4]

There is no evidence that the deans acted, but they may be excused because all energies in the next two years were pressed toward relocation of the campus at

Good Park, and after that the immediate requirements of dealing with the depression and its limitations were foremost in everyone's mind. But a series of annoyances and inconsistencies gave rise to a growing awareness that some of the academic machinery that had been ignored should be refurbished. Accordingly, on September 23, 1930, Professor Simmons moved in a meeting of the University Council that a committee be appointed "to revise the present by-laws and organization of the university and bring together the state laws governing municipal universities for recommendation to the board."[5] It appears that all Simmons had in mind was to clarify tenure and leave policies, academic freedom, and other such matters rather than advocating any reorganization of the curriculum. A Reorganization Committee of University Council was appointed, however, under the chairmanship of Dean Ayer, but the members had a difficult time determining what they were to study.[6] In May, 1931, another council committee was appointed for purposes of studying a divisional organization for the University. Dean Gardner having to decline the chairmanship because of duties with the North Central Association, Richard Schmidt took over leadership of this group which had two members who were also serving on the Reorganization Committee.[7] Almost at once the two committees discovered that their areas of concern overlapped, so they started to meet together. Finally, in December, 1933, the two groups were merged, and the following spring, with its work on tenure and related topics out of the way, it was restructured as the Committee on Reorganization with Schmidt as chairman and Ayer, Spanton, Crecraft, Gardner, Evans, and, later, Bulger as members.[8] It was this group that brought forth the new program.

Their first task was to construct a satisfactory statement of University objectives. It seems strange now that this task had not been undertaken earlier, but Buchtel College probably regarded its purpose—a short statement of which appeared in the catalog—as self-evident, while the role of the Municipal University was frequently enunciated by Kolbe and Zook, even though these objectives were only briefly stated in the catalog. It was the involvement of Dr. Zook and Dean Gardner with the North Central Association that convinced them of the need for a well defined, written statement of objectives, for the North Central was in the process of changing its accrediting procedures so that a school would be judged in terms of how well it did what it said it was doing rather than on some arbitrary quantitative standards.[9]

As a first step in formulating objectives, the committee requested from each instructor a statement of objectives for each of his courses and for himself as an instructor. The answers were separated into three broad categories: the cultural objective, in which content, technique, discipline, and social and cultural background were emphasized; the social-civic-physical objective, focusing on the development of American society, its cultural background, and on character training; and the vocational-professional objective, concerned with preparation for the professions, for vocations, and for advanced study.

As finally written, the University objectives reflected these emphases. On November 27, 1934, University Council adopted this statement of general objectives with the following preamble:

> *The University of Akron is a municipal university supported in large measure by city taxes. It, therefore, aims to devote its efforts to the work of higher education especially for the people of Akron.*[10]

Then followed a statement of the three chief aims which we may condense as (1) giving the students a survey of the chief fields of knowledge, (2) developing and strengthening a sense of social responsibility in students and (3) preparing students for greater social and individual effectiveness in public service, in commerce and industry, and in the professions. And then as a further aim, the University would "provide expert advice for various civic and educational agencies; . . . furnish a scientific testing service for commerce and industry; . . . offer education programs for the dissemination of culture and knowledge."[11]

The program constructed around these objectives was built with the special mission of the municipal university very much in mind. In the opinion of Dr. Zook and many of the faculty, Akron had lost sight of its special area of service by becoming too much like any private university that maintained selective admissions standards, treating all its students as though they could and should finish a conventional four-year degree program in four years in preparation for conventional jobs in business and the professions. In some mysterious way, the student should know at entrance what it was that he wanted to spend the rest of his life doing. Put in terms of a positive program, if Akron were to fulfill her mission of public, urban education, then her admissions policies would have to be liberalized to take a broader spectrum of applicants; programs of less than four years duration would have to be developed to accommodate the student who could not afford the longer course and to accommodate the student who would be better off in a vocationally oriented program of less than four year's duration; and, finally, a good, responsible counseling system would be needed to place students where they had a realistic prospect of success, if not in a full four-year curriculum, then in some suitable alternative. Running through all these considerations was the conviction that, regardless of program, each student should take courses designed to prepare him for effective citizenship.

The endless debate that characterizes major curriculum changes caused the committee to go off into all sorts of blind alleys as it attempted to formulate a wholly new program that would achieve the objectives they had set forth for the University. To help keep themselves at the task, the members set a deadline of February, 1935, for reporting to University Council. At the committee's suggestion, a Faculty Educational Conference was held in December during which Dr. John Dale Russell brought the faculty up to date with the general education movement as it was progressing nationally, but more important, it gave the faculty a preview of the thinking and work of the local committee.[12] Some of the opposition expressed to specific proposals for Akron were useful in causing the committee to recast its thinking along lines more acceptable to the faculty. The committee pressed on with its work and met its self-imposed deadline. Its recommendations were presented to Council in a series of five meetings held in February and March, 1935, each meeting dealing with selected portions of the total report.

The first of these Council sessions was devoted to a paper, prepared by Dean Evans, which argued the theoretical reasons for changing in the direction of general education. In later sessions specific recommendations were adopted. The admissions procedure was changed so that an applicant had to be a graduate of a senior high school or have equivalent training, his four-year high school average had to be such as to establish "a reasonable probability of success in college," and his ratings in psychological and achievement tests also had to give "reasonable probability of success."[13]

The next portion of the work—recommendations concerning the curriculum of the "lower college"—was presented by Dean Spanton. The purpose of the lower college (freshman and sophomore years), said the report, was to furnish a general cultural education for students who planned to enter the "upper college" (junior and senior years) and earn an academic degree, and also for students who desired approximately two years of general education but who did not desire to enter upper college or were unable to. Further, it was to furnish pre-professional courses and terminal courses of an occupational nature to students who did not desire to enter upper college or were unable to.

Ordinarily, the work of the student in the lower college would cover two years, but the abler student could shorten this time by taking examinations for credit. General education courses required of all students were:

1.	English, oral and written	6 hrs.	first year
2.	Hygiene, physical and mental	4 hrs.	first year
3.	Introduction to Social Sciences	6 hrs.	first year
4.	Introduction to Natural Sciences	6 hrs.	first year or second
5.	Introduction to Humanities	6 hrs.	first year or second
6.	Mathematics, Accounting or Foreign Language	6-7 hrs.	first year or second

The lower college was also to offer pre-professional courses and technical courses of an occupational nature—secretarial science, engineering, home economics, applied art, commerce—for students who could not, or would not remain at the University.[14]

The lower college, or as it soon came to be known, the General College, was intended to function as a sort of a training ground for the specialized work carried on in the upper colleges. The upper colleges were the degree-granting College of Liberal Arts, College of Engineering, and College of Education. These upper colleges, each with its respective dean and faculty, were divided initially into divisions, but the divisional arrangement was eventually confined to the College of Liberal Arts alone, where a Humanities Division, a Social Sciences Division, and a Natural Sciences Division were organized, each with its chairman who had responsibility for advising divisional majors and for coordinating curricular and other matters of concern to the division. During the reorganization, commerce and secretarial science moved to the Social Sciences Division of the College of Liberal Arts from the College of Engineering, and psychology was placed in the College of Education. An early sentiment to place mathematics and the physical sciences in engineering as a separate division died in committee.[15] A student with an arts and sciences major had to complete a distributive requirement that kept him from confining his courses solely to the division in which he was carrying his major program.

A source of later conflict was the requirement that to be eligible for "admission" to the upper colleges, a student had to complete at least 64 semester credits, including all the required general courses and the prerequisites of his particular program, and maintain a "C" average for all work attempted. One effect of this rule was to practically guarantee that any student admitted to an upper college had the ability to make it all the way through to a degree.

It may be well to digress a moment and say a word about the counseling and advisement of students. Heretofore there had been only haphazard student advisement. Either the admissions officer served as an informal adviser, especially with freshmen, or a lucky student might find a sympathetic and well informed faculty member who would give him the benefit of his counsel. Prior to 1935, the Dean of Men and the Dean of Women had no formal responsibility for academic counseling; but, as a matter of fact, a growing number of students made their way to these offices in an effort to find someone willing and able to give academic direction. Faculty members started to send confused students to the deans for help.[16] The "student deans," as we may call them, also maintained personal records for most students which sometimes revealed personal and family problems that were factors in a student's ability to perform satisfactorily.

Dean Gardner was well informed about the student personnel movement developing on some campuses where trained advisers were available to assist students. In 1935, Gardner, Mitchell, and Schmidt were given responsibility for advising General College students. With the resignation of Dean Marjorie Mitchell, student services were consolidated in a new Dean of Students Office, and in the spring of 1937 Donfred Gardner was appointed dean. He was assisted by an Adviser of Men and an Adviser of Women. His staff then took on the responsibility of academic advisement of freshmen and sophomores (i.e. General College students), after which time the student went to the head of his major department for academic advisement.

Academic advisement was seen as but a portion of the need to help the student realize his potential in every aspect of college life. Dean Gardner quickly consolidated the student personnel program. He had established a freshman orientation program in 1926 and in 1933 had added the practice of using upper classmen as freshman counselors during the orientation period. Complete personnel files were maintained in the Dean of Students office. In addition to personal information, the file contained a picture, high school record, health record, outside work experience, and scores made on psychological tests. These forms were filled out by an adviser in the Dean of Students Office during an initial interview with the incoming freshman. Periodic grade checks in the first semester and thereafter indicated to the counselor when it was time to call a student in and have a chat with him concerning his progress.

Other student services centered in this office. Responsibility for the entire extracurricular program, including the fraternity system, focused there. Even as old Buchtel felt it part of its charge to help students achieve social graces, so did the Dean of Students' staff. In this effort they instituted lectures on social customs, advised students on proper dress, and, to achieve results, worked through classmates and sometimes even parents or pastor. The Dean of Students Office also ran a part-time employment agency for jobs both on and off campus. It also handled placement of graduates. The Health Service and University physician, first introduced in 1929 in the physical education department, became a responsibility of the office. In short, everything that touched the lives of the students was of interest to the personnel counselors since they operated on a philosophy that looked toward developing the fullest possible growth of the student in all aspects of his life, not just the academic.[17]

With the new machinery fairly well identified and approved by the Council, an enormous amount of work remained to be done during the spring and summer to prepare the new courses for the class entering in September, 1935. Marjorie Mitchell was given responsibility for preparing suitable adaptations of the English courses, Dr. Jay O'Hara was to prepare the Introduction to the Social Sciences, Dean Gardner the Humanities, Richard Schmidt the Natural Sciences, and Dean Evans and Hjalmar Distad the Hygiene courses.[18] The first task of each was to determine the format his course would take, and at this point the limited physical facilities came into consideration. The only room large enough to handle big lecture sections was the basement of the First Church of Christ Scientist, a long block away from the campus. Use of this room was a temporary expedient pending completion of Simmons Hall. Simmons 155 was to be well known to every Akron student for many student generations. Lack of laboratory space compelled those who formulated the Introduction to the Natural Sciences to rely on a lecture-demonstration presentation. English would continue to be taught in small sections while the common format for humanities, hygiene, social science, and natural science was the lecture-discussion method. Most courses used the two lecture, one discussion per week format with the discussion sections limited to approximately 30 students. Testing was initially done largely in the discussion sections although later this was modified.[19]

Work on the courses progressed through the summer. Syllabi were prepared, mimeographed, bound, copyrighted, and sold at cost by the University. Required readings were chosen and discussion leaders assigned. The social science course was designed to avoid the "problems approach" and focus instead upon a study of human nature, the complex of social forces, attitudes and organizations that comprise our modern social order, and to awaken the student's capacity for constructive criticism on social questions.[20]

The natural sciences treated such broad topics as the origin and meaning of science, man's knowledge of the universe, changes in the earth's surface since its origin, the nature of matter, man's application of science in relation to the necessities of life, and life on earth.[21]

The humanities focused on the major contributions to our culture of previous civilizations with an emphasis on literature, religion, art, and music. Attention was also given to a study of the close relationship between man's physical and mental development, and to the development of the student's sense of appreciation, and his critical and sympathetic outlook. It was clear that there was to be no effort to indoctrinate student thinking. A source book prepared by the staff was accompanied by Harry Elmer Barnes' *History of Western Civilization.*[22]

The hygiene courses were divided: physical hygiene in the first semester and mental hygiene in the second. The content of physical hygiene is self-evident. In mental hygiene, a noble effort was made to help the student understand himself, his motivation, his abilities, and his limitations with respect to certain norms of our society. Its inability to accomplish what it set out to do is a matter for later comment.[23]

As this program of introductory survey courses developed over the years, a number of personnel changes occurred. Dr. Roy Sherman soon replaced Jay O'Hara as Director of the Introduction to the Social Sciences and became the principal lecturer. His folksy manner was a byword with students. In dealing with social issues at an explosive time in our nation's history, it is not surprising that Dr. Sherman became embroiled in his share of controversies for he was not a man to back off easily when he favored an idea. Active involvement in Republican politics also kept the pressure on him to demonstrate his objectivity. Master of the long pause, at one time or another he battled the Catholic church, the University administration, and the Democratic party.

Meanwhile, upon his assumption of new advisement responsibilities, Dean Gardner moved out of the humanities picture and his role as director and lecturer was assumed by Don A. Keister, Class of '31, who honed the lectures and the course content to a fine edge of efficiency and effectiveness over the years. With a sharp, incisive, critical mind, two jumps ahead of those with slower mental processes, he brought informed, articulate direction to the course. As is true of all effective teachers, he was the embodiment of those intellectual virtues he purported to teach.

The natural sciences course, started under Richard Schmidt's direction, was taken over by Professor Dwight Gray. An able physicist, he managed the difficult feat of placating his science colleagues, led by the inimitable Walter Kraatz in biology, who decried a science course with no laboratory instruction.[24] Here inadequate facilities clearly dictated that pragmatic considerations prevail over principle, for there was no chance of accommodating this course in the sorely limited lab space then available on campus. Gray's successor, Dr. Paul Acquarone, was long identified with the course and brought to it a breadth of competence in the sciences that few of his captive students were able or willing to appreciate.

The introduction of general education produced adjustments in other areas of academic life. For the first time since old Buchtel College days, all students were required to take the same package of core courses so that every student in the school had some classes and professors in common with every other student. In other words, general education provided a core of common experience with which any graduate or student could identify. The best known instructors were the lecturers in the survey courses—Sherman, Keister, Acquarone, *et. al.* Whether engineer or arts major, each student had heard about pithecanthropus erectus from Dr. Sherman or St. Augustine's *City of God* from Dr. Keister. Like it or not, the bond was there.

One heartening sign of the influence of the introductories was the notable increase in library usage that accompanied their establishment. To gain more space in the library, the women's league room was remodeled as a reading room for the General College introductory courses. The librarian reported that in 1935–36, under the General College plan, 155,906 books circulated as compared with 82,329 the previous year.[25] What the report could not show was the frantic activity this near doubling of usage involved for the staff. Crowded facilities and wear and tear on materials became a major concern. It was found that occasionally a lecturer in one of the introductory courses would suggest that a particular article would be helpful and, as soon as class was over, a flood of students would descend on the library, each seeking the one copy of the appropriate journal. As often as not the latecomers would find part or all of the article torn from the journal by a selfish student ethically unfit to be in a university. This bane of the professional librarian is, unfortunately, still at work even though strenuous efforts have been made in recent years to minimize loss by making it easy and inexpensive for students to have material copied.

During the academic year 1936–37, chairmen were appointed for each of the divisions in the Buchtel College of Liberal Arts—Charles Bulger, Humanities; Earl Crecraft, Social Sciences; and Fred Householder, Natural Sciences. Dean Spanton was pleased with the working of the new procedure at the end of its first year. He felt that the "New Plan," as he called the restructuring, "although far from perfect is justifying itself." Spanton seemed particularly pleased with the "great advance in care in dealing with students in the first two years." Students were better advised, and they were treated with greater consistency. With respect to the introductory courses, Spanton wrote: "Basing my opinion only on student opinion expressed concerning the worth of these courses, I should be inclined to list them in the order of Humanities, Natural Science, Social Science, Hygiene."[26]

This optimism for the promise of the reorganization at an early stage must be tempered somewhat by one of the most basic and enduring problems faced by any college or university—the inability or unwillingness of many instructors to change their customary way of doing things in order to maximize the student's experience. Charles Bulger helped formulate the new plan. He was imbued with the spirit of possibilities that pervaded the thinking of the committee members as they strove to bring the student alive to his full range of possible achievement and to remove old barriers to such achievement. But in June, 1937, he had to report in his capacity as Chairman of the Humanities Division:

> At the upper college level few instructors have grasped the possibilities of adjusting the courses to the capabilities of the individual. The instructors are still proceeding on the traditional classroom attendance and specified number of courses program. The criterion seems still to be hours of classroom attendance rather than knowledge of subject matter. Judged by what instructors do, there seems to be no faith that a student can learn anything anywhere other than in a classroom. This continues the characteristic neglect of the really alert and worthwhile student.[27]

While obviously unfair to those dedicated, talented, and imaginative members of the faculty who were not slaves to petty conformities, this harsh indictment was probably deserved in all too many cases. Judging from what goes on in classrooms all over the country, it is optimistic in the extreme to believe that teachers do not need to free themselves from tyrannies of form and conventional thinking that have limited their ability to communicate with students. For the Akron story, the point is simply that no form of reorganization or restructuring of the academic machinery or curriculum can remove the deficiencies of certain instructors. What *can* be accomplished by reorganization is to arrange the academic program and machinery so as to minimize the impact of instructional inadequacies on student morale and progress.

Early assessments of the new program were available. Studies were made of student progress through the General College and of instructional costs, both studies being made in the spring semester, 1937. With regard to student progress, of the 439 students entering as freshmen in September, 1935, 10 percent had been dropped for inadequate grades, 8 percent withdrew for various reasons, 23 percent did not return to school, though eligible, and 39 percent were still enrolled. Of the 39 percent still enrolled, only 44 percent were right on schedule toward meeting requirements for "promotion" to the upper colleges by the end of their sophomore year. Another 108 students were below the "C" average required for promotion, and since the University was primarily a degree-granting institution, the Committee on the General College, who made the study, wondered whether or not "the funds and resources of the university should be expended on such students."[28]

This development was of great concern to President Simmons, particularly the requirement that a student have a minimum "C" average to qualify for promotion to the upper colleges. Students doing inadequate work in the required introductories might do much better in courses of their own choosing in the various specialized fields. "I believe," said Simmons, "that our present requirement of the same quality standard for promotion to the Upper College as that required for graduation is not sound." He suggested the Committee on Admissions and Advanced Standing study the matter. The study was made. It had the virtue of indicating again that the standards of performance expected in the new introductory courses were as demanding, as far as grades were concerned, as were those in the old program, but the committee found no convincing reason to change its position with respect to the "C" average for promotion. In this matter of education policy, care had to be taken not to place "too much emphasis . . . upon the concept of cost."[29]

Cost was a major concern of the president, and he had frequently expressed a desire to increase the size of upper college classes to achieve operating efficiency. A cost study in 1937 showed that the cost per student credit hour for 1936–37 ranged from a low of $1.46 in the introductory courses to a high of $7.37 in advanced engineering courses.[30] It was proper for Simmons to call attention to this disparity, but it was equally proper for the committee to place its priority with the maintenance of standards. To his credit, President Simmons accepted the committee's decision, but through the remaining years of his tenure, he continued to try from time to time to convince the faculty to abandon the promotion requirement.

Since it appears that the faculty and administration were in a mood to assess the new program in the spring of 1937, it is not surprising that an Appraisal Committee was appointed at council's request. Members of the Appraisal Committee were persons other than those on the Reorganization Committee (which was discharged in 1939), and they were charged with making an appraisal of the entire reorganization plan "in order to ascertain the good and the bad points."[31]

Under the chairmanship of Howard Doutt, this hard-working committee brought in a "Preliminary Report" to the University Council in May, 1938. A tremendous amount of data had been collected from faculty and students, most of it through use of a questionnaire that was much more carefully and scientifically structured than most instruments of that description. With a 74 percent return from the faculty and near 100 percent from students (because of close controls imposed by the registrar) the committee had an unusually complete expression of opinion with which to work.

The report was highly critical of the divisional plan.[32] The impression reported earlier by Spanton and Evans that the divisional system was functioning satisfactorily was not at all representative of majority opinion. Since the deans maintained their traditional functions and powers, there was "neither the simplicity of a small college, where everything is settled by one faculty, nor yet the moderate complexity of a large university; but an extreme complexity which is altogether unjustified by the exigencies of the situation." The same ground was covered at least three different times by many faculty members—in division, college, and University Council (they might have added department). Either the colleges or the divisions should go, and since Buchtel College of Liberal Arts had to be maintained as part of the agreement made with the Buchtel College trustees, the divisions would be sacrificed. Council voted to discontinue the administrative activities of the divisional chairmen, and once again the department heads were to deal directly with the deans.[33]

With respect to the division's legislative powers, council referred that matter to the College of Liberal Arts for recommendation since it was the only body affected. In November, 1939, the college recommended that the legislative powers of the divisions be retained, and council accepted this recommendation.

The Appraisal Committee also recommended that the functions of the Committee on the Administration of the General College be distributed and the committee abolished. This was done, the bulk of the functions passing to the University Examiner and the Dean of Students who were now responsible for admission and retention procedures in the General College. Council adopted this recommendation, but not an accompanying one that suggested appointment of a director for the general college introductory courses.

With respect to the introductory courses, the data gathered by the Appraisal Committee showed that all things being equal (which they were not) the faculty favored the "old plan" of course requirements over the large introductories; but, with a bow toward reality, the faculty favored retaining the introductories because of their cost efficiencies. Since salaries had just experienced another slight setback, the faculty was understandably alert to cost considerations. Although not convinced that the introductory courses were "effective introductions to courses in their departments," faculty members strongly favored retaining the new plan, but only if certain changes and modifications were introduced. There was no ground swell of sentiment for a return to pre-1935 conditions. As a corollary to these opinions, the faculty approved of the new way in which student advisement was being handled in the General College.[34]

The restructuring process received a serious blow in October, 1937, when a report from the Engineer's Council for Professional Development (the chief accrediting group in engineering) "criticized the facilities, curricula, salary scale and faculty loads." The difficulties inherent in adjusting the facilities, salary, and load needs have been indicated elsewhere, but the criticism directed at the curriculum was pointed at the General College plan and the introductory courses. As interpreted by Dean

Ayer, the accrediting team found that the professional curricula departed "rather widely from the customary pattern of American engineering colleges, apparently because of the necessity of fitting into the broad program of the General College."[35] Put another way, the accrediting team was saying that were it not for involvement in the General College plan and the introductories, the Engineering College would have a more conventional curriculum. The difficulty was placed before University Council which responded on February 24, 1938, by granting permission to the Engineering College to waive any part, or all, of the introductory courses in Humanities, Social Science, and Hygiene (Natural Science already having been waived). For the time being, "the Engineering College was . . . out of the general education program."[36]

This revealing incident demonstrates the degree to which the best-laid plans of a university for restructuring its effort can be thwarted by external pressures. Vested professional interests have often stood in the way of colleges as they attempted to fulfill their function in a manner that to them, at least, seemed to offer advantages. Paradoxically, when another accreditation team from the same engineering society visited in the late 1950's, the College of Engineering was criticized for not having gone far enough in the direction of general education although the college was once more a part of the general education program and was finding it difficult to fit all of its requirements into a five year co-op program.

In the year following the Preliminary Report of the Appraisal Committee, a substantial amount of tinkering with the academic machinery was undertaken to offset some of the criticisms leveled at the new program. During that year much additional information was collected from students, and an analysis of this material formed the body of the Second Report to University Council in May, 1939.

The most revealing results of the student opinion poll were in relation to the introductory courses. Fifty-five percent of the students polled preferred general introductory courses covering wide fields of knowledge rather than specific courses in each field. However, by a 10 percent margin they opposed the idea of requiring all students to take all of the general introductories, but by a 3 to 1 margin they endorsed the idea that students should take the general introductory course most relevant to the field in which they intended to specialize. A substantial majority indicated that they approved of the lecture-discussion method of presentation, they believed that lectures, discussion methods, and tests should be improved. At the risk of over-generalizing, it might be said in summary that there was no great hostility to the General College plan and the introductories as such, but there was a strong desire for more flexibility in the new program, and there was agreement that the teaching and testing could be improved.[37]

Also revealed by the Second Report was the fact that the lecture-discussion teaching method in the introductories saved 112.7 teaching hours per week. At this time in the University's life, there was a frank recognition that cost considerations were an important part of the rationale for general education. At a later time, when the University was much more affluent than it ever dreamed it would be in 1939, those who wished to consider abandoning the introductory courses were confronted with the fact that to revert to a pre-1935 program of selective requirements in each of the basic fields of knowledge would be prohibitively costly, particularly in the sciences where there was insufficient lab space to accommodate the hordes of students that would descend upon science departments.

One final body of data analysed in the Second Report should be mentioned. It had always been thought within the University that an extraordinary number of students changed their programs and their prospective majors after their freshman year. No figures were available on the situation nationally, so it was impossible to know whether the condition at Akron was an abberation or simply a normal manifestation of youthful indecisiveness. In truth, it was probably both. The report showed that of the seniors graduating in 1939, some 56 percent had changed their objectives at least once since admission to the University. Of the junior class that year, 50 percent did not know what their career objective was.[38] Spot checks in later years would indicate that the 1939 test was not exceptional. This high level of change stemmed partly from a lack of ability to achieve the goal originally set. Any number of boys who had their ambition set upon engineering, for example, discovered that they had confused their mechanical aptitude and interest with the theoretical and abstract work essential to the engineer. Many would-be doctors foundered in chemistry. The toll was particularly heavy in courses that required competence in mathematics and abstract reasoning. Although the General College did not help students decide what they wanted from college, it did facilitate adjustments to student programs.

General Education is a continuing story at The University of Akron. At the time of this writing it remains the keystone of the curricular structure. In the post-World War II years the pattern underwent substantial change in detail, but the objectives remained essentially as they were in 1935. In its place, we shall discuss the changes and restructuring that took place in 1955 under the direction of Dean Donfred Gardner who remained the most effective and articulate proponent of general education in the years after Spanton, Bulger, Evans, Schmidt, and others who had strongly supported it had left the campus. We shall reserve for that time a summary assessment of the strengths and weaknesses of this concept that has been at the heart of the University's program for more than three decades.

NOTES

[1] Daniel Bell, *The Reforming of General Education: The Columbia College Experience In Its National Setting* (New York, 1966), p. 19. Although principally an account of Columbia's experience, Bell's book provides the best account and analysis of general education yet written.

[2] Don A. Keister, "General Education at the University of Akron," TS in UArch., box 20/0/33 #2. Hereafter referred to as Keister, "General Ed."

[3] University of Akron, Publications, 1926.

[4] Spanton to Zook, Nov. 28, 1927, UArch., box 4/8a/99.

[5] Keister, "General Ed.," p. 15.

[6] In his own inimitable fashion, Dean Ayer wrote a humorous parody of the work on University reorganization. Some of his colleagues failed to see any humor in it. UArch., VF (Committee Reports).

[7] Council Mins., May 26, 1931.

[8] Keister, "General Ed.," pp. 20–21.

[9] Interview with D. H. Gardner, ca. 1966; Keister, "General Ed.," p. 21.

[10] *Ibid.*, p. 25.

[11] *Ibid.*

[12] *Ibid.*, p. 40.

[13] *Ibid.*, p. 46.

[14] *Ibid.*, p. 47.

[15] *Ibid.;* President's Report, 1935, pp. 12–13.

[16] Interview with D. H. Gardner, April, 1968.

[17] President's Report, 1937, p. 13.

[18] Keister, "General Ed.," p. 53.

[19] *Ibid.;* President's Report, 1935, p. 13.

[20] Keister, "General Ed.," p. 55.

[21] *Ibid.*, p. 62.

[22] *Ibid.*, pp. 64–66.

[23] *Ibid.,* p. 67.
[24] *Ibid.,* p. 45.
[25] President's Report, 1936, p. 11.
[26] Dean's Report, Buchtel College of Liberal Arts, 1936–37, University of Akron Publications, 1937.
[27] UArch., 21/1/VF.
[28] Keister, "General Ed.;" p. 68.
[29] *Ibid.,* pp. 69–70.
[30] President's Report, 1937, pp. 8–9.
[31] Keister, "General Ed.," p. 73.
[32] Preliminary Report, Appraisal Committee, UArch., VF (Committee Reports).
[33] *Ibid.*
[34] Keister, "General Ed.," pp. 76–7.
[35] *Ibid.,* p. 89.
[36] Council Mins., Jan. 20, Feb. 24, 1938.
[37] Second Report, Appraisal Committee, May, 1939, UArch., VF (Appraisal committee).
[38] *Ibid.*

XVI

Student life: protests, prizes, and perseverance (1930–1939)

The majority of students in the Municipal University were from families that had little to spare for their child's college education. By familial sacrifice, but especially through their own work, thousands of "poor" students have passed through the University. And they came when there were virtually no scholarships or other monetary aids available. Motivation and hard work were the secrets of their success; what the sociologists call "upward social mobility" drove the student, often with the backing of his family, to seek the skills and background that a university could provide. The distinguishing characteristic of the Municipal University was that it made it possible for the student to live at home, thus keeping the cost of his education to a minimum. Earlier it was noted that in 1929, at the height of what was supposed to be a boom economy, 75 percent of the Akron high school graduates who went on to college chose their local University, many out of financial necessity.[1] By far the largest number of students came from what were then still referred to as the "working classes."

Despite overcrowded campus facilities, and despite the deep depression both of dollars and of spirit that enmeshed Akron during the early thirties, enrollments continued to rise. By 1935, 2,520 students, day and evening, made Akron the fifth largest university in the state.[2] "While it always seems possible to admit one more student," said President Simmons, "we have now reached the point where . . . we must limit the enrollment."[3] The limitations imposed involved a slight tightening of an already selective admissions policy. By 1939, some 3,050 students were registered, and despite the addition of Simmons Hall to campus facilities, classes spilled over into nearby churches and Spicer School.

Even while one-third of Akron's citizens were unemployed, or dependent upon an unemployed head of the household, a considerable percentage of University students had jobs, most of them part-time, and all of them at relatively low pay. This was the condition in 1932–33; three years later a survey by the Dean of Men revealed that 47.6 percent of the freshman men were working at outside jobs, of which some 30 percent were in rubber shops. The average work load for this group was 25 hours per week.[4] Many of the girls also worked off campus. There was much embarrassed explaining to do when the *Times-Press* published the calling cards of local prostitutes, cards which read, "I am working my way through Akron University." Solemn denials from University officials set the record straight.[5] Meanwhile, always quick to make a virtue out of necessity, the student newspaper editorialized that Akron students were showing a new spirit in educational values by getting away from a concern with making money and by "using their opportunity for education to learn how to live."[6]

The first substantial relief for many hard-pressed students came with the introduction in February, 1934, of the Federal Emergency Relief Administration's (FERA) part-time employment plan for college students. Some 89 students, 40 of them coeds, were in the initial group of participants. They were to be paid not less than 30 cents an hour for work about the campus. These students averaged about 50 hours of work per month in clerical jobs, research, library work, maintenance, and special assignments. The next fall, 146 students were employed at a 40-cent minimum, some of them being assigned to jobs in public agencies off campus.[7]

In 1935 the FERA program gave way to the National Youth Administration

(NYA). The new agency permitted the University to enlist up to 12 percent of the full-time enrollment in a work program; and 156 students were enlisted in the first group. They received an average pay of $15 per month, but it would have been impossible for many of them to continue in school had it not been for this aid. Among the group were "some of the best students enrolled at the University."[8] A year later fewer students were applying for NYA aid, probably because improving economic conditions made it possible to get jobs, but also because the quota was reduced—by 1938 only 9.3 percent of the enrollment of 1936 could be accepted into the program. Signals were changed again in 1939 and Akron's NYA dollar allotment was increased to a level that made it possible to create nearly 20 new jobs. The program closed after the 1941–42 session as the nation moved to a wartime economy.[9]

Some NYA students were engineers. The depression revealed one of the problems faced in cooperative educational practice; when jobs are unavailable, the co-op student is left high and dry. The brief, one year experience of 1920–21, when a similar job scarcity had created problems for the co-ops, had not prepared anyone for the prolonged crisis of the early thirties. Early in 1933, only one-fifth of the engineers who should have been on co-op jobs could be placed.[10] To meet the emergency, the hours required for co-op work were reduced; Goodyear and some other plants offered Saturday use of their shops; local industries helped the University set up its own industrial shop; and in time the city's engineering department funneled what work it could to the engineering students. By 1934 the worst of the crisis was past, but placement continued to be a major concern for some years to come.

As was true of all federal work programs, there were complaints from various people that the FERA and NYA programs were "make work" programs, hence wasteful and unnecessary. It is true that some of the tasks assigned were not of major consequence. One student was an "umlaut putter-on."[11] His task was to place the two little dots over appropriate letters in the manuscripts used in German classes. Most of the work was clearly worth doing, however, and with the perspective that 30 or more years gives us, these programs appear sensible even if the rear guard of "rugged individualists" saw waste, extravagance, or even a plot concealed therein.

For all the difficulties associated with the depression, student life went on, somewhat curtailed in its more formalized portions, perhaps, but nevertheless as vital and frenetic as ever. Prior to the opening of the Student Building in 1939 the main campus eateries and hangouts were the "Buchtel Eat," presided over by Nick Yanko who soon went on to bigger and better things, "Ted's Akron U. Confectionery," presided over by Theodore Topalu, and "Schroeder's." As with student hangouts the world over, these places were immortalized in song and story, some of them unrepeatable, and they became part of the tradition on the Hilltop. Periodically they were in trouble; in 1934 Yanko and Topalu were fined for operating gambling machines on their premises. (The *Buchtelite* turned them in and was never forgiven by some students for this defection to the enemy.)[12] The proprietors fared better in a most interesting decision handed down in 1936 by Judge Ray B. Watters of the Municipal Court who dismissed charges against Yanko and Topalu for violating the city ordinance prohibiting sale of beer or liquor within 300 feet of a "public school." The Judge ruled that Akron University did not fall into the class of "public school" because it was not supported entirely from public funds and it did not receive appropriations from the general school fund.[13]

The Buchtel Eat was familiarly known as "The Greek's," apparently because students assumed that Nick Yanko was Greek. A little clever sleuthing revealed, however, that Nick was a Macedonian, his wife was Hungarian, and of those who worked for him, two were Scots, two Croatian, and there was one each of Italian, Bulgarian, Serbian, and French extraction. For several years after Nick closed the

Buchtel Eat, Topalu retained an establishment on Buchtel Avenue. To more recent student generations it was known as "Terry's." It was nearly the last haunt of the student (or faculty member) who preferred risking a thumb in his beer to the relative cleanliness of the Student Building, and those insights that flow most readily in the presence of mild alcoholic stimulation could not be turned on in the dry confines of the Student Building.

Throughout the decade, the old cry of "no school spirit" was raised again. Class organization died, and with it class rivalry. Efforts to reinstitute the class rush and other related activities were unsuccessful. An intensification of student political activity in campus elections helped fill this vacuum. But then a scandal of sorts, involving some ballot box stuffing in the 1931 May Queen election, caused the administration to forego that election for a year. Some heated election battles were fought over Student Council seats and the presidency of the student body. The old charge of fraternity domination of campus politics was raised periodically; and indeed this domination did occur, because the "Greeks" were more interested and better organized than the Independents.

The election of 1936 generated this objection: political parties should be abolished since they served only to put fraternity people in office thereby gaining status for certain fraternal groups at the expense of the larger student body. "Neither the old-line combines, the Buktal and Zipper parties has ever contributed an iota to the welfare of the student body," claimed a *Buchtelite* editorial.[14] In the '36 contest Paul Bagwell (Buktal) won the presidency of the student body over Wilbert "Dick" Wright (Zipper) which may have had something to do with his decision years later to run for the governorship of Michigan. (He was well equipped vocally: Professor Donald Hayworth tested student voices and found Bagwell's the loudest. On a calm day, according to Hayworth's calculations, Bagwell could be heard at a distance of a mile and a half.)[15]

If the student wanted to get away from campus events and hangouts for a while, there were things to do in town. He could catch the stage show at the Palace. The big bands of the age of swing came through Akron on a regular basis. In 1936, Ted Lewis, Jan Garber, Jimmy Dorsey, Henry Busse, Little Jack Little, Eddie Duchin, and others appeared, to be followed shortly by Benny Goodman, Tommy Dorsey (featuring a skinny kid named "Frankie"), and even Glen Miller. One of the cultural high points must certainly have been the appearance of Phil Spitalny and his All Girl Band, featuring "Evelyn and Her Magic Violin." On campus as elsewhere the dance craze was the "Big Apple," and parents were concerned that their children were going to come to no good end with such foolishness.

In 1939, excitement ran high over a beauty feud between Akron and its near neighbor, Kent State. A "beauty team" of seven coeds from each school was chosen on the basis of good looks and charm. Edgar Martin, creator of the comic strip "Boots and Her Buddies," was brave enough to judge the contest; the poised and pretty Akron girls walked off with a victory. Some enthusiasts wanted to make it an annual affair, but fortunately it didn't catch on. That same year marked an important addition to University tradition, however, when Fred Waring, at the request of the *Buchtelite*, wrote "a distinctive song" for Akron. First played over Waring's NBC hookup on November 17, "The Akron Blue and Gold" was well received. The *Buchtelite* said the song was "swell," and told Waring "we intend to use it a lot."[16] This prophecy proved accurate, and the "Akron Blue and Gold" remains a favorite.

Some of the old rigidities of campus conduct were modified in this turbulent decade. An effort had been made by each college generation since the early 1920's to have the ban on smoking removed. Times had changed since those early Buchtel College days when a "godless youth from Oil City" caused a Kappa to cry by smoking in her presence. Earlier efforts to remove the ban failed. Claiming that Akron was one of the last of the "up-to-date" schools to have a no-smoking rule, one student commentator inquired, "Is our university in Ohio or in Tennessee?"[17] Since this comment was made in 1927 one must assume the student had in mind the Scopes Monkey Trial when he chose Tennessee to represent the epitome of backwardness and non-modernity. When the issue was again brought to a student vote in 1933, the no-smoking tradition was upheld by a narrow margin, 385 to 363. President Simmons let it be known that so far as he was concerned smoking on campus was "mainly an economic question" because the buildings were old and the insurance rates high! Dean Howard Evans, representing the rule's defenders, objected to the campus being cluttered up with cigarette butts. Inexorably things moved to a predictable conclusion. The restriction—this "blot on the university"—was removed in 1934.[18]

Concurrent with the debate over the smoking issue, another restriction—or rather, a compulsion—was fought over. In the first days of the Municipal University, daily chapel exercises had been reduced to a two-a-week regimen. Later, chapel was held every Friday morning, but the programs were not religious in character; indeed, gatherings were assemblies rather than chapels. When, in 1930, student attendance was required at a morning assembly that was part of a "Religious Emphasis Week," some students petitioned the faculty for relief. "The idea of making religion compulsory is futile," said one protester.[19] The grievance against compulsory attendance was wider than that, however. Even though educators of note and leading speakers of the day were featured, many students ("at least three-fourths of them") studied and slept during the program. It might be well to drop the programs in the interest of economy, said one student commentator, since "cutting down expenses seems to be the favorite indoor sport of late."[20] Finally, in the fall semester, 1934, the Faculty Council ruled that chapel attendance would no longer be compulsory, and a policy to make assembly programs so appealing that students and faculty would voluntarily attend was recommended as a goal. By February, it was apparent that attendance did not justify a continuance of the weekly programs, and student assemblies were discontinued for an indefinite period. President Simmons had a point when he said "an institution of our character has no other way of creating institutional spirit except through at least frequent assemblages of the entire student body."[21] Predictably, once the program was discontinued for lack of student support, a significant sentiment for re-establishing assembly programs arose. But compulsory attendance was dead, although in later years, after an abortive attempt to revive it, various devices would be found for assuring respectable crowds at certain University functions.[22]

During the 1930's as in no previous period of the University's existence, there was campus debate on issues of the day—and active protest by concerned students. In part, the campus merely reflected the wider society in its questionings and protests, but the students spent less time than their parents damning the bankers and the "rubber barons" and more time condemning war, compulsory military training, and other forces that impinged upon their ideals of how society should be ordered.

Generally speaking, Akron students have not been effective protesters. It may be that the scarcity of off-campus hangouts of the kind attractive to students with an "anti-establishment" bent accounts for this in part—there was no place to hatch a plot or organize a cabal. The fact that, until recent years, Akron had no dormitories, and nearly all students lived at home and had to go home and face mom and dad at the end of the day had something to do with it. A student personnel operation that was unusually close to the student pulse and which moved to head off certain kinds of "unhealthy" protest played a part in minimizing dissident activity. Only during the 1930's, when the climate of the larger society was also one of protest, did student disenchantment flower into meaningful movements on the Akron campus.

Certainly one reason the students were heard was due to the able direction given to the *Buchtelite* by the faculty adviser, "Bus" Vance, and a succession of able, imaginative, and courageous student editors. They identified the issues, gave space to the whole spectrum of opinion on these issues, conducted spot polls of student opinion on various subjects of concern to the campus, took a stance editorially, and in a responsible and sustained manner carried the fight to the faculty, administration, and even to the Board. The twenties and thirties represent the "golden age" of student journalism on the Akron campus; most other periods fall far short of that mark.

Before focusing on specific issues that became the center of student protest and debate, it might be well to give a brief insight into campus response to the political and social issues of the day. In 1932 the principal interest politically was the presidential race between Herbert Hoover and Franklin D. Roosevelt. The city of Akron was not so much pro-Roosevelt as it was anti-Hoover. In time the majority of the city's people became "true believers" in FDR and his New Deal but, at first, he seemed a weak reed to lean on in a period of unparalleled crisis in domestic affairs. Nationally, the trend in college polls showed a preference for Hoover. A poll conducted on Akron's campus gave Hoover 365 votes while FDR could manage only 175, but this did not begin to tell the story. The hard-working Socialist Club had been pushing their candidate effectively, so much so that Norman Thomas received 336 votes.[23]

Something happened to Norman Thomas between 1932 and 1936 as a campus vote-getter. In the straw balloting of 1936 he garnered only 20 votes while FDR received 310 and Alf Landon 280.[24] The campus was much less wedded to the Democratic administration than was the city of Akron. In 1940, a *Buchtelite* poll found students 4 to 3 in favor of Wendell Wilkie over Roosevelt.[25] Indeed, students favored Republican candidates for all offices contested that year. It is unlikely that the Republican surge was totally the result of students coming from well-to-do families. Only a minority of Akron students came from such a background. One of the marked phenomena that distinguished the sons and daughters of the working man was the eagerness with which many identified with the management class which they aspired to join upon graduation. They had already adopted much of its economic and political faith. Further, after years of listening to their fathers excoriate the rich, and praise FDR, the New Deal, and the unions, the sons and daughters of working men were sick of the sound, and with the rebelliousness of the young, they turned against the enthusiasms of their parents.

Among the social issues of the 1930's prohibition and its repeal played a prominent role nationally, but on campus "repeal" was less fervently welcomed than one might think. The student paper summed up the case pretty well when it stated that drinking, long an escape for complex-ridden individuals, would now "become a means of socializing students" rather than "giving them something to bluster about in the eight o'clock class the morning after." Further, repeal would be "the death knell of alleged humor magazines who believe themselves at their funniest when they portray a college student with a flask in one hand and a pennant in the other. This will be welcomed."[26]

On other social fronts, the Oxford Movement (a moral uplift movement), came and went, briefly impressing a few students and faculty members, but leaving no considerable heritage, even though much of Akron society took it to heart.[27] Then there were petitions: typical of them was one urging the removal of Huey Long of Louisiana from his seat in the United States Senate. Started at Harvard, the movement spread across the nation's campuses but, like nearly all such endeavors, it proved a futile gesture. On two fronts, however, student opinion went well beyond the petition stage, and led to a serious discussion of problems very much worth discussing. The first of these was the problem of compulsory ROTC.

From its inception on campus in 1919 there had been periodic outbreaks of dissent to the compulsory feature of ROTC training. These were small scale protests, however, such as that of 1925–26, which had more the character of a debate than a protest. By 1931, some local students who were aware of protests on other campuses, including Cincinnati's where the compulsory feature was abolished, felt that Akron's policy should be examined.[28] When interviewed about the compulsory feature, Hadley Ensign, a senior, said, "If this was Russia or the Sudan, I'd say O.K. but the idea of a progressive nation and a non-militant institution making ROTC a requirement to such an extent that it can remove a student from school is preposterous. It should by all means at least be optional."[29] The other view, or more precisely, *an* other view was represented by a junior coed: "I think compulsory ROTC is a good thing, especially for the incoming freshmen who need discipline. Besides, they look nice in the uniforms."[30] Believe it or not, more than 30 years later "they look nice" was still being used in justification of compulsory ROTC.

The discussion was generally on a higher level than these comments might suggest. Late in 1931, a student group called the League Against Compulsory Military Training at Akron University was formed to stage an active campaign to make ROTC optional. Paul Zeis was the group's able president. He was assisted by an executive board composed of Chalmers Stewart, Preston Bergin, Branko Widick, Herman Rabe, Robert Kinney, Harold Mikolashek, Arthur McDowell, and Nick Syracopoulos. They issued a statement pointing to a definite trend away from compulsory military training in American schools. "This trend against compulsory drill is not ascribed to a decline in patriotism, but rather to an increase in intelligent loyalty and to a better understanding of the issues involved." According to War Department information, said the statement, Akron was the only municipal university in the United States requiring military training. The only other schools in Ohio to require it were Ohio State, Dayton, and Wilberforce. Compulsion was the responsibility of the University administration, not of the government. The statement denied that any physical benefits accrued from ROTC training that could not just as easily be secured through physical education classes; and as for the argument that ROTC supplied needed discipline, the statement read that "The underlying principles of military organization—unquestioning obedience to established authority—is diametrically opposed to the cardinal principle of a university: a free, untrammeled quest for truth." Additionally, the statement rejected the argument that ROTC taught patriotic and enlightened citizenship and that it was necessary for "preparedness." In sum, the statement rejected compulsory ROTC because 1) it was incompatible with the ideals of American university education, 2) it perpetuated the war culture, and 3) it was incompatible with the ethos and Christian ideals of American society.[31]

It was only a matter of days until a group formed to advance the cause of compulsory ROTC. This group accused the League officers of being "sociologically inclined" and claimed they were motivated by egotistical impulses.[32] The new group was promptly dubbed the "anti-anti" group. But they were not nearly so spirited as the League, whose members approached the mayor for support, circulated petitions seeking student signatures, sought faculty support, and appealed directly to the Board.

By early spring, the issue was debated in the community. The American Legion of Akron firmly backed compulsory ROTC while supporters of the League to Abolish Compulsory ROTC included the Akron Ministerial Association, League of Women Voters, National Conference on the Cause and Cure of War, the Y.M.C.A.'s National Student Council, the *Buchtelite*, and the *Cleveland Plain Dealer*. Such organizations as the Association of Land Grant Colleges, the National Student Federation, and an informal group of 327 college presidents, deans, etc. who petitioned Congress that the War Department withdraw from the field of education, were cited by the League in support of the cause.[33]

Through it all, the military instructors on campus said nothing for public consumption. "We have nothing to say" was the "cold, concise" but unsatisfying comment of the commanding officer, Major Coates.[34] President Zook's role in the dispute was a cautious one. While not condemning the League's position outright, he reminded everyone that there had to be at least 100 men enrolled in ROTC to keep a unit on campus, and should training be made optional, there was a good chance this minimum could not be maintained. Zook appointed a faculty committee to study the matter, and the committee decided to poll their colleagues.

Results of the faculty polling became known in March. Of the 37 voting, two wanted to continue compulsory ROTC, 19 wanted to continue compulsory ROTC with liberalized exemptions, 15 wanted optional ROTC, and one wanted it abolished altogether. After this sampling of faculty opinion, the Faculty Council voted 22 to 7 to recommend to the Board of Directors that compulsory ROTC be continued, but "with such exemptions as may be made by the council from time to time."[35] This vote was the backbreaker for the League's cause. On April 6, the directors voted to retain the existing plan of military training. Only Mr. Lee Ferbstein objected for the record.[36]

For more than a year the ROTC issue lay dormant, but the protest slack was taken up by occasional student attacks, verbal in every case, against those they thought fostered the militaristic spirit in America. A *Buchtelite* editorial pointed out that the American Legion, "that band of jingoists," and several other organizations of ex-servicemen were "rallying around the Constitution, Nordic superiority, the D.A.R., and a huge army and navy." It was the desire of militarists for preparedness, said the editorial, that caused the World War of 1914–18. "We do not care to make another world safe for democracy when all the democracy there is, is hypocrasy *[sic]* and we do not care to fight another war to end war, because we did that once and the result is all too indicative."[37]

These thoughts, published in 1934 when Akron afforded much visual evidence that the old systems and slogans were shopworn, did not seem out of place to a reasonable man—even though he might disagree with the analysis—and they would not seem out of place to many students of a later generation facing the Vietnam war and a troubled condition within America. In support of these sentiments, William Grampp, a sophomore in the College of Liberal Arts, headed a petition drive whose purpose was to have Akron students indicate their unwillingness to participate in any war involving the invasion of foreign soil. This group was careful, initially, to keep its identity separate from another student group that was about to revive the fight against compulsory ROTC, but shortly the forces came together in a renewed protest.[38]

If one reads between the lines of reports of the rebirth of interest in the fight against compulsory ROTC, he is likely to get the same impression the *Buchtelite* got, that the Akron Ministerial Association, with the "zealous" aid of downtown reporters, effectively reopened the ROTC question.[39] For the clergy, the fight was led by Dr. Noble S. Elderkin, pastor of the First Congregational Church, who claimed in sermon and column that the DuPonts and other "merchants of death" were behind compulsory ROTC, and that a youth wanting an education at Akron University was "compelled to learn how to serve the financial interest of the DuPonts." He even blamed the DuPonts for the University's abandonment of compulsory chapel.[40] The *Beacon Journal* had advised the community to allow the students to "thresh the thing out" in the earlier protest, but now it applauded Dr. Elderkin's desire to see compulsory ROTC abolished at Akron although the *Beacon* did not subscribe to his theory about the DuPonts and munitions makers.[41]

In this protest revival the group which called itself the League for Voluntary Military Training led by Louis Haberman became submerged in an anti-compulsory group led by William Grampp. The 1934 protest employed direct tactics and the solicitation of support from the community to a greater degree than the 1931 movements. Students sought support from national groups and from local ones like the Summit County Central Labor Union, the League for Industrial Democracy, the League Against War and Fascism, the Y.M.C.A., the National Student League, and the Akron Ministerial Association which petitioned the Board on behalf of making ROTC optional. Some groups volunteered support, solicited or not. The Communist Party communicated to the Board its opposition to compulsory training.[42]

Once more veteran's organizations and D.A.R. chapters led community support for retaining compulsory ROTC. President Simmons—by this time Dr. Zook was at his new job in Washington—did nothing to encourage the protestors, nor did he forbid them their right to protest. He must have been embarrassed, however, when the League for Voluntary Training adopted as a slogan words he had used in a student assembly: "Human nature revolts against compulsion."[43]

With battle lines drawn, a replay of the earlier protest unfolded. A student poll revealed a substantial majority of men favoring optional ROTC. The septuagenarian mayor, "Honest Ike" Myers, after being briefed at a Board meeting, said that compulsory military training was not "nearly as bad as pictured;" it was simply a form of physical education! Again, only Lee Ferbstein voted against retaining compulsion when the matter came before the directors. It was thought he might be joined by a new member of the Board who had not voted on the matter two years earlier, but the new man felt the University got some advantages from ROTC—government-furnished band equipment, for example.[44] The Board stood firm against sporadic sniping which lasted until the issue was stilled by United States involvement in war with the Axis powers.

The issues of war and peace soon supplanted the ROTC issue which, said the *Buchtelite,* should be separated from the peace demonstrations then appearing on American campuses. The paper was "heartily" in favor of a student peace demonstration scheduled for November, 1935.[45] The Student Council assumed some of the initiative for a peace drive based on four points: 1) support genuine neutrality legislation, 2) relate education to crucial problems of war and peace, 3) support "necessary national defense," and 4) go to war only to repel invasion of the United States.[46] The National Student League criticized the Student Council for making no effort to support the Nye-Kvale Bill which provided for voluntary ROTC where such training was then compulsory. More than 500 students and faculty members attended the peace rally in front of Buchtel Hall. Paul Bagwell's speech caught the isolationist mood of the meeting: "The American flag should stand for peace and should never be planted on foreign soil."[47]

The peace movement took a bizzare twist in the spring of 1936 when a chapter of the "Veterans of Future Wars" was organized under the leadership of Sol Radam. Its platform was to secure a government bonus payment in advance, before its members were killed in war. Originally created as a gag by a Princeton student who was parodying payment of a bonus to veterans of World War I, the movement became a focus for anti-war sentiment and propaganda. It was an elaborate put-on that some took seriously. A local post of the Veterans of Foreign Wars sent a letter of protest to President Simmons and the Board. The editor of the campus paper said that if the V.F.W. wanted to take seriously the student's "little satire on war" that was their responsibility, but "when you throw a rock into a pig pen it is always the pig who gets hit that squeals the loudest."[48]

By the end of the spring semester, some of the fun had gone out of the various protest movements. An anti-war group of approximately 150 students tried to "strike" against war. Their demonstration was not widely popular, however, for the word "strike" had an unhappy connotation in Akron where the rubber workers were in conflict with management in a series of "sit-down strikes" that would find the industry organized in America's first successful implementation of industrial unionism on a large scale. Hecklers threw firecrackers at the student strikers; the *Buchtelite* editorialized against their efforts. When the academic year 1935–36 drew to a close, the discussion of America's role in international affairs and the issues of war and peace were returning to a less emotional base.[49]

Shortly before Akron men started to leave for military training in earnest under the terms of the Burke-Wadsworth Act of 1940, there were still other student objections to United States involvement in foreign wars. President Roosevelt's support of arms shipments to Europe, and his "cash and carry" program were opposed in *Buchtelite* editorials. President Simmons favored FDR's position, but he said he would in no way interfere with the student editor's right to oppose. At this time, a campus poll revealed that three-fourths of the male students questioned said they would not fight on foreign soil for their country's interests, and a somewhat larger percentage of the coeds said they would not consider their boy friends cowards for this refusal.[50] Within months, Pearl Harbor made these sentiments mere vaporings. The same student who had argued so persuasively against involvement was apt to be first in line at the recruiting station, and the young man disqualified from military service was pitied. There is surely something worth pondering by critics who are all too ready to see in student protests a denial of fundamental values. Students hate cant and sham, but when real issues are on the line, they appear to be willing to fight for them.

There is a tendency by social commentators of a later time to interpret the turmoil of the thirties, both on campuses and in the nation at large, as being essentially Communist-inspired. This makes about as much sense as the charge of the

1960's that rioting in the city ghettoes was the responsibility of "outside agitators." It is certainly true that the troubles of both decades attracted the engaged attention of agitators, whatever their affiliation, but they were swept along by the tide of general discontent rather than controlling it. The Communist Party organization, small and underfinanced locally, did lend overt support to the anti-compulsory ROTC movement in 1934, but much more in the way of leadership came from the Akron Ministerial Association. In her book, *Industrial Valley,* relating Akron's cruel plight during the depression, Ruth McKenney reveals the role that the Communist organization played in urging the rubber workers of Akron to unionize; but to charge, as many Akronites did in the 1930's, that the strikes came about as a result of Communistic activity is to lose sight of reality.[51] On the Akron campus, student protests of this decade were almost always local manifestations of national student movements, some of which were supported in part by "front" organizations. But those leaders on the Akron campus who took a position on rational grounds, who sought support by legitimate means, and who carried their cause to appropriate persons deserve commendation. They were the "thinking men" that universities claim they seek to produce. It is interesting to note that, almost to a man, the student protest leaders of the turbulent thirties are now well established business and professional men, pillars of society, and a long way from being destroyers of the American dream.

It is now amusing, therefore, to note that late in 1938, when the Dies Committee on Un-American Activities was pursuing subversives, Ohio Congressman-at-Large Harold C. Mossier, reported to be in charge of investigating "red" activities in Ohio, told a *Buchtelite* reporter that the committee was not planning an investigation at The University of Akron. The Oberlin College paper claimed that investigations would be conducted at Oberlin, Western Reserve, Ohio State, and Akron, but Mossier had indicated that Akron was out of it, all of which led the *Buchtelite* to lament "aren't our reds as good as theirs?"[52]

With the enormous difficulty President Simmons faced in keeping the University alive during this decade, it is a great credit to him that he made no effort to deny the students their right to sound off, to protest, to be heard. He certainly must have experienced embarrassment with some of his conservative Board members when they were rankled by student protests and pressures. As noted, some persons in the community were unhappy at student attitudes and activities, and in Akron this was always a concern, for the University's fate rode on citizen support at the polls. Even so, there is no evidence in the records that this fact was used to intimidate the students in any way.

Always working behind the scenes was the astute and resourceful Dean of Men, Donfred Gardner, whose insight into students was enviable. His interest was not to deny a student from taking a position on important public issues, but to make as certain as he could that in the process the student did not expose himself or the University to ridicule. He was more a counselor than a censor although no one was ever left in doubt when he felt the bounds of decency or rationality were being transgressed. During this restless decade, his advice, assistance, and accessibility to students proved to be of value in reconciling issues. Though his was a key role, many other faculty and administrative officers proved wise friends to students and good servants of the University.

Before leaving this consideration of student attitudes and University response in the thirties, a word should be said about discrimination. Before World War II, Akron had few Negro students. As far as can be determined, the first Negro student attended classes at Buchtel College well before the turn of the century, but not until 1921 was there a Negro graduate. In the 1930's the city had a small Negro element in a population whose make-up was overwhelmingly white and of recent southern origin. The Ku Klux Klan was an active force in Akron. Such Negroes as may have hoped to get a college education locally may well have thought twice because of the backlash such action would trigger. In the 1930's few Negro families could secure the funds needed for fees, books, clothes, and the other expenses of going to college. Admission requirements from 1923 to 1945 worked to the disadvantage of children who came from educationally deprived backgrounds. Not until World War II brought a large Negro migration to Akron, and the G. I. Bill provided funds for schooling, did the campus have a substantial number of Negro students.

A more pervasive prejudice in the Akron community during the twenties and thirties was directed against Jews. In Akron the issue was intensified by the hate activities of the Klan, by the suspicious fundamentalist outlook with its distrust of alien ideas, by resentful business competitors, and by racist propaganda emanating from the Third Reich but finding some true believers in Akron. To a lesser extent, there had been a certain amount of Catholic exclusion in the community as well.[53]

On campus there were few overt signs of discrimination. Fraternities and sororities must bear the brunt of responsibility for making it perfectly clear that there were indeed some organizations whose membership was based on considerations completely irrelevant to the quality of the individual. In all other activities, there appeared to be no formal barriers, although a *Buchtelite* editorial in November, 1941, asserted that an ROTC student officer was demoted because he signed a handbill which charged that a "silent conspiracy" existed to deny Negroes the right to take advanced military training.[54] In response to a bulletin of the Akron Federation of Teachers charging anti-semitism and anti-catholicism on the Akron campus, President Simmons replied that "there is absolutely no race prejudice at the university." He went on to ask, "How could there be race discrimination? Why there are two Catholics and one Jew on the board of directors."[55] To contemporary ears his remarks have a quaint and a dated ring—the association of "race" with religious belief and the unconscious defense of the quota system with token representation on the Board have an antique quality about them that tempts the present generation to label them hypocritical. But in expecting more, we are asking of that earlier generation a wisdom that it has taken the public an additional thirty years to begin to acquire.

While the 1930's provided a backdrop of events that stimulated campus discussion, severe financial limitations restricted the scope of organized student activities during much of the decade. In 1929–30 a forward step in the financing of student activities was taken with the introduction of a Student Activity Fund. Heretofore, extracurricular activities were regarded as "outside" activities, and officers of student organizations had to spend much time and ingenuity collecting student dues and fees. Now a student activity fee was introduced. This source of income went into a fund administered under the supervision of University officials. Eligible student organizations had to prepare budgets of their needs to present to the Fund's administrators for support.[56] Student Council, publications, theater, and other organizations were thus put on a more businesslike basis. The failure of the First Central Trust Company in 1933 froze the activity funds and forced temporary cancellation of some student activities. It is a credit to the directors that even in the face of other critical financial considerations, every effort was made to minimize interruption of the student program. A greater drag was the unavailability of any facilities for student activities. More than any one act, the opening of the Student Building in 1939 marked a new coming of age for extracurricular activities on the Akron campus.

Although it is impossible to mention the contribution to campus life of each club and organization, some notice should be taken of activities embracing a large cross section of the student body's interests. Just as babies continued to be born although at a reduced pace during the depression, so clubs and organizations continued to sprout anew on the campus even though funds were in short supply. Ironically, a new military honorary, the Olin Rifles, later the Pershing Rifles, made an appearance during the height of the anti-compulsory ROTC furor. While the Rifles made their appearance despite the climate, an attempt to reactivate the long extinct German Club in 1934 as the *Freunde Deutscher Kultur* failed because of the "blaring of one of the city's so called patriots" who started a rumor that the organization was to be a Hitler club. Some students jeered the news of a German Club and the furor caused its sponsors to withdraw from the effort.[57]

The Akron chapter of the National Student League appeared in 1935 in time to play a role in the various protest movements. Also representative of new interests was the Cloud Hoppers Club for aviation enthusiasts. It secured its own plane, competed in meets, suffered a minor crack-up of its aircraft, and ultimately faded into the broader interests of a federal Civilian Aeronautics Authority pilot's training program which Akron, along with many other colleges, introduced in 1939. President Simmons worked hard to secure this program for Akron. It never attracted as many, nor as dedicated student fliers as hoped and was finally disbanded as war preparation took precedence.[58]

Other activities went their normal way. The Speech department had an unusually vital and successful program. University Theater, formed in 1928 by students participating in drama activities, survived despite the lack of a suitable stage for its performances. This lack was remedied in the new Student Building. Meantime the group wrote and performed many radio plays which were favorably received. The debate team scored well throughout the decade. Indeed, it won the first Ohio Debate Conference tournament it entered after being accepted to membership in 1930. For a moment in 1934 the men's dramatic club, "Laughing Masque," was revived, but again succumbed before accomplishing anything of interest. In 1938–39, Herbert Bracken, a senior, won the Ohio Intercollegiate Oratorical Contest and went on to finish second nationally. His topic, "The Economic Color Line" reflected certain problems of the Negro community of which he was a part. As the first Akron winner since "Bob" Tucker in 1890, Bracken was honored at a student assembly where he received the praise and commendation of his fellow students and President Simmons.

The *Buchtelite*, under the sponsorship of its faculty advisor Ulysses Vance, was possibly the most uniformly vital and successful activity of the period 1926–41. In the former year it organized the Ohio Intercollegiate Newspaper Association at a convention held in Akron, and in 1927 it won the first prize offered by the group for the best college paper in Ohio. Also in 1927 the Association's News Bureau, located at Akron, began operation with Sherril Leonard, *Buchtelite* editor in 1926–27, as its first director. Mr. Phillip Dietrich was editor in 1930 when the paper was voted the best semi-weekly college paper in Ohio. This led Professor Charles Bulger to give the staff a little perspective. "The present editors have a soft snap," said Bulger who edited the paper in 1906 and 1907. "Why, we were responsible for the paper financially and otherwise. The editor's job was to fill up space at any cost even if we had to sit down and write the stories ourselves. If we lost any money on the paper it was our hard luck and if we made any money that was luck too."[59]

A contest was held in 1933 to select a new name for the *Buchtelite* since that name was no longer as representative as it had been in Buchtel College days. A new high school named Buchtel contributed another source of confusion. The winning suggestion, *The Akronian*, was submitted by both Mr. Edgar Roberts, Instructor in English, and freshman William Grampp. They split the $25 prize, but a poll of 91 students revealed that only three favored changing the paper's name; so the *Buchtelite* it has remained.[60] Having dominated Ohio college journalism, the *Buchtelite* won an impressive string of national awards including selection as a "pacemaker" which meant that it was chosen as a model operation from among the best papers in national competition.

Not everyone approved of the paper. Miss Helen Redner, "former peace striker" and reported to be chairman of a campus Socialist Club, reportedly charged the *Buchtelite* with being "the organ of the administration" and saw it as an impediment to progress charging that it "has obstructed every progressive movement on the campus."[61] This criticism was hardly accurate or fair. However, U. S. Vance thought journalism at Akron was still an "unwanted child." The paper was a success despite being limited to a second-hand print shop and a small office in the basement of Buchtel Hall; but the lack of a journalism department was what really hindered the effort. Such journalism courses as there were found a tenuous home in the English department. Success with the paper, said Vance, came because of the student's "try anything once" policy.[62] The *Buchtelite* continued its award-winning ways well into the 1940's, and although Professor Vance finally secured his journalism department, it apparently came too late, when the fires of journalistic triumph had cooled and student interest was insufficient to justify a program; and so, in the 1950's, the department was disbanded and journalism courses returned to the English department curriculum.

Some new traditions that had taken root on campus prospered mildly throughout the depression. As early as 1926, the engineers had celebrated St. Patrick's Day with campus clowning and a march through the city. The occasion became formalized as Engineer's Day and was a feature of early spring. Periodically the celebration got somewhat out of hand and then the administration would attempt to tame it. A favorite part of the day for many students, and some faculty, came in the morning when St. Pat, the "original rivet slinger," would rise from a coffin and lead a noisy and motley throng through the hallways, emptying classes of their captives.

Some professors never learned the art of accepting this in good grace. They would shout horrible threats to the invaders, one of them going so far as to hurl chalk and erasers at them. The engineers retaliated by barricading the door with chairs making escape from inside impossible. The fire marshal would not have liked it, but the fire marshal was not there. Other activities involved repelling raids by liberal arts students intent on capturing the engineers' flag, painting dogs, or an occasional freshman, lofting coeds' skirts with an air jet installed outside a busy doorway, and then an afternoon of contests—spitting, beard raising, etc. The evening was capped by the Engineer's Brawl at some local retreat. Like the publication "Engin-Ears," banned by Simmons for its "ribald humor," Engineer's Day too has passed into history as a result of administrative action in the early 1960's. The modern campus is nearly devoid of tradition, and many persons feel it can ill-spare "E Day."[63]

One of the most pleasant campus traditions, Song Fest, was first held in the spring of 1933. Separate contests for fraternity men and sorority women were held with Phi Delta Theta and Zeta Tau Alpha the winners of the first of these annual affairs. In quite another area of endeavor, the Women's Athletic Association emerged in 1938 out of the Women's Physical Education Club started ten years earlier. Consideration was also given to having women cheerleaders—an innovation in the thirties. Most students favored the idea, but one sophomore girl said, "Women cheerleaders look silly. A woman may smoke, bob her hair, and work as well as a man; but to be a cheerleader is to lose her last iota of effeminacy."[63] So completely did the girls take over, however, that in time a move would be required to recruit some males for the cheerleading corps to redress the balance.

The strong fraternity interest that had characterized Buchtel College carried over to the Municipal University. The first new "Greek" group to emerge after transition was Sigma Beta fraternity which organized in 1914. Five years later it was chartered as Zeta chapter of Lambda Chi Alpha. The early 1920's, witnessed a spurt of fraternity growth with Alpha Sigma Omicron (1920), Sigma Beta Nu (1923), Phi Kappa Rho (1923), and Alpha Epsilon Pi (1924). The Commons Club was organized for men who had no fraternity affiliation (1921). The girls meanwhile were busy founding Sigma Delta Theta (1921), Omega chapter of Alpha Gamma Delta (1922), Kappa Alpha Sigma (1922), which became Zeta Tau Alpha (1928), and Chi Lambda Phi (1928) which was installed as Sigma chapter of Theta Phi Alpha (1931). The financial crisis stopped temporarily the forming of new groups.

Not until 1927 did any sorority have its own house. Although Phi Kappa Delta had occupied part of a house, the Phi Mu's were first to have their own full-sized quarters, located nearby on Buchtel Avenue. The fraternities, of course, had long been in off-campus lodgings. In the beginning they occupied rooms in the business section of Akron, well removed from watchful eyes, but by the 1920's fraternities had located east and north of campus in some of the great mansions once occupied by Akron's wealthy families along the old "gold coast" residential district. A combination of limited funds, excessive wear and tear, and high maintenance costs made it impracticable for some groups to keep up these properties in suitable style, and for years the University was the target of complaints from neighbors of the "Greeks." New housing in the 1960's finally provided a partial answer to this problem, although fraternity and sorority housekeeping and groundskeeping is still never all that it might be.

By their very nature, fraternities and sororities are competitive. They battle each other for pledges and prestige. Occasionally they join in mutual interest to battle for their existence against the unaffiliated students or the public at large whom they feel misunderstand or misrepresent their purpose and their actions. It is easy for the outsider to attribute all sorts of unworthy motives to the fraternal groups. Most of these charges grow out of misunderstanding or a lack of information on the critic's part, but any organization that practices a closed membership policy, that recruits its new members in such a way as to suggest that some candidates are "better" than others, and which rests this determination on considerations other than intrinsic merit, leaves itself open to suspicion and resentment. It must be said that all too often the fraternal groups stand justly accused. Add to this consideration their propensity to engage in initiation high jinks and destructive bursts of high spirits and one can see that they had an image problem. This problem was particularly acute in 1914–15 when it appeared that attitudes tolerated in the private school were not going to be acceptable in an institution responsible to the public.

Throughout the fall semester of 1914 criticism had been rising against the fraternities. Dissension directed both inwardly, one group against another, and outwardly against the students at large marked the conflict. It is no longer possible, if indeed it ever was, to unravel the threads of dissension, but the Board of Directors of the Municipal University wanted it stopped. In February, 1915, they informed the faculty that they "viewed with rising alarm the internal dissension among the men's fraternities . . . as reported by current talk among our citizens and even by articles in the local papers." While disclaiming any desire to infringe upon the faculty's right, along with the president, to control internal policies, the directors felt "a careful examination should be made of the conduct of the college fraternities, their influence upon student life and especially their alleged detrimental influence upon the activities of the whole student body." The Board had no desire to forbid fraternity activity on the campus, but "should repeated efforts fail to bring about improved conditions . . . fraternities should be abolished for the best welfare of the whole student body." The faculty was requested to investigate and report.[64]

The faculty found no reason to abolish fraternities, but the purpose of the inquiry was served in that the fraternal groups toned down their particularism although there seldom was a time during which they were not charged with putting their own interests above the University's.[65] Slowly, however, many of the irregularities were smoothed over as the faculty, and later the Dean of Men, took a hand in restraining excesses. Much was accomplished in establishing constructive controls over fraternity activities during the twenties and thirties.

A closed rushing season was adopted in place of the old catch-as-catch-can operation that created constant bickering over prospective pledges and which had certain students in an uproar throughout the school year. In 1923 the Interfraternity Council, formed to organize "Greek" activities along cooperative lines, determined that a man must complete 12 credit hours of work before he was eligible for rush. The system of closed bidding used by the sororities was adopted by the fraternities. The rushing season was limited to the first two weeks of the second semester. Something appears to have gone wrong with the adoption of the new system, for in 1926 the Men's Pan-Hellenic Council passed a rule prohibiting rushing or pledging of high school students until the day after their graduation from high school.[66]

In January, 1927, a new Interfraternity Council (IFC) was formed. Fraternities were divided into regular and probationary status, the groups in the latter category having five years to meet requirements for regular status. Rushing, bidding, and pledging were confined to regular University students only and were to take place at a stipulated time (initially, six weeks after the start of the fall semester). A student court was established to try infringements of the constitution of the IFC. Each fraternity was to have a faculty adviser. The *Buchtelite* said this was a unique system among American colleges, particularly in that it permitted freshmen some consideration in choosing fraternities.[67]

Among the time-honored customs of fraternities and sororities is initiation, and probably no one facet of their activity caused these groups so much adverse publicity. In 1925 there was some local sentiment for a regular "Hell Week," during which time the fraternities could concentrate their informal ceremonies instead of prolonging them at irregular times through the year. This was done; but a decade later there was a mild outcry for abolishing "Hell Week" completely because it caused public humiliation to pledges and interrupted their studies. The most constructive years of fraternal activity still lay ahead for Akron.

For much of the general public, and for some of those associated with the University, the principal topic of interest in the University's life is its record in intercollegiate athletics. For the most part this is a legitimate and healthy interest since it is on the playing field that much of the drama, spirit, color, and excitement of collegiate life unfolds. There are, of course, occasional embarrassments, ranging from inept team performances to charges of professionalism that cause even the most faithful momentary disillusionment; but the craving for excitement, the competitive spirit, the need for heroes finally prevails, and the enthusiast returns to his allegiances with renewed fervor. And whatever benefit the spectator and armchair quarterback receive from their vantage point on the sidelines is magnified many times in benefits to the players themselves. While it is true that schools and alumni have exploited athletes on occasion, for every young man thus exploited, there must be many who profit in poise, self-esteem, and sense of accomplishment from participation in varsity athletics.

In this history, only limited and proportionate space can be devoted to intercollegiate athletics. This requires a degree of generalization that will not permit examination in detail. Fortunately for local sports enthusiasts, the *Akron Beacon Journal*'s able sports editors take their readers back with some frequency to the great moments of athletic achievement in times past. Mr. Phil Dietrich's fine columns dealing with Akron's athletic greats are particularly fruitful sources of sports lore, and it is to them, and to similar blow-by-blow accounts, that the true enthusiast will have to turn for satisfaction.

From the point of view of the educator, intercollegiate athletics forms but the peak of the physical training iceberg whose base is comprised of the Department of Physical Education, charged with responsibility for an extensive number of courses, some of which every student must take in order to fulfill graduation requirements. The coaching staffs have regular teaching duties within this department. Some coaches must feel on occasion that this important work, which engrosses much of their time, is given insufficient measure against that given their coaching duties.

Under the administration of Mr. Fred Sefton, the Municipal University established from the beginning a respect for physical training as a part of each student's experience. While varsity athletics were in no sense ignored—indeed, some of the finest teams in the University's history marked the early years—Fred Sefton was a believer of physical fitness for all.[68] In 1916 the physical education program was completely reorganized. A physical examination and a statement of the health history of each student was provided the physical education instructor so that he might prescribe exercises of greatest benefit to the individual student. The new organization required sophomores as well as freshmen to take physical education courses. Commenting on this development, the *Beacon Journal* said that the many National Guard rejections for physical disability revealed the need for better programs of physical fitness. The special wartime programs had emphasized physical fitness, and the carry-over of that enthusiasm into the postwar period assured that Akron students would have sufficient opportunity for physical training. By 1935 physical education was safely ensconced in the general education requirements so that all students not excused would have at least a year of physical education.[69]

In time, the duties first handled by Charles Bulger as Faculty Manager of Athletics fell to the coaches, particularly to Fred Sefton; however, it was realized that the task of coaching, preparing teams for intercollegiate athletic contests, and supervising the management of athletics was too much for one man; therefore, the position of Faculty Manager of Athletics was reactivated in 1934. Mr. Jean Smith, Class of '27, was appointed to that position and charged with the entire management of intercollegiate sports. It was, however, the appointment in 1939 of Mr. Leslie Hardy as Director of Athletics that finally modernized the organizational end of intercollegiate sports. He brought a degree of order and stability to the intercollegiate program that paved the way for the work of the next three decades. The University at that time had just concluded its first modest move in the direction of big-time football, and the problems involved were proving insurmountable.

President Simmons was ready to advocate an athletic program that would keep varsity athletics in proportion to the entire physical education program:

> *A sound athletic program does not need to be intercollegiate in character. It should be the by-product of a thorough, well-planned course in physical education where the most proficient in all athletic sports of an institution may engage in contest with the students of other institutions that have similar programs. . . . The university is attempting such a program internally in the organization of its Physical Education Department, and externally it is attempting to arrange intercollegiate competition with institutions having similar plans. . . .*[70]

But even as Simmons promulgated this view, he was aware of the University's inability to adhere to it. "Unfortunately," he said, "this is not the present accepted idea."[71] If one could wipe the slate clean and build anew, there might be hope that such a plan would be adopted by many, if not all, of the schools of the country who are chronically overextended in the area of varsity athletics, but there is too much investment—plant, equipment, scholarship, public relations, alumni sentiment—to expect that any radical change will transpire in the foreseeable future.

"To the average person," wrote President Simmons in 1940, "college athletics means intercollegiate football." Akron's experience to that time would largely bear out the president's assertion, although locally, at least, basketball was an important challenger for primary interest and allegiance in the years between world wars. But football was still number one. A combination of factors was responsible: colorful coaches and players, some good teams, the intimacy of Buchtel Field which made the spectator feel close to the action, worthy opponents that stretched but seldom outclassed the local boys, lack of competition from other entertainment sources, and an occasional furor over eligibility or some other touchy subject that kept football in the news.

A turning point in competition was reached in 1919–20 when Akron teams, heretofore losers more often than winners, discovered the joys of winning on a regular basis. The football squad of 1919 lost to Wooster and tied Case, but swept past six other opponents for Akron's best season on the gridiron. Meanwhile, the basketball team, which had had a great 1917 season and a fair 1918 season, swept to an undefeated record of 14 wins in 1919, taking the Ohio Conference championship in the process and having several of its players recognized with all-Ohio honors. Men like Art Knowlton, Eddie Wentz, "Red" Daum, Bruce Bierce, Tommy Tomkinson, and others provided a depth of talent that Akron teams could seldom boast.

The concentration of talent led to some accusations and questions. Case broke off football relationships in 1922 after the Case faculty representative charged Akron with "unsavory football." The game officials denied that Akron had engaged in any questionable practices. When Case then offered to come to Akron another season if guaranteed $500 rather than the customary $300, Akron's faculty representative, Charles Bulger, broke off relations in football.[72] Earlier that year the issue of "professionalism" in college athletics had been discussed with reference to the local situation. Coach Sefton said "this university is absolutely free of anything like professionalism. There is no chance for it, as we have no tuition, and expenses are low. Our athletes do not have to play professional football or basketball in order to support themselves." Bulger, however, did think that some professionalism existed in the Ohio Conference and charged it largely to alumni influence, athletic scholarships, and loosely administered loan funds. Although he cited no money involvement at Akron, he did feel there was "too much question of what material reward" the athlete would receive "even in this institution." He mentioned a letter to President Kolbe from the father of a football-playing son asking in effect whether Akron would care to buy his son's services.[73]

Much of Akron's sudden success must be attributed to Coach Sefton. He was a driver who "constantly urges his men on to the last minute." The *Beacon Journal* called him "the idol of AU" and reported that "his word is taken as law." Other schools coveted his services, but he chose to remain at Akron where his contribution to coaching was exceeded only by his devotion to the whole spectrum of physical education activities, clean living, and the virtues that flow therefrom.[74]

Two developments made 1923 significant for Akron athletics. The new grandstand with a seating capacity of 5,500 plus room for another 1,500 in bleachers was dedicated at Buchtel Field making it a fine facility for watching football. In 1927 the "A" Association collected $1,000 with which to provide facilities at the stadium so that the football team could sleep there three nights a week in the practice season. Since the players lived all over the area and had no common gathering place off the field, this bringing together of teammates cultivated "an excellent spirit" among them. The first stadium bonds were paid off in 1927 when excellent gate receipts provided a surplus, and by 1930 the debt had been reduced to $28,000 from the initial $35,000.[75]

The other development of long range interest was Board approval of a plan proposed by Carl Leffler and backed by Student Council, to increase the student activity fee by $5 and in return provide students with a season ticket good for all athletic events played in Akron. Students supported the plan 396 to 15.[76]

Student Council which favored the activity fee also backed a proposal to set aside a special day for an athlete of particular accomplishment, and so "Red Daum Day" was proclaimed in 1921. The following year, however, it was decided to honor the whole football team by staging a Migration Day to Wooster. Since 1922, migrations have been held occasionally but they never caught on as a tradition.[77]

Certainly one of the unique features of Akron athletic teams is the nickname by which they are known. Many loyalists have complained over the years that "Zippers" seems inappropriate as a name to inspire heroic deeds. Some irreverent associations suggested by the name have been mentioned by its detractors. But the name persists, and for good reason. First, it is unique; no other college boasts the same name, and those who think this unimportant might remember the recurring unhappiness over the fact that Akron's Alma Mater is set to the tune of the Cornell Hymn which it shares with hundreds of schools. Second, over the years the contraction "Zips" has supplanted the full name. This name has an abundance of onomatopoeia. It is readily adapted to the needs of newspapermen, fits easily in the limited space of headlines, banners, and announcements, and lends itself to cheers.

The name "Zippers" was suggested in 1927 by Margaret Hamlin as part of a contest to choose a name for Akron's athletic teams. The B. F. Goodrich Company had a copyright on the name "Zippers" which they had just given to a popular style of overshoe, but it consented to let the University use the name. It certainly is more distinctive than some of the other suggestions submitted—"Golden Blue Devils," "Bisons," "Rubber Soldiers," "Hill Billies," and "Kangaroos."[78]

The nickname is well fixed in sentiment as witness the repeated and uniformly unsuccessful attempts to change it. A serious effort was made in the early 1950's under the leadership of Robert Savoy, All-American diver and President of Student Council, to select a new name and find a mascot for Akron teams. After considerable thought, Student Council came forth with "Kangaroos" as an alternative. The movement died for lack of support, and the "Zips" continue to ride high although "Zippie" the kangaroo has appeared as a mascot since 1954.

In 1926 Mr. George R. Babcock was appointed head football coach. He was soon replaced by Howard "Red" Blair who built a succession of fine teams and in the process earned the affection and support of a wide segment of the Akron sports public. Two of Blair's outstanding athletes were Kenneth "Red" Cochrane and Harold Frye, both of whom were honored for their outstanding play. Cochrane was possibly the greatest all-around athlete in Akron's history. He won practically every sports letter available. In 1929 he was an all-Ohio halfback and in 1930 was chosen the best back in Ohio. While still a sophomore he won the mile race in the Big Six track meet. He was the heavyweight boxing champion of the University in 1929–30 and won the heavyweight championship at Fort Knox during ROTC summer encampment. Unlike many athletes, he was heavily involved in non-athletic activities being a regimental commander in the ROTC, president of Lambda Chi Alpha, and member of ODK, Interfraternity Council, and Scabbard and Blade. When he returned to his Alma Mater in 1948 as Director of Athletics, he was welcomed back to the fold where he has since infused the athletic program with a zest and spirit that has carried it to new heights of effectiveness and comprehensiveness. In the highly charged competitive world of sports where in every contest someone has to come out a loser, "Red" Cochrane has maintained the respect and good wishes of a cross section of coaches, players, fellow faculty members, alumni, and community supporters.

As in so many other phases of the University's life in the early thirties, things were looking up athletically when the effects of the depression started to eat into the program and cut off promising growth. Spring football practice was introduced in 1931 but proved abortive. The prospect of varsity athletes being granted some course credit for their long training and effort, just as credit was given for glee club and musical work, was scotched by fortune's turning. Attendance at football games fell, thus curtailing income and forcing cancellation of the baseball season in 1933. Even in 1936 the school did not have the $100 required to field a baseball team despite the efforts of President Simmons, himself a former catcher and captain of the Buchtel nine, to find money.[79] Other schools, harder hit than Akron, had to cancel all spring sports so that Akron could not arrange a schedule for baseball and had difficulty in so-called minor sports where expenses generally were low.

The teams and coaches had zest for their sport, but that old bugaboo, lack of school spirit, was as much an issue in the depression as it had been in relative prosperity. One of the more irascible local newspapermen, Jim Schlemmer, sports editor of the *Beacon Journal,* made a point of jabbing the needle into Akron students for their lack of school spirit. In 1932 he suggested that if only some Akron students were thrown in jail for celebrating a football victory, it would be a most happy sign that some genuine school spirit was being developed on the Hilltop. Yet Schlemmer was but one in a long and—on the whole—honorable line of sports writers who lamented the lack of "Joe College" spirit. After needling and prodding for many years, he turned over the task to others while he went off to seek solace following the Cleveland Indians.[80] In 1933 a Loyalty Gang was formed to encourage support of athletics. Similar efforts had failed before because of weak organization, and this effort also failed to elicit a response.

Through all the years of effort to generate a lasting spirit in support of athletic teams, the administration gave strong and continuing assistance. Not since Orello Cone had a president failed to show appreciation for the role of intercollegiate athletics in college life, even though a good many of their problems were connected with varsity sports activity. Simmons was a football enthusiast in 1933, and though he cooled somewhat by 1940, having experienced how the public relations surrounding football could harm as well as help, he stood behind the athletic effort during his administration.

One of the difficulties faced by Akron teams, according to a *Buchtelite* columnist, was that most Ohio Conference schools looked upon Akron with an "across-the-tracks" attitude.[81] He thought this was due to Akron's municipal character and to its lack of collegiate environment. That it was businesslike in comparison to the small private schools that constituted the rest of the conference cannot be questioned. Institutional snobbery is an enduring phenomenon in American higher education; even old Buchtel College felt she was snubbed at times by the patronizing attitude of Oberlin. Most Akron athletes worked full- or part-time at jobs that were in no way tailored to minimize the effort required. This was not the case with many jobs for athletes at Akron and elsewhere in the post-World War II period. Many of the varsity footballers worked a full six-hour shift in the rubber shops in order to stay in school. It is little wonder that Akron coaches have been frustrated for years because their players were working when they were supposed to be practicing, or they were so tired from their jobs that they had little to give to football, basketball, or track.

In keeping with President Simmons' conviction that the best way to put the school before the public was through football, steps were taken in 1933–34 to boost attendance. A more vigorous sports promotional effort was launched. The Akron-Kent game in 1934 was sponsored by the Junior Chamber of Commerce. This contest, the first night game played at Buchtel Field, was a success as far as the 26 to 0 Akron victory was concerned. That same season, Goodyear sponsored the Akron-John Carroll game. It took many years, however, before sponsored games paid off in a big way. Other efforts to stimulate interest involved playing up the "cowbell" rivalry with Wooster, initiated in 1920 by "Weeds" Mason, and by building up the neighborhood rivalry with Kent State Normal, soon to be a university, but still outclassed in its athletic rivalry with Akron.

The principal effort to stimulate football attendance came with the hiring of Mr. James W. Aiken as coach and Athletic Director. Immediately following the 1935 football season, the able Howard Blair resigned from his positions as Athletic Director and coach of the football, basketball, and track teams. Blair had been criticized by the newspapers, but he had support within the University. The students appeared sorry to see him leave and reacted caustically to "Blair's loud-mouthed grandstand assistants" who had yelled criticisms from the stands during the season just finished. Simmons emphasized that Blair had not been forced out, and his resignation was accepted "with great regret" by the directors. When one is familiar with the forbidding difficulties under which he labored, it is fair to say that he compiled a good record in won-lost statistics, his teams winning 140 and losing only 65. Of the 20 schools in the Ohio Conference, only Mount Union had a better record in these years. There was general campus agreement that he epitomized the fine qualities that coaches are supposed to possess. Student sports editor Jack Carroll summed up campus feeling. Blair, he wrote, was "the victim of many unfair accusations in the past few years, and we congratulate Mr. Blair for the fine spirit he has displayed in the face of all these criticisms, most of which are unfounded. He has proven himself a real man."[82]

"Jimmy" Aiken brought color, dash, and excitement to Akron football; indeed, as it turned out, a little more excitement than was comfortable. Aiken came from the Ohio River country, long the producer of hard-nosed football players. He was an All-American end on Washington and Jefferson's Rose Bowl team of 1920–21 and had played professional football with Steubenville and other Ohio teams in the cradle of professional football. When appointed to the Akron position, he was coaching the Canton McKinley Bulldogs, annually one of the state's strongest high school teams. This was his first job on the college level although he had been approached for the Kent job the year before and had turned it down because the plant and program were inadequate.

Aiken lost no time recruiting players. More than any previous Akron teams, the Aiken teams drew on boys of all national and ethnic backgrounds, and the local sports pages were soon to make household names out of Abdulla, Zazula, and Monzo. Aiken's melting pot would have done justice to Notre Dame, which sometimes had a difficult time finding a son of Erin among the Fighting Irish.

There was some suspicion on the campus that Aiken's success as a recruiter was resented and feared throughout the Ohio Conference. This feeling may have been partly responsible for a ruling handed down on October 5, 1936, at an Ohio Conference meeting in Columbus. In the heated, five-hour session five Akron players—Al Abdulla, Stanley Junius, Carl Lee, Harold Hartline, and Andy Garcia—were ruled ineligible because they carried less than a full classroom load (11 hours in the fall semester and 11 hours in the spring semester). The "full course" rule had been adopted by the conference in May, 1936. The conference now made the ruling retroactive, an act which caught the five men short of hours. Dean Ayer, Akron's representative, protested the retroactive feature: "If we quit on this thing now you can readily see what kind of 'tool' they have to work with," he warned. Loss of the five, all backfield men, would leave the Zippers with but two backfield players.

In the furor that followed, Akron focused attention on the retroactive feature of the rulings. Dr. Ira T. Wilson, President of the conference and a faculty member at Heidelberg College, issued a statement in which he appealed to an observance of the spirit of the law. In sum, he argued that Akron should have known that a "full college course" involved the student's being registered for at least 11 credits each semester even though this precise definition was not made until May, 1936. Wilson said that "Akron University athletic officials are attempting to build a team and remain in the conference by stretching the conference rules beyond all reason and the interpretation built around the letter of the rules by tradition and practice."[83] The University's charge that they were the victims of an *ex post facto* ruling persuaded the conference to permit the suspended players to compete pending the December meeting. But Akron was angry, and there were many persons on campus and off who advised withdrawal from the conference. In Jim Schlemmer's view, Akron was angry because "the conference, in its concentrated effort to keep Jimmy Aiken from being too good a coach and turning out too powerful teams had had to turn to the present channels of mudslinging, as Dr. Wilson did. . . ." The *Buchtelite* joined the local papers in calling for Akron's withdrawal from the "unwieldly and outmoded" Ohio Conference. The decision was taken out of local hands, however, when the conference voted in December to expel Akron.[84]

The University took the position they were just as well off out of the conference. When, at the conclusion of the academic year, 10 athletes were among those students dropped from school for scholastic deficiencies, the *Buchtelite* editor wrote that, while regretting the fate of the students involved, and of the fall football program, "we are . . . rather relieved in being thus decisively vindicated in our contention as to the calibre of student work done here." This should prove to all, he said, to those voting ouster from the Ohio Conference and to the general public, that they were wrong to doubt the seriousness of the academic effort required of athletes.[85] As for Jimmy Aiken, he was given a new three-year contract in December, 1937.

There can be little doubt that Aiken brought exciting football to Akron. His first game, a 33 to 0 victory over Detroit Tech, brought Stanley Junius, Al Abdulla, quarterback Bill Sturgeon, Mike Krino, Carl Tsaloff, and many other talented players to the fore. The fans became used to watching a succession of fine athletes on Aiken's teams; many of them now hold useful positions in the community, and for some, it was the chance that football gave them that channeled them into productive lives and careers.

In July 1939, Aiken resigned to become head coach at the University of Nevada. Thomas M. Dowler succeeded Aiken as head football and basketball coach. Otis Douglas was appointed an assistant in both sports, and two years later he succeeded Dowler as head football coach. The basketball chores were assumed by Russell Beichly in 1940. Of this trio, Beichly coached longest and established the best record with a succession of fine teams that gave Akron an enduring winning tradition in this sport.

The attempt to build strong varsity teams in football and basketball was accompanied by a desire for better playing facilities. The basketball team used Goodyear gym for its home games, and though it was a fine court, it was too far removed from campus to provide the best access or a collegiate atmosphere. Their drive for a student building having succeeded, ODK opened its guns on old Crouse gym and tried to rally support for its replacement, but another decade and a half were to elapse before a new gym was built.

Football did find a new home. In the fall of 1940, Akron started to use the Akron Municipal Stadium, better known as the Rubber Bowl, for its home games. This fine football stadium seemed the solution to the inadequacies of Buchtel Field whose grandstands were deteriorating and whose dressing rooms, lack of parking, and many other problems discouraged attendance. "Buchtel Field is dead," said the *Buchtelite*, "Let us all unite in one mighty moan and lay her gently to rest."[86] But the Rubber Bowl created a new psychological problem for spectators. The same number that had comfortably filled Buchtel Field looked embarrassingly lonesome in its cavernous interior; the old intimacy of Buchtel Field was gone, and only the throngs that in later years swelled in to watch the Acme-Zip contest filled the bowl to a degree that generated excitement.

While football and basketball captured the lion's share of attention, a number of so-called "minor sports" were developing on the varsity level. Although there had long been interclass track meets at Buchtel, the first varsity track team was formed in 1916. But track's fortunes were sporadic. Some years no team was formed, and it was not until the post-World War II period that Akron developed a strong program in track. An abortive effort to establish a tennis team was made in 1920, but this too was a marginal activity until much later. Boxing did not become a varsity sport although the University had intramural tournaments and assisted in preparing boxers for the Golden Gloves Tournaments.

The new wrestling team made its appearance in 1931 with a 40-0 loss to Case followed by another one of the same magnitude to Kent State. With little to work with, and an 18 by 18 foot room to practice in, the wrestlers had to wait for some years for their fortunes to improve. The spring of 1933 also found the University organizing its first gymnastics team under the direction of Walter Lipps. The first competitive effort was a losing one to Kent State. No sustained interest could be generated for support of a varsity team, and this demanding sport never flourished at Akron. Golf also made its appearance in 1933 when the new team managed an 8-8 tie with Ashland in its first match. By the 1950–60 period, Akron teams would be the class of the Ohio Conference. Finally, varsity swimming started in 1936. A team coached by "Bus" Gladwin and captained by Bill Fretz won its first Ohio Conference victory over Kent, 48-44, in the YMCA pool, having previously been dunked by Fenn College. Nearly two decades were to pass before a pool would be built on campus to provide a home for the swimmers.

Athletics always suggest alumni. Alumni activity and support were solicited on behalf of University projects other than athletics, and it is appropriate to look briefly at some of them. The tight-knit unity of sentiment and purpose that had characterized the graduates of Buchtel College had its counterpart in the first few classes graduating from the Municipal University, because they were still small, the faculty was known to all, and campus life was a more exclusive focus for their interests and energies than would be true by the late 1920's and thereafter.

Kolbe, Spanton, Simmons, Bulger, and C. R. Olin were not only at the heart of University operations, they were equally at the heart of alumni activities. Parke and Lydia Kolbe returned to the campus frequently after they had left for new fields of service. One faculty member recalls that Kolbe would suddenly appear in his office, unannounced, just wandering around to see how things were going. There is no record of what George Zook thought about his predecessor prowling the premises, but Zook was the imperturbable kind who probably took it in stride.

The appearance of *The Alumni Quarterly* in 1914, published by the Buchtel College Alumni Association, unleashed a flood of sentiment for the old school as scores of former Buchtelites wrote of their memories and their current activities, and sought information about their classmates. As is true of all such enterprises, once the initial flood of enthusiasm quieted, it was difficult to get contributors to write and pass on news. In time, a professional editor would be required to sustain an alumni publication.

In 1922 the Buchtel Association voted to change its name to the Alumni Association of the University of Akron. They engaged an alumni secretary, Miss Juliette Allen, Class of '14. At the same time, their magazine was renamed the *Akron Alumnus.*

Another important event of 1922 for alumni was the publication of *Fifty Years of Buchtel, 1870–1920,* edited by Dean Albert I. Spanton. Many former students had contributed material to the book. It was erratic in organization, uneven in contribution, repetitious, and thoroughly delightful. There will never be another like it for it contained virtually every name—student, faculty, trustee, donor, and friend—associated with the school, and it had the easy intimacy and informality of presentation that has meaning only for the members of the society it described.

During Kolbe's last years as president, the Alumni Association started to organize neighborhood clubs for alumni living in Akron and vicinity. These were not successful, but the effort to establish alumni clubs in other cities was. Municipal universities as a group were notoriously inept at alumni affairs and private fundraising. Akron made a start in both activities in the twenties, but the economic collapse, followed by years of war, precluded much dramatic success along these lines. Not until Norman Auburn brought his determination and tightly disciplined program to the task would Akron emerge as a front-runner among municipal schools in alumni organization and in securing private money for essential University needs.

The solicitation of donations to the stadium fund in 1922–23, the organization of Akron Day in the community, the sterling support of the relocation effort given by the Alumni Association under Alfred Herberich, the formation of an Endowment Association have all been mentioned in their place. But one of the most significant forms of support provided by alumni in Akron's behalf was the voting strength and influence they could exercise at the polls. In this work, Mr. Sherman O. Schumacher, Class of '27, was a leading spirit. He had done an outstanding job in organizing the campaign on behalf of campus relocation in 1928–29, and in recognition of his work, he was appointed Alumni Secretary in 1930. Alumni activities were curtailed during the depression, yet the ground work done in these early efforts paid dividends in support and concern in later years.

NOTES

1. *Beacon Journal,* Oct. 4, 1929.
2. *Buchtelite,* Oct. 17, 1936.
3. President's Report, 1935, p. 10.
4. *Buchtelite,* Oct. 17, 1936.
5. Ruth McKenney, *Industrial Valley* (New York, 1939), p. 186.
6. *Buchtelite,* April 7, 1933.
7. *Ibid.,* Feb. 17, 1934; President's Report, 1934, p. 14.
8. *Ibid.,* 1935, p. 12.
9. *Ibid.,* 1936, p. 10; Council Mins., Sept. 12, 1938; *Beacon Journal,* Oct. 26, 1939.
10. *Buchtelite,* Feb. 15, 1933.
11. *Ibid.,* Feb. 21, 1934.
12. *Ibid.,* March 3, 1934.
13. *Ibid.,* Oct. 7, 1936.
14. *Ibid.,* Sept. 26, 1936.
15. *Ibid.,* Jan. 8, 1937.
16. *Ibid.,* Nov. 22, 1939.
17. *Ibid.,* Sept. 23, 1937.
18. *Ibid.,* Oct. 28, 1933, Oct. 13, 1934.
19. *Ibid.,* April 4, 1930.
20. *Ibid.,* May 19, 1931.
21. President's Report, 1935, p. 14.
22. The most common method of assuring an audience was to require certain classes—English, speech, ROTC—to attend. Also, the Student Center and the library were closed, but students who were reluctant to attend could still manage ways to avoid it.
23. *Buchtelite,* Oct. 29, 1932.
24. *Ibid.,* Oct. 3, 1936.
25. *Beacon Journal,* Nov. 5, 1940.
26. *Buchtelite,* Dec. 9, 1933.
27. *Ibid.,* Jan. 25, 1933; McKenney, *Industrial Valley,* p. 54.
28. *Buchtelite,* Feb. 10, 1931.
29. *Ibid.*
30. *Ibid.*
31. *Ibid.,* Dec. 4, 1931.
32. *Ibid.,* Dec. 8, 1931.
33. *Ibid.,* various issues, 1932.
34. *Ibid.,* Dec. 11, 1931, Jan. 8, 1932.
35. *Ibid.,* March 11, 1932.
36. Board Mins., II, 261.
37. *Buchtelite,* Feb. 14, 1934.
38. *Ibid.,* Feb. 17, 1934.
39. *Ibid.,* Feb. 21, 1934.
40. *Beacon Journal,* Oct. 1, 1934.
41. *Ibid.,* Oct. 2, 1934.
42. *Ibid.,* Oct. 5, 1934; *Buchtelite,* Oct. 6, 1934; Board Mins., II, 365.
43. *Buchtelite,* Oct. 10, 1934.
44. *Ibid.,* Oct. 6, 1934; *Beacon Journal,* Oct. 2, Nov. 30, 1934.
45. *Buchtelite,* Nov. 2, 6, 1935.
46. *Ibid.,* Nov. 6, 1935.

[47] *Ibid.,* Nov. 9, 13, 1935.

[48] *Ibid.,* April 4, 18, 1935. A course planned for "future Generals" was "How to keep as far behind the battle-line as possible."

[49] *Ibid.,* April 22, 24, 1936.

[50] *Ibid.,* April 28, May 2, 24, 1940; *Beacon Journal,* Sept. 28, 1939.

[51] McKenney, *Industrial Valley,* pp. 122, 198, 345.

[52] *Buchtelite,* Dec. 6, 1938.

[53] See, for example, McKenney, *Industrial Valley,* pp. 8, 9, 13, 22.

[54] *Buchtelite,* Nov. 12, 1941.

[55] *Ibid.,* May 18, 1938.

[56] President's Report, 1930, p. 10.

[57] *Buchtelite,* Feb. 17, 1934.

[58] *Ibid.,* Oct. 23, 1935, Oct. 11, 1939.

[59] *Ibid.,* Dec. 19, 1930.

[60] *Ibid.,* May 5, 13, 1933.

[61] *Ibid.,* May 22, 1937.

[62] *Akron Times Press,* June 13, 1937.

[63] *Buchtelite,* Oct. 9, 1931.

[64] Board Mins. (1913–24), p. 33; *Buchtelite,* June 20, 1917.

[65] Board Mins. (1913–24), p. 40.

[66] *Buchtelite,* March 7, May 16, 1923. High school graduates were being pledged as they marched across the platform at commencement.

[67] *Ibid.,* Jan. 7, March 22, 1927.

[68] *Ibid.,* April 2, 1925, March 10, 1934, March 4, 1936.

[69] *Beacon Journal,* July 26, 27, 1916; President's Report, 1934, p. 11.

[70] *Ibid.,* 1940, pp. 6–7.

[71] *Ibid.*

[72] *Akron Alumnus,* Dec., 1922.

[73] *Buchtelite,* Feb. 8, 15, 1922.

[74] *Beacon Journal,* June 14, 1919.

[75] President's Report, 1927, p. 7; *ibid.,* 1930, p. 10.

[76] Board Mins. (1913–24), p. 217.

[77] *Buchtelite,* Oct. 14, 1930.

[78] *Ibid.,* Jan 8, 15, 1926.

[79] Zook thought that "in the distant future" credit would be given for varsity athletics. He considered athletics as "laboratories for molding the character of the players." *Buchtelite,* Oct. 2, 1931, Dec. 10, 1932.

[80] As reprinted in *Buchtelite,* Nov. 5, 1932.

[81] *Ibid.,* March 10, 1934.

[82] *Ibid.,* Dec. 6, 1935, March 4, 1936; Board Mins., II, 405.

[83] *Akron Times Press,* Oct. 6, 1936; *Beacon Journal,* Oct. 7, Nov. 5, 1936.

[84] *Ibid.,* Nov. 5, 1936; *Buchtelite,* Nov. 11, 1936.

[85] *Ibid.,* June 30, 1937.

[86] *Ibid.,* Sept. 20, 1940.

War came to the University in the '40's and due to the scarcity of rubber for tires, many students traveled on two wheels instead of four.

XVII

Out of the depression and into the war (1939–1945)

Every so often in the life cycle of a social institution there appears a period of relative quiescence when no substantial changes are in progress and the course of events flows along in familiar and predictable channels. It is easier for the historian to identify such periods in retrospect than it is for contemporaries who are experiencing them.

The years following the worst of the depression and preceding World War II were such a time in the life of the University of Akron. During this brief period no new buildings were constructed; the curriculum experienced only minor accretions and adjustments; student advisement procedures and the sympathetic direction given to extracurricular activities helped iron out student problems; athletics were withdrawing from a brief flirtation with the big-time; but most important of all, the attention of campus and nation was drawn increasingly toward Austria, Czechoslovakia, and Poland where the Nazi war machine was remaking the map of Europe. "Blitzkrieg" was added to the nation's vocabulary.

Summarizing the 1939–40 year, President Simmons indicated that the academic house was being put in order and recent gains consolidated: "While we have no outstanding accomplishent to announce," he wrote, "yet we have had one of the most successful years in our educational existence."[1] Enrollment was at a healthy level. With 3,265 credit students—1,763 of them in the regular day session—Akron ranked sixth among the 48 colleges in Ohio. Enrollment in the evening program was up 14.2 percent over the previous year due to the "improved economic conditions of the city," and 496 persons were enrolled in the non-credit courses of the Community College. Another 328 students were enrolled in special courses being offered at the B. F. Goodrich Company. Summer Session enrollment was up over previous years.[2]

Despite relative quiet, the University was never static, and adjustments continued to be made in its programs and in its services. In June, 1940, the Guggenheim Institute became an integral part of the College of Engineering, and its staff was given faculty status. This was done, said President Simmons, because "we are fully aware that air transportation is now past the experimental stage," and as a municipal university in a city that was "air-minded," it was "the duty of the institution" to provide training in this new form of transportation.[3] Thus, aeronautical engineering became a new option in the Department of Mechanical Engineering and, for a brief time, it was one of the most popular engineering programs.

The College of Engineering acquired another source of strength at this time. In 1941 it was accredited by the Engineer's Council for Professional Development making it only the fourth of Ohio's nine engineering programs to secure this recognition. That same year the chemistry department was accredited by its professional body, the American Chemical Society; it was the sixth Ohio department to attain that status. While sometimes impatient of the demands imposed on the institution by these accrediting bodies, the University was nevertheless pleased by these outside evidences that its programs were of acceptable quality.

In some other curricular areas, much needed to be done to provide high quality programs. In the developing field of psychology, an attempt to upgrade the program was led by a student, Bert Wolin, who urged that the Board of Directors be petitioned to establish an experimental psychology laboratory at Spicer School. The department had only a small supply of home-made apparatus. Wolin believed that "the psychology department has been married to the College of Education so long that it doesn't have any value by itself."[4] Though Wolin had the backing of Professor George Hayes, who taught most of the psychology then offered, he was unsuccessful in his crusade, and the psychology program remained undernourished for another 20 years. While supporting Wolin's efforts, the *Buchtelite* said of the psychology reformers, "We wish them luck. They'll need it."[5]

This tone of skepticism reflected the *Buchtelite's* frustration in trying to secure a Department of Journalism on the Akron campus. Success for this effort was still in the future, but in the meantime, the paper went on winning national and state recognition for its excellence. In 1940, for the fifth consecutive year, the paper was awarded a coveted "All-American" rating from the Associated Collegiate Press. The paper was informative, well written and carefully edited, and it took a positive position in supporting causes to its liking, but it did this in a rational and responsible manner. During this time it was less inhibited than it would be in the future years. Indeed, the *Buchtelite* had great fun chiding the University of Michigan for controls that it had placed on the *Michigan Daily,* one of the country's fine collegiate papers. "The *Buchtelite* is not as big as the *Daily.* It is not as famous. It is not, unfortunately, as good," admitted the local editors. "But at least the *Buchtelite* is free."[6]

Among the campus innovations of this period were several that started Bierce Library on its way toward more up-to-date services. The librarian commenced a cooperative cataloging program with her counterparts at Kent, Hiram, and Mount Union. Experience gained in this work made Akron one of the more informed Ohio schools when attempts were made in the 1960's to establish a state-wide central cataloging system. The first microfilm readers were introduced in 1940, but the library was slow in developing this facility. An important assist in the library's work was given by the newly established "Friends of the Library." This group, formed in conjunction with the Alumni Association, provided modest financial support for special collections. Over the years it helped greatly in building collections on the American Indian, Negro history and culture, Far Eastern history, and many other special interests.

For the first time since Old Buchtel flourished, scholarship money started to flow to the University. Private money sought since 1913 had been scheduled for use in capital improvements; little was said about the need for scholarships. Indeed, as long as the University managed to keep close to its intended character as a school free to the sons and daughters of Akron taxpayers there was no need for scholarships. But as we have seen, financial circumstances forced the University far away from this posture to the point where students were paying more than 50 percent of the cost of their education. Most impressive of the new scholarship money was the $25,000 Knight Memorial Education Fund established by the Beacon Journal Publishing Company in honor of C. L. Knight, its former head. This was not a University scholarship fund, although many awards went to Akron students. The Fund was called "one of the greatest boons to highly qualified students ever to be created in Akron."[7]

Although no large increase in faculty size was possible to accommodate the large enrollment, new faces continued to be seen among the faculty. The students were particularly pleased when one of the new faculty members, Dr. Robert Thackaberry, married another recent arrival, Miss Helen Saunders. Following the wedding ceremony they were driven to Cleveland by a colleague in the English department who later was mis-quoted as saying, "They talked about *ceramics* all the way up."[8] What they really had talked about was *semantics,* which somehow seems more appropriate for English teachers, even if it appears somewhat odd for newlyweds.[9] Within a short time, Dr. Thackaberry would be one of a considerable number of faculty members off to war.

It became increasingly obvious to Americans, after 1940, that the nation was moving toward belligerent status. Those on the Akron campus who remembered the adjustments that World War I had brought to the University's program had some appreciation of what lay in store. President Simmons reminded the Board of Directors what to expect:

The European conflict has had its effect upon the thinking of our faculty and students. As the year progressed and the events were recorded, it has been interesting to note the similarity of the pattern now being formed and the one that developed in the last World War. Out of that previous experience we should do the best job of teaching possible, for when peace comes to the world, we shall need the best trained minds to lead us through the reconstruction phase that will follow.[10]

Of course there had already been much speculation about America's role in a foreign conflict. Faculty opinion had been sampled in the spring of 1940 by the *Beacon Journal* which found that many professors agreed with their colleague who said: "Let us remember that we can afford to be calm because of our isolated position."[11] This illustration merely confirms the truism that college teachers and administrators have little special insight to offer, as a group, when it comes to predicting the course of events. Of greater moment than casual prediction was the "one all-compelling thought" that President Simmons called to the board's attention: "What effect will the War have upon the University?" Simmons did not know the answer yet, but he did know that it was "no time to slacken our efforts."[12]

One of the principal effects was not long in coming. The selective service program—the draft—made its appearance in the fall semester, 1940. In its early phases, before the nation was at war, the draft had a disruptive effect on college campuses. The uncertainties associated with a call-up kept college men off stride. They never knew whether or not they could finish the semester's work, employment prospects dimmed when potential employers learned that the student might soon be drafted, courtships were disrupted, and life suddenly was filled with uncertainties. To help counteract the tendency of male students to abandon their studies or to "take a last fling," President Simmons continually urged them to stay in school until called. "When this country needs the aid of her young men and women they freely give their service, but until you are informed that your duty is to your country, your duty is to yourself," he said.[13] A letter from President Roosevelt making the same case was read to entering freshmen in 1940.

In preparation for the draft, the Board of Directors voted to refund all fees to students who were called for a year of military duty under the conscription act.[14] For a year? That is how long the first young men conscripted in 1940 were committed to serve. But those who marched off singing the pop hit of the day—"Goodbye Dear I'll Be Back In a Year, Cause I'm In the Army Now"—would soon discover that the "year" turned out to be the "duration and six months." In November, the moment everyone had been anticipating arrived; nine Akron men, faculty and students, were selected in the first draft lottery. The war had come to the Hilltop.

There would be no consensus about America's role in world events until after December 7, 1941. Every attitude from demoralization about the political climate to happy-go-lucky acceptance could be found on campus. A local reporter observed that scholarship had declined modestly and that an increasing number of students were leaving to take jobs in industry on a temporary basis. Most of the latter went to Akron factories or the Ravenna Arsenal where they were engaged in war production. One Akron coed was unhappy at the prospects; "War is a waste of time—and it certainly will be boring around here when we have nobody to associate with but other women," she said. Dr. DeGraff was convinced that many students didn't know what they were supposed to be defending, and this contributed to their unrest, but DeGraff, like his fellow instructors, thought the students were patriotic and loyal. Dean Gardner put it succinctly: "Students want to do their duty but they don't quite see where their duty lies."[15] To those who have pondered student reaction to the Korean and Vietnam conflicts, these words have a familiar ring.

There were the "eat, drink, and be merry" students who either sought escape from war threats or used them as an excuse for a little fun. This attitude was especially noticeable in the spring semester, 1941. During the summer session the atmosphere took on a new note of seriousness as the war threat increased. Students were busy at war jobs; the student building was little used. With the coming of the fall semester, a definite trend toward freshmen enrollment in evening classes was attributed to student employment in preparedness industries.[16]

No protests against compulsory ROTC were heard now. The campus unit was ordered to work with the Fifth U. S. Army Corps in an effort to interest students in military training, with special emphasis on aviation training. At the end of a 35-week training period, qualified students would be commissioned as Second Lieutenants in the Army Reserve.[17]

Campus life went on much as usual, although a shortage in certain supplies was beginning to be a problem, but President Simmons could still secure the Black Jack chewing gum of which he was so fond. Students still politicked: and little did anyone realize that the skinny boy named John Ballard who had just been elected to the Dance Committee would one day parlay his new-found political acumen into the Mayor's office. With their minds elsewhere a good part of the time, and with many engaged full time in defense work, the football players managed to win two games and tie two, one of the losses being a heartbreaking 6-0 defeat by a strong Western Reserve team in the first game Akron played in the Rubber Bowl, the new home field of the Zips. Russ Beichly started his winning ways, which even the war failed to stop, when his first Akron basketball varsity registered 13 wins against 6 losses. In student government, a popular independent, Gordon Hagerman, presided over Student Council. Fraternities and sororities, music organizations, theater groups, and the many other campus activities continued through 1940–41 with minimal interruptions.

The effects of war preparation spread over the campus with interesting results. It suddenly seemed that everyone was getting married. Couples who would have been content to prolong courtship, drinking "Cokes" in the student building while listening to "The White Cliffs of Dover," now discovered that draft call-ups, involving long periods of separation, were a great stimulus to matrimony. Knitting made its appearance as a staple female activity. Without tires for their automobiles, professors and students took to bicycle riding. A student-faculty "share-the-ride" program was introduced. And students rediscovered the Akron Transportation Company. Sororities sold war savings stamps, visited USO installations, and gladly accepted defense stamp corsages in lieu of flowers. Drives were initiated to save tin cans; exams were written on the blackboard to save paper; signs in the cafeteria reminded coffee drinkers to take it easy on the sugar. Though Akron was still a civilian school, ROTC uniforms were soon to give way to army khaki as preparations were made to receive military trainees on campus.

In this mixture of normality and nascent war preparedness, the balance was swinging away from normality. As early as the spring of 1940, the University had been asked to submit a plan to the federal government showing how facilities might be secured to train workers in industries essential to the national defense. By 1941, more than 2,500 persons had enrolled for courses in Akron's Engineering Defense Training program under the auspices of the U. S. Office of Education. One of the specialized programs Akron was uniquely prepared to offer was ground training for blimp pilots. Men trained in this program would later man the blimps that performed so well on anti-submarine patrols and in other vital tasks.[18]

Within a short time, America would experience a problem of enormous importance to its survival when it appeared certain that its chief supply of natural rubber would be cut off by the Japanese. A crash program, centered in Akron, was developed to produce commercially feasible synthetic rubber, and much of this vital work was carried on by chemists and engineers trained by C. M. Knight and "Hez" Simmons in the little rubber chemistry labs in Knight Chemical Laboratory. Through the cooperation of the various rubber companies, secrets were shared, talents pooled, and success achieved. Synthetic rubber saved the day and reshaped the future of the industry. Dr. Knight just missed seeing this most dramatic fulfillment of much that he had worked to achieve, for he died in 1941, age 93, after a lifetime of service to rubber science and to the school he had cherished so long.

December 7, 1941, ended any ambivalence the campus may have had about the draft and war preparations. The same unity of purpose that the larger society experienced in the wake of Pearl Harbor was found on campus. From this point, an all-out effort would be made to contribute to the nation's success in its struggles around the world. On December 12, President Simmons called the faculty's attention to the imperative need for "a twelve-month, year-around educational program."[19] University Council voted to preserve the various curricula, but to shorten the time required to complete them. This was to be done by introducing a 12-week summer session, so structured that a student attending year-round could complete a four-year degree program in three years. The emphasis was now on speed, efficiency in instruction, and flexibility.

On February 20, 1943, a cadre of Army Air Corps personnel under the command of Captain Ned Garten, arrived in Akron. They were an advance unit sent to prepare a reception for the first 125 student trainees enrolled in the Army Air Force College Training Program. President Simmons had worked long to secure Akron's participation in such a program. It was an appropriate way for the University to be of service, and it was also a great boon in providing support of the regular, ongoing programs. Instructors were employed, administrators had tasks to fulfill, facilities were kept operative through use, and the life of the campus was enriched by the presence of the trainees. The air cadets took a five-month course consisting of 60 hours of training in each of several subjects—English, mathematics, history, and geography. They were also given 180 hours of instruction in physics and 289 hours of physical and military training. Since they were all eventually to be flight officers —pilots, bombardiers, or navigators—each cadet received 10 hours of flight instruction at the Akron Municipal Airport. Their training schedule was not to interfere with the regular college curriculum, but on a tight-knit campus like Akron's this was more a hope than a promise.[20]

The first unit of 125 men arrived early in March from a five-week tour of basic training at Miami Beach. It is a testimony to the capacity of the young and vigorous to adjust that the cadets survived the transition from the balmy climate of Florida with little trouble. Little trouble, perhaps, but much griping. Akron was happy to see them: "The presence of these boys should add incentive to our war effort," said the *Beacon Journal* in a welcoming editorial. Part of the incentive offered was to a hopeful group of coeds, some of whom had shown their unhappiness with the male depletion by placing a sign reading "Hilltop School for Girls" on the front lawn. But, to the disappointment of all, the cadets were kept so busy, and their schedule kept them so segregated, that it was difficult even for the most enterprising to fraternize extensively.

The University was responsible for housing and feeding the trainees. Crouse gym, ancient relic of bygone days, was judged by the army to be unsuitable for use as a barracks. As had been the case in World War I, off-campus facilities had to be found for housing the cadets. A building located at the corner of Main Street and E. Buchtel Avenue was secured, and the lines of trim young men, marching up the hill to campus, became a familiar sight to Akronites.[21] The student building cafeteria was taken over to feed the cadets. With these arrangements complete, a second group of trainees appeared in April to swell the number to respectable size.

In September the first contingent of 125 men in the Army Specialized Training Program (ASTP) arrived in Akron. These men were to take a three-term course of pre-engineering subjects, each term to be 12 weeks in length. This ASTP Program was conducted independently from the Air Cadet program. The ASTP trainees were billeted in the old Sweeney Funeral Home on East Market Street. It was inevitable that the men would refer to their barracks as "the morgue."[22]

Much campus effort went into these training programs. Richard Schmidt acted as coordinator of the Air Cadet Program while Dean Fred Ayer performed a similar function for the ASTP. Faculty members taught courses for both programs, and the University was reimbursed by the federal government for their salaries. But no sooner had the campus adjusted to the new programs than they ended. In the spring semester, 1944, both programs were phased out.

One belated training program brought 121 seventeen-year-olds to the campus in the summer of 1944. These students received pre-induction training which was to keep them in reserve until their eighteenth birthday at which time they would be reassigned. This program terminated September 30.[23]

Suddenly the campus was again quiet; no marching ranks singing cadence, no uniforms in the student building, and no "Kiwi," the shortlived supplement to the *Buchtelite* put out by the air cadets and named, appropriately, for the little flightless bird. Akron was given a high rating for its training activities, and the programs had been well conducted. In a day before close cost accounting was established, it seems likely that the University lost money on these programs, but if that were indeed true, it must be counted as still another contribution to the nation's cause.[24]

The disappearance of the military trainees left a distinct vacuum, so much so that President Simmons found it necessary to squelch rumors that came "floating" into his office from faculty members and students indicating that there was "a question in the minds of some people that the university might be closed next year." He stated emphatically that it would *not* close. There were plenty of civilians even though the military units were gone.[25]

Many colleges could boast of war service rendered through the training of military personnel, but not many could match Akron's contribution to the equally essential but less glamorous activity of upgrading the skills of laboring men and women employed in war industries. In proportion to its size, Akron possibly had as wide an impact in this vital activity as could be found in the nation. To demonstrate that these wartime services were but an adaptation of established procedures to new ends, we should review briefly the University's contribution to adult education in pre-war days.

The University had always considered itself the servant of the community. In good times and bad it responded to calls for service and help from industry, business, government, social agencies. and other community interests. The community had come to take for granted the University's response to the needs of its citizens and to regard the University as its servant rather than its guide. We have already noted examples of campus-community cooperation ranging from the comprehensive evening program of credit courses, supplemented with special adult education courses in the non-credit program, to the assistance rendered community agencies in the solution of specific problems.

During the two decades preceding American entry into World War II, courses were offered in industrial teacher training at the request of the Ohio Department of Education; in production engineering at the request of local industrialists; short courses were offered for the Short Story Institute, the Purchasing Institute, and the Retail Credit Institute; an economics program was offered at the request of local labor unions; courses in social work were offered for the convenience of the Family Service Society; courses in Instructor-Foreman training were complemented by a Conference on Leadership Training for men in local industry; Employment Training programs were carried on for the Ohio Board of Vocational Education; and so on.

Some of these programs were innovative; some were marked by their magnitude. The program of general courses offered at the B. F. Goodrich Company in 1935, for example, enrolled 446 students that year and was reported to be the largest program of general education subjects ever offered in an industrial plant.[26] These courses were non-credit, but they were not job-oriented in a narrow sense. Most were taught by regular faculty members although considerable part-time instruction was also used. Other such programs existed briefly at General Tire, Quaker Oats, and the Firestone Tire and Rubber Company. This was "grass roots" education with a vengeance. Years later, when local industries requested that the University set up credit courses in the factories, much caution was exercised to make certain that the kind of work offered was appropriate to the setting. In other words, courses requiring ready library access would be avoided in favor of courses that relied heavily on a standard text, class lectures, and discussions. When such courses were offered, students were registered and processed in the normal way, so that the University did not fall into the trap of violating its own self-imposed admission and retention standards. The later programs, however, tended to stress a "beefing up" of skills and knowledge already basically acquired. Courses designed to keep engineers, chemists, or accountants abreast of evolutionary movements within their own specialties were also offered in the plants.

The machinery needed to organize and supervise the adult education effort evolved during the twenties and was refined during the thirties. The thoroughness of the commitment was enunciated best by George Zook in 1929:

> The keynote of an institution of this type [municipal] is the direct correlation of the educational program of the institution with the needs of the city. Inasmuch as these needs, both cultural and technical, are at our very doors they are easily identified and we can make our plans accordingly. We train our teachers for the Akron schools, our engineers for the Akron industries, our chemists for the rubber industries, our Commerce students for the Akron business firms, and our home economics students for local employment.
> ... We believe that it is our duty to cooperate with local civic and social agencies and with other municipal agencies for mutual benefit.
> We believe that the education of so-called regular college students is only a part of our task. There are many more adults beyond normal college age who should be reached with part-time evening education than there are full-time students between the ages of 17 and 22.[27]

The first full-time Director of Adult Education, Mr. Leslie Hardy, was appointed in 1934. Three years later the old extension course concept was updated into the "Community College" in which a wide variety of non-credit courses was made available to the public at minimal cost.[28] Most of these courses were offered on the campus in a setting just like that used for regular credit work. The *Beacon Journal* praised the newly created Community College, and the paper's publisher, John S. Knight, could say in good conscience that same year that the University was "one institution upon whose merits all classes of our citizenship seem to agree."[29]

The depression years saw a new kind of cooperative community-campus venture when the University entered directly into attempts to ameliorate acute social problems. Home Economics instructors set up demonstrations of how to cook with optimum effect the predominantly starchy foods many families had to subsist on. Courses in government were designed to foster civic pride in a day when Akron was conspicuously lacking in that essential ingredient of a healthy city. A teacher's institute sponsored by the WPA was organized and run by University personnel. The census tract maps were handled through the Sociology department because the city could not afford to hire suitable personnel. Sociology students followed through on investigations of court decisions to see that the sentence was carried out when it required the offender to change certain environmental conditions. Sample voter registration surveys were put into the hands of Professor David King in 1940 because the Board of Elections feared there would be charges of tampering with the data. They picked the right man; anyone who knew Professor King's passion for accuracy and accountability could attest to this. It might be said that the University had become the city's only true "neutral ground" where parties, mutually suspicious, could find an arbiter that would command respect and stand above the partisan battle.

This partial review of Akron's experience with adult education reveals that a quick and natural diversion of this experience to wartime needs was likely. Isolated courses pertinent to war preparedness had been offered for some years when, in 1942, the University embarked on a broad program of service to Akron's wartime needs. Many credit courses were tailored to make them relevant to war conditions; 10 such courses were introduced by the College of Engineering in the spring semester. At the same time, nine courses specially designed for the war effort were introduced by the Community College.

A major effort was the Training Within Industry (TWI) program which taught industrial squad leaders, supervisors, and foremen how to teach great numbers of new workers in a short span of time to become efficient and skilled producers. Classes were held in the plants under the tutelage of 231 persons certified in job instruction training, job methods training, and job relations training. This effort was supplemented by the Engineering, Science, and Management War Training Program (ESMWT) directed by Leslie Hardy. Courses ran for 12 weeks and were designed to provide a practical education in specific areas of need. Students attended classes in the evening after a full day's work. Only a high school diploma was needed to qualify. Akron's group of 3,567 students was the largest among the 15 Ohio programs.[30] Heretofore, the costs of the program were absorbed by the federal government, but when the TWI and ESMWT programs were terminated in June, 1945, the directors voted to continue these courses on a fee basis.[31] Over 11,000 persons were trained in these courses which proved so valuable that portions of them were retained as part of the Community College program.[32]

The war period found the University fulfilling one of its most cherished dreams, one that went back to Dr. C. M. Knight and his interest in rubber chemistry. This was the establishment of an Institute for Rubber Research under the direction of the University and in cooperation with the rubber companies of Akron. President Kolbe favored the idea, as did George Zook, who actually had the wheels turning in 1930 when plans were nipped by the financial crisis.[33] Simmons was vitally interested in the project, and in 1942, under the spur of wartime exigencies, the plan he submitted to the Board of Directors for development of a Rubber Technical Institute to be sponsored by local rubber companies was adopted, and Mr. James Schade was appointed Director effective February 1, 1942. Schade's salary accounted for all except $2,500 of the modest budget set aside for this purpose. The University was to provide facilities to research men designated by the companies supporting the program.[34]

A year later the first substantial contract was received—$29,000 from the Rubber Reserve Company for research in synthetic rubber. This work was carried out under the direction of Dr. George Stafford Whitby, Professor of Rubber Chemistry since 1942 and an eminent scientist in the field of rubber and its associated technology.[35] After a most diversified career that had taken him through all aspects of the rubber business from plantation to laboratory, Dr. Whitby brought to Akron the talent, vision, and respect which caused the rubber research program to flourish and endure. Just as important in smoothing the way for this specialized program was his profound feeling for, and knowledge of, the fine arts and the humanities; for this liberally educated man so obviously belonged on a college campus that the scientific research he was engaged in seemed appropriate too.

In 1943 another important development in rubber research grew out of an agreement made by the University with the War Production Board (WPB) to operate

a synthetic rubber pilot plant and research laboratories built by the federal government on Wilbeth Road. Mr. James Schade was named manager. The almost insurmountable problem of staffing the laboratory was solved by the Rubber Director of
the WPB, Mr. Bradley Dewey, through whose efforts 32 chemical warfare officers
were assigned to duty at the plant.[36] Even before the formal opening of the pilot
plant in June, 1944, samples were run. During the remainder of the war period, effort
concentrated on improving the quality of synthetic rubber so crucial to the war effort.
Some 209 persons were employed in this research in 1945. After VJ Day, emphasis
shifted to the problem of reducing costs without impairing the quality of the product.
President Simmons, an old rubber chemist himself, described details of the program
with loving care, probably telling the Board of Directors more than they could absorb
about the details of the work.[37]

At mid-year, 1947, the budget of the pilot plant and laboratories was reduced
approximately 40 percent.[38] It was only a matter of time until the government would
lose interest in maintaining basic research in this area, for private companies were
developing great research organizations that could do the work as effectively. Slowly,
as the cramped and inadequate resources of the University would permit, the research effort was focused more and more on campus. In 1947 the library of the
Rubber Division of the American Chemical Society was located on the Akron campus. This central comprehensive library became an important adjunct to the research
program—and later the instructional program—in rubber and polymers.[39] The appointment of Dr. Maurice Morton to the staff of the Institute of Rubber Research, as
the program was now identified, brought to Akron the man who would carry on the
important work started by Dr. Whitby and his associates. This continuing development will be outlined in a later chapter.

While rubber research waxed, aerospace research at the Guggenheim Institute
waned. The sudden and dramatic demise of the lighter-than-air industry had virtually
terminated the enterprise before it was well launched. When the California Institute
of Technology withdrew from further participation in the Institute's work at the end
of its five-year contract, support fell entirely to The University of Akron and the
Institute itself. It continued to be a money-maker in a modest sense during most of
the pre-war period, but it was increasingly clear that aircraft technology, so acutely
accelerated by the war effort, had made the Guggenheim obsolete. In 1942 the
Institute was integrated into the financial and instructional program of the University.
Dr. Troller was named Director of Research while Mr. Curtis C. Myers became
resident Director of the Institute.

The Institute was involved in the war effort, one of its contributions being
associated with the development of Azon, a steerable bomb. By 1945 it was running
at an annual loss of $34,000. Four years later, obsolescence of equipment and inability
to win contracts caused the Board of Directors reluctantly to approve President
Simmons' recommendation to terminate the program and close the Institute. In 1950
City Council transferred the title to the Guggenheim property to the University. The
buildings were then leased for one dollar a year to the Akron Board of Education for
use as a training facility. Finally the buildings were sold to Goodyear in 1956.[40]

These major efforts overshadow other important wartime contributions.[41]
Courses in sanitation and bacteriology were revamped under government direction
to stress the bacteriological and sanitary problems of wartime. Students completing
these courses were enrolled as auxiliary personnel in the public health division of the
medical section of Civil Defense. Courses were introduced in sugarless cooking and
meat substitutes, in navigation, meteorology, aircraft drafting, camouflage, first aid,
and "Contemporary Thought and Policy." Akron was named one of six Ohio "key
information centers" by the U. S. Department of Education. This involved establishing a large "war library" of materials concerning defense. A speaker's bureau was
initiated to spread the word about American war aims and to provide speakers
equipped to deal with topics of current interest. The musicians, not to be left out,
organized a "morale division" of civilian defense to sing at nearby military installations, patriotic rallies, and at twilight summer concerts. Also introduced as a war
measure was a cooperative nurses training course operated in conjunction with local

hospitals. Later on, of course, this kind of University-hospital cooperative program, which was claimed to be the first in Ohio, would be a standard part of the curriculum.

In addition to the fact that special programs were established to meet wartime needs, the regular curriculum was modified in response to war conditions and also in response to the normal flow of pressures that work for change. Shortly after Pearl Harbor, President Robert Hutchins of the University of Chicago announced that his institution would award bachelor's degrees to students who had completed just two years of college study. When asked how he viewed the Hutchins plan, Hezzleton Simmons replied that he agreed with Hutchins on the fundamental point that time alone was no measure of education and with the idea that the student who could not profitably proceed beyond two years should be able to leave the university with respect, but Simmons differed with Hutchins on details. Akron, said Simmons, eliminated those not fit for college work through its entrance requirements, and further, it "has never had a place for the Joe College type which regards college as a lark."[42] He thought that high school graduates could become competent engineers and chemists with only two years of college—a strange idea to the present generation that argues for an additional year on the engineer's five and the chemists' four—but he opposed granting the degree that early because it would handicap the student in later competition. He favored two-year, terminal curricula in practical courses such as secretarial science, but the resources to start more such programs were not available.

Early in 1945 considerable discussion was generated about these additional terminal or "certificate" programs of two-year duration. Nothing of substance was accomplished because other priorities crowded the issue into the background. While never relinquished, the terminal course idea was essentially dormant until the great push in Ohio that led to the establishment of technical education revived the issue and brought the University to a full-fledged involvement. But even as the war drew to a close, the College of Education responded to an acute need for public school teachers by instituting a two-year certification program of teacher training. These "cadet" teachers were rushed into the elementary school classrooms. There was never any substantial body of support for making this a permanent program, and it was abandoned in the early 1950's when the flow of four-year degree teachers once more became adequate to handle the instructional load in the public schools. The College of Education had no wish to jeopardize the accreditation it had earned in 1942 from the American Association of Teachers Colleges.[43]

A new division of the Buchtel College of Liberal Arts was formed in wartime. In 1944, the Applied Arts Division was established consisting of the Departments of Art, Home Economics, Commerce, and Secretarial Science.[44] This was done in response to the need for increased specialization in those fields. Dean Bulger called the new division an attempt to solve, at least temporarily, "the problem that arises from the demands on an urban university to contribute trained people to the industries and business enterprises of the city." The old liberal arts college, he said, "put the emphasis on broad training, and instilling the will to learn, the ability to improve oneself. . . . It was taken for granted that graduates would learn the specific tricks on the job."[45] A further adjustment in the arts college was the development of a program in psychology which heretofore had offered a major only in the College of Education.[46] It would be some years yet until the department would change locus from education to arts, but recognition was growing that the discipline's impact was universal and spread well beyond the confines of any professional program.

Elsewhere in the curriculum, the war brought changes. As happened in the depression of 1920–21 and again in the 1930's, the cooperative engineering program became a temporary casualty. To speed the supply of engineers to a hungry war economy, the five year co-op plan was modified into a straight four-year academic course.[47] Meanwhile, courses offered in 1945 in the field of industrial management, largely with an eye toward the post-war development of Akron, grew in popularity until they became important in the commerce curriculum.[48] As business administration developed into full collegiate status after the war, the Department of Industrial Management would be the largest unit in that college.

The acceleration of activity during World War II had additional impact on campus schedules and programs. The buildings were used 14 hours a day. Coal shortages required a complete plant shutdown on Saturdays. The old heating plant boilers were in a critical state of disrepair and were scarcely able to maintain steam in all classrooms and offices at the same time. While the class schedule was speeded up, so was the process of awarding degrees as first January commencements and then September commencements were introduced. This practice was abandoned at war's end not to be reestablished until class sizes forced adopting a mid-year commencement in 1967. Through it all, the boilers held, the buildings withstood their buffetings, and resources, stretched to the breaking point, were adequate.

Aside from plant and curricular matters, the critical concern in maintaining the high level of activity in wartime was the securing and retaining of competent personnel to administer and to teach. From 1942 to 1944, President Simmons was gone from the campus most of the time on assignment as Associate Chief of the Rubber Branch of the War Production Board. His weeks were spent in Washington and most of his weekends on the campus. Not only did Simmons contribute to the war effort in this role, but he was convinced that he had gained "some valuable experience which . . . may prove to be of value to the university as well."[49] During the early part of his absence Dean Bulger was charged with the running of day-to-day business.[50] In 1943, Mr. Les Hardy was appointed Assistant to the President and began to relieve Simmons of certain detail work.[51] Dean Howard Evans left for military service as did Dean Donfred Gardner, who was commissioned a major in the U. S. Army and placed in charge of officer procurement for northern Ohio. Other faculty members leaving for military service kept up a steady exodus from campus. It was difficult to realize that many who left would not return; few became war casualties, but several sought post-war positions on other campuses or in other activities.

In addition to those entering military service, several of the faculty had special skills that were much in demand in civilian war work. Professor Warren Leigh, for instance, was a rubber consultant in the Office of Price Administration, Mr. Frank Simonetti became a Labor Market Analyst for the War Manpower Commission, Dr. Orville Hitchcock held a position with the Office of War Information, Dr. Dwight Gray became Research Associate in the Underwater Sound Laboratory at Harvard, Professor John Adendorff worked for the War Manpower Commission, and so it went.

In the spring of 1942 the Board of Directors approved President Simmons' recommendation that members of the faculty who entered military service be granted a leave of absence without compensation from the time of their induction to the time of their eligibility for discharge. Upon expiration of this leave, every effort would be made to restore the person to his previous position or one for which he qualified.[52] This policy worked satisfactorily and there was no difficulty in fitting men and women back into their familiar teaching and administrative positions, for with the end of the war came an accompanying surge of enrollment that created an acute shortage of experienced faculty.

The sense of loss that pervades an institution when many of its familiar faces depart was deepened during the war years by the untimely death of Miss Helen Battrick, who had been an able and well liked Adviser of Women. Professor Rolland Fox, since 1921 a member of the biology staff, also died unexpectedly leaving a notable gap in the teaching ranks. Early in 1942 word came of the death, in Phila-delphia, of Parke Kolbe, so much a part of all that had transpired on the campus he did so much to shape. Another familiar campus personality, Miss Gladys Weeks, longtime Secretary to the President and one-time registrar retired.

But the oldest enduring tie with the past was cut when Albert Spanton, Professor of English and Dean Emeritus of the Buchtel College of Liberal Arts, retired in 1943. His advice to the last student generation he would teach was "live your lives richly and fully, so that at the close you can say, 'How good is man's living.' "[53] In his honor, the Albert I. Spanton Collection of English and American Literature was established by friends. This expanding collection contains hundreds of important volumes including many rare ones. It is a fitting memorial as is the Spanton Room, a quiet haven in the busy Student Center, and Spanton Hall, a dormitory.

It is easy for faculty and staff to overlook the significance of changes in the Board of Directors because few have direct contact with Board members. Certain changes, however, have considerable consequence. One was the retirement of Mr. John W. Thomas in 1942. His work as Chairman of the Board of the Firestone Tire and Rubber Company was most difficult during the wartime crisis, and he had already served the University as a director for some 23 years, 16 of them as chair-man. He, more than any other director of that time, was leaned upon by President Simmons who found in this fellow chemist, rubber expert, and old Buchtel classmate a common bond of understanding, although there were times when the essentially conservative position of Mr. Thomas forced a cautious approach to problems that should have been met with a broader sympathy or more vigorous initiative.

A poor boy who made good, John Thomas represented the "establishment" of an earlier age. Had he remained on the Board into the post-war era, he would have been unhappy at the radical departure from earlier truths that higher educa-tion was embarked upon. The appointment of Mr. Phillip Hartz, campaign manager of Mayor George Harter, was one of the Board's relatively rare political appoint-ments. In later years appointments of a similar kind were made by other mayors, but far from being a catastrophe, some directors so appointed served ably and counter-balanced the disproportionate industrial representation on the Board. In 1943 Mr. Harry L. Besshardt, an electrician for the B. F. Goodrich Company, was the first appointee to be drawn from the ranks of labor.[54]

Predictably, the war years brought a curtailment of campus life. The initial panic following Pearl Harbor, when President Simmons warned "we expect Akron to be bombed—and we expect it in 1942," gave way shortly after to a matter-of-fact approach to the business of ending the war.[55] The majority of day students—women outnumbering men for the first time—were working, many of them in war-related industries. Grades showed no appreciable decline. There was little horseplay on campus. Most courses were slanted to contribute to an understanding of the war and how to cope with the changes it required. Many of the most experienced professors had left, leaving an increasing proportion of the teaching load to be handled by younger and less experienced teachers. This was a source of mild student displeas-ure, particularly when one of the newcomers affronted the dignity of a college student by requiring a notebook or some other stricture that reminded the students of their high school days. Thoughts were elsewhere, and although grades remained up to previous standards, class cutting was more common and threats by the faculty and administration went unheeded.

Student activities were seriously reduced. The marching band did not finish out the 1942 football season and was disbanded for the duration. The *Buchtelite* was reduced to one edition per week and was short of staff, paper, money, and everything essential to production. The *Tel-Buch* disappeared, was reborn in the 1944 edition, but died again and did not reappear until 1948.

The war hurt fraternity membership. For a time, the "Greek" men kept their operations relatively healthy by concentrating on new freshmen and younger students who were not yet draft-eligible, but as the manpower pool was depleted and these younger students were eligible, they refused to put their money into fraternities when it was doubtful that they would have time to enjoy their investment. The brothers who did remain on campus were largely engaged in war work. All of the fraternities survived this membership crisis even though social programs and other activities were seriously curtailed. In contrast, the sororities were never healthier; with little else to do, the girls pledged in record numbers and sought the companionship that was otherwise lacking.

The athletic program was curtailed. In the reorganization of the University's program to conform to wartime conditions, Leslie Hardy was relieved of his duties as Athletic Director and assigned other responsibilities. He had brought order out of the chaos of 1939, and now he passed his duties on to Otis Douglas, football coach, raconteur, fabulous eater, and a colorful leader who, when he tired of the college game, won a position with the professional Philadelphia Eagles at an age when most players hang up their cleats.[56] The shortage of eligible players resulting from the military's decision in 1942 to call all enlisted reservists to active duty, caused the University Council to permit freshmen to participate in varsity athletics.[57] Wartime restrictions forced a return of Akron football to the friendly, but time-worn confines of Buchtel Field. And in still another move that marked a return to friendly confines, the Ohio Conference welcomed Akron back into the fold in December, 1943. As far as the football effort went, this was all academic, for the University discontinued competition in that sport until 1946.

Basketball continued to be played throughout the war years, and Russ Beichly's teams were always tough. Under the freshman-eligible rule, Beichly came up with a prize player from Akron South. Fritz Nagy was certainly not the picture of grace, but once he had the ball in his hands, his hook shot from the pivot was unstoppable. He led the charge as Akron went to the fringes of big-time basketball competition. Akron's ambitious schedule created difficulties when the Zips became involved in a game at Madison Square Garden against Brooklyn St. John's; a game that New York gamblers had fixed. Although totally innocent, Akron decided not to risk its reputation and Beichly accepted no more bids to the Garden. Nagy was mentioned on several All-American teams for his outstanding play.

Meanwhile, that old whip of university athletics, the *Beacon Journal's* Jim Schlemmer, berated Akron's wartime athletic program. In 1942 he answered a letter from a former Buchtel coach, Frank Haggerty, who recommended a return to the athletic policies of an earlier time, by writing, "Akron U today is operated as a sideline indulged in by boys in off hours when they are not on their jobs in industry or in bed resting from their labors." He claimed Akron had lost much ground athletically under the current administration and that most high schools had more bond between administration, faculty, and athletic department than did Akron University. The administration at Akron University couldn't make up its mind about athletic policy, he claimed, and the basic question that needed to be answered was, did Akron University desire to continue in varsity intercollegiate athletics? The answer, of course, could not be given to that question until the post-war circumstances were known and assessed.[58]

The modest student sacrifices asked of those who stayed home—curtailment of social and athletic activities, taking courses from less experienced instructors, sharing of facilities with military trainees—were not of the same magnitude as the sacrifices required of those who left familiar places for distant dangers. It is fruitless to attempt a summary of the total contribution made by Akron students in World War II. Too much of the story is hidden from view. Yet one stark figure inevitably emerges as a measure although it reveals nothing of the anguish associated with each loss. Most Akron men and women who went off to war knew that some must die that others might live; they knew about Bunker Hill, Gettysburg, San Juan Hill, and Belleau Wood. And now, 121 of them—former students all—had joined those who through the generations had made the ultimate sacrifice for their country.[59]

NOTES

[1] President's Report, 1940, p. 5.

[2] *Ibid., Beacon Journal,* Nov. 13, 1940.

[3] *Ibid.,* June 26, 1940; Board Mins., III, 22.

[4] *Buchtelite,* Jan. 9, 1940.

[5] *Ibid.,* Jan. 12, 1940.

[6] *Ibid.,* Jan. 10, 1941.

[7] *Ibid.,* Sept. 20, 1940. This issue lists 21 of the first recipients. Included in the list are two members of the current Akron faculty and two former members.

[8] *Ibid.,* March 12, 1940.

[9] Mrs. H. Thackaberry to author, August 8, 1967.

[10] President's Report, 1940, p. 3.

[11] *Beacon Journal,* May 26, 1940.

[12] President's Report, 1940, p. 12.

[13] *Beacon Journal,* Sept. 10, 1940.

[14] Board Mins., III, 31.

[15] *Beacon Journal,* March 30, 1941.

[16] *Ibid.,* July 8, Sept. 8, 16, 18, 1941.

[17] *Ibid.,* Sept. 26, 1941.

[18] *Ibid.,* June 6, Oct. 20, 1940; President's Report, 1941, p. 3.

[19] *Ibid.,* p. 3.

[20] Board Mins., III, 161–62; *Beacon Journal,* Feb. 11, 20, March 11, 1943.

[21] *Ibid.,* Feb. 27, March 10, 1943; Board Mins., III, 168.

[22] *Ibid.,* 187; *Beacon Journal,* Sept. 12, 1943.

[23] *Ibid.,* Oct. 26, 1943, Jan. 30, 1944.

[24] Board Mins., III, 260.

[25] *Buchtelite,* March 16, 1944.

[26] *Ibid.,* Nov. 2, 1935.

[27] George F. Zook, "The University of Akron," in *National Education Association Journal* (Oct., 1929), reprint in UArch., VF (History).

[28] *Buchtelite,* Sept. 17, 1937.

[29] *Ibid.,* Nov. 10, 1937.

[30] *Beacon Journal,* July 25, 1943, Sept. 3, 1944.

[31] Board Mins., III, 320.

[32] *Beacon Journal,* Sept. 12, 1945.

[33] UArch., box 4/8a/8.

[34] Board Mins., III, 106.

[35] *Ibid.,* 132, 161.

[36] President's Report, 1944, p. 5.

[37] *Ibid.,* 1945, p. 7; 1946, p. 13.

[38] *Ibid.,* 1947, pp. 10–11.

[39] *Beacon Journal,* Nov. 23, 1947.

[40] Board Mins., III, 90–1, 387, 623; *Ibid.,* V, 152; *Ibid.,* VII, 96, 116; *University Bulletin,* Dec. 11, 1945.

[41] Descriptions of the war effort may be found in *Beacon Journal,* various issues throughout the spring and summer, 1942; in Board Mins. for the same period; and in the President's Reports through the war years.

[42] *Beacon Journal,* Feb. 15, 1942.

[43] *Ibid.,* April 8, 1942.

[44] BCLA Mins., April 19, 1944.

[45] *Buchtelite,* May 4, 1944.

[46] BCLA Mins., Dec. 12, 1945.

[47] *Beacon Journal,* Jan. 14, 1943.

[48] *Ibid.,* Sept. 28, 1944.

[49] *Ibid.,* July 25, 1942; President's Report, 1944, p. 3.

[50] Board Mins., III, 133.

[51] *Ibid.,* 186.

[52] *Ibid.,* 123.

[53] *Beacon Journal,* June 7, 1943.

[54] For Thomas, see President's Report, 1942, p. 10; for Hartz see *Buchtelite,* Jan. 9, 1942; for Besshardt see *Beacon Journal,* Dec. 17, 1943.

[55] *Buchtelite,* July 8, 1942.

[56] Board Mins., III, 104.

[57] *Beacon Journal,* Dec. 17, 1942.

[58] *Ibid.,* Oct. 28, 1942.

[59] *Ibid.,* March 29, 1946.

Central campus in late 1950's.

XVIII

Opening wide the doors (1945–1951)

Before the end of World War II, The University of Akron was already involved in the process of converting to peacetime conditions. Perhaps the appearance on campus of the first of thousands of veterans marked the beginning of the post-war era. Under the terms of Public Law 16, Akron agreed to cooperate with the Veterans Administration's vocational rehabilitation program by enrolling veterans who had received medical discharges. By October, 1944, the directors had indicated a willingness to cooperate in all educational programs for veterans, especially that conducted under the "G. I. Bill" (Public Law 346,) the wisest, most socially useful federal assistance to higher education since the Morrill Act of 1862.[1]

The advent of VE Day in May, 1945, followed three months later by VJ Day, made it certain that American campuses would be deluged by returning servicemen during the spring semester, 1946. Taking note of this impending flood, President Simmons told a community gathering that the veterans would be "a challenge to every professor and the entire system of education." Akron, he continued, would have to "provide something for them that is on a higher level than ever attempted before" since the veterans would "stand up in class and intelligently tax a professor's knowledge to the breaking point."[2] Simmons' prophecy was fulfilled; the effect of the veterans on the Akron campus, as on campuses all over the land, was as he said it would be.

Although many of the regular faculty returned from their military assignments in 1946, enrollment shot up so fast—to 5,600 day and evening students in September, 1946—that additional help had to be found. There was a national shortage of fully qualified instructors, and it was necessary to find expedients that normally would not have been resorted to, including the hiring of a number of minimally trained instructors. In some cases, a strong undergraduate student who had just received the bachelor's degree would start the next semester as an instructor. This situation produced instruction similar in quality to that which would prevail at a later time when the use of graduate teaching assistants became commonplace. But the ex-G.I. was the most mature and demanding student American colleges had ever seen, and there can be little doubt that his demands were often beyond the capacity of the novice instructor to fulfill. This writer remembers an economics class comprised entirely of male veterans which was "taught" by a bright and comely young lady with her baccalaureate degree barely in hand. Every student in the class had more experience in the "real world" than she, even though she may have known more about formal economic theory. Her good sense, good humor, and lack of pretentiousness helped redeem what could have been a farcical situation.

Students felt keenly the loss of trained and experienced instructors who took positions at other schools. An editorial entitled "This Way Out" appeared in the *Buchtelite* during the 1946 summer session. "Dr. Organ, Dr. Duncan, Dr. Young, Dr. Ford, Dr. Hamilton, Dr. Caine, Miss Kemler. Will this exodus never end?" it asked. "Will the University continue to lose its topflight professors?" To maintain an impressive faculty, said the writer, the University needed attraction and appeal. "No one," he said, "can blame a professor for leaving if he has an opportunity for a better, higher salaried position elsewhere. But why can't The University of Akron do the luring?"[3] We shall try to answer the editor's question further along in this account.

In the absence of these experienced teachers, help came from the large number of part-time instructors. More than 100 were hired in 1947; among them were city officials, scientists, businessmen, welfare workers, journalists, musicians, linguists, public school teachers, and people in many other fields. A great source of strength to the University, then and later, was the reservoir of mature, trained professionals in the community who were available for part-time teaching and who appreciated an opportunity to teach. Many of them proved to be most effective; the evening program in particular would be hard-pressed without them.

Many adjustments were required to accommodate the plethora of students. Heroic measures were needed to handle the paperwork especially for the veterans, whose needs were coordinated through the Veteran's Office directed by Mr. Robert Pealy. He worked in close conjunction with Registrar Richard Schmidt, Dean of Students Donfred Gardner, and Treasurer Maxwell Boggs. Mr. Al Banyar ably handled a heavy portion of the load in the bookstore, as did Mr. Robert Berry in his position as Business Manager. The faculty, too, had additional paperwork as a result of the veterans, but they didn't complain much because they were helping a group of students eager to help themselves. The older faculty members still regard the post-war years as the golden era insofar as student interest, motivation, and accomplishment were concerned.

The ex-G.I. fulfilled his academic promise. (The veterans tested for admission in the spring semester, 1946, raised the median score 10 points.) In the spring of 1947, male students compiled the second highest all-men's average (82.79 percent) since records were started in 1914. Professor Summerfield Baldwin III, Head of the History Department and an uncompromising scholar, noted that the veteran's work was generally of high quality.[4] Each year's graduating class was larger than the one before indicating that a healthy percentage of the veterans were completing their degree programs in a reasonable time span. Indeed, if anything, they accelerated the normal pace for a degree, many feeling that they had already lost enough time out of the mainstream of the "normal" world. But just as the veteran had some catching up to do, so did the University whose needs in plant, campus expansion, maintenance, and financial base claimed priority attention.

Long-range planning to meet the physical needs of an expanding university is a tricky business. Akron's one big pre-war effort along these lines—the proposed relocation at Good Park—indicated how a thoroughly rationalized, vigorously pursued plan could come to naught simply because circumstances conspired against it. The great stock market crash undid in a moment all that the University community and its friends had worked to accomplish over a four-year period.

President Simmons had guided the Board through the bureaucratic riptides of federal funding in order to meet the urgent needs of the thirties, and in 1942–43, he began to urge the directors to consider immediate campus needs which would have to be met as soon as wartime restrictions lifted, and to coordinate them with longer range projections that would prepare the physical plant to accommodate its anticipated load through the next quarter century.

With the advice of the Executive Committee, Simmons produced a list of building priorities that contained the usual Akron triumvirate—library, gymnasium, and recitation hall—but was headed by a power plant. A document, "Long Range Plans 1942–1971," was drawn up in support of the building priorities just established.[5] This plan is worthy of comment only because its projections were grossly conservative, and had this projection been made operative, the University would have been stuck for years with inadequate buildings. The local planners were not incompetent; even national projections at this time were consistently in error on the conservative side. No one, in the early 1940's, could see around the corner of time with precision.

By March, 1944, the directors were convinced that it would be wise to have a firm post-war expansion plan in hand in case a federal funding program was available after the war. To this end, they negotiated a contract with the Akron Allied Architects, a consortium of local architects who were hired because of the Board's time-honored procedure of giving the University's work to local interests. Money to finance the expansion plan came in part from the Endowment Fund Association and in part from a special fund.[6]

This project—the drawing up of a sort of "master plan" for campus development—was viewed as the University's contribution to the City of Akron's post-war planning effort which was proceeding under the direction of a mayor's committee. Higher education was but one of the 12 areas in the community planning effort. It is hard to keep the record straight because some of the University planning was intended to be part of the community effort, and some appears to have been independent of other connections. Further complications arose from the fact that there were two funding tracks; one for the community effort and another for the independent University effort. It is not necessary to follow the details since a general account will reveal the significant features of the efforts.

In May, 1945, the plan evolved by the Akron Allied Architects was unveiled. The *Beacon Journal* ran a special rendering of the campus showing the location of the proposed structures. As conceived by the planners, the campus would be confined to the large block between Buchtel, Sumner, Carroll, and Brown Street (extended). A gymnasium, auditorium, library, chemistry building, recitation hall, and heating plant would be located on the edges of the block leaving an internal quadrangle to give some small feeling of campus to those safely inside the protecting wall. One of the buildings had an archway through its middle; otherwise they were severely functional and unimaginative in design.

It is almost too easy to look back from a later and more prosperous plane and criticize what was proposed at an earlier time. The strains of the moment, the gap between need and funds, the inability of any generation to read the future accurately, all conspire to give the second guesser an unfair vantage point. At the risk of being unfair, it should be pointed out that the 1945 expansion plans convey the feeling of having been drawn with the least common denominator in mind. Little in the prospectus lifted the imagination. This pattern of physical dullness was not overcome until very recent years, and dullness of surrounding is all too likely to lead to dullness of spirit. As described in a special edition of the *Akron Alumnus*, the campus would not be "spacious." And for good reason. There was no federal urban renewal available in 1945; as yet, there was not even a capital improvements levy from the voters of Akron. Every cent of capital funds that could be anticipated would have to go into buildings leaving nothing for real estate. Probably this limitation was responsible for another interesting fact; the new plans made no provisions for parking![7]

The initial effort to finance this proposed campus expansion took the form of a private fund drive under the newly formed University of Akron Memorial Foundation, established in memory of those "who gave their lives for the Four Freedoms," and as a tribute to the returning men and women "who helped secure our way of life." In introducing the Memorial Foundation to the citizenry, President Simmons reminded them that "In the past, Akron has provided excellent facilities for the Y.M.C.A., Y.W.C.A., Boy Scouts, and hospitalization—but never has the city provided adequate facilities for its university. Akron has not turned its efforts to the financial backing of the university in an effort to bring it up to the level commensurate with the position our industry holds."[8] The scolding was deserved, but as we have seen, Akron had never experienced a prolonged period of stable prosperity since the Municipal University was formed in 1913. What she would have done, given a stable environment, can't be known, but it is true that the University had rated a low priority with local donors.

But change was in the air in 1945. The war appeared to be drawing to a successful close. There was growing optimism that the post-war conversion to a civilian economy could be managed without the disastrous setback Akron industry received following World War I. There was a veritable flood of veterans set to descend upon American campuses and Akron was certain to get her share. Psychologically the time was ripe for a fund drive.

The Memorial Foundation set a goal of $1,000,000 that it hoped to raise from local industry. Akron's six substantial rubber companies gave the drive a good sendoff by subscribing $605,000. In two months the remainder was subscribed from some 1,600 smaller companies, and on January 18, Founder's Day, President Simmons, "in an emotion-choked voice," announced that the campaign's first million dollars was "in" making possible the immediate beginning of the building work. The announcement was received by "a polite hand-patting," which caused one observer to lament: "A million dollars! That's something to get excited about . . . . It should have brought everybody to their feet shouting with joy."[9]

While this important initial goal was being achieved, the plans for securing more extensive funds were reformulated several times, finally emerging in February, 1946, in the form of a $2,500,000 program approved by the mayor's Post-war Planning Committee as part of the total community effort. This money was to be secured by private donation and public tax levy. The private subscription drive focused in an alumni effort to raise $500,000 through the Memorial Foundation, but this total was never secured, due in part to the success of the other arm of the fund raising effort.

At the general election of November, 1946, a tax levy in the amount of 68 hundredths mills was submitted to the voters of Akron. This levy was designed to bring in approximately $1,250,000 over a five-year span from 1947 to 1951 inclusive. It carried in all but four of the city's 217 precincts, the most complete endorsement the community had ever given the University to that time. Gratifying as this was, it represented a much reduced version of what was initially sought. The board had hoped to raise twice that amount only to discover that the 1.37 mill levy they originally proposed was illegal in that it exceeded the amount that state law permitted the taxpayers to spend on municipal universities. The success of this levy can be attributed primarily to the mood of the times and to the acceptance of a message that had been put before the citizens many times before; "The University of Akron belongs to Akron's voters. It is not only their obligation but to their own selfish good to support it."[10] With nearly $2,500,000 assured for capital purposes over the next five years, the time had finally come when the Hilltop campus could expect the first systematic development it had enjoyed since 1900.

Even before the tax levy was passed the two most urgent improvements were well advanced. In April, 1945, clearance was obtained from the War Production Board for construction of a new heating plant. The fact that scarce boilers, piping, and other essential materials were released for this building indicate the seriousness of the need. The old plant could not provide enough steam to heat all the buildings at once. Since 1936 there had been frequent crises involving the plant, and added to that was an expected 20 percent reduction in the amount of coal the University was authorized under rationing restrictions which would force a closing of operations. After the usual delays, ground was broken in September, but the new plant was not ready for operation until the fall of 1947. In 1946 federal loans made possible the planning of a library addition, gymnasium, chemistry building, and recitation building. Of these, the library addition had first priority, and in 1946 the directors contracted with the Akron Allied Architects for an extension of Carl Kolbe Hall. They also authorized construction of an engineering building, and old Phillips Hall, the former President's House and the oldest building on campus, was razed. Shortly thereafter, the crumbling grandstands at Buchtel Field were torn down in preparation for construction of a new athletic services building to contain locker rooms, a first-aid room, offices, conference rooms, and rest room facilities. In March, 1949, bids were authorized for a new chemistry building. Among other things, it would house the Institute of Rubber Research and thus fulfill a long-time ambition of Knight, Kolbe, Zook, and Simmons by locating that activity in an appropriate campus facility.

When classes opened in September, 1949, the new engineering building, appropriately named Ayer Hall, was ready for occupancy as was the library annex and the athletic service building. In addition, a home management house for the home economics curriculum had been secured thanks to the efforts of the University Women's Committee. A great deal had been accomplished, but a look around would have convinced any observer that many needs were still to be met. An array of temporary buildings and "make-do" arrangements confronted the eye, on campus and off. Credit is due those who were resourceful enough to find any haven for the many activities squeezed out of regular campus facilities.

The earliest of the temporary expedients had been taken in 1942 when the building on Center Street that formerly housed "the Greeks" was leased for classroom and office space for the music department which moved in from temporary quarters in Spicer School. The facility was promptly dubbed "Hamburg Hall" by the students. President Simmons was aware of its shortcomings, even as a temporary haven, but, as he said, "we have provided the best facilities which the music department has ever enjoyed."[11]

As the veterans swarmed to the campus the Dean's Committee (Cherrington, Evans, Gardner, Landon) recommended that options be secured on more off-campus classroom space. The old wooden portion of Spicer School was put to maximum use. Two Sunday school rooms at the nearby United Brethren Church were rented as classrooms as was similar room at the First Church of Christ Scientist. Central High's auditorium was used for special programs, the Akron armory for commencement, Goodyear Gym for basketball, Jennings School's track for spring sports, the Y.M.C.A. pool for swimming, and the Akron Rubber Bowl for football. The University was practically a community project. The administration even purchased, and converted into a classroom and testing service office building, a small, single-story eating spot across Carroll Street from Spicer School. These efforts were supplementary to other temporary measures taken to provide space on campus.

Most in evidence was a quonset hut which stretched unbecomingly some 144 feet across the most visible spot on the campus. It contained the bookstore and faculty offices. Cordially disliked by the students, the "Dream Hut" was an unpleasant reminder to the ex-G. I.'s of the sort of thing they had been looking at for three to five years.[12] Just to the east of Buchtel Hall, a barracks-like temporary building was erected for the psychology department and College of Education offices. It was attended by a similar structure in front of Olin Hall which served as an electrical engineering lab. Much to the credit of the Board and the administration, the moment these buildings became expendable, they were removed and their sites restored to the tiny campus. In this regard Akron was well in front of most public universities around the country many of which are still using these "temporary" relics of World War II and the great G. I. bulge.

Before the decade was out, a growing concern about parking space would take its place near the head of the list of campus problems. The small area in front of the quonset hut and Buchtel Hall and around other buildings was totally inadequate. Most students parked along the streets that formerly crowded in the campus, particularly to the south across Carroll Street, and in the neighborhood of the fraternity and sorority houses. By 1940, however, the first properties were being acquired for parking—between Center and James Streets. A plan to relieve traffic congestion by making Buchtel and Carroll one way streets was hailed as an improvement when put forward in 1951. The little traffic "triangle" at the intersection of Buchtel and Center, used only as a location for a news rack containing the paper of the Socialist Workers Party, was beautified. Despite University protests, the Haven of Rest mission constructed a building on Buchtel Avenue. It was asserted by the president and his associates that future campus expansion would move in that direction, but it would have been hard to convince most faculty and students that they would see the day it would reach the Haven of Rest. The prophecy was amply fulfilled, of course, and the Haven now crouches in the western shadow of the huge Auburn Science and Engineering Center.

The conversion of old Knight Hall into the Education Building, coupled with the dedication of the new Knight Hall with its chemical laboratories and Institute of Rubber Research, marked the final achievements of the Simmons years. Preliminary planning had been accomplished on a new gymnasium, plans were extant for a building to replace the quonset hut and provide space for the still-wandering art department, the temporary education office structure was scheduled to come down, but the fulfillment of these plans came in the succeeding administration. The University was firmly committed to remain in the heart of Akron and, as if in confirmation of this fact, the last 12-acre parcel of land in Good Park was sold in 1948 for $21,800 which was added to the building fund.[13]

As new buildings crowded the tiny campus, concern was expressed that the last green spaces were disappearing. President Simmons was not at all bothered by this concern since his interest was to put all classes into University buildings for the first time in 20 years.[14] Many students were encouraged by the progress being made toward that goal. The editor of the *Buchtelite* could write that "slowly but surely" Akron was overcoming "the obstacles of decrepit buildings and deficient space." He went on to praise the "inner, intangible spirit that has marked both our mother Buchtel College and her present offspring," and perhaps the day was not too far in the future "when we can . . . point with pride to a really beautiful University of Akron campus."[15] That day is infinitely closer than anyone might have dreamed in 1951.

The University was having trouble enjoying its modest post-war prosperity; some second thoughts were expressed on campus and in the community to the effect that building costs were too high and that it might be unwise to construct any more buildings until it was known what enrollment would be once the veterans departed. There was even talk of a recession. To these fears, President Simmons had the proper answer. "The whole history of building," he said, "shows it must be done when the need for it exists. Delay eliminates the building but not the need for it." As for an economic recession and decreased enrollments, Simmons reiterated the notion that Akron was known for its ability to increase enrollment in depressed times when other schools think of retrenching. "Those who might have gone elsewhere come to us because they can't afford to go away," he said.[16]

Nevertheless, as early as 1947 consideration was being given to admitting all students who had graduated from high school. The Admission Committee felt that the University might do for the city what state universities did for the state in this regard. However, University Council was not ready to consider an admissions policy change at the moment because the veteran bulge was still in full flood and figures projected on existing enrollments would be distorted. One evidence of this thinking is revealed in a 1949 study of area population growth and its influence on University enrollment. This study, worked out "with industrial representatives on the Board of Directors," indicated that Akron should prepare for an "ultimate enrollment" of 2,500 day and 4,000 evening students.[17] Simmons believed the greatest growth would occur in the evening.

With the advantage of hindsight we can well ask, what were they thinking of? The conservatism of this study may well be a carryover of the "depression psychology" that characterized Akron, for two years earlier, in 1947, there were already 3,200 day students enrolled, and even though the veteran factor was included in that figure, the projectors should have seen that the "war-baby" boom would arrive on college campuses in the late 1950's. The limitations of municipal financial support should not have required that low a projection since studies made in the late fifties were also predicated on municipal support, yet they were much more realistic and provided a far better reading for their time than did those of the late forties.

Thus the close of "Hez" Simmons' career found him pushing a building program geared only to meet the accumulated backlog of need and to prepare for an enrollment topping out at about 2,500 day students. Concurrently, fear of the loss of veterans without a corresponding influx of regular students contributed to a coordinate push for a completely open admission policy, with a high school diploma the only requirement. This policy was finally adopted by the Board on the recommendation of University Council in the spring of 1950. Indeed, fears engendered by an immediate fall-off in enrollment, temporary though it might be, gave rise to various recruiting efforts designed to lure additional students to the Hilltop. An open admission policy, however, was consistent with the proper role of a municipal university. Open admission, President Simmons said, was "a further extension of the university's service to Akronites."

The predicted fall-off in enrollment actually came about in 1950, and the decrease had serious impact on the budget. The decline in veterans, coupled with a reduction in the number of new freshmen, brought on by a temporary decline in the number of high school graduates, reduced the student body to such an extent that income from student fees in 1950 dropped about $100,000 below the previous year. Enrollment was also affected adversely by the number of young men of draft age who were enlisting in the military services as the Korean "police action" developed into a full scale conflict. By voluntarily enlisting, these young men were able to choose the branch of service in which they served. This flow of volunteers threatened such havoc on collegiate enrollments that Dean Gardner joined with 14 other midwestern deans in 1951 to urge the Defense Department to stop voluntary enlistments and rely henceforth solely on the draft for necessary manpower.[18]

In the experience of Buchtel College and The University of Akron administrative changes seemed to come in bunches. At the conclusion of World War II, such a period was experienced again. Fred Ayer, who had served as Dean of the College of Engineering from its inception, retired from his administrative post in 1946. Although never a Buchtel College man, Ayer was so close to Parke Kolbe and Hezzleton Simmons that he imbibed the flavor of that heritage. His personalized style of doing things was consistent with a small school where his individuality was marked and largely appreciated. His successor was Ransom D. Landon, another Cincinnati man, who assumed his duties in 1946. Like his predecessor, Landon supported the co-op program of engineering education. He was more conservative than Ayer, and by the time he arrived on campus it was already becoming difficult for the engineering dean to play as large a part in University operations as Ayer had been able to do.

Another significant change occurred in 1948 with the retirement of Charles Bulger as Dean of the Buchtel College of Liberal Arts. He retained his role as Graduate Dean and Head of the Department of Modern Languages until retirement from the University in 1951. Bulger had long been a tower of strength. He was that rare person who, when he sees a job to be done, takes on the responsibility even though it could be avoided without stigma. A demanding teacher, he was liked and respected by his students. He was well known in the community, and in the years following the death of his contemporaries at Buchtel College, he became identified by alumni and the older faculty as the embodiment of the spirit of old Buchtel with its emphasis on the liberal arts, scholarship, responsibility, and service. His zest for learning never abated, and he graced nearly every important University gathering with his genial presence.

The new Dean of the Buchtel College of Liberal Arts was Ernest H. Cherrington, Jr., the first scientist to hold the position since Dr. C. M. Knight was given the title, if not the functions, in 1897. Dean Cherrington was impatient with the many loose ends that characterize the academic fabric. In seeking more orderly processes he took a strong and courageous stand in defense of the principle of consultation before action. A master of logical exposition, his memoranda were so precise that it was difficult to argue with them even if one disagreed with the spirit of the argument.

He was willing to consider any proposal on its merits, but he was innately conservative on academic matters, and there were procedures in the fast-changing aura of a growing university with which he never felt comfortable. A strong defender of the arts and sciences, he supported the entire spectrum of campus activities.

Cherrington's initial challenge was the unenviable task of trimming the faculty to accommodate declining enrollments after 1949, and enforcing the new policy of hiring only "men of Ph.D. caliber."[19] Full-time staff members who lacked this terminal degree were encouraged to complete the necessary work. It was claimed that faculty trimming was being done on a quality rather than a seniority basis. No one left an account of just how quality was measured, and it is a pity since that problem has plagued the academic world from time immemorial. The dean was not the only one interested in faculty quality. In 1950, it appeared that students would evolve a faculty rating scale and that initiative had passed from "those students sincerely interested in the problem along constructive and sound lines" to a little group of "student agitators insistent upon action."[20] The Dean's Committee took no action against the "agitators" since their interference would aggravate the situation. As the deans had guessed, the students failed to sustain enough enthusiasm to put a rating plan in action.

Meanwhile, some additional restructuring was taking place in the administrative group. The premature death of Treasurer Max Boggs was the occasion for creating the new position of Financial Vice-President which Les Hardy assumed in January, 1951. At the same time, Cecil Rogers was named Treasurer and Robert Berry took the new title of Business Manager. These two men, and all others involved in the financial and business side of the operation, reported to the Financial Vice-President.

It is interesting that there was no concurrent development of an academic vice-presidency. The record does not show why the academic side was not thought to need a focus of responsibility on the vice-presidential level, but a number of factors seem to have influenced this lopsided development. It is always easier for management people in the academic world to spot weaknesses in the business structure of the institution than it is for them to see weaknesses in the academic structure. Budgets and balance sheets are far more tangible things to work with and evaluate than are faculty performance, the amount and quality of learning taking place in various classrooms, the adequacy of the curriculum to meet the needs of students and society, and all related questions. Perhaps it was evident to the president that he needed constant close and trusted advice in financial matters, whereas he might be tempted to feel that he was as well equipped as the next man to make judgments in the academic realm without similar advice.

Still another consideration bearing on this point is the fact that Les Hardy was very versatile and useful, and over the years Simmons had relied on him to an increasing degree, sometimes to the consternation of the deans who felt that Hardy had the president's ear in a way they did not, and that his judgment prevailed over theirs in too many instances. This feeling grew out of a belief that during Hardy's tenure as Director of Adult Education he had run the evening session too much as an independent fiefdom with resulting double standards for day and evening students. When it was announced that Mr. Hardy was to be Financial Vice-President, the Dean's Committee made it known that they assumed his former duties in the evening session would be kept entirely separate from the new position and that "the Deans of the respective colleges will be responsible for the entire instructional program in all sessions of the university."[21]

The main burden of discontent with the new arrangement in financial administration grew out of a belief that a move of such importance had implications for the academic program and should have been made only after consultation with the deans. In a long letter to Simmons in January, 1951, the Dean's Committee (Evans dissenting) expressed its concern over the manner of this appointment. "As in the case of certain previous administrative decisions," said the deans, "it has been assumed by the Faculty that the Deans, by virtue of their responsibilities and membership on University Committees, had been consulted and had voiced their approval of these decisions." The fact that there had been a series of such incidents about which most of the administrative officers and the faculty had not been consulted, was "dangerously threatening the effective operation of the university." If this decline in morale and loyalty of the faculty and staff continued, it was the "considered judgment of this committee that grave days are ahead."[22]

On the specific issue of the administrative restructuring, "It seems," the committee continued, "that there is not sufficient recognition on your part of the relationship of quality of instruction, curricular opportunities, faculty cooperation and morale on the one hand, with financial policy and procedural decisions relating thereto on the other hand. In the opinion of this committee, most administrative difficulty arises from the failure to properly integrate financial and educational policy." While recognizing that the president would "lay down . . . official burdens in a few months," the issue was so fundamental to the proper ordering of the institution that the deans felt compelled to bring the matter forward at that time.[23]

The letter was aimed at a particular abuse—failure to consult with the persons whose responsibilities would be most affected by restructuring the administrative machinery—but it brings into the open one of the basic difficulties in administering a university. Decision-making power, applied unilaterally or arbitrarily by the president, can destroy the sense of participation that is essential to the professional self-respect of faculty and administrative staff. In a profit making operation one is prepared to accept the "right" of the boss to make decisions without prior consultation or without much thought as to who was going to resent it. Only a foolish boss would operate this way, but it has been known to happen. Such an approach in the academic world cuts to the heart of the university's image of itself as a community of scholars and learners, as a congeries of professionals. The hallmark of the professional is the right to have a part in making decisions that affect his ability to carry out his function. Thus the doctor is consulted before the hospital changes the rules about patient care, and the minister (except in the most authoritarian churches) is likely to be consulted about how the money received is to be used.

Universities cannot be run too literally on a chain-of-command principle without sacrificing the climate of mutual participation, the practice of operating as professional equals who, for the sake of efficiency, give primacy to certain individuals in the performance of certain duties. It is awkward and somewhat inefficient to operate on the basis of professional consensus, yet the effort must be made or the inevitable tendency of the decision maker is to expedite the job and in the process bypass many of those who should have been made party to the decision.

These arguments, of course, apply primarily to academic considerations—curriculum, faculty standards, admission and retention standards, criteria for professional advancement, etc.—but even though most faculty are more than willing that operational decisions be made by administrative officers, they reserve the right to be heard and considered when these operational matters affect the climate of teaching and learning.

One way in which the faculty attempted to make certain that their opinion was given adequate representation—since there was little confidence that it was well represented in University Council—was to form a new committee to supplement the work of the AAUP in presenting matters of concern to the proper authority. The Akron faculty had always been professionally docile—never had it risen up in anything approaching united protest. The AAUP had been little more than another group holding meetings, and it held no real power as a molder of faculty opinion and action. In 1946, therefore, a local organization, the Faculty Committee on University Improvement (FCUI) was started largely as a means of communicating faculty interests more effectively to the administrative group.

The FCUI did not intend to be a "grievance committee," but inevitably it tended to become just that. There were, in fact, a number of legitimate faculty grievances which did not seem to be getting the kind of hearing at the administrative level that faculty sought. In 1949, the establishment of a "special problems committee" was viewed with "grave misgivings" by the deans who "deeply resent the implication that members of their respective faculties who may have what are believed to be grievances against the administration now stand in need of an agency to represent them in a formalized effort to secure redress."[24] The need was related to the feeling of faculty members that they were ineffectual in dealing individually with "the administration." Many felt as though they were dealing with an unyielding power structure whose decisions appeared to be arbitrary.

At no time, however, did this committee have enough united support to sustain an effective role in getting that hearing they sought. Neither the FCUI nor the AAUP were effectively involved in protecting faculty interests. Late in 1949, for instance, Dr. Charles A. West, recently hired by the political science department after a career in government, was warmly criticized by an influential member of Akron's business community for his participation in an election campaign. After thoughtful deliberation, the directors suggested the faculty be made aware of the need to adopt "self-imposed limitations" on activities that might embarrass the University. West resigned in January, 1950, for reasons apart from this incident, but there is no record that the larger issue of faculty rights and responsibilities was served by the FCUI or AAUP.[25]

The FCUI was successful, however, in drawing up a Faculty Personnel Policy which was adopted by the Board in 1948. It also made a number of studies aimed at identifying areas where improvements should be made. Its major effort, and its major success was in focusing pressure on the Board for significant salary increases.[26] Not since 1919 had there been such concerted expression of faculty sentiment on the salary issue. The totally inadequate salary base in the post-war years was a matter of intense concern nationally. Teachers in general fared poorly compared with other occupations, and the Akron scale compared poorly with teacher's salaries generally.

A general salary increase averaging 6 percent was authorized for the 1946–47 academic year, but even then only some 45 percent of the 1946 budget was marked for instructional costs in contrast to the later experience when over 70 percent of a much larger budget would be devoted to them. In 1947 the University had its first million-dollar budget; of that $1,332,000, only $475,000 was for instructional costs and only $15,000 for books, periodicals, and binding, an amount so negligible that it is difficult to credit it.[27] The faculty, even after considerable agitation by the FCUI, got only a $200 across-the-board cost-of-living increase at the beginning of the year supplemented later by another $200 increment. Still another cost-of-living increase up to a maximum of $200 was authorized in 1948; but the following year income was down and additional raises were not possible.

The five-year, quarter-mill operating levy was renewed in 1949, but it brought no additional income, and the administration was faced with a continuing need to economize. The deans proceeded on the assumption that they must seek "the utmost efficiency" in the academic departments in order that the "unit cost" in the University could be "reduced to the smallest figure possible without appreciable reduction in the effectiveness of teaching."[28] This would mean eliminating off-cycle courses and the frequent repetition of small enrollment advanced courses. With such economies, it was possible to set aside enough money for merit raises, some of them up to $400. As an interesting sidelight it might be noted that this period is the only one where there is evidence that the coaches' salaries were out of line with those of other faculty. The deans were aware of this and resented it, and one would gather from their records that the decision on coaches' salaries had been made at a higher level.[29]

The decline in income resulting from smaller enrollments made it necessary to secure additional funds to maintain services. Since the state code set a limit on the millage a municipal university could secure, there was no possibility of appealing to the voters for more tax income. The alternative was to get more money from student fees. Reluctantly—such moves are always made reluctantly despite what many students and their contributing parents may think—the Board approved an increase of $21 a year in the maintenance fee. Akron had not raised this fee since 1930. Although it represented an increase of 47.2 percent, this was still well below the national average (a 65.2 percent increase by 1949 over the 1936 level). The increase in fees did not keep pace with the increase in costs which had risen 54.6 percent in the previous decade.[30]

Students are realists when candidly presented with the facts. There was no substantial resentment of this fee increase, and had they known that the deans submitted budget requests for 1951 which were below the actual expenses of 1950, they would have known that every effort was being made to hold down costs. The conviction that a municipal university should be as widely serviceable to its community as possible meant keeping the door open to as large a segment of the city's students as could benefit from higher education; hence the need to keep fees low to prevent shutting students out on financial grounds.[31] More sympathy for this philosophy could be found on the Board and in the administration than in the faculty at large. While aware of the desirability of keeping fees at a minimum, faculty members favored fee increases if that is what it would take to ameliorate their salary plight.

In the spring of 1951 measures were taken to bring a greater degree of stability and predictability to the University's financial base. Akron City Council was asked to provide additional tax millage within the city charter which would bring in an additional $100,000 or more in operating revenue. This would make it unnecessary to go to the voters every five years for operating funds. The millage was needed just "to hold the line" in the face of rising prices.[32] Leslie Hardy, who presented the case before the Taxes and Assessments Committee of City Council, said that the University was losing strong faculty and was having a hard time attracting replacements. He also pointed out that over the years a diminishing portion of the operating money came from taxes. In 1914, 74 percent of the operating funds came from taxes, while in 1950 only 39 percent came from that source.[33] Ben Baldwin, chairman of the committee, said: "I have known for some time that the tax structure of the U keeps everything there in turmoil. They don't know where they're going from year to year."[34]

Predictability was not the only issue. As finally adopted by the City Council, the charter amendment called for an additional 2 tenths mills thus raising Akron's millage to the limit permitted under state law. Much difficulty resulted, however, from a reapportionment of the millage so that one full mill of the 1.45 allowable under state law would be used for operating purposes and the capital improvements millage would be reduced from 68 hundredths mills to 45 hundredths mills. This maneuvering undoubtedly caused confusion among the voters; they were left with the impression that the University was asking for an *additional* 45 hundredths mills when in fact the new money would amount to only 2 tenths mills.

Although he retired in August, President Simmons was appointed director of the campaign for passage of the charter amendment. On the same ballot appeared the renewal of the five-year building levy. The building levy passed while the charter amendment failed by 1.1 percent of the vote. It was a bitter blow to Simmons who had taken the lead in Ohio to secure from the state legislature permission for municipal universities to use a full mill of their allowed 1.45 for operational purposes.[35] It was a blow as well for the new president who stepped into this partial rejection by the voters.

The academic program was largely stable in post-war years. Clearly the pressing issues of buildings, finance, staffing, and related issues were so evident that there was little time or energy left to experiment with the academic program. The result was a mixed bag. There was little need for radical adjustment in specialized, Upper College courses. But in the survey courses that introduced students to the specialized fields of knowledge, enough change had occurred in the natural, physical, and social sciences to make some of these surveys outdated. The war had a tremendous accelerating effect on the growth of knowledge and methodology in many fields. With professional meetings reduced and travel to them restricted, it was not easy for a faculty member to keep up with the most recent developments especially when he worked overtime to keep his normal activities in hand. The result was that the ex-

G. I.'s found their instructors couldn't take them as far as they wished to go with the newer concepts and methods, and this led to student disenchantment with particular courses and instructors.

The introductory courses received the most criticism. They were the most exposed, most vulnerable, and they were taught in large lecture sections that reminded the veteran of his recent unhappy experience as part of a crowd. The Humanities course, because it was most traditional in its approach, because it was easy for a student to see its potential importance to his social competence, and because it was well taught, came out best in student evaluation. Introduction to the Natural Sciences met with a rather neutral reaction. It reminded students of the popular song, "I know a little bit, about a lot of things, but I don't know enough about . . . [physics, chemistry, biology, astronomy, geology]." As in previous years, Mental Hygiene (veterans were excused from Physical Hygiene) came in for the largest amount of criticism; it promised much but delivered little to a skeptical student group. Introduction to the Social Sciences was disliked nearly as much. It didn't seem to be concerned with the "real world," all the drama and fascination of man was drained out of its theoretical approach.

The deans were aware of the criticisms. They were aware of the validity of some of them, but it seemed the wrong time to innovate. On the other end of the academic continuum, in graduate work, there was also a reluctance on the part of University Council to investigate graduate policies. Students thought they must take leadership if any changes in curricular structure were to occur in time to do their generation any good: "the time has come for us . . . to actively participate in bringing about the establishment of new courses and additional scopes of study here on the campus," editorialized the *Buchtelite*.[36] President Simmons had emphasized to the students his desire for student action and opinion regarding additional courses. But these desires were clearly in conflict with the contemporaneous drive to reduce curricular offerings in the interest of savings. The *Buchtelite* won one of its old battles when a Journalism Department was established in 1947; but few other curricular adjustments of significance were introduced at this time.

The most significant departure from traditional curricular programs during the post-war years was the development of the so-called "basic studies" program. Although its emergence was intertwined with the entire business of curricular reevaluation, it has in retrospect a kind of separate identity that enables us to review it as though it were a separate phenomenon.

For antecedents of the basic studies concept, one would have to go back at least to pre-World War I days when Parke Kolbe was advocating the Municipal University ideal of total service to the supporting community. Following that war, Kolbe suggested developing a number of two-year terminal courses in practical, vocationally oriented subjects. Secretarial Science was introduced as a two-year program and it was hoped that others would follow as resources permitted. But resources did not permit an expansion of this effort. George Zook took up the verbal urging where Kolbe left off, and his promises of action in the development of short vocational courses were part of the rationale for seeking relocation of the campus where space would be available to build the facilities to sustain additional programs.

Hezzleton Simmons was not prepared to abandon that dream. "Our sole purpose," he wrote in 1948, "is that of providing good education for the residents of our city." A month later he told University Council: "Every graduate of every high school in the community who wants to attend the university should be given the opportunity to do so. Not every student who wants to enter should be regarded as a prospective graduate, but we could render a real service to those people who could take advantage of an education beyond the high school level." Then, in the kind of phrase that reads better than it holds up in practice he said: "We should never drop a student. Students drop themselves."[38]

Four months later, in an interview with the student paper, Simmons said of the University's academic standing: "We've maintained a pretty high one, and we want to keep it that way."[39] It may be unfair for later investigators to quote a man against himself, but these presidential pronouncements do not comprise the total evidence, and it is apparent from the council minutes and the Dean's Committee minutes that Simmons' desire to have it both ways was but part of a rather general confusion. Everyone was in favor of maintaining good academic standards, whatever those are, but academic standards had traditionally been linked by an unbreakable bond to admission and retention standards and to the nature of the curriculum. To favor admission of all Akron high school graduates to programs including vocational short courses and "basic studies" was an honorable position; but to maintain at the same time, as the president did, that this would not adversely affect academic standards bordered on wishful thinking and sophistry.

The instrument for bringing a plan of curricular reorganization before the faculty was an Appraisal Committee consisting of the deans—Cherrington, Evans, Gardner, Landon—plus professors Distad, Duffy, and Griffin. This committee met regularly throughout 1948–49 to study the report of President Truman's Commission on Higher Education (drafted by a group headed by George Zook) to see how The University of Akron was meeting the Commission's recommendations and to investigate how the University might better serve the community as a whole.[40]

On Founder's Day, 1950, the Appraisal Committee presented the faculty with a plan resulting from its study of Akron's responsibility for educating students beyond the high school. Because it has had a decided impact upon the University in subsequent years it is worth setting it forth in full. The recommendations provided:

1. *That students henceforth be admitted to the University of Akron on the basis of graduation from an accredited high school or equivalent preparation. However, admission to specific curricula is to be restricted according to standards set by the University Council.*

2. *That suitable curricula and courses be established to meet the needs of students who desire:*

   A. *Programs of general and specialized education culminating in academic degrees.*

   B. *Programs of general education and specialized training.*

   C. *Specialized and/or cultural courses to be taken on the adult level for the purpose of advancing themselves in their business or profession or for the purpose of enriching their lives.*

3. *That a program of measurement be established to determine the abilities, aptitudes, and interest of the students for counseling and placement in a suitable educational program.*[41]

In reporting these recommendations to the faculty, Dean Ernest Cherrington, Chairman of the Appraisal Committee, said: "We feel that it is most appropriate for a municipal university to admit all who apply. We must see that each receives as much education and training as he can assimilate."[42]

In the discussion that followed presentation of these proposals, Dr. Roy Sherman asked where the money was coming from to serve a larger number of students; they could not be served with the present staff. President Simmons answered that Akron would be fortunate to maintain its enrollment on the existing level and that it would be faced with a reduction in faculty in the next three years. Akron was serving a smaller percentage of Akron high school graduates than it had served five years earlier. Although he did not want to "weaken" the present curricula, Simmons said he was "perfectly" in accord with the Appraisal Committee, and he urged adoption of its proposals as quickly as possible. Dean Howard Evans said what was on many minds when he claimed that the admission of more students with lower high school averages would "encourage mediocrity and discourage high achievements" unless there were a "division of classes." Dean Gardner responded that the largest reason for failure was not ability, but attitude. He advised: "Key your program to the major group. Then advance the better students more rapidly."[43]

After a salubrious airing of the issues, the Appraisal Committee reconsidered its recommendations and then brought them to the University Council for approval. University Council did approve the recommendations substantially as presented. However, one important new ingredient which won council approval was the "basic courses" concept. The "basic courses" comprised certain remedial courses available to students with inadequate high school preparation. Immediate steps were taken to implement this part of the plan. The academic deans were well aware that this remedial work must be handled with care if they were to avoid accusations of establishing a "dumbbell college."[44]

The "experimental program" as the basic courses came to be known officially, was adopted by University Council June 1. It consisted of Basic Mathematics, Basic Language Skills, Business Records, Survey of Business, Family Living, and Orientation. Through the summer, syllabi were developed in each course. Top faculty members in each field wrote the syllabi although they generally did not teach the courses once they were safely launched. Students admitted to the experimental program were those who had a high school average below 77 percent and a psychological index on the American Council on Education tests of below 25. Typically their initial course load would consist of basic mathematics, basic language skills, physical education, ROTC (for men), Orientation, and a choice of one vocational subject from a list approved by University Council, or an "elementary degree credit course" which the appropriate department head would be willing to accept.

The deans tried to forestall the possibility that the basic courses would become "mere content-centered departmental courses." They felt the emphasis should be functional. The best insurance of this would be the selection of instructors who were "thoroughly sold on the principles of general education" and who were "enthusiastic about the freshman or subfreshman courses" they were assigned to teach. The deans asserted, correctly one assumes, that the Ph.D.-type instructor would probably fail at that task.[45]

The important measurement arm of the experimental program was put into operation in 1950 when a Testing Center was established; its director reported to the Dean of Students in whose office all academic counseling for entering students, including those in the experimental program, centered. Experience gained with the Veteran's Counseling Service had prepared the way for a relatively smooth inauguration of the Testing Service. It is somewhat unusual that the Testing Service was not set up as an adjunct of the Psychology Department. This was not done because it would have introduced some interests that appeared to the deans to take attention away from the main focus of student advisement and academic programming.

The impact of the experimental program is difficult to assess with confidence because its impact is concealed within the mixed nature of Akron's academic records. It might be said, first of all, that Akron's program was a positively motivated attempt to do something to provide for the demonstrated need, outlined in the Truman Commission's report, of the high school graduate who lacked the academic skills to profit by a four-year degree program of a conventional sort. The Appraisal Committee kept this truth in mind and responded courageously to this need. In the second place, Akron was not alone in pursuing the idea of offering "remedial" work to those who might have a successful experience in college if some basic deficiencies were overcome. Many other public universities across the nation were involved in "subfreshman" courses, and not all of them demonstrated the integrity and restraint that Akron did in refusing to allow basic or remedial course credits to count toward a regular four-year degree.

Of great local significance is the fact that this program was the first fully rationalized step toward the University's later success in operating a two-year, vocationally oriented Community and Technical College totally within the University structure. The progression led from the "basic course" concept, to the two-year Associate Degree Program which introduced regular curricula in a number of vocational areas, to the Community and Technical College with its full-time staff and total access to University resources. The Community and Technical College program will be described later. Also of local importance was the reminder this program, and the debates surrounding its inception, stimulated about the role of the Municipal University in a day when the pressures were building to make Akron like every other public university—more concerned for those who could rise to the top than for those who could go only part way, and that along a different road.

The other side of the story is less happy. There was a definite note of expediency creeping through the inaugural phases of this program. Put directly, the institution needed more students to provide income and to keep the staff fully employed. In addition, there were a lot of Akron voters whose sons and daughters could gain admission to college only if admission requirements were minimal and remedial work were available. Another shortcoming was the practice of registering "basic" students for courses in a regular degree program at a time when, by Akron's own definition, the student was not qualified for such work. This was not a widespread abuse, but it gave credence to those who argued that the presence on campus of doubtfully qualified students inevitably had a deleterious effect on the level of some courses in the regular curriculum. It tempted the instructor to "talk down" to the least common denominator of student ability in his classroom. The other alternative when dealing with a class that had a number of basic students enrolled was to keep the presentation on a high level and eliminate the basic students. As much as anything, this argument persuaded some who had initially favored the program that the experiment had failed. When it was phased out in the mid-1950's, there was little regret on campus and in the community.

Harvard, mother of American colleges, comes in for her due share of praise in the academic world for the innumerable accomplishments she can legitimately boast. Sometimes, however, she is given credit that better belongs elsewhere. In this light it is amusing to note that the *Beacon Journal* in commenting on the University's innovative programs in general education spoke with reverence of the fact that Harvard president, James B. Conant, had long emphasized the need for two-year programs of general and/or vocational education. Would that the *Beacon*'s reporter had known that Akron's own Parke Kolbe was on this trail long before Conant, and that The University of Akron, though it never told its story effectively, actually tried more programming along these lines than Harvard.

We noted earlier in this narrative that many of the fine teachers and scholars of the pre-war years were gone from campus. Brilliant young scholars like Morton Bloomfield (English) were off to more fruitful academic fields where their passion for scholarly investigation received the backing necessary for serious work. The popular and able political scientist, Paul Zeis, left academe for the business world. Established men and women of more senior rank like Orville Hitchcock (speech), Harlan Hamilton (English), and Dwight Gray (physics), found better positions and larger challenges elsewhere. But their replacements were hired, many of them while the war was still in progress, and among them were some of the finest teachers and scholars Akron had ever boasted.

Among those who gave the University many years of service and who were generally recognized for their contribution to teaching and scholarship was Summerfield Baldwin III, Professor of History and Head of the Department. A brilliant scholar, he was a teacher who violated all the rules of pedagogy and yet was for most serious students of history the "best teacher I ever had." With jet black hair, piercing eyes under dark brows, and a hook nose, he looked like a bird of prey ready to pounce. He was sarcastic, required students to keep notebooks ("historical records"), and picked on the weak member in each class. The faint-hearted stayed away, but those who remained (and in the days of the G. I. Bulge, there were a lot) tended to become "disciples" and most went on to success in professional or graduate school.

A gentler scholar, Charles Duffy, arrived during the war years to become Pierce Professor of English and Head of the Department. His whimsical outlook on the academic scene, which he loved intensely, made him a gentle critic of all that tasted of perversion of the intellectual life, a life which he understood to be at the heart of a university. Also gentle in demeanor but fierce in gentlemanly intellectual combat was Emile Grunberg, Professor of Economics and Head of the Department. His European background placed him among those brilliant émigrés from Naziism who have done so much for American scholarship. His zest for ideas represented the true spirit of inquiry that should characterize the University.

Still others who came to the faculty in the thirties and forties stand out for their excellence or their service. A number of them were women, Ruth Putman, Helen

Saunders Thackaberry, Florence Whitney, Ruth Raw, and Julia Anich Hull (English), Dr. Emily Davis (Head of the Art Department), Charlotte Packan (art), Mary Wilson (home economics), Dr. Clara G. Roe (Professor and later Head of the History Department), Phyllis Bacheldor Hardenstein (speech), Lucy Self (secretarial science), Dr. Helen Painter (elementary education), Dr. Margaret Mauch (mathematics), Evangeline Witzeman (psychology), Lucille Lamkin (physical education), Mary Vernon Slusher (accounting), Helen Park (biology), Irene Grunberg (modern languages), Nellie Whittaker (piano), and Ebba Larson, Assistant Registrar, who for many years was an indispensable keeper of student records.

Among the women who played a key role in developing the academic resources of the University none was more important than Dorothy Hamlen. As Librarian, she presided over her rapidly growing responsibility with professional competence, with efficiency and humaneness. A faculty favorite for her honesty and candor, she brought the library into the main stream of the academic program where, of course, it belonged but had not always been.

None of the women appointed during this time had more influence on the University than did Dr. Mabel Riedinger. She came to the University after a fine career as a teacher of literature in Akron high schools. She expressed herself in a forthright way that clarified issues, and this capacity was put to use on campus and also in the community where for many years she served as a member of the Akron Board of Education, several of these years as president. When Dr. Riedinger told her students how to prepare for a teaching career, they knew that she was giving them a firsthand account. In 1965 she was one of the first faculty members appointed to the new rank of Distinguished Professor. In addition, she was Head of the Department of Guidance and Counseling and did much to formulate its program.

Several of the able faculty men who came to Akron before World War II, who have not already been accounted for, made strong contributions in their fields of teaching. Among them were Hjalmar Distad (Professor and later Head of the Department of Elementary Education), Walter Cook (Professor and Head of the Department of Chemistry), Elmer Ende (music), Donato Internoscia (Spanish), Paul Smith and Earl Wilson (engineering), Kenneth Sibila (Professor and later Head of the Electrical Engineering Department), Ernest Tabler (mathematics, and also Assistant Director of the Evening and Adult Education Division), Donald Varian (speech, later Head of the Speech Department), and John Stein (voice).

The war years and those immediately following brought important additions to the staff including Dallas Riddle and Ossian Gruber (business administration), Frank Simonetti (industrial management, later Head of the Department of Industrial Management), Dennis Gordon (accounting, later Head of the Department of Accounting), Louis Ross, Louis Rodabaugh, and Richard Davis (mathematics), Vaughn Floutz and Alvin Wolfe (chemistry), Boris Boguslavsky (Professor and Head of the Department of Civil Engineering), Lester Weinberg, John Fairburn, and Paul Huss (engineering), E. Kenneth Hamlen (engineering and Director of Co-operative Engineering Placement), William Petry (engineering, later Head of the Department of Mechanical Engineering), William Painter (education), Darrel Witters and Clarenz Lightfritz (music), Paul Twining (Professor and Head of the Department of Psychology), Wesley Alven (psychology), Andrew Maluke (physical education), James McLain (economics), Raymond Nelson (philosophy), Theodore Duke (Classics, later Head of the Department of Classics), John Hull (English), and Edward Jones (geography). No suitable generalization can cover the work of these diversely talented people. Some served longer than others; some were effective in the classroom and some were not; some related well to students and some did not. But all gave of their best to the University. This was primarily a teaching faculty. Graduate work was still in an infant stage insofar as the amount of energy directed toward that end was concerned. There had been no need for a publishing faculty in order to assure good teaching for undergraduates. Nevertheless, there were within this group a number who had published significantly or who were well known among their professional colleagues. One thinks of Summerfield Baldwin whose publications in the area of early modern European history were scholarly standards, of Emile Grunberg whose studies in economic theory were widely known and highly regarded, and of Sam Selby whose texts and tables in mathematics brought him recognition and reputation far beyond the campus. Dennis Gordon wrote accounting texts and articles that gave him a substantial national reputation in that field while Helen Painter's work in children's literature brought her attention beyond Akron. No one in the faculty was better known professionally than G. Stafford Whitby whose career spanned the diverse periods of rubber science and technology. His assistant, Maurice Morton, who later succeeded Whitby as Director of the Institute of Rubber Research, also had a distinguished reputation for his investigations in polymers. It is important to note that publication is not the only test of scholarly capacity and contribution, and the singling out of those who did publish substantially in no way implies that their colleagues lacked this capacity. They may have lacked the opportunity or the particular kind of drive that distinguishes the contributor to professional literature.

One could argue that even though they published, Walter Kraatz, Paul Acquarone, and Ted Duke did more for scholarship by turning out, year after year, superbly trained undergraduates who went on to highly successful graduate and professional careers. Any graduate program in the Classics would be delighted to get a Duke-trained student. The distinguished record established by Akron's pre-med students as they went on in medical schools around the country attests to the excellence of the undergraduate work under Kraatz and Acquarone.

It is risky in the extreme to try to compare the faculty strength of one institution with another. Yet a general feeling or impression about faculty quality is apparent to perceptive and knowledgeable observers of the academic scene. Just as it is reasonably certain that old Buchtel College of the 1880's had as good a faculty as most schools of its kind, so it is reasonably certain that the tenured Akron faculty in the late 1940's compared favorably with the faculties of other small and medium-sized public universities. At that moment, it was several cuts above the level of the former state normal schools which were just emerging into a period of growth toward comprehensive university status.

One of the few measures of faculty quality—inadequate though it might be—has traditionally been the number of terminal degree holders within a faculty. Due in part to the emergency push to hire faculty in 1945–46, and in part to poor economic conditions on the Akron campus, the percentage of terminal degree holders was below the norm of that time. Simmons and Cherrington were determined to reverse that pattern and to concentrate on hiring persons with the doctorate and to encourage those lacking it to complete their work for this badge of scholarly accomplishment. In a very few years this push would gain added impetus through the rapid development of graduate work which requires a professionally active staff of fully qualified teachers and researchers who themselves have gone the full route in graduate education.

Not since the old community surrounding the Buchtel College campus started to disintegrate in the 1920's had there been much faculty cohesiveness within the institution. Scarcely anyone lived within walking distance. Faculty residences were scattered to all points of the compass from the school's central location. Too often instructors left the campus immediately following classes, just as the students did, with the resulting feeling of desertion that closed down upon the operation every afternoon around three. Things came alive again with the arrival of the evening clientele, but it was difficult to find much of the atmosphere that one imagines as characteristic of a campus. This "feel" of the campus had a dampening effect upon faculty recruitment that was not dissipated until a decade later when great improvement in the physical setting coupled with a desire of young faculty to come to urban areas "where the action is" once again put the University in a favorable position to attract quality staff.

NOTES

1 President's Report, 1945, p. 8.

2 *Beacon Journal,* Jan. 20, 1946.

3 *Buchtelite,* July 19, 1946.

4 *Ibid.,* Nov. 21, 1947; Dean's Report, BCLA, 1947–48, p. 11.

5 "Long Range Plans 1942–1971" in UArch., VF.

6 Board Mins., III, 232, 244; President's Report, 1944, pp. 6–8.

7 *Akron Alumnus,* July, 1945.

8 President's Report, 1945, p. 8; *Beacon Journal,* May 13, 1945.

9 *Ibid.,* Oct. 28, 1945; Board Mins., III, 343; *Univ. Bulletin,* Feb. 4, 1946.

10 Board Mins., III, 368, 410; *Beacon Journal,* Oct. 27, 1946.

11 *Buchtelite,* August 5, 1942; President's Report, 1942, p. 8.

12 *Buchtelite,* July 19, 1946.

13 Board Mins., III, 537.

14 *Beacon Journal,* March 27, 1949.

15 *Buchtelite,* June 29, 1951.

16 *Beacon Journal,* March 27, 1949.

17 Council Mins., June 19, 1947; *Beacon Journal,* March 27, 1949.

18 President's Report, 1950, p. 3; *Beacon Journal,* Jan. 16, 1951.

19 *Ibid.,* April 3, 1949.

20 Dean's Committee Mins., Feb. 28, 1950, in UArch.

21 *Ibid.,* Dec., 1950, Jan. 22, April 23, 1951.

22 *Ibid.,* Jan. 22, 1951.

23 *Ibid.*

24 Council Mins., Sept. 25, 1946; Dean's Committee Mins., Nov. 17, 1949.

25 Board Mins., IV, 71; *Beacon Journal,* Jan. 24, 1947.

26 Board Mins., III, 348, 588–89.

27 *Ibid.,* 443.

28 Dean's Committee Mins., Oct. 11, 1949.

29 *Ibid.,* Dec. 6, 1949.

30 *Beacon Journal,* March 24, 1950.

31 Dean's Committee Mins., Nov. 20, 1950; *Beacon Journal,* March 30, 1950.

32 *Ibid.,* May 18, 1951.

33 *Ibid.*

34 *Ibid.*

35 *Ibid.,* August 5, Sept. 15, 1951; President's Report, 1951, p. 5.

36 *Buchtelite,* Dec. 17, 1946.

37 *University Bulletin,* Sept. 23, 1948.

38 Council Mins., Oct. 21, 1948.

39 *Buchtelite,* Feb. 18, 1949; Board Mins., IV, 70.

40 Dean's Committee Mins., Sept. 27, 1949; interview with D. H. Gardner, 1967.

41 UArch., VF (Appraisal Committee, 1951).

42 *Beacon Journal,* Jan. 19, 1950.

43 *Ibid.*

44 Dean's Committee Mins., May 31, 1950.

45 *Ibid.,* June 6, July 27, 1950.

XIX

Ex-G.I.'s and "Fact Finders" (1945–1951)

Student life in the postwar era was influenced greatly by the preponderance of veterans on campus. One might guess that this more mature group of students would be impatient of participation in clubs, fraternities, athletics, and publications, but this was not uniformly true. If anything, there was a certain eagerness among many of the veterans to tune in on that kind of activity from which they had been excluded by military life. The big difference they brought was an unwillingness to be intimidated from stating their views, a propensity for direct action, and a disinclination to participate in the more infantile types of fraternity initiations, hazing, etc.

But the veterans were not above horseplay when it was of their own making and direction. The classic instance of horseplay involving both the veteran and non-veteran undergrad was the elaborate farce known as "Nippy's Nook." An abandoned 8 x 14 construction shed located beside the Education Building, was taken over by three art majors—Jim Larsen, Tom Schenz, and Gene Tucker. With their claim tacitly recognized by the Dean of Students, they "beautified" their property by adding a kitchen and decorating the shack in unique fashion including a chartreuse door. New members were initiated in a knighting ceremony during which the new initiate was dubbed with an oversize mallet. Several faculty—prudently, these art majors included the art faculty—were honored with membership. This welcome intrusion of irrationality into the business-like campus atmosphere livened up student elections when the Nook's candidate, with no organized support, swamped his opponents in a campus-wide election.

The classic diplomatic coup of 1949 was consumated when Nippy's Nook, "Cradle of Progressive Aesthetics," and Sigma Omicron Beta (SOB) "Society of Omnipotent Buchteliteers," signed the "North Campus Pact" for defense against their mutual foes, the engineers and their satellites, the commerce majors, who were identified as "the regressive pathetics."[1] It was great fun, but as so often happens with imaginative undertakings, once the initiators of the spoof graduated—and, despite all the time spent amusing the campus and themselves, they did graduate—the movement collapsed.

There are two great certainties one might confidently expect to find at any point he cares to dip into student life on the Akron campus. One is lament about lack of school spirit; again in 1947 the *Buchtelite* editor, Harry Hollingsworth, was convinced that spirit had fallen off since the war. The other was the formation of an Independent Student Association, which, like its many predecessors, was an attempt to provide those who had rejected fraternity life (or who had been turned down by the fraternities), some of the sense of identification that association brings to a student. Had the Independents been militant, had they attacked the fraternity system where it was then vulnerable—on the exclusion provisions in their charters—they might have survived, for there is a certain vitality in combat. But this student militancy was conspicuously lacking and the Independents failed to prosper. Nor could outsiders rouse militancy: When Mr. Henry A. Wallace spoke to a local labor gathering in 1947 he stated that "The Progressive students at Akron University should get together." He thought "The leaders should organize for real political action."[2] Such clarion calls for serious social protest had no impact on the postwar generation.

Homecoming decorations.

Jim Larsen and Gene Tucker preside over Nippy's Nook, 1948.

Air Cadets form in front of Curtis Cottage, 1944.

Torchlight Rally, 1965.

Political action on the Akron campus continued to mean the annual jousting of two or three student political combines for the Student Council presidency and seats on the council. In 1948 what everyone knew was possible happened. The engineers decided to vote in a bloc for a candidate of their own, Andrew Slezak, and they elected him President of Student Council. The voting power of the engineers was not particularly strong; they simply demonstrated that when most students failed to vote, it was easy for any substantial bloc to put its man in office. It would be interesting to know how many of those who organized this victory at the polls carried the lesson with them as they later considered their place in the political structure of the larger community.

Within the fraternities a prosperity of numbers afforded marked contrast with recent experience. A few of the groups took the progressive step of translating "Hell Week" into "Help Week" and put their pledges to work on useful projects. Some seemed to feel that the sophomoric hazing traditionally associated with fraternity initiations was necessary to bind their members together, thus reviving the old argument used by those who wanted to maintain freshman hazing and the class rush of old Buchtel days. One reason for moving away from hazing was that new pledges were often veterans who had experienced enough physical discomfort and personal debasement and simply refused to join unless excused from that kind of initiation.

The Dean of Students Office worked closely with the fraternities and sororities. Through the Interfraternity Council and the Panhellenic Association representatives from each group gathered to recommend common policies and regulations governing rushing, grade requirements for pledging and going active, and associated subjects. Fraternity housing, much of which was in rather poor shape, was inspected by the Dean's office and by local fire marshals. Efforts were made to minimize the discomfort caused to residents of the area by virtue of their proximity to fraternity and sorority houses. In short, much was being done to assist the groups to live up to their purposes. These efforts would pay off handsomely within a few years through the recognition won by various chapters for outstanding performance within their national organizations.

The Akron fraternity system as a whole was soon to receive very favorable attention nationally for its strong and constructive nature. This was indeed remarkable since the urban setting, housing inadequacies, lack of resident students, and similar circumstances would appear to work against a successful system. Probably the secret, if there was one, was that the Akron fraternal groups worked with the University rather than against it. Their membership provided a disproportionate number of campus leaders and supporters; their grade averages exceeded the all-student average consistently; the campus would be poorer without their influence despite the fact that pain and damage resulted on occasion from their selective membership practices. None of the Akron groups now adhere to the past rigidities with regard to membership eligibility.

Despite "spirit" vs. apathy, and independent vs. "Greek," a questionnaire circulated by the Psychology Club found student morale to be "good" in the fall of 1947.[3] Complaints hadn't stopped. The University's lack of stimulating assemblies was cited as an unhappy condition. A few students wanted to rate faculty because some instruction was inadequate. But the resumption of student activities curtailed by the war—the marching band, football, and the *Tel-Buch* among others—helped offset complaints in other areas. A plan introduced in 1949 whereby each department head would hold a general meeting of all his majors in an effort to develop a closer relationship with them and provide more effective counseling seemed to promise relief from one substantial student complaint.

Among the perennial issues, objections were raised once more that the Alma Mater was shared by too many other schools, and that no one could sing "Close beside Cuyahoga's waters, stream of amber hue" without the image of a polluted stream crossing his mind. In the fall of 1950, Parke Kolbe's "Men of Akron" was proposed as the new alma mater. President Simmons said he would support the change only if a majority of the students wanted it. No majority was forthcoming; indeed, the whole movement collapsed for lack of interest.

In the late 1940's and early 1950's, the Cold War with its debates over the proper American stance in foreign affairs created a mood of caution in some quarters. The full impact of McCarthyism would soon be felt with its accompanying pall on controversy. There was surprisingly little debate and concern among students on these issues—at least the records are relatively barren of evidence of such discussion. The Akron campus was never in the forefront of student political activity. Part of the reason rested in the nature of the student body, but part of the quietude was the result of the cautious policy of the Board of Directors who sought to exclude controversy from the campus. This attitude was not effectively challenged by the president, administration or faculty. In 1950, an election year with a University levy on the ballot, both Senator Robert A. Taft (R) and Representative Walter B. Huber (D) were barred from campus speeches because someone in the community might be offended and fail to support the University at the polls. The *Beacon Journal* was correct in claiming that University officials were "timid to a fault" in thus depriving students an opportunity to see and hear important political figures.[4] It's little wonder that political awareness was difficult to find on the Hilltop.

Student discontent was evident in the early 1950's. But it was an apathetic discontent. The onset of the Korean conflict again created an aura of uncertainty among the student body. There was much rhetoric expended during these years about the inadequacies of American higher education. Many of the inadequacies did indeed exist, and this knowledge was used by students to challenge old ways of doing things. Even the *Buchtelite,* a fine college paper for many years, now assumed a carping tone rather than one of helpful criticism. The deans talked among themselves of the "deplorable deterioration" of the paper whose writers seized every opportunity to create issues and belabor the administration, usually "upon the basis of partial fact or erroneous rumor."[5]

The athletic program particularly came in for a large amount of student criticism. The athletic program was largely a wartime casualty. Basketball had flourished, but little else. Indeed, it was at this time that basketball definitely supplanted football as the favorite of the Akron fans, a position that it still holds. The program was brought to a new vitality as soon as men returned to campus in large numbers, but when the football team took the field in 1946 for the first time in four years it did not have enough success to win back the affection of the fans. The basketball skills of Henry "Hank" Vaughn, Bobby Walker, "Whitey" Wahl, Cal Moore, and the massive presence of "Big Bill" Mohr helped the roundballers retain the interest generated by the wartime teams. They won against stiff competition, for the schedule had been beefed up significantly. The annual clashes with Duquesne, a nationally-ranked power through these years, provided the season's emotional high point. And for the first time in their long rivalry, the Zips found themselves with some regularity on the short end of the score in contests with Kent State which had started to produce exceptionally strong teams in basketball.

The effort to revive football with a winning flourish was doomed to disappointment. Head coach Paul Baldacci, hired in 1943, had to wait three years before building a team. The men he worked with were a mixture of young new recruits and veterans whose football skills were often somewhat rusty, or whose combativeness was not adequately complemented with football savvy. The old difficulties of Akron football were still present. Recruiting of top prospects was minimal due to the extremely small amount of grant-in-aid money available and to the stringencies of the Ohio Conference. And the fact that Akron was not a glamorous place, having little to offer in attractive surroundings or in athletic plant, made it necessary to rely almost exclusively on local talent already acclimated to the school's environment. Add to these realities that other enduring problem, the need of many varsity players to work in the factories or in other heavy labor, and it is apparent that Akron's head coach was potentially in trouble.

With expectations high, the postwar team returned to the not-so-friendly confines of the Rubber Bowl. Psychologically this was a poor place to play because the 35,000-seat stadium looked deserted with the "crowds" of 3,000–5,000 fans that generally attended. The fans tended to be critical from the first, and they found little on the field to cheer about except for the heroics of Gene "Scooter" Scruggs, an exciting runner. Countering some of the apathy over the team's performance was pride in the best marching band the school had produced. It featured a huge, rolling bass drum. A large lug-type tractor tire revolved around a bass drum, mounted inside the tire; it was described as "the most original piece of band equipment ever devised for use in band maneuvers on football fields or in public parades."[6] Even more attention was received by the "Zipperettes," (later the "Zippettes") whose attractive presence and routines were sure attention getters.

When the 1947 football squad won just two of its eight games and in the process appeared to be outclassed by schools smaller than Akron, the situation was ripe for protest. Two stimuli contributed to its outbreak, first of which was a rumor that weaker opponents would be scheduled henceforth in football. Just before the end of the season in November, Jim Schlemmer pointed to this trend. Although Athletic Director Russ Beichly claimed he knew nothing about it, evidence existed, said Schlemmer, that weaker opponents were being scheduled for the football team. Schlemmer felt that one of three choices must soon be made: strengthen the football team, weaken the schedule, or give up football.[7]

Close on the heels of this analysis came the second stimulus to protest. The 1947 football contest between Akron and Kent State was marked by excessive and dangerous student horseplay. Things had gone far beyond the stage of painting college letters on each other's campus. An editorial in the *Buchtelite* described some of the action under the lead: "Cancel Kent Series or End Horseplay."[8] "The annual shenanigans preceding the Kent State game . . . were more than 'red-blooded American fun.' Property was destroyed and human lives were endangered." There were several fast, dangerous auto chases. An auto from Kent and one from Akron were hit by gunfire. An Akron student admitted firing a pistol at a pursuing Kent car. Several Kent men had their hair trimmed and were painted, one man's face being painted with indelible ink. Kerosene was poured on an Akron fraternity lawn and paint, pitch, and horse manure were thrown around campus. A Kent student was apprehended for carrying a concealed weapon and another for inciting a riot. A smoke bomb was thrown in front of the Akron band during its halftime show. Both the Akron and Kent student newspapers recommended a severing of athletic relations in the wake of such violence. Incidentally, Kent won the football game 6–0, and after absorbing 10 straight defeats capped by a decisive 58–18 shellacking in 1954, Akron severed its football rivalry with the Golden Flashes and in the process lost its best draw at the gate.

With these developments in the background, a swell of student dissatisfaction with Akron's athletic policies surfaced in the form of a semi-spontaneous meeting of campus organizations. They unanimously favored a student-directed probe of university athletics with special reference to football. The call for action was supported by the Student Council. On November 19, some 600 students jammed a mass meeting at which 10 questions concerning the University's posture in athletics were asked. The questions ranged from "Does the University of Akron have an athletic policy?" to "Why can't Akron compete on equal terms with similar Ohio schools?"[9] A task force of 18 students under the chairmanship of George Wilson undertook the job of finding answers. Members of the task force emphasized it was not their intention to secure the ouster of any athletic coach, but rather they were intent on securing facts about the conduct of athletics on the Hilltop. This student-generated movement met with an initial "no comment" from President Simmons. Coach Baldacci called the initial gathering a "fine meeting" while Dean Howard Evans, Chairman of the Athletic Committee, assumed a somewhat patronizing tone: "It is nice for the students to have their fun."[10]

Wilson pushed the investigation with the same energy he was later to display as Governor Rhodes' first Director of Development. The "Fact Finders," as the investigators came to be known, discovered that Akron did indeed have a written athletic policy adopted in 1939 by the Athletic Committee.

The University of Akron wants to continue an athletic program which pro-

vides good intercollegiate competition with institutions in our class which maintain similar athletic standards and hold like traditions.[11]

Obviously this broad generalization was of little help in determining how the machinery actually functioned, but it provided a starting point for further investigation.

Late in November, over 200 alumni, former varsity "A" men, and other interested parties met in the Mayflower Hotel to hear a review of progress from the Fact Finders. While generally endorsing the effort, the "A" men withheld their specific support until they were satisfied that the Fact Finders were not leading a drive to oust Coach Baldacci.[12] The athletic committee of the Alumni Association, headed by ex-athletic great Verlin Jenkins, presented President Simmons with a seven-point proposal in support of the Fact Finders. The proposal endorsed the 1939 statement of athletic policy, but urged that there be no de-emphasis in the strength of the football opponents scheduled.[13]

Early in the protest movement, Russ Beichly had said that the movement "is a good sign." At least, he said, "students are interested and that's important. We'll listen to whatever suggestions they wish to make!"[14] The suggestions were ready on January 10 when the Fact Finders submitted their report to President Simmons. It contained 39 recommendations within its 28 pages and represented the results of some 44 meetings. Predictably, the first reaction to the report was negative: the Athletic Committee which had a share of the responsibility for inadequate programs was reluctant to review the report and spent the first review meeting criticising it instead of trying to determine whether or not its recommendations made sense. And it is easy to understand this reaction when one realizes that the Fact Finders were quite critical of the committee's handiwork and its two strongest voices—Dean Evans and Russ Beichly.[15] Most of the immediate reaction centered on the recommended removal of Baldacci. He was to be the "fall guy" of the athletic setup said the report's critics. In explaining the Fact Finders' recommendations, George Wilson said that the student committee was of the opinion that Baldacci has been designated as the "fall guy" by the administration even before the report was made. He had no documentation for this charge and there was considerable speculation as to who had so marked him. Apparently there was a tendency to believe Wilson's charge. Probably the position taken by the *Beacon Journal* in an editorial comment on the report came close to stating the position of most observers. The editorial subscribed to Jim Schlemmer's position that the Fact Finders were unfair in requesting the firing of Coach Baldacci: ". . . it hardly seems right to demand Baldacci's scalp because he has failed to overcome apathy toward football which is evident in the administration, the faculty, and the athletic department and among the students and alumni." The editor continued:

Without pretending to know how many of the committee's recommendations are sound, we'll agree—and most Akronites probably will also—that the present state of sports affairs at the University is unsatisfactory. If Akron is going to have football teams at all, they ought to be teams that the students and townspeople can be proud of.[16]

Coach Baldacci was in the most exposed position for receiving criticism. It was only natural that he should attempt to reveal some of the difficulties he labored under. He thought the Athletic Director (Beichly) was out to make him look bad, that he was interested in keeping basketball preeminent over football in public favor. He claimed that he was unable to get into sessions of the Athletic Committee. He was particularly incensed by charges that he was inactive in recruiting talent, pointing out that he had the respect of area high school coaches, and that he had succeeded in interesting good players in Akron only to have his efforts blocked by President Simmons and Dean Evans. He claimed he was not permitted a voice in scheduling opponents.[17] George Wilson reported that the Fact Finders were not convinced that Baldacci was a good enough coach even if everything else was made right, and they were distressed that the "fall guy" issue took attention away from the basic problem. The Baldacci issue, he said, was "overshadowing" the more important one of "arousing sentiment against the top administration."[18]

Public reaction as evidenced by letters to the editor of the *Beacon Journal* was mixed. One writer wanted the University to develop better teams. It was not the turning out of rubber chemists that brought reputation to the Hilltop, he said, but the reputation of the basketball team and formerly the football team. Typical of the other side of the ledger was a letter from an alumnus who congratulated his Alma Mater for not making athletics the sole emphasis in the University. The writer hoped that "the ranting and ravings of the misnamed fact-finding committee have no effect whatsoever on the present policies." The *Beacon Journal,* said the writer, showed "very poor judgment" in giving prominent space to such a "mediocre cause."[19]

Finally, in early February, the Athletic Committee and President Simmons made public the action they proposed to take on the 39 recommendations. Coach Baldacci would be relieved of his duties as football coach, the office of Athletic Director was to be divorced from a coaching assignment, the "minor sports" program was to be improved, alumni support in recruiting was to be sought, grants-in-aid were to be more effectively used within the limits allowed by the Ohio Conference, better schedule coordination with classes would be worked out, and other procedural details of this sort would be more efficiently handled. Some modification of the membership on the Athletic Committee would be entertained, and in time would be implemented. Recommendations outside the province of the Athletic Committee were referred to appropriate offices for consideration, such things as new facilities for practice, a new gymnasium, and so forth. Simmons promised speedy action wherever possible and thanked the Fact Finders for the "earnest manner in which the investigation was conducted."[20]

There was no intention in all of this to push Akron into a much stronger level of competition than it had faced before. The money and resources simply weren't there even if the intent had been. At a gathering of influential men in the community, Simmons said: "We are not providing Akron with a professional team. If such a team is wanted—the citizens of Akron will have to provide it," and he didn't mean at the University.[21] Meanwhile it was announced that William "Bud" Houghton, head coach at Massillon Washington High School, perennial state power, would be the next head football coach at Akron. Another important change found Russ Beichly relinquishing the athletic directorship while retaining his position as head coach of the basketball team. As the new Athletic Director, the University selected one of its own former sports greats, the popular, able, and dynamic Kenneth "Red" Cochrane under whose imaginative and enthusiastic direction Akron varsity sports were to achieve a comprehensiveness, an orderliness, and an overall success that exceeded anything in the school's experience.

The new football coaching regime was no luckier than the former. Akron teams continued to be beaten soundly by smaller Ohio Conference rivals. Apathy was expressed by trouble at the turnstiles, and the athletic program ran a deficit of $23,500 in 1950–51 and another deficit in 1951–52. The ex-G.I.'s who had fueled the earlier protests were gone. Concern over the athletic situation was no longer more acute than concern over the outlook for the University generally in a period of falling enrollments and inadequate income. One can't help but suspect that "Hez" Simmons, who had entered the presidency in 1933 with a determination to win support for the University through football, was pleased by 1951 that he no longer had to deal with that troublesome "game."

After 18 years as head of the University the time had come for Hezzleton Simmons to retire. His intention to retire had been announced 18 months earlier so that the Board would have plenty of time to initiate the search for a successor. Lee Jackson was appointed chairman of the Selection Committee and he was joined by fellow directors, Besshardt, Hoyt, Schrank, Roetzel (ex-officio), and Albrecht (ex-officio) and by Dr. Hjalmar Distad, Dr. Jay O'Hara, and Mr. Ken Sibila of the faculty. While the search was under way for his successor, it is appropriate to make a few observations concerning Simmons' style as president.

To understand Hezzleton Simmons it is necessary to remember how much he and his wife, Agnes, were a part of old Buchtel College with all of its loyalties and traditions. As president, Simmons was paternalistic in the same sense that old Buchtel was paternalistic. In his first years in office, while the influence of Spanton, Bulger and Ayer was strong, and while Parke Kolbe, his summer neighbor in Canada was still around for counsel and advice, he appears to have talked over his intentions and procedures quite fully with these men who were his equal in experience and knowledge of the campus and its problems. In the postwar years, however, with an increasing number of his close administrative associates newcomers to the campus, he became more arbitrary in judgment. The strong protest from the deans already cited shows how isolated the decision-making process had become in his last years in office.[22]

That the students saw him as a friend is a matter of universal testimony. He told the students repeatedly that his door was always open to them. He meant it; they believed him; and they often dropped by to tell him what they were up to and to seek his advice or support. Although he got things done, often under extremely trying circumstances, he did not convey the impression of cool efficiency that George Zook, for example, conveyed, a coolness which tended to hold people off at a distance. Indeed, the more one talks with the wide variety of people who knew him well, and the more one reads his own statements, the more it becomes plain that "Hez" Simmons was a teacher—not a manager, a fund raiser, a politician, but a teacher—sitting in the presidential chair.

His own assessment of himself tends to confirm this. "I am inclined to the belief that my greatest contribution was made as a teacher," he said a few months before retirement. "Here I came into the closest contact with students, and it is for their welfare that I have given all my energies." He went on to say what most who have run a complex organization would say in their own way:

> *As President, I have felt a loneliness for the lack of that close friendship that exists between teacher and student. In this position I have never known the individual student with the intimacy that my heart has longed for. There is a loneliness that comes with being regarded as 'the boss' which is a characteristic of this position and which is absolutely foreign to my way of life.*[23]

A close friend from early days made the same point while refusing to become a candidate for an Akron deanship: "Let us be honest, Hez, the teaching profession lost more, in my opinion, when you left it, than a dozen colleges could gain by your administration." He then anticipated Simmons' own remarks: "I . . . have a hunch, deep in your heart you have longed to be back, standing before eager students, gaining their respect and admiration because you inspired them."[24] Compatible or not, "Hez" Simmons played the presidential role, and in so doing moved his University through depression, war, and the G. I. Bulge in a way that a lesser man could not match. Without ever experiencing a day of prosperity, he left the school well along the path it was destined to pursue toward fulfillment of the municipal university ideal, and beyond.

NOTES

[1] *Buchtelite,* May 5, 1948, April 8, May 10, 1949.
[2] *Ibid.,* Nov. 18, 1947.
[3] *Ibid.,* Nov. 21, 1947.
[4] *Beacon Journal,* March 2, 1950.
[5] Dean's Committee Mins., Feb. 18, 1950.
[6] *Buchtelite,* August 8, 1946.
[7] *Beacon Journal,* Nov. 13, 1947.
[8] *Buchtelite,* Nov. 18, 1947.
[9] *Beacon Journal,* Nov. 18, 20, 1947.
[10] *Ibid.,* Nov. 20, 1947.
[11] *Ibid.,* Nov. 22, 1947.
[12] *Ibid.,* Nov. 30, 1947.
[13] *Ibid.,* Dec. 1, 1947.
[14] *Ibid.,* Nov. 18, 1947.
[15] *Ibid.,* Jan. 11, 1948.
[16] *Ibid.,* Jan. 14, 21, 1948.
[17] *Ibid.,* Jan. 14, 1948.
[18] *Ibid.,* Jan 14, 1948.
[19] *Ibid.,* Jan. 16, 21, 1948.
[20] *Ibid.,* Feb. 4, 1948.
[21] *Ibid.,* March 31, 1948.
[22] See Dean's Committee Mins., May 23, 1950.
[23] *Buchtelite,* May 18, 1951.
[24] J. Breitenbucher to Simmons, March 10, 1948, Simmons Papers.

President Auburn, right, and Dr. Maurice Morton, left, accept electron microscope
donated by Goodyear Tire & Rubber Co., represented here by Ralph Dinsmore,
center.

XX

Norman P. Auburn: an infusion of "executive energy"

In contrast with the short search that culminated in the appointment of Hezzleton Simmons to the presidency, the Board of Directors took well over a year to find his successor. More than 50 people were seriously considered, and at one point an offer was about to be made when the candidate under consideration withdrew his name. As usual, the students felt left out. "I wonder who's choosing him now?" asked the *Buchtelite,* arguing that students should be kept better informed about the progress of the search.[1] Finally, late in June, 1951, several members of the selection committee visited Norman Paul Auburn at the University of Cincinnati where he was Vice-President and Dean of Administration. They were impressed with what they saw and heard, and upon their recommendation the Board of Directors selected him unanimously for the presidency, effective September 1, 1951.[2]

Norman Auburn, a native of Cincinnati, had spent virtually all of his 46 years in that city. He was a graduate of Norwood High School where he had served as President of the Senior Class. In 1923 he entered the University of Cincinnati, edited the semi-weekly student newspaper, and graduated in 1927 with the B.A. degree in political science. He was then employed by the Associated General Contractors of America as editor of their weekly trade journal. In the evenings he attended the University's College of Law. From the time he graduated he was active in the Cincinnati alumni association and edited their publications. In 1933, when the depression wrecked the building trades venture, he became Executive Secretary of the alumni association. By 1936 he was Assistant Director of the Evening College with the rank of Assistant Professor, and in 1940 he was appointed Dean of the Evening College. He assumed the position of Vice-President and Dean of Administration in 1943 while Cincinnati was struggling with the emergency caused by World War II.

Throughout his career Norman Auburn had the support and assistance of his wife, the former Kathleen Montgomery whom he married in 1930. Daughter of a college president, Kay Auburn's warm sympathies and ready wit made her a favorite on campus and in the community. She was a gracious and relaxed hostess whose home was open to an incredible number of social gatherings in support of the University. Their daughter, Ames, and sons Richard, Mark, and David were used to the great demands made on their parents in their new position.

It would have been difficult to find anyone more thoroughly imbued with the municipal university ideal than Norman Auburn. As a graduate of a great municipal university, and as one who had held positions that enabled him to experience at first hand the many diverse interests of municipal education, he did not need to be oriented to Akron's mission. From the beginning of Parke Kolbe's efforts to convert Buchtel College into a municipal institution, Cincinnati had served as the model. The leaders of the two schools had worked together over the years to secure changes in the state code for the benefit of municipal education. What the new president found in Akron was a smaller, less comprehensive, and less affluent version of the University of Cincinnati.

PRESIDENT NORMAN AUBURN (1951–   )

The qualities that he brought to his new responsibility were exactly those needed at the time. Conditions within the University had sunk to a nadir by 1951. Enrollment was down; income was reduced; faculty cutbacks were necessary and the salaries of those who stayed on were disgraceful; operating money for the newly enlarged plant was desperately needed; the morale of the administration and the faculty was at an ebb. President Simmons had made a total effort to ameliorate conditions, but as so often happens in the academic world, a president about to retire does not command as much influence over events as he might at an earlier point in his career; this was Simmons' experience.

What was needed most in 1951 was new blood, new enthusiasm, a break out of the depression psychology that still lay upon the city of Akron, the Board of Directors, and University personnel who had done without too long. Norman Auburn brought "executive energy" to this unpromising situation. With supreme confidence in his own judgment, with a drive and determination that exceeded anything Akron had known, with a desire to know the University to its smallest detail, with an organized, retentive, resourceful mind, Auburn had the equipment to shake things up constructively—and he did!

Demanding of himself, he was demanding of his associates; there were times, indeed, when he failed to realize that most persons were not geared to as unrelenting a pace as he set for himself, but he seldom failed to extract maximum effort from them. Although he was to do far more than anyone else for faculty welfare, and although he truly believed his frequent assertion that a university was no better than the quality of its faculty, his own lack of experience in the teaching and research role made it difficult for him to empathize with certain inefficiencies that are intrinsic to faculty procedures. It was difficult to identify those academic procedures that could be made more "efficient" without sacrificing educational values, and in trying to determine this, the president sometimes seemed to have priorities different from the faculty's. If this led occasionally to faculty disenchantment, the fault was partly with a faculty that made little effective effort to state its case clearly, if indeed the faculty as a whole could be said to have had a "case."

Because funds were so tight, the new president decided that there would be no formal inaugural ceremony for introducing him to his new role. The revelation of educational philosophy that usually marks a new president's inaugural address must be sought elsewhere. In his first appearance before the student body, President Auburn stressed the importance of maintaining a balance between society's technological advances and the cultivation of the art of human relations. His address, entitled "Enlarging Humanity's Beachheads," urged students to be participating citizens, to seek constantly to advance the cause of education, and to "serve your God as a good Christian or a good Jew."[3]

The Board's introduction to the new president must have been reassuring, for he displayed from the first an ability to identify problems and to suggest plausible solutions to them. In his first report to the Board, he warned that enrollment in the fall semester would be 12 percent below the level of 1950; the loss of income therefrom made passage of the charter amendment providing additional operating money essential, as was the levy for new capital money. To make optimum use of these anticipated funds, long-range planning was essential.

On the academic side, a restudy of the general education program should be made. Above all, in all of its activities the University must move forward confidently.[4] There had been enough negative thinking; it was time to forget past frustrations and get on with the task of building.

Since all else hinged on it, the problem of maximizing income demanded first attention. The University was already committed to a vote on additional tax revenue so this source of money received top priority from the new administration. It was especially crucial that the charter amendment pass since it would bring in additional operating money. Unfortunately, as things turned out, the charter amendment issue was coupled with an effort to renew the building levy, and there can be little doubt that the voters became confused at the manner in which the package was presented on the ballot. As outlined to the faculty the issue was easy enough to understand:[5]

	For operations	For buildings	Total
We now get	.80 mills	.65 mills	1.45 mills
We need and are requesting	1.00 mills	.45 mills	1.45 mills

Despite the preliminary explanations circulated to the voters, and despite the hard work of the campaign committee chaired by President Emeritus Simmons, the charter amendment to increase operating funds was defeated. In its postmortem the *Beacon Journal* called the defeat a "disappointment and a surprise," and attributed the setback to the cumbersome ballot wording which required the voter to wade through a lengthy title and 162 words before reaching the first, and only, mention of Akron University. The building levy, on the other hand, passed handily suggesting that it was not disenchantment with the University that accounted for the defeat, nor was it voter resistance to taxes since the Akron Board of Education's 12-mill levy—an increase of 3.15 mills—was approved.[6]

This was a bitter introduction for President Auburn. Every effort had been made to secure passage, and from this experience he gained renewed determination to see that in future attempts at the polls, the ballot wording would be as clear as public officials could be persuaded to make it, and that the campaign effort would spare no pains for success.

Never one to take "no" for an answer when the University's interests were at stake, Auburn urged the Board to try again with the charter amendment on the May, 1952, primary ballot. The directors supported this recommendation, and they also requested City Council to levy an emergency .214 mills for current operating expenses for the year 1952. The $95,000 additional operating money the charter amendment would have provided was critical and, in requesting help pending another vote, Board Chairman Cletus Roetzel said, "I hope Council can find a way to give us some help without crippling city services."[7]

A new era in city-University relations was dawning. In the past, the directors and University officials had been diligent in their efforts to secure from the city all that they could in the way of financial support, but there had always been such obvious needs for funds in other municipal services that once the city said it could do nothing for the University, that had generally closed the matter. Now, under the skillful and persistent prodding of President Auburn, city council would be reminded time after time that they had a responsibility to the University. City officials should consider the University as an "essential service" to Akron when preparing the 1952 budget. "We want them to review the entire city financial picture and consider the University along with other necessities," said Les Hardy.[8]

There was no question about the legitimacy of the need. President Auburn described the faculty as "demoralized" over the salary situation resulting from the defeat of the amendment. Akron would "have trouble in hanging on for the next five years." It was especially galling to know that public school teachers were likely to earn starting salaries of $3,000. "It doesn't help our faculty morale to have an instructor making $2,800 a year teaching students who will begin at $3,000," Auburn said.[9]

Meanwhile, every internal economy was examined. University Council heard suggestions for putting more of the burden of education on the learner as a means of reducing faculty size. A suggestion to discontinue intercollegiate football proved unacceptable as did a proposal to abolish the Measurement Service (Testing Service). In view of the "serious conditions," the deans recommended that consideration be given to the suspension of plans for new buildings since money needed to operate them would diminish the amount available for the academic program.[10]

If the deans hadn't known it before, they found out then that President Auburn was adamant about expediting buildings. Nothing short of a strike and work stoppage would ever convince him to slow down on construction plans, and even the work stoppages were fought tooth and nail. Some resentment of the president's intransigence on this point was bound to arise as other persons supported different priorities, but in the long run his position was probably correct. He maintained that the public tended to judge a university by what they could see. Their support at the polls was essential, and it followed, therefore, that the physical plant be improved and modernized so that the community would take favorable notice of the school. Voters would support a winner at the polls faster than a down-at-the-heels institution. "It is more important educationally to maintain an able, loyal and conscientious faculty than it is to purchase brick and mortar," said the president, but the quality of the faculty would be only as good as the resources of the institution permitted, and the resources must be cultivated by winning popular support for the University. Ultimately, faculty would be attracted to the campus if it had good facilities for them to work in.

The problem of supplementary income was placed before the Citizen's Finance Committee, an advisory group to the Mayor of Akron. The University revealed that its preliminary budget for 1952 was running at a deficit of $150,000 some $90,000 of which resulted from the fall-off in student fees. No provision had been made for salary adjustments although the need was urgent.[11] In fact, the AAUP soon submitted to the president a resolution calling for a $600 across-the-board salary increase which was the amount they expected Akron public school teachers to realize from their successful tax levy. The faculty was also anxious that salaries be adjusted in line with other publicly-supported universities.[12] In forwarding this request to the Board, President Auburn said the salary increase was "completely justifiable" inasmuch as the University had been unable to increase faculty compensation in line with rising costs of living.[13] Apparently initiative by the AAUP was a new phenomenon to some directors, for the president had to explain its functions to them.

On December 17, the Board adopted a budget calling for an increment of $330 for all full-time staff, but there were no funds for merit increases. The budget anticipated a year-end deficit of $112,000 unless City Council provided interim funds or unless the charter amendment passed in May. Under this budget, the lowest-paid instructor would receive $3,000, but the highest-paid professor would receive just $5,830.[14] Although President Auburn recognized that the $330 increment was "inadequate in the light of rising living costs" it was granted despite the fact that the budget was thereby thrown badly out of balance.[15] This, he said, was evidence that the administration and the Board were doing all in their power to increase salaries.

The Citizen's Finance Committee, meanwhile, was examining the request for interim financing; its members believed a major policy decision must be made concerning Akron University. John Davies, Research Director at the Akron Chamber of Commerce, pointed out that Akron and Kent were too close to each other. Whereas Kent had the great taxing powers of the state behind it, Akron was hard-pressed to secure operating funds. Some committee members suggested that perhaps Akron could be run as a subsidiary of Kent or that some form of merger could be worked out.[16] This suggestion was totally unacceptable on the Hilltop. From Akron's viewpoint, it would mean that the much older institution, the one with more tradition and the more comprehensive concept of public service would play second fiddle to a normal school which had but recently grown to strength. It was clearly out of the question on the Akron campus, and there is little doubt that President Auburn felt a need to demonstrate anew to Akronites the merit of their Municipal University and its right to better support. The Citizen's Committee did not press the issue.

There was to be no sitting around waiting for someone to bail the school out of its problems. "Let's face facts," said Auburn; "the financial picture in the years ahead is grim indeed."[17] The deans were admonished to scrutinize schedules and eliminate marginal classes and to consolidate multiple-section courses. The alumni fund drive for 1952 was to be directed toward reducing the anticipated deficit.

Strict economies in the operating budget were instituted and some of these caused misunderstanding, largely because the control of expenditures which had already been approved for each college was left in the hands of the business office rather than in the hands of the academic deans. This practice had started under President Simmons and so angered one dean that he prepared a letter to Simmons that he never sent because he "could not approach the subject in a rational mood."[18] While the financial crisis lasted this centralized control of expenditures was accepted as necessary, but the deans believed that the practice continued on past the time when it was justified.[19]

To this day, The University of Akron has an extraordinarily centralized system of budget planning and preparation and while it makes for business efficiency, it has the unfortunate effect of removing the deans from meaningful participation in the important assignment of priorities for the University as a whole. And since the ultimate control over expenditures centered in the presidential and vice-presidential levels, everything of moment came to this level for decision which meant that virtually everything that the University did had the personal stamp of the top administrative group on it.

The need for operating money was desperate as a renewed attempt was made to secure passage of the charter amendment in the May, 1952 election. Despite a full-scale campaign effort, the issue was again defeated, a defeat that President Auburn attributed to a "protest against soaring taxes" rather than to "any dissatisfaction with the university's educational services to the community."[20] Perhaps, as some persons thought, a municipal income tax would be the answer to the financial needs of the city and the University.

Because the margin of defeat was small, the Board, upon the recommendation of the president, had the issue placed on the November ballot. Again all the elaborate campaign machinery was put into gear. A citizen's committee under Judge Thomas Powers took care to educate the citizenry to the University's need. They pointed out that Akron's request was modest; that the University's costs were rising in a manner consistent with national experience. Some support was gained for the charter amendment by pointing out that hundreds of veterans of the Korean conflict would be coming to the local campus soon. And once more the *Beacon Journal* urged that the University—this "asset of incalculable worth" to Akron—be properly supported.[21]

This time all the effort was rewarded; the charter amendment passed by a margin of some 4,000 votes. The campus was jubilant: "We look upon this vote as a mandate to adjust our educational program to meet the needs of the people of Akron," said the president.[22] This victory marked "a turning point in the history of the University of Akron."[23] The president's words were prophetic; the difficult times had finally bottomed-out; the long-awaited salary increases could be made; the 1953 budget was balanced; and for the first time since 1948, a real spirit of optimism returned to the Hilltop.

With operating income secured in the city charter at a one mill level, and with the five-year building levy safely renewed, the needs of the moment could be met with some assurance. In the fall semester, 1953, the University was in the best financial health it had enjoyed in 25 years.[24] But it was important to find additional income to support the growth that was sure to come as the "war-baby" boom hit the college campuses. Between the Ohio Code's limitations on tax levels permitted municipal universities on the one hand, and the public's sense of having reached a tax-saturation point on the other, there appeared to be little prospect of additional operating income from tax sources. Operating funds would have to come from supplementary sources. Money collected in the 1953 Akron University Fund drive was used for general expenditures, but it was not enough to keep pace with the need. And so it became necessary for the Board to raise student fees.

The fee increase took effect September,1955, and it was of a magnitude that put Akron's fees "in line with other municpal colleges in Ohio."[25] It was estimated that students would pay less than half the cost of their education, but a 1957 study revealed that they were paying 52 percent.[26] Not only was the student paying much more of the cost than his counterpart in the land-grant institutions, but that important concept of municipal higher education that required the University to minimize cost to the "consumer" was seriously compromised. It was difficult to persuade the public that the student should not bear most of the cost of his education or to persuade the public that an educated young adult was a community asset, that the benefits of higher education did not accrue solely to the selfish advantage of its recipient because his expertise was helpful, indeed essential, to the well being of all.

With students paying a large part of the cost of their education, more operating funds could be acquired through larger enrollments. Even though an increase in students meant an increase in operating costs, it was clear to the administration that Akron was operating below its optimum size. The enrollment of about 1,000 Korean veterans in 1954 provided a temporary influx of students, but, it was clear that efforts should be made to achieve long-range growth.[27] To this end, President Auburn instituted aggressive recruiting policies.

A Faculty Committee on Enrollment was charged with finding ways to get more than the 22 percent of Akron high school graduates currently attracted to the University.[28] The "crusade for scholars" that the committee implemented included high school visitations by committee members and various other direct approaches. With the initiation of High School Day in 1954, programs designed to bring high school students to the campus for visitations were undertaken. The Buchtel College of Liberal Arts sponsored a series of science lectures which brought outstanding high school juniors and seniors to Saturday morning lecture-demonstrations of a sort to challenge the brighter students. It was hoped that some in the audience might also be attracted to the University and eventually enroll there. Later the series was expanded to include lectures in the social sciences and the humanities. Another effort to increase familiarity with the University involved the annual dinner given by the College of Education for the principals and counselors of the high schools of Summit County.

While these efforts were underway, President Auburn started as early as 1955 to prepare the public for the wave of students that would soon appear. More students meant a need for more money. "It is now evident," he told the Board, "that the University, like the public schools, is being expected to perform a rapidly expanding service which requires added support over and above that provided by an enlarged tax duplicate. We shall have to be alert to finding new ways to finance educational services to which the students and adult people of Akron are entitled."[29] One place to seek new financing lay just beyond the city limits.

The "flight to suburbia" in the postwar era was part of the national experience. Municipal universities were particularly hard hit by this flight since it put a damper on the expansion of city tax duplicates and deprived the universities of considerable support at the polls, for many who moved were from the socio-economic group that traditionally supported taxes for educational purposes. It seemed natural, therefore, that The University of Akron consider expanding its tax base by extending to the county the same fee benefits that Akron residents enjoyed in return for which it would receive appropriate tax millage from the county. The Summit County Commissioners were interested in the proposal as were many influential citizens groups including PTA's. "With the spread of population from the city into the county and the blurring of municipal lines," said a *Beacon Journal* editorial, "it seems entirely logical that the facilities of the University of Akron will sometime be offered to the people of the whole county."[30]

State Representative Thomas L. Thomas, an Akron alumnus, joined with his legislative counterparts from Lucas and Hamilton counties to introduce enabling legislation that would permit a county-wide tax base for Ohio's municipal universities.[31] When the enabling act passed in the spring of 1953, the directors were confronted with the problem of determining whether or not to ask that an appropriate measure be put on the ballot. They examined a report on city and county population, school enrollment, high school graduates, and tax evaluation and concluded that it was too risky to proceed immediately along this course. Exploratory meetings were held with city, township and county officials. Everyone appeared to have some reservations. A quiet sampling of voters, taken by the University, revealed that the plan would be defeated if voted on at that time. There was more support for the idea in the southern and western townships of Summit County than there was in the eastern and northern, and for a very plausible reason. Persons living east and north of Akron could drive to Kent as readily as to Akron. Without increasing their taxes a penny, their sons and daughters could attend Kent at approximately the same cost they would be assessed were the county to tax itself to secure a fee break at Akron.

Although this idea of a county-wide tax base didn't die completely, it never blossomed into a realistic prospect. Probings of voter sentiment suggested to University officials that perhaps certain townships or school districts outside Akron might be willing to join the city in the University taxing district. Again an Akron graduate, Representative Frances McGovern, joined with Senator Oliver Ocasek (an Assistant Professor at the University), and with Cincinnati legislators to introduce permissive legislation enabling a county or any taxing district within a county to join a municipal university taxing district. This legislation passed in 1959. Coventry school district, Stow, and Munroe Falls considered joining the tax district, but nothing came of it.[32] By this time, there had been a lot of talk and some action toward securing state assistance for Ohio's three municipal universities.[33] It was the start of such assistance shortly thereafter that put this issue to rest.

While the wooing of county voters went on, there was no let up in the search for other public funds. Some of the directors were distressed by the state law limiting the amount a city could tax itself in support of its university. "By what right does the state tell Akronites how to spend their money?" said one, while Lee Ferbstein felt "the people of Akron should be the ones who set the limit."[34] Akron's situation differed from Cincinnati's and Toledo's; they each had a chance to secure funds from payroll taxes, this money being in addition to the state limitation of 1.45 mills.[35] Nevertheless, Akron's sister institutions were ready to join in a plea to the legislature to raise the state tax limit.

One statistic points up dramatically the problem facing Akron's university. By 1957 the city tax duplicate was increasing about $15,000,000 annually, but the one mill of operating money received by the University from this growth amounted to only $15,000 or about what it would cost to pay the salaries to two instructors for a year. This was insignificant when set against the need. But perseverance paid. In the spring of 1957, the Ohio legislature passed a bill permitting cities to tax themselves up to three mills in support of their universities.

The Board of Directors took immediate steps to implement this permissive legislation by requesting City Council to put a charter amendment providing an additional mill of tax income on the November ballot. Before council would act, a clarification of the University's tax position was secured from William Saxbe, Attorney General of Ohio, who ruled that Akron could run its tax levies for more than five years at a time, thus making it possible to seek a permanent millage under the city charter.[36] With this point clarified, council approved placing the charter amendment on the ballot, and once again all the familiar campaign machinery was put in motion ranging from citizen's committees to student workers at the polling places. A most effective tactic in encouraging support was the detailing of the cost of this millage to the "average" property owner. The owner of a $15,000 home, appraised at $6,000 would pay $3 semi-annually which was less than two cents per day. It was anticipated that the new millage would bring in about $700,000 annually for operations.[37]

In supporting the charter amendment, the *Beacon Journal* pointed out that in the last 10 years, the University had kept slightly ahead of increasing numbers of students by a "combination of planning, financial manipulation and administrative skill." This combination could not work much longer, and Akronites could either help the University or some Akron students would have to go elsewhere to college, or forget about it. Akron had a "decidedly lopsided" financial situation with students paying 55 percent of the operating costs. Student fees could not be increased further without pushing some students out of school. Finally, the *Beacon* pointed to what was described as a "practical" angle for supporting the school. Akron area schools needed more teachers and industry needed more engineers and technicians, and the University could supply these needs. "In effect it is a reciprocating proposition," said the paper.[38]

President Auburn, meanwhile, placed emphasis on America's need for trained manpower to compete with the USSR which had just launched its Sputnik, much to the consternation of the western world whose patronizing attitude about Russian science and technology was dramatically punctured. To meet the Soviet challenge which had successfully breached America's supposed "Maginot line of atomic supremacy," the only "logical course," said President Auburn, was "to nourish the educational institutions which train the manpower and carry on the scientific research needed to keep this nation strong." And The University of Akron had a role to play in this national commitment. It couldn't move effectively, however, without additional resources, especially for faculty salaries. "It is paradoxical that our democratic society has so far tended to penalize the very profession on which it depends most for its continued existence and welfare," he said.[39]

The voters remained unconvinced. The amendment carried only three of Akron's 10 wards and secured only 45.8 percent of the vote. It was the poorest showing the University had made, but in spite of the discouragement the president insisted that the issue would have to be resubmitted to the voters "at the first propitious time."[40] Student reaction was more indignant than on the occasion of previous defeats. Ten students signed a letter to the editor of the *Beacon Journal* pointing out the improbability of keeping good faculty and attracting others unless more funds could be found. They wondered "how much longer people with the training and ability necessary for this task will sacrifice for the seemingly ungrateful people of Akron."[41] There appear to be two reasons why students responded with more heat than usual to defeat at the polls. First was genuine concern about the scientific accomplishment of the USSR. Second was the fact that the University was visibly on the move, it was becoming stronger daily despite limited resources, and students resented any threat to its continued progress.

Having been turned down at the polls the directors reluctantly took the only other alternative to secure money; they raised student fees by about 10 percent, an amount that seemed inadequate to some observers. The new non-resident tuition was now so high it "virtually restricts enrollment to Akronites" which was unhealthy in creating the best climate for learning.[42]

The new fee structure was incorporated into the 1958 budget, and tax income accounted for only 34 percent of that budget.[43] Akron was rapidly approaching the fee condition of a private school which was, of course, the farthest thing possible from the ideal of municipal education. An unhappy letter writer complained, especially about the high fees assessed students from outside Akron, and said that if fees continued to go up colleges would not have to worry about future enrollment increases because no one would be able to afford to go to college.[44]

The fee increase prompted some citizens to wonder about the efficiency of Akron's operations. Higher education had expanded into all sorts of activities not previously a part of the accepted roles of colleges and universities, and this sometimes did result in embarrassment. There was much comment in the public press about "educational frills." The *Wall Street Journal*, for instance, carried an article charging universities with inefficiency in handling their business operations and their budget dollar. Commenting on this article, President Auburn wrote: "By and large I believe colleges have stretched their all-too-limited dollars more efficiently than most industrial concerns."[45] Certainly Akron had stretched its dollars efficiently. Over and over again, the University was cited by state examiners, accreditation teams, and review teams as a model in stretching the public dollar to maximum usefulness. One commentator said that the institution was a "highly efficient educational plant." It was doubtful, he said, if there was "another institution of higher education anywhere in the country" that got "as much mileage out of its buildings and equipment as does the University of Akron." He went on to say "there probably are few other communities in the nation that get as much return on their investment as do the citizens of Akron."[46] In the late 1960's when state status was in the offing, Governor Rhodes, himself a former auditor, publically complimented the University on several occasions for its wise use of public tax dollars and stated that no other unit of the state system did better. This was important since in order for Akron's appeal for new tax money to be effective, the Akron voter had to be convinced of the University's stewardship of its money.

It appeared to those on campus that they were spending a good portion of their time preparing campaigns and manning the polls to get out a favorable vote on money issues. Procedures followed on these occasions were rather well set through practice; indeed it is doubtful that there was another university in the country that had more experience along these lines. Since the campaign to secure an additional mill of operating income through a charter amendment had failed in 1957, an all-out effort was mounted in its behalf in 1958—the greatest effort since the relocation issue of 1929—and since it involved every device commonly used in money campaigns, it might be well to describe briefly the scope of this effort.[47]

A Citizen's Committee of 446 prominent Akronites was formed to support the charter amendment.[48] They represented every important segment of civic life. Mayor Leo Berg served as honorary chairman while two directors, Mr. E. J. Thomas, Chairman of the Board of the Goodyear Tire and Rubber Company, and Mr. L. S. Buckmaster, President of the United Rubber Workers, served as general co-chairmen of the campaign. Mr. Thomas Ferns, widely known insurance executive and civic leader was the campaign director. Nearly all of the labor involved in mounting the campaign was handled through regular University departments and personnel. The expenses incurred, some $19,000, were underwritten by private gifts including $12,000 from the Akron Chamber of Commerce. No public tax money was used.

Campaigns are usually marked by a symbol and a slogan. In this campaign the symbol was an oil lamp of a style common to biblical days—the "lamp of learning" —and a large gas torch with a two-foot flame burned on top of the Student Center throughout the campaign as a visible reminder of the slogan, "Keep the Lamp of Learning Burning." A successful effort was made to secure public endorsements from business, labor, fraternal, and civic groups. Conversely, great tact and foresight were used to prevent alienating any significant voter group or creating any sort of organized opposition.

On the evening of October 21, a two-hour alumni campaign to ring 3,000 doorbells was undertaken. A week later 3,000 simultaneous meetings in homes throughout Akron brought seven or eight people together in each home to hear a radio-television simulcast on the importance of the charter amendment. Some 20,000 waxed paper cups, decorated as torches, were to be lighted on sidewalks in front of supporters' homes on the eve of election day. And, of course there was the usual Speaker's Bureau supporting the effort; campus tours for interested parties; and extensive literature passed out at every gathering on campus and at many off-campus gatherings as well. All faculty and staff members were urged to preface any speeches they delivered during the campaign period with a short plea for support. Student speakers from speech classes appeared in each classroom to remind students to vote for the amendment or to encourage their parents to do so. On election day, each of Akron's 427 precinct voting places was manned through voting hours by relays of students and faculty passing out literature to those approaching the polls.

Such effort should be rewarded, but it appeared that it would not be, for when the 95,626 votes were counted, the charter amendment had been defeated by 64 votes. The bitterness of such close defeat after so much effort is hard for anyone to imagine who hasn't experienced it. It didn't help the mood on the Hilltop when the *Beacon Journal,* while lamenting the defeat asked, "Could these votes have been won with another ounce or two of effort?"[48]

President Auburn, never one to take defeat easily, listed for the faculty some five ways in which defeat could have been avoided.[49] One of these was an old sore point: if every faculty member living outside the corporate limits of Akron had lived inside the city and had voted for the amendment, it would have passed. Many persons attributed defeat to the work of "sudden citizens," those habitual non-voters who turned out to vote, this time against Ohio's proposed "Right to Work" amendment to the state constitution which purportedly would have broken labor union power in Ohio.[50]

While the official count of votes was being made, the president was meeting with Board members and with selected faculty and staff to plot a strategy should the official count confirm defeat. This being the case, the decision was made to request a recount of the vote in some 149 precincts chosen because the results in those precincts seemed most likely to be in error. No recount had ever changed election results in Akron's experience, and President Auburn warned the Board that chances were "very, very slim indeed in this recount." Defeat, he cautioned, was almost a "certainty," and it would be a "miracle" if the issued passed.[51]

The "miracle" came to pass! In the 30,000 votes recounted, there was a shift of 326, enough to put the charter amendment in the winner's column by 262 votes.[52] Once more there was jubilation on the Hilltop! Once more perseverance paid; the University's leadership had pulled finances above a mere subsistence level. In the joy and relief of the moment no one was saying what some knew all too well; that the charter amendment was a stop-gap only. Within a distressingly short time, still more public monies would be required to keep the University abreast of the times and its mission. Nevertheless, it was true that "the future suddenly looks much brighter for the University of Akron."[53]

A recount showing such wide disparities as this one did tends to shake the public's faith. Votes were gained in 86 precincts, lost in 42 precincts, and remained the same in 21 precincts. However, Board of Election members were convinced that no dishonesty was involved in the original tally. They attributed the changes to routine errors, but this implied an unacceptable degree of sloppiness in counting the votes, and the Board of Elections promised to make a check of booth workers.[54]

Some disgruntled Akronites had their own theories. The "dubious wide margin" struck more than one as being a little fishy, while many failed to understand how some precincts could be recounted without recounting them all. If matters were left with only a partial recount, it would "smell to high heaven," and the Akron taxpayer would become the "goat" for those who could get tax money by foul means. These doubters were given reassurance that the recount technique was legal and that the amendment had passed "fairly and squarely," but one doubts that this reassurance converted any doubters into believers.[55]

Still another hurdle remained to be jumped before the full sweets of victory could be savored. County Auditor C. L. Bower claimed the amendment was an "outside" levy, meaning that it was not a permanent one, but only of five years duration. He was supported in this view by County Treasurer Clyde Weil while the third member of the County Budget Commission, Prosecutor John Ballard, said the City Charter had been legally amended and that the levy was permanent. Ohio Attorney General William Saxbe, the City Law Department, Akron City Council, and the University Directors all thought the levy was permanent.[56] After City Council voted 11–0 to request the County Budget Commission to reconsider its action making the levy an "outside" levy, and after the ruling from Columbus supported the interpretation of permanence, the levy was ruled valid as an enduring feature of the city charter.[57]

To put the financial picture in better focus for the future, the fiscal year was changed from the calendar year to the academic year (September 1 to August 31), and the first budget constructed on this calendar totaled $2,217,000.[58] Faculty members received a substantial raise in January, 1959, and a smaller supplementary raise effective September, 1959 so this most urgent of needs was well met. With a maximum salary of $11,100 for full professors and a minimum salary of $4,300 for the newest of instructors, Akron salaries compared favorably for the first time with similar institutions around the country and in Ohio.[59] Toledo, which paralleled Akron much more closely in size and constituency than did any other school, had a similar experience at the polls in the fall of 1959 when its effort to secure two mills of operating money succeeded by less than one half of one percent of the total vote. While Toledo would receive about $1,729,000 annually for operations, Akron would get about $1,500,000. Cincinnati did not have the two-mill tax income, but its one mill of operating income was supplemented annually by the City Council, and Cincinnati also had a substantial endowment which both Akron and Toledo lacked.[60] It was not only in the area of operating income that Akron could now hold her head high with respect to her sister institutions, for during that struggle the campus was undergoing a continuation of the face-lifting operations that had started in 1946.

If there was one part of his responsibilities that President Auburn pursued even more effectively than he did the financial undergirding of the institution, it was the development of the campus and its facilities. His direction and determination helped turn the campus into a modern and much more attractive place than it had been since old Buchtel Hall and Crouse Gym sat on their shaded five acres during the "Gilded Age" of the eighties and nineties. Three financial instruments were used to accomplish campus improvements—building levies renewable every five years, gifts, grants, and loans both from private sources and appropriate government agencies, and loans in the form of Board-issued bonds. In addition to these three instruments, Akron used the federal Urban Renewal program with spectacular success.

It was the building levy renewal in the fall of 1951 that gave President Auburn his first victory at the polls. The 45 hundredths mill levy was renewed successfully in 1955, 1960, and for the last time in 1965. Usually the victory margin was comfortable, and it was obvious that the voters understood where the building money was going in contrast with the more difficult task of demonstrating where the operating funds were going. The president was right; in the voter's mind the University was what he saw when he visited or passed the campus. Therefore, a vigorous and continuing effort was needed to make the campus as attractive as possible while also making it as functional as possible in serving educational needs.

While the public tax dollar was assiduously pursued, a quiet campaign got under way in May, 1952, to raise $1,200,000 from Akron industry and business, to be followed somewhat later by another $300,000 to be raised from individuals and foundations. This million and a half, when added to the $1,250,000 expected from the 1951 building levy during the five years of its viability, would produce a total of $2,750,000 to underwrite Akron's "second cycle" expansion program.[61]

At a kick-off dinner at the Portage Country Club for 125 Akron community leaders, Mr. Lee Jackson, President of the Firestone Tire and Rubber Company, former Buchtel College football great, and Chairman of The University of Akron Board of Directors, referred to contributions to the expansion program as "dividends"—a paying investment rather than a "mere contribution to a good cause." President Auburn scored with this economically conservative group by emphasizing that without financial support from the private sector of the economy, colleges would be forced increasingly to turn to the federal government for help, and a dollar sent to Washington was a "much watered-down dollar" when it came back to Akron. Adequate contributions from industry could "help limit the growing encroachment of government."[62]

The first two corporate gifts to come in—totaling $450,000—prompted a suspicious citizen to ask: "Is Big Business 'buying' into education at the university level?" There might well be reason to ask that question since historically in America what business paid for business tried to control.[63] But persons who thought that business was "buying" the University were unaware that the analogy to earlier business attitudes was a false one. It was true that contributions from business and industry were in their own self-interest. Indeed, President Auburn and his associates had gone to great lengths to convince businessmen of this truth. The Municpal University had always held this fact up as a clear illustration of its character in serving the community in every aspect of its life. If there was anything new in this relationship of university and business it was simply that business was becoming increasingly convinced that what the institution had been saying all along was abundantly true; that Akron had in its University a tremendously valuable source of expertise and trained manpower capable of moving into local business to the advantage of the business and the community.[64]

The confusion in some minds may have grown out of what seemed superficially to be contradictory positions claimed by the University. It must be remembered that during the 1930's, Akron had experienced what amounted to an economic class war which centered in the unsuccessful attempts of the rubber industry to fight off industrial unionism.[65] The bitterness and suspicion that was part of the struggle was slow in dying. While seeking voter support of various levies the University was prone to emphasize the extent to which the institution was a "workingman's university" because to a large extent it was, and more voters were "workingmen" than corporate managers. In private fund raising efforts it was prone to emphasize its essential service to industry and business because it provided this service, and more private money was controlled by corporate managers than by "workingmen."

The important point was that Akron took the sons and daughters of the "workingman," counseled, taught, and trained them, and then sent them into the world prepared to join the ranks of management or the professions. No one wanted that more than the so-called "workingman" did. As America became the "affluent society" there was less chance of misunderstanding, for the skilled worker with a small investment—perhaps an apartment house—enjoyed an income and had a life style that compared favorably with that of a young professional man or anyone in "middle management" or below in the great industries of the city. Thus the former owner-worker, or manager-worker dichotomy was lessened.

The skeptic's concern that business and industry would dictate educational policy to the University was ill-founded. No one at the University ever suggested they could, and few in the business community made the effort. The happy fact was that the citizens' attitude toward their University had matured. They had come to believe in a convincing way—through no-strings-attached monetary support—that Akron University was indeed an "essential service" for a healthy and progressive community. In this instance, what was good for the University was also good for the community and for business.

By September, the industrial and business quota had been reached, and about a year later the campaign for individual gifts was completed successfully. For the first time in a major fund-raising effort, the University reached its entire goal without compromise or modification of its initial targets. The money for this "second cycle" was to be used for Memorial Hall, an addition to the Student Center, and for an arts and sciences building. The education building originally scheduled for a portion of these funds had to be delayed.

An important new campus facility was acquired as part of the gift campaign. The Harvey S. Firestone family gave $165,000 for the purchase of the buildings formerly occupied by St. Paul's Episcopal Church and their remodeling into a conservatory of music.[66] The buildings, consisting of an older unit suitable for offices, classrooms, and practice rooms, and a newer auditorium that would seat about 350 people, were located three blocks northeast of the campus on East Market Street. This facility permitted a dramatic upgrading of the music program which had been in rather pitiful shape despite the presence on the faculty of some talented musicians. The gift of a $36,000 Moeller pipe organ by the Firestone Foundation in 1958 gave another lift to the department members and moved them closer to the leadership role in Akron music activities that they had long coveted.

Work on the "second cycle" proceeded expeditiously. At the close of 1952 plans for the physical education building were approved; ground was broken on April 8. It was an interesting coincidence that just the night before groundbreaking, old Crouse Gym suffered a $15,000 fire as though hurrying its successor along.

The new building was the first beyond the old eastern limits of the former Buchtel College campus. Located at the corner of Carroll and Brown (which had been cut through the block between Carroll and Buchtel), it occupied an area of over 33,000 square feet. It contained a gymnasium with permanent seats and concealed bleachers that gave it a seating capacity of over 3,000 for basketball games, a women's gym, swimming pool, dance rooms, wrestling and weight rooms, offices for the athletic and physical education staffs, and a number of classrooms. In April, the directors voted to name the building "Memorial Hall" and dedicate it as a memorial to men and women from Akron and Summit County who gave their lives for their country in World War II.[67] Since 1945, the Memorial Foundation had this in mind, but no suitable opportunity to fulfill the idea had previously appeared. Red granite plaques containing the names of more than 1,500 Summit County men and women who died serving their country in World War II were erected on the walls alongside the main entrances.[68] The solemn dedicatory services were most appropriate, and observers agreed that the building provided a fitting memorial for Summit County's heroes.

The Board immediately made the building available to the public on a rental basis, and Memorial Hall replaced the old Akron Armory as a favored gathering place for large groups. It was impossible to design the building so that its use as an auditorium was as satisfactory as its use as a gymnasium. Nevertheless it was the only floor that would accommodate major University gatherings and programs aimed at a large public. The acoustics were poor, and the atmosphere simply wasn't right for cultural programs, but it has been made to serve nevertheless. Over 100,000 people attended events in the hall in 1957–58, the first time a count was made, and usage has increased considerably since that time.[69]

The second building financed by the "second cycle" was the arts and sciences building. Named Parke R. Kolbe Hall, this building was opened in September, 1955. It contained facilities for biology, speech, and English. A fine little theater seating 250 and containing a full size stage finally gave the University Theatre a splendid home. Certain Board members balked at the idea of using so much space for a stage, but they were persuaded to go along with the plan after President Auburn and some of their colleagues stressed that it was as important for the arts to have facilities as it was for engineering, chemistry, and "practical" curricula.[70] Placed immediately in front of Memorial Hall, the outstanding feature of the building was a great central colonnade through which the facade of Memorial Hall was visible from the Buchtel Avenue approach. At night, with its lights aglow, the Kolbe arch forms an attractive frame for the visitor approaching Memorial Hall.

These buildings and other urgent campus improvements absorbed nearly all of the money available for building, and the earlier expectation of using some of the funds for an addition to the Student Center was dropped. In 1956, however, a $550,000 loan was negotiated with the Federal Housing and Home Finance Agency to build the addition.[71] Completed for use in 1958, this splendid center was expected to meet student needs for the next decade. Well before that time, however, the building would again be enlarged, but the alumni of an earlier day who had nothing more than a small lounge in the basement of the library to call a "student center" were amazed at the extent and attractiveness of the new building.

In tracing the development of a particular fund drive, tax levy campaign, or building construction, there is a tendency to forget that many of these things were going on simultaneously. They did not simply follow one another in orderly sequence as would appear from describing them. Therefore it is not surprising that tax levies and private fund raising efforts for new construction should be accompanied by a drive to raise private monies for operating purposes.

President Auburn had stated this need frequently in speeches throughout the community. "We cannot turn out topflight personnel for industry," he told a group of alumni chemists, "unless we have topflight teachers. We cannot hold promising young faculty members whose senior students command starting salaries in excess of our own."[72] Like the private colleges, municipal colleges needed private money to supplement their income from taxes. And when the Ford Foundation made its widely heralded grant of $500,000,000 to private colleges, hospitals, and medical schools, he objected to the *Beacon Journal*'s handling of the story because it seemed to suggest that municipal universities had sources of support that made private philanthropy unnecessary. The state code definitely set a limit to what they could expect, and to rise above this subsistence level private gifts were essential.[73]

The president's plea found at least one receptive listener. Late in 1956 the Pittsburgh Plate Glass Foundation announced that it was establishing a Columbia Southern Professorship of Chemistry, supported by a $15,000 grant, renewable annually. The first designate was Dr. Thomas Sumner, Head of the Chemistry Department, the first Akron University professor to hold a chair supported by outside funds since the beginning of the Municipal University.[74]

At about the same time, Mr. Joseph Thomas suggested to his fellow Board members that a program similar to one in use at Case be initiated for private fund raising. The program, to be called "AU Associates," was aimed at persuading Akron business and industrial firms to subscribe a modest amount annually in return for which they were identified as members of the "Associates" group.[75] It was hoped that most firms would regard $5,000 as a normal contribution with some companies giving more and some less. The "AU Associates" group was formed immediately and proved successsful from the start although a great deal of cultivation of these contacts was required. Income from the program was used at the Board's discretion, but by far the greatest portion of it has gone to support scholarships for talented students; the presence on campus of a large number of superior students is due in considerable part to this plendid program.

Every effort to raise money or elicit support for the University involved public relations work. President Auburn was experienced in this type of activity and brought the first professional public relations effort that Akron had known to a high peak of effectiveness. Efforts that had been disjointed and overlapping were consolidated into the office of University Relations under the leadership of the Director, Mr. George Ball, assisted by John Denison who had wide contacts in the community and among alumni. Ball had responsibility for the Alumni Office, the News Bureau, Publications, Radio and TV, the planning of special events, and many other functions. An unprecedented flow of printed materials poured out of the University Relations operation. It cost a considerable amount, but President Auburn was a firm believer in the adage that you "have to spend money to make money." And it was clear the Municipal University had to spend money to elicit voter support. Campaign funds always derived from non-tax sources.

Another means President Auburn used for getting the University's story circulated through the community was through informal citizen's advisory committees to the various collegiate units. Because Akron had a Board of Directors of just nine members, it was helpful to extend, in an informal structure, the number of influential local people that had some first-hand connection with the University, who could communicate its needs and its accomplishments. A somewhat more socially oriented group, the "Hilltoppers," was also formed with this thought in mind. The success of all these efforts can be seen in the growing support the University experienced in all of its endeavors.

NOTES

[1] *Beacon Journal,* June 10, 1951; *Buchtelite,* June 1, 1951.

[2] Board Mins., IV, 220.

[3] *Buchtelite,* Sept. 28, 1951.

[4] Board Mins., IV, 233–35; *Beacon Journal,* Oct. 6, 1951.

[5] *University Bulletin,* Oct. 8, 1951.

[6] *Beacon Journal,* Nov. 8, 1951.

[7] *Ibid.,* Nov. 10, 1951.

[8] *Ibid.,* Nov. 15, 1951.

[9] *Ibid.,* Nov. 10, 1951.

[10] Dean's Committee Mins., Dec. 7, 1951.

[11] *Beacon Journal,* Nov. 20, 1951.

[12] *Ibid.,* Dec. 1, 1951.

[13] Board Mins., IV, 250–51.

[14] *Ibid.,* 278.

[15] Dean's Committee Mins., Feb. 14, 1952.

[16] *Beacon Journal,* Feb. 3, 1952.

[17] Dean's Committee Mins., March 17, 1952.

[18] *Ibid.,* Dec. 13, 1951.

[19] *Ibid.,* Dec. 7, 1951.

[20] *Beacon Journal,* May 7, 1952; Board Mins., IV, 327.

[21] *Ibid.,* 334; *Beacon Journal,* Oct. 17, 26, 1952.

[22] *Ibid.,* Nov. 5, 1952.

[23] *University Bulletin,* Nov. 8, 1952.

[24] *Beacon Journal,* Sept. 30, 1953.

[25] Board Mins., IV, 207; *Beacon Journal,* Dec. 16, 1954.

[26] President's Report, 1957, p. 7.

[27] Board Mins., IV, 252.

[28] *Beacon Journal,* Sept. 23, 1954.

[29] Board Mins., VI, 179.

[30] *Beacon Journal,* April 11, 1953.

[31] *Ibid.,* May 14, 1954; March 5, July 8, 23, 1959, March 10, 1960; Board Mins., X 156.

[32] *Beacon Journal,* July 11, 1959.

[33] *Ibid.,* Dec. 16, 1955.

[34] *Ibid.*

[35] Board Mins., VI, 17; *Beacon Journal,* Jan. 6, March 30, July 25, 1952.

[36] *Ibid.,* Oct. 28, 1957.

[37] *Ibid.,* Oct. 30, 1957.

[38] *Ibid.,* Oct. 28, 1957.

[39] Board Mins., VIII, 193.

[40] *Beacon Journal,* Nov. 10, 1957.

[41] *Ibid.,* Nov. 16, 18, 1957.

[42] Board Mins., VIII, 236.

[43] *Beacon Journal,* Feb. 26, 1958.

[44] *University Bulletin,* May 12, 1958.

[45] Ray Sutliff in *Beacon Journal,* Oct. 2, 1955. An example of commendation by state examiners may be found in *ibid.,* Dec. 27, 1957.

[46] See for example, *ibid.,* Nov. 15, 1958.

[47] Details of campaign organization may be found in *ibid.,* Sept.–Nov., 1958.

[48] *Ibid.,* Nov. 6, 1958.
[49] *Ibid.,* Nov. 7, 1958.
[50] *Ibid.,* Nov. 20, 1958.
[51] Board Mins., IX, 200ff.; *Beacon Journal,* Nov. 25, 1958.
[52] *Ibid.,* Nov. 25, 1958.
[53] *Ibid.,* Nov. 28, 1958.
[54] *Ibid.,* Nov. 28, 29, Dec. 4, 7, 1958.
[55] *Ibid.,* Dec. 17, 1958.
[56] *Ibid.,* Dec. 23, 1958.
[57] Board Mins., IX, 191.
[58] *Ibid.,* X, 126, XI, 25.
[59] *Beacon Journal,* Oct. 11, 1959.
[60] *Ibid.,* May 9, 1952.
[61] *Ibid.,* May 9, 14, 1952.
[62] *Ibid.,* June 19, 1952.
[63] Board Mins., IV, 350; *Beacon Journal,* Sept. 13, Oct. 18, 1952.
[64] *Ibid.,* June 19, 1952; Board Mins., IV, 353.
[65] Files of the *Beacon Journal* and the *Times Press* reveal this clearly. See also McKenney, *Industrial Valley.*
[66] *Ibid.,* IV, 437.
[67] "Program of Dedication, December 11, 1954," UArch., VF (Buildings).
[68] *Beacon Journal,* May 30, 1958.
[69] *Ibid.,* March 22, 1952, July 25, 1958.
[70] *Ibid.,* August 11, 1954.
[71] Board Mins., VII, 91.
[72] *Beacon Journal,* April 16, 1955.
[73] *Ibid.,* Dec. 18, 1955.
[74] Board Mins., VII, 210.
[75] *Ibid.,* VII, 209, 223.

XXI

Toward true University status (1951–1960)

Every phase of University life depended upon the development of a sound financial base. Once this base was guaranteed it was possible to give attention to curricular development, to the extension of public service activities, to faculty salaries and benefits, to faculty recruitment, and to other areas where needs had accumulated over the years. But in order to move efficiently in these matters, an extension and restructuring of the administrative machinery was required.

At the heart of the University's operation was the Board of Directors. Composed of nine local citizens, the Board was available for instant consultation as situations developed, and President Auburn wisely took full advantage of that fact. At times, he was in daily communication with the chairman and with members of key committees. When, for example, a building project or urban renewal project had to be expedited through the federal bureaucracy the directors could be consulted on short notice and emergency meetings called with a minimum of difficulty. It was reassuring to the president to know that he had Board sanction for decisions that could not wait for the regular monthly meetings.

To keep the directors up to date on fast-moving developments President Auburn flooded them with information concerning everything of significance and of potential interest. The same organizational power, the same ability to muster convincing arguments in logical sequence that he used so successfully with those who had business with the University were employed in his presentations to the Board. Typically he prepared a substantial report which was mailed to each director about a week before the regular monthly meeting. This report was full of detailed information and accompanying recommendations and was an admirable summary of what was going on in the University. The day before the Board was to meet, each director received a supplementary report covering things that had transpired since the earlier report was compiled. In most cases the Board "approved the President's report" and its accompanying recommendations, and in this fashion expedited a great amount of business. Although they appreciated this thorough preparation, there were occasions when the unending flow of information seemed overpowering to a Board member or two; on one occasion a director was heard to mutter somewhat facetiously, "President Auburn tells me more than I want to know about the university."

There was one potentially serious drawback to this procedure. The president's reports were so thorough, and his recommendations followed so logically from the material presented that it deterred the directors from challenges and from free-wheeling discussion of important academic matters. Of course, since none of the Board members were professionally involved in education they tended to accept the interpretation of educational questions given to them by the president; and perhaps it was just as well, for many an institution has suffered at the hands of zealous trustees who overruled the educators.[1] Yet the "give and take" in Board meetings was usually minimal; Lee Ferbstein appears in the record as a director who would "think otherwise" with some regularity although others questioned specific items of special concern to them. Under its By-Laws, all communication with the Board was through the president only; the alternatives presented to the Board were generally the president's alternatives, the priorities were his priorities although others were consulted in arriving at them. There are few "checks and balances" in most University administrative structures. At Akron, as elsewhere, as far as the general public and the Board of Directors were concerned, the University tended to be what the president said it was.

The membership of Akron's Board of Directors reflected the great corporations that dominated the city's most important industry—rubber. From the first years of the Municipal University the strong men of that industry had great influence. Frank Seiberling, John Thomas, Paul Litchfield were among the decisive, often arbitrary men whose influence in the city and in its university was profound. In the 1950's the industry was represented by Lee Jackson, E. J. Thomas, Ward Keener, Charles Jahant, Joseph Thomas, Harry Schrank, and later, Arthur Kelley. Cletus Roetzel who retired from the Board as its chairman in 1951 after 24 years of service was a lawyer as was Lee Ferbstein. Business interests outside rubber were represented by Hurl Albrecht, Sherman Schumacher, and Kurt Arnold. Mrs. Walter Hoyt represented the distaff side; she was a faculty favorite because of her close personal interest in people and her faithful attendance at campus functions. Organized labor was represented by H. L. Besshardt and later by L. S. Buckmaster, President of the United Rubber Workers.

Board members served overlapping three-year terms, three being appointed every other year. They were appointed by the mayor, usually after consultation with University officials, but not always. In 1948 Mayor Charles Slusser was distressed when City Council, led by Councilman Edward O. Erickson, requested that he reconsider three Board appointments, none of whom represented the majority party on council. After some sparring, council members endorsed the three appointees.[2] Also in the late 1940's, the Akron Labor Youth League asked Mayor Slusser to appoint a Negro to the Board, but that was not to happen until 1967 when Mr. W. Howard Fort was named by Governor Rhodes as one of the first trustees of the State University.[3]

In 1954, Mayor Leo Berg raised a real storm by appointing Kurt Arnold, a widely known East Akron jeweler who had served as Berg's campaign manager. Council charged Berg with paying off a political debt, to which the mayor replied, "The man has the ability. He probably has the best qualifications of anyone ever appointed to the board." City Council later confirmed Arnold 11–2.[4]

This was not the first time a close mayoral associate had been appointed, nor was it to be the last. In 1942 Mayor George Harter named his political adviser and former Democratic campaign manager, Phil Hartz, to a directorship, and upon Hartz' resignation replaced him with Robert Azar, another well-known Democrat and Assistant Prosecuting Attorney for Summit County.[5] As for the future, in 1962 Mayor Edward Erickson failed to reappoint Lee Ferbstein after 30 years of outstanding service, and in his place, the mayor appointed a close political adviser, Mr. Bernard Rosen, Class of '39. The *Beacon Journal* felt that "political considerations should not enter into the selection of men and women to be directors of the university," but Rosen, a prominent Akron attorney, was well qualified and during his five-year term was regarded by the faculty as one with great concern about the educational process.[6]

Those who served as Chairmen of the Board during Auburn's tenure included Cletus Roetzel, who retired at the end of 1951, Lee Jackson who served through 1954, Hurl Albrecht, who served until 1961, and Harry Schrank, who served until the Municipal University was transformed into the State University at which time he became the first Chairman of the Board of Trustees of the State University. Increasingly through the years the directors played the role one thinks of as typical; they were in the vanguard of fund raising efforts, they paved the way to many important contacts in Washington and elsewhere, and above all they had the confidence of the community which proved invaluable in pursuing the University's interests. Many of them faithfully attended important University functions demonstrating by their presence their interest in its welfare.

In the highly centralized administrative structure that has characterized The University of Akron, there was little opportunity for the administrative group below the vice-presidential level to act with a high degree of independent judgment on matters ostensibly within their responsibility. All important decisions, and a host of minor ones, went directly to the top—to the president and his immediate advisers. Effective control of the budget was in the president's hands at all times, but he delegated significant portions of budgetary responsibility to his vice presidents. Deans did not manipulate a budget independently within their colleges, nor did any department have final control over its funds. While "efficient" in harboring resources, this system tended to keep subordinates from "sticking their necks out" and created an unfortunate timidity and sense of resignation among some men who felt that they should have authority to go along with their responsibility. It is as if the captain of the ship insisted on standing all the watches; no junior officer could then exercise final judgment even on calm seas.

When an executive is "on top of his job," it is difficult for him to know when the entire operation he heads becomes cast too much in his own image. Perhaps in a profit-making business such centralization might be efficient; in a small college it might be traditional; in reorganizing a struggling university it may well be necessary. But what is appropriate to those conditions is not equally appropriate to a strong, multi-purpose university where, by definition, the clash of ideas in civilized discourse should be encouraged; for a university is a place where there is constant tension between the old and the new, between tradition and innovation. It is a place where prevailing social and political dogma should be put to the test, where originality finds congenial surroundings, and where "truth" is pursued even at the expense of conformity.

The difficulty is this: those qualities that President Auburn brought to the task in 1951 were essential to bring order out of impending chaos. But once that monumental task was accomplished, once the financial base was sound, the administration organized, the faculty revived, the voters convinced, it was difficult for him to relax his hold and permit the institution to grow independently of himself in areas like curriculum, standards, degrees, and the many other concerns that traditionally fall to faculty control. Part of the responsibility for perpetuating this high degree of centralization must lie with the faculty and with the deans, whose unwillingness to take concerted action in securing anew those rights that traditionally were theirs, left them to the president by default. Although he could be intimidating in face-to-face exchanges when the subject was not to his liking, President Auburn would always hear out a person with well formulated views, adequately documented, when he knew that this individual was genuinely concerned to make the University a better place. He had little patience, however, with the seemingly endless discussion that a faculty engages in before it talks itself into a consensus. In order to get on with it, the president would sometimes force a decision before it was all talked out, and properly so, but the price he paid for it was to suffer the charge of arbitrariness.

It has been said many times by those within and without the University family that Akron's campus lacks an "intellectual climate," whatever that may be. Though it can't be defined, people sensitive to intellectual processes believe they can recognize its absence. Part of the lack—if indeed it truly is one—grew out of the transient nature of the student body, the lack of faculty community, and the no-nonsense spirit of activity on campus.

The students have an unkind term for this directive atmosphere—"super high school." They have little sense that they are in a special environment. It is less that way now than formerly, for some of the ties bind less closely; the dormitory residents give the campus a sense of continuity of activity, while the wide ranging recruitment of faculty and the special programming that keeps the campus supplied with outside talent from diverse fields of interest combats parochialism. And President Auburn has led in securing these things.

Early in his presidency, Norman Auburn had an administrative group thin in numbers. His determination to spend every penny of the short money supply for faculty raises and new construction kept him from adding new personnel until he had been in office for several years. The first substantial shift in administrative roles came in 1955 when, in order to handle growing enrollments, the new position, Dean of Administration, was created. Dean Donfred Gardner was appointed to this position where his broad administrative talents and his unparalleled knowledge of the University could be more readily brought to bear on the whole spectrum of campus problems. In those years of rapid curricular development, his intimate knowledge of the accreditation process through his long relationship with the North Central Association stood Akron in good stead and smoothed over many a rough spot. Gardner's former title, Dean of Students, was abolished in favor of Director of Student Personnel and into this post went Gordon Hagerman, Class of '41, Gardner's long-time assistant and a born counselor. He was to hold that position but briefly, for following the retirement of Richard Schmidt as Registrar in 1955, the position was filled by an interim appointment for a year following which Hagerman was appointed to the post. Richard Hansford, Class of '49, another experienced assistant in Gardner's operation, was then appointed Director of Student Personnel.

Dr. E. D. Duryea, Jr., Director of Adult Education and Director of Research since 1953, was appointed to the new position of Dean of the Evening and Adult Education Division. His Assistant Dean, Dr. Dominic J. Guzzetta, displayed great talent and drive, and upon Duryea's resignation was appointed Dean in 1956. For some years following Dean Bulger's retirement in 1951, there was no director of graduate work. Ernest H. Cherrington, Jr., Dean of the Buchtel College of Liberal Arts, took on that additional burden and just in time, for the graduate effort was about to grow.[7]

Two new colleges were established in the 1950's: Dr. Warren W. Leigh served as the first Dean of the College of Business Administration, and Stanley Samad was appointed Dean of the new College of Law. More will be said about these important academic units later. Upon the resignation of Dr. Howard Evans as Dean of the College of Education in 1958, Dr. Chester McNerney was appointed to fill that position.

Thus, by 1959, there had been growth and change in the administration, and in that year another basic restructuring took place as the result of a university-wide study just completed by the Committee on the Educational Forecast. To balance the academic program's importance with the financial side of things, a new position, Vice-President and Dean of Administration, was created and Dean Gardner was appointed to it. Another new position was formulated to coordinate the academic programs of freshmen and sophomores, to oversee the General Studies program, the Associates program, and Special Programs. Dominic Guzzetta was the first to be appointed Dean of the General College. His assistant in the Evening Division, William Rogers, succeeded Guzzetta as Dean of the Evening and Adult Education Division.

Akron's chief legislative body was the University Council (formerly the Faculty Council), made up of deans, administrators and department heads. It conducted most of its business through committees; chief among them was the Academic Policies and Curriculum Committee which existed under various names but whose duties involved recommending curricular changes and reviewing and adjusting academic policies. Standing committees on Library, Extracurricular Activities, Assembly, etc. had representation from both faculty and administration, and some had student representation, but they were essentially faculty committees.

The Executive Committee—most powerful of the council committees—was presided over by the president and consisted of the deans and the vice-presidents. No teaching faculty sat on this key group. It was empowered to act when council was not in session, and in all but routine decisions its deliberations were to be reported to council for approval or rejection. This arrangement had a dulling effect on debate, for typically, decisions covering a wide spectrum of business were made by the president in consultation with the Executive Committee, and these decisions were reported to council virtually as *fait accompli*. Theoretically, University Council could reject the Executive Committee's decisions, but it was nearly impossible to do so. There was no agenda for council meetings, and the faculty representatives who, as department heads, were quasi-administrative representatives, found it awkward to raise issues on the floor when they had been studied and acted upon by the Executive Committee with fuller information than the faculty possessed.

Had there been in the fifties, a greater number of secure, vigorous, and resourceful faculty members they might have demanded a more equitable and representative arrangement, since most of the decisions made for them affected the manner in which they could discharge their professional responsibilities. But so little did the faculty demur—at least overtly—that another 10 years would go by before effective steps toward reform would be taken.

The detachment of effective decision-making power from the faculty (or, if you will, the faculty's abdication of its proper role in the decision-making apparatus), proceeded a step further in 1961 with the formation of an "Administrative Committee." The original members of the group were the president, Gardner, Hardy, Ball, Guzzetta, and Dr. Ian MacGregor, newly appointed Assistant to the President. The committee's function lay in "screening ideas" which were to be presented to the Executive Committee.[8] The Administrative Committee arrived at a consensus which in turn was referred to the Executive Committee which, like council before it, now found itself faced with the decision of top administration already well outlined. There was, therefore, seldom any fundamental debate within the Executive Committee.

Early in the 1960's the faculty of the Buchtel College of Liberal Arts, representing about two-thirds of the full-time faculty of the University, indicated its distress at the inability of "grass-roots" faculty sentiment to secure an effective hearing by introducing in faculty meetings matters of interest that concerned them. After vigorous discussions that had the virtue of allowing everyone to speak his piece, resolutions were passed and forwarded to University Council or the proper administrative officer for action. It was natural that the liberal arts faculty would assume leadership in this manner for traditionally it contained persons who were most likely to question the status quo. However, there was little open support—indeed little sympathy—among other collegiate faculties for most of these resolutions. Vigorous faculty recruiting in the late fifties and early sixties brought to Akron a number of young, vigorous, talented, and professionally secure faculty who breathed new life into colleagues whose careers had developed in the shadow of depression, war, inadequate working conditions, depressed salaries, and lack of alternatives—conditions that had bred in many of them a propensity for not rocking the boat.

When all is said and done, there are a number of ways to run a university, and institutions can prosper and grow under most of these alternatives. From largely unstructured Sarah Lawrence to a rigidly structured Catholic girl's school, or from latitudinarian campuses like Antioch to more conformist campuses like those of municipal universities, the business of higher education gets done. No matter what the emphasis—individual freedom, discipline, faculty domination, administrative centralization—each carries certain advantages and disadvantages in its choice of direction. Like those in other walks of life, students, faculty, and administrators want it all, but they are forced to make a choice, and assuming that the values they seek are those inherent in the public, urban university, The University of Akron provides them with an environment conducive to securing them.

The academic program was modified in several important directions during the 1950's. At the heart of the curriculum, both in terms of content and student involvement, stood the "introductories"—the core courses so carefully formulated in 1935 as part of the general education program.

Deans Gardner, Spanton, Ayer, Evans and their associates had assumed that the core courses they established would be reviewed periodically. Indeed, the courses were reviewed in 1937 and again in 1939, but the war intervened before any thorough reorganization was possible. Returning G.I.'s were especially critical of the introductories: they kept them away from courses in areas of their own choosing; they seemed to be superficial; they were too far removed from the realities of life. In their rather pointed way, the veterans made some of the courses the butt of campus jokes. Speaking of this discontent in 1948, President Simmons said: "It would have been a strange coincidence if we had struck upon the ideal formula for General Education in 1935. I believe it is now time for us to make an appraisal of our efforts in this direction, and profiting from our own experience and that of others, take another forward step."[9]

The report of President Truman's Commission on Higher Education pointed out a number of areas in which American colleges and universities were failing to perform services beneficial to society. This report was taken seriously on the Hilltop. An Appraisal Committee [Gardner, chairman, Evans, Cherrington, Landon, Distad (education), Duffy (English), Griffin (engineering)] was appointed in 1948 to survey the curriculum, especially the introductories, and to take into consideration other services the University might well be performing in keeping with the Truman Commission report.[10] The committee did little to revise the general education program with its introductory courses, but it did stimulate development of the so-called "Basic Studies" program of remedial and subfreshman work noted elsewhere.

Following Norman Auburn's arrival in 1951, the Appraisal Committee requested that the president bring a consultant to campus to review the broad impact of the general education program in all its features—financial, administrative, and instructional. It is ironic that the consultant selected was Dr. David Henry, President of Wayne University, for just two decades earlier, the City Colleges of Detroit had employed the consulting services of George Zook to tell them how to organize an effective municipal university; and now that strong young institution was returning the favor. More significant, however, was the fact that Akron had much more experience with general education than did Wayne, but even though his own campus had nothing like it, Dr. Henry was perceptive and astute, and his report presented at least one recommendation that was quickly acted upon—a Director of General Studies was given general supervisory control over the entire general education program. The logical choice, Dean Donfred Gardner, was appointed to this position. He had been the driving force behind general education and would continue to be its foremost advocate until his retirement.[11]

Before Henry's report was submitted, sub-committees of the Appraisal Committee commenced reviewing the introductory courses. They were charged with taking a "utopian" viewpoint for, as Gardner knew so well, the cost savings of the introductories were so considerable that it would be easy to rationalize them on a cost basis alone.[12] Students supported the review. The *Buchtelite* periodically identified aspects of the introductories not to students' liking. An "inquiring reporter" noted that it was doubtful that the general studies (a new terminology which was gradually supplanting the term "introductories" to describe the required core curriculum), were doing their job. He found Humanities the most popular and Mental Hygiene the least popular of these courses. A small poll of students revealed that more than half of those polled (about 12 percent of the entire student body) answered "no" to the question "are introductories important enough to be made compulsory." President Auburn, who had been converted to general education after his arrival in Akron, urged the students to take a more positive attitude toward these courses, but such urging would be in vain unless needed changes were made.[13]

It was again time to remind the campus what general education was all about. At Akron, the introductory courses were not to be considered as the sole instrument for achieving the objectives of general education. The expectation that departments would organize their specialized work to build on top of the introductories in a logical manner had been lost sight of as had the charge to departments to leave flexibility in their major requirements.

The departments, in turn, faced a dilemma even if they were anxious to cooperate fully with the general education ideal. Certain curricula—engineering, chemistry, elementary education, for example—were so tightly packed with required professional courses that there was no room for flexibility. Engineers had no electives in their 155 hours, and chemists had only one three-hour elective in an undergraduate program of 128 hours. Professional accrediting agencies such as the American Chemical Society, or certifying agencies such as the State of Ohio Department of Education, had set up such a heavy undergraduate requirement for professional courses that there was little maneuvering room for the student or his adviser. But even in departments not affected by outside pressures, there was too much of a tendency to force-feed students with courses in their major field and too little tendency to encourage them to broaden their reach.[14]

In the spring of 1953, the Appraisal Committee presented its report the heart of which dealt with a recasting of the core curriculum. "Vehement" objections were raised by the faculty on a number of points.[15] Among them was the enduring one that general education objectives could better be reached by the widely used "group elective" method which required the student to select a certain minimum number of credits in the introductory courses within the departments—so many credits in the sciences, so many in the social sciences, the humanities, etc. When, after four University Council meetings, it was apparent that the faculty was badly split in its reaction to the report, Dean Gardner said the Appraisal Committee had exhausted its ideas and resources and he recommended it be disbanded and a new committee specifically charged with responsibility for recasting the introductory courses be appointed in its stead. The recommendation was approved.[16]

The new Committee on General Education was a faculty committee in contrast to its predecessor, a majority of whose members were deans. Once more Dean Gardner acted as Chairman, but this time he was assisted by Professors Ittner (modern languages), Petry (engineering), Riedinger (education), Rogler (sociology), Simonetti (business administration), and Sumner (chemistry.)[17] It was a talented, outspoken, and congenial group and immediately began the long process of recasting the general education program. They were cheered on by the president's message to the faculty:

The University of Akron has always emphasized liberal education. No student is graduated from any department, even such vocationally directed ones as engineering, chemistry or business administration, unless he has mastered our general education courses in the humanities and the social and physical sciences. Akron U pioneered in general education; it does not now propose to eliminate 'know-why' courses in order to offer more 'know-how' techniques. The University conceives that its obligation is to train the whole man, not merely to equip him with the narrow skills required to perform a routine task.[18]

The committee presented its 80-page report to University Council in December, 1954. Council had previously approved a statement of objectives for general education and the methods for its basic implementation, but now it had to review specific course proposals. Many of the same objections that had been instrumental in scuttling the earlier program were raised again, but this time the supporters of general education closed ranks, and with President Auburn reminding the doubtful of the "consensus" in support of general education that had developed nationally since 1937, the report was approved.[19]

Of the various proposals made over the years for revising general education, the new program just adopted was clearly superior; indeed, on paper it was a beautiful construct. In the first place, the required core curriculum was distributed through all four undergraduate years. Provisions were made to exempt qualified students from those requirements that would force them to go over material previously mastered.

The approach of the old introductories in the social sciences—five weeks of anthropology, five weeks of political science, five weeks of economics,—a "bumpty-bump" sequence of fragments, gave way to an integrated course, Social Institutions in the United States, with the concept of social control as its organizing focus. Similarly, the fragmented science course was replaced by Reasoning and Understanding in Science an integrated course which used the historical case study approach advocated by James Conant in his *Science and the Common Reader.*

The four semesters of Written English stressed effective writing and the subjects upon which students wrote were selected from readings that complemented what they were then studying in the Institutions course (*e.g.* Riesman's *The Lonely Crowd* or Brogan's *The American Character*). In like fashion the subject matter of the English courses was to parallel the subject matter presented in speeches in the two-semester Effective Speaking course.

A semester of mathematics, called Numbers Communication, paid special attention to the fact that numbers were symbols of communication. The course dealt with the historical evolution of number concepts and also featured "practical" mathematics. Any student whose course of study took him into traditional mathematics was exempt from Numbers Communication.

Worthy of special mention because of its uniqueness as a credit course was a freshman requirement, Personal Development. This course reflected Dean Gardner's long-standing hope that some of the impediments in the background and experience of new freshmen could be systematically eliminated or smoothed out so the freshman could work to better advantage throughout his college career, and also that he might be better prepared to fit in socially with his peers. The course had a little of everything in it—interpretation of the student's test scores on ability and interest tests, personal hygiene, social customs, and much more. But the student needs were too diverse, the course could not be taught on a truly academic level, and inevitably it developed the reputation of a "Mickey Mouse" course. To the credit of the Committee on General Education, once the noble idea became a practical failure, committee members had the grace to admit that their experiment hadn't worked and the course was dropped from the curriculum.

These courses, plus Physical Education and ROTC (for men), were hopefully to be mastered by the close of the second year. In the third year the student encountered Western Cultural Traditions, an adaptation of the former Humanities course. With an enthusiastic staff teaching students who represented the culling of two years of University work in a course organized on a traditional chronological model, "Western Cult" became the most successful of the core courses in the new general studies program. Much more demanding than the Western Civilization courses usually required of freshmen on other campus, "Western Cult's" chief drawback was the vastness of the material to be covered even though the emphasis was selectively on art, music, philosophy, religion, in short, on cultural history rather than political history. Within a few years, its counterpart in Eastern Civilizations was introduced at the third-year level.

The frosting on the general studies cake was reserved for another innovative course, Senior Seminar, a one-semester "capstone" course designed to give students a foretaste of their adult roles as participants in social processes. Seniors from every discipline were placed indiscriminately in discussion groups of 12 under the direction of student discussion leaders working with a faculty "resource person." Lectures and readings supplemented the work which focused on effective participation in group discussion. The original plan for bringing top-flight experts to campus regularly to deliver the lectures could not be sustained because of scheduling and monetary limitations. On those happy occasions when the luck of the draw brought a stimulating student group in conjunction with an informed and understanding faculty resource person, the experience could be worth while and exciting. As often as not, however, this happy association failed to materialize, and many seniors came to regard the course as just another hurdle to be jumped.

More public interest was generated by the 1954-55 revision of general education than by the inauguration of the program 30 years earlier when the *Beacon Journal* had misinterpreted somewhat the "revolutionary" two-year general education program just adopted.[20] In response to those among the public (and some Board members as well) who thought it untimely to resist specialization, university spokesmen again had to call attention to the philosophy that generalization and specialization must walk hand in hand so that each graduate would know his major subject well and yet see how it and how *he* fit into the larger scheme of history and contemporary affairs.

This "democracy in education" as Dean Gardner referred to it, was catching on around the nation.[21] Akron could be proud of its early role in developing general education, its work pre-dating by a decade the famous Harvard Report which urged "preparation for life in the broad sense of completeness as a human being, rather than in the narrower sense of competence in a particular skill."[22] With many modifications, the 1955 reorganization is still at the heart of Akron's curriculum.

Assessing any curriculum is perilous because of the infinite number of variables to consider, many of which cannot be adequately known or measured. At its worst, curriculum assessment becomes an exchange of biases and prejudgments about what to transmit to students, and how. All such judgments are highly subjective and are unduly dependent upon a course's general reputation among faculty and students. Yet there is a kind of collective judgment that is worth noting because it helps define what people think they are getting from a course whether in fact they are or not, and if enough people think this is worthwhile then the course has a certain validity aside from whatever "hard" virtues it may possess. As a case in point, Personal Development may have had some real and useful contribution to make, but the vast majority of those who took it failed to see it.

In retrospect one might well argue that Akron's general education program, especially its interdisciplinary courses in science and the social sciences, might better have been oriented toward the Columbia model rather than the Chicago model. In his splendid book, *The Reforming of General Education*, Daniel Bell sees the Columbia concept of general education as historically oriented while the Chicago model was conceptually and theoretically structured.[23] Nearly all of Akron's early advice on general education came from Chicago personnel—Hutchins, Judd, Russell—but the thinking that was appropriate to Chicago's high-powered student body was not equally appropriate to Akron's. It is true that because of selective admission standards, Akron's students were an uncommonly able group for public universities during the thirties and early forties, but the progressive amendment of these standards to the post-World War II position of admitting any Akron high school graduate eroded the general academic quality of the student body, especially the freshman class, until it in no way resembled Chicago's or that of any other highly selective school.

Chicago's idea of general education centered about broad courses that conceptualized and generalized about society and man in abstract terms. The typical Akron freshman had little in his high school background to prepare him with an adequate data base, an adequate possession of the basic facts out of which these generalizations were drawn. Therefore, courses like "Social Institutions in the United States" seemed to be talking about an unreal world. Had the student been conversant with the extensive studies, tests, and factual material that underlay generalizations about the family, the church, the school, the economy, and the state, he might have had a better appreciation of the value of generalization and more eagerness to admit its relevance.

Many Akron freshmen in the fifties and thereafter did not come from college prep backgrounds and as freshmen they simply did not have in mind the historical "facts," the literary awareness, the basic economic, psychological, and sociological "laws' and definitions that would have enabled them to move comfortably into the realm of abstraction. Additionally, Akron students were "practical" in their outlook. They took more readily, and with more conviction, to descriptions of specific phenomena. They appreciated a description of how *a* family operated, but resisted generalizations about *the* family. Many had what might be called in terms of intellectual outlook a "fatal attraction" for the specific, the real, the individual datum.

The most successful integrated course was Western Cultural Traditions which, as we have seen, was organized on the tried and true chronological model and proceeded as a conventional history course might proceed, along a friendly path from painter to painter, school to school, composer to composer, idea to idea. Eastern Civilizations also profited from this familiar procedure. Additionally, those taking these two courses were generally in their third year of college and represented the survivors of the culling and sorting process. They had proved their ability to handle material on the University level. For its freshman and sophomore courses, Akron would have been better advised to stick more closely to the historical approach and then move into the more theoretical once a secure base had been established.

Nothing looks better on paper than an educational plan, impeccable in its order and rationale. By all rights, it *should* work. Unfortunately, colleges seldom have the opportunity to put their schemes through extensive tests the way a manufacturer would a tire or an automobile frame. It was not, therefore, until the whole complex instrument of general studies was fastened upon the University that the stresses and strains, the inadequacies and miscalculations began to appear. And although the concept of general education has been well enough accepted on campus, the fulfillment of its objectives, and the specific program in force at any given time remain favorite campus targets. We have time for only a superficial analysis of the difficulties encountered with general education.

There is little question that general education as practiced at Akron or anywhere else would work as well as other alternatives if one could assume that the students were exposed to inspiring teaching in classes of manageable size. Most of the courses in Akron's general studies program were taught in large lecture sections (some over closed-circuit television, of which more later). They abandoned the required discussion sections that at one time put each student in a small class with a regular full-time faculty member as discussion leader. In the competitive market for faculty, it was impossible for the University to hold bright young scholars if they were to be required to conduct discussions in someone elses' course over material they knew but tangentially. As Akron moved into graduate work in a serious way, the faculty member realized that work in his specialization would bring him quicker recognition and more enduring fame outside his own institution than any amount of participation in a general studies course. Mature graduate assistants were used as discussion leaders after the regular faculty opted out, but despite the excellence of the work done by some of them, they lacked the authority that a full-time professor brings to his task.

Akron has always had a disproportionate number of part-time students. This is characteristic of municipal institutions and is not regarded as unhealthy. Yet no rational, orderly program designed with the full-time student in mind ever applies equally well to the part-timer. Evening students, particularly, had schedule problems that caused them to get the academic cart before the horse, and the careful logic of sequential courses was interrupted beyond repair. It might be noted that the older evening student had an advantage in his confrontation with courses that theorized about society. With his broader experience he often recognized the validity of generalizations which to his younger daytime colleague remained unreal and "academic." The heterogeneity of Akron's freshmen and sophomore classes was such that no single track, however cleverly designed and devotedly pursued, could provide for individual needs.

Graduate aspirations affected students as well as faculty. The great pressure that graduate education put on the undergraduate courses in an effort to have baccalaureate students completely prepared in specific courses of interest to the graduate schools created an awareness in the better students that general studies courses would not get them into graduate programs, but extensive work of high quality in their specialization would. This knowledge made them impatient of time spent outside their major.

One could add other points, some of which are pertinent to general education wherever practiced, and some of which had significance peculiar to Akron's condition. But the purpose of this review is not to condemn. Any alternative that has ever been attempted, locally or elsewhere, has its share of inadequacies, contradictions, and has met with its share of criticism and disenchantment. Akron's experience with general education may be characterized as fully consistent with the school's enduring commitment to the ideals of municipal education (since 1967, to public urban higher education in general since the day of the Municipal University has passed). It demonstrated concern for the whole person. It purported to "educate" rather than merely "train." General education at Akron has been a dependable reference point for the entire curricular structure. It embodied a point of view in action that transcended the accomplishment of American universities whose undergraduate programs are a mish-mash of unrelated courses. Above all, it has been the tool by which a public, urban, practically-oriented university has preserved for all of its students an irreducible minimum of the "liberating arts" without which they would be deprived of the common communicative ties of their heritage and of their contemporary society.

In 1953, the University branched out again into a new program—the first of a continuing flow of curricular additions—with the establishment of the College of Business Administration. The Commerce Department in the College of Liberal Arts had come of age, and important persons in the community were calling for a separate college of business. The directors shared this interest in providing expanded service to the city. The new college opened with four departments: accounting, general business, industrial management, and secretarial science. Ultimately the secretarial science curriculum would be transferred to the Community and Technical College while the general business program became separated into departments of marketing and finance.

The first dean was Dr. Warren W. Leigh, longtime head of the Commerce Department and a man widely known in marketing circles. He had published and consulted with special attention to the interests of the rubber industry and this served him well in organizing Tire Dealers' Conferences and special symposia designed to keep the businessman posted on new developments. He was one of the pioneers in this work which is now so common a part of the academic scene.

In spite of rather limited facilities and resources, Dean Leigh put the new college on a solid footing. Upon his retirement in 1962, he was succeeded by Dr. Richard Reidenbach whose great accomplishment was securing accreditation for the undergraduate program in 1966. In 1968 Dr. Wilbur E. Benson was named dean. Throughout its existence the college has had strong department heads; Dennis Gordon in accounting, Frank Simonetti in industrial management, Charles Poston in marketing and finance which later split, with marketing coming under the direction of Stephen Castle and finance being headed by James W. Dunlap. Completion of the Business Administration-Law Building in 1965 gave the college a fine home in which it continues to grow and develop with special emphasis in recent years upon graduate work.

It would appear that the emergence of a separate College of Business Administration was a matter of concern to some persons. A Board-administration committee reported in December, 1952, that the College of Liberal Arts was "the academic hub about which the entire university revolves," but the committee was convinced that, "as a municipal institution, the University must serve as large a proportion of those intellectually qualified as possible: to do so, greater emphasis should be placed upon vocational and professional programs than heretofore."[24] The creation of the new college, President Auburn said, was "not a step toward further specialization," but rather a step to "provide liberal education under a more efficient administrative setup."[25] And yet the creation of a professional school would inevitably produce its own momentum toward increased and expanded specialization. It was impossible to appease those opposed to a new professional college in these terms, especially when, a month later, the president found it necessary to urge the faculty to guard against "proliferation of courses" and "growing specialization."[26] It furnishes one of Akron's clearer examples of strain inherent within a growing institution.

Coincident with the push for a College of Business Administration came a suggestion from certain Board members that Ayer Hall, with its "excellent facilities in engineering," should enable the University to offer "greater opportunities to industry" through evening courses in engineering.[27] The response to this suggestion was immediate; it was announced that mechanical engineering would offer a complete degree program in the evening session starting in September, 1952, in order to "meet the educational needs of the industrial community."[28] By 1957, an annual grant from Goodyear Tire and Rubber Company and Goodyear Aircraft permitted the College of Engineering to offer a master's degree program with classes scheduled in late afternoon and evening hours. From this start the graduate program was quickly expanded into additional engineering specialties.[29] When the college celebrated its Fiftieth Anniversary in 1963, it was offering extensive service in the graduate field.

Graduate and professional education reached a turning point of primary significance in 1956 with the announcement that Akron would offer a program leading to the Doctor of Philosophy degree in Polymer Chemistry.[30] President Auburn provided the drive to take this significant step. It was the logical place for Akron to break into doctoral level work for it possessed advantages that transcended anything the institution could show in other departments. Akron was truly the "Rubber Capital of the World" with the headquarters and research labs of four of the five largest rubber companies, an existing research program and facility in the Institute for Rubber Research, the library of the Rubber Division of the American Chemical Society, the presence of research men of the caliber of Dr. G. Stafford Whitby, Dr. Maurice Morton, and somewhat later, Dr. Alan Gent, and a competent chemistry department backing them up. Directing the organizational effort was Dr. Thomas Sumner, the 30-year old Head of the Chemistry Department, who possessed a talent for putting the pieces together.[31]

The introduction of Ph.D. level graduate education was destined to change Akron, and, in the process, subject it to all the well-known strains that affect any institution whose primary goals had been oriented toward teaching and service to local needs, and which then finds itself having to extol the virtues of research in support of the doctorate (which is a research degree). Faculty hired while the emphasis was still exclusively on teaching could see that unless they produced publications or research of some significance, they would suffer in salary and promotion with respect to their peers who were more research minded. The strain was not acute until a decade later when several more doctoral programs were added to the curriculum. In Akron's favor it must be said that the disparity in treatment that one finds on many campuses between the faculty publishers and non-publishers was minimized. There was a price to pay for this policy, however, in that some excellent research people would not come to Akron because they were denied preferential treatment that was available to them elsewhere. Another strain introduced by the shift toward doctoral work and research grew out of the heavy outlay of funds required to build suitable facilities and acquire equipment beyond the needs of an undergraduate or master's program.

The first students awarded the Ph.D. degree by The University of Akron received their hoods at the 1959 commencement. Their dissertations had been read and approved by experienced directors of doctoral work from other campuses. Having produced its first graduates, the University was then inspected and approved for accreditation in its new program by the North Central Association. Akron thus became the fifth Ohio university to offer doctoral work, following Ohio State, Case, Western Reserve, and Cincinnati.[32]

With this new level of endeavor in polymers, a new name—the Institute of Polymer Science—was given to the operation. As this academic program became known, students from around the world sought out Akron for training in polymers. Regular conferences and symposia held by the Institute attracted the top investigators in the world. In 1967 the Institute moved into extensive laboratories in the newly opened Auburn Science and Engineering Center, giving it the kind of home its work required.

An unusual opportunity to tell the world about rubber and polymer research and instruction at Akron developed in 1958 when the University celebrated the fiftieth anniversary of the teaching of rubber chemistry on its campus. It would have pleased—though it is doubtful that it would have surprised—Professor C. M. Knight to see how his child had grown, to see eminent scientists from around the world making a pilgrimage to the chemical laboratories named for him to discuss the astounding developments that 50 years had wrought. The culmination of the celebration centered on two awards, one to the living and the other to the dead whose work lived on. Dr. G. Stafford Whitby was recognized with an honorary doctor's degree as was the principal speaker, Dr. Alan T. Waterman, Director of the National Science Foundation, who praised Akron's partnership between the University and local industry.

The recognition of Dr. Whitby was immensely popular for no one who had graced the campus in recent years represented as well as he the broadly educated man, the scientist whose technical contributions were enhanced by his deep appreciation for, and knowledge of, the arts, literature, and the ways of mankind. Other awards went to five of the foremost contributors to rubber science and the technical development of rubber. These men were the first to be installed in the Rubber Science Hall of Fame.[33] Each year another outstanding rubber scientist is added to the Hall's growing ranks. Their portraits hung in the library until 1967 when they were transferred to a room prepared for them in the new Auburn Center. These benefits flowed from the University's determination to enter a new level of academic life, a step that some believed, as did President Auburn, to be "the most important academic achievement in the . . . history of Buchtel College and the University."[34]

The development of Ph.D. work gave the entire graduate program a psychological boost. By the time the first doctorate was awarded in 1959, just 733 "earned Master's degrees" had been awarded by the University since 1920. Buchtel College, of course, had awarded a few earned master's degrees starting in 1880. All except three of these degrees were awarded either in education or in liberal arts, for the first master's degrees in business and in engineering were not awarded until 1959.[35]

The North Central Association's accrediting visitation in 1960 was the catalyst that caused Akron to take organizational steps necessary to administer a growing graduate program.[36] University Council recommended that a Graduate Division be established effective July 1, 1960, that it be administered by a dean, and that a graduate faculty be established to control the curriculum and to implement the North Central's recommendation that the University develop a philosophy of graduate education. The importance of this recommendation lay in the fact that the president was determined to press on toward graduate work in additional areas, but the basic thinking about direction, goals, standards, impact on the remainder of the curriculum, and other fundamental issues had been given but superficial consideration. It was vital that a path be laid out before the University became locked into practices not suitable for maintaining a strong graduate program.

The Board acted with dispatch on these recommendations, appointing Ernest H. Cherrington Dean of the Graduate Division, charging him with organizing selection of a graduate faculty and putting records and procedures in order.[37] The graduate faculty was organized in 1960 and a Graduate Council was authorized to act for it in conducting the main business of the group. Acceptance in 1961 for membership in the Council of Graduate Schools in the United States was yet another sign that a new level of graduate activity had been achieved.[38]

Dean Cherrington could no longer be expected to care for the graduate effort in his "spare time" as formerly. Cherrington's new appointment meant relinquishing the deanship of the Buchtel College of Liberal Arts to Dr. Thomas Sumner. Sumner was well qualified through his experience as Head of the Chemistry Department, organizer of the Ph.D. effort in polymer chemistry, member of the General Education Committee, formulator and teacher of the core course "Reasoning and Understanding in Science." outstanding teacher of chemistry, and adviser to Lambda Chi Alpha, Omicron Delta Kappa, and Alpha Chi Sigma. Just 34 years old, he was the youngest man to hold a deanship on Akron's campus.

During the spring of 1959, while graduate education still held center stage, the Trustees of the Akron Law School offered "to the Municipal University of Akron the assets of every kind and character of the Akron Law School with the sincere request that the . . . University . . . accept the Akron Law School and operate it as an integral part of their University." It was, as President Auburn, remarked, "an intriguing offer."[39]

Akron Law School was founded in 1921 by Charles A. Neale. At the time of the offer to the University it was operating night classes at 105 East Market Street. Three years of college credit were required for entrance and the law course took four years to complete. Judge Oscar A. Hunsicker, Dean of the Akron Law School, had a full-time teaching staff of three, supplemented by a number of part-time instructors, some of whom were outstanding local practitioners. The law school claimed 650 graduates through 1958, and of these the number passing the Ohio Bar Examination was high.

Akron Law School had never achieved more than a hand-to-mouth financial base; its success in preparing students was a tribute to the competence and skill of its faculty and officers and not to its facilities. In 1934, it became a charter member of the League of Ohio Law Schools which was the agency designated by the Supreme Court of Ohio to regulate the teaching of law in the state. In the mid-fifties, the League amended its constitution to provide that member schools must raise their standards to meet American Bar Association (ABA) standards. Akron Law School had voted for this amendment and set about preparing for ABA accreditation which it hoped to receive in 1957. It was unsuccessful in this attempt and in later overtures. It became obvious to the trustees that the school lacked the financial base, the equipment, library, etc. to qualify for ABA approval and so, in 1959, while the school was operating at a loss, with no prospects for improvement in sight, the President of Akron Law School, Mr. Joseph Thomas, also a member of the University Board of Directors, made the motion to offer the school to Akron University.[40]

Reaction from within the University, from most Akron Law School alumni, from the public as represented by letters to the editor, and by the *Beacon Journal* favored the move as logical and necessary to preserve this "valuable asset" to the community.[41] President Auburn promptly formed a committee (Gardner, Cherrington, Guzzetta) to investigate whether such a move would be "academically sound and financially feasible." The committee reported in favor of the takeover but warned that it would be a deficit operation until the law school could be put on a secure footing. This situation was remedied by a gift from Mr. C. Blake McDowell, Akron attorney, of $100,000 payable in amounts of $20,000 per year for five years. This splendid gift covered the difference anticipated between operating costs and income from student fees. The Board of Directors quickly accepted the offer, and the Akron Law School became the College of Law of The University of Akron.[42]

During its first year of University affiliation (1959–60), the college was operated at its old location on Market Street with Donfred Gardner as acting dean until the appointment in 1959 of Stanley A. Samad, formerly Dean of the Franklin Law School in Columbus. Dean Samad was anxious to make ABA accreditation the first order of business, and he took immediate steps toward that end. With a thorough grasp of the problems of legal education, he saw that steps were taken immediately to regularize the teaching staff and the curriculum. Starting in 1960, a regular four-year baccalaureate degree was required for admission. Physical facilities were improved by moving the college to campus buildings and an immediate effort was started to upgrade the holdings of the law library. More than 300 alumni of the Akron Law School were incorporated into the University alumni rolls. Up to this time the program was a part-time evening operation, and until new facilities were available, nothing could be done to start a regular three-year day curriculum. Some accrediting agencies were not too happy with part-time evening education—indeed it was thought the ABA wished to "squeeze out" night programs—and it was Akron's intention to have both, in this manner strengthening the College of Law while continuing to serve the employed man and woman who could get a legal education only in the evening.[43]

These vigorous efforts paid off when, in less than two years' time, the American Bar Association extended tentative accreditation to the College of Law.[44] Finally, after the college occupied new quarters in the Business Administration-Law building, it received full accreditation from the ABA in 1965.[45] Not only did this new graduate professional school add a most important educational enterprise to the University's services, it was also regarded as a victory for the community. It was particularly satisfying "to those of us who as recently as 1956 were defending the very existence of the Akron Law School against critics who thought it ought to be closed," wrote a *Beacon Journal* editorialist. "All who contributed to these notable steps deserve the congratulations and thanks of the whole community."[46]

NOTES

[1] This conclusion is the result of conversations the author has had with a member of the Board and with others who attended Board meetings with some regularity.

[2] *Beacon Journal,* Feb. 3, 10, 1948.

[3] *Ibid.,* Dec. 26, 1949.

[4] *Ibid.,* Jan. 18, Feb. 2, 1954.

[5] *Ibid.,* Jan. 10, 1962.

[6] *Ibid.,* Jan. 9, 1962. See also, Board Mins., VIII, 118.

[7] These appointments are a matter of record in the Board Minutes.

[8] UArch., box 4/10c/52.

[9] *University Bulletin,* Jan. 15, 1948.

[10] Keister, "General Ed," pp. 95–6.

[11] Board Mins., IV, 401.

[12] Keister, "General Ed," p.119.

[13] *Buchtelite,* Nov. 14, 21, 1952, March 14, 1953.

[14] Summarized in "Report of the Appraisal Committee" April 6, 1953, UArch. VF (Appraisal Committee).

[15] Keister, "General Ed," pp. 133 ff.

[16] *Ibid.* For faculty sentiments on "group electives," see Council Minutes, April 6, 1953.

[17] Board Mins., IV, 450.

[18] *University Bulletin,* Dec. 8, 1953.

[19] *Ibid.,* Dec. 6, 1954; Council Mins., Dec. 9, 13, 1954.

[20] *Beacon Journal,* Dec. 15, 1934.

[21] *Ibid.,* Feb. 6, 1955.

[22] *Ibid.,* Oct. 18, 1955.

[23] See Bell, *Reforming of General Education,* pp. 13–36 for a summary of the position of each.

[24] Board Mins., IV, 379–80.

[25] *Beacon Journal,* Feb. 19, 1953.

[26] *University Bulletin,* March 9, 1953.

[27] Board Mins., IV, 352.

[28] *Beacon Journal,* Sept. 17, 1952.

[29] Board Mins., VIII, 19.

[30] *Ibid.,* VII, 95.

[31] *Beacon Journal,* May 25, 1956.

[32] Board Mins., VII, 98, XI, 80.

[33] The first five to be honored were Charles Goodyear, C. Grenville Williams, Carl O. Weber, Henri Bouasse, and Ivan I. Ostromislensky. (*Beacon Journal,* Oct. 3, 1958.)

[34] *Ibid.,* May 25, 1956.

[35] "Forecast Committee Report," March 7, 1960, UArch., box 4/10a/61.

[36] Board Mins., XI, 80–1.

[37] *Ibid.,* XI, 117.

[38] *Ibid.,* 252 i.

[39] Board Mins., X, 63; Akron Law School Mins., March 7, 1959 (UArch.).

[40] The course of development of Akron Law School can be followed in the Akron Law School Minutes (UArch.) and in appropriate issues of the *Beacon Journal.*

[41] *Beacon Journal,* March 31, 1959.

[42] Board Mins., X, 141; *Beacon Journal,* July 15, 1959.

[43] *Ibid.,* April 17, Sept. 18, 1959, March 12 1961.

[44] *University Bulletin,* Sept. 6, 1961.

[45] *Beacon Journal,* Feb. 15, 1965.

[46] *Ibid.*

XXII

"Pinnacle of the
public education system of Akron:"
The Municipal University in full flower
(1959-66)

Universities are places of the intellect where, one would assume, rational men operate along rational lines planned well in advance. Until recent years, however, public universities had developed more by guess than by plan. Those which have to accept all applicants find themselves repeating, year after year, the same frantic endeavor to accommodate the latest surge of students. In short, planning has not been the strong suit of most public universities.

There are obvious reasons for this condition, foremost among them being that public universities are servants of the political world that supports them, and political signals can change peremptorily and frequently. In addition, this condition is traceable to the unpredictable nature of young people whose goals keep shifting. Some will register for classes and never show up; some who intend to be engineers in May end up as business majors in September; some stretch out their undergraduate program to take advantage of work opportunities; some are poorly motivated and find themselves unable to focus their abilities. The numbers in which they come to campus depend on how many alternatives the campus provides. These circumstances by no means exhaust the list of conditions that make planning difficult; and we must add another of great consequence: formerly, most academic administrators were drawn from the ranks of teaching faculty, and they tended to be unacquainted with the principles of management. Planning, for them, was done casually and seldom took into account the degree to which campus conditions reflected conditions in society at large.

Akron was in an unusually strong position to plan intelligently for future growth. Better than most universities, Akron knew what her clientele was and what they were seeking from college. Growth patterns in the community could be determined with considerable accuracy. The Akron tax base was a dependable reference point on which to build financial projections. And because Richard Schmidt, Donfred Gardner, and others had kept careful records, the University knew with fair precision where it was, which, of course, was the first step in knowing where it was going. In previous efforts to project growth the University had fallen very wide of the mark, largely because of the sudden dramatic increase in the percentage of high school graduates going on to college, a phenomenon that took all of American higher education by surprise.

In September, 1957, President Auburn announced the appointment of a Committee on the Educational Forecast (Forecast Committee). The committee was composed of representatives from the Board, faculty, administration, student body, alumni, and the Akron citizenry. Dean Gardner was named Chairman of the Forecast Committee and Dean Dominic Guzzetta was appointed Director of the study it was to make. A grant of $10,000 from the Akron Community Trust underwrote the cost of studying the services the University should render to the community through 1975.[1]

The first major task of the Forecast Committee was to gather data. The members had at their disposal studies that purported to show how Ohio would be affected by the forthcoming "tidal wave of students." They had the results of a local survey made by the University showing that of the Akron parents with children in elementary and secondary schools, 88.6 percent hoped their children would go on to college, and of this number 71.7 percent expected their children to go to Akron.[2] While a small sample, the data revealed the probability that the "tidal wave" would crest locally much higher than national figures predicted, and the committee took warning. Nationally recognized consultants were brought in to review selected aspects of the operation.[3] An extensive "working bibliography" was assembled and the materials therein consulted as required.

Originally the Forecast Committee planned to take two years for the study, but the need for guidelines was so urgent that the president encouraged them to report after one year's work and then supplement the original report with additional information as it became available.

On June 15, 1958, the "First Report on the Educational Forecast of the University of Akron" was issued in some 87 mimeographed pages plus bibliography and extensive appendices.[4] Its 21 recommendations were formulated on the most extensive and accurate data base ever assembled locally for higher educational purposes. Although each of the recommendations had significance for the University, only the most outstanding or useful ones need to be mentioned here.

First, the committee urged that the data collected be added to and reanalyzed annually thus keeping a running account of essential information. Current University objectives were to be maintained as was the open admission policy which sought to offer higher education opportunities to all whose formal education qualified them for admission. An "educational evolution" of the traditional teaching role of the faculty was to be brought about by a new emphasis on teaching aids, especially TV, and by placing more responsibility on students for their own educational attainment. Each college faculty was to reexamine its curriculum in keeping with this "educational evolution" in an effort to "streamline" curricular offerings. University Council should be reformed and reconstituted as a representative body. Two-year technical courses should be instituted immediately; a Dean of the General College should be appointed to administer the first two years of study for all students; counseling and advisement of students in the General College should be done by the Student Personnel Office. A number of recommendations concerned specific reforms or changes in the library and its operation; the fiscal year should be changed to conform to the academic year; schedules should be adjusted to affect maximum utilization of facilities throughout the day; the evening credit program should be designated the Evening College. Finally, and of great importance through the years, the average faculty base salary of 1958 should be doubled by 1970.

The usefulness of the report was in no wise confined to these recommendations, for day-to-day operations were to be greatly affected by what the enrollment projections revealed and by the sources of income anticipated. Although the Forecast Committee dealt only with Akron and its environs, it could not be content with just one projection of enrollment because there were too many variables to consider, the most important of which had to do with assumptions about the percentage of high school graduates going on to college, about fees, about the curricular structure of the university, and above all, about the sources of income. The committee, therefore, calculated four different formulas and based enrollment projections on each of the four formulas. Almost before the ink was dry, it was evident that the growth pattern was going to trend toward the more optimistic projections.

The Forecast Committee issued supplementary reports in 1959 and 1960. The former emphasized the reordering of fiscal policies, acquisition of additional physical facilities, the relationship of the Student Personnel Office to the Dean of the General College, and also the problems of record-keeping. The 1960 report emphasized graduate study, and its recommendations together with those made by the North Central Association's Ph.D. accreditation team supplied the push toward formalizing the administration of graduate work.

Unlike many studies, the Forecast Committee reports were acted upon.

Through the next decade—a time of great change—the University moved with a confidence that it could not otherwise have had. John Dale Russell, consultant to the committee and himself a leader in the new art of educational forecasting, commended the committee on "an excellent piece of work" which provided a model "that might well be followed by many other institutions of higher education."[5] When the enrollment forecasts turned out to be "incredibly accurate," committee members were not surprised. "We feel," said Dean Gardner, "that we are among the first universities applying management principles to education by planning for our future needs."[6] As word got around, some 60 universities requested copies of the comprehensive report. Perhaps the greatest tribute of all was a silent one. There was no faculty sniping at the report or its projections.

Complementing this useful planning on the fiscal, administrative, and academic side of the institution was a pace-setting plan for campus development and expansion of physical facilities. In common with many colleges and universities, Akron had planned and built her campus with a minimum of professional help, relying to a large extent on the president, Board, and administration to do the planning. But with the complexity of modern construction—land acquisition and use, utilities relocation, and a thousand and one additional considerations—it was time for the professionals to take over planning. No longer would a Chairman of the Board do as John R. Buchtel did and point a finger at a campus location and say, "that's where we will build."

Late in 1963 the Cleveland firm of Outcault, Guenther, Rode and Bonebrake was engaged to develop a long-range land-use plan. It was the first time that any extensive work connected with building layout and design had been put in the hands of non-Akronites. They went to work immediately. At nearly every step plans had to be checked with the City Planning Commission and with Citizens For Progress, a local organization helping to redevelop the city. In a surprisingly short time the Development Guide Plan was ready for unveiling.[7] It proved to be spectacular. Buttressed with extensive data on projected enrollments, the plan laid out a step-by-step progression for extending the campus until ultimately it would occupy the 180 acres bounded by E. Market Street, the Akron Expressway, E. Exchange Street, and the railroad tracks. Certain substantial private buildings in this area—churches, apartments, etc—would remain, but the traffic pattern would be changed to clear the campus site of through traffic. It was a bold and dramatic projection, and just enough new development was underway to make it seem feasible even though the scale model, which was avidly studied by interested faculty and students, had a utopian look about it.

Well before the Development Guide Plan was produced, steps had been taken to assure some regularity in the development of the campus area. A committee to inquire into possible areas for campus growth was one of President Auburn's early appointments. In 1956 the Board considered establishing a development fund to handle gifts to the university, and as part of this consideration President Auburn and Vice-President Hardy were requested to prepare a five-year projection of physical needs.

In 1952 the Board took a major step when it authorized the establishment of a University District, designed to limit new construction in the area immediately adjacent to the campus. The idea was first introduced in 1945, but nothing had come of it then. This would prevent further deterioration of the immediate neighborhood and prevent the building of costly structures in an area that the University would require for future expansion. Real estate values were already high, some of the better locations selling for nearly $100,000 an acre in the late 1960's, and the University could not afford to have the appraised value of property soar uncontrolled. The

University possessed right of eminent domain, but it tried to secure property without recourse to court action.

In October, 1954, an area of 46 acres surrounding the campus was identified by the Board as the University District; Akron City Council legislated it into being in February, 1955. As far as could be determined, this marked the first time a university had created a protected zoning district around its campus.[8] The district was extended in 1963 largely to accommodate a pressing need for parking spaces and was again extended in 1966.[9]

Of all of Akron's development efforts, however, the most promising was made possible by participation in the federal urban renewal program as specified under the Federal Housing Act of 1959 which permitted municipal universities to use urban renewal for expansion purposes.[10] The University became a pace setter in the employment of this program to the solution of its space problems. From the beginning its efforts were tied in with the City of Akron's urban renewal plans largely because of President Auburn's conviction that the University could expedite her program in this fashion.[11] And when Leslie Hardy was appointed Chairman of the Akron Urban Renewal Commission, it appeared that coordination of effort was likely to result.

For some years there had been rumors circulating in the residential neighborhood just south of the campus that the University would expand in that direction.[12] By late 1959, plans to extend the campus southward in an area bounded by Carroll, Brown, Exchange, and Sumner Street were formulated. The University had acquired credits through recent campus building to cover most of the local share of the project's cost. It was ready to move ahead.

The City Planning Commission promptly made the University plan a part of the city's master plan although Mayor Berg made it clear that the city had no money to divert toward the University project.[13] Meanwhile, consultants hired by the city recommended that the University project be pursued, but they gave priority to the city's Grant-Washington project. Since Grant-Washington bordered the area that one day would be campus, it worked to the long-range advantage of the University, but, for many months to come, the question of priorities would be argued back and forth.

And what about the 23 acres that the University had mapped out for its urban renewal project? This land on which Buchtel College boys once played baseball and football had been built up slowly until the era of World War I at which time it suffered from overbuilding. Houses were squeezed together on little blind courts; population density was too high. Following World War II, the neighborhood became increasingly integrated. As one of the few integrated areas in Akron, a number of persons, on campus and off, were torn between their desire to see the University expand and their recognition of the price that must be paid in social dislocation.

It is impossible to say what the attitude of the homeowners themselves was for there did not appear to be any solidarity in their position. On one thing they did agree, however; they bitterly resented the designation of their area as "sub-standard" and "blighted." Over 100 property owners jammed City Council chambers in February, 1960, asking first why they had to surrender their property to Akron University, but later directing their ire at those adjectives—sub-standard and blighted—that would make it hard for them to receive full value for their property.[14] Ultimately, these objectionable words were removed from the description. It would appear that there was little residual hostility toward the University among these people. At a meeting in Kolbe Theater, attended by nearly 200 residents of the area, no objections were raised to the University's plans, and in November, 1960, their precincts gave a 63.2 percent favorable vote to a University levy, the highest percentage ever from that area.[15]

As might be expected, those who opposed the University's plan suggested alternate directions in which expansion could go. Most interesting of the alternatives was a suggestion, endorsed by Mayor Berg for political purposes, that the campus grow westward between Buchtel and Carroll. The answer to that was delivered by Ward Keener of the Board of Directors who said that mayor's idea would create a campus that would look "like a hot dog between two buns."[16] The mayor was not adamant. He was trying to placate voters. But while he personally supported University expansion to the south, he would not agree for a moment that this project take priority over Grant-Washington, arguing that the University project was "aid to education" rather than slum clearance. By summer, the mayor had the "reluctant" agreement of University officials to proceed simultaneously with the two projects.[17] Even though there was a possibility that this would slow the University project, it was urgent that the City of Akron show some progress toward improvement of its sadly deteriorated condition or the city would languish to the detriment of all, especially the University.

The Federal Urban Renewal Commission announced in June, 1960, that Akron would receive $50,000 for advanced planning on the University project (designated R-30) and that $1,460,000 had been earmarked for a loan-and-grant contract to clear the land.[18] A year later a gift of $250,000 from the Firestone Tire and Rubber Company was made to help defray the cost of development of the 23 acres.[19] It was fitting that this gift should come from the corporation whose former president, Mr. Lee Jackson, had served 12 years on the University Board of Directors, three of them as its Chairman. This service was in the directors' minds when they unanimously voted to designate the 23 acres the "Lee R. Jackson Field" and dedicate its use to physical education.[20]

With this excellent support the project moved forward to its next critical point. Early in October, 1962, the U.S. Housing and Home Finance Agency approved a $2,117,592 grant and a $2,360,695 loan for the urban renewal projects. City Council applauded when Mayor Edward Erickson, Class of '44, read the confirming telegram.[21] This was the most important University participation in a federal capital program since 1935 when Simmons Hall marked the break in a long drought of new construction. The promise held forth by Jackson Field made the prolonged period of demolition and construction bearable. Through 1963–64 huge bonfires burned across Carroll Street. As the last house blazed like a torch amid surrounding rubble, regret for the passing of the old which held memories for so many was overborne by elation for the new with its promise for generations to come. For the first time ever, Akron's university would have breathing room. The psychological benefits derived from Jackson Field, while not so easily justified to the public, were almost as important as the physical benefits.

Other vitally important additions were made to the campus following completion of the "second cycle" expansion. Paul Litchfield, who had served as a director for many years, gave a red-brick, colonial style house at 856 Mayfair Road to be used as a residence by the University president. A gift of $8,000 from Mr. and Mrs. E. J. Thomas was used to furnish and redecorate it.[22] For the first time since 1925, there was now an official president's residence. The Auburns regarded it in that spirit, and the great number and variety of dinners, receptions, and meetings that they hosted so graciously fulfilled to the fullest its intent and purpose.

The next buildings erected were given priority as a result of the reports of the Forecast Committee whose projections revealed the urgency of building a library and a dormitory. The library was actually an addition to an addition. Carl Kolbe Hall, built in 1916, was totally inadequate for modern needs, so it was determined to raze it and put in its place a new structure tied in with the library annex which was constructed in 1949. The whole was to provide adequate study space and stack capacity for the next decade assuming Akron remained essentially a municipal university. The new library building was dedicated April 16, 1961, with addresses by Edward Weeks, Editor of the *Atlantic Monthly,* and Dr. Louis B. Wright, Director of the Folger Shakespeare Library. "The highest function of this building," said Weeks, "is to put the student in touch with greatness."[23] It was a useful and pleasant addition to the campus, but, as was true of the Student Center and other buildings that experienced increased use in direct proportion to student population, within a few years it was crowded at peak hours; the extension of library hours over a longer period each week helped, but did not solve the problem. Well before the end of the decade plans would be laid for a large new library which was to be the heart of a so-called "learning resources center" that would bring library facilities in line with the expanded curriculum and the growing graduate program.

Few collegiate undertakings are more complicated than moving a library. After supervising the move into new quarters, Miss Dorothy Hamlen, who had served so ably as Head Librarian since 1947, resigned that position to become the first University Archivist, in which position she performed the invaluable service of classifying and caring for both historical and contemporary materials. Under her leadership the library staff finally received faculty status. Through her efforts, the Friends of the Library was revived as a viable organization whose contributions made possible valuable special collections on the American Indian, Negro life and culture, the Far East, and many other vital topics. She worked effectively for inter-library cooperation among Ohio colleges and universities, and a good working relationship with Kent State University was established whereby the two schools attempted to minimize duplicate ordering of expensive and little-used materials. Perhaps her most meaningful contribution was her concern for people and her gift for candor. The library was a place for people, not simply a repository for books, and as such was truly the heart of the academic enterprise. In 1965, she was succeeded as Librarian by Mr. H. Paul Schrank, Jr., who has directed the library into the computerized era.

The second building given priority by the Forecast Committee appears a little strange at first glance. "A dormitory?" some asked. Why compound the University's responsibilities when it took all of its resources to handle those it already had? Was it appropriate for a municipal university to encourage non-residents to attend? The answer to these questions had deep ramifications for Akron's interpretation of its role and function.

Municipal higher education was intensely focused inward. The central theme was always that the Municipal University, in return for tax dollars, would provide the widest possible educational and supporting services to the community that taxed itself for its support. It wasn't enough that non-Akron students paid twice what the Akron student paid. To be true to the ideal of municipal education would require that dormitory students somehow be explained in terms of community benefit, and that is what was done.

The world of the 1950's and beyond was different indeed from the pre-war world. America's commitment was international in scope; young people were addressing themselves to an ever wider spectrum of social, political, economic, and international ideas. To continue to restrict the Akron campus to local students, largely products of the same school system, readers of the same newspapers, subject to much the same social outlook, was to do them a disservice.

In June, 1959, President Auburn told the Board that a men's dormitory was urgently needed to provide housing for out-of-town students who were expecting to enter the science and engineering programs, and within a year, contracts were awarded for a 98-bed dormitory.[24] The dedication ceremony was held in September, 1960. This "milestone," said the *Beacon Journal*, was important "as a symbol of an attitude which points to a greater future for Akron U." Though educating Akron's youth "will continue to be the University's main concern," Akron students would benefit by the introduction to the campus of a more cosmopolitan flavor. The men from 10 states and five foreign countries who were in the first group of residents would indeed help to add this character.[25] Almost overlooked in the dedication were

Buchtel Hall (1900–), is the oldest building on the main campus.

Students now stroll in front of the Gardner Student Center (1968)

Where cars once parked in the 1920's

President's Residence
856 Mayfair Road

Panorama showing the 23 acre
urban renewal area south of
the main campus.

Thompson House and Mitchell House, frame houses converted to use as women's dormitories pending construction of a new building.

The new women's facility was not long in coming. A gift of $175,000 from Owen Orr provided much of the stake required to obtain a federal loan for construction.[26] Another men's dormitory was projected at the same time, and in the fall of 1962 the women's residence hall (Orr Hall) and the second men's dormitory were ready for occupancy. After a few years without names, men's residence hall number one became Ritchie Hall, and men's residence hall number two became Sisler-McFawn Hall thus successfully recognizing a desire by the dormitory residents to give up anonymity for an identity. Temporary men's housing caused by the oversubscription of the dormitories had to be resorted to, and it created problems. A protest by men housed in the old Shaar Apartments had the salubrious effect of slowing down oversubscription of dormitory space.[27] With the completion of the two tower dormitories, more than 1,500 students were to be accommodated in modern dormitory facilities.

There are many difficulties involved in establishing dormitories. The man who filled them was the Director of Admissions and Housing, Mr. Howard Haynes. He and his staff traveled extensively, cultivating good feeder schools and telling Akron's story in areas where it was totally unknown. The first dormitory group represented in part students who could not get into schools of their first choice; but this condition quickly changed. Before long Akron was receiving a strong flow of applications from able students, some of whom had heard good reports from the "pioneers" and had therefore selected Akron as one of their first choices. The dormitory population soon came to have a higher average ability level than the student body at large.

Nearly all that had been hoped for the dormitory program came to pass. The presence throughout the day and evening of a permanent student population gave the campus new life. No longer did the University appear in late afternoon to be a commercial establishment that had just closed its offices. Spirit was a passé concept on American campuses in the 1960's, but the dormitory students came close to bringing that obsolete standard of the college scene back into evidence. Akron finally looked like a university and this was important in helping it to act like a comprehensive, multi-purpose institution.

The Education Building had been superseded in priority by the library and the first dormitory. Construction was started in September, 1961, however, and as the excavation on the front lawn deepened, part of the foundation and walls of Old Buchtel were uncovered. Pieces of dinnerware and crockery were found where they had fallen in the holocaust of 1899. The familiar cycle was again perpetuated on the Hilltop—the old making way for the new. The new Education Building was dedicated in impressive ceremonies in March, 1963, and the College of Education boasted its first home in a building especially designed for its needs.

Even before completion of this job, the president was authorized to proceed with a campaign to raise $1,250,000 for construction of a Business Administration-Law building. By April, 1963, this goal was subscribed by some 1,224 donors.[28] Among the many special purpose rooms named for individual donors, were the C. Blake McDowell Law Library and the Judge W. E. Pardee Moot Courtroom. A splendid auditorium seating 550 persons, the gift of the Beacon Journal Publishing Company, was named the John S. Knight Auditorium. Completed in 1965, the building was dedicated by the Honorable Earl Warren, Chief Justice of the United States Supreme Court.

These buildings came along just in time, for enrollment was booming. In the early 1960's, Akron grew faster than any public university in Ohio.[29] Total credit enrollment went over the 10,000 mark in 1964, but the full-time student equivalent, was still well below that figure. Nevertheless, full time or part time, the students were there and had to be accommodated. Summer enrollment also experienced a marked upsurge. To the regular six-weeks session a second six-weeks session was added. Not only was the total summer enrollment skyrocketing, but it was a more diversified enrollment, no longer dominated by teachers. While the College of Education continued to lead the way, other programs moved forward as year-round enterprises with heavy summer enrollments.

Physical changes on the campus were not accomplished without certain strains. It appeared at times to the uninformed that buildings were torn down indiscriminately. But they were old, inefficient, costly to maintain, and had seen years of heavy service. Just as important, perhaps, was the space they occupied, for the purchase of land outside the immediate campus area was almost prohibitively expensive. As a result, the old buildings had to be sacrificed to the new. In order to put the Business-Law Building where it belonged it was necessary to tear down the old Knight Hall which had been most recently used by the College of Education. Little of the old campus, familiar to earlier student generations, would be left when this building and the curving drive in front of it disappeared. Joseph Thomas urged his fellow directors to save the old building, perhaps by moving it across Buchtel Avenue; but the building would not stand the move. As a caution for the future, however, Thomas reminded his colleagues, "I hope we don't tear down Buchtel Hall too, some day, and leave no tradition at all on this campus."[30] The razing of Crouse gym to make way for another expansion of the Student Center followed closely by the razing of Olin Hall to clear the access way to the Auburn Science and Engineering Center pretty well cleaned out the last of the old. Only Buchtel Hall and Simmons Hall remained of the pre-1946 buildings.

The practice of tearing down an old building every time a new one was created had interesting ramifications, one of them being that not as much new space was gained with new construction as might be supposed because old classrooms were lost to make room for new. Another result was happier; the facilities of the Akron campus were, on the whole, quite modern and functional. Physically, by 1965, Akron was essentially a new university. And the intent of it all—good learning conditions, improved student and faculty morale, community pride—was served. President Auburn's slogan, "good housekeeping is essential for good instruction and research," was the guiding principle.[31]

Though less noticed than new buildings, parking space was almost as essential to the University's growth. Before the end of President Simmons' tenure, the first moves to acquire land north of Buchtel Avenue had been taken. Attempts to extend the lots in this area ran afoul the determination of Mr. T. H. Topalu to keep his short-order restaurant "Terry's Place." The disappearance of the Buchtel Eat ("the Greek's") years earlier left "Terry's" virtually unchallenged for the close-in college trade. Some of the more fastidious had long wanted to remove "Terry's" from the scene, but in 1956, when legal steps to acquire his land were initiated, the *Buchtelite* came to his defense as did a number of letter-to-the-editor writers in the *Beacon Journal*. One angry writer condemned the attempt to "confiscate the livelihood" of Mr. Topalu in order to provide parking. "If the university's only means of attracting students is the capacity of its parking lots rather than the quality of its educational staff," said the writer, "it should close its doors."[32] The writer overlooked the new fact of life that all universities had to live with: *both* good educational facilities and staff *and* adequate parking were necessary. This case dragged out for more than two years before a settlement was reached and the much-needed parking space acquired. With the passing of Terry's Place, only Schroeder's remained near enough to permit a student to drink his beer and dream about the better things he had to look forward to if only he could make himself study.

The most helpful partial solution to the parking problem was embodied in the Development Guide Plan. It provided that new classroom buildings and other selected buildings have underground parking decks. This was possible because of the gentle slope of the land which made excavation and access relatively easy. Even though parking decks added to the cost of construction and maintenance, money could be obtained through bonds issued by the Board and retired by parking fees. The first building to be constructed on this new plan was the first tower dormitory with its adjacent Residence Hall Dining Center. The Auburn Center and Schrank Hall each featured parking decks. While there was no question about the usefulness of this plan in reducing the amount of surface parking required, in getting "double use" of expensive urban land, and in improving the appearance of the campus and neighborhood, the number of vehicles to be parked increased at such a rate that the decks could not keep up with the need.

Those responsible for planning, designing, and constructing public buildings are fated to have their handiwork exposed to generations of users. It is little wonder, therefore, that criticisms occur about everything from the location of coat racks to an uninspiring facade. While Akron's new buildings were functional, and often quite attractive internally, there was nothing on the campus in 1965—save possibly ivy-covered Buchtel Hall—that was exciting or visually pleasing to external view. All sorts of reasons have been advanced for this condition. Some observers attributed it to the architects, but their response was that they designed what they were instructed to design. Others laid the responsibility on the Board or the president. The more informed claimed that Akron's building code was unduly restrictive.

There appear to be two principal reasons for the pedestrian nature of the pre-1965 buildings. First, the Board and administration were determined to squeeze every last square foot of classroom space out of severely limited dollars, and in the process grace and style were sacrificed. Second, no one having the ear of the Board succeeded in providing the aesthetic leadership a university should provide its community by making a determined fight for buildings with external beauty and character. Left to their own judgment, the Board built buildings appropriate to commercial or industrial functions. Only Kolbe Hall with the archway through its middle (a feature some called "waste space") displayed any external originality among the classroom buildings. In an editorial, "Buildings Lack Beauty," the *Buchtelite* said that aesthetic considerations appeared to have been "lost in the shuffle." And then, in a passage that reminds us that the more one gets the more one wants: "Why should the university—so bound and determined to excel in every area to create an inspired academic community, to project a fine image—settle for architecture akin to that used for warehouses and glue factories?"[33]

No doubt such criticism pained those who thought that their efforts were unappreciated and their difficulties underestimated. But better days were ahead architecturally. The new student center was an object of visual pride; the campus approach down the westward incline leading to the massive Auburn Center had impact; Schrank Hall provided interesting elevations and an eye-catching decorative screen; the dormitory-living complex seemed to tie the university to the elevations of the adjacent central city. Most impressive of all were the projections for a new Performing Arts Center which, at the time of this writing (1969), would provide Akron with its first large-scale sample of contemporary architecture—a vivid departure from the early blandness.

The period 1957–67 marks the zenith of the Municipal University. Never before had it come so close to fulfilling the vision of Parke Kolbe and others who had led Akron toward comprehensive service to the community. In only one important area—given its resources—had the university been unable to come close to the ideal; it had to charge the student more for its services than it should.

The old adage that "nothing succeeds like success" describes precisely the University's acceptance by the community in the early 1960's. Although the city had always given lip service to its University and had supported it at the polls on occasion, the level of this support was so modest as to preclude the University from doing more than meeting its most urgent immediate needs. Under President Auburn's aggressive and resourceful leadership, old sources of revenue were used to the hilt, new sources were cultivated, and the money thus secured was used to attract additional support.

And the support came. Leaders of community opinion made flattering comments. Mr. Paul Litchfield wrote, "The university now is the pinnacle of the public education system of Akron and represents the great interest of its citizens in higher education for its use."[34] Some years later John S. Knight could say that "Few institutions of higher learning are serving their constituencies as effectively as the University of Akron. The municipal university is a tremendous asset to our community."[35] Akron's less well-known citizens were no less impressed. They sent their sons and daughters in ever-increasing numbers, they attended the educational and cultural programs devised for their benefit, they responded with votes in support of University levies. President Auburn had these things in mind when he said, "No publicity-supported institution of higher learning is so dependent upon the understanding and support of the citizens of its community as is a municipal university of our type. None is so close to the grass roots."[36]

The educational opportunities offered to the community included regular degree programs, day and evening, informal non-credit courses in the Community College, special conferences, symposia, workshops, lecture courses, cultural courses, extension courses, and other organized presentations. The University also offered the community use of facilities, special services, speaker's bureau, equipment, and professional leadership from faculty and administrative consultants. While other public universities offered many of these same services, Akron's special claim is that in proportion to its size and its budget, it was perhaps as thoroughly involved as any school in the nation.

The University's basic service was the higher education it provided Akron students. Twenty years ago (1948) the local rubber industry employed 1,500 Akron graduates and 3,000 former students. Graduates of the University controlled, or were officers in over 65 local industries other than rubber. Were these figures updated to the present, the number would be much greater. More than two-thirds of Akron's public school teachers in 1955 had taken all or part of their training at the University. Without the doctors, lawyers, judges, dentists, social workers, ministers, and other professionals that the University had trained, the city of Akron could not function. Insurance, real estate, financial institutions, retail sales, and countless other occupations depended heavily on its graduates and former students. In 1958, Goodyear Aircraft chose Akron over Arizona as the site for development of a major contract partly because its managers knew that Akron University provided a dependable flow of "brainpower" whereas they had no certainty that they could draw competent people to Arizona from all over the country. One of the reasons the General Tire and Rubber Company gave for developing its research facilities in Akron was the nearness of the University's resources. "Akron U is a vital asset to us," a company spokesman said.[37] To keep the University abreast of its needs for graduate training, Goodyear Aircraft gave $15,000 annually toward the start of a master's degree program in engineering in the evening session.[38] By the late sixties, the graduate program in engineering had expanded to the doctoral level, thus joining existing Ph.D. programs in Polymer Science, Chemistry, and Industrial Psychology in its direct assistance to industry.

In the non-credit Community College program, a fascinating selection of adult education courses was offered—everything from flower arranging to a sophisticated course in nuclear power systems. Many of these courses were taught by experts drawn from the large talent pool that the Akron community offered. One top-flight electronics engineer said he taught in the Community College as a "community service." The $200 per course he received hardly compensated him adequately for his time, but he found that talking with a class of educated and alert students helped him "to think better on [his] feet" when he had to.[39] If the instructors appreciated the opportunity, so did the students. One group, when finishing a course in Real Estate Law, presented a check to the instructor to be used to further the work of the Community College. The students simply wanted to express their appreciation for the opportunities afforded them.

It is incorrect to think that adult education services, credit or noncredit, were for Akronites only. People commuted great distances for courses. In 1954 more than 65 cities and towns were represented in evening programs as were 500 or more business and industrial firms. Some 36 school districts were represented by teachers taking additional work in the evening credit program.[40] Improved highways extended the University's reach so that similar statistics gathered at a more recent date would reveal an even greater geographic spread in clientele.

In 1953, extension courses were offered in other communities. They were very limited in number and scope; most of them were offered in hospitals in Massillon and Canton. The municipal character of the university did not lend itself to extension work, however, for it put it in the position of using local tax resources for the benefit of persons in other communities, and even though a substantial fee differential helped cover the costs, it still seemed inappropriate somehow. No such barrier existed after state status was achieved.

A special effort was made to improve the meshing of University resources and programs with the needs of the Akron Board of Education. The most interesting of these programs was the development by the University of a plan whereby academically talented high school juniors and seniors in the Akron area could take certain freshman courses at the University. These students received regular credit toward a degree which meant that these credits would transfer to other accredited colleges. The program was financed by a $25,000 grant from the Fund for the Advancement of Education and was called by a knowledgable observer "one of the four or five outstanding patterns developing in this field."[41] The only difficulty with this outstanding program was cost; once foundation support ran out, students would no longer pay the fees the university was forced to charge although occasionally some talented high school student still takes advantage of the opportunity to accelerate his program.

Among the many services offered to the community on a fee basis was the Speech and Hearing Clinic. The University Testing and Counseling Service was also available to the public. Local clubs or sponsoring groups could readily rent appropriate meeting rooms, dining rooms, engage the gymnasium or swimming pool, all for a modest fee. The only problem they faced was to find a time when the schedule was clear and when parking would be available. By the end of the 1960's, nearly 6,000 regularly scheduled student and community events, exclusive of formal classes, were being held annually in campus facilities.

Of all the University programs of service to the community, none was more productive and more imaginative than the Institute for Civic Education. This unusual undertaking grew out of community interest in current affairs and community-related problems and Norman Auburn's commitment to adult education. This interest led to the formation of an Akron Area Adult Education Council. In 1952 the Ford Foundation made Akron's adult education program part of its national survey of adult education. The survey resulted in the designation of 12 "test cities" across the nation. The Ford Foundation's Fund for Adult Education selected Akron as one of the "test cities" to study new methods and techniques in furthering liberal education for adults.

A sizeable grant supplemented by locally subscribed funds enabled the newly formed Akron Adult Education Foundation to engage an executive secretary, Mr. Leo Molinaro, and to initiate a community-wide program of civic and educational projects on public affairs.[42] After three years of independent operation it was proposed in the interest of efficient operation and closer cooperation, that the activities of the Adult Education Foundation come under the aegis of the University. President Auburn reminded the Board that if The University of Akron were a private institution, "it might dare to pass up Adult Education on the assumption that it had no obligation to the community," but as a public institution "the university would be ill-advised if it did not expand and develop its Adult Education program to the limit of its ability."[43]

The Board agreed, and in April, 1956, the Institute for Civic Education (ICE) commenced operation as part of the Evening and Adult Education Division. Throughout its early years, ICE was generously supported by foundation money, although many of its programs operated on a fee basis, thereby extending its reach beyond the limits of foundation support. With the appointment of Mr. Lee Smith as Director, the ICE spurted forward into a wide variety of programs. Creative leadership in the field of adult education is rare indeed, and in Lee Smith the University had one of the nation's true innovators, equally adept at devising imaginative programs and carrying through on the detail and promotional work.

It is an injustice to the ICE merely to list its programs, but space is lacking to tell the complete story. Some vision of the scope of its activities can be gained from a representative sampling of its programs. After World War II, much attention had been given nationally to the "problem" of bringing mature women back into useful activities outside the home. Early efforts introduced by the ICE ultimately merged into and were superceded by a regular, noncredit course, "The Second Half of Your Life" which, under the resourceful Mrs. Kay Motz Hunter, became a model for courses designed to acquaint women with career opportunities. For women already employed, the ICE sponsored a lecture-discussion course, "Liberal Education for Women in Business," which stressed the social sciences and humanities, and was thought to be the first of its kind in the country.[44] It was modeled somewhat along the lines of "A Liberal Education Program for Executives" which introduced those broadening topics relating to public affairs, international relations, social, artistic, and psychological phenomena into the mental armory of business executives.

The ICE again took leadership in establishing courses for retired persons interested in major issues and problems of the day. Both the campus and the community at large were invited to the weekly sessions of the World Affairs Luncheon, the Community and National Issues Luncheon, and the Thursday Breakfast Roundtable. For a select group of faculty men and community leaders, the Friday Conversations provided a place to exchange views in an informal setting over sherry or coffee. All sorts of special series were started, like the five-week seminar on "Communism; Theory and Practice." Special programs were offered for the United Rubber Workers, for the Akron Police Department, for civic officials, and for all types of groups. Often initiative for these programs came from the community sources, but in many cases Lee Smith and his associates were responsible for calling the attention of some group to this means for assisting them in handling some problem in their work.

Some of the ICE's best work was with students. A few were employed as in-service trainees in the Institute. The "Interns in Civic Leadership" program was an imaginative and effective device which placed a student in close association with a city official, councilman, labor leader, or other person involved in community activity. The student followed him on his rounds, observing all that went into that position. In the international field, a Community Ambassador and a College Ambassador were chosen each year to represent the University and the City of Akron in a foreign country. Upon their return, the "ambassadors" were obligated to give talks concerning their experiences to any group requesting them. As for other international involvements, the ICE was the clearing house for handling the steady flow of foreign visitors who came to campus, placing them in homes for brief stays, setting up opportunities for them to get a representative view of the community, etc.

In addition to this kind of service and special programming, the Institute provided help to departments running conferences, workshops, or short courses. Ultimately most of the University's cultural programming for the public came under the ICE's direction. Often a campus visitor who had been brought for a public address could be persuaded to stay on for another day or two and talk to students, visit classes, and make himself available to a wide segment of the University population.

In 1962 the Institute celebrated 10 years of productive activity. Grants totaling $255,000 had been received from the Fund for Adult Education during that decade. ICE had created in the community a focus for ideas, for discussion, for continuing education by adults. And at the height of its success, it became involved in controversy.

The Board had always worked to keep the University divorced from partisan politics. In 1962, however, the ICE agreed to assist in staging a series of "Neighborhood Forums" designed to educate Akron's citizenry to the true conditions within the city with respect to its finances, the functioning of city government and related topics. It was all part of an attempt to convince the voters that a city income tax would be required to provide funds to keep the city from falling any further in arrears in public improvements. Akron was already years behind more aggressive cities in its civic housekeeping. Indeed, the University was virtually the only bright spot where the public could see that things were getting done by a public agency.

The issue developed when it was charged that the city administration was using the University to promote a program that would reflect to its partisan advantage. In 1963, D. E. "Gene" Waddell, Vice-Chairman of the Summit County Republican Central Committee, claimed that the ICE-sponsored Neighborhood Forums were a "tool" of the Erickson administration and that the University was becoming a tool of the Democrats. Said Waddell, "Lee Smith and his staff, by working so closely with Erickson, have made the Forums the reflection of that Administration."[45] The charge was promptly denied.[46] The Neighborhood Forums brought city officials to each city high school where they were available for questioning and comment after the audience had viewed a presentation showing the city's needs and its actual expenditure of resources. It was civic education of a kind most communities only dream about; a kind of "grass roots democracy," a simulation of the town meeting in a complex city where many voters were uninformed and alienated.

The charge that the ICE was a "tool" of the Democrats and the city administration was excessive. As President Auburn explained, he had no prior knowledge that the Erickson administration would advertise in the newspaper in such a way as to involve the University with the *politics* of city finance.[47] There is no question, however, that the University hoped for the passage of the proposed city income tax. The University expected to realize some income from the tax; but even if it did not, Akron desperately needed the money, and it was true that the University could not long prosper unless Akron prospered. If it appeared that this put the University in the Democratic camp, it was only because that was the party currently in power and that party was proposing a course of action that was in the city's interest. The charge of "playing politics" belonged elsewhere.

Nevertheless, this experience was unpleasant. Misrepresentation has long been a part of American politics, and a municipal university cannot afford to be caught in the game. Its very existence is at stake. Therefore, when it was proposed some years later that another round of Neighborhood Forums be instituted to further the city's business, the Board declined to participate. As President Auburn told the Administrative Committee "the university should give its advice and counsel to the city and provide research opportunities," but it should "at all costs avoid an intimate relationship with the city government on an operating level."[48]

It is indeed unfortunate that the political issue was introduced into the neighborhood forums. The idea was widely applauded around the nation by those whose work and responsibilities made them aware of the extreme difficulty of getting the facts before the voters and getting public officials in contact with a significant percentage of the voters. As with the University's excellent planning studies, so with the neighborhood forums; requests for information came in from around the nation. Once again Akron had shown the way to institutions and communities that shared her problems.

Following Lee Smith's departure for another position, the ICE maintained its full range of programs under the able direction of Mr. Charles Blair. In 1968, however, the ICE was caught in the general financial belt tightening. It had to relinquish its quarters to an academic department, its staff was pared, but it managed, nevertheless, to retain a substantial amount of its programming and of its service. One could argue that the shift of the University from municipal to state status relieves it from direct responsibility for adult education directed at Akron's needs, but the Board, the administration, and most of the faculty would reject that interpretation, for the University still serves the public regardless of the size of the political base from which it draws its support.

Buchtel College and The University of Akron had long added to the cultural resources of Akron in a modest way through the work of certain faculty members and students as well as through sponsorship of programs open to the public. Before old Buchtel Hall was destroyed by fire, its chapel could accommodate several hundred persons; interested citizens in the community could come and enjoy a college presentation. From 1899 until the opening of Memorial Hall in 1954, there was no place on campus that would serve adequately for large gatherings.

Concurrent with the opening of Memorial Hall, President Auburn informed the faculty that it was now possible for the University to assume leadership in presenting cultural events in Akron, thus achieving a goal he had consistently pursued. Everyone realized that Memorial Hall was essentially a gymnasium and that it had acoustic and aesthetic limitations for cultural presentations, but despite these concerns programs were developed that have added immeasurably to Akron's cultural range.

The first undertaking combined music, drama, humor, and serious lectures in a "Town and Gown" series open to the public for a modest fee.[50] Bennet Cerf, then at the height of his fame as a TV personality, opened the series before a packed house of appreciative listeners, and although his presentation might not be "cultural" in the narrow sense, it broke the ice effectively. The community would benefit "measurably" from this series, said the local newspaper.[51] As the University extended its offerings in drama and music through other channels, Town and Gown became transformed into a lecture series, and despite competition from television and activities elsewhere in the city, it continues to attract good audiences, particularly when the speaker is in the public eye.

A "University Film Series" was followed by "The World at Our Door," a most successful series of color travel films which capitalized on the public's growing appetite for overseas travel. In the summer sessions various artistic offerings were introduced largely through the initiative of William Rogers, Dean of the Summer Sessions. From time to time traveling art exhibits were hung about campus, but lack of effective gallery space limited what could be accomplished until the spacious areas of the new Gardner Student Center gave room for displays.

In some ways the most successful of the cultural programs was the Fine Arts Festival, originally a three-day affair featuring music, drama, and the visual arts. The festival combined offerings by the world's outstanding professionals with the contributions of the faculty and students. The initial effort culminated with an exciting presentation—the "Voice of Firestone" program featuring Rise Stevens, Heidi Krall, Brian Sullivan and Jerome Hines was televised nationally from Memorial Hall. The tenth anniversary of the festival was celebrated in 1969 and all those who had helped make it a reality over the decade could take immense pleasure from the knowledge that the community had been enriched through their efforts.

Throughout the sixties the Music Department added many new faculty members who were performers. They in turn attracted to Firestone Conservatory talented students, and from this enlarged talent pool came frequent recitals and special programs open to the public. Under Dr. John MacDonald, the University Singers took on a new polish. They added their voices to the Akron Symphony Chorus which, under MacDonald's direction, grew into an excellent organization whose performances were widely admired in the community. The University Orchestra took on new artistic vigor under the batons of Dr. James Lerch and Dr. Andrew Galos. Richard Jackoboice brought musicianship and enthusiasm to his work with the revitalized marching band and symphonic band. Burt Kageff's Opera Workshop took programs to the schools of the Akron area; these schools were further aided by sending their most talented musicians to the Akron Youth Symphony conducted by Dr. Galos. In terms of public awareness and in terms of overt contributions to Akron's cultural climate, the music program had moved to a flourishing growth that promised even greater achievements for the future as new facilities provided the room so desperately needed to accommodate this new vitality.

In drama as in music the University's contribution to the community experienced healthy growth. In former days, the principal output of the drama effort consisted of three plays a year, usually presented in the Student Center lounge. Just one faculty member, Mr. Don Varian, had total responsibility for what was otherwise a student production. The opening of Kolbe Hall with its fine little theater presented new opportunities for work in the drama. To the "standards" favored by Varian were added different, and more experimental, offerings under the direction of Dr. James F. Dunlap. By 1965 the staff had increased, more professional and semi-professional help was available, a broader spectrum of student talent was tapped, and the theater program had grown into an enlarged and diversified operation. As a community service a Children's Theater was operated in the summer. Throughout the year, "Family Plays" were offered to interested groups in the area. These plays were dramatizations of situations that contribute to the tensions and frustrations of modern life. They were sponsored by a grant in the interests of mental health.

The University's FM radio station, WAUP, contributed to the cultural scene. Under the direction of students supervised by Mrs. Phyllis Hardenstein and Dr. Ruth Lewis, good music, drama, lectures, and commentary were emphasized. The broadcasting facilities in Kolbe Hall permitted quite a professional production, while the broadcasting effort was coordinated by the student Radio Workshop.

It is not possible to give adequate credit to all who contributed to Akron's cultural renaissance, nor is it possible to identify the total contribution made to the community's appreciation of music, drama, and the visual arts. The measure of the University's growth in cultural contribution can be appreciated by those familiar with Akron over a 20-year span or longer. In 1948 no one would have looked first to the University for support of cultural activities or for a contribution thereto. By 1968 it was the logical place to look, it had truly come of age in this important part of community life.

Whether in educational programming for adults, in special opportunities for school age children, or in cultural offerings for all ages, Akron's university now touched virtually every segment of the population which had interests outside themselves. To a foreigner this type of involvement was a thing of mystery for it was so completely divorced from the concept of a university's proper role as understood elsewhere in the world. One interesting evidence of this came with a letter from a young lady in Sydney, Australia, who was writing a novel in which one of the characters was portrayed as attending Akron University. She wrote to the University for materials describing the school. What she read about the wide-spread opportunities for admission to higher education, about working students, about involvement of the University in community life, so intrigued her that she decided to give the university a larger play than originally intended. Her interest was the subject of a *Beacon Journal* editorial. The advantages of Akron as a municipal university are so familiar, said the editorial writer, that "we tend to take them for granted." The enthusiasm of this Australian should be noted "for reminding us of our good fortune."[52]

NOTES

1   Board Mins., VIII, 176–77.
2   *University Bulletin,* Nov. 10, 1959.
3   Particularly John Dale Russell who made many visits to the Akron campus. See, for example, *ibid.,* May 9, 1956, and his "Report of a Study of the Financial Administration of the University of Akron," in UArch., box 4/10a/61.
4   Each faculty member received a copy of the report and its later supplements. Copies are in UArch.
5   Russell, "Study," UArch., box 4/10a/61.
6   *Beacon Journal,* Oct. 9, 1960.
7   *Ibid.,* Oct. 18, 1963; Administrative Committee Mins., Nov. 11, 1963, March 9, 1964, UArch., box 4/10a/52.
8   Board Mins., IV, 398, VI, 27; *Beacon Journal,* Sept. 26, 1951, March 11, June 20, 1956; Council Mins., Feb. 10, 1955.
9   *Beacon Journal,* May 7, 1963; Feb. 2, 1966.
10 *Ibid.,* Nov. 12, 1959.
11 *Ibid.,* Nov. 26, 1959.
12 *Ibid.,* May 6, 1957.
13 *Ibid.,* Nov. 26, 1959.
14 *Ibid.,* Feb. 19, 28, 1960, March 8, 1961.
15 *Ibid.,* March 30, 1962, Nov. 27, 1960.
16 *Ibid.,* April 2, 1960.
17 *Ibid.,* April 15, 1960.
18 *Ibid.,* June 25, 1960.
19 Board Mins., XII, 125.
20 *Ibid.,* 144,
21 *Ibid.,* XIII, 288; *Beacon Journal,* Oct. 9, 1962.
22 Board Mins., VII, 141; *Akron Alumnus,* Fall, 1966.
23 *Beacon Journal,* April 17, 1961.
24 *Ibid.,* June 18, 1958.
25 *Ibid.,* Sept. 12, 1958; Board Mins., XI, 186.
26 *Ibid.,* XII, 23.
27 *Buchtelite,* Oct. 23, 1964.
28 *Beacon Journal,* April 11, 1963.
29 President's Report, 1964, p. 3.
30 *Beacon Journal,* April 21, 1963.
31 *University Bulletin,* April 17, 1961.
32 *Beacon Journal,* Feb. 26, 1958.
33 *Buchtelite.* Feb. 4, 1966.
34 Board Mins., VII, 153.
35 *Beacon Journal,* May 6, 1963.
36 *University Bulletin,* Nov. 7, 1955.
37 *Beacon Journal,* Oct. 26, 1958.
38 Council Mins., Feb. 12, 1957.
39 *Beacon Journal,* July 1, 1958.
40 *Ibid.,* March 25, 1954.
41 Board Mins., X, 138; *Beacon Journal,* Dec. 20, 1959, Jan. 16, 1960.
42 "Adult Education Newsletter," I, no. 1, UArch.
43 Board Mins., VI, 168.
44 *Beacon Journal,* Jan. 19, 1958.

[45] *Ibid.,* March 13, 1963.
[46] See, for example, *ibid.,* Sept. 21, 1963.
[47] *Ibid.*
[48] Administrative Committee Mins., Jan. 7, 1963.
[49] *Beacon Journal,* Sept. 19, 1955.
[50] *Ibid.,* May 17, 22, 23, 1959.
[51] *Ibid.,* August 1, 1955.
[52] *Ibid.*

A familiar campus scene of the 1960's:
President Auburn and Governor Rhodes
break ground for a new building.

Dominic J. Guzzetta

Board of Directors, The University of Akron
(municipal), 1962.

"The Dean"
Donfred H. Gardner

XXIII

"We Go State!"

At the same time Akron was maturing fully in the role of the Municipal University, it was apparent that municipal higher education had just about reached its limits. This national phenomenon had nothing to do with how well municipal institutions had performed; rather it was a matter of money. Akron's problem was typical. Even while celebrating the additional mill of operating money won in the disputed election of 1958, steps were being taken to secure support from a broader tax base.

The need for this was evident. The great growth of the Akron metropolitan area was occurring outside the corporate limits of the central city. The tax duplicate of Akron was not increasing fast enough to provide significant improvement in revenues. In addition, political observers were confident that Akron voters would not extend further the limits to which they were willing to tax themselves in support of the Municipal University. In 1963, the city enacted a one percent income tax which was scheduled to include monies for the University, but in spite of vigorous efforts to collect this money, the University found its share diverted to other uses. The passage of the income tax had been accompanied by a reduction in the property tax, and it was this mood for tax reduction that seemed to prevail. Chances for adding new taxing districts to the University's support were as minimal as before. In short, no higher level of income could be expected from the city even though increased enrollments made such support mandatory.

The enrollment projections made by the Forecast Committee were proving accurate; indeed the most optimistic of the four projections was actually coming to pass. The committee felt obliged to recast its projections so that an even more optimistic track was established to hedge against the chance that enrollment growth would get more explosive in the future. Along with the enrollment surge there had been an accompanying budgetary growth reflecting both the increased millage and the larger amounts of income from student fees. More students required more buildings, more equipment, more books, more instructors, and these costs increased more rapidly than income.

In 1956, Akron, Cincinnati, and Toledo reopened their cooperative efforts—first tried more than 30 years earlier—to secure state assistance for municipal universities, and, by 1958, President Auburn was telling the Board that this should be the University's prime objective for that year.[1] Prospects were not encouraging. The state of Ohio was hard pressed for funds, and Governor Michael DiSalle was not at all sympathetic to the municipal universities' efforts.[2] He refused to lend any support to a bill in the Ohio General Assembly that would have provided Akron with about $1,000,000 in state money annually, and this bill was defeated in committee in 1959. Two years later, the effort was renewed.[3]

This new effort called for a state subvention to the municipal universities for each full-time freshman and sophomore and an additional subvention for part-time students through the sophomore year. Testifying before the House Education Committee in April, 1961, President Auburn said the bill provided "the most economical way" for the state to expand collegiate facilities. "I know of no other way," he continued, "in which students can be assured two years of college at a cost to the state of only $300 per academic year per student."[4] If state aid were not forthcoming, said Auburn, Akron would have to restrict enrollment either by increasing fees or by taking only select students.

The gubernatorial campaign of 1962 was a turning point in the 40-year struggle for state aid to municipal universities. The Republican candidate, James Rhodes, said he favored state aid and told Akronites they were being "double taxed" because they supported state universities as well as Akron University.[5] Following his election in November, Rhodes endorsed the bill calling for a state subvention. With his support urging on the large Republican majority in the General Assembly, the bill was passed. On July 1, 1963, Governor Rhodes signed into law this bill making Akron a "state-assisted university."

Through its new relationship to the state, Akron (and also Cincinnati and Toledo) received a subvention that finally amounted to $162 for every full-time Ohio freshman in 1963–64, and $200 for every full-time Ohio freshman and sophomore in 1964–65. For the 1963–65 biennium Akron's subvention amounted to $547,377.[6] In the 1965–67 biennium, $764,800 was received.[7] This income was extremely helpful, and most welcome, but it provided only some 8 to 11 percent of the University's annual operating budget. Financially it was clear that this was but a stop-gap measure, and yet that all-important precedent of state assistance had been won.

Before the ink was dry on the bill granting state assistance, steps were taken to sound out the prospects of a more complete involvement with the state. Constant liaison was maintained with the governor, key legislators, and above all, the Ohio Board of Regents. This body was composed of nine men appointed by Governor Rhodes in keeping with his campaign promise to regularize and assist the business of higher education in Ohio. The Regents had very limited formal powers, the principal ones being the right to limit new degree programs in the state universities and in state-assisted schools, and the power to review budgetary requests from these institutions. However, under their aggressive new Chancellor, Dr. John Millett, former President of Miami University, the Regents extended their influence far beyond these limits. "Guidelines" set forth by this body inevitably had the force of dictum, especially when accompanied by financial implications. As a state-assisted university, The University of Akron was fully bound by the Regents' policies.

The first Chairman of the Board of Regents, Dr. Harold Oyster, was a veteran of Republican politics in Ohio, and for many years was a member of the General Assembly. He ran the Board with efficiency and dispatch. He soon became unusually well versed in the subject of state supported higher education. It was a real coup, therefore, when President Auburn persuaded him to accept a position as Vice-President for Development. With his Columbus connections intact, Oyster did much to pave the way through the political labyrinth as Akron moved toward full state status; and as he worked in the state capital, President Auburn and Chairman of the Board Harry Schrank carried the heavy load of essential "behind-the-scene" chores that forwarded the cause.

In Columbus, meanwhile, the Board of Regents hired a firm of educational consultants, the Academy for Educational Development, to study state-financed higher education in Ohio in relation to its responsibilities, its resources, and its needs.[8] This study, as refined by the Regents, was published as *The Master Plan for State Policy in Higher Education*. In convincing fashion, it demonstrated that the needs of the state (especially the northeastern section) for public higher education would far outrun the capacity of existing state universities. Among their recommendations was the suggestion that Akron become a full-fledged state university, for only with a broadened tax base could she expand her services to care for a proportionate share of the needs outlined in the *Master Plan*.[9]

With the support of the Governor and the Board of Regents assured, plans went forward to convert Akron to a state university. A bill calling for state status was drafted with the help of Dr. Oyster and Dean Samad of the College of Law, and it was introduced into the legislature by the local state senators, Oliver Ocasek (D) and Edward Garrigan (R) as Senate Bill 212. This bill was simply an enabling act setting forth the steps that Akron must take should it press on to state status. As it progressed through the legislative process, the bill came to include Toledo under the same terms as applied to Akron. Sections 3349.28 through 3360.05 of the bill, as amended, provided the essential guarantees that protected the interests of the municipal universities as they transferred to state status.

There were interests in Ohio that did not favor state status for the municipal universities. Democratic members of the legislature expressed concern that the Governor's ambitious plans for higher education would commit the state to operating expenses that could be met only with new taxes. This worried the Democrats because Rhodes had made "no new taxes" a byword of his campaign and seemed disposed to operate on that premise. Understandably, the existing state universities were not eager to see the state financial pie, already seriously limited, cut into more pieces. In Akron itself there were modest grumblings from some alumni who wished to maintain the municipal connection and character and from some parents who worried that Akron students would no longer get preference in admission and that their places would be preempted by students from out of the city. These concerns were stilled by assurances that no qualified Akron student would be turned away, that the University still regarded Akron as the focus of its service, and that the name "The University of Akron" would endure.

Years of planning and effort culminated on July 29, 1965, when the Ohio General Assembly passed amended Senate Bill 212. It was signed by Governor Rhodes on August 12, and thus was Akron enabled to proceed toward state status.[10]

With enabling legislation safely passed, it was time for the directors to come to a decision. It was important that they gauge correctly the mood of the campus, the City of Akron and its residents, those individuals and business firms that contributed to income through gifts, and other interested parties. The compelling fact, however, was there for all to see. Without full state status the cost of attending Akron University would be excessive to a degree that would keep hundreds of deserving students from their chance at higher education.

Financial projections were based on a central assumption—that income from the City of Akron would not rise appreciably in the future. The reasons were obvious. With a municipal income tax recently enacted, there was no chance that Akronites would tax themselves beyond the 2.45 mills they already carried in support of their Municipal University. Growth in the tax duplicate was minimal. Tax districts surrounding Akron were unresponsive on the whole to joining the University taxing base. As of 1965–66, the student was already paying 52.7 percent of the cost of his education, a far cry indeed from the ideal of free higher education for Akron residents that had characterized the first days of the Municipal University movement. The 1965–66 budget of $8,323,684 was entirely too small for a public university with an enrollment of some 11,000 credit students plus 1,700 students in informal, non-credit courses.[11]

The fateful step was taken on December 8, 1965 when the Board of Directors unanimously agreed to convert The University of Akron to a state university. The directors were thoroughly convinced that the amount of state assistance currently received—about 11 percent of the 1965–66 budget—was but a "palliative" and not a solution to long-range needs. President Auburn likened their decision to that of the Buchtel College Trustees in 1913 who changed the character of the institution rather than let it die of financial malnutrition.[12] The change from municipal to state would be far less drastic a change in character. In fact, only those charged with maintaining records and handling business details would see any substantial difference. The concept of municipal higher education required little modification to make it equally appropriate to state higher education—the clientele was larger, and not so immediately present as in the case of the Municipal University—but the key words were still service and opportunity; service to the larger community of the state, and opportunity for young people of the entire state to take advantage of Akron's educational assets to prepare themselves for productive lives which, in turn, would enrich the state.

There were four steps to state status. First, the agreement between the Board of Directors and the Ohio Board of Regents transferring the assets, property, and obligations of the Board of Directors (municipal) to a new Board of Trustees (state), effective July 1, 1967, was approved by the Ohio Board of Regents on January 14, 1966. Second was the unanimous adoption by Akron City Council of an ordinance submitting the conversion to the Akron electorate. Third, was the affixing of necessary signatures to the agreement which took place in the Governor's office with President Auburn and Chairman of the Board Schrank representing the University and Chancellor Millett representing the Ohio Board of Regents with Governor Rhodes signing as a witness.

The fourth step was completed successfully on May 3, 1966, when Akron voters gave the conversion proposal overwhelming approval—36,034 to 4,015. Also approved overwhelmingly—35,142 to 4,665—was the accompanying measure whereby city taxes in support of the Municipal University were to terminate at the end of the tax year, 1967. Election officials thought this to be the most conclusive vote ever recorded in Summit County on an issue.[13] One would assume that its decisiveness reflected the voter's confidence in the move's necessity and also their eagerness to divest themselves of 2.45 mills in taxes. "No one could have been surprised that Akron voters overwhelmingly approved the two issues which convert the University of Akron to state status while reducing local real estate taxes," said a *Beacon Journal* editorial writer. "The benefits to be derived from this evolutionary step," he continued, ". . . were obvious for all to see." It was clear that "not only the physical properties but the student body, the faculty and, most important, the intangible spirit which is the heart of the university will remain unmoved and unchanged right where it has always been."[14]

The consummation came late in the spring of 1967 when the state legislature appropriated operating funds for The University of Akron for the biennium beginning July 1, 1967, and the first Board of Trustees of The University of Akron (state) assumed their duties on that date. "We go state," said the *Buchtelite* headlines with satisfaction.

Norman Auburn was the architect of state status just as surely as Parke Kolbe was the architect of the Municipal University. Like Kolbe, he saw clearly that there was but one viable alternative for a prosperous future, and he had the courage and persistence to press for that alternative. The qualities needed to get the job done, foresight, organization, perseverance, aggressiveness in defense of the University's interests, were qualities President Auburn had in abundance, and in bringing them to bear on the task at hand, he assured himself a place in the vanguard of those who built the University of Akron.

What did the newly established relationship to the state mean for the University? It meant, above all, a broadened tax base and an income that would rise along with enrollment; it meant some loss of autonomy to the Regents; it meant a larger and more diverse student body; but the most visible development was the physical enlargement and growth of the campus and its facilities.

Akron's timing in achieving state assistance in 1963 could not have been better. In November of that year, a state bond issue was passed from which the University of Akron received $6,000,000 for capital improvements. This sum represented more than had been secured from city building levies in the 17 years they had been voted. Such a windfall had no precedent in the school's experience and considerable thought went into determining its use.

In order to honor Governor Rhodes' intention in pushing the bond issue, the directors reasoned that the money should be used for a science and engineering center. Rhodes had stressed the urgency of creating new jobs through industry, and to attract industry Ohio needed highly trained manpower, research facilities, consultants, opportunities for continuing education, and similar assets. Since these priorities fitted in well with Akron's needs, the directors decided to put the money into such a center.

A supporting reason for giving priority to a science and engineering facility was that the $6,000,000 stake could be parlayed into additional funds if the cards were played right. They were played to the lasting benefit of Ohio and Akron with a skill a poker player might envy. The $6,000,000 was the stake that attracted $2,142,336 in a federal matching grant under Title I of the Higher Education Facilities Act of 1963, the largest such grant to any institution in Ohio. Among the factors that counted heavily in Akron's eligibility for such money was its efficient use of space and resources; since the public money was being used to good advantage it seemed proper to commit even more where it would be judiciously used. The following year another $897,745 for graduate facilities was granted by the federal government and another $30,000 for equipment was granted by the National Science Foundation.

More money was secured for the proposed structure when the Board of Directors agreed to issue bonds for the construction of a 350 car parking deck under the building. The bonds could be retired through parking fees, and this decision was consistent with the Development Guide Plan which emphasized underground parking. To these funds were added $1,000,000 from the capital improvements tax levy, thus making the total investment in the science and engineering center some $10,500,000.

The structure that emerged was a giant. Including the parking decks, there were more than five acres of floor space in what was soon described as the largest educational building under one roof in the state of Ohio. It was so easy to get lost in this massive structure that Mr. James Peach (just "Peach" to generations of students), longtime campus custodian and man of all tasks, was ensconced in the lobby to dispense information and directions from his new command post. Actually there were three buildings rising out of a common plaza at campus level built over three levels of parking. Covering the entire space between Buchtel and Carroll just west of Sumner Street, the plaza was connected to the main campus by a wide pedestrian concourse spanning Sumner and joining the campus where Olin Hall once stood. This arrangement permitted a visual extension of the campus to the west well beyond its former confines, giving additional spaciousness to the narrow quadrangle between buildings. It also perpetuated the ease of access that characterized the Hilltop. Visitors from those large campuses that spread for uncomfortable distances always commented on how compact and "handy" the Akron campus was.

Even before the great building was finished in 1967, its new tenants moved in—the College of Engineering, the Institute of Polymer Science, the departments of biology and mathematics, and the Science and Technology Library. The Board had already decided on a name. In recognition of his skillful and untiring efforts in every area of the University's life, but especially in securing the state liaison, bond money, matching funds, and additional construction funds, President Auburn was to be honored, and in impressive ceremonies on April 19, 1968, the new complex was formally named the Norman Paul Auburn Science and Engineering Center. In January, 1969, it won the local "Civvie" award as the best designed building constructed in Akron in the preceding year.

The Auburn Center proved its worth immediately. In addition to much needed classroom, laboratory, and research space (there were more than 200 research labs), the Center allowed room for expanding educational programs and activities. A Ph.D. program in engineering was now possible and this new graduate curriculum went into effect in 1969. Expanded research efforts long anticipated by the Institute of Polymer Science were feasible as was an increase in graduate work in the biological sciences and in mathematics.

In many parts of the United States following World War II, the junior college and community college movement flourished. Not in Ohio, however, where there was still a pronounced lack of interest among state officials for seeking the tax funds required to establish a system in the Buckeye State.

Among the earliest ideals of the municipal university movement was the expectation that "short courses" of less than four years duration would be made available to train young people and old for the many useful tasks required by modern urban society. Parke Kolbe and George Zook had been unusually articulate proponents of these short "certificate" programs, and only acute financial limitations kept them from going beyond the secretarial program and a few shortlived efforts in other fields in providing this work.

The "community college" or the "technical college" here referred to is not to be confused with the non-credit "informal" or "community college" courses offered by Akron as a regular program after 1939. The latter were not structured into programs leading to a certificate or a degree. It had been thought sufficient to provide a few courses that would assist a person to acquire skills or knowledge that would help him secure or improve employment. During the great depression it would have been the salvation of some young people to have marketable skills short of a college degree, but the University was not set up to meet this need despite the favorable attitudes of Simmons, Gardner, and certain other administrators.

As noted earlier, the report issued by President Truman's Commission on Higher Education served as a catalyst for a reexamination of public higher education, and it was strongly supportive of extending post-high school training in job-oriented courses to students having little talent for, or interest in, conventional degree programs. Akron took the report seriously and in her own self-examination focused on her responsibilities in this area of service. With a background of effort and concern stretching back a quarter century, plus the immediacy of the need in the postwar era, Akron had good reason for formulating a program to meet this responsibility.

Akron had not held back from fear that job oriented students would compromise its academic virtue, for there was perhaps a greater threat to that in the so-called "basic" students who seldom had much natural academic ability. But, as has been noted, in order to extend the opportunity for post-high school training to the greatest number, an admissions policy was adopted in 1955 that permitted any holder of a diploma from an accredited high school to enroll as a freshman. Once enrolled, he would be counseled into a program appropriate to his talents and background. A high school graduate with a poor record, said President Auburn, "should have an opportunity at least for a first chance." If this system resulted in "high mortality" (it did), it could be justified since this policy could be effected "without lowering or endangering the standards required for graduation." Those students finding college study too rigorous and thus dropping out "will have profited from what they completed."[15]

Not everyone agreed. Some thought the new admissions procedure was aimed at increased enrollment. They never did explain how that would benefit the University since it received no additional public monies for additional students, and the fees these students paid covered less than half the cost of their education. It is true that more families in Akron would have a selfish interest in voting for University issues, but that seems a risky and unreal faith on which to encourage an increased flow of students. Clearly, encouragement of the open admission policy was based on a belief that it was part of the total responsibility of the Municipal University to its community. "The University of Akron does not exist for the benefit of an intellectual elite," said the *Beacon Journal* in supporting a broad admission policy. "It exists to serve all who have the desire and ability to learn."[16]

Late in 1956 the first step was taken toward developing formalized degree programs in specialized, job oriented courses when a committee was appointed to study this "important educational matter." Both Cincinnati and Toledo had two-year associate degree programs, and the state universities were rushing to establish branches featuring courses which were job related. The Forecast Committee report had emphasized the immediate need to establish technical degree programs. With this evidence before them, a committee under Dean Guzzetta's leadership pushed ahead, and by September, 1959, the first Associate Program was ready.[17]

Two-year programs leading to the Associate Degree in the arts, secretarial science, mechanical design, and industrial electronics were offered in this new package. The programs were designed to meet the need for "practitioners" whose work would lie between the skilled and professional levels in the community. A new Department of Associate Programs of the General College administered the courses, and the first associate degrees were awarded at the 1960 commencement.[18]

For several years the Associate Program ran along as an adjunct operation, enrolling few students and showing little sign of growing appreciably. The next move forward for technical education came in 1963 when the Rhodes administration made it clear that the state and state-assisted universities were to provide technical education for their constituencies. The Regents gave high priority to "promotion of a state-wide system for technical education" in their first annual report. For an ambitious school seeking complete liaison with the state system and seeking simultaneously to extend its educational services, it was both politically wise and educationally desirable for Akron to strengthen technical education.

A key question in expansion plans was, would the community support a total effort in technical education? The existing programs were not drawing well and did not appear popular. Would more students elect technical programs if there were a greater choice? Would there be jobs available for those who completed the work? Would parents cooperate, or would they try to steer their children into more prestigious academic programs? The history of university-related technical education was unpromising on the whole, for invariably an estrangement developed between the traditional curricula and the technical department.

To find answers to these and other questions, a study was conducted by Dr. Aloysius Misko, Director of Associate Programs. He discovered that both students and parents would respond well to technical programs and associate degrees, *if* they were administered as a regular part of the University program and *if* the student were identified as a University of Akron student. It was important that the work be taken on campus so that there was no stigma of inferior status attached to the courses. Largely on the basis of these returns the early assumption that the technical programs would be physically separate from the traditional courses was restudied and the innovative decision to incorporate technical education into the heart of the University system was adopted.

This fully integrated program which permitted students, faculty, and administrators in the technical programs to share classrooms, library, athletic facilities, and even extracurricular programs on a completely equal footing was unique. The committee had been informed everywhere that such integration would not work, that real problems plus academic snobbery would force separation. One national leader in the community college movement said that should Akron's proposal toward a fully integrated program do what it planned to do, it would be a "pioneer in education," and he praised the University for "honestly facing up to its job in the community—taking care of its youth. Here is a recognized municipal university," he continued, "which realized that it was not fulfilling its entire function in the community—and is doing something about it."[19]

As for the survey of job availability, some 400 firms agreed that jobs listed on the questionnaire could be handled by people with less than a four-year degree.[20] They expressed interest in having a manpower pool of persons trained in these jobs. The University was encouraged to move ahead in the confidence that the jobs were available once the men and women were trained.

The Community and Technical College (C & T) was formally established as Akron's sixth degree-granting college in February, 1964.[21] William Petry, long-time head of the mechanical engineering department and subsequently acting dean of the College of Engineering, was appointed Dean. He proved to be an excellent choice, for he was enthusiastic about the new program and committed to its importance; he had fine rapport with local industry and business people, and he was easy to work with. He had the grace of making his point without making excessive claims for his new college, a talent that endeared him to his fellow deans. Within a few years, he and his associates had firmly established the new curricula, offering over a dozen fields of specialization ranging from commercial art and data processing to chemical and industrial technology. As foreseen, the C & T graduates were in great demand by industry and business.

The C & T College had two kinds of students. It had those whose ability was such that they could choose virtually any curriculum in the University but who wanted a program in that college. The larger number were students whose ability test scores and high school records were low. They were required to enter the C & T College, but here they had an option. Either they could take a two-year specialized, job-oriented course, or they could take a more generalized "arts" curriculum, upon successful completion of which they could transfer into a regular four-year degree program. This meant that the student who had the least chance of academic success was put into an environment that maximized his chances. In its first years, it was obvious that the college succeeded better at training adequate students for technical positions than at salvaging marginally-qualified students.

By 1968, there were 3,183 students enrolled in the C & T College. The prediction of the president and others that the day would come when it would boast the largest enrollment on campus did not seem far distant.[22] Early returns on its accomplishment are overwhelmingly positive, but all the evidence is not yet in.

From its inception, the C & T College lived in borrowed quarters. It was squeezed in wherever space was available. Once more a state bond issue came to the rescue. In 1965 Akron received $6,000,000 from the state for a building to house offices, classrooms, labs, and special facilities for the C & T College. Bonds for a parking deck, plus a $1,000,000 grant from the Federal Facilities Act parlayed the building into a $7,500,000 structure. Completed in 1969, it was named Schrank Hall in honor of Harry P. Schrank, Class of '24, Chairman of the Board of Directors of the Municipal University, first Chairman of the Board of Trustees of the State University, and devoted supporter of the institution. The Board had never experienced finer leadership than it did under his concerned and effective direction.

Flanking Jackson Field on the west, Schrank Hall was built astride part of Sumner Street which the city had vacated between Carroll and Exchange. It was the first building to be constructed after it became clear that the most accessible view of the campus was from Exchange Street across the cleared land of Jackson Field, and for that reason it was designed to show the public something better than its backside which was the fate of those older structures lining Carroll Street. It is approached by a pedestrian concourse spanning Carroll Street and connecting Schrank with the Auburn Center.

While designed primarily to house the offices, classrooms, and labs of the C & T College, Schrank Hall was a general purpose building like all the others, available to classes from every unit of the University. It also provided a home for the Department of Art and the Department of Home Economics both of which had been campus wanderers. Art had been suspended on occasion in Buchtel College days because there was no home for the activity; it had been squeezed out of the Municipal University in the early period; when the President's House was converted into Phillips Hall, it was located there until the hall was razed; the Library Annex then provided the department with space until Schrank Hall was built. Home Economics had occupied its "School" in Curtis Cottage, then a house on Buchtel Avenue, after which it moved to Olin Hall, from there to temporary quarters on Exchange Street, and finally into Schrank. The acquisition of a beautiful new Home Management House (1968) located at the corner of College and James Street rounded out departmental facilities and gave the work in "Home Ec" a tremendous boost. As is so often the case, once Schrank Hall was occupied, one wondered how the University ever got along without it.

The increased financial resources resulting from state status permitted the

University to restructure its academic program in certain areas, and also to add to its capacity to serve the community. In the restructuring process one of the first steps was the establishment in February, 1968 of a College of Fine and Applied Arts made up of the departments of Art, Home Economics, Music, and Speech.[23] There was a two-fold reason for setting these departments apart into a new collegiate unit; they had special problems growing out of their traditional modes of instruction which did not work in well with other departments in the College of Liberal Arts, and there was a need to emphasize the work of these departments beyond what had been done to date. Separate identity would have the effect of drawing more attention and resources to them.

The first Dean of the College of Fine and Applied Arts was Dr. Ray Sandefur, formerly Head of the Speech Department, a well liked and competent administrator. His most pressing initial problem was space. Schrank Hall took care of art and home economics, but music had outgrown the Firestone Conservatory and it would be some time before it could be adequately housed in expanded facilities. Speech spread out all over the campus because of its diffuse character. Drama was still centered in Kolbe Hall as was the radio and TV work which had studios in that building. Speech Therapy, however, had to find new quarters in the former Italian protestant church on James Street and later in the O'Connor Building on Center Street. Dr. Elizabeth Hittle, Director of the Speech and Hearing Clinic, succeeded in securing support from federal grants which helped expand the efforts in speech and hearing therapy and extended further the services that this program offered to the community.

Another new academic unit came into being in July, 1967. The College of Nursing, under its new Dean, Dr. Estelle Naes, had to start from the beginning to formulate a regular degree program in nursing.[24] The University's previous experience in nursing education and in the cooperative program with area hospitals gave the formulators of the new curriculum some guidelines, but essentially the college was a new operation. There was a definite need for trained nurses, with competence beyond that required when the profession was younger. Nursing had grown in complexity along with medicine and medical technology. Since this program has yet to produce its first graduates at the time of this writing, it is not possible to assess its impact.

Another important reason for expanding nurses' training grew out of the University's intense interest in securing a medical school. In the 1950's, various state commissions were formed to assess Ohio's needs in higher education, and among the recommendations emanating from these studies was one calling for the organization of additional medical schools to supplement the work of Ohio State, Western Reserve, and Cincinnati. The Ohio Interim Commission on Education Beyond High School, appointed by Governor DiSalle, was expected to recommend additional medical school facilities in Ohio, and in an effort to see that Akron's case was made properly, Mayor Berg, at the urging of the Board of Directors and President Auburn, appointed a citizen's committee to study the feasibility of a medical school attached to the University. The citizen's committee reported in January, 1962, recommending that a school be established in Akron, and presenting a rationale for its recommendation. President Auburn said the University was "ready and eager" to operate a medical school although all the funds would have to come from state and federal sources.[25]

Other Ohio cities, chief among them being Toledo, also wanted a medical school as part of its university. To meet the competition, Berg's successor, Mayor Erickson, appointed the Mayor's Medical School Action Committee to press Akron's case before the Interim Commission and other influential parties. Mr. Paul Belcher was appointed Chairman of the Action Committee and immediately set out to make the case for Akron.[26]

In the spring of 1962, a medical panel from the Ohio Interim Commission held a hearing in the Akron Student Center at which some 75 University and community people presented reasons for locating a new medical school in Akron. To meet one of the main drawbacks, the city indicated that it would provide a 48 acre site northeast of the campus, and that it would obtain this land through federal urban renewal. City Council agreed to vote $1,000,000 toward the purchase of this land as an indication of good faith should Akron get the school. "Getting a medical school for Akron is a once-in-a-lifetime opportunity," said the *Beacon Journal* in endorsing this move, "it is worth any such modest local contribution as a million dollars."[27]

In April, the Interim Commission received a report from its medical panel recommending Toledo as the site. Akron's consolation was that the door was kept open for establishing a second school later on, and it was considered a likely contender for that school. Akron lost out because it lacked a site, and also, strange to say, because its hospitals had such fine intern and resident training programs that they might suffer if patients were funneled off into a University hospital.[28]

The Action Committee fought the issue right on through the legislature, but to no avail. However, the Mayor's Action Committee incorporated itself as the Akron Area Medical College and Educational Foundation, to further the selection of Akron as the site of a possible second medical school.[29] As of this writing, the effort still goes on.

Although medical education was eluding Akron, progress was made in securing a program in yet another area of public concern. At the urging of Lee Smith, a faculty committee under the chairmanship of Dr. George Knepper was appointed to examine how the University might assist in training students for careers in various aspects of urban affairs. The committee's solution called for creation of a center for urban studies which would coordinate the University's efforts in research, teaching, and public service as they related to the needs of the urban area centered on Akron. Support for a move in this direction came from President Auburn. In a speech delivered in January, 1963, he called for the establishment of a department to study urban problems, particularly Akron's, and stated his hope that an endowed "Professorship of Akron" could be established to attract a top-flight specialist in urban problems to the campus. The core of the nation's urban centers was the new frontier, said Auburn, and just as the Morrill Act had developed a farming frontier, so a "twentieth century equivalent" was needed to support the urban university's attack on the problems of the city. As for Akron University, "We shall stretch our financial resources to the limit to aid the city whose name we carry." He then outlined areas of concern that would be served by this new program.[30]

After several false starts, the Center for Urban Studies was established in July, 1965, and in September of that year it entered into its first contract with the City of Akron to study the organization and operation of the city's safety department.[31] Under the leadership of its new Director, Dr. Edward Hanten of the Geography-Geology department, it began immediately to meet those tasks that had so long cried for professional attention. It also started land-use seminars for key people in the Akron area, thus providing a much-needed communicative service. In 1968, the Department of Urban Studies, with Dr. Hanten as its Head, established an academic program leading to the master's degree. The staff expanded rapidly to carry the new teaching responsibilities and to handle the contract work of the center. State status did not change its mission; Akron remained the focus of its interests, but the outlook was not provincial. Instead, much effort was made toward cooperative ventures of a regional character.

An important part of any American university's charge during the last two decades has been the need to remain abreast of the technology that was forcing new techniques into classroom and lab, into library and business office. A faculty committee appointed in 1957, with Dr. Paul Huss as chairman, made the studies and recommendations that led to the establishment of a computer center and data processing operation. The sophisticated hardware acquired by the computer center extended the teaching and research capacity of faculty and staff. But the computer industry was evolving so rapidly that it was impossible to own the latest equipment because of the tremendous costs involved. Nevertheless, for an institution of its size and character, Akron maintained a large computer and data processing center which is now a thoroughly integrated part of its operation.

Another standard technological advance made by American universities in the 1950's was the language laboratory. Again Akron was among the early users of the lab and developed an effective teaching laboratory in "Plato's Cave," the windowless lecture room more properly known as Kolbe 104; it was replaced by an enlarged and modernized lab in the Education Building. Experimentation and development in the language lab was given high priority by Dr. Arno Lepke, Head of the Modern Languages Department, and the rapid development of language lab techniques grew in part out of seminal experiments undertaken by Dr. Ted Mueller in the teaching of freshman French almost entirely from tapes. These excellent facilities, plus Dr. Lepke's skill as an organizer, brought several summer institutes for teachers of French to the campus; it was always a surprise when walking across campus to pass groups in earnest conversation—all in French!

Following World War II, America entered the "Nuclear Age," and it was clear that universities and colleges would have to adjust their teaching in the sciences and engineering to take account of "the urgent need for greater training in the nuclear energy field."[32] Again, equipment was a vital concern, and Akron was most fortunate to receive as a gift from the General Tire and Rubber Company, an AGN 201 nuclear reactor. It was a safe, low-power reactor specially designed for teaching purposes. Although it could be used in a few research applications, it was not high powered enough for widespread use. It was mandatory that the reactor be managed carefully under strict conditions laid down by the Atomic Energy Commission. Courses were designed to train students in its use, but the real excitement came when the cylindrical monster was first installed in the mechanical engineering lab in Simmons Hall. Several faculty members were instructed in its use. Whenever they failed to balance their operations correctly, a red light on top of the tank would flash and a bell would ring. Members of the faculty from non-scientific disciplines whose offices were located in Simmons Hall—historians, business administrators, economists, political scientists—went uneasily about their tasks with many rude jokes about what was going to happen when that red light flashed and the bell rang; indeed, the bell rang with distressing frequency. This $100,000 gift was an excellent asset for a while and then, in common with so much of the newly evolved technical equipment, it became prematurely obsolete. Since it was prohibitively costly to maintain in view of the fact that the University had no curriculum in nuclear engineering or physics, it was dismantled in 1967 when the mechanical engineering lab moved to Auburn Center.

If the postwar period was a nuclear age it was equally the age of mass communication with television leading the way. For many years it had been apparent that television held tremendous promise as an educational tool. Most attention was given to programs on regular commercial stations or on special educational stations. In the spring of 1953, a faculty committee headed by Dr. Robert Ittner was charged with reviewing the prospects for University participation in some sort of televised instruction, whether affiliated with a commercial station or an educational outlet. The committee saw an educational TV network as the best instrument for its needs, but no such network as yet had a place for Akron. The next best thing was then tried in December, 1953, when an adult education program, "Synthetic Rubber—Man's Duplication of Nature" was presented with the cooperation of WAKR-TV.[33] Various series were run in education, military history, etc., but there was no way to measure the impact or effectiveness of this casual broadcasting. The next logical step, therefore, was to offer a credit course, and in 1957, Peter Hampton, Associate Professor of Psychology, presented General Psychology over WAKR-TV.[34] The viewing audience was small, there was a practical limit to the generosity of WAKR in providing time and technical help, and this effort proved abortive.

The best prospect for establishing an enduring program of educational TV appeared in 1954 when President Auburn, as a member of the newly formed Northeastern Ohio Coordinating Board on Educational Television, participated in reserving UHF channel 55 for educational TV under the joint auspices of The University of Akron, the Akron Board of Education, and Kent State University.[35] This action formalized a "Gentleman's Agreement" between Akron and Kent that was made in 1951.[36] Nothing was done for years to operate a program on channel 55 since none of the three parties involved could finance an operation of the magnitude required. But on November 16, 1962, President George Bowman of Kent State announced plans to put an ETV station on the air over a 14-mile viewing radius. Bowman claimed that no basis existed for joint operation of an ETV station by Kent and Akron.[37]

Reaction from Akron was swift. It was evident that Akron felt it was the victim of a misunderstanding. Whatever President Bowman's interpretation of the conditions under which channel 55 had been set aside, the conviction in Akron was that Kent had no right to take "unilateral" action in establishing a station without bringing in the other two parties.[38] The Akron Board of Education backed out of the hassle immediately, but Akron and Kent exchanged a great deal of commentary over their respective interpretations and over the validity and implications of various engineering reports, site prospects, etc.[39] Mayor Edward Erickson became involved as something of an intermediary; he appointed an ETV committee to study the matter.[40] Meanwhile to counter Kent's application to the FCC for permission to operate a station, Akron filed a counterclaim, and the FCC, apparently somewhat piqued by this infighting, told both parties to get together and work out their disagreement.[41] The FCC wished to avoid formal hearings.[42] The situation remained in flux, safely removed from the front pages, as various alternatives briefly appeared and then were shelved.

A way out of the impasse developed when WAKR-TV, a UHF station and Akron's only commercial outlet, decided to abandon channel 49 for channel 23. Channel 49 was thus set aside for Akron University whenever it had the resources to operate an ETV station. An enormous boost toward getting those resources came in the summer of 1967 when the Berk family, operators of WAKR-TV, gave the University equipment valued at $250,000 in memory of S. Bernard Berk, the founder of WAKR. As of this writing, plans are underway to commence broadcasting on a limited schedule just as soon as FCC clearance is forthcoming.[43]

While Akron's efforts toward ETV were held in abeyance, it moved with success into closed circuit television (CCTV) for the production and transmission to its own classrooms of lectures, demonstrations, and other teaching techniques designed for its own students. A good deal of thought had been given from an early time looking to the day when CCTV would be used as an instructional medium on campus. Kolbe Hall was designed with a full-sized, professional TV studio built in.

CCTV was undertaken in the first place out of necessity coupled with a certain amount of experimental fervor which led some faculty to think that the teaching-learning operation could be enhanced through this medium. At a meeting of the Board late in 1959, President Auburn indicated some of the conditions that had caused him to appoint a committee to study CCTV. The rapidly increasing enrollment made it necessary to consider CCTV or one of two alternatives: 1) more buildings to handle increased enrollment, these buildings to have lecture rooms holding up to 250 students each, and hiring additional instructors, or, 2) providing two lecture halls to hold 500 persons each. Either of these alternatives would be far more costly than introducing CCTV, which the president estimated would cost about $60,000.[44]

Experiments with CCTV were not new, and a faculty committee under Dean Guzzetta's chairmanship had plenty of models to look at and consider. In Ohio, Miami University had been a leader, and its installation was visited as were many others in near-by states. The literature on teaching by television was strongly supportive of the medium, especially when the alternative was to put the student in a large lecture hall along with 500 other students where he had no contact with the lecturer, indeed, he might even have trouble seeing or hearing him, both of which problems TV could readily overcome.

The faculty committee reported in favor of instituting CCTV. A generous grant from the Ford Foundation covered the major costs involved in the new operation, and in the spring semester, 1961, four courses went on the air—Effective Speaking, Reasoning and Understanding in Science, Analytical Geometry, and Education in

American Society.[45] Prior to this, a dry-run demonstration lecture had given the students a hilarious introduction to CCTV. The microphone went dead; there was no picture in one of the viewing rooms and the other viewers saw TV Coordinator William Mavrides dashing across the screen on his way to fix the trouble; there were mixed camera shots accompanied by *sotto voce* comments which were not intended for broadcast. All in all, it was a lively dress rehearsal.[46]

The facilities were dedicated in January, 1961, and the main speaker, Dr. Franklin Dunham, chief of radio and television for the U.S. Office of Education, praised the system as "the last word." "It's superb," he said, "the best yet!"[47] Each year the University's commitment to CCTV became greater. Each new building was designed with its needs in mind. From the 1,226 students taking at least one televised course in the spring of 1961, the number rose to 7,266 by September, 1968. Vice-president Guzzetta, described CCTV as "an example of students getting the most for their money."[48] But it wasn't yet clear just what it was the most of.

In the manner of technological innovations, what started as something of a necessity was subtly translated into a virtue. Instead of viewing CCTV as a necessary adjunct to be used when optimum teaching conditions were not possible, there grew up a considerable sentiment dedicated to its extension into new areas. It was true that nearly every study made across the country demonstrated that students taking courses over TV scored as well on traditional tests as those taking the same course in conventional sections. What was not well publicized, however, was that, almost without exception, students engaged in TV instruction preferred a conventional classroom situation to a TV class if such an option were possible. Of course, the alternative to CCTV at Akron was not classes of optimum size, but rather huge lecture sections, just as impersonal in their way as a televised presentation.

CCTV appears now to be so accepted a part of the whole teaching spectrum that it is no longer the subject of vigorous debate. But, through a peculiar sophistry, it has been argued that it increases the possibility for personalized attention. This may be potentially true, but it is hard for a freshman to believe if he finds himself sitting in a poorly monitored viewing room, watching a lecturer he has never seen in person—indeed, there is a good chance he is watching video tape—and taking tests by marking a small box on an IBM punch card to register his answer to multiple-choice questions flashed on the TV screen, questions that will be graded by a machine which will print out his score and rank him on a grade sheet. Most freshmen take more than one CCTV course; several unhappy souls have found that three of their four courses were offered over CCTV. They must have wondered whether they were in a university or on an educational assembly line.[49] Most students and most instructors would probably admit that TV can be a valuable supplementary or special utility tool, or even a completely satisfactory medium when used to best advantage, but to allow its use to penetrate too completely into the educational process, to allow the means to become an end, is to allow an undermining of the teaching-learning structure. Old Buchtel stalwarts like Knight, Kolbe, Bates, Parsons, and Claypole would find it a strange world that removed the student so far from the teacher; but for that matter, some contemporary teachers found it strange also.

One unique use of the medium caught the public fancy. As commencement crowds outgrew Memorial Hall, television sets were set up in the student center lounges and elsewhere so that relatives and friends who could not get into the Hall could view the ceremonies live over CCTV.

Another innovation in the broadcasting field was the inauguration of a regular radio broadcasting outlet over WAUP-FM, employed at Akron as an instructional device. The new station went on the air for the first time in December, 1962.[50] It could be heard within a radius of 20 miles.

Films were another medium that received much attention. Under the direction of Mr. Robert Blankenship, the Audio-Visual Services department provided a wide assortment of films and tapes for classroom use, but Akron's innovation was a decision to produce experimental films to be used in the regular curriculum.

The first effort in this line was undertaken under the direction of Dr. Thomas Sumner, then Head of the Chemistry Department. He was confronted with the problem of limited lab space and a burgeoning enrollment. In an effort to resolve this, short of building new laboratories, he proposed to make color movies of the standard freshman chemistry lab experiments. These films would be used, in lieu of actual lab experience, by freshmen engineers and others who would not be going beyond the freshman level in chemistry. The rationale as worked out in detail was so convincing that the Fund for the Advancement of Education gave the University $23,000 for this experiment in improving science instruction for non-majors.[51]

The films, made in the Knight Hall laboratories with Sumner as the chief commentator and demonstrator, were well done. Great interest was expressed by schools around the country and in several foreign countries. A long article in the *Wall Street Journal* praised the work and called it to the attention of other institutions. Akron's work was a "trail blazer" for science films on the collegiate level.[52] Although they were successfully used on the Akron campus and on others, they were never popular with the students, possibly because the students viewing them were not motivated toward chemistry in the first place, and possibly because students are more enamored of what they can do than by what they see others do. Most of the scientific world was skeptical. "There is no substitute for a student working on his own," was a typical comment from the dissenters.[53] The series was sold to Coronet Films, but it had helped Akron over a difficult barrier at a critical time in her growth.

A similar project was soon undertaken by Dr. William Painter, who used training films as a substitute or supplemental experience for education students observing classes in the grammar schools. His work was supported by a grant of $31,000 from the U.S. Office of Education.[54] Like the chemistry films, they could do the job as well as personal involvement insofar as this could be measured by tests, but skeptics felt that the intangibles, motivation, impressions, point of view, perhaps the most vital part of the educational process, were distorted by removing the student from actual contact with the *activity* involved in his learning. Hence, the chemistry film viewer never discovered how messy and exasperating lab technique could be. He never cut his finger on a shattered test tube, nor fretted away a lab period trying to make a Bunsen burner work properly. In his film world, everything came out neat and proper the first time around, a phenomenon that did not accord at all with the actual experience his contemporaries were having in the lab. In like manner one can say of Dr. Painter's films that the "feel" one gets of a classroom from a film is apt to be quite different from the "feel" one gets while actually sitting in the classroom and seeing the entire range of activity accompanied by the steady background hum of youngsters at work.

On the basis of experience to date, all of the technological developments—computers, TV, films, data processing equipment—should better be regarded as *aides* rather than substitutes. Insofar as the University used them as such and showed restraint in their use, they performed a service for their students. It was the University's good fortune most of the time to have in charge of these technological areas men of discretion and restraint. William Mavrides performed excellent work in the television center, regarding his medium as a tool to be used to support rather than to replace. His creative ability coupled with his down-to-earth realism made him a favorite of those faculty who worked in the TV medium and of the administrators who supported the effort. Robert Blankenship was a resourceful and efficient director of the Audio-Visual Aids center who always went the extra step to be helpful. Robert Hathaway maintained services in the computer field. And, of course, among the unsung heroes of any campus are the assistants, aides, and technicians, many of them very creative people, who labor behind the scenes to make these operations work.

NOTES

[1] *Beacon Journal,* Jan. 21, 1958.

[2] *Ibid.,* Feb. 20, 1959.

[3] *Ibid.,* May 14, 1959.

[4] *Ibid.,* April 20, 1961.

[5] *Ibid.,* Oct. 8, 1962.

[6] President's Report, 1964, 1965.

[7] *Ibid.,* 1966, 1967.

[8] "First Annual Report of the Ohio Board of Regents," 1964, p. 6.

[9] *Master Plan for State Policy in Higher Education* (Ohio Board of Regents, 1966), especially chapters 3–5.

[10] "Conversion of the University of Akron From a Municipal University to a State University as of July 1, 1967. Transcript of Proceedings," in UArch. Since the complete legal record is contained therein, extensive citations to details of the conversion will not be made.

[11] *Ibid.,* pp. 27, 31.

[12] President's Report, 1965, p. 20.

[13] *Ibid.,* 1966, p. 5.

[14] *Beacon Journal,* May 4, 1966.

[15] *Ibid.,* May 31, 1955.

[16] *Ibid.*

[17] *Ibid.,* Jan. 24, 1959; Board Mins., IX, 98.

[18] *Beacon Journal,* July 1, 1959; *University Bulletin,* May 6, 1960.

[19] *Beacon Journal,* October 18, 1963.

[20] *Ibid.,* Nov. 14, 1963.

[21] Board Mins., XIV, 170, 183.

[22] Registrar to author, January, 1969.

[23] Board Mins., XVIII, 261–62.

[24] *Ibid.,* 304–06.

[25] *Beacon Journal,* Feb. 22, 1961, Jan. 21, 1962.

[26] *Ibid.,* Feb. 6, March 7, 1962.

[27] *Ibid.,* March 27, 29, April 9, 10, 12, 1962.

[28] *Ibid.,* April 13, 14, 1962.

[29] Board Mins., XIII, 272.

[30] *Beacon Journal,* Jan. 7, 1963.

[31] President's Report, 1966, p. 9.

[32] *Beacon Journal,* August 9, 1957.

[33] *Ibid.,* Dec. 1, 1953.

[34] Board Mins., VII, 173.

[35] *University Bulletin,* Nov. 8, 1954.

[36] Board Mins., XIII, 328–30.

[37] *Beacon Journal,* Nov. 19, 1962.

[38] *Ibid.,* Nov. 21, 1962.

[39] *Ibid.,* Nov. 18, 1962.

[40] *Ibid.,* Nov. 22, 1962.

[41] *Ibid.,* June 6, 13, 1963.

[42] *Ibid.,* Oct. 16, 1963.

[43] *Ibid.,* July 11, 1968.

[44] *Ibid.,* Dec. 18, 1959.

[45] Board Mins., XI, 128, 149; *Beacon Journal,* Jan. 3, 1961.

[46] Related in *ibid.,* Jan. 6, 1961.

[47] *Ibid.*, Jan. 8, 1961; Board Mins., XII, 8.

[48] *Beacon Journal,* March 7, 1961.

[49] Dr. John Popplestone, lecturer in psychology over CCTV, once taped a lecture and, while it was being shown, made a tour of the viewing rooms. Upon his entering a viewing room, the students looked at him incredulously until their minds registered just how it was that he could be appearing on the screen and in the room at the same time.

[50] *Beacon Journal,* Dec. 6, 1962.

[51] Board Mins., VIII, 106.

[52] *Wall Street Journal,* March 19, 1959.

[53] *Ibid.*

[54] Board Mins., X, 150.

XXIV

The heart of the enterprise: Students and Faculty

Within one 12-month period of 1954–55, Akron experienced another period of concentrated loss when four of its principal teachers and administrators, three of whom were retired, passed from the scene. In December, 1954, President Emeritus Hezzleton Simmons died. The campus and the whole community mourned this loss, and more than 800 persons gathered for a memorial service on Founder's Day. The anxious young lad from LeRoy, Ohio, who had approached his new experience at Buchtel College on old Spicer Hill with apprehension, gave his best to that college and its successor for half a century. As his friend and associate, Albert Spanton, said, "in a very real sense . . . Hez Simmons lives on."[1] And so he does, in the buildings and other physical properties he brought to the campus, in the good will he encouraged within the city, but above all, in the lives of generations of young people whom he influenced.

Dean Spanton could well have been proclaiming his own eulogy, for within a few months he, too, was gone. At the time of his retirement in 1943, Spanton had served Buchtel College and the University for 43 years. As a Universalist minister, he had maintained the old ideals of the "liberal religion" and the sense of man's dignity that it fostered. "The little dean is gone," wrote Jim Jackson, a long-time friend, "but he will ever loom large in the memories of the thousands who have lived a fuller life because of his influence."[2]

The first man that Parke Kolbe reached out for in building the new Municipal University in 1914 was Fred Ayer. His influence and contribution spread well beyond the engineering college with its co-op program. He was a force in the life of the entire University and in the community as well, and his competence was off-set by a certain sly irreverence that lightened many a stodgy occasion. His death in 1955 removed still another of the builders from sight, but not from mind.

Most unexpected of the four deaths was that of Summerfield Baldwin III, Professor of History and Head of the Department since 1945. In his 10 years on campus, he earned recognition as its outstanding scholar. Those who are skeptical about the contagion of real scholarship never sat in a Baldwin class. Though he violated every standard of "good" pedagogy, he was regarded by his many disciples as the best teacher they ever knew. He was not loved by the weak or timid—whether student or fellow faculty member—for to him thought was a discipline to be based on solid information presented in an orderly fashion, and he did not suffer fools gladly. A scholarship in his name perpetuates his influence on the most recent recruits to historical studies.[3]

As had happened many times before, while mourning the passing of the old, the University welcomed the arrival of new faculty members who would serve it well in their time. There is not room or time enough to identify the particular contribution of each, but it is certainly proper to name those who have served well. Among the faculty who arrived after World War II who contributed their talents for a decade or more were Dennis Gordon, Mary Vernon Slusher, and Frances Clark (accounting); Emily Davis, Malcolm Dashiell, and Bernard Weiner (art); Roger Keller and Irene

Horning (biology); Vaughn Floutz and Gerald Corsaro (chemistry); James Harwood and Howard Stephens (chemistry and polymer science); Ted Duke (classics); Emile Grunberg, Robert Black, James McLain, and Annette Seery (economics); Mabel Riedinger, James Doverspike, William Beisel, Kenneth Cochrane, Tom Evans, Anthony Laterza, Andrew Maluke, Wilma Ruman, John Watt, Alfred Johnson, and Helen Becker (education); Michael Bezbatchenko, William Petry, Joseph Edminister, Milton Kult, Kenneth Hamlen, George Manos, and Alvin Richards (engineering); Frank Phipps, Gerald Levin, William Stevens, John Hull, Julia Hull, Edward Paul and Walter Lehrman (English); Charles Poston (finance); Clara Roe, George Knepper, David Riede and Henry Vyverberg (history); Irene Bear, Mary Wilson, and Dorothy Laubacher (home economics); Richard Marshall (law); Frank Simonetti, Donald Becker and Thomas Sharkey (management); Margaret Rogler and Stewart McKinnon (marketing); Ossian Gruber (general business); Margaret Mauch, Louis Ross, and Leonard Sweet (mathematics); Farley Hutchins, Darrell Witters, Henry Smith, and John MacDonald (music); Evelyn Tovey (nursing); Ernest Thackeray (physics); Paul Weidner (political science); Paul Twining, Edwin Wagner, Peter Hampton, Francis Werner, and Howard Maher (psychology); Samuel Newman, Charles Rogler, and Norman Washburne (sociology); James F. Dunlap, Elizabeth Hittle, and Phyllis Hardenstein (speech); Helen Arnett, Barbara Clark, Ruth Clinefelter, Pauline Franks, Mary Grace Harrington, Lois Myers, and Helen Thornberg (bibliography and library); Phyllis Paul and Katherine Vegso (advisement and counseling).

These faculty were joined by many other talented contributors in the first years of the sixties: Dale Jackson, Richard Nokes, and Eugene Flaumenhaft (biology); John Bachmann and Paul Garn (chemistry); Robert McNeil (classics); Kenneth Hoedt, Patricia Taylor, Gordon Larson, James Ewers, Oliver Ocasek, Sarah Orlinoff, and Jerrold Maben (education); Coleman Major and Robert Grumbach (engineering); Martha Hosfelt, Cathryn Taliaferro, David Jones, and John Phillipson (English); James W. Dunlap (finance); Allen Noble and Edward Hanten (geography); James Teeter (geology); Warren Kuehl, Don Gerlach, Jerome Mushkat, and Lester Bilsky (history); Robert Kovach and Marvin Moore (law); Herbert Hayward and Howard Taylor (management); Frederick Manzara (marketing); William Beyer and George Szoke (mathematics); Arno Lepke, Theodore Mackiw and Hugo Lijeron (modern languages); Burt Kageff (music); Charles Wilson and Ronald Schneider (physics); Roger Kvam (political science); Alan Gent (polymer science); John Popplestone (psychology); Edwin Lively (sociology); John Auston (speech); and Agnes Martin (bibliography and library.)

In addition to the large number of faculty members added during the past two decades, there have been many changes in administrative personnel. Old positions have been transformed and new ones created, but it is not the position so much as the man that ultimately determines the effectiveness of any administrative arrangement. We have already noted the most significant adaptations of administrative assignments in the 1950's, but great changes took place in the next decade.

Foremost were those on the vice-presidential level. In 1962, Donfred Gardner announced his intention to resign as Vice-President and Dean of Administration. Although he had not yet reached the age for mandatory retirement, he believed that in the rapidly changing environment of American university life, most administrators should relinquish their posts by age 60 in favor of younger men and women who were, perhaps, more in sympathy with contemporary trends in education. He carefully groomed Dean Dominic Guzzetta as his successor.[4] As the architect of Akron's superior machinery for dealing with student advisement, personal counseling, and control of extracurricular activities; as the most persuasive proponent of general education; as the embodiment and symbol of integrity and of the worth of the "whole man," Dean Gardner's influence upon the University and its students was profound. It was with surprise and pleasure that he received an honorary degree, Doctor of Humane Letters, from the University that he had done so much to build. Even more appropriate, however, was the affixing of his name to the newly enlarged student center, for more than anyone else, he had devoted a professional lifetime to student growth and interests and had been the untiring proponent of a student center long before there was any sign it would be realized. The Donfred H. Gardner Student Center is where the action is, and that is where "the Dean" liked to be.

At the same time that the top academic man was bowing out, the Financial Vice-President was moving into a new challenge. Mr. Leslie Hardy had been an administrative "jack of all trades" early in his career, serving wherever President Simmons and President Auburn had need of his talent for getting things done. He was one of those valuable men who, given a job to perform, did it. As Financial Vice-President in an academic setting where purse strings were tightly held at the top, he was constantly badgered for money and goods, and in this situation it was inevitable that some were disappointed. If they blamed the vice-president, it was in part a failure to recognize that stringent, centralized financial control was the only means of getting balanced growth and securing full value from each dollar spent. It was Les Hardy's job to find ways to reconcile the thousand-and-one demands put upon the financial side of the operation. Like Gardner, he, too, left a unique contribution to University growth and development. He babied the new urban renewal program to completion, and his work made him as knowledgable as anyone in the country about the involutions of this particular program. Indeed, it was this knowledge, coupled with his good organizing capabilities, that led to his departure from the campus, for he was asked to assume the position of Executive Secretary of the Citizens For Progress, a non-profit corporation dedicated to the advancement of the Akron community.[5]

These resignations set off a round of administrative musical chairs. On the academic side, Dr. Guzzetta, as we have seen, became Vice-President and Dean of Administration. His former role as Dean of the General College was assumed by Dr. Thomas Sumner who had served two years as Dean of the Buchtel College of Liberal Arts. Sumner, in turn, was succeeded in Buchtel College by Dr. George W. Knepper, Associate Professor of History and Head of the Department who, as a World War II veteran, had completed his B.A. degree work at The University of Akron.

On the financial and business side, Hardy was succeeded as Financial Vice-President by Dr. Ian MacGregor, a University of Cincinnati man who had served briefly as Assistant to the President. With a Ph.D. in chemistry, this former teacher and researcher had the interests of the academician at heart, and even when his hands were tied by limited funds, the classroom teacher and researcher felt that "Mac" understood his problems. A campus newcomer, Richard Reidenbaugh, was appointed Assistant to the President in which role he did much to lay the groundwork for state status. Upon his leaving two years later, this position was abolished, but some of his duties went to Harold Oyster who was appointed to the new position Vice-President for Development January 1, 1965.

Other important administrative changes of the early sixties involved the College of Business Administration where Dr. Richard Reidenbach succeeded Dr. Warren Leigh as Dean. The college was Leigh's creation, having been nurtured from its struggling state in 1953 into a strong academic unit in a key area of community interest. Another significant change brought Dr. Michael J. Rzasa to Akron as Dean of the College of Engineering, succeeding Ransom D. Landon, who had resigned in 1962, and William Petry, who had spent two years as Acting Dean prior to assuming the deanship of the Community and Technical College.

In the financial office, Robert Peck served as Assistant to the Financial Vice-President and then as Controller, succeeding Carl Hall, who left for another position in 1963. When Peck, in turn, left Akron in 1966, Carl Hall returned as Controller-Treasurer. Mr. R. Wayne Duff was appointed Assistant to the Financial Vice-President in 1963, and later was appointed Business Manager in which position he assumed responsibility for housekeeping operations, land purchases, and many other vital tasks. His strong work was recognized in 1968 with his appointment to the Financial Vice-Presidency. Many other persons served the business side of the institution, among them Earl DeVoe and his successor Robert Paul, as Superintendent of Buildings and Grounds, Donald Bowles, first as Purchasing Agent and then in several other capacities, Alex Banyar as Bookstore Manager, Ralph Larson as Manager of the Student Center and later as Assistant Director of Purchasing, and Cecil Rogers who, as University Auditor, kept watch over it all.

A key figure in making the University machinery function is the Secretary to the President. Since 1951, Miss Caroline Pardee, Class of '32, has provided unusually dedicated and skilled service in this role.

In other important areas of University work, Richard Hansford was promoted to Dean of Student Services, and later (1969) to a Vice-Presidency. Gordon Hagerman left the Registrar's position to become Assistant to the Vice-President and Dean of Administration. Robert Berry was appointed the first full-time Placement Officer to accommodate the increased traffic in employment interviewing and information. The tremendous growth of scholarship, grant, and loan money made it necessary to put a full-time director over that important phase of operations and Mr. Robert Larson assumed these duties. In the Printing and Duplicating Department, Mr. Robert Pye became a familiar and dependable figure, while the Publications Department was efficiently managed by Mr. Robert Sartoris. There can be no end to this shifting of positions and persons, yet The University of Akron has been fortunate to have had the services of these able people over a long period. In no small part, it is their familiarity with the University and their expertise that enables the enterprise to proceed efficiently.

It is difficult for a new president, under the best of circumstances, to take hold of his charge effectively; but when he is confronted with skepticism and disgruntlement in the faculty, his task is doubly hard. We have noted how minimal faculty salaries and benefits were in 1951, and we have also touched briefly upon the improvements that occurred in this crucial area. But building a faculty is a complex and delicate business, many facets of which are ordinarily hidden from public view.

In common with the rest of mankind who must set about making a living, faculty members desire and seek the best salaries and working conditions possible. Part of American folklore is the image of the "dedicated teacher," willing to work for glory and inner satisfaction rather than for a livable wage. Somehow teachers are supposed to be content with less than society readily gives truck drivers, plumbers, and machinists, and no one even gives serious consideration to the proposition that teachers might earn as much as lawyers, dentists, and public officials. There seems to be no objection that teachers earn more, on occasion, than ministers, social workers, nurses, and librarians. Could it be because these professionals are even more "dedicated" than the teachers?

This judgment is not excessively harsh when applied to public attitudes in the early 1950's. The salubrious changes that have occurred since that time for the teaching profession in general, and the university teacher in particular, are dramatic. Even the general public appears more willing than in pre-Sputnik days to admit that the teacher is essential to the nation's well being, and that good working conditions might attract strong people to the profession.

Shortly after his arrival, President Auburn received a letter from Dean Cherrington that put the case bluntly: "The morale of the faculty has been low indeed." On the whole, he said, "we are a melancholy group."[6] Salaries were one of the principal factors in the morale failure, but there were other things disturbing the faculty. They felt that a disproportionate share of operating funds went into maintenance at the expense of salary improvement. There was resentment at the lack of an effective faculty voice in the decision-making process. There was a conviction that faculty were expected to refrain from any comment that would upset influential groups in a community whose support at the polls was assiduously wooed.

In a day when the great national issues were the Korean conflict, the Cold War, and "McCarthyism," there was a notable lack of public commentary emanating from the campus. It may be that the self-selecting process was working—that faculty prone to comment freely on controversial issues chose not to teach at Akron—but whatever the reason, there was little informed opinion or, more important, public instruction on the issues coming from the faculty. The Parkins incident revealed some of these tensions.

Ivan Parkins was hired in 1948 as Instructor in Political Science, but he was better known to many students as the lecturer in Introduction to the Social Sciences. He became involved in local politics to the extent of running as the Democratic candidate for the U.S. House of Representatives in 1954. His difficulties started two years earlier, however, when a local industrial leader took exception to what he interpreted as a pro-labor point of view taken by Parkins in an article, "Government and Labor," written for the *Local Five Air Bag*. Even though all parties would probably agree that the *Air Bag* was not one of America's premiere publications, the local industrialist was incensed enough to complain to the president who quite properly passed it on to Dean Cherrington for comment.

Dean Cherrington wrote a blunt and forceful defense of the position that the social scientist is put in when he publishes his views on contemporary matters:

> *It is most unfortunate that the scholar in the social sciences is almost invariably forced, whenever he makes a contribution, to run the gauntlet of innumerable self-appointed 'experts' who are dead certain that the poor fellow is either a crackpot or an agitator who should be chastised severely. They 'know all about it' because they are people and the social scientist naturally writes about people.*

He went on to ask: "Must we muzzle our scholars in the field by insisting upon completely unbiased (i.e. innocuous) presentation?" He spoke of people using "their wealth or position to bludgeon the school they support into teaching in accord with their particular prejudices. . . .That is exactly what happens when a local industrialist questions the right or propriety of one of our social science instructors to express his views on labor issues. And believe me, I am against any and all such effort to limit our scholars."[7]

It would be pleasant to record that this courageous defense by Dean Cherrington sufficed to clarify the University's position for all time. But academic freedom is won by constant, repeated struggle against people who either do not understand a university's function or who would make it less than it should be because it suits their interests to do so. And when the public whose tax dollars keep the university going take exception to its course, then there are real pressures to temper its stand, a temptation to pray that the faculty keep quiet on controversial issues. The fact that the president and deans have often fought off these pressures when they encroached on academic freedom has been a real service. But the toll it took was to make them cautious about stimulating intellectual exchanges in the public press or in the community.

As for Mr. Parkins, he had yet another round with a special interest group of a different nature. In his campaign for Congress, Parkins was identified as a member of the American Civil Liberties Union (ACLU). This drew a protest from a local newssheet, the "Veteran's News," which said the ACLU was allegedly pro-Communist. It was a popular charge in the suspicion-filled atmosphere of the early fifties, and Mr. Parkins was by no means the only person to come under fire for his present or former affiliations. Commenting on the charge, the *Buchtelite* stated' "With everyone and his brother . . . being accused of Communistic tendencies, it was bound to hit our campus."[8] It did not hit very hard, however, and Parkins appeared to suffer no disadvantage from his ACLU connection.

In Akron's history there is no great *cause celebre*, no academic Dreyfus Case involving faculty fighting for principle against malevolent forces of suppression. Akron does not provide the kind of environmental focus that would have predisposed persons prone to make an effective public stand on principle to come or to stay. There was little that could be interpreted over the years as administrative suppression even though the Board and the president found it prudent to remind faculty about "responsible" behavior. Until the 1960's, when again a spirit of protest rose rather generally throughout higher education, Akron had no effective coterie of professionally secure young professors who were outspoken on social and political issues. The coterie was present by 1965, and although the positions taken by outspoken professors were not always admired, there was a growing recognition that issues were getting a more thorough airing than before and some observers felt the campus was more vigorous and interesting as a result.

Throughout the 1960's, faculty working conditions continued to improve. As late as 1957, President Auburn was describing the faculty as "underpaid and overworked;" but not many years thereafter he was able to report that average faculty salaries and compensation placed Akron among the top 80 schools in the nation out of some 2,000 institutions; and he deserved credit for the accomplishment.[9] The goal set by the Forecast Committee in 1958—to double average faculty salaries by 1970 —remained in force, and progress toward that end kept to schedule. This progress could be measured against national norms because the AAUP published annually a rating scale against which salary schedules of colleges and universities were ranked. The faculty was gratified with the enormous strides that had been made, but for the University the struggle to keep salaries competitive was an enduring one, especially as Akron competed increasingly for scholars to man its expanding doctoral and professional programs.

Along with salary improvement came a generous program of benefits. In 1956, the "Faculty-Employee Welfare Plan" was adopted, giving the faculty and staff adequate protection for the first time.[10] The State Teachers Retirement system and an extensive plan of medical insurance formed the backbone of the benefits program. By the mid-1960's, the University was paying an additional 16 percent of faculty salary in benefits, and this plan compared most favorably with those found in the academic world.

While improved pension plans made retirement less of a threat than before, some faculty members were disgruntled by the rule that required retirement at age 65. The Board has an option to hire any retired faculty member on a year-to-year basis to age 70, but this power has been used with utmost discretion, for to choose some and not others could cause hard feelings and dissension. Prior to 1957, only Fred Sefton and Stafford Whitby had been asked to stay on past retirement age. (This discussion discounts practices of an earlier day when "Daddy" Olin stayed on until age 78.) However, in 1957, Dr. Paul Fall, President Emeritus of Hiram College and a former teacher of chemistry, was hired on a yearly contract to teach freshman chemistry. His work was to be partially supported by a grant.[11]

This move had repercussions. A recently retired faculty member charged that the University was discriminating against its own faculty by refusing to keep them on after age 65 while at the same time hiring a retiree from another institution. Another irate commentator mistakenly charged that the University had bought a house for Dr. Fall on Union Street.[12] Although Dr. Fall had been a superb teacher in earlier times, and although he merely rented the University-owned house on Union Street, this affair turned out to be a tactical error for the University. Dr. Fall, in the meantime, discovered that the teaching of freshman chemistry had changed so completely since he last taught that he had to "work harder" than he ever did in his life to relearn the subject along contemporary lines.[13] This effort contributed to a health condition that prompted him to retire permanently. The larger issue of mandatory retirement at 65 is still debated.

From time to time, questions were raised about The University of Akron's hiring policies as they involved members of minority groups. The University's position has been that it hires faculty and staff according to professional competence and that it takes no account of religion, race, or other social characteristics. For many years the University had employed Negro faculty members on a part-time basis, usually in the evening session. There was no reason other than an acute shortage of fully qualified candidates to prevent the hiring of Negro faculty members on a full-time basis. The first so employed was Dr. Edgar Toppin, Assistant Professor of History, hired in 1959. An extraordinarily talented and resourceful scholar, Dr. Toppin was a great favorite and made an outstanding contribution to the campus during the four years he stayed at Akron. In teaching, coaching, counseling, library, and business offices, Akron has been well served by minority group members.

If the hiring of minority group members was one of the chief national concerns of these decades, another was the academic controversy over "publish or perish." Possibly more useless rhetoric was spilled on this topic than on any other in academe during a brief period of the sixties. Akron has always sought a teaching faculty. This was appropriate when one remembers that undergraduate preparation was nearly the sole responsibility of the institution until well after World War II. Even so, some professors found time and inclination to do research and to publish. But with the advent of a deliberate push toward professional and graduate education, it became mandatory for the University to secure active researchers and publishers. The doctoral degree is a research degree; a doctoral candidate best learns his craft by working with a faculty member on a sort of apprentice-master relationship, and no man can be master of his craft unless he is a practitioner in all its parts. The difficulty comes when the institution expects the same man to teach undergraduates effectively and then, in what amounts to a role change, work individually with graduate students pursuing current research interests. Despite protests to the contrary, very few faculty are either skilled enough to make the transition with full effectiveness or are equally interested in the two levels of instruction. As limited resources are employed to secure graduate-oriented teachers and researchers, undergraduate instruction cannot help but suffer by getting the less well-trained, the less well-paid, the part-time teachers or graduate teaching fellows. There simply is no happy solution to the dilemma short of an unlimited supply of funds.

In 1960, shortly after approval was secured from the North Central Association to offer the Ph.D. program in polymer chemistry, President Auburn told the faculty what this meant for them. "The Deans of all the academic units are naturally going to watch the performance of their faculty members more closely. They are conscious as we all are that scholarly advancement is expected of an institution accredited to award the doctoral degree." He said that this did not mean Akron would adopt a "publish or perish rule." But it certainly meant that the deans would "weigh with greater care than previously the research accomplishments of their faculty members as they make recommendations for salary increases in the years ahead."[15] As one faculty wag put it, this policy would be "publish or languish!"

Akron was no more successful than other schools in bridging this dichotomy completely although it did avoid the extremes experienced on some campuses. The faculty member who combined strong classroom teaching with continuing research and/or publication was prized, and perhaps this is as it should be. There was also advancement, however, for the fine teacher who never published and for the fine researcher who failed as a teacher. Fortunately, as the faculty increased in size, it was increasingly possible to place individuals in situations where their talents were maximized and their shortcomings minimized.

How did this Akron faculty measure up to that of similar institutions? There is no sure way of knowing. Akron could boast that it was well above the national norm in the number of terminal degree holders on its faculty, particularly in the Buchtel College of Liberal Arts and, after 1967, in engineering. Those who were familiar with the national scene judged that it stood up well in comparison. Campus visitors from granting agencies and scholarly associations found the faculty competent. In the final analysis, however, that indefinable rapport that occurs when the right teacher meets a receptive student can never be measured adequately.

In 1964, the professorial rank, "Distinguished Professor," was created. It was to recognize senior faculty who were outstanding classroom teachers and whose contributions to The University of Akron and the academic world were "exemplary and professionally constructive."[16] Award of the title carried an additional salary stipend of $500 which became part of the base salary. The first appointees to this honor were Dr. Mabel Riedinger (education), Dr. Samuel Selby (mathematics), and Dr. Ernest Thackeray (physics). They were joined the following year by Dr. Charles Duffy (English). As long as people of their concern form the heart of the faculty, it will remain healthy in spite of the pressures of the moment that periodically rock the academic world.

World War II was a watershed of sorts in the composition of the student body. Not that there was any dramatic break. Before the war nearly all students admitted to the University had completed a college preparatory curriculum with a record strong enough to warrant admission. There were limited alternatives. The G.I. Bill encouraged some veterans who had no idea prior to the war that they would go on to college; many of these men fulfilled the entrance requirement by amassing a suitable score on the General Educational Development tests devised for that purpose. In the early fifties, Akron's experience with the "basic" program brought to campus a limited number of students who needed remedial work before they were ready for regular freshman courses.

After 1950, it was possible to say that any Akron high school graduate could enter the University although he might be placed in a curriculum not of his own choosing. Placement was done on an individual basis as the result of counseling and testing. This Jacksonian concept of permitting every student a chance to go as far as his capabilities would take him created some problems, but it seemed appropriate to a municipal institution. It was in fact what Kolbe, Zook, and Simmons said a Municipal University was required to do in order to serve completely the community that supported it, and President Auburn was as much in favor of this concept as they. As we saw in regard to the C & T College, the price paid for this practice was the high academic mortality rate in the freshman and sophomore years.

Despite all the effort to help the student at the lower end of the ability and performance spectrum, a good deal of attention was also directed toward the able student. The large increase in scholarships and grants brought outstanding students to campus. Special study groups were organized by Mrs. Phyllis Paul to provide these resourceful and motivated students with the small group discussions in which their intellect could expand by testing their ideas in a critical atmosphere. Each year in the 1960's, the faculty was assured that "this year's freshman class is the best ever" as measured by standard tests. But despite these factors, Akron's student body continued to run the whole range from the very bright to the very slow, although the latter seldom lasted more than a semester.

One of the pleasures of the Akron campus is a student body that represents a cross-section of American society, skewed somewhat toward the urban portion. Akron is no hot house environment where the students reflect a common background or common aspirations and values. If educators mean it when they claim that education should be preparation for life, then where better could one find the mix that one would live and work with than in a heterogeneous student body that reflected all racial and ethnic backgrounds, socio-economic levels, ability ranges, etc.? This campus had no ivory tower, remote-from-this-world feel to it. It was very much wrapped up in this world, possibly too much so for optimum educational conditions, for much that is of value in the educational process cannot be measured in terms of practicality. Akron is still a working campus; even a fair percentage of the dormitory students hold part-time jobs both on campus and off. More than 70 percent of the men and 25 percent of the women in the day session hold jobs involving regular hours (i.e. something other than baby sitting or an occasional repair job), and of course nearly everyone in the evening session is employed, most of them full time. The great majority of Akron students are relatively immune from the criticism that college students lead a sheltered life divorced from the hard realities of life.

Students of the 1950's were characterized as the "apathetic generation." Like all labels, this one slandered a sizable number who were anything but apathetic, yet in contrast to the ex-G.I.'s before them, and the socially conscious students who followed in the next decade, they did appear uninvolved on social and political issues. If they were conformists, however, it was no more so than the society at large during those years.

They had welcomed President Auburn to campus with a plea to faculty and administrators to stop apologizing for Akron University.[17] This plea, typical of each generation of student boosters, overlooked the fact that there was a good deal to be pessimistic about in 1951. The last person to need a pep talk was the new president, for if there ever was anyone to accentuate the positive about The University of Akron, he was the man. One of his favorite sayings was the old saw that the deans' job was to make the school as good as the president said it was, and his half-facetious response to recognition—"you ain't seen nothing yet!—became a campus watchword.

As the decade moved along and the campus became vibrant with activity and constructive development, the students caught the spirit. It was no longer as fashionable as before to knock the school because it lacked acres of greensward, majestic buildings, and the educational resources of Harvard. Some may harbor doubts about the efficacy of the "power of positive thinking," popularized during that decade by Norman Vincent Peale, but it started to work on the Akron campus.

With the exception of a brief period in the early 1930's, Akron's student body had been essentially conservative in its social and political outlook. Eisenhower was the choice over Stevenson in a 1952 campus poll, but it would be a mistake to think that either stirred the hearts and minds of most students. Political consciousness was singularly lacking. One coed when asked by a pollster to indicate whether she favored Ike or Adlai replied, "which one is the Democrat? Put me down for him."

No "beatniks" defiled campus walks, no pickets carried signs. The Korean "police action" was safely removed from Akron, Ohio, and once it was apparent that students would not be drafted in wholesale numbers, little attention was paid to it. Seldom did the student newspaper comment upon its implications or on student attitudes toward war—hot or cold. Eventually, a thousand Korean veterans were to enroll on the Hilltop, and occasionally they would talk of their experiences; but on the whole one would never guess, from the general tenor of the campus, that there was a war on.

Domestic politics of the early fifties were dominated by "McCarthism." Again, there remains little evidence that the Senator's "witchhunt" and all that it implied aroused much student commentary or interest. There were no protest rallies, no hastily printed broadsides condemning the tactics of character assassination by unsupported allegation. The *Buchtelite* finally took a jab at one of the more ludicrous attempts to find "red" spies everywhere when it came to the defense of the "Weavers," a popular singing group that played Akron in that period.[18]

It is always disappointing to those who expect to find a college campus seething with concern about the problems and issues of the day to discover that the great majority of students never speak out in a public way to demonstrate visible evidence of interest. It is always a minority, a small group of articulate and, sometimes, argumentative students who carry the load of forthright commentary about current affairs. They are not always the best equipped intellectually, but they appear to be best equipped emotionally for the open give and take of the coffee house. On the Akron campus it was in the cafeteria that they were most visible; and they tended to revel in that visibility. Each student generation had its group—generally dominated by *Buchtelite* staffers, philosophy students, drama and literature people—which shifted in composition from time to time but nearly always occupied a predetermined portion of the cafeteria from opening time until lights out at 10 p.m.

By friend and detractor alike these students were called the "intellectuals," but that word can be spoken in a range of tones that implies anything—approval, amused tolerance, or a sneer. As long as their barbs were directed at political candidates, U.S.

foreign policy, or similarly distant topics they created no enmity; but on occasion college football, certain courses, fraternities and sororities, and the vagaries of their "square" brethren preempted their discussions at which time they came under counterattack. Some faculty and administrative officials lamented the fact that they did not act like the others—quiet, unobtrusive, well groomed, future "organization men." When the sixties were well advanced, this coterie was absorbed into the larger number of students who had found—largely through concern about civil rights, the war in Vietnam, and political action—an interest and a meaningful role in the world around them. As always, a few students found flamboyant ways to display their rejection of the University and the state of their society.

Why did the Akron student body show in the mid-sixties its first sign of wide-spread interest in contemporary affairs since the depression? No one can really document an answer, but a close observer would have noticed a number of contributing factors. Involvement had become the thing. Concern, demonstration, protest were "in." The witness of personal commitment had been dignified in Selma, Alabama, Memphis, Tennessee, and a hundred other places. More than that, students knew that the national mood was more supportive of change in the interest of securing "rights" than it had been at any previous time. The old absolutes were in retreat, their flying heels nipped by the power advocates seeking everything from "student power" to "black power."

An important explanation for the emergence of outspoken student concern at Akron rises from the changing composition of the student body. The dormitory program had brought over a thousand resident students to campus. They were safely removed from parental oversight, and although they acted with more restraint than did their counterparts on some other campuses, they were less intimidated, perhaps, than the student living at home. And in common with many other campuses, Akron had a number of young faculty members who were personally involved in various kinds of social action. They provided a rallying point for students. By its very nature, protest creates reaction, and some faculty members looked askance at their junior colleagues whom they regarded as "troublemakers." However one regarded the aims and methods of the student activists (and they were still a distinct minority), an open-minded observer who knew the University as of old would have to admit that there was more variety, more action, more inquiry, more skepticism, in short, more intellectual ferment than was evident in the 1950's.

The most constructive and tangible evidence of student concern was their involvement in action programs. For several years the University was a sponsor of the Akron-Summit Tutorial Project which put student tutors together, on a one-to-one basis, with educationally underprivileged pupils in the public school system. Supported by federal funds, the tutorial program was partially administered by University personnel, and many of the tutors were Akron students. Still other students worked on the Center for Urban Studies contracts that gave them a first-hand look at the inner city. Some students were involved in projects sponsored by private organizations which sent them to work with Mexicans, various African peoples, and others who needed so much and had so little. The Peace Corps was attractive. Robert Zimmermann and Charles DeBose, the first Akron students to enter that program, were followed by many others who went to far places of need around the world, while nearer home, "Vista" attracted students to its cause. In former years, the military services had been about the only place where a disenchanted student could find "instant maturation." Now a helpful alternative was available, for maturity comes from accepting responsibility, and these constructive social action programs dispensed responsibility most effectively.

This legitimizing of student idealism was in large part a product of the Kennedy administration. As the first American president since Teddy Roosevelt who seemed to glory in the full range of human activity and who was outspoken in support of the leadership of the young in providing constructive innovations in the social order, John F. Kennedy was much admired on the Akron campus. Although some of the ideas he proposed took form under his successor, there was no great campus enthusiasm for Lyndon Johnson. His manner and style seemed "square" compared with the sense of liberation and excitement that, deserved or not, was part of the Kennedy mystique. However, the revival of student interest in political activity has endured. Active student involvement in political campaigns is a continuing phenomenon; the cynicism of the fifties is, for the moment at least, passé.

An important ingredient in the new outlook was the change that had occurred in the faculty and in the curriculum of several key departments. A talented group of new instructors in political science, sociology, economics, and history were particularly effective in making their courses relevant to the modern mood. Much faculty support has come from departments that have a less direct claim on contemporary social commentary—english, philosophy, physics. As graduate programs develop more fully, the number of mature students with professional interest in contemporary affairs increases. One might say, with more optimism than documentation, that Akron is closer to the ideal of a university than she has ever been; she is on an upward spiral of involvement, concern, and intellectual ferment.

A decade ago, the now-famous "Jacob study" shocked American campuses when it purported to document the "fact" that students do not change their values as a result of their collegiate experience.[19] The study has been challenged and its findings modified, but it remains a goad to faculty who like to believe that students are absorbing from them new truths, new goals, new insights. It seems to this writer that common sense observation of the educational process at Akron reveals considerable modification in the priorities of students, resulting in part at least from their collegiate experience. On this campus where the same instructor is apt to teach both freshmen and seniors, it may be more possible than in another institution to observe the student's progress through the years. And this progress appears to involve more than the capacity to pursue an occupation, it reflects more than "training."

It seems reasonable that an institution that welcomes freshmen from a wide variety of ability levels and economic and social backgrounds would see more change develop in those freshmen over a four or five year span than would be observable on a campus where only the very talented and socially secure, the "winners", were admitted. In the latter circumstances it would be incredible if the graduates were not impressive; one had to be impressive to get in, in the first place. It might be possible for a freshman to "grow" during this college experience without changing his values appreciably—that is, he might grow in competence, or grow in maturity and still retain the same biases and prejudices that he brought with him. These things are difficult to measure; but there is very modest and limited evidence of some attitudinal shifts among Akron students.

While there is a difference between "values" and "tastes," a shift in the latter might indicate a break-away from childhood rigidities and such a break is essential to the change of values. A number of small surveys indicate that the tastes of Akron students in art, music, and dress varies substantially from their parents'. That might simply be a function of age rather than of education, but it is in some cases the combination of emerging independence from family coupled with the new experiences of the campus that trigger the change. If one cannot claim this dawning enlightenment largely for the University, it seems unreasonable to exclude it altogether from the explanation.

A limited survey in 1955 revealed that a substantial majority of the Akron students polled considered their ideas on politics and economics to be different from their parents'. (They did not specify in what way). Yet of this same group only 19 percent said they had different ideas about religion.[20] In the latter case, the students were asked to explain their religious views. (This was done orally in discussion sections of the course Institutions in the United States.) It might have shocked their pastors to discover how completely their young parishoners were disoriented from specific doctrinal beliefs. A questionnaire revealed the lack of centainty on such questions as "Does your church teach a literal interpretation of the scriptures?" Nearly all, whether Methodist, Baptist, Catholic, Presbyterian or what have you, said it did.[21] Apparently, that whale really did swallow Jonah. Some faculty cynics thought this question unrevealing, for they assumed the students did not know what "literal interpretation" meant.

Had similar polls of student tastes, attitudes, and beliefs been taken in the late sixties, one suspects they would have revealed a student belief that their position was far different from their parents', but one might also assume that the position of the parents was shifting more rapidly than in the immediate post-World War II years. The religiosity that had been strong in the fifties, when swelling church membership rolls gave some observers hope for a "return to religion," had faded, and the lament of the sixties was that institutionalized religion was becoming irrelevant. It may be, in fact, that there was more desire on the part of the students to practice religious precepts ("love thy neighbor . . .") in an overt manner than in earlier student generations, and there is little doubt that many felt they could do this better outside institutionalized religion.

Supreme Court rulings on prayer in the public schools dealt a final blow to those who wished to have students fill out religious preference cards as part of registration. Baccalaureate became optional to graduating seniors and faculty after 1966. But these things did not mean that religion was of less interest. It meant rather than compulsion in any form was eschewed. As for the reinforcement of religious values, an important addition to campus life came with the establishment of a chaplaincy for Protestant and Eastern Orthodox students as a counterpart of the Newman Club for Roman Catholic students. Like the Newman Club, its work was supported entirely from outside sources and its offices were located in non-University buildings.[22] But both the Director of the Newman Club and the Protestant Chaplain were welcome at all University functions and were given complete access to its resources. They added an important ingredient to campus life.

Generalizations about student attitudes and values is a tricky and inexact business at best. It is much easier to document student activities because of their formalized character. A growing University would be expected to have a growing program of student activities so it is no surprise that Akron did. In keeping with past experience the main support for campus events came from fraternity and sorority members, but there were also more outlets for the non-affiliates. The existence of these alternatives made failure to join a fraternal group less of a social disaster than it was in earlier days.

Akron's fraternities and sororities compiled an outstanding record, particularly in light of the University's character as essentially a commuter school. This accomplishment was a tribute to good student leadership and enlightened support and direction from the Student Personnel office. Throughout the period of challenge to the rushing and pledging policies of the nationals, the Akron chapters continued to call attention to what they were doing that was constructive while generally supporting efforts to remove restrictive clauses from the national charters. Formal removal of such clauses could not in itself provide immediate relief to excluded students. In 1957–1958, the Sphinx Club, founded by black students, was chartered as Alpha Tau chapter of Alpha Phi Alpha national fraternity. In like manner, the Ivyettes were chartered in 1961–62 as Delta Pi chapter of Alpha Kappa Alpha sorority. Even a decade after all restrictive clauses were removed from fraternity and sorority charters, there appeared to be no rush toward integrated chapters although there were modest breakthroughs.

If the breakdown of exclusivism was the foremost accomplishment of the fraternal system during the fifties and sixties, a close second would have to be their direction away from sophomoric rowdiness toward an emphasis on constructive activities that would help students mature socially and intellectually. Help Week replaced Hell Week in the more enlightened groups although there remained some who thought physical abuse and degradation was necessary for pledges. It would take 10 pictures of pledges painting cottages for tubercular children to offset in the public's mind just one picture of severe hazing or destructive horseplay.

The other area where progress was substantial was in raising the grade point averages of the "Greek" groups. Akron's performance was gratifying. Most local chapters had programs to encourage study and to reward strong scholastic performances by their members. In 1954–55, Akron's seven national fraternities earned a grade average that placed them first in the nation among the 153 colleges reporting. An executive of College Fraternity Scholarship Processing remarked: "Akron U fraternities have done a tremendous job in scholarship, a job that deserves national recognition."[23] Akron later earned the Summa Cum Laude Award of the National Interfraternity Council for the impressive accomplishment of having each of its national chapters score above the all-men's grade average each year for ten years.

Recognitions and awards to individual chapters or to groups within chapters are too numerous to catalog. They would range from the awards won by Phi Delta Theta, Alpha Epsilon Pi, and Phi Kappa Tau for having the outstanding chapters of their nationals, to the selection of the Phi Delta Theta chorus as the official singing group of the national convention. Some of the honors went to advisers as was the case with "Doc" DeGraff, a devoted supporter if there ever was one, of all that was best in fraternity life, whose unselfish involvement over many years was recognized by the Phi award of his fraternity, Phi Kappa Tau.

An "old grad"—that is to say anyone who has been gone five years or more from this rapidly changing campus—would have a difficult time finding his old fraternity or sorority house. The Development Guide Plan identified an area at the eastern fringe of the expanded campus as the location for fraternity and sorority housing. The Lambda Chis, Tekes, and Lone Stars could stay on Fir Hill, but nearly every other group had to move. Phi Sigma Kappa, its mansion on Union Street taken by the University, led the way by building a new house alongside the Akron Expressway which bounds the eastern edge of the future University district. Theta Chi and Alpha Gamma Delta built in this same area. Alpha Epsilon Pi built a house at Buchtel and Fir Hill. There was a time when it appeared that the University might help finance a fraternity row but the chapters were ultimately forced to go it alone. The University contributed help as it could, including building parking lots in the heart of the new district to alleviate the congestion caused by a surfeit of cars, but house rebuilding remains essentially a responsibility of the individual chapters.

Of the many activities sponsored and supported by the fraternal groups, "Greek Week" was outstanding. It was marked by a combination of the serious and instructive on the one hand, fun and games on the other. Each year the outstanding Greek man and Greek woman were selected and recognized for their contributions to the fraternity system. Special support was also given to Songfest, Acme-Zip parades, Homecoming, May Day, and Casbah (Stunt Night). Of all the attention-catching performances at Casbah, none could quite match Carli Palermo's sinuous dance in red leotards—and Carli was an Independent! Songfest was one of the pleasantest of campus events. College songs never sounded better than when sung by the more talented ensembles, but Sigmund Romberg, Victor Herbert, and Hoagy Carmichael would never forgive what was done to their work, on occasion, by the less talented groups. May Day was special; the delightful spectators' gallery made up of little children from Spicer School that used to line the curbs to watch the May Day float parade is no more since the parade now takes place in the evening, wending its way past Children's Hospital where an appreciative group watches, and then on to Stan Hywet where the masterpieces remain on display over the weekend.

Things do not always go well with the "Greeks." A serious misunderstanding in 1957 almost resulted in the national officers closing the Kappa Kappa Gamma chapter. The National President of Kappa, however, apologized for the fact that the sorority's position had been misconstrued. No criticism of the University had been intended; rather, she was impressed with "the excellent facilities, the fine and well-rounded educational program, the high standards, and the plans for future expansion . . ." She then identified the problems that beset the local chapter and advised that a revision of the rushing rules and the quota system would work to its advantage.[24]

President Auburn put strong emphasis on the importance of the fraternity system, especially, he said, in urban universities where dormitory life was lacking and where group working and living together is important. The sorority officers were satisfied: "We are confident in Akron U's future and we are happy to continue our Kappa chapter on the campus."[25] That nadir safely passed, the Kappas recaptured the strength characteristic of them from early days.

The fatal flaw in most student organizations is lack of continuity. Groups tend to prosper as the result of efforts made by a handful of real enthusiasts. While these students remain in school the organization flourishes, but once they have graduated equally devoted students are not always there to take up the slack. Each new student generation has to be educated to the ideals and objectives of the organization. In fraternity life, the continuing education of new leaders was performed largely under the guidance of skillful counselors in the Student Personnel Office, particularly Dean Richard Hansford, Dudley Johnson, Phyllis Paul and Katherine Vegso. Their contacts with national interfraternity and panhellenic organizations kept them abreast of new directions in "Greek" life.

These same persons, along with many others who contributed from time to time, were responsible for starting a number of campus groups whose efforts were directed toward service and the recognition of outstanding campus contributions. For many years Mrs. Phyllis Paul pursued the task of persuading Mortar Board (national women's activities honorary) to grant a charter to Pierian, its local counterpart. When her efforts succeeded in 1964, Akron at long last had the complement of Omicron Delta Kappa. While a great amount of work was done by students in this cause, success would not have been achieved except for Mrs. Paul's determination. Almost without exception, when one finds a successful student organization on the Akron campus, one will find a resourceful and contributing adviser behind the scenes.

Visitors to the Akron campus, some of them from campuses that exert a minimum of control over student dress, were frequently impressed with the good looks and good grooming of the students. Students living at home experienced certain controls on their appearance, but an assist came from the Student Personnel Office which constantly urged good grooming upon student groups. The first dormitory students were required to dress in coat and tie or in a dress and hose before they were permitted into the dining room. Later this rule was relaxed and at this writing dress is much more casual than before, probably reflecting the manners and mores of the larger society.

We alluded earlier to the earnestness with which some defenders of compulsory ROTC supported its continuation by arguing that freshmen men were a motley lot when left to their own devices, and the uniforms, haircuts, and grooming required of them in ROTC were good for them individually and for the campus collectively. It is true that the long ranks of army and air force cadets marching from drill at Buchtel Field or braced at attention while some visiting dignitary made his way to Commissioning ceremonies were an attractive sight, but the question was raised again in the late sixties as to whether the University should require ROTC training. Unlike the earlier protests, this one took place while there was a war on and while there was a growing group of student protestors not easily put off.

Again the president of the University appointed a faculty-administration committee to advise on the question. The faculty of the Buchtel College of Liberal Arts, supported by the College of Law, expressed its support for abolishing the compulsory feature. A few small demonstrations were mounted by students seeking relief from compulsory ROTC. After the 1968 Commissioning ceremonies, General Harold K. Johnson, Chief of Staff United States Army, was presented with a petition bearing student signatures, but this proved little more than a symbolic gesture. While the faculty-administration committee pursued its hearings on the issue, impatience was expressed over its slowness, but finally, during the Fall quarter, 1968, the committee recommended to University Council that the compulsory feature be abandoned, and

The Rubber Bowl could be a gloomy place as in this 1958 game.

Acme-Zip shows the Rubber Bowl at its best as 40,000 people come to cheer.

The great 1965–66 basketball team, veterans of the Evansville tournament trail.

in October council approved the recommendation by majority vote. The issue generated enough interest that, for the first time in council's history, members of the press
and radio, students, and faculty sought admission to the meeting. Their request was
granted by vote of council although one student was kept from bringing a tape
recorder into the room.

The Board of Trustees approved council's action at its November meeting. In
presenting the matter to the board, President Auburn expressed his own preference
for retention of compulsory ROTC, but he recommended that the trustees approve
council's recommendation. Several trustees were also reluctant to abandon the compulsory feature, but only one registered his "nay" when the vote was taken.[26] Thus
ended one of the longest debates ever conducted on the Hilltop, although it is still
to be seen how the decision will affect the ROTC program.

Athletics continued to play a major role in student affairs at Akron although
there was little that could be construed as "over-emphasis" on varsity athletics. A
commuter campus seldom generates the sustained enthusiasm for intercollegiate athletics that characterizes most residential campuses, but the competition remains,
nevertheless, an important focus of student sentiment, pride, and loyalty. The sense
of shared adventure that brought practically the entire Buchtel College student body
out in support of its teams, and led the chronicler of its first years to include in his
book the score of every athletic contest played by the Buchtel boys, is gone. Now
there are hundreds of students who know practically nothing about the fortunes of
Akron teams except when national recognition looms, as in recent basketball seasons,
or when the old stirrings of rivalry with Kent State are touched upon. Yet, even those
students who care little about sports sense in victory some mysterious enhancement
of their University's image.

In athletics as in every other corner of Akron's operation, President Auburn
put his mark. He enjoyed athletics and his intense competitive drive would not
permit him to regard a varsity contest as "just a game." It was a public testing of his
credo that the University must pursue excellence in all it attempted to do. A sloppy
performance on the gridiron was no more acceptable than a sloppy performance in
fulfilling a research contract. As in every other phase of University life, he attended
games faithfully, often at great personal inconvenience, and in this way demonstrated
his support of the teams.

Football continued to be a source of great pleasure and of equally great frustration during the fifties and sixties. The Ohio Conference annually boasted two or three
teams of exceptional strength for schools that had to live within relatively restrictive
conditions of aid. In the fifties, Heidelberg was the terror of the conference to be
succeeded by Wittenberg in the next decade. These schools plus Muskingum and
Baldwin Wallace gave Akron all she could handle, but then the competition dropped
off precipitately. It was an uneven conference and every match involving Akron with
one of the tiny schools with weak teams gave a David and Goliath aura to the contest.

Following the resignation of "Bud" Houghton, "Red" Cochrane assumed the
football coaching duties. Though already burdened by his role as Director of Athletics, Cochrane infused his charges with a winning spirit. Teams that had looked as if
they were simply going through the motions suddenly came alive under his prodding
and zest for the game. While "Red" organized the effort, much of the real teaching
was done by Tom Evans and Andy Maluke. This new found enthusiasm carried over
when a new head coach, Mr. Joseph McMullen, took over from Cochrane in 1954.

McMullen was an extrovert who saw football as a means of teaching young men
to live a disciplined life. His expectations were high and as long as he had good
material to work with his teams performed well. His first team (1954) was the last
Akron team to play arch-rival Kent State. The Flashes won 58–18, but Akron had a

series edge of 11 wins and 9 losses. The explosive 1955 club ran up tremendous scores against Otterbein, Wooster, Mount Union, Oberlin and soundly thrashed Wittenberg and Denison, but Heidelberg and Muskingum were too tough to handle. It took a heady ball player to execute the timing and subtle blocking assignments of the McMullen system. When it worked, it was beautiful; but as every coach knows only too well, there are times when nothing clicks and when this happened McMullen's teams lacked that nose-in-the-dirt drive that sometimes salvages the day when fancier things go wrong.

His successor was an apostle of hard-nosed football. Gordon Larson was familiar with the kind of athlete required for the "three yards and a cloud of dust" football taught by one of his mentors, Woody Hayes of Ohio State. Larson sought out those who could play this brand of ball, but as his players improved in quality he changed to a more exciting style of play. Football fortunes, that had ebbed under McMullen to the point where by 1960 only a win over Wooster brightened an otherwise all-losing season, took a dramatic turn for the better under Coach Larson. His 1961 squad won them all except for a pair of 7–0 losses to Wittenberg and Baldwin Wallace. As of this writing, Larson has never had a losing season although the schedule has become much more demanding. His 1968 team played the toughest schedule ever faced by an Akron team, and its exciting play was rewarded by a trip to the Grantland Rice Bowl where the Zips lost to a strong Louisiana Tech team in a snowstorm. Four members of that squad, Don Zwisler, Dan Ruff, Ken Delaney, and Tony Pallija won Little All-American recognition, the first to do so since John Verdon was recognized in 1954.

One would expect the improved football fortunes of the Akron Zips to be reflected at the gate. Attendance improved modestly from a postwar low, but not in proportion to the increased enrollment. A crowd of 5,000 was an event. All too often games in the Rubber Bowl drew a "crowd" of about 2,500, not all of them paid, where they felt completely overwhelmed by the great empty reaches of the stadium. Attempts to ameliorate this condition by playing a limited number of home games at Clifford Stadium in Cuyahoga Falls or in the Barberton Stadium helped to improve crowd psychology even if it did little to improve total attendance. But one of the many efforts to draw a crowd was successful indeed.

In 1954, "Red" Cochrane, President Auburn, and key men from the Acme stores and from the *Beacon Journal* inaugurated a football promotion that has become the most successful sustained venture of its kind in the nation. The "Acme-Zip" game which they created gave fans a full evening of entertainment for a pittance—buy one ticket for a dollar and get another free. The evening's program started at 4:30 with a soccer match featuring some of the best teams in the country contesting with the perennially strong Akron teams; then came a steady succession of crack high school bands, float parade, sweetheart parade, Shrine and Grotto marching units, Boy Scouts, fireworks, the Akron marching band, and virtually anything else that was handy. Those hardy souls who arrived for the beginning of the soccer match could look forward to seven hours of excitement and entertainment culminated by the football game.

Acme-Zip quickly became a tradition in the community. Any number of local groups staged dinners before the game and then took special buses to the Rubber Bowl. The 23,769 fans who witnessed the first Acme-Zip game in 1954 were joined by others in succeeding years until an all-time attendance record of 43,068 was set for the Rubber Bowl in 1968. All told, some 522,119 persons have attended this contest and the Acme Stores have paid a total of $213,333 to the University (through 1968) in support of scholarships and of its athletic program. Part of the game's popularity in recent years stems from the outstanding performances put on by Larson's teams, the most memorable being a bitterly fought 6–6 tie with Western Kentucky and a 6–0 Zip victory over a tough Tampa team that was considered out of Akron's class.

Basketball maintained the preeminence that it had won in the affection of Akron sports fans. It was identified in the public mind as "Akron's game." After Russ Beichly's impressive coaching career was cut short by illness, his assistant, Anthony

"Tony" Laterza took charge, and the Zips continued on their winning ways. Laterza had much talent at his disposal, most of it consisting of local athletes, for Akron was a hotbed of basketball enthusiasm and it annually produced a bumper crop of talented high school players. The availability of Memorial Hall which could seat 3,200 fans comfortably, and more in a crisis, had a healthy effect on the basketball program. When the great winning teams of the 1960's were in top form, more seats by the thousand could have been sold had they been available.

While the basketball fans of the late 1950's would probably remember the games with Duquesne as the season's high point, later student generations would identify Wittenberg as the team that stimulated the spectator's adrenalin. Perhaps the most dramatic moment in Akron basketball came in the waning moments of the 1964–1965 season. Akron held a slim lead over the incomparable Wittenberg Tigers, scourge of small college basketball and number one college division team in the nation. As the final seconds ticked away, the super-capacity crowd was far from confident since this same team had beaten the Zips 58–38 earlier in the season. With Akron leading 52–51, the Tigers put up a final shot that could have won it all, but Randy Berentz blocked it, the buzzer sounded and hysteria swept Memorial Hall as the Zips claimed the Ohio Conference championship. The new battle cry "NCAA, Akron all the way" would be chanted endlessly until the finals of the NCAA College Division tournament at Evansville, Indiana. In the 1965 championship game, Evansville beat Akron. But for Billy Stevens, Frank Thompson, Randy Berentz, Junior Carroll and their teammates, it had been an unforgettable season. It marked the first of three straight trips that Akron cagers were to make to the national tournament at Evansville as Ohio Conference champions. Never in Akron athletic history had there been such a prolonged period of success as occurred while All-America Bill Turner and his teammates, Don "Stuff" Williams, Frank Thompson, Jerry Sloan, Bobby Smith, and Ken Mackovic were in charge. One may be skeptical about the contribution of athletics to student morale, but the annual "Evansville fever" convinced many erstwhile skeptics that *winning* teams can do much for campus life.

If it is winning teams that the fans like, Akron provided them consistently in two of the so-called minor sports. Most interesting was the development of soccer as a varsity sport. Credit for this goes to Mr. W. Stuver Parry, a former player at Oberlin and an Akron alumnus, who, with the support of "Red" Cochrane, took initiative to form a team, build a schedule, and introduce Akron to a new sport in which the Zips quickly established a winning tradition. It was particularly fortunate that many foreign students found in soccer an outlet through which they could excel. Akron has dominated the sport in Ohio winning the Ohio Collegiate Soccer Association crown nine times in the 11 years from 1958 through 1968. For a while, home games were played in the dramatic setting of Stan Hywet Hall, whose tudor facade and wide green lawns seemed most appropriate to the colorful contest. Home games are now played on Jackson Field. Success in this sport on the Hilltop gave a tremendous boost to soccer interest in area high schools.

In soccer, Akron played with major college and university teams and entered the NCAA university-level post-season competition. Michigan State was the Zips' nemesis in this tournament, having knocked them out of title contention three times. In 1968, Parry's finest team handed Michigan State its only defeat of the season, making the Zips number one in the midwest. The Spartans got revenge, however, with a 2–1 victory in the NCAA tournament. It was Akron's only loss of the season. A number of All-Americas graced Parry's teams. Fritz Kungl was honored three times and Pete Milich, Ford Brunner, and Joe Queiroga were chosen twice for the honor. Ed Long, Ed Bender, Walt Kruppa, and Jim Malcolm were others who won this coveted recognition.

The second "minor" sport in which Zip preeminence was consistent was Riflery. Not a particularly popular sport, it was taken seriously by local enthusiasts. The Lake Erie Conference, organized in 1951, quickly became a Zip monopoly. In 1955–1956 they not only swept the conference, but they also won the National Intercollegiate Tournament at Buffalo. With All-America Robert McMillan leading the way, the riflers won 87 of 88 matches over a four-year span. A two time All-America, Jack

Jones, led the 1967–68 squads, but it was a pretty coed, Jean Linton, who was perhaps Akron's best publicized All-America shooter although she must have wearied of the inevitable references to her as another Annie Oakley.

On many campuses, baseball is the outstanding spring sport, but not on the Hilltop. Poor weather was the special bane of the baseballers. Akron produced outstanding individual players, but it was an exceptional season when the team had a good record. Lefty Dave Young, Ray Glinsky, and Jim Barton were great pitching prospects, but there was never enough depth to produce conference champions. Coach Russ Beichly brought his fiery competitiveness to the task and brought some winning seasons.

Track dominated the intercollegiate scene in the spring. Like the baseball coach and the mentors of the other "minor" sports, Coach Tom Evans had practically no financial assistance to award promising trackmen. He was in the position of having to make do with the talent that gravitated to the Hilltop or, in some cases, with talent recruited primarily for football or basketball.

It is unlikely that any other college track team in the nation suffered the peculiar disadvantage experienced by the Zips. Their practice track at Buchtel Field was more a rectangle than an oval! The curves were nearly ninety degrees. Just how well Akron's sprinters and hurdlers could have performed if they had had a proper track to train on will never be known, but some campus observers theorize that their splendid showing on foreign tracks was the result of the sheer joy and exuberance they experienced from running on a regulation track. When, after much delay, a fine all-weather track was completed at Jackson Field, the team had facilities as good as any in the state, and it remains to be seen whether or not they can stand prosperity as well as they stood adversity.

Coach Evans had the talent and know-how to take men who had been number two in their event in high school and make them number one in collegiate competition. His success in having his team ready for every test was remarkable. In 1961–64, the team went through 28 dual meets undefeated. They swept the Ohio Conference title in 1961, '62, '63, '65, '66 and won the NCAA Mideast Regionals in 1962 and 1963. Among his many standouts, Evans tutored Gary Flinn, Alex Adams, Climon Lee and Bill Heideman to outstanding careers. (Adams, Lee, and Heideman also excelled in basketball.)

The Zips were never a sustained threat in swimming, where they lacked the team depth needed for championships. Memorial Hall's pool gave the swimmers a fine place to practice and compete, and many strong individual performers swam for the Blue and Gold including All-Americas Pete Boggs, Paul Boggs, and two-time winners Pat McDonald and Ed Steinmetz.

In tennis, Coach Bill Beyer suffered his ups and downs. Without home courts for practice and competition until the completion of the superb setup at Jackson Field in 1967, the tennis men had to fight an uphill battle for recognition. The increased popularity of the sport plus fine new facilities promise well for future Zip teams.

Tony Laterza's golf teams were always tough. They were Ohio Conference champions in 1957, 1958, and 1961. They always performed creditably seldom finishing very far behind the leader. In all-Ohio competition the team turned in a number of creditable performances. Like the baseballers, they got into shape with a southern trip during spring recess, for Akron weather was the frustration of spring sports enthusiasts and put Zip teams at a disadvantage in competition with teams that could train in better weather, and this included most of those from the southern portion of the state.

Wrestling, like track, is a sport in which Zip teams have been uniformly strong year in and year out. It too has grown in popularity, and the wrestlers who used to perform for themselves alone in the forties and early fifties suddenly discovered that people were in the stands watching the matches and that these spectators knew some of the finer points. Coach Andy Maluke knew what it took to produce good wrestlers, and he had a knack for getting top performance. The wrestlers won the Ohio Conference title in 1954, '55, and '58, and never finished very far down in the pack. Among the many outstanding grapplers were Ohio Conference champions Mario Russo, Grover Miller, and All-America Pete Guthrie (1965).

Cross Country was another sport in which the Zips excelled. The Akron area produced a large number of outstanding cross country men probably because it was a competition of long standing in Akron high schools, and while many of the top high school performers cast their lot with other schools, enough remained to give the Zips balance and depth. Most successful of coaches was Al Hall whose teams won the Ohio Conference title in 1962, '63, and '65, and in 1963 went on to finish second nationally. Several of the cross country men, George Weatherbee, Charles Young, and Bill Painter among them, were strong performers for the track team as well.

Lacrosse was given a brief trial as a varsity sport in 1955. Under Coach Joe McMullen's watchful eye the green Akron boys started to learn this rugged game, but it did not catch on and after a few seasons it disappeared from the scene.

Although not organized on an intercollegiate basis, women's sports activities have flourished under the sponsorship of the Women's Athletic Association. They sponsored day-long meets which brought together women from many schools for participation in athletic events. High school girls were also encouraged to participate in special activities designed for their interest.

Intramurals were better organized once Memorial Hall became available. A student commissioner was appointed to oversee scheduling and the many other problems associated with this large program. While fraternity teams continued to supply the backbone for intramurals, an increasing number of independent teams appeared, making the IM program more truly a university-wide activity.

A milestone was reached for the intercollegiate program when, on September 1, 1966, Akron's long association with the Ohio Athletic Conference came to an end. For some years several of the weaker schools athletically had been reluctant to schedule Akron although the stronger ones had competed on very even terms with the Zips. The feeling of 30 years earlier that Akron was the "odd man" in the conference was intensified by her state status. Once it became clear that it would be practically impossible to secure a decent schedule within the conference, "Red" Cochrane and his associates started to investigate the alternatives. The "precipitating cause" of Akron's withdrawal was the conference's "insistence" that Akron adopt the College Scholarship Service form as the basis for determining grants in aid to athletes.[27] Akron felt that this so-called "Princeton Form" would be too restrictive; the form seemed better geared to meet the needs of private, selective colleges than public universities. This parting was amicable. Speaking on behalf of the conference, Dr. Dwight W. Berg of Hiram, President of the Ohio Athletic Conference, wrote of his "sincere appreciation for Akron's long association with and total support of the philosophy of the OAC."[28]

As Akron approaches her one hundredth year she is faced with some severe problems in her intercollegiate athletic program. The major problems, the expense of intercollegiate sports and lack of a conference affiliation, are interrelated. While a member of the Ohio Conference, Akron was assured of competing with schools which spent no more on athletics than she, schools which were compactly situated thus minimizing travel costs, and schools that were accustomed to small attendance at games and were thus satisfied with an unusually low guarantee for expenses. As an independent, all these costs soared. By 1967–1968, Akron was spending $300,000 to maintain an athletic program that promised to bring in no more than $75,000 in receipts. It cost each Akron student about $22.50 a year to underwrite varsity athletics. While this appeared high, it was actually modest in comparison with similar schools. Kent students had to pay about $25 apiece to finance that school's program while Toledo students paid $32 each. Akron was unique in taking money for varsity athletics from a variety of budgetary sources whereas most Ohio universities took money for athletics from the general fund only. As a state school, Akron had to keep alert to the sentiments of the Board of Regents which in recent years had started to question the amount of money state schools put into athletics. One of the Regents said "we were searching for non-academic cost areas that could be cut—and athletics stood out like a sore thumb." There is concern that Akron will not soon find affiliation in a conference it can afford. If this is true, some of her happiest days in intercollegiate sport may be behind her.[29] However, in the light of recent experience under President Auburn's leadership, it would be foolish to bet on it.

NOTES

[1] *Beacon Journal,* Jan. 14, 1955.

[2] *Ibid.,* Sept. 1, 1955.

[3] *Ibid.,* Jan. 17, 1955; Board Mins., VII, 27.

[4] *Ibid., XIII, 14; Beacon Journal,* Jan. 17, 1962.

[5] Board Mins., XII, 291.

[6] Cherrington to Auburn, Sept. 28, 1951, in UArch., box 21/1/161. See also Dean's Committee Mins., Dec. 7, 1951, Sept. 22, 1952.

[7] Same to same, May 12, 1952, *ibid.*

[8] *Buchtelite,* Jan. 8, 1954.

[9] *Beacon Journal,* June 21, 1957.

[10] *University Bulletin,* March 6, 1956.

[11] *Beacon Journal,* June 5, 1957.

[12] *Ibid.,* June 6, August 4, 1957.

[13] Conversation with author, ca. Sept., 1957.

[14] Administrative Committee Mins., Feb. 5, 1962, in UArch., box 4/10c/52.

[15] *University Bulletin,* May 6, 1960.

[16] *Beacon Journal,* Jan. 8, 1965.

[17] *Buchtelite,* Sept. 25, 1951.

[18] *Ibid.,* Feb. 12, 1952.

[19] Philip E. Jacob, *Changing Values in College; An Exploratory Study of the Impact of College Teaching* (New York, 1957), p. 58.

[20] *Beacon Journal,* Nov. 27, 1955.

[21] *Ibid.,* Feb. 1, 1956.

[22] Board Mins., VII, 42, 116; Administrative Committee Mins., Sept. 5, 1961.

[23] Board Mins., VII, 20.

[24] *Ibid.,* VIII, 169–70.

[25] *Ibid.*

[26] *Ibid.,* XXII, 479, 485–86.

[27] *Ibid.,* XVIII, 15.

[28] *Ibid.,* p. 16.

[29] *Beacon Journal,* July 1, 1968.

Norman Paul Auburn Science and Engineering Center

Board of Trustees (1968), from left standing, D. J. Guzzetta, Provost, Paul Belcher, Howard Fort, Ben Maidenburg, Joseph Leyden, President Auburn. Seated, from the left, Lisle Buckingham, Joseph Thomas, Chairman Harry P. Schrank, J. Thomas, Arthur Kelly

Artist's conception showing Edwin J. Thomas Performing Arts Hall as planned (1969).

XXV

Adjusting to a wider role

President Auburn greeted the faculty at the beginning of the 1967 academic year with the observation that it was "a good time to 'go state.' "[1] Appropriations for state universities for 1967–68 were 82 percent above the previous biennium, a fact, said the president, that demonstrated Ohio's "determination to increase its support of public higher education."[2] Ironically, at this moment when the financial picture appeared brighter than ever before, the University found itself short of ready cash.

The Board of Trustees was informed at its December meeting that there was a deficit in the operating budget of nearly one million dollars.[3] Although the total University budget was some $3,500,000 above the previous year, a considerable amount of spending had taken place in anticipation of state status, and now the bills had to be paid. The precipitating causes of the deficit, however, were the need to pay the State Teacher's Retirement system some $425,000 which had carried over from the previous year, delay in collection of $250,000 in city tax funds, and the extra "startup" costs of converting to state status. Trustee Ben Maidenburg warned against the temptation to view the state as a big cornucopia of funds. "Perhaps this indicates we have been dreaming of a white Christmas and it isn't going to snow at all," he said.[4]

Tight new budgetary controls were immediately put into effect in an effort to hold the deficit, but it was apparent that additional funds would be required to reduce it expeditiously. Akron had not raised student fees since 1964, and the trustees were reluctant to take this course; nevertheless, the Board of Regents was now approached for approval of an increase. Virtually every other state university also found it necessary to ask for fee increases in 1967–68, but Akron's administration moved so quickly that its request was granted, while those of other institutions which acted more slowly were stalled. This vigorous assault on the problem was responsible for progressive reduction of the deficit until it was completely eliminated by the end of the fiscal year 1969.[5]

It is difficult to cut back an operation at any time, but it becomes especially difficult when it interrupts an expansive and optimistic mood. It was vital to the University's continued growth that the faculty be assured that their interests were secure. While it was possible to survive temporary cuts in equipment, travel, library, and other essential budget items, it was unlikely that the professionally mobile members of the faculty would consent to stay long at Akron if their salary schedule were seriously interrupted. Thus it was that President Auburn pledged regular salary increases, and this promise was redeemed, thereby keeping on the Hilltop many key persons who would have been difficult to replace.[6] The new salary schedule for 1968–69 kept Akron in good competitive position with average salaries ranging from $8,161 for instructors, to $15,491 for full professors; and, of course, the University contributed an additional 16 percent in compensation for pension, insurance, and health plans.[7] Some 52 percent of the total University budget (1968–69) went for instructional salaries and benefits.[8]

As had been true from the time Norman Auburn first came to Akron, a substantial amount of money was committed to physical expansion and improvement of the campus. Its location adjacent to the city's central business district made land acquisition very costly. Urban renewal had been used to good effect with the Jackson Field project (R-30), but a second attempt to employ this program—the University Concourse project (R-104)—ran into difficulties and delays. R-104 was designed to clear an area bounded by East Exchange, Sumner, Center, Hill, Forge, and Broadway. The federal government delayed the project because of its concern that the residents of the area would be unable to secure adequate replacement housing, but, by the winter of 1969, it appeared once more that the project might be funded. It was especially important to the University that this project move ahead, for it was to provide a physical tie between the campus and the community. A broad concourse would span the railroad tracks between the civic center to the west and the new Center for the Performing Arts that was to rise on the eastern end of the concourse.

The Edwin J. Thomas Performing Arts Hall, for which ground was broken July 30, 1969, will provide a fine facility to be shared by the University and the community for the staging of concerts, plays, ballet, and other civic and University events. The building's location—as close to the center city as possible—is visual evidence that the center was designed with the community's interests in mind. Neither Memorial Hall nor the Akron Armory were suitable places for artistic performances, and once the University indicated a willingness to take leadership in obtaining funds and providing management for an auditorium a number of interested parties in the community were ready to donate to the cause. The solicitation of funds was carried out as the major item in the University's centennial fund raising effort known as "Challenge '70." Under the direction of Mr. E. C. "Ted" McCormick, Jr., and with the effective assistance of Mr. James Banks, Challenge '70 planned to raise $10,000,000 in private money by 1970; of that sum approximately $6,000,000 was earmarked for the Edwin J. Thomas Performing Arts Hall, which would make it the costliest building ever erected by private funds on a state campus in Ohio.

Also included in the Challenge '70 fund was $500,000 for the renovation of Buchtel Hall. An alumni campaign under the chairmanship of Mr. Russell DeYoung sought to raise this money. Still another portion of the Challenge '70 fund was to be used for the establishment of endowed chairs, for student scholarships, and for library collections.

Gifts to Challenge '70 were received through The University of Akron Development Foundation, a separate corporation founded June 2, 1966, and created for the benefit of the University. A public university is hard put to do all that it needs to do out of tax money. There are many occasions that require expenditures other than public money, and the institution has to be free from the restraints rightfully placed upon its expenditure of public money. Tax funds and student fees provide only the necessities and leave nothing for certain supportive activities that enhance the University's effectiveness. One of the most successful sources of "private" money was the annual Alumni Fund drive which, by 1969, was bringing in over $100,000 a year, a very creditable record indeed for a university of Akron's size and character.

While the progress of Challenge '70 and the Performing Arts Hall held center stage, desperately needed space was secured through the acquisition of Spicer School which was promptly renamed Spicer Hall and converted into an office building housing the business offices, the registrar, evening and summer sessions, ICE, General College counseling, and many other activities. Additionally, remodeling of Ayer, Knight, and Kolbe Halls at a cost of approximately $1,500,000 converted those buildings into efficient and pleasant work areas. And as always, many new parking spaces were added. By the end of fiscal 1968, the value of the physical plant was $46,787,171 on a campus of 71 acres, which contrasted with a value of $5,601,000 for 22 acres a decade earlier.[9]

There is no question that state status provided the financial resources that made continued growth possible. While recognizing that this was necessary and desirable some persons lamented that the old freedom of operation had been lost. The directors of the Municipal University had been answerable to no one in determining University policy. The legal restraints under which they conducted the University's business rested rather lightly upon the operation. From 1963, when Akron received state assistance, the Board experienced the first modest limitations upon its freedom of action. As defined in the law, the Ohio Board of Regents was charged with presenting to the Ohio legislature the budget requests of state and state-assisted schools and with approving all new degree programs at those schools. Despite these severely limited powers, the regents, under their aggressive Chancellor, Dr. John Millett, were soon asserting their wishes in a variety of additional areas. Each of these moves imposed a degree of uniformity among the state schools and each resulted in additional constraints upon the freedom of action of the boards of those schools. Among these moves, none caused more unhappiness than that which fastened the "quarter system" upon every state institution of higher education.

Several of the largest public universities in Ohio (Ohio State, Kent State, and Cincinnati) were already on the quarter system in 1966 when the regents proposed a uniform calendar for state schools. The regents argued that it would give them a uniform base on which to report information on enrollments, budgets, etc., to the state legislature, and that it would facilitate student transfers among various units of the state system. Those institutions on the semester or "trimester" calendars questioned the need for change in order to attain these goals. It appeared to many faculty members and students that a decision which directly affected the academic process was being imposed for administrative convenience. The faculties were particularly distressed because the boards and administrations of several of the schools publicly stated their intention of complying before the faculties had a chance to express their sentiments on the wisdom of the move. Chancellor Millett explained that no one was to be "forced" to go on the quarter system but, of course, the system used by the regents for calculating the amount of money each institution would receive was so ordered that those which were not on the quarter system were to lose several hundred thousands of dollars for their independence. No board of trustees of a public university can afford to leave itself open to the charge that it is passing up that much money over a calendar matter, and so each school fell into line.

Akron listened attentively to the proposed change. Although it would have been more comfortable to say yes immediately to the regents' proposal, the administration and Board delayed in order that all alternatives could be studied. A resolution from the faculty of the Buchtel College of Liberal Arts alerted the trustees to the faculty's concern with the change. The faculty had little argument with the assertion that the quarter system might lend itself as well to the instructional process as the semester system (although many were strongly predisposed toward the semester system), but they were concerned that the tactics used by the regents and the chancellor appeared coercive and that a decision of significant academic importance was forced on grounds that seemed non-essential.

Since Akron would not become a full-fledged state university until July 1, 1967, it would embarrass the Board to resist the regents' lead, so the directors moved cautiously toward compliance. Nevertheless, at the urging of the faculty and the provost, President Auburn recommended that the Board delay any change in the academic calendar until such time as it could be done efficiently and smoothly. On October 19, 1966, the Board of Directors unanimously adopted the following resolution:

> *That the University should take the necessary steps to convert the academic calendar to a quarter system to become effective on September 1, 1967, but that the University will not necessarily convert to the quarter system on that date, unless it receives an official directive from properly constituted authority to do so.*[10]

When it became evident that the calendar could not be changed by September, 1967, without risk of serious disruptions, the directors voted to adopt the quarter system in September, 1968. The great amount of care and planning that went into this conversion was possible only because local leadership refused to allow premature change. It should be emphasized that Akron was not alone in experiencing the power of the regents to affect them in ways not indicated (and not intended?) in the law. It was a new experience for the established state schools as well, and, as it proved, it was but a foretaste of what was to come. Whether or not one agrees with centralized control over public higher education, any move in this direction takes Akron away from its historic independence. But most observers would appear to assess the situation much as President Auburn did at the general faculty meeting in October, 1968:

> *On balance, I am convinced that we have gained far more from state status than we have lost by coming under the aegis of the Board of Regents.*[11]

The state scene in Ohio was enlivened during the fall and winter of 1968–69 by pronouncements emanating from Columbus. This commentary—from the Governor's office, the state legislature, and the Board of Regents—was precipitated by the strains of attempting to provide adequately in the 1969–71 state budget, the money needed for higher education. An additional complicating factor was the heavy emphasis Governor Rhodes placed on vocational education, both on the secondary and the post-high school levels.

The state university presidents were distressed, some publicly, some privately, at the tendency of the Board of Regents to defend the state legislature at the seeming expense of the universities. "Put yourself in the position of those people over in the legislature," said the regents' chairman; "People don't like to pay taxes and legislators like to get reelected."[12] However, the Ohio Board of Regents was set up to represent the universities' interests to the legislature and not the reverse. And when the regents, without prior approval of the institutions, proposed that student fees be raised approximately $150 a year to a ceiling of $750, and that out-of-state students receive no form of state subsidy, several presidents and boards spoke in opposition to the idea. In a talk to state legislators and executive officers President Auburn said, "You will have to ask yourselves if, since education is an economic asset to the state, it would not be better for the state to assume a larger share of the rising costs to students at Ohio's universities."[13] It is interesting that the president could apply to the state, with equal validity, the same argument that had long been used to encourage the city to contribute to the support of the Municipal University, and one can imagine Parke Kolbe, George Zook, and Hezzleton Simmons breathing a silent "amen" to his argument that a public university is a civic investment which redounds to the selfish benefit of the entire community, be it a city or a state or a nation. At this writing, this issue, and many others that bear on the well being of the institution, are still being debated in Columbus and around the state.

While administrative efforts and liaison with the state pre-empted much time and attention on the Akron campus, there was growing concern that the wave of student unrest so characteristic in the late 1960's of certain California schools, some eastern universities, and one or two major midwestern universities would become more generalized. Ohio had experienced two or three relatively minor attempts by dissident student minorities to disrupt campus activities in order to coerce administrations into making concessions. The two principal moving forces appeared to be the Students for Democratic Society (SDS) and black student pressure organized on some campuses as Black United Students (BUS).

Fearing that the state universities were insufficiently prepared to meet these challenges, the Ohio General Assembly enacted a bill requiring the trustees of each state school to adopt rules governing conduct on university property and defining a number of activities specifically prohibited. Akron's Board complied in June, 1968, when it adopted such rules along with a code of Student Disciplinary Procedures. This code was reviewed and revised during the academic year 1968–69, and Akron was thereby prepared to defend University interests while guaranteeing careful and just procedures in pursuing charges brought against students for alleged misconduct in violation of University rules and regulations. Of special concern in formulating this code was a desire to protect as much of the counseling orientation of University disciplinary practices as possible, but it was evident that in a more militant society such an approach had to be supported by formal codes.

Another important feature of student life at the close of the decade was the interest in securing student representation on University committees and other bodies that formulated policies bearing on the student. It was a pleasant surprise to most who urged greater student participation when Governor Rhodes proposed putting one student and one faculty member on the board of trustees of each state university. Rhodes had in mind non-voting members who would serve to improve communication between faculty and students on the one hand, and the administration and board on the other.[14] Dr. Auburn went the governor one better by urging that the student and faculty representatives be voting members.[15] It is of considerable interest to all to see whether this idea is implemented.

While representation on the Board was being debated, a significant breakthrough was made in another important area. After years of frustration in effecting reform, University Council was reorganized on an elective basis, and provision was made for four student representatives to sit and vote on this key legislative body.[16] In addition, students were appointed to many of the University's standing committees. The president supported the representative principle, but representation alone guarantees nothing, and only time will tell how effectively the faculty and students employ their new opportunities to contribute to University development; but that vital first step has been taken.

To put all of these innovations into effect while carrying on the heavy day-to-day work load placed a heavy demand on many administrative officers. The key person in the administrative group was clearly Dr. Dominic J. Guzzetta whose excellent work was recognized in August, 1966, when the Board appointed him to the new position of Senior Vice-President and Provost. He continued his "splendid service to the University" until February, 1968 at which time he left to assume the presidency of Marian College in Indiana. He was widely liked and admired, personally and professionally, and the University felt keenly the loss of his quick intelligence, his knowledge about current trends in education, his approachability, and his contagious enthusiasm to advance the cause of The University of Akron.

Some of Guzzetta's vice-presidential duties were assumed by Dr. Arthur K. Brintnall who came to the University as Dean of Administration, and then served briefly as Graduate Dean and Acting Dean of the College of Business Administration before succeeding Guzzetta as Vice-President for Academic Affairs (the position was restructured and the title Provost dropped). Dr. Brintnall's steady competence proved most valuable during the period of adjustment to state status. Concurrent with this change, Mr. R. Wayne Duff was appointed Financial Vice-President while Dr. Ian MacGregor shifted roles to become Vice-President for Planning. Dr. MacGregor retained his position as Secretary of the Board of Trustees. A new position, Director of Institutional Research, was created in 1968 and Dr. Charles Poston was asked to develop that responsibility which had as one of its principal functions the accurate and timely reporting of data to the Ohio Board of Regents and other appropriate bodies.

In the academic colleges, Dr. George W. Knepper relinquished the deanship of the Buchtel College of Liberal Arts in June, 1967, in order to resume his teaching role. He was succeeded by Dr. Don A. Keister, Professor of English and long-time member of the faculty. Dean Keister's sharp intelligence clarified many knotty issues, and the arts and sciences continued to make significant progress through a period of great change. Both profited from the able work of the Associate Dean, Dr. Paul Wingard. Meanwhile, in 1968 Dr. Edwin Lively, Professor of Sociology, was appointed Dean of the Graduate School. He immediately set out to focus more effectively the burgeoning efforts in this important portion of the University's work. A particular concern was the need to enhance the research program, and responsibility for this was shared by his Assistant Dean, Dr. Robert Carson.

Direction of the University's adult and continuing education effort changed during this period when Dr. William Rogers, Dean of the Evening College, switched administrative roles; first to become Dean of Administration *vice* Dr. Brintnall, and then Dean of Summer Sessions and Off-Campus Academic Programs. Mr. Charles Blair, Director of the Institute for Civic Education took over the Evening College deanship.

In the College of Education, Dean Kenneth Barker was ably assisted by his Associate Dean, Dr. John Watt. Barker had a second role as Dean of International Programs, a role that indicated the extent of Akron's commitment to international education. For many years the University had been actively involved with the "international dimension"—in its work with the Regional Council for International Education, its programs for water resource engineers funded through the Agency for International Development (AID), its college and community ambassador projects, and in scores of additional ways. President Auburn had a keen interest in this activity. He had made numerous study trips to countries around the world, particularly behind the "Iron Curtain." In 1965, he served in Washington as Special Assistant for University Relations to the Administrator, David E. Bell, in the Agency for International Development for the Department of State. In announcing Dean Barker's appointment, the president had said that Akron, "as a cosmopolitan center" whose industries had "vast involvements overseas," had more than "normal interest in the international dimension of higher education."[17] In short, while the University was struggling with local problems it did not lose sight of the broader arena to which it contributed.

It is obviously beyond the capacity of the historian to assess with unerring accuracy the credit and blame, the praise and censure that accrue to human activities within a complex social institution. It is easy and natural to attribute both the plusses and the minuses of the operation to one person—in the case of a university, to the president. Like the conductor of an orchestra, he takes the public bows for the splendid accomplishments of an ensemble; but he also takes much of the criticism when things go wrong. So it was with Norman Auburn.

It should be evident at this stage of the narrative that he was extraordinarily successful in the presidency. It would be an injustice to point to any one characteristic or talent and say that his success rested on that point alone, yet an editorial writer of the *Beacon Journal* probably came close to the mark when he wrote a flattering assessment of Auburn under the lead "He Gets Things Done."[18] The evidence was overwhelming. (In an unprecedented action, the Board of Trustees, in July, 1969, extended Dr. Auburn's contract for a year beyond normal retirement date, August 31, 1970, with option to renew the contract annually through 1975—a supreme vote of confidence in his talents and accomplishments.)

Since Dr. Auburn's arrival in 1951, Akron has been transformed. In some ways —size and complexity of offerings, for instance—the transformation was as radical as that of 1913. From a wholly inadequate operating budget of $1,147,516 (1951), resting on a narrow municipal tax base, the University now operates on a budget of $19,173,000 (1969-70) which rests on a secure state base. This is the basic truth on which all other evidences of University growth rest. Other gross figures are equally impressive: the value of plant and campus rose from $5,700,000 (1951) to almost $54,000,000 (1969); endowment increased from $165,000 (1951) to about $2,335,000 (1969); alumni giving, scholarship funds, gifts in kind, and many other avenues of support for the University were developed successfully. Perhaps one of the best measures of growth in quality was the strong, self-confident staff that had been assembled; and the fact that Akron's faculty salaries ranked most favorably with those of comparable institutions was a source of great satisfaction to Dr. Auburn. His consistent determination to keep this development a first priority paid off in quality of staff and low rate of turnover.

The 1950's and 60's were prosperous decades for the nation and for Akron, and it is reasonable to assume that some growth and development of the University was inevitable during those years. Certain it was that some public universities prospered despite what appeared to be rather inept leadership, but it does not follow that Akron's progress was assured no matter what the quality of her leadership. The painful step-by-step escalation of financial support won between 1951 and 1967 was the result of masterful planning and vigorous execution. It is inconceivable that it could have happened accidentally as a sort of by-product of a prosperous time.

It was President Auburn who practically forced Akronites to reconsider their attitudes toward the University. Once they saw, with growing pride, what could be accomplished in the public sector of Akron's economy through vigorous University leadership, their response to other sorely needed public improvements became more positive. Public officials were inclined to use the University as an example of what could be accomplished; its new buildings were cited by Mayor Erickson and his associates in support of their goal of redeveloping much of downtown Akron. This thriving campus development right on the edge of the core city has remained a powerful stimulus to new construction in the downtown sector.

When a later historian turns his attention to the Akron story some years hence he will give due praise to John R. Buchtel and to Parke R. Kolbe for their part in guiding Buchtel College and The University of Akron through formative periods, and certain it is that he will add the name of Norman Auburn to form a worthy triumvirate of those who could "get things done." It detracts nothing from hundreds of other deserving people to single out these three as the guiding spirits of the private College, the Municipal University, and the State University.

Was there any philosophic position around which The University of Akron (state) could organize its programs and policies comparable to the focus formerly provided by the municipal university ideal? It is still too early to determine with confidence just what the answer to that question will be. The land grant universities had a specific charge that determined rather well the role they were to play. State normal colleges knew their role. But what of the institution lately come to the role of state university? Could it exert equal claim with the land grant university to a position of statewide influence? And what of its sister institutions and their equally strong claims? It is evident that, once having stepped clear of the municipal corporation line, The University of Akron would require time to find the perimeters of its new area for service. Not that it was reluctant to stake a claim. In May, 1966, President Auburn reported to the faculty and to the Board: "Our aim is to respond to the educational and research needs of the people of this rapidly expanding quadrant of northeastern Ohio."[19] But the existence nearby—in northeastern Ohio alone—of three other comprehensive state universities, two community colleges, and a number of two-year and four-year university branches meant that efforts to exert territorial rights immediately ran afoul of competing interests.

That Akron's interest was now statewide was evident by the increasing enrollment of Ohio students from outside commuting distance, by her support from state tax monies on a par with every other four-year institution, by her need to explain her mission to state legislators rather than Akron legislators (although the latter were kept well-advised of university plans), by her concern with the direction of leadership provided by the Ohio Board of Regents and the Governor's office, by her cooperation in state services and her participation in promulgating state issues, and by her modest removal for the necessity of accommodating every local interest that could influence local elections.

In an effort to define The University of Akron's role as a state university more effectively, President Auburn urged the establishment of a study group whose charge was to chart its course through the decade of the seventies and beyond. It was hoped that this group could emulate the successful work of the Forecast Committee, but its task would be more difficult since the familiar guidelines within which the earlier group operated were now blurred. Accordingly, in the fall of 1967, a Commission on Centennial Goals and Projections was established to "chart the course" for years to come. Its eight committees—academic development, faculty matters, student affairs, research and scholarly investigation, public service, campus facilities, university development, budget and finance—were comprised of board members, administrative officers, faculty members, students, alumni, and citizens of Akron, more than 150 persons in all. As with the earlier Forecast Committee, financial support for the study was received from the Akron Community Trusts, this time in the amount of $33,500, some of which was used for the consulting services of Heald, Hobson, and Associates of New York.

It is fitting to close an account of past achievement on a note that suggests one of the central truths about Buchtel College and the University of Akron. They never became fossilized. Since the private College, the Municipal University, and the State University all responded to the pulse of Akron, the institutional rhythm moved with the changing course of events in a rapidly changing city. Challenge and response may be the condition of civilization as Professor Arnold Toynbee has postulated; there is no question that it describes the life of The University of Akron, already engrossed in preparing to meet tomorrow's need.

NOTES

[1] *University Bulletin*, Sept. 14, 1967.

[2] *Ibid.*

[3] *Beacon Journal*, Dec. 21, 1967.

[4] *Ibid.*, Dec. 20, 21, 1967.

[5] *Ibid.*

[6] *Ibid.*, Dec. 20, 1967.

[7] Auburn to Faculty, Nov. 21, 1968.

[8] C. Hall to author, Feb. 17, 1969.

[9] President's Report, 1968, p. 26.

[10] Board Mins., XVIII, 117.

[11] *University Bulletin*, Nov. 1, 1968.

[12] *Beacon Journal*, Jan. 11, 1969.

[13] *Ibid.,* Jan. 30, 1969.
[14] *Ibid.,* Jan. 14, 1969.
[15] *Ibid.,* Jan. 30, 1969.
[16] *Buchtelite,* Feb. 12, 1969.
[17] Board Mins., XVII, 186.
[18] *Beacon Journal,* June 26, 1965.
[19] *University Bulletin,* Dec. 1, 1967.

Index

The jacket and interior of *New Lamps for Old* were designed by a staff designer, and manuscript production editing was performed by staff editors of Wm. J. Keller Inc. The book is printed on Keller Publishing Text paper. The cover is grade B book cloth over binders board. Jacket and text were printed by means of offset lithography by Wm. J. Keller Inc.

Both headline and body type were set on a RCA Videocomp Model 820 Cathode Ray Tube (CRT), driven by a RCA Spectra 70 computer. The display typeface is News Gothic; body is 10/11 and notes are 9/10 Caledonia. The entire book was typeset in the equivalent of approximately forty minutes. Type set by means of conventional hot-metal process would have required approximately fifteen full working days.

Manufactured in the United States of America.